Lecture Notes in Computer Science 10279

Commenced Publication in 1973
Founding and Former Series Editors:
Gerhard Goos, Juris Hartmanis, and Jan van Leeuwen

More information about this series at http://www.springer.com/series/7409

Margherita Antona · Constantine Stephanidis (Eds.)

Universal Access in Human–Computer Interaction

Human and Technological Environments

11th International Conference, UAHCI 2017
Held as Part of HCI International 2017
Vancouver, BC, Canada, July 9–14, 2017
Proceedings, Part III

 Springer

Editors

Margherita Antona
Foundation for Research
  and Technology – Hellas (FORTH)
Heraklion, Crete
Greece

Constantine Stephanidis
University of Crete and Foundation
  for Research & Technology – Hellas
(FORTH)
Heraklion, Crete
Greece

ISSN 0302-9743   ISSN 1611-3349 (electronic)
Lecture Notes in Computer Science
ISBN 978-3-319-58699-1   ISBN 978-3-319-58700-4 (eBook)
DOI 10.1007/978-3-319-58700-4

Library of Congress Control Number: 2017940388

LNCS Sublibrary: SL3 – Information Systems and Applications, incl. Internet/Web, and HCI

Printed on acid-free paper

This Springer imprint is published by Springer Nature
The registered company is Springer International Publishing AG
The registered company address is: Gewerbestrasse 11, 6330 Cham, Switzerland

Foreword

The 19th International Conference on Human–Computer Interaction, HCI International 2017, was held in Vancouver, Canada, during July 9–14, 2017. The event incorporated the 15 conferences/thematic areas listed on the following page.

A total of 4,340 individuals from academia, research institutes, industry, and governmental agencies from 70 countries submitted contributions, and 1,228 papers have been included in the proceedings. These papers address the latest research and development efforts and highlight the human aspects of design and use of computing systems. The papers thoroughly cover the entire field of human–computer interaction, addressing major advances in knowledge and effective use of computers in a variety of application areas. The volumes constituting the full set of the conference proceedings are listed on the following pages.

I would like to thank the program board chairs and the members of the program boards of all thematic areas and affiliated conferences for their contribution to the highest scientific quality and the overall success of the HCI International 2017 conference.

This conference would not have been possible without the continuous and unwavering support and advice of the founder, Conference General Chair Emeritus and Conference Scientific Advisor Prof. Gavriel Salvendy. For his outstanding efforts, I would like to express my appreciation to the communications chair and editor of *HCI International News*, Dr. Abbas Moallem.

April 2017   Constantine Stephanidis

HCI International 2017 Thematic Areas and Affiliated Conferences

Thematic areas:

- Human–Computer Interaction (HCI 2017)
- Human Interface and the Management of Information (HIMI 2017)

Affiliated conferences:

- 17th International Conference on Engineering Psychology and Cognitive Ergonomics (EPCE 2017)
- 11th International Conference on Universal Access in Human–Computer Interaction (UAHCI 2017)
- 9th International Conference on Virtual, Augmented and Mixed Reality (VAMR 2017)
- 9th International Conference on Cross-Cultural Design (CCD 2017)
- 9th International Conference on Social Computing and Social Media (SCSM 2017)
- 11th International Conference on Augmented Cognition (AC 2017)
- 8th International Conference on Digital Human Modeling and Applications in Health, Safety, Ergonomics and Risk Management (DHM 2017)
- 6th International Conference on Design, User Experience and Usability (DUXU 2017)
- 5th International Conference on Distributed, Ambient and Pervasive Interactions (DAPI 2017)
- 5th International Conference on Human Aspects of Information Security, Privacy and Trust (HAS 2017)
- 4th International Conference on HCI in Business, Government and Organizations (HCIBGO 2017)
- 4th International Conference on Learning and Collaboration Technologies (LCT 2017)
- Third International Conference on Human Aspects of IT for the Aged Population (ITAP 2017)

Conference Proceedings Volumes Full List

1. LNCS 10271, Human–Computer Interaction: User Interface Design, Development and Multimodality (Part I), edited by Masaaki Kurosu
2. LNCS 10272 Human–Computer Interaction: Interaction Contexts (Part II), edited by Masaaki Kurosu
3. LNCS 10273, Human Interface and the Management of Information: Information, Knowledge and Interaction Design (Part I), edited by Sakae Yamamoto
4. LNCS 10274, Human Interface and the Management of Information: Supporting Learning, Decision-Making and Collaboration (Part II), edited by Sakae Yamamoto
5. LNAI 10275, Engineering Psychology and Cognitive Ergonomics: Performance, Emotion and Situation Awareness (Part I), edited by Don Harris
6. LNAI 10276, Engineering Psychology and Cognitive Ergonomics: Cognition and Design (Part II), edited by Don Harris
7. LNCS 10277, Universal Access in Human–Computer Interaction: Design and Development Approaches and Methods (Part I), edited by Margherita Antona and Constantine Stephanidis
8. LNCS 10278, Universal Access in Human–Computer Interaction: Designing Novel Interactions (Part II), edited by Margherita Antona and Constantine Stephanidis
9. LNCS 10279, Universal Access in Human–Computer Interaction: Human and Technological Environments (Part III), edited by Margherita Antona and Constantine Stephanidis
10. LNCS 10280, Virtual, Augmented and Mixed Reality, edited by Stephanie Lackey and Jessie Y.C. Chen
11. LNCS 10281, Cross-Cultural Design, edited by Pei-Luen Patrick Rau
12. LNCS 10282, Social Computing and Social Media: Human Behavior (Part I), edited by Gabriele Meiselwitz
13. LNCS 10283, Social Computing and Social Media: Applications and Analytics (Part II), edited by Gabriele Meiselwitz
14. LNAI 10284, Augmented Cognition: Neurocognition and Machine Learning (Part I), edited by Dylan D. Schmorrow and Cali M. Fidopiastis
15. LNAI 10285, Augmented Cognition: Enhancing Cognition and Behavior in Complex Human Environments (Part II), edited by Dylan D. Schmorrow and Cali M. Fidopiastis
16. LNCS 10286, Digital Human Modeling and Applications in Health, Safety, Ergonomics and Risk Management: Ergonomics and Design (Part I), edited by Vincent G. Duffy
17. LNCS 10287, Digital Human Modeling and Applications in Health, Safety, Ergonomics and Risk Management: Health and Safety (Part II), edited by Vincent G. Duffy
18. LNCS 10288, Design, User Experience, and Usability: Theory, Methodology and Management (Part I), edited by Aaron Marcus and Wentao Wang

Universal Access in Human–Computer Interaction

Program Board Chair(s): **Margherita Antona and Constantine Stephanidis, Greece**

- Gisela Susanne Bahr, USA
- João Barroso, Portugal
- Rodrigo Bonacin, Brazil
- Ingo K. Bosse, Germany
- Anthony Lewis Brooks, Denmark
- Christian Bühler, Germany
- Stefan Carmien, Spain
- Carlos Duarte, Portugal
- Pier Luigi Emiliani, Italy
- Qin Gao, P.R. China
- Andrina Granić, Croatia
- Simeon Keates, UK
- Georgios Kouroupetroglou, Greece
- Patrick M. Langdon, UK
- Barbara Leporini, Italy
- Tania Lima, Brazil
- Alessandro Marcengo, Italy
- Troy McDaniel, USA
- Ana Isabel Paraguay, Brazil
- Enrico Pontelli, USA
- Jon A. Sanford, USA
- Vagner Santana, Brazil
- Jaime Sánchez, Chile
- Anthony Savidis, Greece
- Kevin Tseng, Taiwan
- Gerhard Weber, Germany
- Fong-Gong Wu, Taiwan

The full list with the Program Board Chairs and the members of the Program Boards of all thematic areas and affiliated conferences is available online at:

http://www.hci.international/board-members-2017.php

HCI International 2018

The 20th International Conference on Human–Computer Interaction, HCI International 2018, will be held jointly with the affiliated conferences in Las Vegas, NV, USA, at Caesars Palace, July 15–20, 2018. It will cover a broad spectrum of themes related to human–computer interaction, including theoretical issues, methods, tools, processes, and case studies in HCI design, as well as novel interaction techniques, interfaces, and applications. The proceedings will be published by Springer. More information is available on the conference website: http://2018.hci.international/.

General Chair
Prof. Constantine Stephanidis
University of Crete and ICS-FORTH
Heraklion, Crete, Greece
E-mail: general_chair@hcii2018.org

http://2018.hci.international/

Contents – Part III

Universal Access to Education and Learning

Universal Access to Mobility

Universal Access to Information and Media

Design for Quality of Life Technologies

Contents – Part I

Accessibility and Usability Guidelines and Evaluation

User and Context Modelling and Monitoring and Interaction Adaptation

Design for Children

Contents – Part II

Non Visual and Tactile Interaction

Gesture and Gaze-Based Interaction

Universal Access to Health and Rehabilitation

Universally Accessible mHealth Apps for Older Adults: Towards Increasing Adoption and Sustained Engagement

Christina N. Harrington[✉], Ljilja Ruzic, and Jon A. Sanford

School of Industrial Design, Georgia Institute of Technology, Atlanta, GA, USA
{cnh,ljilja}@gatech.edu, jon.sanford@coa.gatech.edu

Abstract. Mobile health (mHealth) applications are emerging as a convenient approach to monitoring and tracking health informatics and promoting health-related behaviors. Despite proven health benefits of these systems, many are not designed in consideration of older users. Studies report low or inconsistent usage and high abandonment among these applications, often attributed to poor motivation and engagement strategies utilized in the workflow of the application. However, we posit that a lack in the universal access of a mHealth interface may also contribute to low and inconsistent usage, and is an equally important factor of consideration when designing a product. The approach of universal design should be applied when designing, developing, and evaluating mHealth applications as a consideration to making products usable by the general population. The universal design mobile interface guidelines support the design and development of mobile applications that are accessible by all users equally. As an adaptation to these guidelines, we outline a tool for evaluating mHealth applications for usability and perceived usefulness. We also discuss the importance of universally designed interfaces in the adoption and sustained engagement of mHealth applications. Future work in this research area aims to utilize this approach in the evaluation of mHealth apps that target physical activity. This paper contributes to the field of human-computer interaction as it better positions mHealth applications to be adopted by a wider subset of the general population, increasing the likelihood of individuals experiencing associated health-related benefits.

Keywords: Mobile health interfaces · Universal design · Usability · Evaluation · Older adults · Heuristics

1 Introduction

The growth of the older adult population is foreseen to have a tremendous impact on the healthcare industry. Oftentimes, challenges faced in the healthcare domain such as functional limitations preventing independent maintenance of self and onset of chronic illnesses and disabilities could be overcome by such things as healthy diet, routine exercise, and medication adherence. However, many older adults fail to routinely adhere to these activities, and thus are not able to maintain good health as outlined by healthcare professionals [1].

Mobile health (mHealth) technologies have emerged as an accessible and convenient approach to addressing several areas of health and wellbeing for the older adult

© Springer International Publishing AG 2017
M. Antona and C. Stephanidis (Eds.): UAHCI 2017, Part III, LNCS 10279, pp. 3–12, 2017.
DOI: 10.1007/978-3-319-58700-4_1

population, including chronic illness management, nutrition tracking, fitness promotion, and medication management. Oftentimes these technologies appear as mHealth applications (apps) accessed through an individual's personal smartphone or tablet, paired with sensor-based and wearable technologies to allow for real-time activity monitoring. In addition to activity monitoring, these apps often possess the ability to provide tailored feedback through messaging and incentives, based on an individual's data input, vital signs, or patterns of behaviors. Many mHealth apps target health issues through health promotion messaging and analytic infographics. Such advancements in technology suggest mHealth apps as promising interventions for health tracking, promotion, and health-related behavior change.

Despite this recent emergence in mHealth apps, as well as the potential benefits of these systems to improve the health and well-being of their target end users, there are still many barriers to their sustained use as a health behavior intervention. The Pew Research Center reports that nearly 77% of the overall U.S. population currently own a smartphone, with 42% of adults aged 65 and older owning a personal smartphone [2]. Of this population of smartphone owners, 31% use their devices to download mHealth applications to search for health information or track their health status [2] with nearly 165,000 mHealth apps existing across the iPhone, Google Play, and Android platform app stores. However, many of these apps are often abandoned shortly after their download. Previous research studies of mHealth app use suggest that many of these systems often see low adoption rates, inconsistent use and a lack in user engagement for long periods of time [3–6]. In a survey examining the usage trajectory of mobile health and fitness apps, researchers found that 35% of existing apps that are downloaded to personal smartphones or tablets are abandoned within the first three months of that initial download [7]. Such low adoption and utilization rates prevent the actualization of health benefits associated with continued use.

Various factors can be attributed to this low usage, including ineffective system engagement strategies, burdensome workflows, a low system usability associated with a lack of consideration for functional limitations and age-related challenges. Usability has long been an aspect included in the concept of mobile user experience, and is important to consider as having a direct relationship to adoption and sustained engagement. Here we define the concept of usability as the measurement of a product's expected functionality and accessibility, as well as the ability to be considered useful to user needs.

Although existing heuristic evaluations and taxonomies have been utilized to address general mobile interface usability, very few specifically consider the age-related challenges and functional limitations of older users. Failing to evaluate products for this population has detrimental affect not only on the interactions of the older user, but may also mean little consideration to users that span a wide range of ability levels, including those with hearing, vision, or dexterity impairments. This paper looks to examine the importance of evaluating mHealth apps as a part of the process to design and develop health-related technologies that are universally accessible. We discuss universal/inclusive design as an approach to creating usable mobile apps, and identify usability measurement tools that are feasible for this assessment. Additionally, we discuss the utilization of this approach in an evaluation of mHealth apps to assess them as an appropriate intervention for health-related behaviors among older adults.

2 Background

2.1 Issues with mHealth Adoption and Sustained Engagement

Although various mHealth apps exist that target chronic illnesses and diseases prevalent among the older adult population, many of these apps are not considered usable by older users [8]. Various studies report challenges experienced during interactions with interface-based systems, including those expressed by the older adult population [8–11]. Existing mobile apps are often perceived to be too complex [9, 11], move at a pace not conducive to users who require a longer learning time [10], or were not legible to the decreased visual acuity of many older users [9]. In a usability assessment of existing glucose tracking apps, Whitlock and McLaughlin [9] found that apps presented poor visual contrast and small text and button size, having negative implications for older adult use. Similarly, in a heuristic evaluation of healthy eating apps for older adults, Watkins et al. [11] found five nutrition apps to feature, complex navigation and workflow, poor contrast, unfamiliar iconography, and insufficient instructions.

As a result of varying usability challenges, many older adults report abandoning and never adopting potentially useful mHealth apps. Use of mHealth apps decreases with age among adults 60 and older, with only 10% of adults aged 65 and older choosing to adopt the use of these apps [8]. Despite such low use, 42% of older adults reported an interest in utilizing such as technology in a national survey addressing the current use and interest in using mHealth apps [12]. Studies evaluating older adults' experiences with these apps conclude that lower usage rates and lessened likelihood of adoption is often associated with challenges perceived in using these apps [8, 9, 12]. Usability is often not a major consideration in the development of mHealth app interfaces, thus suggesting a need for a design approach more inclusive of older users.

2.2 Universal/Inclusive Design in Mobile Interfaces

To alleviate many of the challenges experienced during older adults' interactions with mHealth apps, designers must consider design techniques that consider the potential limitations of various users. Universal (or inclusive) design is a design approach in which products and environments are designed to be used by the widest range of individuals possible, regardless of disability, impairment, age, race, or gender [13]. By encompassing a wider range of users, this design approach affords for usable products by smaller subsets of the population, including those with a specific functional limitation, or older adults that experience age-related challenges. The seven principles that comprise universal design include: equitable use (design is useful and marketable to people with diverse abilities); flexibility in use (design accommodates a wide range of individual preferences and abilities); simple and intuitive use (using the product is easy to understand regardless of experience, knowledge, language or skills); perceptible information (design communicates necessary information effectively regardless of sensory abilities); tolerance for error (design minimizes hazards or unintended actions); low physical effort (design can be used comfortably with minimum fatigue); and size and space for approach and use (appropriate size and space is provided for the approach or manipulation of the design regardless of a user's body size, posture, or mobility) [14]. Kascak et al. [15] suggests that applying this design approach to the development of mobile interfaces addresses a deficit in existing mobile design guidelines, and integrates concepts of accessibility and inclusion in a new and emerging field of products. This design approach should be considered the most relevant when designing for non-exclusive user groups. General mHealth apps that are more domain specific, or are designed based on a target activity or behavior, should understand usability for the general public, including all demographics.

2.3   Usability Metrics for Interface Evaluation

Although several research efforts have defined and identified heuristic tools and usability metrics to evaluate mobile interfaces, little emphasis is placed on the needs and limitations of older users. Many existing evaluation tools have utilized heuristic measures and testing methods that target the general population, lacking specific consideration to users age-related challenges or (physical or sensory) impairments. The most well-known usability heuristics are outlined in Nielsen's heuristic evaluation tool, which defines ten usability heuristics specifically for mobile interface usability evaluations [16]. Several derivations of this tool have been developed incorporating additional metrics and newer methods of technology interaction such as touchscreen interfaces [17], however these adapted metrics fail to consider the aging population. In line with design criteria relevant to the aging population, there are usability evaluation metrics that must also be defined to be more inclusive of older adults.

Reviewing previous work done in this area we identified four existing tools that define heuristics within a usability evaluation tool or a set of design guidelines specifically for older adults [18–21]. Across these four sets of heuristics and design guidelines, researchers have identified such metrics as 'feature recognition', 'flexibility and efficiency in use', and 'naturalness' as additional measures with which to evaluate system usability. While heuristics defined by Wildenbos et al. [18] and Watkins et al. [19] are more inclusive of a few metrics that consider the limitations of older adults, there are areas such as navigation of the app and appropriate methods of system input that are not addressed. Silva et al.'s list of heuristics [20] along with the Universal Design for Mobile Interface Guidelines (UDMIG) [21] cover a larger set of guidelines addressing design aspects of an interface as it relates to the mental and physical capabilities of older users. Ruzic et al.'s UDMIG v2.1 presents these heuristics as a blueprint for designers to develop universally accessible applications that are considered usable given limitations that may be experienced due to normative age-related changes, chronic illness, or impairment, specifically. Building upon the latter frameworks, we have adapted two tools for the evaluation of mHealth apps; an initial set of heuristics utilized in the design process as a researcher/designer, and a usability assessment tool to discern older adults' perception of the universal access of these products.

3 Application: Evaluating mHealth Apps Based on Universal Design

To validate the outlined design guidelines and usability metrics that afford universal and inclusive access for mobile interfaces, an evaluation of existing mHealth fitness apps is planned to discern the current state of mHealth applications. As a part of a larger research effort to discern effectiveness of mHealth apps for older adults, this evaluation will be leveraged to understand user's experiences and perceptions of system usability. We selected fitness apps as a case study to evaluate heuristics and metrics, and for their relevance to the overall health of all older adults, avoiding chronic illness or impairment specific apps.

We aim to discern how well these existing apps align with universal design guidelines and whether they meet the needs of the older adult population. Here we propose that the more usable an app is, the easier it is to consider an intervention useful, thus increasing the projected usage trajectory and engagement with the system. To confirm this assertion, we have identified an approach to evaluate existing mHealth apps based on usability metrics relevant to the aging population. Here we discuss the importance of examining usability from a researcher's perspective, as well as measuring usability metrics with older users themselves.

3.1 Heuristics for Researchers and Designers to Evaluate Apps for Older Adults

Based on literature that identify usability criteria and guidelines for designing accessible mobile apps, we have synthesized and adapted a comprehensive list of heuristics as those that best meet the needs of older adults. These heuristics have been aggregated and adapted from the existing literature on usability metrics for the general population [16, 17], and heuristics specifically addressing designing interfaces older adults [18–21]. Heuristics that appeared redundant across literature sources were removed, and those that were specific to a specific app were also not included in this list. Additionally, new heuristics have been introduced that represent what we know about designing usable interfaces for older populations [22–25]. Each heuristic incorporates elements of the original universal design principles and have been adapted with language that applies specifically to the design of system interfaces and the interactions that would be associated with this context. Twenty-one heuristics are outlined to assess the universal and inclusive access of mobile interfaces for the older adult population. These heuristics have been organized into 4 higher level categories of design principles: *Perceptible Information, Navigation, Appropriate Cognitive Affordance*, and *Accessible Interaction*. Table 1 lists these heuristics by the higher-level category of design principle that they address. New heuristics are denoted with an asterisk.

Perceptible Information/Output encompasses guidelines that address the necessity to effectively present information in a way that is perceptible to users regardless of their sensory abilities. This considers users that may have low vision associated with age. Navigation as a design principle highlights ways to make the system workflow easy to maneuver for all individuals. Appropriate Cognitive Affordance speaks to the design of the app considering memory and learning of the older adult population, as well as

Table 1. Comprehensive list of universal heuristics inclusive of age-related challenges

Perceptible information/output	
P1	Provide adequate contrast between background color, images, and text
P2	Make the most important information readily available or present on the home screen
P3	Allow adjustments to change the brightness and contrast of the display
P4	Use font styles appropriate for older adults including size and type (sans serif, non-italic, 12–14 size)
Navigation	
N1	Keep navigation structure narrow, simple, and straightforward
N2	Make navigation keys visible and easy to discern from other elements
N3*	Avoid the use of multiple gesture motions to navigate through screens
N4	Use consistent navigation for each screen
N5	Utilize visible a "Back" button
Cognitive affordance	
CA1	Communicate user status in a way that is visible and readily available
CA2*	Minimize the number of tasks occurring at the same time
CA3	Minimize the need for working memory and memory recall
CA4	Utilize prompt messages, warnings, and proper button placement to avoid unintended actions
CA5	Provide feedback to signify correct use of app such as auditory, visual, and vibrotactile feedback when pressing a button
CA6*	Allow users to adjust the pace of their interaction
CA7*	Make instructions clear and present them without distraction
CA8*	Avoid screen clutter and large bodies of text. Present information in smaller chunks
CA9	Provide different modes of feedback such as audio, tactile, or visual feedback
Flexible inputs	
FI1	Provide alternate methods of interaction such as speech input, hands-free, or eyes-free interaction
FI2	Buttons, keys, and icons should be large enough for to select without error (at least 14 mm square)
FI3	Minimal amount of physical force required to perform actions

presenting information at a pace that is comfortable or adjustable to older users. Lastly, Flexible Inputs relates to the way in which older users can physically interact with an app, keeping in mind challenges with dexterity and precision.

The process of evaluating existing apps is a two-stage approach: screening apps across multiple app platforms, and evaluating them based on the heuristics mentioned above. Apps will be identified through a systematic search in the iTunes and Google Play stores. Researchers will perform this search directly from platforms stores and not previous databases found in literature for apps that are currently supported and available for download. Terms included in this search are any combination of "physical activity", "fitness", "fitness for elderly", "fitness motivation", and "coaching".

3.2 Usability Metrics to Evaluate Apps with Older Adults

Since the guidelines presented in the UDMIG best address potential usability challenges specifically for older users, these guidelines have been adapted into an evaluation tool to be administered with older users. Table 2 displays metrics adapted from Silva et al.'s 35 heuristics and the UDMIG v2.1, separating metrics for universal access of the design, and usefulness of system features.

Table 2. Usability metrics for mHealth app evaluation with older users

Universal access of app design	
UD1	This application provides alternate means of interaction such as speech input, hands-free, or eyes-free interaction
UD2	I am able to find the information I am looking for easily
UD3	The design of this application minimizes the occurrence of unintended actions (e.g., prompt messages, button placement, etc.)
UD4	This application provides informative feedback (e.g., a beep when pressing a key, an error message, etc.) that I am using it in the right way
UD5	I am able to tell that I have successfully completed an action in this app
UD6	This application provides different modes of feedback such as audio, tactile, or visual feedback
UD7	I can easily reverse my actions if I make a mistake in using this application
UD8	The design of this app appeals to me
UD9	The interface of this app is easy to understand and not complex
UD10	This app provides adequate contrast between background colors, images, and text
UD11	Fonts and images are legible in this app
UD12	Navigation in this app is easy - I can easily find my way from one screen to the next
UD13	I can easily understand the terms and language used throughout this app
UD14	I am able to change the size and brightness of the display in this app
UD15	The amount of force required to perform actions in this app is adequate
UD16	Buttons, keys, and icons are large enough for me to select without error
UD17	I feel comfortable with this app regardless of my previous experience with mobile apps
Usefulness of system features	
SF1	I find this app useful to my health needs
SF2	I am able to tell my status throughout the use of this app
SF3	This app features an appropriate pace of interaction for me
SF4	Interaction in this app is consistent with my expectations
SF5	This app will improve my overall health
SF6	Interacting with this app will improve my ability to keep track of my health

Usability metrics adapted from Silva et al. [20] and Ruzik et al. [21].

The usability evaluation of each app will involve a systematic assessment of a user's agreement of each of the adapted metrics as detailed above. Each metric will be assessed on a Likert scale of "strongly agree" to "strongly disagree". We expect that apps that are rated as being more universally accessible will be considered more useful, thus see more sustained engagement from older users.

4   Discussion

In this paper, we discuss the importance of considering usability and universal access in the design and evaluation of products targeting older adults, specifically mobile health interfaces. Usability is an important construct when evaluating interactive technologies such as mobile interfaces and this construct should be given consideration throughout the entirety of the design process. Defining system features and engagement strategies often take priority in the early stages of a software product with designers strategizing system workflows and scenarios to build strong products. However, the end utility of a product is dependent on usability, regardless of how well the information content is designed and implemented. Universal access is also important for its tie to product usefulness and the relation to the actual content of what the app does. Despite the method of engagement, apps deemed non-useful, frustrating, or burdensome will ultimately not be used by the end user. Universal and inclusive design present an approach to enhance system usability, incorporating the cognitive and physical needs of various special populations including older adults. This design approach emerges as the most relevant for apps that are not targeting a specific user group and thus should be inclusive of the general population. This concept is essential in the development of health-related mobile apps, as proper design of apps that target health and wellbeing create opportune health interventions for the general population. By designing non-stigmatizing products for a population that has been shown to have the most difficulty in learning and adopting new technologies, we may be able to develop products that are usable and thus adopted by a large subset of the general population. Such improvements in system acceptance has grave value to the fields of design and human-computer interaction because it promotes products that will see long-term and widespread success.

Specifically, examining and improving usability of mHealth applications could have significant positive impact on an individual's experience with using these applications, increasing the likelihood of consistent and sustained user engagement. We hypothesize that enabling better usability of mHealth apps has the ability to not only make for a better user experience with these systems, but will also promote positive changes in health-related behaviors (i.e. better adherence to medication regimens, increased physical activity, proper hydration, calorie management, etc.). Thus, users will be more likely to experience sustained health-related benefits associated with these systems, which has great significance to the aging population as these benefits enable a healthier state of aging.

Identifying a standard approach to designing and evaluating usability for mobile apps also has great value to designers and developers. Having a universal language within the design community will help to streamline the design process and create products that are deemed universally accessible by all end users.

4.1   Usability as a Factor of System Adoption and Engagement

It is appropriate to examine system usability as a factor of adaptation and sustained engagement in addition to other factors related to system design (engagement strategies and content of system features). Constructs of the Technology Acceptance Model [26, 27] suggest that both usability and functionality of apps play a major, if not the most important, role in the actual use of a product [28]. Davis [26, 27] outlines in the Technology Acceptance Model that both cognitive response of perceived ease-of-use and system usefulness lead to the act of using a system; increasing or improving usability measures should thus have a positive effect on use of a product. Usability has great influence on a user's initial attitude toward using a product, as well as the intent to continue to use the product in the future.

4.2 Future Work

This evaluation serves as a part of a larger research effort to determine the potential effectiveness of mHealth apps for older adults in changing health-related behaviors. We are currently in the process of evaluating existing mHealth apps with other experienced researchers in the field of design and HCI. Future work in this research area looks to evaluate existing mHealth apps utilizing the adapted version of the UDMIG with older adult users. As a part of a larger research effort, we are curious to understand the interaction effect between system usability and engagement strategy, and assess whether mHealth apps that rate better on measures of usability are more effective than those that are perceived to be more engaging. Long-term future research efforts look to refine the measurement variables used to evaluate system usability specifically for the older adult population, and translate these measurement variables into guidelines to be used during system design. This tool will aid researchers and developers in gaining user feedback of mHealth applications, and incorporating universal or inclusive design as an iterative approach to system development.

References

1. Schiller, J., Lucas, J., Peregoy, J.: Summary health statistics for U.S. adults: national health interview survey, 2011. Vital Health Stat. **10**(256), 5–11 (2012). National center for health statistics
2. Pew Research Center: U.S. Smartphone Use in 2016: Who Owns Cellphones and Smartphones. Pew Research Center, Pewinternet.org (2016)
3. Bickmore, T., Schulman, D., Yin, L.: Maintaining engagement in long-term interventions with relational agents. Int. J. Appl. Artif. Intell. **24**(6), 648–666 (2010)
4. Bort-Roig, J., Gilson, N.D., Puig-Ribera, A., Contreras, R.S., Trost, S.G.: Measuring and influencing physical activity with smartphone technology: a systematic review. Sports Med. **44**(5), 671–686 (2014). doi:10.1007/s40279-014-0142-5
5. Burke, L.E., Ma, J., Azar, K.M., Bennett, G.G., Peterson, E.D., Zheng, Y., et al.: Current science on consumer use of mobile health for cardiovascular disease prevention: a scientific statement from the American heart association. Circulation (2015). doi:10.1161/CIR. 0000000000000232
6. Klasnja, P.V., Consolvo, S., McDonald, D.W., Landay, J.A., Pratt, W.: Using mobile and personal sensing technologies to support health behavior change in everyday life: lessons learned. In: AMIA (2009)
7. Murnane, E.L., Huffaker, D., Kossinets, G.: Mobile health apps: adoption, adherence, and abandonment. In: Adjunct Proceedings of the 2015 ACM International Joint Conference on Pervasive and Ubiquitous Computing and Proceedings of the 2015 ACM International Symposium on Wearable Computers, pp. 261–264 (2015)
8. Dahlke, D.V., Ory, M.: mHealth Applications Use and Potential for Older Adults, Overview of. Springer, Singapore (2016)

9. Whitlock, L.A., McLaughlin, A.C.: Identifying usability problems of blood glucose tracking apps for older adult users. In: Proceedings of the Human Factors and Ergonomics Society Annual Meeting 2012 Sep, vol. 56, no. 1, pp. 115–119. SAGE Publications, Los Angeles (2012)
10. Isaković, M., Sedlar, U., Volk, M., Bešter, J.: Usability pitfalls of diabetes mHealth apps for the elderly. J. Diab. Res. **2016**, 9 pages, Article ID 1604609 (2016). doi:10.1155/2016/1604609
11. Watkins, I., Kules, B., Yuan, X., Xie, B.: Heuristic evaluation of healthy eating apps for older adults. J. Consum. Health Internet **18**(2), 105–127 (2014)
12. Barrett, L.L.: Healthy@Home 2.0. AARP (2011). http://assets.aarp.org/rgcenter/health/healthy-home-11.pdf. Accessed 23 Jan 2017
13. Sanford, J.A.: Universal Design as a Rehabilitation Strategy: Design for the Ages. Springer, Heidelberg (2012)
14. Mace, R.: What is universal design. Center Univ. Design North Carolina State Univ. **19**, 2004 (1997)
15. Kascak, L.R., Claudia, B.R., Sanford, J.A.: Integrating Universal Design (UD) principles and mobile design guidelines to improve design of mobile health applications for older adults. In: 2014 IEEE International Conference on Healthcare Informatics (ICHI), pp. 343–348 (2014)
16. Nielsen, J.: Heuristic evaluation. Usability Inspection Methods **17**(1), 25–62 (1994)
17. Inostroza, R., Rusu, C., Roncagliolo, S., Rusu, V.: Usability heuristics for touchscreen-based mobile devices: update. In: Proceedings of the 2013 Chilean Conference on Human-Computer Interaction, pp. 24–29. ACM (2013)
18. Wildenbos, G.A., Peute, L.W., Jaspers, M.W.: A framework for evaluating mHealth tools for older patients on usability. In: MIE, pp. 783–787 (2015)
19. Watkins, I., Kules, B., Yuan, X., Xie, B.: Heuristic evaluation of healthy eating apps for older adults. J. Consum. Health Internet **18**(2), 105–127 (2014)
20. Silva, P.A., Holden, K., Jordan, P.: Towards a list of heuristics to evaluate smartphone apps targeted at older adults: a study with apps that aim at promoting health and well-being. In: 2015 48th Hawaii International Conference on System Sciences (HICSS), pp. 3237–3246. IEEE (2015)
21. Ruzic, L., Lee, S.T., Liu, Y.E., Sanford, Jon A.: Development of Universal Design Mobile Interface Guidelines (UDMIG) for aging population. In: Antona, M., Stephanidis, C. (eds.) UAHCI 2016. LNCS, vol. 9737, pp. 98–108. Springer, Cham (2016). doi: 10.1007/978-3-319-40250-5_10
22. Shneiderman, B.: Universal usability. Commun. ACM **43**(5), 84–91 (2000)
23. Fisk, A.D., Rogers, W.A., Charness, N., Czaja, S.J., Sharit, J.: Designing for Older Adults: Principles and Creative Human Factors Approaches. CRC Press, Boca Raton (2012)
24. Pak, R., McLaughlin, A.: Designing Displays for Older Adults. CRC Press, Boca Raton (2010)
25. Harrington, C.N., Hartley, J.Q., Mitzner, T.L., Rogers, W.A.: Assessing older adults' usability challenges using kinect-based exergames. In: Zhou, J., Salvendy, G. (eds.) Human Aspects of IT for the Aged Population. Design for Everyday Life, ITAP 2015. LNCS, vol. 9194, pp. 488–499. Springer, Cham (2015)
26. Davis, F.D.: A Technology Acceptance Model for Empirically Testing New End User Information Systems: Theory and Results. Massachussets Institute of Technology, Sloan School of Management, Cambridge (1986)
27. Davis, F.D.: Perceived usefulness, perceived ease of use, and user acceptance of information technology. MIS Q. **13**, 319–340 (1989)
28. Legris, P., Ingham, J., Collerette, P.: Why do people use information technology? A critical review of the technology acceptance model. Inf. Manag. **40**, 191–204 (2003)

Achieving End User Acceptance: Building Blocks for an Evidence-Based User-Centered Framework for Health Technology Development and Assessment

Matthias R. Hastall[1(✉)], Christoph Dockweiler[2], and Juliane Mühlhaus[1,3]

[1] Faculty of Rehabilitation Sciences, TU Dortmund University, Dortmund, Germany
{matthias.hastall,juliane.muehlhaus}@tu-dortmund.de
[2] Faculty of Health Sciences, University of Bielefeld, Bielefeld, Germany
christoph.dockweiler@uni-bielefeld.de
[3] Department of Applied Health Sciences, Hochschule für Gesundheit, Bochum, Germany

Abstract. Innovative healthcare services and technologies show great promises for reducing individual and societal burdens, but predominantly fail to attract sufficient end user acceptance and usage. This renders the aspect of technology adoption as key weakness of most health technology development endeavors, but also as most promising area for implementing changes that can dramatically increase the likelihood of project success. The purpose of this paper is to discuss some core assumptions of a user-centered process framework for technology adoption that addresses three major weaknesses of many current adoption models: First, the inadequate consideration of the process character of health technology adoptions. Second, the restricted view of human motivation, information processing, and behavior as being primarily rational and utilitarian in nature. And third, the insufficient attention to situational and social influences, and the role of individual differences. Theoretical, methodological, user inclusion-related and communication-related implications of the proposed prespective changes are discussed.

Keywords: Health technology · Adoption · Acceptance · Theory · User participation

1 Introduction

Understanding the adoption and acceptance of health technologies is crucial for optimizing design choices, application selections, and educational as well as marketing strategies. Adoption, acceptance, and sustained use are essential for achieving the core aims of health technology development such as reducing individual burdens, increasing physical and psychological well-being, facilitating healthy aging in familiar places, ensuring social participation, and minimizing demands on health care systems. Yet, most technological innovations fail to attract sufficient levels of end user acceptance and usage [1, 2]. This renders the aspect of technology adoption as key weakness of most health technology development endeavors, but also as most promising area for implementing changes that can dramatically increase the likelihood of project success. Several

© Springer International Publishing AG 2017
M. Antona and C. Stephanidis (Eds.): UAHCI 2017, Part III, LNCS 10279, pp. 13–25, 2017.
DOI: 10.1007/978-3-319-58700-4_2

technology adoption models have been proposed (e.g., Theory of Planned Behaviour (TPB), Theory of Interpersonal Behaviour (TIB), Technology Acceptance Model (TAM), Unified Theory of Acceptance and Use of Technology (UTAUT) [3]). We argue that a better understanding of individuals, of the process of technology adoption, and of factors driving individuals' preferences and behaviors can greatly enhance the chances for meaningful user inclusion and technology adoption. Several building blocks for revised and more comprehensive models of technology acceptance are presented below, followed by a discussion of their implication for user inclusion, effectiveness evaluations, and dissemination activities.

2   Building Blocks for a Refined Understanding of Adoption

Acceptance describes a highly subjective positive attitude of an individual towards a technological innovation and towards its potential or actual use. It consists of several dynamic psycho-social processes within an individual. Acceptance can thus be understood as the result of a complex decision-making process involving cognitive and affective appraisal processes, which is also substantially affected by social and situational influences [4]. Our impression is that several technology acceptance models (e.g., TAM, UTAUT) fall short of adequately mirroring this dynamic and multi-determined process. Three major weaknesses were identified and are discussed below in more detail: First, the inadequate consideration of the *process character* of health technology adoptions. Second, the restricted *view of human* motivation, information processing, and behavior as being primarily rational and utilitarian in nature. And third, the insufficient attention to *situational and social influences*, and the role of *individual differences*.

2.1   Stages of Health Technology Adoption

It is rather rare that developers and designers are capable of creating a health technology product so attractive that it triggers automatic impulse purchases. Instead, technology adoption typically occurs in distinct *stages*, which are characterized by different knowledge, motivation, and informational demands. Several stage models have been proposed [e.g., 5, 6]. For the purpose of our discussion, it seems fruitful to distinguish at least seven stages: (1) Not being aware of an innovation, (2) forming an opinion about it, (3) intending to try or to use it, (4) initial use, (5) purchase (if applicable), (6) sustained use, and (7) stopped use or disengagement. Ideally, an individual passes through the stages one to six. The seventh stage is usually only desirable if the objective of technology use was attained (e.g., after full recovery).

If one accepts that technology acceptance and adoption occur in a dynamic process consisting of distinct phases, three implications become evident. First, on the individual level, each phase is characterized by different set of affective, cognitive, and behavior-related processes and motivations that require consideration. Second, the type and impact of situational and social influences can also vary greatly in each phase. Third, as a result, each phase requires a distinct and phase-specific (i.e., tailored) communication approach in order to foster or maintain adoption. A comprehensive model of health technology adoption should therefore incorporate adoption phases, and specify adoption-fostering as well as inhibiting factors for each phase.

2.2   Underlying Views of Human Functioning

At least implicitly, many theoretical and empirical approaches towards technology adoption presume that humans are rational utilitarian beings who make decisions based on rational information processing, and who are capable of relatively accurately predicting future behaviors. Yet, research indicates that a large portion of humans' attention allocation, information processing, learning, attitude formation, mood states, and behavioral responses are initiated outside individuals' awareness [7]. From this perspective, it is not surprising that individuals typically have little insights into their higher-order cognitive processes, and that they may be unaware of occurring attitude and behavior changes as well as the stimuli that caused them [8]. In contrast, we presume everyday user behavior to be considerably driven by emotions such as anxiety, excitement, or hope, and furthermore by unconscious motivations that may have an evolutionary foundation [e.g., 9]. It is also worth noting that individuals' attention allocation and information processing is usually strongly biased, particularly when they are confronted with threatening information such as health-related information. These perceived physical or ego threats are likely to produce defensive motivations [10, 11], which are a very plausible explanation for individuals' notable avoidance of health technology interventions, and also for the substantial gap between individuals' self-reported intentions and behaviors (e.g., [12]).

It appears self-evident that a more accurate understanding of humans that integrates unconscious and conscious modes of thinking, experiencing, and motivation can greatly advance the development of technologies that are perceived as valuable by their target groups. Such an understanding should also facilitate more meaningful ways of user inclusion and more valid user acceptance testing. For further discussion, we distinguish three classes of adoption-relevant influences: *individual-related factors*, *social and environment-related factors,* and *technology-related factors*. These factors are highly interrelated and affect each other in dynamic and reciprocal ways. Yet, for the purpose of an organized discussion, it seems helpful to address these aspects first separately before discussing how they can be integrated in a more comprehensive framework of health technology adoption.

2.3   Individual Factors

Individual factors are as manifold as individuals are, and can be described on several levels. For understanding technology adoption, it seems useful to distinguish, on a very basic level, factors that motivate *approach behavior* (e.g., information seeking, tryouts) from those that trigger *avoidance behavior* (e.g., information avoidance, negative emotional and behavioral reactions, disengagement). Both behavioral impulses are strongly linked to positive respective negative affect. They are initiated by separate neural systems that react to rewarding respective aversive stimuli, and were termed *behavioral activation system (BAS)* and *behavioral inhibition system (BIS)* by Gray [13].

As both systems operate in parallel and can be triggered simultaneously by the same information, it seems valuable to clearly distinguish between adoption-facilitating (i.e., BAS-activating) and rejection-inhibiting (i.e., BIS-deactivating) factors. Evidently, development processes should aim for maximizing adoption-facilitating cues while simultaneously reducing rejection-facilitating triggers. This, however, requires a profound knowledge about the target group. Some factors that are deemed to be particularly influential are discussed below.

2.3.1   Motivation

Motivation is an important aspect of humans' interaction with technologies, but so far neither included in technology acceptance models nor systematically integrated in technology design [14]. Motivation-based technology design facilitates a sustained and enjoyable user acceptance by avoiding triggers for disengagement. Motivational effects are well defined in psychology, and just recently received greater attention in the context of health technology use [15]. It also seems overdue to have a closer look at health behavior models beyond the theory Theory of Planned Behavior (TPB: [16]). Parallel-response models (e.g., [17]), stage models (e.g., [18–20]), and approaches from positive psychology (e.g., [21]) offer valuable additional insights into the wealth of factors that drive human decisions and behaviors. Finally, modern evidence-based marketing approaches are a valuable resource to understand why awareness for innovations is critical, how it can be achieved, and which product communication strategies are actually motivating [22].

2.3.2   Knowledge and Literacy

Informing individuals about technological innovations is far from being simple or straightforward, but requires educative approaches that fit both the specific adoption phase and the individual (e.g., [23]). Not only do target groups regularly have little technology- and health-related foreknowledge, also access to information can be an issue. The term "digital divide" describes the paradox that the increase of available digital technologies and information can increase existing gaps in knowledge between different socio-economic groups instead of reducing them [24]. Yet, the use of health-related information and communication technologies requires appropriate knowledge, experience, and user competences, and therefore likely knowledge about effective motivating education strategies. Adequate ways of informing people about health-related information, and for empowering individuals to make adequate health-related decisions, can be also derived from the "shared decision-making" (SDM) literature [25].

2.3.3   Emotional Processes and Risk Perception

Human behavior is to a large extent driven by emotions, especially in the context of health applications. While it seems intuitively plausible to assume that individuals should be interested in health-related information and solution, especially those that may help them to maintain or improve their health status, it is not unlikely to observe avoidance behavior instead [26]. Attempts to inform about relevant health threats may result in worsened health behavior (boomerang effect: [27]) and reactance [28]. It is also rather the rule than the exception that people have very distorted risk perceptions [29], and that they tend to down-play their vulnerability to health threats (e.g., [17]). Such defense mechanisms are reactions towards threatening thoughts about sickness and death, and help individuals to maintain their self-esteem [11]. It is important to note that these mechanisms tend to prioritize ego threats over physical threats. Or, put differently, that individuals are not unlikely to risk physical health problems in order to maintain high levels of self-esteem. Drastic warnings (i.e., fear appeals) are therefore not unlikely to further increase defensive reactions, including boomerang effects [17]. Positive emotions, in contrast, may help to encourage the non-defensive processing of risk-related information [30]. It is important to understand these – occasionally unintuitive – effects, the complexity of emotional reactions, and individuals' priorities for emotion regulation. It is also worth noting that the interplay between positive or negative affect and health is complex, and that subjective well-being includes way more dimensions than just affect (e.g., [31]). To sum up, when developing health technologies, it is not just sufficient to make sure that approach impulses outweigh avoidance triggers. Developers should also be aware of the critically roles that emotions play when being confronted with topics such as sickness and death, and need to carefully implement this knowledge in the innovation design process and in innovation-related communication.

2.3.4 Individual Differences

It is obvious, that individuals differ greatly from each other, and that such differences can have profound influences on their decisions to adopt a technological innovation. Demographic difference such as sex, age, education, and income are partly incorporated in existing technology adoption frameworks (e.g., [32]). Yet, psychologists distinguish hundreds of personality traits, and it is still largely unclear which of them are most influential when it comes to health technology adoption. Different sensitivities for rewarding and aversive stimuli, which are linked to BAS and BIS activity (e.g., [33]), might be one reason why individuals react differently towards health technology inno-vations. Openness for new experience, dispositional anxiety, sensation seeking, and many more are similarly likely to underlie individuals' interactions with new technology (e.g., [34, 35]). It should be noted that the knowledge about relevant personality char-acteristics is not only important to develop attractive health technology solutions, but also critical when deciding how to communicate the intervention to different target groups (e.g., [36]).

2.4 Social and Situational Factors

Social, organizational and situations factors likewise play an important role for tech-nology adoption. They provide information about the benefits and difficulties of inno-vations, signal social validation or sanctioning, and exhibit various further supporting or inhibiting influences. Several social aspects surrounding technological innovation are discussed in the literature as factors for increasing the chances of adoption. These include, among others, dimensions of social support und social networks, organizational factors, cultural influences, laws and regulations, and situational triggers.

2.4.1 Social Network

Social networks provide friendship, advice, communication, and support among members of social systems. They create trust, reduce uncertainty, and mitigate the information ambiguity. The influence of personal and peer attitudes towards innovations such as colleagues of friends is considered in several health technology adoption models [37]. The family is one of the central reference points for patients in the adoption of health technologies [38]. Relevant factors are expected support within the social network or implications of technology adoption for family life. Just as important is the perceived attitude of the physician, especially when family networks are missing, when patients are older, or if high degrees of physical impairment exist. It can be concluded that the perceived benefits of adopting technology are higher if many adopters already exist in a social network, due to increased information flow, support, and similarity of beliefs [39]. The influence of social networks also depends greatly on the perceived competence of the user [38].

2.4.2 Organizational Factors

It is increasingly accepted that the diffusion of technology within complex organizational systems such as, for example, companies or healthcare organizations, is not a linear process. This is in part due to the large human, organizational, and financial capital involved, but also the result of complex management structures with different hierarchies and regulations. Individuals act and decides within this organizational framework. Perceptions of organizational complexity, competitive pressure, control beliefs, participation and perceived behavioral control, the image of innovations within the organizational subsystems (e.g., close colleague) or the perceived organizational readiness for change play a decisive role in the adoption of new health technologies within organizational structures [40–42]. Furthermore, organizational leadership is a crucial factor of technology adoption. Organizational leaders who possess digital skills and have prior experience with health technology are likely to develop a vision that comprises a long-term commitment to technology use [43]. Economic concerns about the implementation of health care technologies also play a major role (e.g., [44]), for example fear of high cost, increased administrative burden, modest cost-benefit ratios, accountability and available financing options (e.g., through health insurance). All in all, organizational influences on technology adoption are manifold and deserve a stronger consideration in health technology adoption models.

2.4.3 Cultural Determinants

Cultural patterns are shared within a social environment such as nation, ethnicity or profession. Present models of health technology acceptance, however, largely disregard norms and values shared within a culture. Stable patterns of thinking, feeling and potential acting strongly vary within national and professional cultures [45]. Cultural patterns like individualism (vs. collectivism), uncertainty avoidance, masculinity (vs. femininity) or long-term orientation [46] are not unlikely to affect individuals' adoption decisions. In addition to direct links between culture and the adoption of health technologies (e.g., language), culturally shaped behavioral preferences could affect the process in diverse ways. From a physician's point of view, socialized professional values (e.g., the helpful nature of medical professionals, or fears of "dehumanized" care) can have an impact on the perception of performance and effort expectations of health technologies [47]. The socialization within a specific culture determines relationship to technology as well as to medicine. Culture also shapes our understanding of how we can affect health [48]. Consequently, questions of cultural views and norms deserve a more prominent place in health technology adoption models.

2.4.4 Geographic Challenges

Barriers and facilitators of health technology adoption can also stem from geographical factors. Literature has constantly noted the under-serviced nature of healthcare in remote areas as a consequence of numerous system-related barriers, including availability, continuity, delivery, acceptability, lack of information exchange, and coordination difficulties [49]. The experience of care (from the perspectives of patients and physicians) in rural areas also plays a role in the assessment of individual advantages of using information health technologies [38]. While the use of telemedicine reduces geographic boundaries in medical care, adequate coverage of the underlying digital technologies (e.g., broadband connections, UMTS, LTE) can still be an issue.

2.5 Technology Factors

This last category encompasses factors that are mainly the result of the development process. The crucial questions are: How do health innovations (including innovation-related communication) fit to the aspects discussed above? In which aspects is the possession and use of the technology perceived as rewarding (e.g., emotionally, socially, culturally, financially, goal-related, or self-esteem-related)? And which innovation aspects are perceived as negative or threatening (e.g., costs, difficulty to use, stigmatization potential, reminders for sickness or death)? Put differently, to what extend are behavioral avoidance impulses triggered, and to what extend approach impulses? Relevant technology factors encompass the optical and tactical appearance, perceived simplicity, perceived effects on self-esteem and social inclusion, functionality, joy of use, anxiety-arousing potential, reliability, costs, and many more. Again, it should be noted that the *perceived* characteristics are more relevant for individuals than the actual characteristics, which are often unknown or can only be inferred from provided communication, the appearance of the solution itself, or social reactions towards it. This again emphasizes the role of professional and tailored communication for the success of health technology innovations.

3 Implications and Outlook

Several factors that can influence the adoption (or avoidance) of health innovations are discussed above. A consideration of these factors and principles has implication for the conceptualization, measurement and communicative accompaniment of adoption processes, which are outlined below.

3.1   Perspectives on User Participation in Research and Development

In order to promote user orientation in health technology research and development, it is crucial to integrate the attitudes, perceptions, needs, traits and the social frameworks of tomorrows' users early into the development cycles of health innovations. This requires new forms of cooperation between practice and science, the co-production of knowledge and the participation of relevant user groups in a process of open innovation. This is a paradigmatic shift away from the traditional assumption that exclusively health care professionals are able to devise, develop, and disseminate innovative concepts in health care. As a result, open innovation processes in health care are more accepted by users than traditional technology development [50]. For this purpose, methods of participatory health research are particularly relevant.

Participative research follows the principle of "knowledge for action" and not (only) "knowledge for understanding" [51]. Interventions are designed to be participatory, quality-assured, life-oriented, and setting-based to include the relevant personal and social variables of technology adoption. However, the understanding of "participation" is very divergent [52], but can be understood as a continuum between the poles of pure "information" and "inclusion in decision-making" [53]. In this continuum, participation characterizes the relationship between the researchers as well as the participants in a bilateral sense: On the one hand as the participation of the participants in the research process, on the other as the participation of the researchers in the processes and social references of the examined settings [54]. For research practice, this means that the main interest of research is defined by the interplay of two (possibly incongruent) perspectives – science and practice. The aim of a participatory design of research processes is the promotion of an individual and collaborative learning process within practice and science, to make action strategies more relevant to practice [55]. In addition, participation in (application-oriented) research is intended to avoid the emergence of critical barriers in the diffusion of technologies in health care.

The interdependence of the perspectives of science and practice required in the framework of participative research is not simply determined by the decision to participate. Rather, it is a methodologically challenging procedure, which only gradually develops during the actual research process through the encounters, interactions and communication processes. This understanding breaks with traditional roles within research and thus requires fundamental changes in the research processes – and in the involved parties. In particular, the concept of co-researchers [56] seems promising for a process of open innovation. In this understanding, co-researchers are members of a relevant group (e.g., patients) or have an institutional or occupational group-specific affiliation (e.g., doctors, therapists or employees in the field of technology development). They have an individual knowledge (e.g., about relevant actors in the research field) and research-relevant social contacts (e.g., for the planning and organization of interviews). Co-researchers should carry out their own research tasks within the framework of participatory research. For this purpose, adequate trainings (e.g., for the development of questions, construction of interrogators, conducting surveys) is an unconditional prerequisite.

3.2 Methodological Implications

The co-researcher approach just described already constitutes a fundamental change in innovation-related methodological assessments. Yet, even in this constellation, it still can be challenging to avoid the risks of obtaining invalid (e.g., speculative) or biased (e.g., social desirability bias) responses. Asking questions about the acceptance of planned products or future behavior is largely ineffective, as individuals are little aware of the factors (e.g., emotions, situational and social cues) that drive their behavior (e.g., [8]), and furthermore tend to give socially desirable responses. People also cannot be expected to correctly report their knowledge levels [57] or anxiety [58]. Most notably, individuals completing adoption-related questionnaires typically are in a "forced exposure" situation, in which they were deliberately brought into contact with the innovation. In reality, however, most innovations already fail at the level of getting sufficient attention. This increases the likelihood that forced-exposure responses are a methodological artefact rather than valid evaluations [59]. Taken together, new approaches are needed that reduce the risks of obtaining invalid data. The major challenge will be to measure the stage-specific adoption determinants in a methodological sound way that reduces biased and inadvertently invalid responses, and also in a way that acknowledges the crucial role of attention and awareness processes for project success.

3.3 Communicative Implications

Professional communication should be perceived as an integral part of technology development, and as definitive prerequisite for project success. Not just with regard to internal project communication, which is not discussed here, but with regard to informing and persuading potential end users. It is vital that this communication matches the relevance frames, foreknowledge, and language of end users, and that it is adoption phase-specific. Achieving sufficient awareness for the solution, emphasizing rewarding aspects, and reducing or positively re-framing threatening or aversive aspects is likely among the most important goals of strategic innovation communication. As biased risk perceptions, defensive motivations and boomerang effects are commonly observed in the area of health promotion, these unwanted effects should be conceptually considered in the development process and minimized through adequate motivational and communication strategies. A suitable user inclusion is essential for learning about the perceived benefits and problems of the innovation, as well as learning about alternative use scenarios. Not only the development process profits greatly from valid user feedback, these insights are particularly beneficial for effective marketing strategies.

3.4 Outlook

Considering the dissatisfying low rate of health technology adoption, it seems essential to look for new ways for improving the development process and of facilitating adoption. Three general approaches were discussed in this paper: A more realistic understanding of human functioning and decision-making, a consideration of different stages of technology adoption, and a stronger focus on social, organizational and situational determinants. Broadly distinguishing individual, social/situational and technological factors as well as facilitating and inhibiting factors, several building blocks for more comprehensive and user-centered adoption models were elaborated. Implications for user acceptance assessment, user inclusion, and strategic communication were also discussed.

Although many of the suggested dimensions are already integrated in some existing models, a comprehensive theory that incorporates all these dimensions is still missing. Our hope is that this examination stimulates the discussion about adequate and inadequate conceptualizations of the process of health technology adoption, and about the significance of adequate communication strategies. Unsuccessful technology adoption is, after all, most likely the result of dysfunctional communication during or after the development process, and to a lesser degree a technological problem. We believe that technological excellence needs to be accompanied by communication excellence. Both skills require a realistic view of humans, sufficient knowledge about the process of technology adoption, and a decent understanding of the range of relevant determinants. Besides, this approach encourages transdisciplinary discourses between social sciences and technology research and development, and hopefully also an enhanced user inclusion in all relevant development processes.

References

1. Standing, C., Standing, S., McDermott, M.L., Gururajan, R., Mavi, R.K.: The paradoxes of telehealth: a review of the literature 2000–2015. Syst. Res. Behav. Sci. (2016). Advanced Online Publication. doi:10.1002/sres.2442
2. Zanaboni, P., Wootton, R.: Adoption of telemedicine: from pilot stage to routine delivery. BMC Med. Inf. Decis. Mak. **21**, 1–9 (2012). doi:10.1186/1472-6947-12-1
3. Venkatesh, V.: Technology acceptance model and the unified theory of acceptance and use of technology. Manag. Inf. Syst. **7**, 1–9 (2015). doi:10.1002/9781118785317.weom070047
4. Niklas, S.: Akzeptanz und Nutzung mobiler Applikationen [transl.: Acceptance and use of mobile applications]. Springer, Heidelberg (2015). doi:10.1007/978-3-658-08263-5
5. Rogers, E.M.: Diffusion of Innovations. The Free Press, New York (1983)
6. Kollmann, T.: Attitude, adoption or acceptance? Measuring the market success of telecommunication and multimedia technology. Int. J. Bus. Perform. Manag. **6**, 133–152 (2004). doi:10.1504/IJBPM.2004.005012
7. Bargh, J.A., Morsella, E.: The unconscious mind. Perspect. Psychol. Sci. **3**, 73–79 (2008). doi:10.1111/j.1745-6916.2008.00064.x
8. Nisbett, R.E., Wilson, T.D.: Telling more than we can know: verbal reports on mental processes. Psychol. Rev. **84**, 231–259 (1977). doi:10.1037/0033-295X.84.3.231
9. Al-Shawaf, L., Conroy-Beam, D., Asao, K., Buss, D.M.: Human emotions: an evolutionary psychological perspective. Emot. Rev. **8**(2), 173–186 (2015). doi:10.1177/1754073914565518
10. Barbour, J.B., Rintamaki, L.S., Ramsey, J.A., Brashers, D.E.: Avoiding health information. J. Health Commun. **17**(2), 212–229 (2011). doi:10.1080/10810730.2011.585691
11. van 't Riet, J., Ruiter, R.A.C.: Defensive reactions to health-promoting information: an overview and implications for future research. Health Psychol. Rev. **7**(Suppl. 1), 104–136 (2013). doi:10.1080/17437199.2011.606782

12. Nistor, N., Göğüş, A., Lerche, T.: Educational technology acceptance across national and professional cultures: a European study. Educ. Technol. Res. Develop. **61**(4), 733–749 (2013). doi:10.1007/s11423-013-9292-7

13. Gray, J.A.: The Neuropsychology of Anxiety: An Enquiry into the Functions of the Septo-hippocampal System. Oxford University Press, Oxford (1982)

14. Szalma, J.L.: On the application of motivation theory to human factors/ergonomics: motivational design principles for human-technology interaction. Hum. Factors **56**(8), 1453–1471 (2014). doi:10.1177/0018720814553471

15. Dewar, A.R., Bull, T.P., Malvey, D.M., Szalma, J.L.: Developing a measure of engagement with telehealth systems: the mHealth technology engagement index. J. Telemed. Telecare **23**, 248–255 (2017)

16. Ajzen, I.: The theory of planned behavior. Organ. Behav. Hum. Decis. Process. **50**, 179–211 (1991). doi:10.1016/0749-5978(91)90020-T

17. Witte, K.: Putting the fear back into fear appeals: the extended parallel process model. Commun. Monogr. **59**(4), 329–349 (1992). doi:10.1080/03637759209376276

18. Prochaska, J.O., Redding, C.A., Evers, K.E.: The transtheoretical model and stages of change. In: Glanz, K., Rimer, B.K., Viswanath, K. (eds.) Health Behavior and Health Education: Theory, Research, and Practice, pp. 97–121. Wiley, San Francisco (2008)

19. Schwarzer, R.: Modeling health behavior change: how to predict and modify the adoption and maintenance of health behaviors. Appl. Psychol. **57**(1), 1–29 (2008). doi:10.1111/j.1464-0597.2007.00325.x

20. Weinstein, N.D.: The precaution adoption process. Health Psychol. **7**(4), 355–386 (1988)

21. Deci, E.L., Ryan, R.M.: Self-determination theory. In: van Lange, P.A.M., Kruglanski, A.W., Higgins, E.T. (eds.) Handbook of Theories of Social Psychology, vol. 1, pp. 416–459. Sage, London (2012)

22. Armstrong, J.S.: Persuasive Advertising: Evidence-Based Principles. Palgrave Macmillan, New York (2010)

23. Hargie, O.: The Handbook of Communication Skills. Routledge, New York (2006)

24. Robinson, L., Cotten, S.R., Ono, H., Quan-Haase, A., Mesch, G., Chen, W., Stern, M.J.: Digital inequalities and why they matter. Inf. Commun. Soc. **18**, 569–582 (2015). doi:10.1080/1369118X.2015.1012532

25. Kiesler, D.J., Auerbach, S.M.: Optimal matches of patient preferences for information, decision-making and interpersonal behavior: evidence, models and interventions. Patient Educ. Counsel. **61**(3), 319–341 (2006). doi:10.1016/j.pec.2005.08.002

26. Case, D.O., Andrews, J.E., Johnson, J.D., Allard, S.L.: Avoiding versus seeking: the relationship of information seeking to avoidance, blunting, coping, dissonance, and related concepts. J. Med. Libr. Assoc. **93**(3), 353–362 (2005)

27. Byrne, S., Hart, P.S.: The 'Boomerang' effect: a synthesis of findings and a preliminary theoretical framework. In: Beck. C.S. (ed.) Communication Yearbook, vol. 33, pp. 3–38 (2009)

28. Rains, S.A.: The nature of psychological reactance revisited: a meta-analytic review. Hum. Commun. Res. **39**(1), 47–73 (2013). doi:10.1111/j.1468-2958.2012.01443.x

29. Bischoff, H.-J.: Risks in Modern Society. Springer, New York (2008)

30. Das, E.: Rethinking the role of affect in health communication. Eur. Health Psychol. **14**(2), 27–31 (2012)

31. Hastall, M.R.: Well-being in the context of health communication and health education. In: Reinecke, L., Oliver, M.B. (eds.) Handbook of Media Use and Well-Being: International Perspectives on Theory and Research on Positive Media Effects, pp. 317–328. Routledge, London (2016)

32. Dockweiler, C., Wewer, A., Beckers, R.: Alters- und geschlechtersensible Nutzerorientierung zur Förderung der Akzeptanz telemedizinischer Verfahren bei Patientinnen und Patienten [transl.: Age- and gender-sensitive user orientation for promoting acceptance of telemedicine from the patients' perspective.]. In: Hornberg, C., Pauli, A., Wrede, B. (eds.) Medizin - Gesundheit – Geschlecht [transl.: Medicine – Health – Gender], pp. 299–321. Wiesbaden, VS (2016)

33. Cooper, A., Gomez, R., Aucote, H.: The behavioural inhibition system and behavioural approach system (BIS/BAS) scales: measurement and structural invariance across adults and adolescents. Pers. Individ. Differ. 43(2), 295–305 (2007). doi:10.1016/j.paid.2006.11.023

34. Rahman, M.S.: Does personality matter when we are sick? An empirical study of the role of personality traits and health emotion in healthcare technology adoption decision. In: Proceedings of the 50th Hawaii International Conference on System Sciences, pp. 3357–3366 (2017). http://hdl.handle.net/10125/41565

35. Svendsen, G.B., Johnsen, J.A.K., Almas-Sorensen, L., Vitterso, J.: Personality and technology acceptance: the influence of personality factors on the core constructs of the technology acceptance model. Behav. Inf. Technol. 32, 323–334 (2013). doi:10.1080/0144929x.2011.553740

36. Hirsh, J.B., Kang, S.K., Bodenhausen, G.V.: Personalized persuasion: tailoring persuasive appeals to recipients' personality traits. Psychol. Sci. 23(6), 578–581 (2012). doi:10.1177/0956797611436349

37. Gagnon, M.P., Desmartis, M., Labrecque, M., Car, J., Pagliari, C., Pluye, P., Frémont, P., Gagnon, J., Tremblay, N., Légaré, F.: Systematic review of factors influencing the adoption of information and communication technologies by healthcare professionals. J. Med. Syst. 29, 241–277 (2012). doi:10.1007/s10916-010-9473-4

38. Dockweiler, C.; Filius, J.; Dockweiler, U.; Hornberg, C.: Adoption telemedizinischer Leistungen in der poststationären Schlaganfallversorgung: Eine qualitative Analyse der Adoptionsfaktoren aus Sicht von Patientinnen und Patienten [transl.: Adoption of Telemedicine Services in Post-Hospital Stroke Care: A Qualitative Analysis of Factors Influencing the Adoption from a Patient's Perspective]. Akt. Neurol. 42(2), 197–204 (2015). doi:10.1055/s-0035-1548876

39. Bandiera, O., Rasul, I.: Social networks and technology adoption in Northern Mozambique. Econ. J. 116(514), 869–902 (2006). doi:10.1111/j.1468-0297.2006.01115.x

40. Cresswell, K., Sheikh, A.: Organizational issues in the implementation and adoption of health information technology innovations: an interpretative review. Int. J. Med. Inf. 82(5), 73–86 (2013). doi:10.1016/j.ijmedinf.2012.10.007

41. Holden, R.J., Karsh, B.-T.: The technology acceptance model. Its past and its future In Health Care. J. Biomed. Inf. 43(1), 159 (2010). doi:10.1016/j.jbi.2009.07.002

42. Keshavjee, K., Bosomworth, J., Copen, J., Lai, J., Kucukyazici, B., Lilani, R., Holbrook, A.M.: Best practices in EMR implementation: a systematic review. In: AMIA Annual Symposium Proceedings/AMIA Symposium, p. 982 (2006)

43. Ingebrigtsen, T., Georgiou, A., Clay-Williams, R., Magrabi, F., Hordern, A., Prgomet, M., Li, J., Westbrook, J., Braithwaite, J.: The impact of clinical leadership on health information technology adoption: systematic review. Int. J. Med. Inf. 83(6), 393–405 (2014)

44. Leppert, F., Dockweiler, C., Eggers, N., Webel, K., Hornberg, C., Greiner, W.: Financial conditions as influencing factors for telemonitoring acceptance by healthcare professionals in Germany. Value Health 17(7), 422–423 (2014). doi:10.1016/j.jval.2014.08.1045

45. Hofstede, G.: Culture's Consequences: Comparing Values, Behaviors, Institutions and Organizations Across Nations. Sage, Thousand Oaks (2001)

46. Hofstede, G., McCrae, R.R.: Personality and culture revisited: linking traits and dimensions of culture. Cross-Cult. Res. **38**(1), 52–88 (2004). doi:10.1177/1069397103259443

47. Dockweiler, C., Hornberg, C.: Die Rolle psychologischer und technikbezogener Persönlichkeitsmerkmale sowie individueller Wissensbestände von Ärztinnen und Ärzten für die Adoption des Telemonitoring in der medizinischen Versorgung [transl.: The Role of Psychological and Technology-Related Personality Traits and Knowledge Levels as Factors Influencing Adoption of Telemonitoring by Medical Professionals]. Gesundheitswesen (2015). doi:10.1055/s-0035-1564266

48. Knipper, M.: Verstehen oder Stigmatisieren? Die Krux mit der "Kultur" in Medizin und Public Health [transl.: Understanding or stigmatizing? The crux with "culture" in medicine and public health]. Pub. Health Forum **23**(2), 97–99 (2015). doi:10.1515/pubhef-2015-0036

49. Zayed, R., Davidson, B., Nadeau, L., Callanan, T.S., Fleisher, W., Hope-Ross, L., Lazier, L.: Canadian rural/remote primary care physicians perspectives on child/adolescent mental health care service delivery. J. Can. Acad. Child Adolesc. Psychiatry **25**(1), 1–24 (2016)

50. Bullinger, A., Rass, M., Adamczyk, S., Moeslein, K.M., Sohn, S.: Open innovation in health care: analysis of an open health platform. Health Pol. **2**–3(105), 165–175 (2012). doi:10.1016/j.healthpol.2012.02.009

51. Cornwall, A.: Unpacking 'Participation' models, meanings and practices. Commun. Develop. J. **43**(4), 269–283 (2008). doi:10.1093/cdj/bsn010

52. Von Unger, H.: Partizipative Forschung: Einführung in die Forschungspraxis [transl.: Participatory research: An introduction to research practice]. Springer, Wiesbaden (2014)

53. Wright, M.T., von Unger, H., Block, M.: Partizipation der Zielgruppe in der Gesundheitsförderung und Prävention [transl.: Participation in target groups for health promotion and prevention]. In: Wright, M.T. (ed.) Partizipative Qualitätsentwicklung in der Gesundheitsförderung und Prävention [transl.: Participatory Quality Development in Health Promotion and Prevention], pp. 35–52. Hans Huber Verlag, Bern (2010)

54. Bergold, J., Thomas, S.: Partizipative Forschungsmethoden: Ein methodischer Ansatz in Bewegung [transl.: Participatory research methods: A methodological approach in motion]. Forum Qual. Soc. Res. **13**(1), 1–24 (2012). http://www.qualitative-research.net/index.php/fqs/article/view/1801/3332

55. Blackstock, K.L., Kelly, G.J., Horsey, B.L.: Developing and applying a framework to evaluate participatory research for sustainability. J. Evol. Econ. **60**(4), 726–742 (2007). doi:10.1016/j.ecolecon.2006.05.014

56. Mockford, C., Murray, M., Seers, K., Oyebode, J., Grant, R., Boex, S., Staniszewska, S., Diment, Y., Leach, J., Sharma, U., Clarke, R., Suleman, R.: A SHARED study-the benefits and costs of setting up a health research study involving lay co-researchers and how we overcame the challenges. Res. Involvement Engagem. **2**(8), 1–12 (2016). doi:10.1186/s40900-016-0021-3

57. Kruger, J., Dunning, D.: Unskilled and unaware of it: how difficulties in recognizing one's own incompetence lead to inflated self-assessments. J. Pers. Soc. Psychol. **77**(6), 1121–1134 (1999). doi:10.1037/0022-3514.77.6.1121

58. Sparks, G.G., Pellechia, M., Irvine, C.: The repressive coping style and fright reactions to mass media. Commun. Res. **26**(2), 176–192 (1999). doi:10.1177/009365099026002004

59. Hastall, M.R., Knobloch-Westerwick, S.: Caught in the act: measuring selective exposure to experimental online stimuli. Commun. Methods Meas. **7**(2), 94–105 (2013). doi:10.1080/19312458.2012.761190

Ergonomic Evaluation of the Portal of the Repository in the Health Area of UNIFESP: Proposal of Specifications and Ergonomic Recommendations for Its Interface

Wilma Honorio dos Santos[1(✉)], Luciano Gamez[2(✉)], and Felipe Mancini[3(✉)]

[1] Department of Informatics in Health, UNIFESP, São Paulo, Brazil
wilma.honorio@unifesp.br
[2] UAB, UNIFESP, São Paulo, Brazil
lucianogamez@gmail.com
[3] Department of Informatics in Health, UAB, UNIFESP, São Paulo, Brazil
fmancini@unifesp.br

Abstract. The Internet, together with the Digital Information and Communication Technologies (DICT), make it possible to create digital documents (DD) that are responsible for the preservation of cultural heritage, dissemination of information and strengthen the construction of knowledge. These DD allow a wide production, dissemination and preservation of information and, with the help of DICT, enable the communication between researchers and scientists, especially regarding the sharing of research results. Digital repositories are informational environments for managing and controlling the scientific and academic production of institutions and/or communities. They offer advantages such as unrestricted access, data interoperability and long-term information preservation. However, they may have gaps such as browsing failures, poor usability and accessibility, limited searches, poor disclosure of the environment, and little or no use of customizable services. In 2015, the institutional digital repository of the Federal University of São Paulo (UNIFESP) was implemented the digital repository in the health area of UNIFESP (RDUNIFESP). Their construction was not user-centered, prototyping tests were not performed, the authors felt difficulty in their navigation and, therefore, it is important to apply an ergonomic evaluation in the RDUNIFESP using the inspection techniques and usability tests, with the objective of supporting users in the development of their activities in a productive, intuitive and safe way. In this way, this work will evaluate and identify points of suitability and inadequacy of usability in RDUNIFESP, and propose specifications and ergonomic recommendations and contribute to the improvement of its interface.

Keywords: Ergonomics · Usability · Institutional digital repositories

1 Introduction

The use of the internet as an educational support tool is increasingly frequent and its application supports the teaching-learning process. The internet, together with the

© Springer International Publishing AG 2017
M. Antona and C. Stephanidis (Eds.): UAHCI 2017, Part III, LNCS 10279, pp. 26–38, 2017.
DOI: 10.1007/978-3-319-58700-4_3

Digital Information and Communication Technologies (DICT), make it possible to create digital documents (DD) [1–3]. The DD, according to the United Nations Educational, Scientific and Cultural Organization (UNESCO) are responsible for the preservation of cultural heritage and defined as cultural constructions and contain views and worldviews for current and future generations [4]. Thus, they enable the dissemination of information and strengthen the construction of knowledge [1–3].

These DD allow a wide production, dissemination and preservation of information and, with the help of DICT, enable the communication between researchers and scientists, especially with regard to the sharing of research results [3, 5–7].

In order to ensure the preservation and access of these DDs, digital repositories (DRs) have emerged, which make it possible to store, organize, manage and access scientific and academic production, manage communities and scientific collections [8].

Institutional digital repositories (IDRs) provide insight into the institution, data interoperability, control and storage of scientific output, long-term information preservation, self-archiving, open access, decreased publication costs [8].

According to Camargo and Vidotti [8]; and Soares [9] or the construction of an RD should be considered navigation requirements, usability and accessibility, searches, disclosure of the environment and customizable services. Therefore, DRs should be evaluated in terms of ergonomics and usability in order to obtain an effective interaction between the user and the material available in an digital repository (DR) and its interface [9, 10]. Among the different tools available to assist in the DR assessment is Possible to evaluate the ease, speed and degree of satisfaction of the users in front of the DR interface [9–11].

Often, its construction was not user-centered, prototyping tests were not performed, so it is important to apply an ergonomic evaluation [12–14], In the Institutional digital repository (IDR) using the inspection techniques and usability tests, with the objective of supporting users in the development of their activities in a productive, intuitive and safe way [15].

Traditionally recognized as a specialized institution in the field of Health Sciences, the Federal University of São Paulo (UNIFESP) was created on December 15, 1994, resulting from the transformation of the Escola Paulista de Medicina (founded on July 15, 1933). It has until that date 6 campuses and 54 courses in the areas of human sciences, exact and biological.

In 2015, the IDR of UNIFESP was implemented as a result of the implementation of a project of the UNIFESP Library Network Coordination (CRBU), the digital repository in the health area of UNIFESP (RDUNIFESP).

2   Theoretical Reference

2.1   Digital Documents (DD)

UNESCO defines DD as cultural constructions and contains world views and visions for current and future generations and is responsible for the preservation of this heritage [4].

The concern with the preservation of DD in Brazilian institutions arose at the beginning of this century, around 2001, with the restructuring of the Technical Chamber of Electronic Documents of the National Council of Archives (CTDE/CONARQ). In 2010, this Technical Chamber published *e-Arq Brasil*, adopted by the National File System (SINAR), which details requirements and fundamental metadata for the development of computerized systems for DD management [16].

DD preservation must be grounded in planning, resource allocation, application of conservation methods and technologies necessary to ensure the original and inherent characteristics of the archival document so that it remains accessible in usable in the long term [17].

In this context, strategies should be applied to preserve these DD to guarantee access, reliability, and integrity of documents [3, 18].

Thus, the creation of a DD preservation policy assumes importance and goes beyond the presentation of only technical and definitive solutions. The DD preservation and management policy must have the ethical commitment to preserve, from public interest criteria, explicit and open for general consultation, documents and their accessibility [4, 17]. This involves information, management and archiving policies of the institution [19].

2.2   Digital Repositories (DR)

With the increase in the production of information in DD format, it becomes important to guarantee its availability and preservation over time. This concern involves both the data producers and the bodies holding this information [3].

In this context the DRs were created, which are informational environments for the storage and management of DD that allow the organization and access of scientific and academic production, the management of scientific communities and collections [20]. These facilitate the implementation of preservation policies and strategies [21].

According to the National Council of Archives (CONARQ) [20], the DR should: manage documents and metadata in accordance with archival practices and standards, specifically related to document management, multi-level archival description and preservation, and protect the characteristics of the archival document, especially authenticity (identity and integrity) and relationship Between documents.

The DR have processes and functions similar to those of digital libraries and also allow the self-archiving and interoperability between various information systems due to the collection of metadata in open files [8].

A reliable digital repository must be able to comply with archival procedures, keep digital materials authentic, preserve them and provide access to them for as long as necessary, and fulfill that mission according to the report "Trusted Digital Repositories: attributes and responsibilities" [20].

An DR can be: Thematic (TDR), when it focuses on a certain area of knowledge or Institutional (IDR), when it is a set of services offered by a certain institution, focused on the dissemination of local scientific production, Research and teaching of academic communities, theses, dissertations, etc.

Regardless of the type, the DRs must be able to organize and retrieve the DDs in order to maintain the organic relationship between them. In this sense, they should support the hierarchical organization of the DD, based on a classification plan of documents, and the multilevel description, in accordance with the international standard for archival description, the International Standard of Archival Description (ISADG) and the Brazilian Standard Of Archival Description (NOBRADE) [20].

DRs are one of the strategies proposed by the Open Access Movement to promote scientific literature in a freeway and without access costs. The number of institutional and thematic repositories created by the world is increasing. In Brazil, this growth was accelerated by the IBICT-FINEP/PCAL/XBDB project, which enabled the implementation of 40 institutional repositories in several universities and institutions of research. With the dissemination and consequent awareness of the Open Access Movement to scientific information, several Brazilian institutions have been dedicated to the creation of open access digital repositories. The project had its first public announcement launched in 2009 and included 27 institutions, in addition to five of the pilot project. Other edicts have since been launched to assist research institutions and universities in building their own institutional or thematic repositories [22].

Among the advantages of DRs are that they provide visibility for the institution, data interoperability, control and storage of scientific production, long-term preservation of information, self-archiving, free access, reduction of publication costs [8].

2.3 Institutional Digital Repositories (IDRs)

According to Leite [23], Academic institutions around the world use RDI and open access to manage and provide scientific support for scientific information from research and teaching activities. In this sense, they have been intensely used to: improve the internal and external scientific communication of the institution; Maximize the accessibility, use, visibility and impact of the institution's scientific output; Feedback on scientific research activity and support teaching and learning processes; Support the institution's electronic scientific publications; Contribute to the preservation of scientific or academic digital content produced by the institution or its members; Contribute to increasing the prestige of the institution and the researcher; Provide input for the evaluation and monitoring of scientific production; And, to gather, store, organize, recover and disseminate the scientific production of the institution.

Like universities, IDRs are now rated by rankings. Being well positioned in a ranking leads to greater visibility and prestige. This prestige can facilitate the development of the repositories, in terms of internal management and obtaining external resources. The Web of Repositories Ranking is a system of most known rankings today and evaluates the DRs of scientific information. In addition to producing data for measuring and comparing system development, rankings have produced quality indicators that should be considered [24].

Still according to Leite [23], The adoption and effective use of RDI functionalities can result in a number of benefits that are perceived by different segments of the target audience (researchers, academic administrators, librarians, department heads, the university as a whole, the community Scientific, among others).

2.4   Digital Repository in the Health Area of UNIFESP (RDUNIFESP)

In 2015, the IDR of UNIFESP was implemented, resulting from the execution of a project of the Coordination of the Network of Libraries of UNIFESP. It is the digital repository in the health area of UNIFESP (RDUNIFESP), a portal for the storage and access to intellectual production of UNIFESP.

RDUNIFESP is available on the *url:* http://www.repositorio.unifesp.br in Portuguese, English and Spanish. Contains publications from 1939 and until the beginning of 2017, more than 40,000 scientific papers, more than 8400 master's dissertations, more than 6300 doctoral theses are stored and available to access, among other publications such as biographies, letters, editorials, errata, Books and news and allows the search of publications by date, author, title, keyword and communities of UNIFESP.

This IRD uses the DSpace platform (Digital Institutional Repository Building System) that allows the creation of digital repositories with storage functions, management, preservation and visibility of intellectual production, allowing its adoption by other institutions in federated consortium form. The system is customizable and allows the management of scientific production in any type of digital material.

The Fig. 1 below shows the IRD Ranking of Universities in Brazil and those that precede the position of UNIFESP.

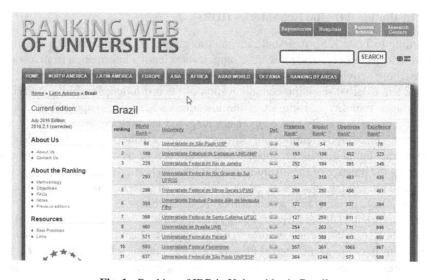

Fig. 1.   Ranking of IDR in Universities in Brazil

The Figs. 2, 3 and 4 show the position of RDUNIFESP in the ranking of IDR: in Brazil, America, Latin America, Brincs and worldwide.

Brazil

Ranking	World Ranking	University	Det.	Country	Presence	Impact	Openness	Excellence
11	637	Universidade Federal de São Paulo UNIFESP			364	1244	573	588

Fig. 2. Position of UNIFESP in the IDR ranking of Universities in Brazil

America

Ranking	World Ranking	University	Det.	Country	Presence	Impact	Openness	Excellence
223	637	Universidade Federal de São Paulo UNIFESP			364	1244	573	588

Latin America

Ranking	World Ranking	University	Det.	Country	Presence	Impact	Openness	Excellence
20	637	Universidade Federal de São Paulo UNIFESP			364	1244	573	588

Brics

Ranking	World Ranking	University	Det.	Country	Presence	Impact	Openness	Excellence
65	637	Universidade Federal de São Paulo UNIFESP			364	1244	573	588

Fig. 3. Position of UNIFESP in the IDR ranking of Universities in the Americas, Latin America and BRICS

WORLD RANKING

World Rank	University	Det.	Country	Presence	Impact	Openness	Excellence
637	Universidade Federal de São Paulo UNIFESP			364	1244	573	588

Fig. 4. Position of UNIFESP in the IDR ranking of Universities in the world

2.5 Ergonomics

The term ergonomics means the study of the laws of labor and can be defined as the scientific study of the relationship between man and his means, methods and work spaces, and how senses and motor skills enable people to use machines and tools [9, 25].

Its objective is to elaborate, through the contribution of several scientific disciplines that compose it, a body of knowledge that, from an application perspective, should result in a better adaptation to the human being of the technological means, of the work and life environments [15, 25]. And seeks to reduce or eliminate occupational hazards to health and also improve working conditions, in order to avoid an increase in fatigue caused by the high global workload in its various dimensions: physical load, derived from muscular effort, load Psychic and cognitive load [12].

2.6 Cognitive Ergonomics

With the wide use of computers, the study of ergonomics was expanded to analyze the mental capacity that enables people to produce, retrieve and understand information generated by the DICT and gave rise to cognitive ergonomics [9, 12], And it is concerned with the aspects of the mental activity performed by the user in a given activity and seeks to optimize the effort expended to understand and develop the task, as well as to facilitate the mental process for decision making and execution of a given action [12, 15, 26].

2.7 Mental Load of Work

All elements of the interface should reduce the cognitive and perceptual load of the user, and increase the efficiency of the dialogue. Thus, the greater the mental workload, the greater the likelihood of making mistakes and the fewer actions required, the faster the interactions [9].

2.8 Usability

Interfaces are computational resources that allow the interaction of the user with the system, that is, allow its use in different tasks and its usability is considered a critical factor of success and acceptance of the product by its users [15, 27].

According to Nielsen, usability is a requirement of software quality required and required to achieve the quality of a computer system allowing it to be usable and easy to learn. A system that has good usability rates allows its users to use it in a satisfactory, pleasant and productive way and thus, reaches its goal [13] And its main goal is to ensure that devices and systems are tailored in ways the user thinks, behaves and works, and thus provides usability [12, 15].

There are three standards that specify usability characteristics.

- ISO 9241 defines usability as the ability of an interactive system to offer its user within a specific context of accomplishing their tasks with effectiveness (completeness), and efficiency (better resources) and satisfaction (user well-being) [28].
- ISO/IEC 9126-1 defines the quality of use of a software product used in a context-specific environment and makes it possible to quantify whether user objectives have been achieved in the software environment [29].

- ISO 13047 standard defines a design process and dictates guidelines for the software to be developed focused on the user, facilitating the user's operation and, consequently, a greater usability of the software [30].

An interface that has good usability avoids that its user has to learn complex procedures, helps in memorizing the activities in the system, guides in the exploration of its content, protects against errors and facilitates procedures and reduces the physical and mental load of the user, the time taken to perform a task [12].

2.9 Repositories, Cognitive Ergonomics and Usability

In order to obtain an effective interaction between the user and the material available in an DR, its interface must aggregate usability concepts, which is the quality related to ease of use and learning, and ergonomics, which is the quality of adaptation of An interface to the user profile [5, 8, 9, 14, 17, 21, 26, 31–33].

A high degree of usability of an interface reflects on users performing tasks with ease, speed and satisfaction [10, 12, 13, 15, 26, 31].

Studies carried out in DRs show that they may have gaps such as navigation failures, low usability, limited searches, poor disclosure of the environment, and little or no use of customizable services [5, 8, 17, 21, 34–36].

2.10 Methodologies for Usability Evaluation

The usability evaluation can be performed in two ways: usability testing and usability inspection.

The usability test refers to systematic activities with the objective of verifying how a person or a group of people interact with the application and how it interferes positively or negatively in their activities, i.e., its main intention is to verify the interaction capacity Provided by the user interface [12–14].

These tests enable the evaluator to identify problems of system interaction with the user and, in most cases, with the participation of people directly involved with the use of image and verbalization (Think Aloud) [12, 13]. And are performed in the form of interaction scenarios where the user follows specific and predetermined tasks [31].

The usability inspection refers to activities that aim to verify if an interface conforms to a certain quality standard such as the Ergonomic Criteria of Dominique Scapin and Christian Batien [26] or the Heuristics of Jackob Nielsen [13] and is performed through checklists.

2.11 Population and Sample

It is important and fundamental that the sample intentionally determined by convenience, with the selection of users whose profile contemplates the frequent use of the informational system [37–40].

Besides that, Landauer and Nielsen [41] Show that the number of usability problems encountered (n) in a usability test with users, when evaluating an already developed and deployed information system is:

$$n = N(1 - (1 - L)^N)$$

Where N is the total number of usage problems at creation and L is the proportion of usage problems detected during a single user test. In several studies, these authors found an average L value of 31%. In this context, we have as the determination of the curve of L = 31% the following result in Fig. 5:

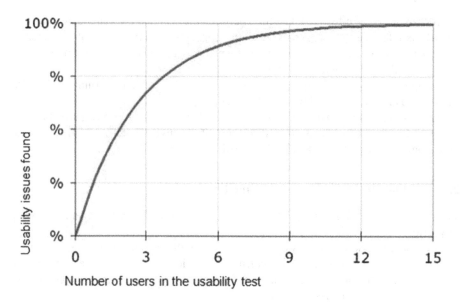

Fig. 5. Usability evaluation according to number of participating users

The first user who performs the usability test shows nearly one-third of the usability issues of the informational system. The second user will display the same information system usability issues encountered by the first user and some other problems.

So, it happens with the third and fourth user and finally we have the fifth user, which makes it reach the mark of finding 100% usability problems of the informational system.

Therefore, the authors of this study recommend that 5 users participate in the evaluation, according to them, this number presents the best cost-benefit ratio, considering users of a group with a single profile [41].

When users of more than one profile category participate in the usability test, 3 users must be chosen for each profile category to ensure coverage of the diversity of behavior within the group [41].

3   Materials and Methods

A qualitative research can be used, with a case study approach to apply usability (predictive) and usability (experimental) and quantitative techniques, also with a case study approach, in the usability test to evaluate The time spent by each user of the sample population to complete each task.

3.1   Apply the Usability Inspection Technique in RDUNIFESP

The step of applying the usability inspection technique in the RDUNIFESP can be performed with the application of the ergonomic inspection checklist, determined from a list of ergonomics criteria, in order to previously analyze the interface of this system and identify points of low Usability in RDUNIFESP to subsidize the next step.

3.2   Apply the Usability Test Technique in RDUNIFESP

The application of the usability test technique in RDUNIFESP is based on the results obtained in the previous subsection. Interaction scenarios are created with tasks to be performed by frequent users of this IDR.

An empirical qualitative research, centered on the user, the evaluation of the experimental analysis is performed on the collection of the data obtained in the observation of users, considering requirements to be fulfilled in the tasks created in the interaction scenarios.

An experimental quantitative evaluation of user observation data collection will be performed as described in ISO 924 [28] On the time taken to complete each task from the screen capture logs.

The quantitative evaluation of the time spent by each user of the sample population to complete each task allows greater precision in the analysis and interpretation of the results, thus trying to increase the confidence margin regarding the inferences of the results found [12–14, 37].

3.3   Identify Points of Suitability and Unsuitability of Usability in RDUNIFESP

The identification and listing of points of suitability and unsuitability of usability in the RDUNIFESP will be accomplished through the qualitative experimental analysis, obtained in the previous subsection.

3.4   Suggest a Set of Specifications and Recommendations for Improving the Usability of IDR

This step to suggest a set of specifications and recommendations for improving the usability of the IDR is performed based on the list of suitability points and usability mismatches obtained in the previous subsection.

4   Contributions

The main technological contributions are the identification and listing of points of adequacy and inadequacy, as well as to suggest a set of specifications and recommendations for improvement of the usability of IDRs.

The main scientific contributions are the dissemination of empirical results with the approach and focus on the usability evaluation, and the creation of a set of specifications and recommendations for the creation and evaluation of IDRs.

References

1. Bartholo, V.F., Amaral, M.A., Cagnin, M.I.: Uma Contribuição para a Adaptabilidade de Ambientes Virtuais de Aprendizagem para Dispositivos Móveis. Rev. Bras. Informática Na Educ. 17(2), 36–47 (2009)
2. Silva, J.B., Rochadel, W., Marcelino, R.: Utilização de NTIC's Aplicadas a Dispositivos Móveis. IEEE-RITA 7(3), 149–154 (2012)
3. Arellano, M.A.: Preservação de documentos digitais. Rev. Ci Inf. 33(2), 15–27 (2004)
4. Funari, P.P.A.: Gestão, preservação e acesso a documentos digitais: patrimônio cultural e diversidade. Rev. Cad. Ceom. 18(22), 213–230 (2014)
5. Ferreira, S.M.S.P.: Repositório institucional em comunicação: o projeto REPOSCOM implementado junto à federação de bibliotecas digitais em Ciências da Comunicação 10.5007/1518-2924.2007 v12nesp1p77. Encontros Bibli Rev. Eletrônica Bibl. E Ciênc. Informação 12(1), 77–94 (2007)
6. Gonçalves, L.S., Scandelari, V., Peres, A.M.: Competências em informática em enfermagem em cenários da prática profissional: uma revisão integrativa. In: Anais e Programação do Simpósio Internacional em Informática em Enfermagem – SIIEnf. São Paulo (2012)
7. Marin, H.F.: Nursing informatics education in the South: a Brazilian experience. IMIA Yearb. 5, 68–71 (2010)
8. Camargo, L.S.A., Vidotti, S.B.G.: Uma estratégia de avaliação em repositórios digitais. In: XV Nacional de Bibliotecas Universitárias, São Paulo (2008)
9. Soares, S.: Elaboração de materiais científicos educacionais multimídia na área da saúde utilizando conceitos de design gráfico de interfaces, usabilidade e ergonomia (2015). http://dspace.c3sl.ufpr.br/dspace/handle/1884/38174. citado 2015 out 29
10. Afonso, A.P., Lima, J.R., Cota, M.P.: A heuristic evaluation of usability of web interfaces. IEEE Information Systems and Technology, CISTI 2012, pp. 1–6
11. LABIUTIL/UFSC: Laboratório Util. Universidade Fed. St. Catarina. www.labiutil.inf.ufsc.br
12. Cybis, W., Betiol, A., Faust, R.: Ergonomia e Usabilidade: conhecimentos, métodos e aplicações, 2º edn. Novatec, São Paulo (2010)
13. Nielsen, J.: Heuristic evaluation. In: Nielsen, J., Mack, R. (eds.) Usability Inspection Methods. Nova Iorque (EUA), pp. 25–62. Willey, New York (1994)
14. Rogers, Y., Preece, J., Sharp, H.: Design de interação: além da interação homem-computador. Bookman, Porto Alegre (2013)
15. Gamez, L.: A construção da coerência em cenários pedagógicos online: uma metodologia para apoiar a transformação de cursos presenciais que migram para a modalidade de educação à distância (2004)
16. Innarelli, H.C.: Preservação digital: a influência da gestão dos documentos digitais na preservação da informação e da cultura. Rev. Digit. Bibl. E Ciênc. Informação 8(2), 72–87 (2011)

17. Santos, H.M., Flores, D.: Repositórios digitais confiáveis para documentos arquivísticos: ponderações sobre a preservação em longo prazo. Perspect. Em Ciênc. Informação 20(2), 198–218 (2015)
18. Ferreira, A.M.A.: Proposta de implantação de uma estrutura de armazenamento por objetos para preservação documental no Tribunal de Contas do Estado do Tocantins (2014)
19. Almeida, M.B., Cendón, B.V., Souza, R.: Metodologia para implantação de programas de preservação de documentos digitais a longo prazo. Rev. Eletrônica Bibl. E Ciênc. Informação 17(34), 103–130 (2012)
20. Conselho Nacional de Arquivosnal de arquivos (CONARQ). Diretrizes para a implementação de repositórios digitais confiáveis de documentos arquivísticos (2014)
21. Sayão, L.F.: Repositórios digitais confiáveis para a preservação de periódicos eletrônicos científicos. PontodeAcesso 4(3), 68–94 (2011)
22. IBICT: Instituto Brasileironde Informação em Ciência e Tecnologia. Repositórios Digitais [Internet] (2016). http://www.ibict.br/informacao-para-ciencia-tecnologia-e-inovacao%20/repositorios-digitais/historico. Citado 13 mar 2016
23. Leite, F.C.L.: Como gerenciar e ampliar a visibilidade da informação científica brasileira: Repositórios institucionais de acesso aberto. IBICT, Brasília (2009)
24. Leite, F.C.L., Amaro, B., Batista, T., Costa, M.: Boas práticas para a construção de repositórios institucionais da produção científica. IBICT, Brasília (2012)
25. IEA: International Ergonomics Association. What is ergonomics [Internet]. http://www.iea.cc/browse.php?contID=what_is_ergonomics. Citado 28 out 2015
26. Scapin, D., Bastien, J.M.C.: Ergonomic criteria for evaluating the ergonomic quality of interactive systems. Behav. Inf. Technol. BIT 16(4), 220–223 (1997)
27. Coleti, T.A.: Um ambiente de avaliação da usabilidade de software apoiado por técnicas de processamento de imagens e reconhecimento de fala (2014)
28. ISO: International Organization for Standardization, ISO 9241-11. Define a usabilidade como uma medida que indica o quanto um produto de software pode ser utilizado para alcançar os objetivos do usuário de forma eficaz, eficiente e com satisfação dentro um contexto de uso específico (1998)
29. ISO: International Organization for Standardization. ISO/IEC 9126. Define a qualidade de uso de um produto de software (2001)
30. ISO: International Organization for Standardization, ISO 13047. Define um processo de projeto em que o software a ser desenvolvido deve ter o usuário como o foco central, facilitando a operação do software (1999)
31. Prates, R.O., Barbosa, S.D.J.: Avaliação de Interfaces de Usuário–Conceitos e Métodos [Internet]. In: Jornada de Atualização em Informática do Congresso da Sociedade Brasileira de Computação, Capítulo (2003). http://homepages.dcc.ufmg.br/~rprates/ge_vis/cap6_vfinal.pdf. Citado 3 dez 2015
32. Winckler, M., Pimenta, M.S.: Avaliação de usabilidade de sites web. Esc. Informática SBC SUL ERI 2002 Ed Porto Alegre Soc. Bras. Comput. SBC 1, 85–137 (2002)
33. Rodrigues E, Almeida M, Miranda Â, Guimarães AX, Castro D. RepositóriUM: criação e desenvolvimento do Repositório Institucional da Universidade do Minho (2004). http://repositorium.sdum.uminho.pt/handle/1822/422. Citado 27 out 2015
34. Sales, E.S.M., Bezerra, E.P., Pereira, H.B.D.B.: Biblioteca digital SCOL: organização, gestão e difusão do conhecimento científico através de objetos de aprendizagem SCORM. Digital library SCOL: organization, management and diffusion of the scientific knowledge through learning objects SCORM [Internet] (2013). http://repositorios.questoesemrede.uff.br/repositorios/handle/123456789/634. Citado 12 nov 2015

35. Bohmerwald, P.: Uma proposta metodológica para avaliação de bibliotecas digitais: usabilidade e comportamento de busca por informação na Biblioteca Digital da PUC-Minas. Ciênc. Informação Brasília **34**(1), 95–105 (2005)

36. Veiga, V.S.D.O., Pimenta, D.N., Machado, R., da Silva, A., da Silva, C.H.: Repositórios institucionais: avaliação da usabilidade na Fundação Oswaldo Cruz. XIV Encontro Nac. Pesqui. Em Ciênc. Informação ENANCIB 2013 GT 11 Informação E Saúde [Internet] (2013). http://www.arca.fiocruz.br/xmlui/handle/icict/8599. Citado 2 mar 2016

37. Baptista, S.G., da Cunha, M.B.: Estudo de usuários: visão global dos métodos de coleta de dados. Perspect. Em Ciênc. Informação **12**(2), 168–184 (2007)

38. Martins, A.I., Queirós, A., Rocha, N.P., Santos, B.S.: Avaliação de usabilidade: uma revisão sistemática da literatura. RISTI-Rev. Ibérica Sist. E Tecnol. Informação **11**, 31–43 (2013)

39. Fernandes, P., Rivero, L., Bonifácio, B., Santos, D., Conte, T.: Avaliando uma nova Abordagem para Inspeção de Usabilidade através de Análise Quantitativa e Qualitativa. In: VIII Workshop Latino Americano de Engenharia de Software Experimental pp. 67–76 (2011)

40. Scomparin, S.E.M.H.: Definição de requisitos para montagem de um laboratório experimental de avalição de Interação Humano Computador. http://www.especializacaoemweb.uem.br/site/files/tcc/2005/Selma%20Elaine%20Marques%20Hidae%20Scomparin%20-%20Definicao%20de%20Requisitos%20para%20Montagem%20de%20um%20Laboratorio%20Experimental%20de%20Avaliacao%20de%20Interacao%20Humano-Computador.pdf. Citado 2 mar 2016

41. Nielsen, J.: Why you only need to test with 5 users [Internet] (2000). http://www.useit.com/alertbox/20000319.html. Citado 1 mar 2016

Hearables in Hearing Care: Discovering Usage Patterns Through IoT Devices

Benjamin Johansen[1]([✉]), Yannis Paul Raymond Flet-Berliac[1],
Maciej Jan Korzepa[1], Per Sandholm[3], Niels Henrik Pontoppidan[2],
Michael Kai Petersen[1,2], and Jakob Eg Larsen[1]

[1] Department of Applied Mathematics and Computer Science,
Technical University of Denmark, Building 321, 2800 Kongens Lyngby, Denmark
benjoh@dtu.dk
[2] Eriksholm Research Centre, Rørtangvej 20, 3070 Snekkersten, Denmark
[3] Oticon A/S, Kongebakken 9, 2765 Smørum, Denmark

Abstract. Hearables are on the rise as next generation wearables, capable of streaming audio, modifying soundscapes or functioning as biometric sensors. The recent introduction of IoT (Internet of things) connected hearing instruments offer new opportunities for hearables to collect behavioral data that capture device usage and user intents and thereby provide insights to adjust the settings of the device. In our study 6 participants shared their volume and interaction data capturing when they remotely changed their device settings over eight weeks. The data confirms that the participants preferred to actively change programs rather than use a single default setting provided by an audiologist. Furthermore, their unique usage patterns indicate a need for designing hearing instruments, which as hearables adapt their settings dynamically to individual preferences during the day.

Keywords: Hearables · Quantified self · Usage patterns · Behavioral data

1 Introduction

Hearables may be the wearable of the future. They fit on or in the ear, providing audio playback, soundscape argumentation, and integrate biometric sensors [6]. More than $28 million have been raised from crowdfunding for hearables since 2014 [5] showing an increased interest in hearables. However, many start-ups have struggled to deliver, and have been forced out of the market in the process. Nick Hunn projects that the market for hearables within 2 years will increase to more than 230 million units, with a market revenue of more than $30 billion [5].

Hearing instruments are a medical device subcategory of hearables, which offer advanced capabilities for augmenting listening scenarios, including amplification, noise reduction and speech enhancement. The latest generation of hearing instruments connects to smartphones through Bluetooth, enabling them to communicate with other apps or cloud services supporting the IFTTT standard, effectively making them IoT connected devices.

© Springer International Publishing AG 2017
M. Antona and C. Stephanidis (Eds.): UAHCI 2017, Part III, LNCS 10279, pp. 39–49, 2017.
DOI: 10.1007/978-3-319-58700-4_4

Hearing instruments primarily support enhanced speech intelligibility in challenging listening scenarios characterized by speech in noise or multiple talkers. However, only a small fraction of the 360 million people suffering from severe hearing loss [12], including 48 million Americans (20% of the populatioon) [9] suffering from hearing loss, use hearing instruments.

In a previous study, Laplante-Levesque et al. [7] investigated the usage of hearing instruments, and compared self-reported use, and historical summarized use from the hearing instrument (average on/off time). It was found that there are two distinct types of behaviors associated with hearing instrument usage. Users wearing the device from morning to bed, and users using the hearing instruments when needed. The hypothesis of this study is that each participant have a unique behavior, and that there may be more than one usage pattern. They furthermore concluded that the average wear of a hearing instrument averaged 10.5 h. This is well beyond the battery capacity of current hearables, with Apple AirPods claiming up to 5 h play on a charge [1] and technologies with binaural microphones, such as the Doppler Labs Here One and the Bragi Dash claims 3 h of use on a battery charge [3,4]. In comparison, current hearing instruments batteries can sustain a week of use, or more, before the need for changing batteries.

This paper investigates the usage patterns of hearing instrument users based on user initiated program and volume changes through a pilot study of 7 weeks. These adjustments are converted into time series data saved in the cloud using IFTTT to transfer data. Previous studies have primarily used summarized historical data retrieved from the hearing instrument software, whereas IoT devices may potentially learn from usage data, such as volume and program interactions, to dynamically adapt the hearing instruments to behavioral patterns. In this article hearing instruments will also be referred to as hearables.

2   Method

6 participants (median age 61.8) with more than 5 years experience of hearables were recruited for the study. Half of the participants were retired, while the other half are still working. Participants were equipped with two Oticon Opn^{TM} hearing instruments connected personal iPhones using Bluetooth. All user initiated program selection or volume changes were recorded as time series data stored over a 7-week period. All participants were provided with a Google Drive account used for data collection, allowing them to retain full ownership of the data. The hearing instruments were fitted based on audiograms by an audiologist to provide individualized frequency dependent amplification for each subject. Rather than a single optimized setting the hearables were fitted with four alternative programs from the Oticon OpenSound Navigator^{TM}.

These programs are trade-offs between speech and noise balance, i.e., speech intelligibility, and of background sound amplification. The OpenSound Navigator works with three modules to analyze the sound, these are described by Le Goff et al. [8] as: Analyze, analyzes the sound environment both omnidirectional, and backward, estimating where a noise sources are placed. This simulates how sound normally are perceived by the human ear, with more sound attenuation from the back and the sides of the listener. Balance, which determines speech sources and attenuate noise sources between speech sources. This balances the signal-to-noise ratio (SNR). And, noise removal, which attenuate noise sources and amplifies speech above the hearing threshold.

Each of the programs gives various support depending on the context, from simple environments such as speech in quiet to more complex environments with multiple talkers and ambient background noise, such as an outdoor cafe.

The four programs are:

- *P1*: Resembling an omnidirectional perception with a frontal focus. Sounds from the sides and behind the listener are slightly suppressed to resemble the dampening effect of the pinna.
- *P2*: similar to P1 but gently increasing balance and noise removal when encountering complex listening environments.
- *P3*: similar to P1 but increasing balance and noise removal even in simple listening environments.
- *P4*: similar to P3 with high sensitivity to noise increasing balance and noise removal in all listening environments.

2.1 Participants

6 participants were recruited for the study (6 men). The median age was *61.8 years (std. 11.1 years)*. All participants have used hearables for more than 5 years. All have an iPhone 4S or newer. Half of the participants are retired, and the other half are working. The hearing loss ranges from mild (26–40 dB), moderate (41–60 dB) and severe (61–80) as described by the WHO [11]. Two participants were not included in the study due to lack of data or missing data. A short summary of each subject is provided in Table 1.

Table 1. Demographic information related to 4 subjects

Subject	Age group	Hearing loss	Experience with OPN	Occupation
1	50–59	Moderate-severe	No	Working
2	70–79	Moderate	No	Working
5	50–59	Mild	Yes	Working
7	70–79	Mild-moderate	No	Retired

The study was carried out in Denmark in the autumn of 2016, and follow up in January and February 2017. Participants were instructed at Eriksholm Research Centre.

2.2 Apparatus

Each participant were equipped with two Oticon Opn^{TM} hearing instruments, stereo Bluetooth low energy (BLE) 2.4 GHz, Near-Field Magnetic Induction

(NFMI). All participants used (personal) iPhone 4S or newer models, Bluetooth 4.0 (or newer). The data streamed by the hearables consist of any user initiated program change or volume changes (-4 to 8) accompanied with a time-stamp of the interaction, stored in the cloud on a test subject owned Google spreadsheet and shared via Google Drive. The hearing aids were fitted with four audio profiles P1, P2, P3 and P4, described earlier.

The participants were provided with a private test user Google account prior to the experiment. The account was used for data collection, and the participants have full ownership of the account and data. Data was collected over a 7-week period.

2.3   Procedure

Participants were fitted with OPN hearing instruments. The hearing instruments were fitted based on a unique frequency dependent volume amplification for each subject, by an audiologist. User initiated program and volume changes are collected trough the ON app, which in combination with the IFTTT app collects and store usage patterns as time series data. Each user initiated action is stored as a row on a private Google drive spreadsheet. 10 IFTTT recipes[1] were installed on the participants smartphone. The participants were encouraged to explore the hearables and their functionality with no further instruction provided in which scenarios the programs would be best suited. Participants could then test the device, while the researcher and an audiologist were present. The participants were informed that data would be continuously streamed for the duration of the experiment. Each participant was fitted with four programs, through the Genie 2.0^{TM} fitting software using the OpenSound Navigator. Follow up consultations with an audiologist was planned for the end of the study. These consultations included an interview about the use of the hearables along with: Usage history collected by the device compared with the collected cloud data. Secondly, inquiring into the usage of specific programs to further understand the users preferences and intents in various scenarios. Leading to defining new program settings for a follow up study. The aim would be to tease apart the need for increasing attenuation of ambient sound sources, noise removal and improving speech intelligibility associated with different scenarios.

3   Weekday Program Usage over 24 Hours

The program patterns in Figs. 1 and 2 ranging from P1 (beige), P2 (brown), P3 high (light blue), to P4 (dark blue), illustrate the large differences between users, their contrasting needs throughout the day, as well as their changing preferences for weekday vs weekend activities. General trends towards increased support during the day can be seen for users 1, 5 and 7. Conversely, less need of support in the evening is reflected in the behavior of user 2. In addition, the bright

---

[1] Accessible online: https://ifttt.com/p/benjaminjohansenphd/shared.

sound represented by the P2 (brown) versus the full sound of P3 (light blue) may indicate how preferences for the P2 increases speech intelligibility, whereas P3 provides a less intense listening experience. Likewise, the program usage on weekdays could be driven by the demands of work related activities, while the preferences on weekends might to a larger degree reflect individual baselines defining their cognitive processing needs [2, 10].

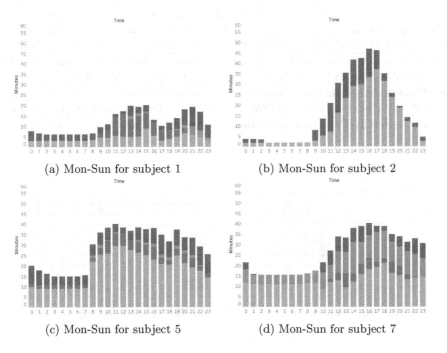

(a) Mon-Sun for subject 1

(b) Mon-Sun for subject 2

(c) Mon-Sun for subject 5

(d) Mon-Sun for subject 7

Fig. 1. Aggregated average program time. The time is displayed in minutes for each hour, and is aggregated for the full data collection period. The use of P1 (beige), P2 (brown), P3 (light blue), and P4 (dark blue), varies for each test subject as well as over the course of the day. (Color figure online)

4 Changing Preferences in the Weekends

4.1 Weekends as a Baseline

In Fig. 2a comparison between weekday usage (left side of the figure) and weekends (right side of the figure) is illustrated for subject 2 and 5. It can immediately be noticed that the behavior pattern varies from weekdays compared to weekends. A clear trend of preferring P1 in the weekend is evident. The preference for a more natural sound in the weekend can be due to a less challenging context, compared to weekdays (and working days). It can also be observed that the weekends have a later onset of the day.

From these observations it seems as the weekend reflects a baseline state where the user prefers natural sound and does not need the enhanced speech intelligibility and noise reduction associated with the P4 program.

4.2 Varying Context Creates Different Needs

An interesting observation from Fig. 2a and b for subject two, is the distinct pattern of removing background noise from morning to late afternoon. In a follow up interview, this subject indicated that he works in the transportation industry, and indeed works between 8AM and 4PM. The choice of this program is to reduce noise. This subject along others, indicated that the weekends have the least troublesome scenarios, and a more natural sound, such as the one provided by P1, is preferable in these contexts.

Subject 7 have a distinct pattern using the automatic and supportive programs, especially P3. These programs increase speech intelligibility and have a

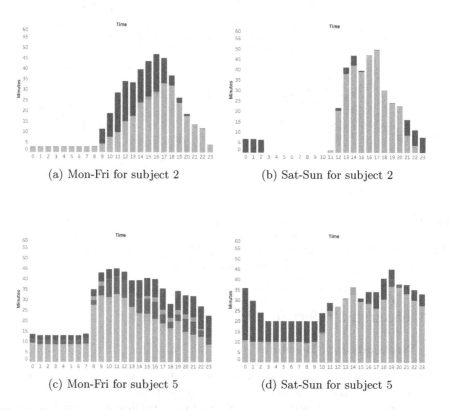

(a) Mon-Fri for subject 2   (b) Sat-Sun for subject 2

(c) Mon-Fri for subject 5   (d) Sat-Sun for subject 5

Fig. 2. Comparison of weekday and weekend patterns for subject 2 and 5. The data is aggregated over the full study period, and is displayed as an average minute per hour. Notice the distinct pattern of less support in the weekends (brown and teal colors are preferred). P1 (beige), P2 (brown), P3 (light blue), and P4 (dark blue). (Color figure online)

higher sensitivity to background noise. This subject play cards 2–3 times a week for several hours. Due to the nature of the card game and a room with poor acoustics, the P2 and P3 program increases speech inteligibility.

Both of these subjects mentioned that the weekends contains less challenging scenarios. Anecdotal, the reason for wearing the hearables later in the day is caused by reading the newspaper in the morning. The newspaper creates an uncomfortable sound environment containing rattling and sharp noises, where a quiet environment is preferred.

5   Program Use over Several Weeks of Use

From Fig. 3 the preferences for program use over several weeks can be observed. Due to some weeks without data, caused by a lack of Internet connection (e.g., in outdoor environments), some subjects have fewer weeks represented than others. It can be observed that the majority of the subjects uses two or more programs the first 3 weeks. While at the end of the pilot study they seem to prefer two programs, typically P1 and a program that assist in challenging listening environments. This indicates that over time the participants become aware of the capabilities of the hearables, in which scenarios it can support them as needed, and at which times it performs the best. From the figure it is visible that a

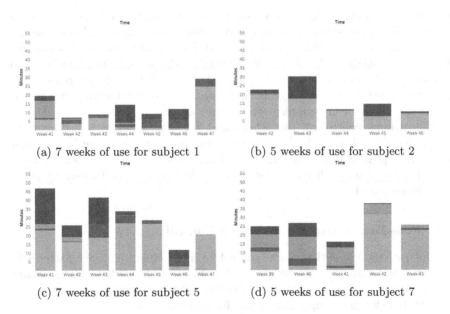

(a) 7 weeks of use for subject 1   (b) 5 weeks of use for subject 2

(c) 7 weeks of use for subject 5   (d) 5 weeks of use for subject 7

Fig. 3. Preference of using the hearing aid over time. The data is aggregated and averaged per week of collected data. Notice how the first weeks include use of more programs, while this decline towards the end of the data collection period. This indicates that the user finds a "preferred" setting over time. Some subjects have missing data due to lack of Internet connection (outdoor environments).

preference for the more open and natural sounding P1 is used most frequently. This indicates that the participants prefers a natural sound, and when a challenging scenario occurs, they change to a supportive program.

A second observation indicates that the preference between the changes in many cases includes two contrasting programs. Over time a preferred supportive program for the subject emerges.

5.1 Perceived Sound Quality

The perceived sound quality is a motivator for behavioral use of hearables. The primary focus from the established hearing aid industry have been on increased speech intelligibility and dealing with challenging listening scenarios. However, from interviews of the subjects in this study, the majority of the wear time is not spent in challenging environment. The natural open characteristics of P1 seems to provide a natural sound environment, which provide sufficient amplification in most listening scenarios, involving only few speakers and less background noise. As confirmed by accumulated usage history, the P1 is used to reproduce a natural sound up to 75% of the time.

6   Program Duration and Volume Changes

The program changes can explain part of the behavioral patterns of each of the subjects. The programs can be observed as macro settings modifying a soundscape by adjusting the noise removal and attenuation of ambient sound sources. As earlier mentioned, P1 has the least effect on the soundscape, with a frontal focused omnidirectional producing a natural sound, while P4 has increased noise removal and attenuation of ambient sound sources. The interaction between programs and volume can be interpreted as user intents.

The volume control on the other hand works as a micro adjustment. By controlling the volume gain the user can zoom in or out of a soundscape, alternating how present in the current context they wish to be. This does not affect the reproduced sound from the programs, only the gain and intensity of the reproduced sound.

6.1 Fine-Tuning Using the Volume Control

To illustrate the use of the volume control for fine-tuning, the usage patterns for subject 2 and subject 7 can be observed in Fig. 4. In Fig. 4 the average change in volume gain is displayed, with respect to the two contrasting programs of P1 and P4, blue for decreasing and orange for increasing gain.

Figure 4a indicates a unique pattern for subject 2 of a need for an increase in volume, around meal times. In the weekend, shown in Fig. 4b the volume is primarily decreased, and only increased in the late evenings on weekends. This pattern is contrasting with subject 7 s pattern, seen in Fig. 4c where the volume

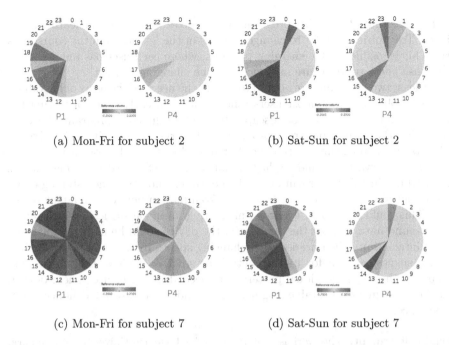

(a) Mon-Fri for subject 2   (b) Sat-Sun for subject 2

(c) Mon-Fri for subject 7   (d) Sat-Sun for subject 7

Fig. 4. Comparison of volume interactions with respect to weekdays (left figures) and weekends (right figures) for subject 2 (top) and subject 7 (bottom). Notice the distinct difference in volume patterns between the two subjects. Observe the contrasting volume changes for weekdays versus weekends. (Color figure online)

is always decreased in P1. In P4 there is a contrasting volume change from evening meal time, and just after this meal time.

Comparing just these two programs for two subjects with respect to volume shows how the subject intentionally uses a combination of a program and a volume to adjust the auditory experience. Furthermore, it highlights the difference between usage pattern between two subjects. One prefers to primarily increase volume, while the other prefers to decrease volume. These changes also occurs at different time intervals, indicating a need for personalized hearables.

7 Conclusion

These results show how user generated volume and program interaction data may capture preferences for personalizing the listening experience to the changing context. The usage patterns highlight individual needs for selecting contrasting programs rather than a medium one size fits all setting often provided by default. The shared user generated data might potentially be used to learn behavioral patterns enabling the devices to automatically adapt their settings and thus optimize the user experience of hearables.

It seems that at least two programs are needed to optimize the hearing experience. Test subjects prefer to change settings of the hearables in the course of a day. This is visible in the emerging patterns, where each user has unique usage patterns. These patterns are influenced by the changing context.

At least two programs are needed to satisfy the needs of the users of hearables. It can be observed that most users tend to have an early onset of testing the various modification of the soundscape observed by changing programs. Later in the period they find a preferred program that works in most situations. For all subjects this is program P1, the one that reproduces sound most naturally.

These observations could be the foundation for the future design of hearables. The findings in this paper can be used to optimize, not only the listening experience, but also how the devices can learn from human behavior to adapt to the user. This could lead to a "I forgot I'm wearing an in-ear device", which reproduces sound naturally. At the same time, the device could be used to enhance a social interaction, when needed, by enhancing speech intelligibility.

We suggest a need for better control, or smarter devices, that learns and adapts to the users individual patterns are needed in the future. These devices can be used in any hearable augmenting sound, to create an enhanced user experience.

Acknowledgment. This work is supported by the Technical University of Denmark, Copenhagen Center for Health Technology (cachet) and the Oticon Foundation. We would like to thank Eriksholm Research Centre and Oticon A/S for providing resources and access to test subjects, devices, clinicians, developers and researchers.

References

1. Apple Inc.: AirPods (2016). http://www.apple.com/lae/airpods/
2. Borch Petersen, E., Lunner, T., Vestergaard, M.D., Sundewall Thorén, E.: Danish reading span data from 283 hearing-aid users, including a sub-group analysis of their relationship to speech-in-noise performance. Int. J. Audiol. **2027**(April), 1–8 (2016)
3. Bragi GmbH: Bragi support: check the battery status (2016). https://support.bragi.com/hc/en-us/articles/203178431-Check-the-battery-status
4. Doppler Labs Inc.: Here one: how long does the battery last? (2016). https://support.hereplus.me/hc/en-us/articles/221655867-How-long-does-the-battery-last-
5. Hunn, N.: The market for hearable devices 2016–2020. Technical report November, WiFore: Wireless Consulting, London (2016)
6. Kissner, S., Holube, I., Bitzer, J., Technology, H., Sciences, A.: A smartphone-based, privacy-aware recording system for the assessment of everyday listening situations. In: Proceedings of the International Symposium on Auditory and Audiological Research, vol. 5, pp. 445–452 (2015)
7. Laplante-Levesque, A., Nielsen, C., Jensen, L.D., Naylor, G.: Patterns of hearing aid usage predict hearing aid use amount (data logged and selfreported) and overreport. J. Am. Acad. Audiol. **25**(2), 187–198 (2014)
8. Le Go, N., Jensen, J., Pedersen, M.S., Callaway, S.L.: An introduction to penSound Navigator^TM, pp. 1–9 (2016). https://www.oticon.com/~/media/OticonUS/main/DownloadCenter/WhitePapers/15555-9950-OpnSoundNavigator.pdf

9. Lin, F.R., Niparko, J.K., Ferrucci, L.: Hearing loss prevalance in the United States. Arch. Otolaryngol. Head Neck Surg. **171**(20), 2011–2012 (2014)
10. Lunner, T., Rudner, M., Rönnberg, J.: Cognition and hearing aids. Scand. J. Psychol. **50**(5), 395–403 (2009)
11. World Health Organization: Grades of hearing impairment (2011). http://www.who.int/pbd/deafness/hearing_impairment_grades/en/index.html
12. World Health Organization: WHO global estimates on prevalence of hearing loss (2012). http://www.who.int/pbd/deafness/estimates/en/

The Privacy, Security and Discoverability of Data on Wearable Health Devices: Fitness or Folly?

Vishakha Kumari and Sara Anne Hook[✉]

Department of Human-Centered Computing, Indiana University School of Informatics and Computing, 535 W. Michigan Street, Indianapolis, IN 46202, USA
vkumari@umail.iu.edu, sahook@iupui.edu

Abstract. With data from wearable health devices increasing at a rapid rate, it is important for lawmakers to make sure that this data remains well protected. This paper will question the perceptions of people with respect to current and future use of wearable health devices, especially if the security and privacy risks to their data are more commonly understood, and particularly if this data is discoverable and admissible in court. It will explore the electronic discovery issues with data from wearable health devices in the context of litigation and examine how the current rules of court procedure and evidence would be applied. The paper will review the federal and state legislation that may or may not provide protection for data from wearable health devices. The authors intend to use their paper as a vehicle to advocate for stronger statutory protection and greater clarity about the use of and potential risks to this data, including when the data becomes evidence in litigation.

Keywords: Wearable health devices · Fitness devices · Internet of Things (IoT) · Privacy · Security · Electronic discovery · Legislation

1 Introduction

Wearable health and fitness devices are emerging at a rapid rate and the lives of people are being impacted by them. On one hand, these wearable health devices help a user to achieve his/her health goals and improve overall health by constantly tracking and monitoring health data. However, the lack of clear legislative protection for the privacy and security of this data can put individuals at risk. What the future of this industry will be like is not known. However, it will be interesting to evaluate if this technology will have a positive or negative impact on people's lives. To narrow the scope of this paper, it will specifically focus on fitness trackers rather than trying to cover the full range of health devices that are available.

The paper will first review the federal and state legislation that may or may not provide protection for data from wearable health devices and advocate for either new legislation or amendments to existing statutes that would offer at least some level of security and privacy over this data. It will explore the electronic discovery issues with data from wearable health devices in the context of litigation and examine how the current rules of court procedure and evidence would be applied. It will highlight the

© Springer International Publishing AG 2017
M. Antona and C. Stephanidis (Eds.): UAHCI 2017, Part III, LNCS 10279, pp. 50–64, 2017.
DOI: 10.1007/978-3-319-58700-4_5

perceptions of people with respect to current and future use of wearable health devices, especially if the security and privacy risks to their data are more commonly understood, and particularly if this data is discoverable and admissible in court. The authors hope to raise the awareness of the HCI and health informatics communities so that these professionals will be more mindful of the issues when designing and testing wearable health devices and in using these devices themselves. They intend to use their paper as a starting point to advocate for stronger statutory protection and greater clarity about the use of and potential risks to this data, including when the data becomes evidence in litigation.

2   Wearable Health Devices and Their Data

It has been estimated that one in every ten Americans over the age of eighteen owns an activity tracker [1]. The wearables market has shown impressive growth over the years and is expected to increase to 35% by 2019 [2]. This growth rate speaks to the growing interest in wearable technology. The wearables industry is promising a healthier future with devices capable of monitoring daily activities, calories burned, sleep patterns, body temperature, step counts, heart rate, oxygen levels, hydration levels and blood sugar levels, to name but a few [3]. These wearable health devices perceive and record information about users continuously and discreetly. With every second, the amount of health-related data available through the Internet is increasing. Wearable health devices are considered as being part of the Internet of Things (IoT), which "involves not only the connection and integration of devices that monitor the physical worlds – temperature, pressure, altitude, motion, proximity to something else, biometrics, sound, images, and so forth – but also the aggregation, relationship and analysis of the information those devices create in order to take action on the situation, and the business and technology

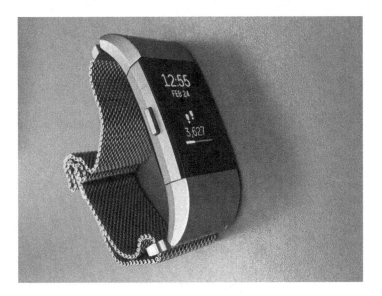

Fig. 1. Example of a Fitbit

changes required to use the data and analyses" [4]. As indicated in Fig. 1 of this report, the Internet of Things "stack" can be represented as a triangle, with local sensing at the bottom, then data integration and analytics of things, with cognitive action at the top of the pyramid [4]. As the authors note in their discussion of what this means for an IoT application, "[w]ithin the activity tracker industry, for example, the end-state vision should address how consumers, the health and fitness industry, and the health insurance industry will make use of the devices, functions, and data" [4].

2.1 Advantages of Health Data from Wearables

The advent of these wearable health devices offers the potential to dramatically alter the way that health care services are delivered because of the opportunity for users and providers to more easily capture, compare and respond to even small changes in a person's medical status, hopefully before the person's condition worsens. These devices can reduce the visits to clinics and hospitals and can perhaps reduce overall expenses on health care. These devices allow remote health monitoring, which is particularly worthwhile for chronic conditions and elder care. Wearable health devices not only benefit the consumer, but they can also help health care service providers to facilitate and improve the quality of care. If the data can be aggregated, it has the potential to bring a health revolution and transform the health industry. Aggregated data from wearable devices can provide valuable insights into the overall health of the population and the collective data can be used to plan for the facilities, personnel and expenditures that

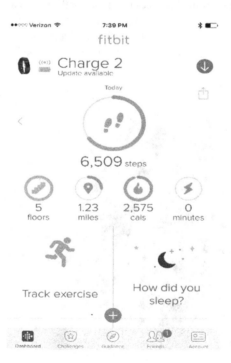

Fig. 2. Screenshot of user's cellphone with Fitbit data

will be needed in the future. Moreover, many of these wearable health devices, particularly fitness trackers, are attractive and easy to use and provide a very simple view of the user's data on his/her cellphone (Fig. 2).

2.2 Concerns with Wearable Health Devices

In 2015, personal health information breaches affected 113 million individuals and with the wearable market on the rise the breach rate is bound to increase if measures are not taken [5]. The reason for this is that health information is 50 times more profitable on the black market than Social Security numbers [6]. Also, the use of wearable devices brings the possibility of this data being exposed to the black market since these devices tend to be easy to compromise in a socio-technical sense. The data collected by these devices are either stored locally, or if collected ubiquitously, then stored in a cloud. There can be physical theft, malware attack or loss of local data and these devices are not yet sophisticated enough to provide a secured flow of the data to the cloud, which can act as another hacking point [7].

2.3 Security and Privacy Concerns

Wearable devices generate and store confidential health information about the user, because of which there is a high chance of misuse if the privacy and security of this data are not ensured. The scenario that the decision to promote someone was based on the data collected by a fitness tracker that was given to an employee by his/her employer is now a possibility. As has been seen with other high-profile information security breaches, inadequate protection of this data can put people who use wearable devices at greater risk for becoming victims of identity theft, profiling, stalking, extortion or discrimination at a personal and professional level [8]. Bad credit, inaccurate health records, higher premiums and loss of insurance coverage are a few other examples of problems which may arise [7].

2.4 Electronic Discovery

Although questions about evidence in digital format were raised in cases as early as the 1980s and 1990s, the emerging area of law known as electronic discovery (e-discovery) did not begin to find its way into the typical lawyer's lexicon until the mid-2000s. Two major events occurred during this time that marked the true beginning of the field of e-discovery and that continue to form the foundation of how the process is handled today. In *Zubulake v. UBS Warburg*, Judge Shira A. Scheindlin articulated major principles and themes regarding e-discovery, including the responsibilities of lawyers and clients, sanctions for spoliation of evidence and what constitutes accessible versus inaccessible data [9]. In 2006, the Federal Rules of Civil Procedure were amended to incorporate Judge Scheindlin's rulings and to establish the discoverability of Electronically Stored Information (ESI) as an umbrella term intended to encompass both current and future technology and the data that it generates. E-discovery is something that impacts everyone, whether they know if or not, because it deals with the proper collection, preservation, analysis and production of evidence in digital form. To put it bluntly, in the United States, if you are sued, the opposing party's lawyer will request nearly every piece of digital evidence in any format that might be relevant to the case, including email, text messages and information from social media sites. Anyone can find himself/herself needing to comply with requests for potentially relevant evidence – in electronic or paper/hard copy form. There are various steps in an e-discovery process which are best understood by reviewing the Electronic Discovery Reference Model (EDRM).

As indicated by the EDRM below, the duty to preserve potentially relevant ESI begins at the time that litigation can reasonably be anticipated rather than when actual notice is received about a lawsuit, investigation or audit. Ideally, an organization - or even an individual - will be managing its information appropriately even beforehand so that the actual e-discovery process will be as streamlined as possible. For users of wearable health devices that generate data that may be relevant to a case, the challenges will be knowing that they need to preserve this data, how to identify the data that may be requested and then how to properly collect this data. Of course, the lawyer representing the user should be able to offer guidance. The scenario of needing to obtain information from a user's wearable health device can be compared with that of information from social media sites. Although it would be tempting to think that data from wearable health devices can be requested and received from the vendors of these devices or cloud computing services that might be storing this data, in the context of social media, commentators suggest that it is best to first make the requests for information from the actual users or from other users ("friends") who may have access to this data. Thus, it will be interesting to see what procedures are developed for requesting data from wearable health devices, particularly the valuable information that might show trends in a user's medical status, activity levels or location (Fig. 3).

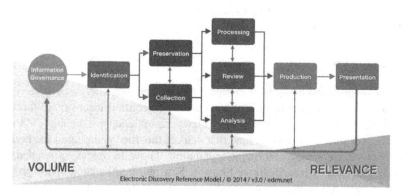

Fig. 3. Electronic Discovery Reference Model (edrm.net)

The Federal Rules of Civil Procedure were amended again in December 2015 to shorten the timeframes for various stages in an e-discovery process, to place a greater emphasis on proportionality and to provide clarity on when and what kinds of sanctions the court can impose for spoliation of evidence [10]. Courts are already applying the amended version of the Federal Rules of Civil Procedure, which means that an e-discovery process must now be completed in a significantly reduced period of time and with greater specificity required for requests and objections [11]. The e-discovery process becomes increasingly complex as lawyers and clients deal with wearable devices and the Internet of Things, which create and store even more potentially relevant electronic evidence in a wider variety of files and formats [12, 13].

Thus, another concern with data from wearable health devices is that it will usher in a new era of digital forensics because these devices present a rich repository of potentially relevant evidence that can be requested and used as part of litigation. As with other Electronically Stored Information (ESI), courts are already allowing data from these devices to be discovered and admitted in trials [14, 15]. Even though data from wearable health devices is discoverable, it must still meet the tests for admissibility as outlined in the Federal Rules of Evidence and corresponding state court rules. One of the issues with the data generated by wearable health devices is its reliability, especially since studies indicate that the readings may not be entirely accurate [16, 17]. The variety of wearables available in the market have their own algorithms to track and capture data. For some, even moving one's leg while seated is captured as a step taken, while other devices give a different result because the wearable was probably too tight or loose on the wrist to record the data properly. Determination of deep from light sleep has different parameters for each of the fitness tracking devices. For data which lacks standardization to be used as evidence can be perilous to the objectivity of the judicial system. Similar to concerns with social media, one of the special issues with data from wearable health devices is authenticity, since it would have to be proven that the person to whom the device is attributed was actually the one using it [18].

As previously indicated, the data from a fitness device was used in the case of a 44-year-old woman who claimed she had been awakened and sexually assaulted at around midnight. The data from her fitness device showed she was awake and walking at the alleged time of the crime. She first claimed to have been wearing her fitness device during the time of the attack, but later changed her story to having lost her wearable device during the attack [19]. Later, it was shown that she falsified the entire incident and was ordered to serve two years of probation and complete 100 h of community service. Another case was of a Canadian law firm which collected the fitness data of its client to compare that to other wearers of her age and profession to show that the plaintiff's activities were reduced from what would normally be expected due to the injuries she sustained in an auto accident [20, 21].

Concerns have also been raised about instances where employers and insurance companies have provided wearable devices such as fitness trackers under the auspices of promoting the health and wellness of employees and insureds [22, 23]. Although seemingly benevolent at first glance, is such data collection over-intrusive and would it result in either adverse employment actions or denial of coverage for illnesses or injury if someone could point to a lack of physical activity as a rationale? Although wearable health devices, which collect data continuously, might be able to give a picture of what might have happened, they may fail to collect the exact details of the particular moment. However, the data from wearable health devices including fitness trackers does present a rich repository of potentially relevant evidence, particularly for cases involving personal injury, medical malpractice, employment disputes and any other type of litigation where someone's health status is at issue. Trend data will be especially valuable. Lawyers have been searching for and requesting information from social media sites for several years, looking for data about opposing parties, the lawyers who represent them, potential jury members and judges and even their own clients so it is unlikely to be any different with data from wearable health devices. One of the authors has been publishing articles and book chapters and giving presentations on e-discovery for 10 years. Most recently, she reviewed a number of recent cases that considered a wide variety of files and formats of information in digital form, including social media, email, video surveillance, chats and instant messages [24]. It is clear that data from wearable health devices will be considered Electronically Stored Information (ESI) for purposes of discovery. However, data from wearable health devices will still need to meet all of the other requirements outlined under the Federal Rules of Evidence and comparable state court rules in order to be admissible in court.

3   What U.S. Federal Legislation May Apply to Fitness Devices?

There is an urgent need for the legal framework to catch up with the speed of technology development; the gap between the law and technology continues to widen. Unfortunately, research suggests that neither the Health Information Portability and Accountability Act (HIPAA) - nor any other federal or perhaps even state law - seems expansive enough to protect the health data collected by these devices. The wearables industry is such a rapidly-evolving field that there are no specific sets of laws that cover it. The public seems unaware of the security and privacy risks posed by wearable health devices; however, this may change if there are some high-profile instances of misuse of this data. Fortunately, experts are calling for new regulations, including legislation that would cover the health and fitness data of employees [25].

3.1   HIPAA and the HITECH Act

Health information that is captured and stored by wearable health devices such as fitness trackers is likely not considered protected health information under federal or state law unless the information is shared with doctors, hospitals or any third-party vendors (Business Associates) of these entities. Because these devices are not covered under the Health Care Portability and Accountability Act (HIPAA), there can be little to no expectation of privacy or security provided under this legislation. Interestingly, one major vendor of wearable devices indicates that its devices are HIPAA-compliant, raising questions about why this vendor chose to incorporate HIPAA considerations into its products when other vendors have not done so [26]. Without adequate statutory protection, questions remain about whether the use of wearable health devices actually promotes fitness or is folly.

In addition, the advancement in technology today makes it very easy to re-identify data and link it back to the person. However, under HIPAA, the data falls out of the protection scheme once it is de-identified, since protection is only available for "individually identifiable data" [25].

In 2009 another law, known as the HITECH Act, considered a more refined version of HIPAA, was passed to "addresses the privacy and security concerns associated with the electronic transmission of health information" [27]. However, even the reforms to this law do not encompass data from wearable health devices and thus this data falls out of the protection provided by these laws.

Concerns about the security and privacy of individually identifiable health information are not confined to the wearable devices industry, but are more broadly considered whenever technology is used to create, store and transmit health data. Indeed, Rockwell notes that "[t]he telemedicine industry is especially vulnerable to exposing private patient information given its reliance on electronic data collection and storage and frequent distant data transfer" [28]. The author examines the application of HIPAA and the HITECH Act of 2009 in the context of telemedicine, noting that the question of "whether a patient-facing telemedicine technology vendor is a HIPAA business associate subject to these regulations is a complex question depending on a number of variables" [28]. Additionally, she observes that "[e]lectronic health records, video storage devices, telemedicine devices, and any other data-generating or receiving device involved in the telemedicine interaction carries the potential to collect and store protected health information" [28]. As she concludes, "[c]ollection and storage of that information as well as any use or disclosure are subject to federal HIPAA and HITECH laws [28]. It is fairly easy to apply the same approach to the collection and storage of data from wearable health devices.

3.2 Federal Trade Commission (FTC)

The Federal Trade Commission (FTC) ensures that consumers should be able to enjoy the benefits that technology brings without having to worry about the privacy risks involved. Though not specifically directed towards health data, the FTC sets guidelines for protecting consumer data. In the future, it can play an important role in protecting the data from wearable health devices. The federal rules will have to be adjusted to encompass wearable devices and to ensure that consumers are not misled about the privacy protections in place for their data. As is clear from a number of FTC enforcement actions, vendors and other third parties that are part of the wearable health devices industry will have to be careful not to "overpromise" about the security and privacy practices that are used to safeguard the data that is generated, stored, transferred and shared about consumers. Particularly worrisome to many consumers is the specter of "secondary use" of their data by third parties without permission or without an opportunity to "opt out" of certain activities such as data collection and analysis and offers for additional services from third party vendors.

3.3 Food and Drug Administration (FDA)

The Food and Drug Administration (FDA) is another U.S. agency charged with protecting and promoting public health through the control and supervision of regulated medical devices. Fitness trackers likely would be placed into the category of "low risk general wellness" devices and thus do not require FDA oversight [29]. However, when the use of fitness trackers is recommended by physicians, they would fall under FDA's purview as now they can be classified as medical devices and thus could be regulated by it.

The FDA has made it clear that it does not intend to regulate "low risk" devices, but as wearable technology delves deeper into the realm of tracking and monitoring as part of bona fide medical services to maintain a patient's health, there is a need to regulate these devices as well [30].

4 Representative Examples of State Legislation that May Apply to Fitness Trackers

The authors chose three states to examine to see whether there is legislation available that could potentially provide more protection for the security and privacy of data from wearable health devices such as fitness trackers than what is available at the U.S. federal level.

4.1 Indiana

The authors are currently located in Indiana, so they were first interested in reviewing the potential legislation that might be available in this state that would offer a greater level of protection for the security and privacy of data from wearable health devices than what is provided under federal law. Indiana Code 24-4.9 covers the disclosure of a security breach, which includes definitions for terms such as breach of the security of data, data base owner, encrypted data, "person" and personal information, requirements for disclosure and notification of a breach, the duties of a database owner, the methods of disclosure, penalties for disclosure and the actions that can be taken by the Attorney General [31]. Indiana Code 4-1-6 features its Fair Information Practices and Privacy of Personal Information [32]. Finally, Indiana Code 4-6-14 is devoted to the protection of health records and identifying information [33].

4.2 Massachusetts

The law in Massachusetts was the second state of interest to the authors. Many experts consider the laws in Massachusetts that deal with information security and privacy to be the best among all of the states in the United States. Moreover, these experts advocate for other states to adopt what Massachusetts has in place, hopeful that it can be a model not only at the state level but also the federal level. The law in Massachusetts includes regulations on the protection of personal information. Its definitions for "persons" and "personal information" are expansive [34]. Its Standards for the Protection of Personal Information of Residents of the Commonwealth cover purpose and scope, definitions, duty to protect and standards for protecting personal information and a deadline of March 1, 2010 for compliance [35]. Interestingly, this statute includes computer system security requirements, making it particularly compelling as guidance for implementing a comprehensive security program [35]. Among the provisions within this section of the statute are secure authentication protocols and secure access control measures that include education and training of employees [35].

4.3 Washington State

Fortunately, as this paper was being developed, a comprehensive examination of the personal health data privacy laws that would apply to wearable fitness devices was published in the *Seattle University Law Review* [30]. The author first provides an explanation for why fitness devices are so popular, including the medical and social benefits of these devices and the commercial benefits [30]. The author then discusses the current federal law, including HIPAA and the HITECH Act and the regulations from the Federal Trade Commission (FTC) and the Food and Drug Administration (FDA), characterizing them as a "limited landscape" [30]. He proposes a statutory framework, including state constitutional amendments and legislation, that Washington State should develop to protect consumers from privacy violations through wearable fitness devices [30].

The Uniform Health Care Information Act, enacted in 1991, is Washington's state primary health data protection legislature. It recognizes the patient's interests in privacy and health care and states that "[h]ealth care information is personal and sensitive information that if improperly used or released may do significant harm to a patient's interests in privacy, health care, or other interests" [36]. It also focuses on the rights to access health care information, stating that "[p]atients need access to their own health care information as a matter of fairness to enable them to make informed decisions about their health care and correct inaccurate or incomplete information about themselves" [36]. Washington State's current health information protection laws provide protection similar to HIPAA for traditional health care information and the state constitution is considered one of "a handful of state constitutions that explicitly protects privacy" [30]. However, the law needs to expand and be more definitive in order to provide better protection for personal health information and the processes associated with fitness devices.

5   Recommended Next Steps

The rate of growth of the wearable industry demands a quick update in the design and legal framework of these devices to avoid the misuse of this data. In this part of the paper, the authors will cover design considerations and legal reforms which would help to ensure the health data remains secure and can act as permissible digital evidence if needed. They consider what other approaches that can be taken to provide greater comfort to users of wearable health devices and to the vendors and third parties who provide these devices or handle the data generated by them.

5.1 Design Amendments

Security should be a prime concern for the professionals designing wearable health devices. The responsibility to make sure that data is safe should rest upon the hands of consumers as well as the designers, makers and vendors of these devices. The industry can show respect for a user's data by making the private settings as the default settings of these devices and giving users the freedom to choose otherwise. The user's expectation that his/her data is safe and not being shared with third parties without his/her consent should be met. Secondly, how often has it happened that the user did not understand a vendor's Terms of Service or Privacy Policy, and yet agreed its terms and conditions just for the sake of obtaining the devices or using the software application. It is unlikely that in such cases the user will pack up his/her wearable health device and return it. The designer's intervention is needed in fashioning an application where the user has the choice to opt out of any terms and conditions, yet he/she will still retain the basic functionality of the device. Wearables provided to users as medical devices is a potential solution, but again there should be an update on the legislative side.

In addition, keeping users informed about the specific data being generated and stored and how this data is going to be shared with any third party would be an important step forward. This can be accomplished during the initial setup; however, the design should always allow users to go back, check and change their information sharing settings and other preferences whenever they choose.

5.2 Law Amendments

The law must keep pace with the growth and innovation in the wearable health devices industry. It is still unclear what laws and regulations apply to this ever-evolving field. There is a need for specific laws targeted towards the "wearables" which will ensure that the privacy, security and discoverability of this data is clearly defined. It is important that protocols for requesting, collecting and preserving health data from wearable health devices be clarified, likely through court cases as well as amendments to federal and state court rules, so that clients and their lawyers handle this data properly throughout the e-discovery process, but particularly during the identification, preservation and collection stages.

Previously, the authors discussed the definitions of "covered entities," "individually identifiable health information" and "third parties." To extend HIPAA protection to data from wearable health devices, it is necessary to expand the above-mentioned definitions of this terminology, such as including device manufacturers as covered entities, and encompassing in the definition of business associates all of the involved third parties that store, share and analyze the data from these devices. In addition, broadening the scope of "individually identifiable health information" to include the data from the wearable devices and mobile health applications will prepare data from wearables for being admissible and discoverable in the digital age.

5.3 Other Options

Interestingly, insurance companies are now providing coverage for devices and data falling under the broad umbrella heading of the Internet of Things (IoT). As indicated by Reuhs, the "internet of things" appears to "represent the next wave of new liabilities: cars being remotely controlled by hackers; medical devices being used as access points for theft of medical records; baby monitors being used as spying devices; a software update pushing bad code that disables a fire sprinkler system; and TVs being rendered useless by malware" [37]. The article continues with a description of general liability policies and what they might cover and exclude related to IoT devices and the data they capture and store. As he indicates, since 2014, nearly all commercial general liability polices have excluded coverage for non-physical loss arising from data breaches (whether from IoT devices or not) [37]. He then discusses whether first-party losses would present more interesting insurance issues, noting that because all of these issues may not be solved in a larger sense, it is important to read policies carefully and understand the risks [37].

There is an overall lack of awareness about what kinds of data are being generated by wearable health devices and who can access it. The relative newness of this technology has not yet offered users with an opportunity to explore and become more vigilant about the protection of their data, especially given the variety of privacy threats that can emerge because of the continuous collection, storage and sharing of this data. The ubiquitous nature of these devices makes it difficult for users to be able to perceive the potential risks. The lack of privacy awareness in ubiquitous systems was a problem identified in early research; however, controlling privacy had been the prime focus rather than increasing privacy awareness of users [38, 39]. The design of these wearable health devices should be such that the visibility of information transfer is more transparent. One way to do this is by making an intuitive and easy to access user interface featuring relevant privacy information. Adding data control filters would be another way to ensure that users have some decision-making power over what data is collected, when it is collected, how much will be collected and shared and who will have access to it. This will make users more conscious of the data that is being shared and give them more control over the data that they prefer to share, making the data sharing process a more intentional act. A society that is well-informed and updated on the privacy and security issues that might arise because of wearable health devices will provide an incentive for designers, manufacturers and vendors to incorporate security measures as an integral part of their wearable health device systems.

Another important facet of addressing the risks with wearable health devices such as fitness trackers is user education. Although Fitbit provides extension information on its privacy policies, it is unlikely that users either read or understand what these policies mean [40, 41]. One of the authors was twice offered a free fitness tracker as part of the wellness programs on her campus, which she refused because of concerns about privacy, security and e-discovery. Participants were not provided with any information about these issues nor with suggestions for how to secure their data. Moreover, the leaders of the wellness program were shocked when the author told them that the data from fitness trackers was already being requested as evidence as part of litigation. Some options for increasing a user's awareness of the risks that might be posed by wearable health devices include clearer and more succinct privacy policies posted on vendor websites and training that accompanies the distribution of these devices as part of medical, health and wellness initiatives. The information on the Fitbit website is noteworthy in that the first set of information is in summary form in non-legal language that the public can easily understand [40]. More detailed information is then included as part of the company's detailed Privacy Policy [41]. Fitbit also provides its policies on other legal issues in its Terms of Service [42].

6   Conclusion

The question remains whether the privacy, security and discoverability risks to wearable health devices such as fitness trackers outweigh the benefits that these wearables can provide. There is a need to balance the privacy and security concerns against the potential improvements that can be made with respect to the health and wellness of consumers, the health care system and society as a whole. Given the as yet unsettled issues with the privacy and security of data from wearable health devices, the clear indication that this data will be requested and admitted as evidence in litigation and the lack of true understanding by users of the risks that these devices may pose, leads the authors to question whether the use of these devices is fitness or folly.

References

1. Ledger, D., McCaffrey, D.: Inside wearables: how the science of human behavior change offers the secret to long-term engagement. Endeavour Partners, LLC (2014). http://endeavourpartners.net/assets/Endeavour-Partners-Wearables-and-the-Science-of-Human-Behavior-Change-Part-1-January-20141.pdf. Accessed 19 Oct 2016
2. Marr, B.: 15 noteworthy facts about wearables in 2016 (2016). http://www.forbes.com/sites/bernardmarr/2016/03/18/15-mind-boggling-facts-about-wearables-in-2016/. Accessed 24 Feb 2017
3. Pricewaterhouse Coopers: The wearable future. In: Consumer Intelligence Series (2014). http://www.pwc.com/us/en/technology/publications/assets/pwc-wearable-tech-design-oct-8th.pdf. Accessed 28 Feb 2017
4. Davenport, T.H., Lucker, J.: Running on data: activity trackers and the Internet of Things. Deloitte Rev. **16**, 5–15 (2015)
5. The Office of the National Coordinator for Health Information Technology: Breaches of unsecured protected health information (2016). https://dashboard.healthit.gov/quickstats/pages/breaches-protected-health-information.php. Accessed 28 Feb 2017
6. EMC Corporation: Cybercrime and the health care industry (2013). http://www.emc.com/collateral/white-papers/h12105-cybercrime-healthcare-industry-rsa-wp.pdf. Accessed 28 Feb 2017
7. Goh, J.P.L.: Privacy, security, and wearable technology. Landslide **8**(2), 30–33 (2015)
8. Hunt, A.: Experts: wearable tech tests our privacy limits. USA Today, 5 February 2015. Available at http://www.usatoday.com/story/tech/2015/02/05/tech-wearables-privacy/22955707/. Accessed 24 Feb 2017

9. Zubulake v. UBS Warburg, 217 F.R.D. 309 (S.D.N.Y. 2003); Zubulake v. UBS Warburg, 216 F.R.D. 280 (S.D.N.Y. 2003); Zubulake v. UBS Warburg, 220 F.R.D. 212 (S.D.N.Y. 2003); Zubulake v. UBS Warburg, 229 F.R.D. 422 (S.D.N.Y. 2004)

10. Federal Rules of Civil Procedure As Amended to December 1, 2016. Available via Legal Information Institute at https://www.law.cornell.edu/rules/frcp. Accessed 8 Feb 2017

11. Fuchs, J.L., McLean, C.G., Fiorentinos, I.S., et al.: Noteworthy trends from cases decided under the recently amended Federal Rules of Civil Procedure (2016). Available via Jones Day at http://www.jonesday.com/noteworthy-trends-from-cases-decided-under-the-recently-amended-federal-rules-of-civil-procedure-09-06-2016/. Accessed 28 Feb 2017

12. Nelson, S.D., Simek, J.W.: The internet of everything: what it means for lawyers (2014). Available via Sensei Enterprises at https://senseient.com/articles/the-internet-of-everything-what-it-means-for-lawyers/. Accessed 28 Feb 2017

13. Gottehrer, G.: "Connected" discovery: what the ubiquity of digital evidence means for lawyers and litigation. Richmond J. Law Technol. **22**, 1–27 (2016)

14. Odendahl, M.: Fitness trackers add to flood of digital evidence in court (2016). Available via The Indiana Lawyer at http://www.theindianalawyer.com/fitness-trackers-add-to-flood-of-digital-evidence-in-courts/PARAMS/article/41112. Accessed 28 Feb 2017

15. Matthews, D.R.: Electronically Stored Information: The Complete Guide to Management, Understanding, Acquisition, Storage, Search, and Retrieval, 2nd edn. CRC Press, Boca Raton (2016)

16. Evenson, K.R., Goto, M.M., Furberg, R.D.: Systematic review of the validity and reliability of consumer-wearable activity trackers. Int. J. Behav. Nutr. Phys. Act. **12**, 159–181 (2015)

17. Weintraub, K.: Wearable health monitors not always reliable, study shows, 12 October 2016. Available via USA Today. http://www.usatoday.com/story/news/2016/10/12/wearable-health-monitors-not-always-reliable-study-shows/91922858/. Accessed 28 Feb 2017

18. Chauriye, N.: Wearable devices as admissible evidence: technology is killing our opportunity to lie. Catholic Univ. J. Law Technol. **24**(2), 495–528 (2016)

19. Hambright, B.: Police: knife, vodka used to stage scene report debunked: crime woman alleged she work up to man assaulting her; officers say Fitbit device conflicted with story. LNP (Lancaster, PA), 20 June 2015, p. 3 (2015)

20. Murphy, P.: Wearables: e-discovery's new frontier? (2015). Available via Rhode Island Lawyers Weekly at http://rilawyersweekly.com/blog/2015/05/14/wearables-e-discoverys-new-frontier/. Accessed 28 Feb 2017

21. Schetzer, A.: Look who's minding your step count. The Sun Herald (Sydney, Australia), 28 December 2014, p. 15 (2014)

22. Kuitenbrouwer, P.: Your fitness tracker could be a snitch. Financial Post, 5 May 2015, p. FP5 (2015)

23. Hitchcock, H.: Who's keeping track of workers' fitness trackers? The Western Mail, 5 August 2015, p. 20 (2015)

24. Hook, S.A.: Real-world examples, handy how-to's and sample screen shots. In: How to Get Your Social Media, Email and Text Evidence Admitted into Evidence (and Keep Theirs Out). National Business Institute, Eau Claire (2016)

25. Brown, E.A.: The Fitbit fault line: two proposals to protect health and fitness data at work. Yale J. Health Policy Law Ethics **16**(1), 1–49 (2016)

26. Fitbit Press Release (2015). https://investor.fitbit.com/press/press-releases/press-release-details/2015/Fitbit-Extends-Corporate-Wellness-Offering-with-HIPAA-Compliant-Capabilities/default.aspx. Accessed 28 Feb 2017

27. U.S. Department of Health and Human Services: HITECH Act Enforcement Interim Final Rule (2009). https://www.hhs.gov/hipaa/for-professionals/special-topics/HITECH-act-enforcement-interim-final-rule/index.html?language=es. Accessed 28 Feb 2017
28. Rockwell, K.L.: The promise of telemedicine: current landscape and future directions. Michigan Bar J. **96**(2), 38–42 (2017)
29. Sullivan, T.: FDA device guidance: general wellness policy for low risk devices (2015). Available via Policy and Medicine at http://www.policymed.com/2015/01/fda-device-guidance-general-wellness-policy-for-low-risk-devices.html. Accessed 28 Feb 2017
30. Spann, S.: Wearable fitness devices: personal health data privacy in Washington State. Seattle Univ. Law Rev. **39**, 1141–1432 (2016)
31. Indiana Code 24-4.9, Sections 1-5: Disclosure of security breach. https://iga.in.gov/legislative/laws/2015/ic/. Accessed 28 Feb 2017
32. Indiana Code 4-1-6, Sections 1-9: Fair information practices; privacy of personal information. https://iga.in.gov/legislative/laws/2015/ic/. Accessed 28 Feb 2017
33. Indiana Code 4-6-14, Sections 1-15: Health records and identifying information. https://iga.in.gov/legislative/laws/2015/ic/. Accessed 28 Feb 2017
34. Nelson, S.D., Ries, D.G., Simek, J.W.: Locked Down: Practical Information Security for Lawyers, 2nd edn. American Bar Association, Chicago (2016)
35. Appendix F. Massachusetts Regulations – Personal Information Protection. In: Nelson, S.D., Ries, D.G., Simek, J.W. (eds.) Locked Down: Practical Information Security for Lawyers, 2nd edn. American Bar Association, Chicago (2016)
36. Medical Records – Health Care Information Access and Disclosure. Available via Washington State Legislature at http://app.leg.wa.gov/RCW/default.aspx?cite=70.02. Accessed 28 Feb 2017
37. Reuhs, N.: Insurance coverage for the Internet of Things. The Indiana Lawyer 27:8 (2017)
38. Königs, B., Schaub, F., Weber, M.: Who, how, and why? Enhancing privacy awareness in ubiquitous computing. In: 2013 IEEE International Conference on Pervasive Computing and Communications Workshops (PERCOM Workshops). IEEE, pp. 364–367 (2013)
39. Motti, V.G., Caine, K.: Users' privacy concerns about wearables. In: Brenner, M., Christin, N., Johnson, B., Rohloff, K. (eds.) FC 2015. LNCS, vol. 8976, pp. 231–244. Springer, Heidelberg (2015). doi:10.1007/978-3-662-48051-9_17
40. Let's talk about privacy, publicly. Available via Fitbit at https://www.fitbit.com/legal/privacy. Accessed 27 Feb 2017
41. Privacy Policy. Available via Fitbit at https://www.fitbit.com/legal/privacy-policy. Accessed 27 Feb 2017
42. Terms of Service. Available via Fitbit at https://www.fitbit.com/legal/terms-of-service. Accessed 27 Feb 2017

Design and Usability Evaluation of Speech Rehabilitation APP Interface for Patients with Parkinson's Disease

Hsin-Chang Lo[1]([⊠]), Shih-Tsang Tang[2], Wan-Li Wei[1], and Ching-Chang Chuang[1]

[1] Department of Product Design, Ming Chuan University, Taoyuan, Taiwan
{lohc,wanliwei,ccchuang}@mail.mcu.edu.tw
[2] Department of Biomedical Engineering, Ming Chuan University, Taoyuan, Taiwan
sttang@mail.mcu.edu.tw

Abstract. Most patients with Parkinson's disease suffer from speech disorders which can be effectively improved through continuous speech therapy. However, there are very few speech therapists in Taiwan, so the patients do not have enough access to rehabilitation therapy, thereby contributing to poor rehabilitation outcomes. Based on motor speech disorder therapy and the service design process, this study proposed a Speech Rehabilitation mobile application software (App) interfaces for patients with Parkinson's disease. The sound interface usability is verified by the actual operation of two patients, and the pronunciation is significantly improved after a short-term use. In the future, the results could be extended to develop long-distance rehabilitation services, expecting to enhance the rehabilitation motivation and effectiveness of patients.

Keywords: Parkinson's disease · Speech rehabilitation · App interface design · Usability evaluation

1 Introduction

Approximately 60–90% of patients with Parkinson's disease (PD) will experience speech disorders, which include monopitch, feebleness, slowness, incoordination, hoarseness and irregular articulatory breakdown [1]. The current solution to speech disorders is to combine levodopa with speech therapy. According to speech and language therapist (ST) planning, patients with PD will receive a series of face-to-face corrections, such as Lee Silverman Voice Treatment and Pitch Limiting Voice Treatment [2], including pronunciation exercises, control the speed of speech, articulation exercises, emotion expression, intonation exercises, volume control, breathing regulation, etc. Besides, auditory feedback device, amplifiers, rhythm boards and other auxiliary equipment are used based on the actual needs [3, 4]. However, speech therapy is a highly personalized and time-consuming course of treatment [5]. It was mentioned that at least 26.2 STs were required for every 10 million people, but this ratio is relatively low (only 1.6 STs for every 10 million people) in Taiwan. In addition, most

© Springer International Publishing AG 2017
M. Antona and C. Stephanidis (Eds.): UAHCI 2017, Part III, LNCS 10279, pp. 65–75, 2017.
DOI: 10.1007/978-3-319-58700-4_6

of the STs worked in medical centers or rehabilitation institutions in cities. As a result, patients with PD cannot receive sufficient treatment from STs, leading to reduced rehabilitation effectiveness. After returning home, only a few patients can follow the ST's instructions and independently carry out related training. Moreover, the repeated, monotonous and drab traditional rehabilitation movements lower the patient's rehabilitation willingness, and worse still, the effectiveness of patients' self-exercises at home is difficult to control [6].

In recent years, because of the immense advances in intelligent mobile devices digital contents can be efficiently transmitted and presented to the users, hence also providing a more convenient way of rehabilitation. In the era of "Time is Brain", mobile devices can provide patients with information and images, assisting them in overcoming space-time barriers, and enhance the motivation and effectiveness of home-based rehabilitation [7, 8]. In other words, mobile devices have become an integral part of telemedicine. Therefore, this study aimed to design the Speech Rehabilitation APP interface and conduct the usability evaluation for patients with PD.

2   Empirical Study

2.1   Operation Task

Three patients with PD (Hoehn-Yahr stages I to III) were recruited to participate in the empirical study. The detailed information was shown in Table 1.

Table 1. Description of the subjects

	Sex	Age	Education	Visual ability	Tablet experience	Stages
1	Male	78	Less than high school	Presbyopia, cataract	No	I
2	Male	84	Bachelor	Presbyopia, cataract	No	III
3[a]	Male	62	Bachelor	Presbyopia	Yes	II

[a]Received deep brain stimulation

They were asked to operate two types of Apps related to speech therapy and three types of voice recording APPs (Figs. 1 and 2) using Sony Xperia™ Z4 tablet computer (Android 5.0, 10.1″, WQXGA 2560 × 1600 pixel). The researcher observed the subjects' operational behaviors and inquired them about their reflections on operation task (Fig. 3).

2.2   Results of Empirical Study

From the empirical study, we found some defects when subjects operating above speech therapy and voice recording APPs:

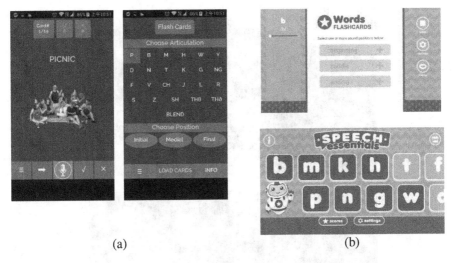

Fig. 1. Speech therapy Apps. (a) Speech therapy word list; (b) speech essentials therapy.

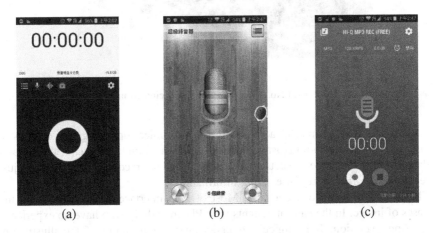

Fig. 2. Voice recording Apps. (a) ASR; (b) sound recorder; (c) Hi-Q MP3 voice recorder

1. Inconvenient APPs download and installation process: the researcher asked subjects download assigned APPs to the Tablet from the Google Play store. All of the subjects could not complete this task. Then, researchers ask the subjects to operate the installation process after assisting download the specified APPs, they still could not successfully complete the task, especially in fill in basic information in the registration stage.

2. Inconvenient recording process: the researchers asked the subjects facing the tablet computer microphone and said a passage. But the subjects did not know the location of the microphone. After reminding the location of the Tablet computer, the subjects move the device to the mouth side and then talk. However the subjects represent that they could not see the screen content, and not sure whether complete the task successfully.

(b)

Fig. 3. Subject (a) No. 2 and (b) No. 3 participated in this study.

3. Cannot find past records: In addition to ask the subject operating above APPs, it also asked the them to find just recorded files. It was found that even if there was a date and time code, the subjects were unable to find the recorded files that were just recorded in a few pieces of existing information.
4. The icon is difficult to understand: Most of App interface were designed on the bases of image. In the case of patients with PD are elderly who have no experience on App operation. It is difficult to understand the meaning of the illustration, therefore affects the fluency and efficiency at the time of operation.
5. Lack of explanation: For aesthetic reasons, APP interface design significantly reduce the text explanation that led to the operation of the user inconvenience. Subjects represent that they would like to have a written description of the APP.

3   Interface Design

3.1   Operation Process

According to those defects, we build the speech rehabilitation service blueprint for patients with PD. Through the interaction, visible and internal interaction lines, the whole service process was divided into four sections: Customer Action, Front-of-stage, Back-of-stage, and Support Process, respectively (Fig. 4). This service blueprint focused on the speech rehabilitation service actions and were classified into the traditional rehabilitation, the pre-therapy stage, the therapy course, and the post-therapy stage.

Then, the speech rehabilitation service process was conducted. The most important stage is the therapy course, which includes: pronunciation practice, monophonetic practice (including the exercises of volume, persistence, high pitch and low pitch), phrase practice, and sentence practice (mainly including the exercises of volume and

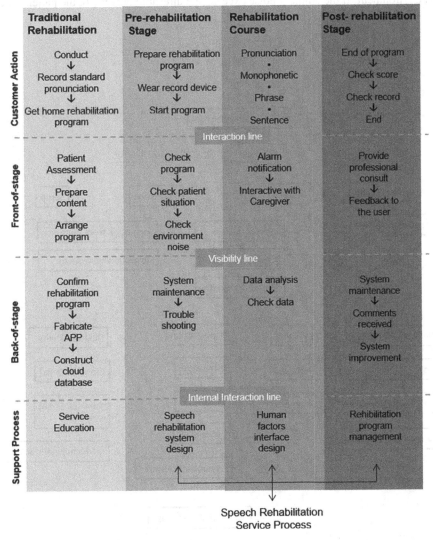

Fig. 4. The service blueprint of Speech Rehabilitation for the patients with PD

intelligibility). At the end of practice, it would provide the patients with the evaluation data of rehabilitation effects. It was expected to provide the comprehensive score (weighted from the volume level and intelligibility scores) as a reference for the user. The rehabilitation results would also be recorded.

3.2 Interface Design

The framework of the Speech Rehabilitation APP for patients with PD is presented in Fig. 5:

When the users starts the App, the software will first test the background noise of field environment. If the ambient noise exceeds the threshold 50 dB [9], the patients are

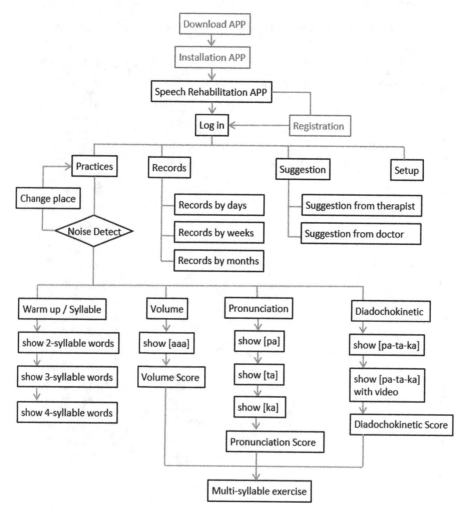

Fig. 5. The framework of the Speech Rehabilitation App

recommended to exercise in other rooms. If the background noise is within the acceptable range, then it will be go to the main menu. Then, the patients choose a. Volume, b. Pronunciation, c. Diadochokinetic, d. Syllable exercise or other exercises. a. Volume exercise means that users are asked to utter long sound of a-a-a. The louder and longer the sound is, the better it is. Such exercise is designed to record whether the patients' sound frequency is stable. b. Pronunciation exercise means that patients are

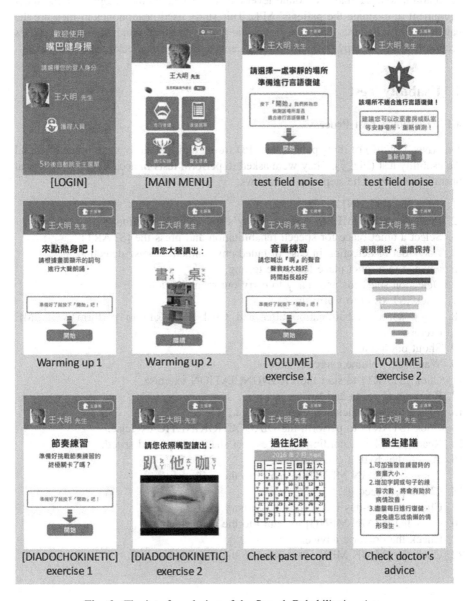

Fig. 6. The interface design of the Speech Rehabilitation App.

asked to quickly move their lips and to continuously emit such sounds as pa, ta, and ka. c. Diadochokinetic exercise means that patients are asked to quickly move their lips and to continuously emit the sound pa-ta-ka. d. Syllable exercise means that patients are asked to read words of 2, 3, and 4 syllables, and aims at warming up. Some interface design of the APP were shown in Fig. 6.

The mean and duration of the patient's sound pressure level (SPL) are important indicators of evaluating the degree of speech disorders. In the visits to the department of rehabilitation, ST may use sound level meter, chromatic tuner, stopwatch and other equipment to evaluate the patients' SPL. This study used headphones to measure the patients' SPL. Patients can repeat the same exercises or conduct other exercises according to the therapy program. Both patients and STs can check records and scores.

4 Usability Test

4.1 Usability Test Process

Two (No. 1 and 2) of three patient with PD from empirical study were invite to attend the usability test (Fig. 7). They were asked to perform tests in accordance with typical operational tasks. The steps are as follows:

1. Press the [LOGIN] to log in.
2. Press the [RESUME] to perform today's speech rehabilitation.
3. Select a quiet place for speech rehabilitation and press the [START].
4. Carry out re-detection in case of failed environmental noise detection.
5. Change to a quiet place for noise testing.
6. Detection succeeds and ready to carry out rehabilitation.
7. Click [START] to warm up.
8. Begin speech rehabilitation after and Click [START] to perform VOLUME exercise.
9. Shout out a-a-a.
10. Watch the volume exercise score.
11. Click [START] to start the PRONUNCIATION exercise.
12. Read aloud pa, ta and ka.
13. Watch the pronunciation exercise score.
14. Click [START] to perform the DIADOCHOKINETIC exercise.
15. Read [pa-ta-ka] according to the correct shape of lips and speed.
16. Watch the rhythm exercise score.
17. Click the [MAIN MENU] to return to the main menu.
18. Check past records.
19. Check the one-day record of 11 February 2016.
20. Click the [MAIN MENU] to return to the main menu.
21. Check the doctor's advice.
22. Click the [MAIN MENU] to return to the main menu.

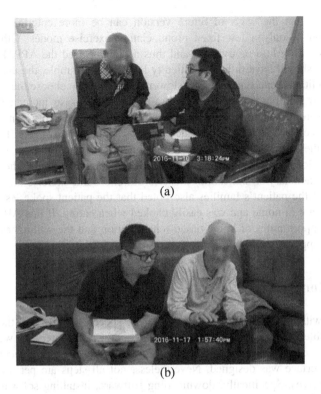

(a)

(b)

Fig. 7. Subject (a) No. 1 and (b) No. 2 operate the Speech Rehabilitating APP.

The first round of interviews was carried out after the completion of typical operational tasks. After the interview was completed, the subjects were allowed to freely operate this APP, then have the second round of interviews.

4.2   Results of Usability Test

It is found from the first round of interviews that the Speech Rehabilitation APP interface is designed by combining icons and texts. The subjects indicated that most of the tasks were performed by reading texts, and believed that icons facilitated use. The icons and text descriptions were large enough during operation, so there was no difficulty in reading, recognizing, or touching icons. Additionally, this APP provides static icon guidelines, dynamic visual feedback and video. Subjects suggested that the way of video demonstration was the easiest way to learn. However, the subjects pointed out that during the task operation, the step "19. Check the one-day record of 11 February 2016" was difficult to complete. The researchers speculated that the presentation methods of the past records do not meet the subjects' mental model.

During the second round of interviews, the subjects suggested that more interesting ways such as singing can be added in the warm-up stage, or that other more interactive ways can be added to prevent the patients from feeling bored. In the meantime, they also mentioned that the ways of future version can be more entertaining or more diverse, instead of only a few fixed pronunciation exercise modes. Otherwise, the patients would easily lose motivation, and thus no longer used the APP. Diadochokinetic exercises should have different difficulty levels. For example, the users who just start the rehabilitation can start from the slower speed, and can choose the faster modes after they grow familiar with the exercises. Besides, they also indicated that when completing exercise, on top of APP can show performance scores and encourage words, sound feedbacks may also be added, such as applause and cheers. This not only can increase the patients' sense of accomplishment, but can promote the patients' motivation of long-term use. Apart from above recommendations, the users also indicated that their larynx and mouth muscles did exert and exercise after task completion. One of the patient's families also noted that the patient spoke less frequently due to the disease at home and was easily choked when eating. If this APP can boost the patient's opportunities of home-based rehabilitation and the willingness to speak, they will be happy to see.

5 Discussion

The patients with PD were invited to operate the speech therapy and the recording APPs using tablet computer. The site-observation and in-depth interview were adopted to develop the service blueprint and operation process and then the Speech Rehabilitation APP interface was designed. Nevertheless, not all steps are performed by the patients themselves. Specifically, downloading software, installing software, registering personal data and other functions (shown in gray box of Fig. 5) require the assist of STs or caregivers. Especially, the registration function involves the input of Chinese and English names, the choice of gender and the choice of date of birth, which are difficult to complete by patients with PD (middle-aged and elderly).

For the interface design, the minimum font size of the APP in this study presented on a tablet is about 14 pt and the minimum icon is about 1 × 1 cm. Although the subjects suffered from presbyopia, they did not argue that they could not see or could not clearly see the work descriptions. As a result, visual degradation does not affect their operation of the APP. At the same time, this study used icon and text to make redundant code to guide the users, so there are few identification errors. However, the button click is not smooth. The button will the visual feedback of becoming larger and moving to the lower right corner when correctly pressed, but due to the lack of tactile feedback, the users do not know whether they click the button correctly and hence press the screen hard. Tactile degradation is a common problem with operation of tablet computers, and if necessary, may be addressed in other ways.

In addition to the aforementioned interface usability problems, the subjects also indicated that their larynx and mouth muscles did exert and exercise after task completion. Furthermore, the researchers observed that within a short term of about 15–20 min from typical task operation, the patients' voice is significantly louder and their pronunciation is clearer. These prove that the APP does help the patients to exercise their laryngeal muscles.

6 Conclusion

Speech disorders of patients with PD will deteriorate over time, and only through uninterrupted exercises can degradation be slowed down. This study is based on motor speech therapy and proposes Speech Rehabilitation APP interfaces for patients with PD. The interface usability of the APP is verified by the actual operation of two patients, and the pronunciation is significantly improved after a short-term use. In the future, it is hoped that patients with PD can continue to use the APP for independent exercises after receiving ST treatment, and should be able to reach the effect of delaying laryngeal muscle degeneration. In the future, the research team will extend the results and make use of information and communication technology and cloud computing technology to develop long-distance rehabilitation services, expecting to enhance the rehabilitation motivation and effectiveness of patients.

Acknowledgements. The authors appreciate Chang Ching-Min and the participations. This work was sponsored under grant MOST 105-2410-H-130-034 - and 105-2632-E-130-001 - by the Ministry of Science and Technology, Taiwan.

References

1. Weiner, W.J., Singer, C.: Parkinson's disease and nonpharmacologic treatment programs. J. Am. Geriatr. Soc. **37**, 359–363 (1989)
2. Cynthia, F., Georg, E., Lorraine, R., Shimon, S.: LSVT LOUD and LSVT BIG: behavioral treatment programs for speech and body movement in Parkinson disease. Parkinsons Dis. (2012). Article ID 391946
3. Aronson, E., Bless, M.: Clinical Voice Disorders. Thieme, New York (1990)
4. Enderby, P., Pickstone, C.: How many people have communication disorders and why does it matter? Int. J. Speech Lang. Pathol. **7**, 8–13 (2005)
5. Hall, E.: 'Joined-up working' between early years professionals and speech and language therapists: moving beyond 'normal' roles. J. Interprof. Care **19**, 11–21 (2005)
6. Ellis-Hill, C., Robison, J., Wiles, R., McPherson, K., Hyndman, D.A.: Going home to get on with life: patients and careers experiences of being discharged from hospital following a stroke. Disabil. Rehabil. **31**, 61–72 (2009)
7. Fan, Y.J., Yin, Y.H., Xu, L.D., Zeng, Y., Wu, F.: IoT-based smart rehabilitation system. IEEE Trans. Ind. Inform. **10**, 1568–1577 (2014)
8. Al-Razgan, M.S., Al-Khalifa, H.S., Al-Shahrani, M.D., AlAjmi, H.: Touch-based mobile phone interface guidelines and design recommendations for elderly people: a survey of the literature. In: Proceedings of 19th International Conference on ICONIP 2012, Part IV, pp. 568–574 (2012)
9. Baken, J., Orlikoff, R.F.: Clinical Measurement of Speech and Voice, 2nd edn. Singular Thomson Learning, San Diego (2000)

Game-Based Speech Rehabilitation for People with Parkinson's Disease

Juliane Mühlhaus[1,2(✉)], Hendrike Frieg[2], Kerstin Bilda[2], and Ute Ritterfeld[1]

[1] Department of Language and Communication, TU Dortmund University, Dortmund, Germany
{juliane.muehlhaus,ute.ritterfeld}@tu-dortmund.de
[2] Department of Applied Health Sciences, Hochschule für Gesundheit, Bochum, Germany
{hendrike.frieg,kerstin.bilda}@hs-gesundheit.de

Abstract. Neurodegenerative syndromes such as Parkinson's disease usually lead to speech impairments. Reduced intelligibility of spoken language is treatable with Speech and Language Therapy. A successful speech therapy implements the principles of frequency, intensity and repetition. Consequently, patients need to be highly motivated for the exercises to keep up with their training. We argue that game-based technology are prone to support patients in partaking in a self-sustained high frequency training. Furthermore, studies demonstrate that game-based interventions have the potential to enhance motivation for rehabilitative exercising in patients with neurological disorders. Building on these insights we apply successful principles of gamification to enhance impaired speech in patients with neurogenerative syndromes. With the ISi-Speech project ('Individualisierte Spracherkennung in der Rehabilitation für Menschen mit Beeinträchtigung in der Sprechverständlichkeit' (in German) [individual speech recognition in therapy for people with motor speech disorders]) we further integrate psychological motivation theory (self-determination) and user driven design into the developmental process of a rehabilitation tool for patients with Parkinson's disease.

Keywords: Parkinson's disease · Speech therapy · Self-determination theory · Gamification · Game-based intervention

1 Introduction

Some neurodegenerative syndromes result in substantial speech impairments reducing intelligibility of spoken language and hereby affecting everyday communication and eventually contributing to social isolation [1]. For example, dysarthria is a speech motor impairment that results from neuromuscular control disturbance and is a symptom of Parkinson's disease. In this case, speech therapy can help to support communication when frequency and intensity is given [2]. During sessions, therapists introduce and monitor exercises for treatment of articulation, prosody and pitch range, speech rate, vocal volume, or resonance. High frequency of exercises is in need of additional intensive training besides the speech therapy sessions. As therapists cannot supervise all training, they need to give patients control over self-regulated training. Only in this case, the necessary redundancy of several exercise units a day can be ensured.

© Springer International Publishing AG 2017
M. Antona and C. Stephanidis (Eds.): UAHCI 2017, Part III, LNCS 10279, pp. 76–85, 2017.
DOI: 10.1007/978-3-319-58700-4_7

Since such exercises are often strenuous, monotone, repetitive and boring many patients lack the necessary motivation to keep up with their training [3]. In addition, self-awareness of speech quality is often reduced in patients with Parkinson's disease. They need accurate and immediate feed-back, for example via automatic speech recognition, in order to evaluate intelligibility and progress. Game-based technology might be able to provide these patients with the adequate tool for independent and high frequency training, tapping into the empowerment of the patient [4]. In the R&D project ISi-Speech ('Individualisierte Spracherkennung in der Rehabilitation für Menschen mit Beeinträchtigung in der Sprechverständlichkeit' (in German) [individual speech recognition in therapy for people with motor speech disorders]), we are joining efforts to develop a digital training system for people with dysarthria in an interdisciplinary team of engineers for speech signal processing and informatics, media designers, and researchers from the fields of speech pathology and psychology. The challenge is to develop an automatic speech recognition system applicable to distorted speech and to integrate this system into a speech therapy application that incorporates the motivational potential contributing to frequent and autonomous usage. Therefore, motivation theory related to a game-based context will be applied.

2 Gaming Motivation

Games show the potential to satisfy psychological needs and provide deeper and long-lasting experiences for players [5]. Motivational theories such as self-determination theory (SDT) have been applied to games, the motivation of players and the well-being outcomes of play. SDT assumes that all humans are driven by the basic psychological needs for competence, autonomy, and relatedness [6]. While the need for autonomy reflects a desire to engage in activities of one's choice, the need for competence implies a desire to interact effectively with the environment. The need for relatedness involves the feeling of being socially connected. Tapping into these components technology–and particularly game-based interventions–suggest a tremendous potential to facilitate health behavior [7, 8]. The beneficial effects of enhancing the components autonomy and competence have already been observed for features of the gaming environment and in the context of acceptance of video game play [7–9]. Specifically, features such as flexibility, choice, and structured rewards support a sense of autonomy. The feeling of competence may be supported by game features such as intuitiveness, optimal challenges or adequate feed-back. Social elements such as avatars or agents as well as real players connected through a game are supporting the experience of relatedness.

Szalma [5], for example, recently suggested factors for game design that effect human needs in technology use based on SDT. Such factors are for example choice setting, informational feed-back, accountability for performance outcome, acknowledgement of the user's experience, meaningful rationale for tasks as well as an explicit acknowledgement that a specific task may be experienced as uninteresting. In a large study, evidence was accumulated for six clusters of players' motivation such as action, social, mastery, achievement, creativity, and immersion [10]. Knowing that players have different motivations resulting in different profiles can help to implement adequate motivational elements to the game context. Peng and colleagues [11] implemented game features based on SDT in the context of video games. For example, features such as character customization, treasure collection, and different strands of conversation are recognized as support for players' perception of autonomy. Furthermore, system adaption, heroism meter or achievement badges are designed to enhance satisfaction of competence. Finally, context information and supportive dialogue were intended to increase relatedness.

What can be learned from gaming studies for the health context? Health games become increasingly popular (e.g. [4, 12, 13]). They incorporate design elements in a non-game context and are therefore defined as gamification [14]. Health games, specifically applied to intervention format, represent for example an opportunity to meaningfully engage patients and improve enjoyment of training. But most of health technology still neglects the potential of motivational elements and its supportive character [3]. The goal of a supportive environment will be to overcome the boredom of repetitive and monotonous tasks and to engage the users by giving them a contextualized meaning for the repetitive task. The inclusion of motivational elements in the task, the interface or the context offer opportunities to satisfy the core human need for autonomy, competence and relatedness. Within this paper we want to assign insights from both, SDT and game-based studies to ISi-Speech as a therapeutic game.

3   Therapeutic Games

Mader and colleagues [3] defined therapeutic games as "games that produce a direct, expected, and intended therapeutic effect on patients playing them. This therapeutic effect may be to alleviate, to improve or to heal the specific condition of the patients" [3, p. 1]. This means for example, that the therapeutic effect of a better intelligibility of spoken language derives from the loudness adaption and not directly from the game session.

Sustaining a patient's motivation for therapy in chronic conditions is one of the most difficult long-term challenges [15]. The combination of game and therapy is very promising to maintain the motivation of patients to follow their exercises in speech therapy. Over the last years a broad body of research could be accumulated on the positive effects of play in the health context [4, 16–20]. Researchers discussed the potential of games offering therapeutic benefits to various subgroups of people and conditions to use them appropriately. One of the most important challenges of therapeutic game design is the complex development process combining game action and therapeutic competence [3]. How to choose therapeutic games wisely, i.e. based on evidence, has been proposed by speech and language therapists (e.g. [21, 22]). Hereby, the authors suggest a procedure for an evidence-based selection of apps that integrates both, the classical evidence-based approach to the selection of therapeutic methods and the evaluation of apps as well as their integration into the individual therapy setting.

4   Embedding Self-determination Theory into Game-Based Speech Rehabilitation

In this section we want to argue for the necessity to combine both, the evidence of gaming motivation based on SDT and the knowledge on health gaming in order to develop a therapeutic game such as ISi-Speech.

Evidence suggests that interventions based on theoretical approaches are more effective than ad hoc developments (for a review see [23]). As mentioned in Sect. 2 a successful example of linking theory to health intervention designs is the SDT (e.g. [24, 25]; for a summary see [26]). Furthermore, any rehabilitation training technology needs to match the therapeutic intervention. Without explicit attention to theory health behavior intervention might fail.

Within the health domain, game-based interventions are increasingly shown to indeed enhance motivation (e.g. [18, 27–29]) and motor control (e.g. [30, 31]) in patients with neurological disorders. While a few systematic reviews focusing on physical activity examined the effectiveness of game-based interventions (e.g. [32]), studies investigating game-based tools for speech intervention are scarce (e.g. [33]). As a result, interventions seem to enhance the selected therapy goal, but the effect of such interventions in the longer run is not clarified yet. Gamification elements such as feed-back, adaptability, motivational elements, and monitoring are identified as important features for games used as rehabilitation tool (e.g. [34]).

Within ISi-Speech we assigned gamification elements to the patients' need for autonomy, competence and relatedness as described in SDT (Table 1). This theory based approach allows for a better understanding how technology and psychology need to closely work together in order to prompt a usage of the system that will eventually result in effectivity. The first column contains the operationalization of autonomy, competence and relatedness within the context of digital interactive media. Column two defines the goal to be achieved within the therapeutic game. The last column finally gives examples how this goal is supposed to be attained within ISi-Speech as a tool for the improvement of speech in patients with Parkinson disease. These examples are driven from a script implemented in ISi-Speech in which a patient is supposed to order coffee and cake in a bakery. This script was designed to facilitate common interactions in a rather public space.

4.1   Autonomy

Allowing choice as much as it is practical in exercising has been demonstrated to be an important feature supporting autonomy [5]. In ISi-Speech, for each training session the patient will have the choice between activities within the task. For example, the choice whether s/he needs an auditory repetition of the word s/he has to produce.

Another control feature is based on different strands of conversation resulting in true interactivity. If patients can choose between options that result in different interactions, conversation styles are personalized, too [35].

Table 1. Implementing SDT-based gamification elements into ISi-Speech.

SDT related features	Goal	Examples of SDT-based gamification elements in ISi-Speech
Autonomy		
Choice	The patient has choice in activities and goal selection	The patient can choose whether s/he needs an auditory repetition of the word s/he has to produce
Conversation	Achieving credibility of the system via personalized messages	The dialogue path of the virtual coach depends on the item selection of the patient within the task
Rewards	The patient chooses between different reward systems and receives reinforcement for a desired action	The patient has to decide between earning two more points for completing the minimum amount of speech exercises required a day or ten more points to unlock the next level and receive an award
Competence		
Feed-back	The patient receives highly specific and individualized, visual and acoustic feed-back on his/her performance. In addition, improvements over time are communicated	The patient has to order a piece of cake and a cup of coffee by her/his own choice within the participation task. Immediately s/he gets the information from the system that her/his choice of cake was well articulated but the type of coffee wasn't
Achievement	The patient receives information on her/his power gain	The patient can browse for an achievement menu provided by the system
Adaption	The patient continues engaging with the exercise as s/he progresses through it with increased difficulty	The patient is asked to articulate five words above 60 dB in order to unlock additional points
Relatedness		
Virtual coach	The patient forms a long-term meaningful relationship with the virtual character. S/he offers companionship and support and invites for para-social relationship	At the beginning of the ISi-Speech training the patient is instructed to select gender, age and personality of her/his virtual coach that will accompany the patient throughout the training
Competition	The patient evaluates her/his performance by comparing it to others. The comparison drives the patient to perform better on the task	Patients are ranked on a leaderboard by the amount of exercise units they logged within a day
Collaboration	The patient experiences encouragement from other patients and is part of a group effort	To unlock the next articulation level patients must work as a team to achieve the intervention goal of speaking ten words in a clear articulation

Furthermore, the experience of autonomy could be reached by giving patients a choice in the reward system [11]. ISi-Speech will implement extrinsic and performance-based rewards to provide incentives to patients in order to reinforce the desired response. Social and individual norms will be both used as anchors for comparison. Goals are made transparent and associated with the reward, for example how many points can be earned for completing minimum specific amount of speech exercises per day. Positive evidence with respect to the implementation of (social) rewards systems in the game sector [12] encourages us to apply those motivational components to ISi-Speech.

4.2 Competence

The most important motivational design element in ISi-Speech is the feed-back component. Feed-back is given an additional role to forestall the tendency of patients with Parkinson's disease to falsely attribute problems in communication to others (e.g. to attribute hearing loss to their conversation partner rather than acknowledging that they speak too soft and therefore not intelligible enough themselves). In this case, tailored feed-back facilitates the patient's experience of competence during exercising. We implement an automatic speech recognition system that has been shown to be effective in patients with dysarthria [33]. Feed-back that utilizes play-back combined with accurate and specific evaluation of recorded speech will guide towards more adequate self-perception.

The achievement component seems to be highly important for the patients' satisfaction of competence as well. ISi-Speech will incorporate various types of achievement badges per exercise. Throughout all of exercises patients can browse for example in a specific achievement menu [11]. To support the perception of progress, ISi-speech will make the advancement of each user constantly visible [36]. Thus, patients will be able to easily inform themselves about progress and power gain online.

Another competence supporting element is highly adaptive to the performance of the user. In this case, the ISi-Speech mechanism will adjust constantly along with the user's performance in the exercise. For example, when a patient successfully exercises a predefined number of task items, s/he will be offered the next task unit both, immediately and when all task items are completed. Variables such as time and number of repetitions per task are important measurements for a subsequent adaption. However, there is still discussion how incremental levels have to be designed in health games in order to impact health behavior [37].

4.3 Relatedness

We aim to develop a so called para-social relationship between the patient user and ISi-Speech by implementing a virtual coach (VC). Through building a tutor character, we aim to reach a personalization of the system [11, 36, 38]. This VC can be a constant companion during the training. If patients are given the tools to choose her/his features such as gender, voice, age and personality as well as the character's appearance learner motivation will be enhanced [39–41]. Para-social propositions are shown to have a huge potential for the feeling of social inclusion [42]. For example, the VC can fulfill the desire to form long-term meaningful relationships with others [38] and might facilitate motivation and outcome when the valence of social cues is taken into account [39]. Especially when the VC is self-made and implemented in a social dialogue, exercises might be perceived as more pleasant [40, 43] and VC acceptance is higher [44]. In addition, information about the tasks in the exercises will create an environment for users that enhances the experience of social presence [11]. Based on this evidence, the implementation of a virtual coach in ISi-Speech will strengthen the patient-VC-relationship (relatedness) and thereby support the patients' need of being respected and understood and consequently, feeling socially included.

Other components of ISi-Speech are competition and collaboration. Studies demonstrated sustainable usage when competition was included as an element (e.g. [45]). In collaborative teamwork situations, patients might derive satisfaction by the perception of being part of a group effort [38]. ISi-Speech will provide users with social support that encourages them to engage with the speech therapy exercise. For example, patients are assigned teams within an exercise for clear and exaggerated articulation of words. In order to unlock the next articulation level on the articulation exercise of phrases, patients must work as a team to achieve the therapy goal of speaking ten words with clear articulation. Hereby, the automatic speech recognition system implemented in ISi-Speech will support the patient in achieving her/his goal. In collaborative teamwork situations patients could have an interest in helping and chatting with others [38]. In contrast, the competition will enable each patient her/his own performance on the exercise by comparing it to other patients. The patient's motivation is based on her/his focus on a challenge and a competition with others in the exercise. Patients will be ranked on a leaderboard by the amount of speech exercises they logged over a day and different training sessions.

5   Summary and Conclusion

We reported how we use the potential of gamification elements to develop ISi-Speech as a rehabilitation tool in speech therapy based on SDT. The core principles of SDT such as autonomy, competence, and relatedness will facilitate activity, engagement and social interaction in our potential user group - patients with Parkinson's disease. We assume that the ISi-Speech training tool for individuals with Parkinson's disease increases the motivation for self-sustainable usage when intervention components are linked to those three core elements of SDT. Patients' autonomy will be reached by enabling the patients to be independent from others (e.g. family) while training with ISi-Speech. The experience of competence requires a comparison with previous achievements, others or a goal during training. We aim to reach relatedness in ISi-Speech facilitating the connectedness to other users as a source for feeling embedded. The incorporation of SDT during the development process of ISi-Speech as a game-based intervention promises acceptance and effectiveness of training in patients with Parkinson's disease. We envision being hereby able to substantially empower patients with impaired speech and contribute to their social inclusion.

Acknowledgements. The 'ISi-Speech' (grant agreement no. 16SV737/3-7) project is supported by the Federal Ministry of Education and Research under the Program 'IKT 2020 - Research for Innovations'.

References

1. Gage, H., Grainger, L., Ting, S., Williams, P., Chorley, C., Carey, G., et al.: Specialist rehabilitation for people with Parkinson's disease in the community: a randomised controlled trial. Health Serv. Deliv. Res. **2**(51) (2014). doi:10.3310/hsdr02510
2. Fox, C., Ebersbach, G., Ramig, L.O., Sapir, S.: LSVT LOUD and LSVT BIG: behavioral treatment programs for speech and body movement in parkinson disease. Parkinsons Dis. **2012**, 391–394 (2012)
3. Mader, S., Levieux, G., Natkin, S.: A game design method for therapeutic games. In: Paper presented at the 2016 8th international conference on games and virtual worlds for serious applications (VS-GAMES) (2016)
4. Ritterfeld, U.: Von videogames zu health gaming. Eine Einfuehrung. [From video games to health games. An introduction.]. In: Dadaczynski, K., Schiemann, S., Paulus, P. (eds.) Gesundheit Spielend Foerdern. Potentiale und Herausforderungen von Digitalen Spieleanwendungen fuer die Gesundheitsfoerderung und Praevention, pp. 173–190. Beltz Juventa, Weinheim (2016)
5. Szalma, J.L.: On the application of motivation theory to human factors/ergonomics: motivational design principles for human-technology interaction. Hum. Factors **56**(8), 1453–1471 (2014)
6. Deci, E.L., Ryan, R.M.: Self-determination theory. In: van Lange, P.A.M., Kruglanski, A.W., Higgins, E.T. (eds.) Handbook of Theories of Social Psychology, vol. 1, pp. 416–459. Sage Publications, London (2012)
7. Przybylski, A.K., Rigby, C.S., Ryan, R.M.: A motivational model of video game engagement. Rev. Gen. Psychol. **14**, 154–166 (2010)
8. Ryan, R.M., Rigby, C.S., Przybylski, A.: The motivational pull of video games: a self-determination theory approach. Motiv. Emot. **30**, 344–360 (2006)
9. Przybylski, A.K., Deci, E.L., Rigby, C.S., Ryan, R.M.: Competence-impeding electronic games and players' aggressive feelings, thoughts, and behaviors. J. Pers. Soc. Psychol. **106**, 441–457 (2014)
10. Yee, N.: The gamer motivation profile: what we learned from 250,000 gamers. Paper presented at the proceedings of the 2016 annual symposium on computer-human interaction in play, Austin, Texas, USA (2016)
11. Peng, W., Pfeiffer, K.A., Winn, B., Lin, J.H., Suton, D.: A pilot randomized, controlled trial of an active video game physical activity intervention. Health Psychol. **34s**, 1229–1239 (2015). doi:10.1037/hea0000302
12. Breitlauch, L.: Computerspiele als Therapie. Zur Wirksamkeit von "Games for Health" (Computer games for therapy. Evidence of "games for health"). In: Freyermuth, G.S., Gotto, L., Wallenfels, F. (eds.) Serious Games, Exergames, Exerlearning.Zur Transmedialisierung und Gamification des Wissenstransfers (Serious Games, Exergames, Exerlearning. Transmedialization and Gamification of the Transfer of Knowledge), pp. 387–398. Transcript, Bielefeld (2013)
13. Ratan, R., Ritterfeld, U.: Towards a psychological classification of serious games. In: Ritterfeld, U., Cody, M., Vorderer, P. (eds.) Serious Games: Mechanisms and Effects, pp. 10–24. Routledge/LEA, Mahwah NJ (2009)

14. Deterding, S., Dixon, D., Khaled, R., Nacke, L.: From game design elements to gamefulness: defining "gamification". Paper presented at the proceedings of the 15th international academic MindTrek conference: envisioning future media environments, Tampere, Finland (2011)
15. Sabate, E.: Adherence to Long-Term Therapies: Evidence for Action. World Health Organization, Geneva Switzerland (2003). http://www.who.int/chp/knowledge/publications/adherence_report/en/
16. Astell, A., Alm, N., Dye, R., Gowans, G., Vaughan, P., Ellis, M.: Digital Video Games for Older Adults with Cognitive Impairment. In: Miesenberger, K., Fels, D., Archambault, D., Peñáz, P., Zagler, W. (eds.) ICCHP 2014. LNCS, vol. 8547, pp. 264–271. Springer, Cham (2014). doi:10.1007/978-3-319-08596-8_42
17. Baranowski, T., Buday, R., Thompson, D.I., Baranowski, J.: Playing for real: video games and stories for health-related behavior change. Am. J. Prev. Med. **34**(1), 74–82.e10 (2008). doi:10.1016/j.amepre.2007.09.027
18. Kato, P.M.: Video games in health care: closing the gap. Rev. Gen. Psychol. **14**, 113–121 (2010)
19. Thompson, D., Baranowski, T., Buday, R., Baranowski, J., Thompson, V., Jago, R., Griffith, M.J.: Serious video games for health how behavioral science guided the development of a serious video game. Simul. Gaming **41**(4), 587–606 (2010). doi:10.1177/1046878108328087
20. Thompson, D.: Designing serious video games for health behavior change: current status and future directions. J. Diab. Sci. Technol. **6**(4), 807–811 (2012). doi:10.1177/193229681200600411
21. Wakefield, L., Schaber, T.: The PICO template for reviewing speech-language therapy apps: a decision-making tool for SLPs [Press release] (2011)
22. Starke, A., Mühlhaus, J.: Evidenzanspruch in der Anwendung von Applikationen in der Sprachtherapie (Demand on evidence for the use of applications in speech and language therapy). In: Bilda, K., Mühlhaus, J., Ritterfeld, U. (eds.) Neue Technologien in der Sprachtherapie (New Technologies in Speech and Language therapy), pp. 110–116. Thieme, Stuttgart (2016)
23. Glanz, K., Bishop, D.B.: The role of behavioral science theory in development and implementation of public health interventions. Annu. Rev. Public Health **31**, 399–418 (2010). doi:10.1146/annurev.publhealth.012809.103604
24. Deci, E.L., Ryan, R.M.: Self-determination theory: a macrotheory of human motivation, development, and health. Can. Psychol. **49**, 182–185 (2008)
25. Deci, E.L., Ryan, R.M.: Self-determination theory. In: van Lange, P.A.M., Kruglanski, A.W., Higgins, E.T. (eds.) Handbook of Theories of Social Psychology, vol. 1, pp. 416–459. Sage Publications, London (2012)
26. Ng, J.Y.Y., Ntoumanis, N., Thogersen-Ntoumani, C., Deci, E.L., Ryan, R.M., Duda, J.L., Williams, G.C.: Self-determination theory applied to health contexts: a meta-analysis. Perspect. Psychol. Sci. **7**, 325–340 (2012)
27. Primack, B.A., et al.: Role of video games in improving health-related outcomes: a systematic review. Am. J. Prev. Med. **42**, 630–638 (2012)
28. Rahmani, E., Boren, S.A.: Videogames and health improvement: a literature review of randomized controlled trials. Games Health J **1**, 331–341 (2012)
29. Swanson, L.R., Whittinghill, D.M.: Intrinsic or extrinsic? Using videogames to motivate stroke survivors: a systematic review. Games Health J. **4**, 253–258 (2015)
30. Barry, G., Galna, B., Rochester, L.: The role of exergaming in Parkinson's disease rehabilitation: a systematic review of the evidence. J. Neuroeng. Rehabil. **11**(33), 1–18 (2014). doi:10.1186/1743-0003-11-33

31. Burke, J.W., McNeill, M.D.J., Charles, D.K., Morrow, P.J., Crosbie, J.H., McDonough, S.M.: Optimising engagement for stroke rehabilitation using serious games. Vis. Comput. **25**, 1085–1099 (2009)

32. Pakarinen, A., Parisod, H., Smed, J., Salantera, S.: Health game interventions to enhance physical activity self-efficacy of children: a quantitative systematic review. J. Adv. Nurs. (2016). doi:10.1111/jan.13160

33. Yılmaz, E., Ganzeboom, M., Bakker, M., Boschman, D.-S., Loos, L., Ongering, J., Beijer, L., Rietveld, T., Cucchiarini, C., Strik, H.: A serious game for speech training in neurological patients. In: 41th IEEE International Conference on Acoustics, Speech and Signal Processing in Shanghai, China (2016)

34. Jaume-i-Capo, A., Martinez-Bueso, P., Moya-Alcover, B., Varona, J.: Interactive rehabilitation system for improvement of balance therapies in people with cerebral palsy. IEEE Trans. Neural Syst. Rehabil. Eng. **22**, 419–427 (2014)

35. Moreno, R., Mayer, R.E.: Personalized messages that promote learning in virtual environments. J. Educ. Psychol. **96**(1), 165–173 (2004)

36. Yee, N.: Motivations for play in online games. Cyberpsychol. Behav. **9**(6), 772–775 (2006). doi:10.1089/cpb.2006.9.772

37. Baranowski, M.T., Belchior, P.P., Chamberlin, B., Mellecker, R.: Levels in games for health. Games Health J. **3**, 60–63 (2014)

38. Yee, N.: The gamer motivation profile: what we learned from 250,000 gamers. Paper presented at the proceedings of the 2016 annual symposium on computer-human interaction in play, Austin, Texas, USA (2016)

39. Domagk, S.: Do pedagogical agents facilitate learner motivation and learning outcomes? J. Media Psychol. **22**, 84–97 (2010)

40. Krämer, N.C., Rosenthal-von der Pütten, A.M., Hoffmann, L.: Social effects of virtual and robot companions. In: Sundar, S.S. (ed.) The Handbook of the Psychology of Communication Technology, pp. 137–159. Wiley, Chichester (2015)

41. Mayer, R.E.: Principles of multimedia learning based on social cues: Personalization, voice, and image principles. In: Mayer, R.E. (ed.) The Cambridge Handbook of Multimedia Learning, pp. 201–214. Cambridge University Press, Cambridge (2005)

42. Yee, N., Bailenson, J.N., Urbanek, M., Chang, F., Merget, D.: The unbearable likeness of being digital: the persistence of nonverbal social norms in online virtual environments. Cyberpsychol. Behav. **10**, 115–121 (2007)

43. Pütten, Astrid M., Hoffmann, L., Klatt, J., Krämer, Nicole C.: Quid pro quo? Reciprocal self-disclosure and communicative accomodation towards a virtual interviewer. In: Vilhjálmsson, H.H., Kopp, S., Marsella, S., Thórisson, Kristinn R. (eds.) IVA 2011. LNCS, vol. 6895, pp. 183–194. Springer, Heidelberg (2011). doi:10.1007/978-3-642-23974-8_20

44. Dunsworth, Q., Atkinson, R.K.: Fostering multimedia learning of science: exploring the role of an animated agent's image. Comput. Educ. **49**, 677–690 (2007)

45. Forsberg, A., Nilsagård, Y., Boström, K.: Perceptions of using videogames in rehabilitation: a dual perspective of people with multiple sclerosis and physiotherapists. Disabil. Rehabil. **37**, 338–344 (2015)

User Evaluation of an App for Liquid Monitoring by Older Adults

Zaidatol Haslinda Abdullah Sani and Helen Petrie[(✉)]

Human Computer Interaction Research Group, Department of Computer Science,
University of York, York, UK
{zas508,helen.petrie}@york.ac.uk

Abstract. This paper reports on a user evaluation with 20 older adults of a paper-based prototype of an app for tablet computer and smartphone platforms to support older adults in monitoring the amount of liquids they consume, to avoid dehydration. The tablet version revealed 214 usability problems, the smartphone version only three problems. The problems were categorized based on previous work by Petrie and Power into four major categories of usability problems: Physical Presentation, Content, Information Architecture and Interactivity. Lessons learnt and implications for the future design of mobile applications for older adults are discussed.

Keywords: Usability evaluation · Mobile apps · Tablet computers · Smartphones · Older adults · Liquid monitoring

1 Introduction

Dehydration is a serious health problem, especially for older adults. A four year survey by Public Health England and the Food Standards Agency found that the average daily non-alcoholic liquid intake of people aged 65 and above in the UK was only 1.2 L for men and 1.3 L for women [1]. This is well below recommendations provided by the British Nutrition Foundation (BNF) that men drink 2 L of non-alcoholic liquids per day, and that women drink 1.6 L [2].

Dehydration can lead to extreme tiredness, poor mental performance, low blood pressure, physical weakness, dizziness and increased risk of falls [3, 4]. Unfortunately a lack of knowledge of which liquids are appropriate for avoiding dehydration (e.g. whether coffee and tea are appropriate) and the failure to drink liquids late in the day (to avoid trips to the toilet at night), means older adults are particularly prone to dehydration. If left untreated, dehydration can have severe consequences, including long hospital admission, increased morbidity and mortality rate [5].

Currently, there is much research about using "apps" on smartphones and tablet computers to support older adults in a range of healthcare areas. For instance, older adults can use apps to monitor their diet [6], to support themselves in engaging in physical activities [7], to remind them to take medications [8] or to improve their cognitive abilities [9]. These studies have shown that the use of apps can promote positive behavior change among the older adults, leading to better health and well-being.

© Springer International Publishing AG 2017
M. Antona and C. Stephanidis (Eds.): UAHCI 2017, Part III, LNCS 10279, pp. 86–97, 2017.
DOI: 10.1007/978-3-319-58700-4_8

However, to the best of our knowledge, no work has been undertaken on apps to support older adults in monitoring their liquid intake.

Our preliminary work of two focus groups with a total of nine older adults showed that they were aware of the importance of keeping hydrated. However, they had concerns about drinking sufficient liquid, particularly water. The focus groups showed that the older adults lacked knowledge about the recommended daily amount of liquid to drink, the importance of drinking plain water, and the choice of other appropriate liquids to keep hydrated. The focus groups also showed that the older adults were interested in using computers and new mobile technologies such as smartphones and tablet computers. Although only one participant in the focus groups currently owned a tablet computer, the other participants saw themselves using tablet computers in the future.

On the basis of information from the focus groups and a literature review, we have developed an app, MyDrinkApp, to support older adults in monitoring their liquid intake, with versions for smartphones and tablet computers. A collaborative heuristic evaluation (CHE) [10] was conducted on initial prototypes of both versions. On the basis of that evaluation, refined versions of the app have been developed.

This paper will report the next step in the develop of MyDrinkApp, a lab-based user evaluation of the refined prototypes using a think-aloud protocol [11].

2 Method

2.1 Participants

20 older adults participated in the evaluation, 10 women and 10 men, with a mean age of 71 years (standard deviation: 4.7; age range 65–82 years). Six participants lived alone, the rest lived with a partner. Two participants had a highest education level of primary school, seven had secondary school, three had a bachelors degree, one had a post-graduate degree, and four had professional qualifications. Nineteen participants were retirees, one worked part-time. In addition, 16 participants were Internet users with experience of using the Internet from 2 years to more than 20 years (mean: 12 years; standard deviation: 7.9). Twelve participants were computer users with experience of using computers from 5 months to more than 30 years (mean: 12 years; standard deviation: 11.8). Thirteen participants were tablet computer users with experience of using the device from 4 months to 5 years (mean: 2.9 years; standard deviation: 1.4).

2.2 The MyDrinkApp

Paper based low-fidelity prototypes of MyDrinkApp, to support older adults in monitoring their liquid intake were designed for smartphone (iPhone) and tablet computer (iPad) platforms. The prototypes were designed using Lucidchart[1] and followed guidelines for the development of apps for older adults provided by Silva et al. [13] and

---

[1] https://www.lucidchart.com.

Watkins et al. [19], as well as other research on use of touchscreens and mobile devices for older adults [12, 14–16]. For the tablet computer prototype, the features consist of the ability to set a profile, add liquid intake, view profile, view intake progress, set reminders and read tips related to hydration. To suit the more limited context of use of smartphones, only the adding liquid intake feature was designed.

For the iPad prototype, the font size for the text was at least 24px. For the iPhone prototype, the font size for the text was at least 16px. The target size for button for both prototypes was at least 1.5 cm (height) × 1.5 cm (width) each [12]. The gap in between targets was at least 5 mm [17]. All text for both prototypes was black on a white background. To maintain consistency, avoid confusion and reduce mental workload, there were only one task per page [13], and numerous instructions and messages were also given throughout the app [14]. In addition, the design of the features for adding a liquid intake was similar in both prototypes.

To set a user profile, the user has to provide personal information such as their weight, physical activity level, daily liquid target, email address and password. After setting their profile, the user could update their details, if needed, at a Profile page.

To add a liquid intake, three alternative options were offered to users for evaluation. The layout of the options is similar except for the image that represents the intake amount. The first option used is an image of an empty bottle (see Fig. 1a), which then fills up as the user adds liquid during the day. When the bottle is full, the daily target liquid intake has been reached. The second option consists of a measuring jug with a measuring scale on its side (Fig. 1b). The third option consists of six mugs, which

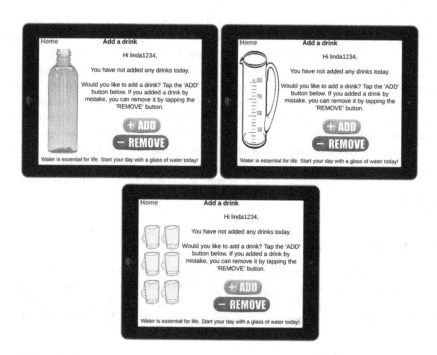

Fig. 1. (Clockwise from top left): (a) add intake option 1, (b) add intake option 2, and (c) add intake option 3

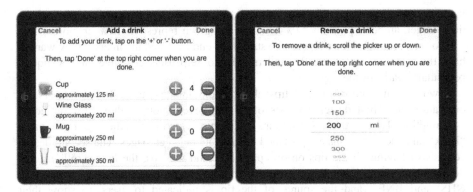

Fig. 2. (From left to right): (a) add intake via buttons, and (b) add intake via picker for the iPad prototype

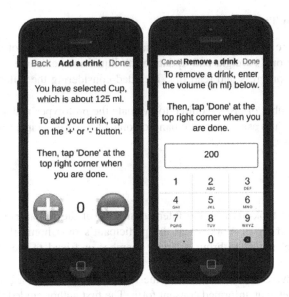

Fig. 3. (From left to right): (a) add intake via buttons, and (b) add intake via keypad for the iPhone prototype

when full represent the daily intake target. To add an intake, the user taps on the "+ Add" button. and can then update their intake via two options offered to users for evaluation. For both prototypes, the first option uses buttons (Figs. 2a and 3a). The second option for the iPad only, uses a picker (Fig. 2b). The second option for the iPhone, to suit the small screen, is a keypad on which the user enters the amount of liquid directly (Fig. 3b).

There are two options to view one's progress towards the daily liquid intake goal. The first option is a colored list showing all liquid intakes. The second is a colored list showing all intakes and the average amount of liquid consumed. The traffic light metaphor [15, 16] was used to represent progress, red represents 0% to 50% of the daily target, amber represents 51% to 70%, and green represents 71% or more.

To set a reminder, the user sets the start time, end time and the interval they want to have the reminder messages. Reminders were to help users consume enough liquid, particularly early in the day.

Two designs option to read tips about liquid intake were offered to users for evaluation. The first design consists of having several topics about tips on liquid consumption. To read the tips, user taps on a topic, which brings them to a new page. "Back" and "next" buttons are provided to navigate between pages. The second design consists of having all the tips on one page. To read the tips, the user scrolls up and down. The tips used in the prototypes were from reliable sources in the UK, such as the NHS[2] and BNF[3] (and the source of the tip is indicated to users, to show their reliability).

2.3   Evaluation Tasks

Twenty tasks were designed to allow evaluation of all the features of the prototypes, including setting one's weight and updating the liquid intake. Three of the tasks, the add intake, view progress and read tips, included considering the different alternative design options.

Given the number of tasks required to evaluate the prototypes and an evaluation of a reasonable length to ask each participant to conduct, each participant performed only four different tasks.

2.4   Procedure

The study session took place in the Interaction Labs of the Department of Computer Science, at University of York, or at the participant's own home if they preferred. Participants were invited to bring a family member or friend to the session, if they wished.

Participants were first briefed about the study and invited to ask any questions. They then completed an informed consent form. The first author guided the participants through the iPad prototype first, followed by the iPhone prototype (as the iPhone had only a subset of features, and could only be used once a profile had been set up on the iPad). Multiple breaks were given throughout each session, as the participant needed.

Participants were asked to "think aloud" as they went through the prototypes, articulating their thoughts about what they were doing, problems they were encountering and pointing out features they liked. Each time a participant proposed a problem, they were asked to briefly explain the problem.

For each task with different design options, participants were asked to choose which option they prefer or they could suggest other possible designs.

---

[2] http://www.nhs.uk/pages/home.aspx.

[3] https://www.nutrition.org.uk.

After completing the think-aloud session, participants were asked whether or not the prototypes would be useful, whether they had any worries or concerns with the prototypes and completed a short demographic questionnaire. Participants were then debriefed and invited to ask any questions about the study. Participants were offered a gift voucher worth £25 (approximately USD36) to thank them for their time and effort.

Each session was audio-recorded for later detailed analysis. Each session lasted approximately 75 min.

2.5 Data Analysis

A list of usability problems identified in each prototype was created (views on the design alternatives were considered separately and are not discussed in this paper). A content analysis [18] was conducted to categorize the usability problems. The first author conducted the first round of content analysis with an a priori set of categories, those developed Petrie and Power [10]. However those categories were developed with younger users and for interactive websites, so we were very open to need for new or different categories. To ensure the reliability of the categorization, the second author went through all the usability problems to check the categorization.

3 Results

214 usability problems were identified in the tablet computer (iPad) prototype and only 3 problems were identified in the smartphone (iPhone) prototype. Therefore only the problems with the tablet computer prototype will be presented. These problems are summarized in Table 1 which shows the distribution of problems into major categories and specific categories within those major categories, the number of participants who encountered them and the total frequency of each problem.

The four major categories from the Petrie and Power [10] categorization were found, being Physical Presentation, Content, Information Architecture and Interactivity. Over half the usability problems (57%) were found in Interactivity category, and over one third (35.9%) were found in Content. Less than 10% were found in Physical Presentation or Information Architecture.

The specific categories of problems found were compared to those found by Petrie and Power (Table 2). Petrie and Power had a total of 34 specific categories, whereas in the current study only 17 were found. However, one of those was a category not found by Petrie and Power, "Inconsistent interaction between elements/pages" in the Interactivity category.

The breakdown of usability problems into the four major categories had some strong similarities and some differences to the Petrie and Power dataset (see Table 2). As with the current study, Petrie and Power found over half the problems were in the Interactivity category. The second most frequent category in both datasets was content problems, although for Petrie and Power this only accounted for 17.0% of problems compared to 35.9% for the current dataset. The third most frequent category in both datasets was Physical Presentation, although in this case it accounted for more

Table 1. Categories of usability problems identified in the tablet computer prototype with percentage/number of users who encountered them and frequency of the problem category (f)

Category	Examples	Users % (N)	f % (N)
Physical Presentation 5.1 (11)			
Inappropriate colours/patterns	the colours for the history page is a bit worrying because my husband is colour blind (P5)	15 (3)	1.4 (3)
Text/interactive elements not large/clear/distinct enough	It's not clear that there are five buttons (P11)	15 (3)	1.4 (3)
Changes to content/interactive elements not noticed	I didn't realize where was the next button (P7)	25 (5)	2.3 (5)
Content 35.9 (77)			
Too much content	when I read it I don't know the answer (P15)	40 (8)	6.5 (14)
Content not clear enough	by looking at the name are you looking into all aspects of fluid intake ... the name is not clear (P10)	50 (10)	9.3 (20)
Content not detailed enough	asking for weight was a bit confusing as this app is for monitoring liquid intake ... why asking for weight (P1)	65 (13)	13.0 (28)
Content not suitable for the users	the image of ice ... [we] shouldn't be drinking ice water (P17)	30 (6)	4.7 (10)
Contradictory content	I don't understand the two options because above you talk about the cups glasses and mugs while at the bottom you gave fluid ounces and this is confusing (P12)	20 (4)	2.3 (5)
Information Architecture 1.8 (4)			
Content not in appropriate order	I actually don't know where is this going ... I honestly don't know the measurement of this mug (P18)	20 (4)	1.8 (4)
Interactivity 57 (122)			
Concerns about how to proceed	adding a drink is confusing for the first time ... looking at it I thought that we can only use it once (P6)	70 (14)	13.5 (29)
Labels/instructions/icons on interactive elements not clear	what is removing a drink ... [is it] removing the daily target (P2)	80 (16)	12.6 (27)
Excessive effort required by user to complete a task	why do I have to press the plus button 10 times to add 10 cups of tea in a day (P11)	55 (11)	13.0 (28)
Input format is unclear	how many letters are there for the password ... do we need alphanumeric (P1)	35 (7)	3.7 (8)
Design and sequence of interaction elements illogical	now it takes me to login and not sign up ... (P13)	5 (1)	0.4 (1)
Options not logical/complete	I don't have an email address or password [so I] couldn't do task ... I'm lost when it comes to this (P9)	75 (15)	11.2 (24)
Interaction not as expected	even this page is not asking for my weight (P20)	15 (3)	1.9 (4)
Inconsistent interaction between elements/pages	the bottle and jugs just probe me ... I didn't know where would I go with the bottles and jugs ... that completely threw me (P8)	5 (1)	0.4 (1)

Table 2. Comparison between the usability problem categories proposed by Petrie and Power [10] and those found in the current study with the tablet computer

Petrie and Power	Current tablet computer
Physical presentation	
13.4%	5.1%
Page does not render properly	–
Poor, inappropriate color contrast	Inappropriate colours/patterns
Text/interactive elements not large/clear/distinct enough	Text/interactive elements not large/clear/distinct enough
Page layout unclear/confusing	–
Timing problems	–
Key content/interactive elements, changes to these not noticed	Changes to content/interactive elements not noticed
"Look and feel" not consistent	–
Content	
17.0%	35.9%
Too much content	Too much content
Content not clear enough	Content not clear enough
Content not detailed enough	Content not detailed enough
Content inappropriate or not relevant	Content not suitable for users
Terms not defined	–
Duplicated or contradictory content	Contradictory content
Information architecture	
8.6%	1.8%
Content not in appropriate order	Content not in appropriate order
Not enough structure to the content	–
Structure not clear enough	–
Headings/titles unclear/confusing	–
Purpose of the structures not clear	
Interactivity	
61.1%	57%
Lack on information on how to proceed and why things are happening	Concerns about information on how to proceed
Labels/instructions/icons on interactive elements not clear	Labels/instructions/icons on interactive elements not clear
Duplication/excessive effort required by user	Excessive effort required by user
Input and input formats unclear	Input formats unclear
Lack of feedback on user actions and system progress	–
Sequence of interaction illogical	Design and sequence of interaction illogical
Options not logical/complete	Options not logical/complete
Too many options	–

(continued)

Table 2. (*continued*)

Petrie and Power	Current tablet computer
Interaction not as expected	Interaction not as expected
Interactive functionality expected is missing	–
Links lead to external sites/are PDFs without warning	–
Interactive and non-interactive elements not clearly identified	–
Interactive elements not grouped clearly/logically	–
Security issues not highlighted	–
Problems with choosing and validating passwords	–
Error messages unhelpful	–
–	Inconsistent interaction between elements/pages

problems in the Petrie and Power dataset, 13.4%, compared to only 5.1% in the current dataset. Finally, only 1.8% of problems in the current data set were related to Information Architecture, compared to 8.6% in the Petrie and Power dataset.

4 Discussion and Conclusions

This paper reports on the user-based evaluation with 20 older people of the prototype of an app to support older adults in monitoring their liquid intake. The tablet computer prototype produced 214 instances of usability problems, a disappointingly large number. The smartphone prototype produced only three usability problems, but had a much more limited functionality compared to the tablet computer prototype.

Both prototypes were designed following heuristics proposed by Silva et al. [13] and Watkins et al. [19], specifically for apps for older people. However, both these sets of heuristics were developed from reviewing the literature rather than on empirical work with older people. It was clear from the comments made by participants and the usability problems they encountered, that our interpretation of some of these heuristics lead to a prototype that was not suitable for this group of older people, who were quite typical of British people in their 60s and 70s living independently.

For example, the first heuristic proposed by Silva et al. is "Focus on one task at a time instead of requiring the user to actively monitor two or more tasks, and clearly indicate the name and status of the task at all times" (H1). We followed this heuristic by only presenting one task per screen in the tablet version of app. However, a number of the problems in our category of "Excessive effort required by user to complete a task" related to only having one task per screen (9 problems encountered by 6 of our participants). Participants commented that they were losing their focus in using the prototype because the task was spread over too many screens and there were too many clicks to get through the screens to complete a task.

Another heuristic from Silva et al. is "Give specific and clear instructions and make help and documentation available. Remember that it is better to prevent an error than to recover from it" (H7). Of our excessive effort problems, 10 problems (encountered by 7 participants) were related to the effort of reading too many instructions and messages. These participants commented that they did not need so many instructions. In pages that required participants to read text or instructions on how to complete a task, they would just skim the text and not read them thoroughly. This is different from the conclusions from Hollinworth and Hwang [15] that older adults need more instructions to successfully executive computer tasks.

These two issues mean that the majority of the 28 problems in the category of "Excessive effort required by user to complete a task" could have been avoided if we had put several tasks on a screen and cut down the amount of instructions. In fact, our older participants seemed very similar to younger users, they wanted to get on with things quickly, did not like having to navigate through a lot of screen with a lot of clicks and only skimmed through instructions.

To provide the fundamental task of adding and removing liquid intake, we followed Silva et al. [13] heuristic "Use simple and meaningful icons" (H33) and Watkins et al. [19] heuristic "Use icons with symbols and text that clearly indicate the icon's function" (R1) (see Fig. 1a–c). We also labeled our buttons with verbs as recommend by Silva et al. "Make sure they are descriptive and use meaningful words and verbs when requiring an action". However, all the problems (27 problems encountered by 16 participants) in the specific category of "Labels/instructions/icons on interactive elements not clear" related to this issue. Participants often commented that the labels and icons for the interactive elements were not obvious in their meaning and if the prototypes were to be in a real system, they would need to explore by try-and-error to figure out what each interactive element did.

In addition, there were two lessons learnt from this evaluation which did not relate to the heuristics used. Firstly we found that when choosing between a number of options, the older participants preferred to choose from a list than a set of buttons. This was slightly surprising, as buttons afford selecting more clearly. However, the readability of the items was clearer in a list form than as the labels on buttons, and reading down a list may be more natural as the cognitive precursor to making a selection than reading the labels on an array of buttons.

Secondly, one of our Interactivity categories of problems was "Concerns about how to proceed" where 14 participants encountered a total of 29 problems. Of these, 7 problems (encountered by 7 participants) were related to the use of the picker. Although the picker is a common input technique for touchscreen devices, the participants in the current study found the picker difficult to use. These participants commented that their physical abilities, such as poor vision and hand tremor, caused them to have difficulties in controlling the picker.

The categorization of usability problems started from the set of categories developed by Petrie and Power [10], although it was expected that there would be some considerable differences in the current set of problems, as the Petrie and Power set were based on the evaluation of e-government websites by younger people, a different type of application with a different user group. Nonetheless, the Petrie and Power categories proved useful, with only one new category needed, that of "inconsistent interaction between elements/pages". However, a number of the Petrie and Power categories were not needed. Some of these were because they were irrelevant to the app under evaluation in this study, such as "links lead to external sites/are PDFs without warning" (there were no external links in this app) and "problems with choosing and validating passwords" (no passwords were used in this app). Others were problems that simply did not appear in this particular app, although there is no reason why they might not appear in other apps from older users (e.g. "page layout unclear/confusing", "terms not defined" or "too many options").

Overall, although the tablet computer version of the app revealed a disappointing number of usability problems, a number of interesting issues were highlighted by this evaluation. In particular, researchers should be wary of heuristics which make broad assumptions about the capabilities and preferences of older users. Older people are more heterogeneous than younger people in their capabilities and possibly in their preferences in relation to computing devices and apps. As the "baby boomer" generation ages, successive cohorts of older computer users will be more familiar with computing conventions and in exploring how to learn to use new devices and apps. This change can already be seen in this evaluation, with older participants only skimming instructions and being almost over-eager to get on with their task, behaviour usually associated with younger users. However, researchers and developers do need to be cautious about new developments which challenge the physical capabilities of older users. The resistance to the picker in this study is an interesting case in point.

Acknowledgements. We would like to thank all our participants for their time and effort to take part in the study. The first author would also like to acknowledge her sponsor, Majlis Amanah Rakyat (MARA), Malaysia.

References

1. Bates, B., Lennox, A., Prentice, A., Bates, C., Page, P., Nicholson, S., Swan, G.: National diet and nutrition survey results from years 1, 2, 3 and 4 (combined) of the rolling programme (2008/2009–2011/2012): a survey carried out on Behalf of Public Health England and the Food Standards Agency (2014)
2. Healthy Hydration Guide - British Nutrition Foundation. https://www.nutrition.org.uk/healthyliving/hydration/healthy-hydration-guide.html
3. Masento, N.A., Golightly, M., Field, D.T., Butler, L.T., van Reekum, C.M.: Effects of hydration status on cognitive performance and mood. Br. J. Nutr. **111**(10), 1841–1852 (2014)
4. Frangeskou, M., Lopez-Valcarcel, B., Serra-Majem, L.: Dehydration in the elderly: a review focused on economic burden. J. Nutr. Health Aging **19**(6), 619–627 (2015)
5. El-Sharkawy, A.M., Virdee, A., Wahab, A., Humes, D.J., Sahota, O., Devonald, M.A.J., Lobo, D.N.: Dehydration and clinical outcome in hospitalised older adults: a cohort study. Eur. Geriatr. Med. (2016). doi:http://dx.doi.org/10.1016/j.eurger.2016.11.007
6. Hakobyan, L., Lumsden, J., Shaw, R., O'Sullivan, D.: A longitudinal evaluation of the acceptability and impact of a diet diary app for older adults with age-related macular degeneration. In: Proceedings of the 18th International Conference on Human-Computer Interaction with Mobile Devices and Services, pp. 124–134. ACM, New York (2016)

7. Silveira, P., van de Langenberg, R., van het Reve, E., Daniel, F., Casati, F., de Bruin, E.D.: Tablet-based strength-balance training to motivate and improve adherence to exercise in independently living older people: a Phase II preclinical exploratory trial. J. Med. Internet Res. **15**(8), e159 (2013)

8. Mira, J.J., Navarro, I., Botella, F., Borrás, F., Nuño-Solinís, R., Orozco, D., Iglesias-Alonso, F., Pérez-Pérez, P., Lorenzo, S., Toro, N.: A spanish pillbox app for elderly patients taking multiple medications: randomized controlled trial. J. Med. Internet Res. **16**(4), e99 (2014)

9. Chan, M.Y., Haber, S., Drew, L.M., Park, D.C.: Training older adults to use tablet computers: does it enhance cognitive function? Gerontologist **56**(3), 475–484 (2016)

10. Petrie, H., Power, C.: What do users really care about?: a comparison of usability problems found by users and experts on highly interactive websites. In: Proceedings of the 30th International Conference on Human Factors in Computing (CHI 2012), pp. 2107–2116. ACM Press, New York (2012)

11. Lewis, C.: Using the "thinking-aloud" method in cognitive interface design. IBM TJ Watson Research Center, New York (1982)

12. Kobayashi, M., Hiyama, A., Miura, T., Asakawa, C., Hirose, M., Ifukube, T.: Elderly User Evaluation of Mobile Touchscreen Interactions. In: Campos, P., Graham, N., Jorge, J., Nunes, N., Palanque, P., Winckler, M. (eds.) INTERACT 2011. LNCS, vol. 6946, pp. 83–99. Springer, Heidelberg (2011). doi:10.1007/978-3-642-23774-4_9

13. Silva, P.A., Holden, K., Jordan, P.: Towards a list of heuristics to evaluate smartphone apps targeted at older adults: a study with apps that aim at Promoting Health and Well-being. In: Bui, T.X., Spragur Jr., R.H. (eds.) Proceeding of the 48th Annual Hawaii International Conference on System Sciences, pp. 3237–3246. CPS, California (2015)

14. Hollinworth, N., Hwang, F.: Learning how older adults undertake computer tasks. In: Proceedings of the 11th International ACM SIGACCESS Conference on Computers and Accessibility, pp. 245–246. ACM, New York (2009)

15. Grimes, A., Kantroo, V., Grinter, R.E.: Let's play!: mobile health games for adults. In: Proceedings of the 12th ACM International Conference on Ubiquitous Computing, pp. 241–250. ACM, New York (2010)

16. Doyle, J., Walsh, L., Sassu, A., McDonagh, T.: Designing a wellness self-management tool for older adults–results from a field trial of YourWellness. In: 8th International Conference on Pervasive Computing Technologies for Healthcare, pp. 134–141. ICST (2014)

17. Jin, Z.X., Plocher, T., Kiff, L.: Touch screen user interfaces for older adults: button size and spacing. In: Stephanidis, C. (ed.) UAHCI 2007. LNCS, vol. 4554, pp. 933–941. Springer, Heidelberg (2007). doi:10.1007/978-3-540-73279-2_104

18. Krippendorff, K.: Content Analysis: An Introduction to Its Methodology, 3rd edn. Sage, London (2013)

19. Watkins, I., Kules, B., Yuan, X., Xie, B.: Heuristic evaluation of healthy eating apps for older adults. J. Consum. Health Internet **18**(2), 105–127 (2014)

SmartGym: An Anticipatory System to Detect Body Compliance During Rehabilitative Exercise

Arash Tadayon[✉], Ramesh Tadayon, Troy McDaniel, and Sethuraman Panchanathan

Center for Cognitive Ubiquitous Computing, Arizona State University, Tempe, Arizona, USA
{arash.tadayon,ramesh.tadayon,troy.mcdaniel,panch}@asu.edu

Abstract. Training and exercise programs, under the guidance of skilled therapists and trainers, have become important tools during the rehabilitation process.
Traditionally, these programs have been difficult to perform at home due to the need
for a trainer to observe and provide feedback on body compliance during the
performance of exercises. To address this difficulty, we've created the SmartGym:
an intelligent modification to the Total Gym Pro that monitors an individual's
performance during exercise and provides feedback through haptic, auditory and
visual cues. The system is evaluated for effectiveness in a case study involving an
individual who is undergoing exercise rehabilitation for Cerebral Palsy.

Keywords: Anticipatory computing · Exercise compliance · Motion capture

1 Introduction

Training and exercise programs, under the guidance of skilled therapists and trainers,
have become important tools during the rehabilitation process. Traditionally, these
programs have been difficult to perform at home due to the need for a trainer to observe
and provide feedback on body compliance during the performance of the exercises. Non-
compliance caused by impaired proprioception can result in serious injuries and slow
the progression of motor learning if left uncorrected during exercise performance. As a
result, research is actively seeking new automated methods for the detection and intervention of non-compliance in unsupervised environments. There are two main sub-
problems that together comprise the problem of non-compliance prevention:

- **Anticipation**: how does a system anticipate the occurrence of non-compliance?
- **Intervention**: how does a system intervene to correct the behavior of the individual
  to prevent prolonged non-compliance?

In this project, we introduce an anticipatory system to detect and intervene before
non-compliance or compensation occurs. Although prior work has looked at detection
of body states during exercise, it is important to explore anticipation since any time spent
in a non-compliant state could harm the individual. Once it is determined that the user
may be at risk, the system provides multimodal feedback through auditory, visual and
haptic cues to correct the harmful behavior before it results in injury.

© Springer International Publishing AG 2017
M. Antona and C. Stephanidis (Eds.): UAHCI 2017, Part III, LNCS 10279, pp. 98–107, 2017.
DOI: 10.1007/978-3-319-58700-4_9

As an initial application, the area of exercise rehabilitation for cerebral palsy is used to provide a context to demonstrate the effectiveness of the system in anticipating and correcting body position. In this paper, we present the SmartGym, an intelligent Total Gym Pro that monitors an individual's performance and provides feedback through haptic, auditory and visual cues. An overview of related work in Sect. 2 shows the need for an effective tool for anticipation, rather than detection, of potentially dangerous body states, which we explore in our design of the SmartGym. In Sect. 3, we differentiate anticipation from prediction and give an overview on how this is achieved within the system. In Sect. 4 we describe the details of our implementation and justify our design decisions in the feedback that the system provides. In Sect. 4 we evaluate our initial prototype for both usability and effectiveness in a case study involving an adult with cerebral palsy who has developed a hemiparetic lower extremity and her physical trainer. We deploy the system within the subject's regularly scheduled training and present feedback to test the effectiveness of replicating the trainer's feedback. We conclude in Sect. 5 with directions for future work.

2   Related Work

Because of the importance and impact of at-home exercise during rehabilitation, much work has been done in the area of remote rehab through sensors to provide the performance feedback that a trainer would physically provide to individuals in clinic.

2.1   Microsoft Kinect for Remote Rehabilitative Exercise

The Microsoft Kinect (Fig. 1) has proven to be an important tool in these applications since it is an effective tool at gathering motion data and is much cheaper than traditional solutions. Prior work has demonstrated the effectiveness of this sensor in this domain by showing its ability to measure the position and trajectory of each joint, the working envelope of each body member, the average velocity, and a measure of the user's fatigue after an exercise sequence [1].

Fig. 1. Microsoft Kinect sensor

In Physio@Home, the authors explore the use of a Kinect camera to prevent re-injury during at-home rehabilitative exercises [2]. The system takes a multi-camera approach in order to provide the individual with visual feedback to guide them in the performance of finer-grained physio exercises. The user is shown wedges that indicate the direction and angle that the specific movement requires and are expected to perform those movements while keeping their arm within the wedge. Similarly, other approaches have looked at using the Kinect to affect balance ability in injured athletes [3]. In this approach, the authors used a Kinect intervention to enhance balance ability and compared this to traditional physiotherapy. The proposed intervention provided feedback through a gaming interface that increased in difficulty over a 10-week period.

2.2 Wii Balance Board for Remote Rehabilitative Exercise

The Wii Balance board (Fig. 2) has also proven to be a useful and cost-effective solution for obtaining accurate measurements of foot pressure and center of balance [4–6]. In evaluating the accuracy of the board, research has shown that it is best used for relative measures using the same device and should be used for low-resolution measurements [4].

Fig. 2. Wii Balance board

In [5], the authors explore the use of the Wii Balance Board as a gaming interface to improve balance for children with cerebral palsy. The study found a significant improvement based on the Trunk Control Motor Scale in the subjects' trunk control and balance. Similar results were found in studies that looked at the effectiveness of a Wii Balance Board intervention for balance improvement in patients with acquired brain injury as well as individuals with Parkinson's Disease [6, 7].

2.3 Anticipatory Computing in Health Applications

Although much of the work in the area of health intervention has leaned more towards predictive rather than anticipatory, Pejovic and Musolesi have proposed the potential for applications of anticipatory computing within the emerging field of digital behavior change interventions [8]. The authors have referenced UbiFit [9] and BeWell [10] as two applications that have taken very rudimentary steps towards the inclusion of anticipation in mobile health applications as well as provided potential architectures for future applications in this domain [11]. UbiFit is a personal health application that was designed to monitor user's weekly activity and provide subtle feedback if he or she has not had enough activity. The app shows a garden that thrives if the user is meeting activity goals and remains barren if the user has remained inactive for too long. BeWell is a mobile application that monitors a user's health along three dimensions: sleep, physical activity and social interaction. Much like UbiFit, this application provides intelligent feedback to the user to promote better health through an ambient display of an aquatic background that becomes more active the healthier you are.

2.4   Limitations of Prior Work

The major limitation of prior work has been that it has used these sensors in applications that solely provide feedback regarding past or current performance of exercise tasks. In traditional behavior change interventions, the therapist relies on self-reported experiences and progress to guide the intervention. In digital behavior change interventions, the interventions are personalized in real time, responding to the immediate user's context. In anticipatory digital behavior change interventions, however, interventions are modified based on the model of the predicted context [8]. Because the concept of anticipation within behavior change applications is so new, few applications exist that are truly anticipatory and thus the literature is lacking. This is important since injury can very easily occur the moment an individual's body position becomes non-compliant. Being able to anticipate this past prediction takes a step towards a more preventative approach to re-injury in the rehabilitation domain. SmartGym looks to build upon existing work by predicting a user's future context and intervening to prevent unsafe states.

3   Proposed Approach

The proposed approach has two main objectives:

1. Anticipate when a user is going to become non-compliant before injury occurs
2. Provide multimodal feedback to an individual so that they can correct their body in real-time

3.1   Anticipation of Non-compliance

Robert Rosen defines an anticipatory system as one that "contains an internal, predictive model of itself and its environment, which allows it to change state at an instant in accord with the model's predictions pertaining to a later instant" [12]. It is important to first differentiate prediction from anticipation since the two are often incorrectly used interchangeably. Predictive applications are those that simply build predictions of the user's current or future context. Anticipation is set in the domain of action that is based on the predictions of future context in order to impact the future to the benefit of the user [13].

To achieve the goal of anticipation, the system breaks down the problem of non-compliance by looking at sensing events that occur before risk of injury. In determining the risk of an accidental fall from the Total Gym machine, the system looks at center of balance and postural stability as both of these are key attributes that worsen gradually throughout the individual's exercise routine. In considering center of balance, the SmartGym measures pressure placed by each foot against the landing plate of the Total Gym Pro and warns the user when compensation occurring between the affected limb and unaffected limb is sensed. Compensation can lead to early fatigue and can also lead to the individual being imbalanced before the start of a movement leading to injury during landing. Secondly, the system considers postural stability by looking at body alignment and warning the user if he or she is leaning to one side while lying down on the machine. By sensing these two indicators, the system can anticipate that the user is going to enter a non-compliant state and provide feedback to correct this before injury.

3.2 Feedback and Actuation

In order to provide feedback to the individual, three modalities are used: auditory, visual, and haptic. The three feedback channels were chosen to map to the feedback that is given by the instructor during supervised exercise. The instructor begins by verbally informing the individual to correct posture or balance. They will then visually show the correct body positioning themselves so that the individual can mirror this. Lastly, they will physically touch the limb or area of the body that is out of position to shift it back into place. This methodology is emulated in the SmartGym since the system begins by making an auditory tone, then displaying a visual feed of their body superimposed on top of what the correct posture should be, and finally vibrating the Total Gym board to inform the user of the direction that they need to shift (Fig. 3).

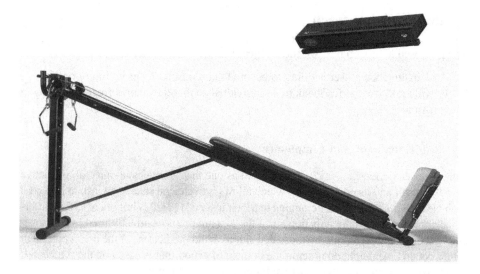

Fig. 3. SmartGym system design

4   Implementation

The SmartGym has been built and integrated with the Total Gym Pro (a commercially available piece of exercise equipment). The system consists of a Wii Balance Board, a laptop with Bluetooth communication, a Microsoft Kinect, an array of pancake motors, an Arduino Uno and a webcam. The laptop serves as the central link between all the devices and uses information from each of the sensors to anticipate when the user is going to enter a non-compliant state.

The Balance Board is positioned on top of the landing platform of the exercise equipment and is used to detect pressure applied by the feet. Each of the user's feet has two pressure sensors under it to measure the difference between pressures put on the ball of the foot versus pressure put on the heel. This pressure is used to determine balance throughout the exercise motions. The system is able to detect if the user is compensating by using one foot more than the other or, similarly, if the user is compensating by prioritizing the ball or heel of one foot. A webcam is also placed facing the individual's feet to give a heads-up display indicating where the user's feet are positioned on the Balance Board to avoid false positives because of incorrect alignment of the feet. This is an important factor given that impaired proprioception is a common side-effect within our target user population.

The Kinect is positioned above the exercise equipment and faces down toward the user to measure joint and skeletal position. This measure gives insight into postural stability during movement and warns the user when his or her body exits the threshold for compliance. Measurements are collected for the shoulders, elbows, wrists, hands, hips, knees and feet. Before starting the exercise, the user is asked to hold a neutral state in which all joints are lined correctly for the upcoming motion. The system captures these positions and uses them to create a bounding box around each of the joints that determines the threshold for compliance. This threshold is set as a variable within the system and can be adjusted by the trainer to become smaller as the individual progresses within their exercise routines. All information from these sensors is streamed to the laptop, which handles all of the processing and gives the auditory and visual feedback.

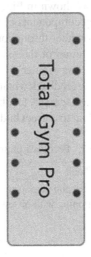

Fig. 4. Vibration motor placement

Two arrays of six pancake vibration motors were embedded onto the Total Gym Pro's padded board and placed horizontally spanning the outside edges of the board as shown in Fig. 4. Each of these motors has a pressure sensor connected to it which will detect if the user is beginning to lean or slide to one side of the board before or during the exercise. These motors and pressure sensors were connected to an Arduino Uno which served as the logic unit for this feedback mechanism. If the pressure sensors pass a certain threshold, the haptic motors are activated and are used to guide the user back to a neutral state where they are balanced on the board. Twelve motors were used in order to fully span the area on the board that a user's body could encompass. This allows the device to detect shifts from the shoulders all the way down to the user's hips. The motors will continue to vibrate until the user shifts his or her body to rectify their postural stability. Given the information that is gathered through the Kinect and presented on the visual interface, this information can sometimes be redundant, but serves to offer the user multiple modalities of feedback that they can choose between. Occasionally, a user's vision might be pre-occupied with an alternate task and thus haptics can be an effective method of providing knowledge of performance.

Fig. 5. Squat exercise

The system was designed for use by an individual with cerebral palsy during rehabilitative exercise. Specifically, we look at an exercise where the individual starts with their feet against the landing plate, as shown in Fig. 5, and presses off to slide up and then lands back on the plate. The key components of this exercise are to ensure that the individual has both knees and feet together throughout the entire exercise and to make sure that they are positioned on the center of the exercise equipment in order to avoid falling off or injuring themselves. The trainer's role is to monitor the individual throughout this exercise and to provide feedback whenever they are breaking these safety guidelines. We have mapped the interface and feedback to the same protocol that the trainer uses in instructing the individual to correct body positioning as shown in Table 1.

Table 1. Feedback protocol

Behavior	Trainer feedback	SmartGym feedback
Uneven feet	Tell the subject and demonstrate correct positioning with his own body	Show heat map with differentiating colors to show which foot is uneven. Camera on the user's feet to also augment lack of proprioception.
Imbalanced	Tell the subject to align their body	Circle shown which changes to green once proper balance is achieved
Sliding off of platform	Tell the subject to move back to the center of the board. If that doesn't work, physically help the subject by pushing the non-compliant body part back onto the equipment	Red points shown on body map to signify which joints are out of position. Tone played until body is compliant. Haptic signals also used to guide the user

For the purposes of this system, we are only considering individuals with moderate, hemiparetic cerebral palsy as these individuals can often gain better motor control through rehabilitative exercises. However, this design can also be used in many other domains where hemiparesis can occur such as in stroke since the same principles of body compliance and compensation play major roles.

4.1 Interface Design

The graphical interface has been designed to give feedback on several metrics at one time. As shown in Fig. 6, the pressure information is displayed to the user as a heat map to show what areas of the foot might be getting too much or too little pressure. The center of gravity is shown as a circle on top of this display that shifts with the user's pressure changes. When the circle is in the center of the interface where the target zone is shown, it switches to green to inform the user that they are centered and may proceed with the exercise. Another section of the interface shows the joint positions of the user that is being captured by the Kinect throughout the exercise. Joints that are outside of the threshold for compliance show up as red and a tone is also played until the desired body position is achieved. Haptic motors embedded within the total gym system also inform the user when they are starting to slip off of the Total Gym System so that the user can correct his or her posture.

Fig. 6. Interface design

5 Conclusion and Future Work

The SmartGym shows great promise in offering an at home solution for individuals to carry out their rehabilitative exercise programs. Through the detection of center of balance and postural stability as indicators for non-compliance, the system looks to reduce risk of injury while the user is not under the supervision of a trained professional.

Future work will look to augment the current anticipation of falls and balance issues with other detrimental cues that could lead to injury during exercise. As a first step, we plan to consider cues for muscle fatigue, as these can also be important factors that cause involuntary non-compliance or compensation. The system will also undergo a much more rigorous evaluation as to the long-term effectiveness of an anticipatory application within this domain. We look to have a subject complete a 6-week exercise program using the system for their at-home training to compare outcomes between traditional physical therapy and the proposed anticipatory approach.

Acknowledgments. The authors would like to thank the National Science Foundation and Arizona State University for their funding support. This material is partially based upon work supported by the National Science Foundation under Grant No. 1069125.

References

1. Gauthier, S., Cretu, A.M.: Human movement quantification using Kinect for in-home physical exercise monitoring. In: 2014 IEEE International Conference on Computational Intelligence and Virtual Environments for Measurement Systems and Applications (CIVEMSA), pp. 6–11 (2014)
2. Tang, R., Yang, X.-D., Bateman, S., Jorge, J., Tang, A.: Physio@Home: exploring visual guidance and feedback techniques for physiotherapy exercises. In: Proceedings of the 33rd Annual ACM Conference on Human Factors in Computing Systems, pp. 4123–4132. ACM, New York (2015)
3. Vernadakis, N., Derri, V., Tsitskari, E., Antoniou, P.: The effect of Xbox Kinect intervention on balance ability for previously injured young competitive male athletes: a preliminary study. Phys. Ther. Sport **15**, 148–155 (2014). doi:10.1016/j.ptsp.2013.08.004
4. Clark, R.A., Bryant, A.L., Pua, Y., McCrory, P., Bennell, K., Hunt, M.: Validity and reliability of the Nintendo Wii Balance Board for assessment of standing balance. Gait Posture **31**, 307–310 (2010). doi:10.1016/j.gaitpost.2009.11.012
5. Bonnechère, B., Omelina, L., Jansen, B., Jan, S.V.S.: Balance improvement after physical therapy training using specially developed serious games for cerebral palsy children: preliminary results. Disabil. Rehabil. **39**, 403–406 (2017). doi:10.3109/09638288.2015.1073373
6. Gil-Gómez, J.-A., Lloréns, R., Alcañiz, M., Colomer, C.: Effectiveness of a Wii balance board-based system (eBaViR) for balance rehabilitation: a pilot randomized clinical trial in patients with acquired brain injury. J. NeuroEng. Rehabil. **8**, 30 (2011). doi:10.1186/1743-0003-8-30
7. Esculier, J.-F., Vaudrin, J., Bériault, P., Gagnon, K., Tremblay, L.E.: Home-based balance training programme using wii fit with balance board for parkinson's disease: a pilot study. J. Rehabil. Med. **44**, 144–150 (2012). doi:10.2340/16501977-0922
8. Pejovic, V., Musolesi, M.: Anticipatory mobile computing for behaviour change interventions. In: Proceedings of the 2014 ACM International Joint Conference on Pervasive and Ubiquitous Computing: Adjunct Publication, pp. 1025–1034. ACM, New York (2014)
9. Consolvo, S., McDonald, D.W., Toscos, T., Chen, M.Y., Froehlich, J., Harrison, B., Klasnja, P., LaMarca, A., LeGrand, L., Libby, R., Smith, I., Landay, J.A.: Activity sensing in the wild: a field trial of ubifit garden. In: Proceedings of the SIGCHI Conference on Human Factors in Computing Systems, pp. 1797–1806. ACM, New York (2008)

10. Lane, N.D., Mohammod, M., Lin, M., Yang, X., Lu, H., Ali, S., Doryab, A., Berke, E., Choudhury, T., Campbell, A.: Bewell: a smartphone application to monitor, model and promote wellbeing. In: 5th International ICST Conference on Pervasive Computing Technologies for Healthcare, pp. 23–26 (2011)
11. Pejovic, V., Musolesi, M.: Anticipatory mobile computing: a survey of the state of the art and research challenges. ACM Comput. Surv. **47**, 47:1–47:29 (2015). doi:10.1145/2693843
12. Volpe, S., Demers, D., Simpanen, E., Chabot, E., Simpson, C.: Balance board rehabilitation device for ankle proprioception assessment. In: 2015 41st Annual Northeast Biomedical Engineering Conference (NEBEC), pp. 1–2 (2015)
13. Rosen, R.: Anticipatory systems. In: Anticipatory Systems, pp. 313–370. Springer, New York (2012)

"The *Sum* of All Our Feelings!": Sentimental Analysis on Chinese Autism Sites

Tiffany Y. Tang[1(✉)], Relic Yongfu Wang[2], and Carl Guangxing Chen[1]

[1] Media Lab, Department of Computer Science, Wenzhou Kean University, Wenzhou, China
yatang@kean.edu, ChenGuanxing316@wku.edu.cn
[2] Department of Computer Engineering, Northwestern University, Evanston, USA
yongfuwang2018@u.northwestern.edu

Abstract. Autism Spectrum Disorder (ASD) is a neurodevelopment disorder affecting 1 in 68 individuals in the US according to the latest Center for Disease Control (CDC) report. In Asia, however, the diagnosis, assessment and intervention of ASD is significantly lagging behind its western counterpart: there is no systematic prevalence study in China yet as to how many of its population has been affected by ASD. In this paper, we present our study, the first of its kind, to offer some preliminary, yet early valuable insights into the practices, knowledge and public awareness of ASD through lexical-affinity based emotion analysis on textual contents extracted from a notably well-known Chinese support site on ASD and one enormously popular social media site-Weibo. Mixed results were obtained. The 'sum' of our feeling is potentially positive and encouraging; yet the data obtained from Weibo are in line with previous works that public awareness of ASD is very low in China and the Asia Pacific region. Thanks to the increasing Chinese government supports and more research and development in this area, it is our 'collective' hope that more HCI community can engage in such efforts in China.

Keywords: Sentimental analysis · Emotion lexicon · Experiment · Collective behaviors

1 Introduction and Background

Despite the fact that an increasingly overwhelming attention in the knowledge discovery in data community has been on social media and its enormous volume of big data, little research has been on the autism-related data till [1] published in 2014. The present study, the first of its kind, was using the public data from Twitter to extract the linguistic and semantic usage patterns to enrich our understanding of the public knowledge on autism as well as the public awareness of it. To the best of our knowledge, there is no published English works on Chinese autism community; this study, the first of its kind focusing on Chinese autism society, attempts to offer unprecedented window of opportunities to examine the collective behaviors and patterns such as public collective sentimental on autism, the linguistic pattern, etc., in China.

© Springer International Publishing AG 2017
M. Antona and C. Stephanidis (Eds.): UAHCI 2017, Part III, LNCS 10279, pp. 108–116, 2017.
DOI: 10.1007/978-3-319-58700-4_10

1.1 Autism Spectrum Disorder and the Current Research and Development Landscape in China

Individuals with Autism Spectrum Disorder (ASD), a neurodevelopment disorder, have marked impairments in social interaction and communications, prone to restricted interests, demonstrate stereotyped repetitive behaviors, exhibit difficulty interpreting others' mental states [38]. It is known that early intervention might lead to improved social skills and increased quality of life and independence when they grow into adolescence [38]. Compared to the plenty of research efforts on the assessment, diagnosis and intervention of ASD, similar works in Eastern Asia lag alarmingly far behind [39], especially in China. Autism was not officially recognized as a disorder until the early 1980s in mainland China, and till now, it is unclear how many of China's population (including adults and children) are with ASD [39, 40].

1.2 Study Motivation

Decades of prior works have consistently affirmed that public and personal mood states play a crucial role in influencing human decision-making [2–4, 7, 29–31]. Among these, Taquet et al. [29] called for researchers in the big data and collective behavior areas to recognize the importance of emotional factors in understanding the collective human behaviors in the big data era. It is notably known the emotional variable sometimes outshadow other variables in the human decision-making cycle [28].

On the other hand, an exponential body of research has been given to the role of big data in understanding human's collective behavior in various real-life applications (refer to [12] for a complete review). Some attempts have been made to link the impact of such collective behavior as manifested by public emotional states or mood for predictive analysis [13, 14], which motivates our study. Specifically, due to the relatively low public awareness (not to mention the subsequent published English works on the assessment, diagnosis and intervention of ASD), our studies, in the long run, could potentially push for public's understanding of the corpus of knowledge of ASD among both the medical community and the general public; greatly facilitating our understanding of the current practices in ASD.

While our work provides more insights about the link between the temporal and collective public sentiment on ASD and its public awareness in China, its findings might also pave the way for further investigations that are beneficial to both raising public awareness and executing public policies on autism education and medical care for thousands of millions of 'undocumented' individuals and their loved ones living in ASD.

2 Related Work

2.1 Data Mining in Social Media for and in Healthcare Application

Numerous prior works have been carried out on the adoption of data mining in healthcare (a few recent among many [1, 11, 15–20, 22–24]). Some also have pointed out that the importance of understanding the demographics of users of online social networks in healthcare applications [11, 21]. Among these, one notable work by Ginsberg et al. [27] has revealed that geographically localized health-related search queries can bring extremely effective level of estimate of influenza-like illness in the United States: with a startlingly one day lag—much faster than the estimated by CDC. These findings have collectively painted a picture of the evolving benefits and practices surrounding big data analytics.

2.2   Data Mining in Social Media on ASD

Despite the fact that an increasingly overwhelming attention in the knowledge discovery in data community has been on social media and its enormous volume of big data, little research has been on the autism-related data till [1] published in 2014. The study, the first of its kind, using the public data from Twitter to extract the linguistic and semantic usage patterns, and enriched our understanding of the public knowledge autism as well as the public awareness of it. The authors later continue to pursue down this path to probe into the autism community. To the best of our knowledge, there is no published English works on Chinese autism community.

2.3   Sentimental Analysis and Social Media

Prior studies have applied indirect assessment of public sentiment from the results of soccer games [8] as well as weather conditions [9]. However, due to the sensitivity of the chosen correlation indicators, the accuracy of these assessments remains unsatisfactory [5]. Recently, there have been many research extracting public mood states directly from large volumes of rich public data such as blogs [6, 10], and twitter (a few recent among many others [21, 25, 26]).

3   Our Study

3.1   Data Collection and the Corpus

The data was collected from one of the most famous autism support site in China[1]. A java free open-resource web crawler was sent to go through over 400,000 pages in the site; advertisement page, blank page and non-textual contents were cleaned resulting in a total of 19,014 pages. The second set of the data comes from Weibo, a Chinese version of Twitter which takes social media by storm in China. We first used keyword-based searching to filter out non-ASD related posts; a total of 19 commonly adopted keywords were applied including "自闭症谱系障碍 (ASD)", "来自星星的孩子(star children)", "埃斯伯格综合症 (Asperger Syndrome)" etc. The automatic data collector was programmed using the open-source Weibo API; data collection period is between November 3, 2015, and November 22, 2015 in 20 consecutive days; a total of 270,750 Weibo posts had been collected during the aforementioned time period.

---

[1]   http://www.guduzheng.net/.

3.2 Emotion Lexical-Affinity-Based Sentimental Analysis

Following the common practices suggested in [32–34, 37], we conduct the sentimental analysis based on two emotion lexicons. One is the Chinese translation of the notable NRC Emotion Lexicon[2] [37]; another is DUTIR[3] (adopted in [32]). Since the former is a translated Chinese version of the original NRC English version using Google Translate[2], and due to the complicated intrinsic natures of Chinese words especially in their rich and subtly different semantic features (for example, Chinese words are notoriously known to bear sentiment ambiguity [36] or the same words might carry multiple emotions [35], we speculate that the Chinese version of NRC emotion lexicon might not be reliable as a basis.

3.3 Study Results and Discussions

Study 1: Emotion Lexicon-Based Study on the Chinese ASD Support Site. Our analysis was performed on the 19,014 pages from the autism support site. The widely adopted Chinese word segmentation- the Natural Language Processing Information Retrieval (NLPIR)[4] was used to segment the words. Figure 1 shows the total emotions shown in the site. Results showed that positive and negative contents have no significant differences; fear, surprise and sadness emotion, and the disgust emotion (against prejudice on people with ASD and their family members) combined might out-shadow other emotions in the public, which is aligned with the relatively low awareness and public acceptance of ASD in the community [39]. The *trust* emotion could spark hope to call for public awareness of ASD. Overall, the results only showed an aggregate emotional landscape of ASD as reflected from the pages and failed to capture more finer grained emotional responses from the articles. We attribute it to the richness of Chinese words in expressing delicate emotions, thus, next, we will show the results obtained from a popular native Chinese emotion lexicon.

The NRC Emotion lexicon contains two labels of negative and positive emotion as well as eight emotions (as shown from left to right in Fig. 1), while DUTIR has richer emotion labels and each word must be associated with a major and minor emotion labels. To simplify the data pre-processing without compromising the outcome, we adopted weighted emotion calculation to again compute the aggregate emotion labels. Figure 2 shows the same output using this emotion lexicon.

---

[2] http://saifmohammad.com/WebPages/NRC-Emotion-Lexicon.htm.

[3] http://ir.dlut.edu.cn/.

[4] http://ictclas.nlpir.org/.

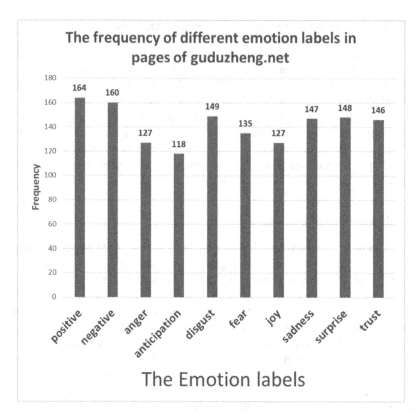

Fig. 1. The frequency of different emotion labels in pages of guduzheng.net based on NRC Emotion Lexicon (Chinese)

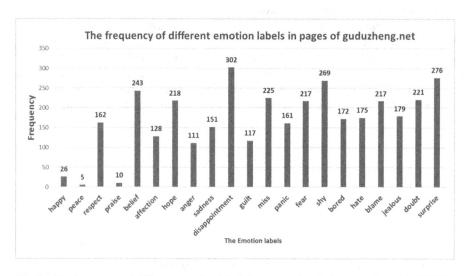

Fig. 2. The frequency of different emotion labels in pages of guduzheng.net based on DUTIR

The result clearly includes more varied and finer-grained emotions as reflected in the site. Among the emotions, the five most heavily moods are disappointment, shy, surprise, belief, miss accordingly. The 'sum' of these emotions is generally in line with those from Study 1, which vividly illustrates the current emotions the public might hold for this population.

Study 2: Emotion Lexicon-Based Study on Weibo posts. Similar analysis had been performed on this set of data. Due to space limitation, we will only report the aggregate moods using the NRC emotion lexicon. Figures 3 and 4 depict the emotion frequency collectively from these Weibo posts related to ASD.

Fig. 3. The frequency of different emotion labels in Weibo posts based on NRC Emotion Lexicon (Chinese)

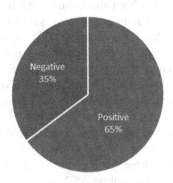

Fig. 4. The frequency of positive and negative emotions in Weibo posts based on NRC Emotion Lexicon (Chinese)

Positive emotions such as trust, joy, and anticipation combined depicted an encouraging mood in the public; due to the enormously popular of Weibo (dubbed as the Chinese Twitter), the results are more interesting.

Out of 270,750 Weibo corpus, we found merely ten posts (about 0.0039%) are closely related to autism; among the ten, 90% of the posts are related to keyword "自闭症" and the rest (one post) is related to keyword "孤独症". As for the geographic location, we found most of the Weibo posts vary from different provinces across China. No correlation among the location and the keywords are found. Interestingly, one post was released by a user from Japan. The extremely unexpected low number of posts might, from another perspective, reflect the low public awareness and interest in this population, which might not be surprising. Since in the Chinese society, having children with mental disabilities such as ASD is regarded as a family shame and failure [41], and thus should be kept as secret and further negatively affect their help-seeking.

Discussions. Compared with the results obtained from the two emotion lexicons (Figs. 1 and 2), the one using the DUTIR emotion lexicon yields more fine-grained results which thus offering us with richer information regarding public emotions on the ASD population. The results are thus consistent with our speculations the Chinese version of NRC emotion lexicon might not be reliable as a basis due to the sophisticated nature of Chinese words [35, 36].

During data cleaning, we also found out that a large number of posts were removed due to the fact that autism was cited as a reclusive personality trait which is different from the word use in English. The unexpectedly low number of posts related to autism might explain the extremely low awareness of ASD in China despite recent government efforts to overcome this increasingly serious issue [39].

4   Concluding Remarks

In Asia, the diagnosis, assessment and intervention of ASD is significantly lagging behind its western counterpart: there is no systematic prevalence study in China yet as to how many of its population has been affected by ASD. In this paper, we present our study, the first of its kind, to offer some preliminary, yet early valuable insights into the practices, knowledge and public awareness of ASD through lexical-affinity based emotion analysis on textual contents extracted from a notably well-known Chinese support site on ASD and one enormously popular social media site-Weibo. Mixed results were obtained. The 'sum' of our feeling is potentially positive and encouraging; yet the data obtained from Weibo are in line with previous works that public awareness of ASD is very low in China and the Asia Pacific region [40, 41]. Thanks to the increasing Chinese government supports and more research and development in this area, it is our 'collective' hope that more HCI community can engage in such efforts in China.

While our work provides valuable, yet preliminary, insights on the link between the temporal and collective public sentiment on ASD and its public awareness in China, its findings might pave the way for further investigations that are beneficial to both raising public awareness and executing public policies on autism education and medical care for thousands of millions of 'undocumented' individuals and their loved ones living in ASD.

References

1. Beykikhoshk, A., Arandjelović, O., Phung, D., Venkatesh, S., Caelli, T.: Data-mining twitter and the autism spectrum disorder: a pilot study. In: Proceedings of the IEEE/ACM International Conference on Advances in Social Networks Analysis and Mining, pp. 349–356 (2014)
2. Swinyard, W.R.: The effects of mood, involvement, and quality of store experience on shopping intentions. J. Consum. Res. **20**(2), 271–280 (1993)
3. Gardner, M.P.: Mood states and consumer behavior: a critical review. J. Consum. Res. **12**(3), 281–300 (1985)
4. Holbrook, M.B., Gardner, M.P.: Illustrating a dynamic model of the mood-updating process in consumer behavior. Psychol. Mark. **17**(3), 165–194 (2000)
5. Bollen, J., Mao, H., Zeng, X.J.: Twitter mood predicts the stock market. J. Comput. Sci. **1**, 1–8 (2011)
6. Mishne, G., Rijke, M.D.: Capturing global mood levels using blog posts. In: Nicolov, N., Salvetti, F., Liberman, M., Martin, J.H. (eds.) AAAI 2006 Spring Symposium on Computational Approaches to Analysing Weblogs, pp. 145–152. The AAAI Press (2006)
7. Dolan, R.J.: Emotion cognition, and behavior. Science **298**(5596), 1191–1194 (2002)
8. Edmans, A., García, D., Norli, O.Y.: Sports sentiment and stock returns. J. Finance **62**(4), 1967–1998 (2007)
9. Hirshleifer, D., Shumway, T.: Good day sunshine: stock returns and the weather. J. Finance **58**(3), 1009–1032 (2003)
10. Dodds, P.S., Danforth, C.M.: Measuring the happiness of large-scale written expression: songs, blogs, and presidents. J. Happiness **11**(4), 441–456 (2009)
11. Culotta, A., Kumar, N.R, Cutler, J.: Predicting the demographics of twitter users from website traffic data. In: Proceedings of Twenty-ninth National Conference on Artificial Intelligence (AAAI 2015), pp. 72–78 (2015)
12. Moat, H., Preis, T., Olivola, C., Liu, C., Chater, N.: Using big data to predict collective behaviour in the real world. Behav. Brain Sci. **37**(1), 92–93 (2014)
13. Papaioannou, P., Russo, L., Papaioannou, G., Siettos, C.: Can social microblogging be used to forecast intraday exchange rates. Netnomics Econ. Res. Electron. Network. **14**, 47–68 (2013)
14. Schwartz, H.A., Eichstaedt, J.C., Kern, M.L., Dziurzynski, L., Ramones, S.M., Agrawal, M., Shah, A., Kosinski, M., Stillwell, D., Seligman, M.E.P., Ungar, L.H.: Personality, gender, and age in the language of social media: the open-vocabulary approach. PLoS ONE **8**(9), e73791 (2013)
15. Beykikhoshk, A., Arandjelović, O., Phung, D., Venkatesh, S., Caelli, T.: Using twitter to learn about the autism community. Soc. Network Anal. Min. **5**(1), 1–17 (2015)
16. Beykikhoshk, A., Arandjelović, O., Phung, D., Venkatesh, S.: Overcoming data scarcity of twitter: using tweets as bootstrap with application to autism-related topic content analysis. In: Proceedings of IEEE/ACM International Conference on Advances in Social Networks Analysis and Mining (2015)
17. Chew, C., Eysenbach, G.: Pandemics in the age of twitter: content analysis of tweets during the 2009 H1N1 outbreak. PLoS ONE **5**(11), e14118 (2010)
18. Culotta A.: Towards detecting influenza epidemics by analyzing twitter messages. In: Proceedings of the ACM Workshop on Social Media Analytics, pp. 115–122 (2010)
19. Harshavardhan, A., Gandhe, A., Lazarus, R., Yu, S.H, Liu, B.: Predicting flu trends using twitter data. In: Proceedings of the IEEE Conference on Computer Communications, pp. 702–707 (2011)
20. Himelboim, I., Han, J.Y.: Cancer talk on twitter: community structure and information sources in breast and prostate cancer social networks. J. Health Commun. **19**(2), 210–225 (2014)

21. Mitchell, L., Frank, M.R., Harris, K.D., Dodds, P.S., Danforth, C.M.: The geography of happiness: connecting twitter sentiment and expression, demographics, and objective characteristics of place. PLoS ONE **8**(5), e64417 (2013)
22. Paul, M.J., Dredze, M.: A model for mining public health topics from twitter. Health **11**, 6–16 (2012)
23. Prier, K.W., Smith, M.S., Giraud-Carrier, C., Hanson, C.L.: Identifying health-related topics on twitter, an exploration of tobacco-related tweets as a test topic. In: Proceedings of the International Conference on Social Computing, Behavioral-Cultural Modeling, and Prediction, pp. 18–25 (2011)
24. Scanfeld, D., Scanfeld, V., Larson, E.L.: Dissemination of health information through social networks: twitter and antibiotics. Am. J. Infect. Control **38**(3), 182–188 (2010)
25. Agarwal, A., Xie, B., Vovsha, I., Rambow, O., Passonneau, R.: Sentiment analysis of twitter data. In: Proceedings of the Workshop on Language in Social, Media, pp. 30–38 (2011)
26. Baucom, E., Sanjari, A., Liu, X., Chen, M.: Mirroring the real world in social media: twitter, geolocation, and sentiment analysis. In: Proceedings of the International Workshop on Mining Unstructured Big Data Using Natural Language Processing, pp. 61–68 (2013)
27. Ginsberg, J., Mohebbi, M.H., Patel, R.S., Brammer, L., Smolinski, M.S., Brilliant, L.: Detecting influenza epidemics using search engine query data. Nature **457**, 1012–1014 (2009)
28. Bentley, R.A., O'Brien, M.J., Brock, W.A.: Mapping collective behavior in the big-data era. Behav. Brain Sci. **37**(1), 63–76 (2014)
29. Taquet, M., Quoidbach, J., de Montjoye, Y.-A., Desseilles, M.: Mapping collective emotions to make sense of collective behavior. Behav. Brain Sci. **37**, 102–103 (2014)
30. Berezin, M.: Emotions and the economy. In: Swedberg, R., Smelser, N.J. (eds.) Handbook of Economic Sociology, 2nd edn, pp. 109–127. Russell Sage Foundation and Princeton University Press, New York (2005)
31. Berezin, M.: Exploring emotions and the economy: new contributions from sociological theory. Theory Soc. **38**, 335–346 (2009)
32. Wen, S.Y., Wan, X.J.: Emotion classification in microblog texts using class sequential rules. In: Proceedings of AAAI 2014, pp. 187–193 (2014)
33. Chang, P.C., Galley, M., Manning, C.: Optimizing chinese word segmentation for machine translation performance. In: Proceedings of the Association for Computational Linguistics (ACL) Third Workshop Statistical Machine Translation (2008)
34. Mohammad, S., Turney, P.: Crowdsourcing a word-emotion association Lexicon. Comput. Intell. **29**(3), 436–465 (2013)
35. Quan, C., Ren, F.: An exploration of features for recognizing word emotion. In: Proceedings of the 23rd International Conference on Computational Linguistics (Coling 2010), pp. 922–930 (2010)
36. Rao, Y.H., Li, Q., Mao, X.D., Liu, W.Y.: Sentiment topic models for social emotion mining. Inf. Sci. **266**, 90–100 (2014)
37. Cambria, E., Schuller, B., Xia, Y., Havasi, C.: Knowledge-based approaches to concept-level sentiment analysis: new avenues in opinion mining and sentiment analysis. IEEE Intell. Syst. **28**, 15–21 (2013)
38. Baron-Cohen, S.M.: An Essay on Autism and Theory of Mind. MIT Press/Bradford Books, Boston (1995)
39. Tang, T., Flatla, D.: Autism awareness and technology-based intervention research in china: the good, the bad, and the challenging. In: Proceedings of Workshop on Autism and Technology - Beyond Assistance & Intervention, in Conjunction with the CHI 2016 (2016)
40. Wang S.: China's uncounted children with autism. Wall Street J. (2015). Accessed 17 Oct 2016
41. Sue, D.W.: Asian-American mental health and help-seeking behavior. J. Couns. Psychol. **21**, 167–178 (1994)

Design of an Innovative Assisting Device for Knee Osteoarthritis

Fong-Gong Wu[✉] and Hsien-Chi Kuo

Department of Industrial Design, National Cheng Kung University, Tainan, Taiwan
fonggong@mail.ncku.edu.tw, chiboboy6300232@gmail.com

Abstract. Osteoarthritis is usually found in weight-bearing joints. Since medial knee joints bear most of the loading during gait, osteoarthritis is especially common in these joints. For early osteoarthritis patients, unloading or increasing muscle strength through exercise is the most fundamental healing approach. The use of assistive devices during exercise can relieve pain and thus increase patient motivation or improve on the duration. However, long-term use of assistive devices may cause discomfort or even side effects and in turn make matters worse. Hence, the purpose of this study includes (1) Developing an innovative assistive device that reduces medial knee loading; (2) Aiming for this device to relieve knee pain caused by OA; (3) Aiming for this device to be free of knee and peripheral muscle movement restrictions and thus increase comfort.

To design an innovative assistive device, this research obtains design criterions through reviewing existing products and expert focus groups. Design concepts are generated in co-design activities following these criterions and eventually converged into one final design with morphological charts. Finally, prototypes are built according to the final design. The results of the experiments show that this innovative assistive device can significantly reduce medial knee loading on both legs, and that the satisfaction scores of design criterions are able to reach an acceptable level.

Keywords: Knee osteoarthritis · Assisting device · Design

1 Introduction

Knee osteoarthritis (KOA) is one of the crucial health issues among the elderly around the world. It is considered the leading cause of disability amongst the elderly, especially those who are above 55 years old [1]. With osteoarthritis, all tissues around the knee joints are affected [2]. Quadriceps dysfunction decreases the protection around the knee joints and periarticular tissues [3]. These local biomechanical factors are particularly important in weight-bearing knee joints and therefore are risk factors of KOA [4]. Additionally, direct injury to cartilage may cause biochemical changes and induce chondrocytes to apoptosis. Thus, previous trauma, incorrect knee movements, and overweight are also risk factors of KOA [5]. Other than that, systematic factors like gender, age, or race that predispose to KOA should also be considered.

© Springer International Publishing AG 2017
M. Antona and C. Stephanidis (Eds.): UAHCI 2017, Part III, LNCS 10279, pp. 117–125, 2017.
DOI: 10.1007/978-3-319-58700-4_11

Using aids to decrease the intensity and frequency of impact or change knee alignments efficiently help reduce pain found in patients with mild to moderate KOA [6]. Although aids like bracing and wedged insoles can improve knee functions or reduce pain, Risberg, Holm, Steen, etc. (1999) found significant quadriceps strength decrease after long-term usage [7]. This indicates that bracing may actually improve knee biomechanics but may also limit quadriceps contractions and impedes leg movement. Additionally, other negative impacts including flexion contracture, peripheral vascular disease and intractable contact dermatitis [8]. These disadvantages are largely caused by how traditional bracing works, existing bracings are bound to fix tightly around knee in order to stabilize or realign joint.

The purpose of this research is to develop a new assisting device, which can relief painful symptom of KOA by improving knee biomechanics. By utilizing an innovative assisting approach that allows natural muscle contractions, negative impacts caused by traditional aids may be decreased. This will eventually increase the quality of life among KOA patients.

This research focuses on the design and evaluation of the prototype. Specific procedures are listed below:

(1) Investigate the relationship between knee biomechanics and painful symptoms of KOA, and establish the basic architecture of proper assisting method.
(2) Review traditional and novel aids and set further design criterions including comfort and aesthetics aspects.
(3) Develop an innovative assisting device based on proper assisting methods and design criterions.
(4) Evaluate the efficiency of final design through objective and subjective methods.

2   Methods

From literature review, we have learnt that unloading of medial knee compartment during one-legged stance is the key to relief pain and to slow progression of knee osteoarthritis. Also, correct alignment is crucial to medial to lateral load distribution. The improvement of disproportionate medial load can be achieved by several mechanisms including expending support base, realigning knee loading axis, supporting corresponding muscles, and using compensatory gaits. However, these mechanisms should not increase knee flexion moment to avoid following ascension of contact force. As for the improvement of comfort level and aesthetics in assisting devices, lightweight and material softness are possible directions for a better design.

2.1 Development of Design Criterions

In order to develop an innovative assisting device, specific design criterions such as in-depth understanding of unloading mechanisms and appropriate directions for development are necessary. These criterions are obtained through expert focus groups and reviewing of existing aids in this research.

2.2 Expert Focus Group

Four experts from KOA related fields in National Cheng Kung University are invited to attend the focus group. The professional background of these experts includes fields of biomechanics, orthopedics, engineering, and wearable device.

After an explanation of the whole process and self-introduction of participants, possible unloading mechanisms are introduced together with current research progress. These include expending support base and unload symptomatic joint, realigning malaligned loading axis, supporting corresponding muscles, and the use of compensatory gaits. The discussion focused mainly on the effects of each unloading mechanism and possible directions for future development.

Besides their own viewpoints, the consensus of all experts include: Avoid prolonged use of assistive devices to prevent side effects. Assistive devices should only be used in cases of serious discomfort or in cases of large amount of activities. Additionally, assistive devices should be used with core treatments such as exercises and weight management. Improvement of medial loading can be assessed by joint space since it is defined in the criteria of severity. Also, it is unnecessary and difficult to find a new unloading mechanism. It would be more practical to improve on existing products or using existing mechanisms to create innovative applications. As for applications of assistive devices, combining sensors, big data and customization is more flexible and suitable for different user groups. Since knee joint degeneration is irreversible, the developing direction should aim towards prevention and delaying deterioration.

2.3 Review of Existing Aids

Extra in-vitro structures are necessary and will increase overall size of the product and decrease user acceptance. Being the most effective orthosis, unloading braces combine wearable design and realigning function. It should be noted that comfort is important and related to adverse effects. As for the third assisting way, protecting joints from adverse movements may be beneficial but relatively passive. Additionally, design direction should focus on the use of light and soft materials to improve comfort and aesthetics. In conclusion, direct unloading of symptomatic joint is the most effective mechanism. While in terms of structure size consideration, realigning may have a higher application potential.

2.4 Design of Assisting Device

After preliminary design criterions are confirmed, the development of design concepts can begin. The forming of final design depends on the output of concept designs and morphological charts. Ultimately, the final design transforms from detailed sketches to tangible and functional prototypes through repetitive improvement and is ready for efficacy evaluation.

Concept Design

Design is conducted according to design criterions obtained from expert focus group and review of existing aids. The aim of design is to generate as many different concepts as possible. Six graduate students from Department of Industrial Design NCKU are invited to attend the concept design procedures.

In the beginning of concept design, background information on KOA and its relationship with unloading is explained to participants. After that, existing assistive devices, unloading mechanisms, and the feedbacks from the expert focus group are introduced.

Among different unloading mechanisms, increasing loading base is the most preferred due to it is the only method that can distract loading of knee joints. Also, it is a more compatible solution and works for most of the patient cases. However, how to increase the loading base while keeping the assistive device compact and small will be a big challenge. Thus, wearable assistive device designs become the mainstream concept in order to reduce product size. After a period of development, several design concepts are generated after co-design.

The detail mechanisms of these concept designs are explained below:

(1) An exoskeleton-like device that can assist corresponding muscles according to user's gait characteristics.
(2) An innovative insole that can adjust loading axis according to plantar pressure under different situations.
(3) A wearable device which will remind users to maintain unloading gait pattern.
(4) A wearable device that shows loading distribution synchronously and allows user to compare with their subjective feeling.
(5) A wearable device that coordinates with walking aids and warns the user in cases of excessive or insufficient loading on the knee.
(6) A wearable structure that will distribute loading out of the knee.
(7) An inflatable device that will support knee joints.

Final Design

Design concepts mentioned above are then deconstructed along with existing assistive devices to set the components and parameters of morphological charts. Converged with the design criterions set up, components of the assistive device are divided into unloading mechanism, assisting basis, usage, position and material. These components are listed according to their importance in the formation of an innovative assistive device, while parameters are listed according to efficacy of existing products or ideal design directions acquired previously.

In order to limit the divergence and increase efficiency, front row parameters will be combined preferentially. Although ideal designs should be the combination of front row parameters, unreasonable results may still be produced. For example, the first row of parameters can form a plantar wearable device which can increase loading base according to knee loading. However, located at plantar is inconsistent to its function of distracting knee loading. Other contradictions include knee loading are impossible to measure directly, and soft material is ineffective in increasing the loading base.

In order to reduce the size of innovative assistive device and increase comfort, the mechanism for increasing the loading base is eventually abandoned as it requires a hard structure to achieve maximum effect. Thus, realigning loading axis, assisting during stance phase, wearable device, and soft material becomes the parameters with priority. After a variety of combination trials, these parameters are combined with full leg positioning and developed into an innovative assistive device.

2.5 Prototype

The building of prototype starts from detailed sketches, enhancing to rough models, then refined to final models. Detail sketches are used to arrange explicit structures, materials and appearances, while putting into consideration the functions, usability, and the manufacturing process.

Rough models are direct implementations of the detailed sketches. They are first built with paper templates before moving onto fabrics. They are used to verify the structures and arrangements of sketches, and determine whether a revision of the detailed sketch is required before continuing with the proofing process (Fig. 1).

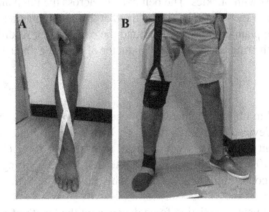

Fig. 1. (A) Paper template and (B) fabric rough model

Inevitably, many errors and corrections were made during the proofing process. Versions of sketches and rough models were also developed. For example, the first rough model was designed to use elastic bands to form assistive abduction moment. Also, the elasticity of the bands prevents them from becoming loose and droopy during knee flexion. However, the elasticity turned out to offset the force yet increase the difficulty of wearing (Fig. 2).

Final model make references to popular sports leggings to avoid the stereotypical bulky and rigid appearance of aids. It uses inelastic nylon belt of a variety of lengths between flexion and extension of knee to create an assisting force. Because of this mechanism, it is able to provide dynamic assistance force only at stance phase and low flexion. Also, the adjustable nylon belt length is able to produce different assisting force magnitudes.

Fig. 2. Tilted views of first rough model

By moving connection points to waist and foot, no tightening is required around thigh and calf and hence will not restrict muscle contraction. Each end of the nylon belt is fixed on the waist with buckles. The belt extends across the thigh and through a ring located on the side of the knee. The ring is fixed at the end of another black nylon belt that runs across the plantar and is sewn around the calf section. Additionally, a device is screwed beside the ring and act as the conductor of assisting abduction force.

2.6 Pilot Study

Pilot study is used to objectively determine whether the final model is comparable to existing assistive device. The data is drawn by built-in serial plotter of Arduino Integrated Development Environment with vertical axis presents force (N) and horizontal axis presents time (0.1 s). The process of pilot testing includes sitting for ten seconds, walking for ten seconds, and then stand for ten seconds. The variations of force are clearly visible.

Since the adjustment of assisting force depends on the length of the belts, the data are respectively recorded at 15 and 20 cm long to present different force magnitudes. 15 cm is the minimum length to prevent the belt from becoming too loose when seated, and it provides a mean force of about 5.5 N. Additionally, the prototype can provide a mean force of about 9 N when the belt length is 20 cm. As for existing products, Rebel Reliever (Townsend, CA, USA) was chosen. It is an unloading brace with mechanism that allows a maximum angle adjustment of 18°, and the data was collected under two degree settings. At a setting of relatively small angle, this unloading brace provides a mean force of about 7 N. In sum, the result of the pilot test shows that the new design is able to provide comparable assisting force to existing unloading brace at a low to medium angle setting. This means the chosen mechanism and structure are functional and ready for evaluation experiments.

3   Results

Medial knee loading is assessed by the frontal plane lever arm variation in this research. If the lever arm is lengthened due to assisting abduction force, the medial knee loading is relatively unloaded. As for pain relief, the visual analogue scale is used to record acute pain intensity.

In the objective evaluation experiment, gait data were recorded by camera while test subjects walk on the treadmill at their own chosen speeds. Reflective markers are located at three points: most lateral superior iliac crest, medial knee joint line and medial malleolus. Gait recording were respectively conducted before and after the belts are put on, to compare the efficacy of assisting abduction force.

However, the results need to be normalized before analyzing against paired sample t-test due to offset caused by body size differences. Divided by another vector of the same test subject, frontal plane lever arm magnitudes can be converted into the same ratio. In this research, we choose thigh vector $\left| \left(\vec{AB} \right) \right|$ as comparison (Fig. 3). The recorded gait data were converted into ratio of frontal plane lever arm magnitude to thigh using equations mentioned above. The descriptive statistics are shown in Table 1.

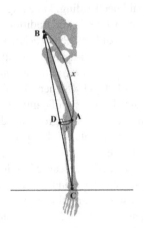

Fig. 3. Vectors and angle relationships of lower extremity markers

Table 1. Lever arm and thigh ratios before and after using innovative assistive device

		N	Mean	SD
Left leg ratio	Before	8	.084	.016
	After	8	.103	.024
Right leg ratio	Before	8	.099	.018
	After	8	.118	.024

Mean ratio of frontal plane lever arm magnitude to thigh increased after using the innovative assistive device. The variations of both legs were further analyzed with paired samples t-test (Table 2).

Table 2. Paired samples t-test results of ratio variation

	Mean	SD	95% confidence interval	T	df	p-val.
Left leg ratio variation	.019	.012	.007 to .029	4.58	7	.003*
Right leg ratio variation	.018	.013	.009 to .029	3.82	7	.006*

4   Conclusion

The purpose of this research is to develop an innovative assistive device which relieves painful symptoms of knee osteoarthritis by reducing medial knee loading. By utilizing an innovative approach with assistance that allows natural muscle contractions, we aim to reduce negative impacts caused by the use of traditional aids and increase comfort.

In order to achieve the research purpose, we first investigate the relationship between knee biomechanics to establish a thorough understanding of assistive methods. These include the importance of medial knee loading, knee alignment, and avoid the increase of overall contact force. Moreover, we reviewed traditional and novel aids to set further design criterions including comfort and aesthetics aspects. After that, innovative assistive device was developed through a co-design activity and morphological charts. Finally, objective and subjective evaluation experiments are conducted to verify whether medial knee compartment is unloaded and whether the pain is notably relieved. Current experiment result shows that the device significantly reduced medial knee loading. However, it did not reduce pain to a notable degree. Besides, overall satisfaction of the current prototype has reached an acceptable level, especially the free movement degree of the lower limbs and its appearance.

To sum up, the current prototype in this research is able to bring benefit by providing assisting abduction moment at stance phase and low leg flexion to reduce medial knee loading. It also allows natural muscle contraction and increase the comfort by utilizing soft, elastic and breathable materials and move the connection points to waist and plantar. Also, its current appearance is well accepted but closer to the preferences of young people. Thus, a customized appearance with functional inner structure may be the direction of future development. Additionally, the current assisting force adjusting mechanisms are highly affected by body sizes. Combining with sensor technology may simplify the process and standardize the assisting force among different users.

Acknowledgements. The authors would like to thank the Ministry of Science and Technology in Republic of China for financially supporting this research under Contract no. MOST 104-2420-H-006-018-MY3.

References

1. Peat, G., McCarney, R., Croft, P.: Knee pain and osteoarthritis in older adults: a review of community burden and current use of primary health care. Ann. Rheum. Dis. **60**(2), 91–97 (2001)
2. Felson, D.T.: Osteoarthritis of the knee. N. Engl. J. Med. **354**(8), 841–848 (2006)
3. Slemenda, C., Brandt, K.D., Heilman, D.K., Mazzuca, S., Braunstein, E.M., Katz, B.P., Wolinsky, F.D.: Quadriceps weakness and osteoarthritis of the knee. Ann. Intern. Med. **127**(2), 97–104 (1997)
4. Felson, D.T., Lawrence, R.C., Hochberg, M.C., McAlindon, T., Dieppe, P.A., Minor, M.A., Weinberger, M.: Osteoarthritis: new insights. Part 2: treatment approaches. Ann. Intern. Med. **133**(9), 726–737 (2000)
5. Musumeci, G., Aiello, F.C., Szychlinska, M.A., Di Rosa, M., Castrogiovanni, P., Mobasheri, A.: Osteoarthritis in the XXIst century: risk factors and behaviours that influence disease onset and progression. Int. J. Mol. Sci. **16**(3), 6093–6112 (2015)
6. Lafeber, F.P., Intema, F., Van Roermund, P.M., Marijnissen, A.C.: Unloading joints to treat osteoarthritis, including joint distraction. Curr. Opin. Rheumatol. **18**(5), 519–525 (2006)
7. Risberg, M.A., Holm, I., Steen, H., Eriksson, J., Ekeland, A.: The effect of knee bracing after anterior cruciate ligament reconstruction a prospective, randomized study with two years' follow-up. Am. J. Sports Med. **27**(1), 76–83 (1999)
8. Segal, N.A.: Bracing and orthoses: a review of efficacy and mechanical effects for tibiofemoral osteoarthritis. PM&R **4**(5), S89–S96 (2012)

Universal Access to Education and Learning

Applying Movie and Multimedia to the Inclusive Learning and Teaching in Germany: Problems and Solutions

Ingo K. Bosse[✉] and Annette Pola

Faculty of Rehabilitation Research, University of Dortmund, Dortmund, Germany
`ingo.bosse@tu-dortmund.de`

Abstract. The focus of the study is on the didactic and methodological implementation of inclusive education through multimedia with a focus on film. The data was provided by teachers using media in their lessons incorporating inclusive forms of learning. The whole project consisted of phase I and II. The educational homepage "Planet School" by the public broadcaster WDR was used as an example. For this purpose, different types of schools worked with "Planet School" in inclusive education. Using guidelines based on the findings of the first phase, the public broadcasting organization WDR made four films for use in geography lessons, as well as additional media and materials for inclusive education. The focus of phase II is on the didactic and methodological implementation of inclusive education using film as a medium. The question is examined: How successfully can pupils learn using films and materials designed using inclusion guidelines? The existing films and materials were tested by eight inclusive classes. Based on these tests, an understanding of how media should be designed to acquire knowledge in inclusive education was achieved. The results of data analysis underline the relative satisfaction of students and teachers. The systematic comparison of the different data sources was made along deductively and inductively developed categories. These example of a personalised learning with a blended learning platform show not only how media based education can enhance everybody's ability to learn, but also that special education can be a key driver in proliferating media related learning.

Keywords: E-inclusion · Blended learning · Broadcasters · Inclusive education · Inclusive multimedia learning materials

1 Introduction

In view of the fact that nowadays, moving images are with us always and everywhere, our knowledge of the world can be seen both in and through them. "Pictures explain the world and influence our ethical and normative ideas. They are used for communication" [1]. For children and adolescents, images are not only moving pictures of reality. They are an essential means of self-expression. The presented study reveals the significance of image-based information and how it is used for blended learning in inclusive classrooms.

Comparative international studies, e.g. ICILS 2013 [2] show how social challenges, such as participation and handling heterogeneity at school, can be addressed through

© Springer International Publishing AG 2017
M. Antona and C. Stephanidis (Eds.): UAHCI 2017, Part III, LNCS 10279, pp. 129–142, 2017.
DOI: 10.1007/978-3-319-58700-4_12

media. The research presented here is part of a project (reported in [3]) with the overall aim of investigating the design and use of blended learning for inclusive education. The whole project consisted of phase I and II. The here described project is the second phase with a focus on the didactic and methodological implementation with a focus on movies.

The main focus was how individualized and personalized blended learning can succeed in inclusive education? Thereby, the research questions are: How does learning with movies and blended learning materials, designed according to the in phase I developed design guidelines succeed? How can students with different learning conditions use movies and learning materials?

This research project aims to show how inclusive education with these movies and learning materials can succeed and what influence different design elements (such as animations) have on learning.

2 State of the Art

In research on evidence-based design of learning materials for inclusive education, the question: "What characterizes good learning materials?" must first be clarified. If this is to be achieved, one should first define what effective teaching and learning involves. The most prominent international study on this issue is the study Visible Learning by John Hattie [4]. He ranked 138 influences that are related to learning outcomes from very positive effects to very negative effects. Hattie found that the average effect size of all the interventions was 0.40. Among the first positions in the ranking are the following factors:

1. Teacher Clarity $d = .75$
2. Feedback $d = .73$
3. Teacher-student-relationships $d = .72$
4. Meta-cognitive strategies $d = .69$
5. Repeated reading programs $d = .67$
6. Peer Tutoring $d = .55$
7. Classroom Management $d = .52$ [4]

Evidence base educational research show that the differences in competences between western and eastern states can be explained by the schoolbooks and its related learning cultures [5]. That's the reason why in many countries learning resources have to be authorized through a scientific evaluation. Based on his research on the design of textbooks Wellenreuther derived the following consequences:

- Emphasis on deeper understanding; different approaches,
- Critical points, typical errors – little internalization of processes
- Fewer topics, thinner books
- More scope for explanations
- Comprehensibility: step-by-step development of solutions
- Clear structure: Presentation of the process - guided practice - use in tasks
- Full explanations in textbooks: textual – visual - symbolic
- Activation of learners

– Related information are presented together (divided attention effect)
– Numerous explicit examples of solutions (cf. [5]).

Although there is few data about it so far, the importance of the design of digital media for the learning success of students is often discussed among teachers and the scientific community. But there is just a short tradition to use these results for inclusive education [3].

Furthermore the evidence based research about the design of learning materials show that the following conditions lead to successful inclusive learning: 1. Deliberate and meaningful use of differential instructional materials, 2. Encouragement and facilitation of active and student directed learning, 3. Mutually agreed and effective cooperation of regular and special education teachers and 4. The alignment of general classroom instruction and diagnostically founded, individually prescribed and intensive instruction in cases of special needs. The learner's self-direction is an accessory skill. Due to the fact that self-directed learning means a big challenge for persons with learning difficulties, their teachers have to pay special attention to train this skill [6].

So far, the research on evidence based design of learning materials for inclusive education focused classic teaching materials such as textbooks in particular. However, the here presented project takes moving images and digital into account, which are part of the everyday life of students, growing up nowadays.

As an example the education platform "Planet School" was used. It is a multimedia joint project of the public broadcaster west (WDR) and south (SWR). This platform offers media-based learning and teaching tools for teachers, students and all others, who are interested in education. But, not all parts of this homepage are directed towards students. First, the homepage provides teachers with material for preparing lessons. The focus are moving images. The WDR and SWR broadcast these movies. Those movies as well as multimedia and worksheets can be downloaded from the platform in various formats. Thus, offers different ways of use during the lessons. Many schools are using these offers in various subjects. "Planet School" is not specifically designed for inclusive education. But in 2013 they started to design offers according to the needs of students with special needs. A first research project (2013/2014) addressed the question: What design principles can be used to create materials for blended learning in inclusive education. In phase I data on contemporary forms of inclusive education from the media-didactical perspective of teachers and producers of the educational homepage "Planet School" was conducted.

The educational homepage "Planet School" by the public broadcasters WDR and SWR was used as an example, because the producers developed a blended learning content that was created according to the design standards developed in phase I. The main outcome of the first phase was the development of principles for designing inclusive teaching- and learning media.

The developed guidelines contain eight factors that are essential for the creation of inclusive learning contents with digital media. These include:

1. Text and language
2. Individualization and personalization
3. Same learning subjects

4. Respect for the complexity of lived-realities
5. Cooperative/collaborative learning
6. Activity-oriented instruction
7. Web accessibility and universal design
8. General design principles

On that basis, the WDR created directives and checklists for the design of inclusive teaching- and learning materials specifically for the different types of media. Additionally, guidelines were developed which describe individual measures more detailed. Thus, both instruments aim at quality assurance. These instruments are the working basis for everyone who is involved in a new production [7]. According to these directives and checklists a first teaching unit was designed.

3 Method

Findings from phase I showed that complex language is one of the greatest barriers for inclusive learning. According to these findings, a further focus of this research are students with migration history.

This research project is supposed to generate universal findings for the development of movies, media and learning materials for inclusive education. Hattie concludes from his study: "If the teacher's lens can be changed to seeing learning through the eyes of students, this would be an excellent beginning" [4]. Following this idea, the perspectives of the students was central for the development of the research design.

3.1 Selection of Participants and Procedure

Using guidelines based on the findings of the first phase, the public broadcasting organization WDR produced four movies for use in geography lessons, as well as additional media and materials for inclusive education. Within the here described research we analyzed how individualized and personalized learning in inclusive education as exemplified by "Planet School" (www.planet-schule.de) can be successful. The focus is on the didactic and methodological implementation of these media for inclusive education.

For this project we chose a variety of schools to work with "Planet School" in inclusive education ("Hauptschule", "Gesamtschule", "Sekundarschule", "Förderschule"), because we wanted to know how successful the lessons are in different kind of schools. Five schools and eight classes with a range of heterogeneity were part of the second phase of the study. They worked at the beginning of the school year 2016/2017 in geography lessons on the topic "City, countryside, river". All schools are experienced in teaching students with special needs. In all classes, there was a great variety of students body, including students with various special needs, such as learning, language and communication, learning difficulties, physical-motor development and social-emotional development as well as German as a second language. The total sample involves 160 students as well as eight teachers with different professional background. Usually, the teachers educate on their own, two classes have team teaching and in four out of eight classes an assistant teacher supports the teacher.

During this intervention the following question is examined: How successfully can students learn by using movies and other blended learning materials designed using guidelines for inclusive design?

The methodology follows the approach of systemic perspective triangulation [8]. Triangulation implies that one investigated object is looked at from different perspectives. In our project we conducted the perspectives of students as well as of teachers. These different perspectives are conducted with different methods. Next to perspective triangulation, a data triangulation [8] is applied. From different sources information is generated. Furthermore, data triangulation implies a combination of differing types of data [9]. The data triangulation should be linked to the perspective triangulation.

Four movies for this teaching unit were produced, according to guidelines for geography in grade 5 and 6:

1. Life in a village and in the city
   In this teaching unit the students learn difference between life in a village and in the city. They learn what impact a different infrastructure has on everyday life. The students compare the living situations of the protagonists in the movie to their own. Based on this comparison, they form an opinion on where they would prefer to live.
2. From village to city
   This teaching unit deals with the spatial structure of cities and villages. While working with the movie, one key element of this teaching unit is the work with maps. The movie is built upon the movie "Life in a village and in the city" in terms of its content.
3. Leisure time and tourism
   In this teaching unit the students perceive that certain location factors and structural conditions shape leisure- and vacationing behavior. Additionally, they deal with occupations in the tourism- and leisure time sector.
4. The change of landscapes
   As a special form of land usage, the students get to know brown coal mining, as a special form of land usage. At the same time, the students reflect the situation of the residents as well as the effects on the landscaping.

Each movie exists in two versions, with and without animation. Five classes watched movie 1, four classes movie 2, five classes movie 3 and six classes movie 4. Six of the 20 movies were watched without animation.

3.2   Survey Instruments

The main approach is the evaluation of contributions to the geography series "City, countryside, river". The evaluation takes the form of a final assessment of the quality of the learning unit.

In our data analysis we referred to:

Flash Feedback
Flash feedback is a data collection method, which is also often used as a method for reflection in lessons [10]. Directly after watching the movie, the teachers conducted a

short flash feedback with their students. During the flash feedback, the students express their opinions on the movies freely. These free expressions were written down directly or from memory. This method allows to gather impressions directly after watching the movie. Totally, 20 of these flash feedbacks were conducted.

Quantitative Survey with Students

The questionnaire consists of closed questions with a six-point Likert scale. The even number of answer options is supposed to force the students to make clear choices. Additionally, this corresponds to the German grading system from one to six and therefore is already known by the students. These quantitative surveys were conducted by the teachers. They were able to react immediately to contradicting statements and had the opportunity to clarify these. The questionnaire covers the following subjects: evaluation of the movies, evaluation of the language, especially the comprehensibility, evaluation of the animations, evaluation of the protagonists and evaluation of the imagery. These aspects were also covered during the group interviews. The collected data was entered in SPSS and analyzed quantitatively.

Participatory Observations in Lessons

In order to conduct characteristics of students, teachers and lessons which affect the development of expertise and social, personal competences of the students a systematic participatory observation of the lessons was conducted. During the participatory observation we focused on individual learning processes and group processes. Chosen students were particularly observed [11]. In close consultation with the teachers one top-performing child, one child performing on an average level, one weaker student, and one child with German as a second language as well as two children with different special needs were selected. Due to the aspiration that the movies and materials are supposed to meet the challenges of students with heterogeneous needs, these students were particularly observed.

This collects data in terms of categories previously defined on conceptual grounds and refined in pilot work. (...) Criticisms of systematic observation have usually centered on validity issues (e.g., Delamont and Hamilton 1986), but it can be a useful research tool when answering specific research questions for which data are needed on relatively easily observed [11].

As main categories for the participatory observation served: methodology and didactic/differentiation, Design of material/reaction to material, design of the movie/reaction to the movie, comprehensibility of language and text, motivation, increase of expertise and collaborative work.

Group Interviews with Students

The group interviews with students were conducted with one top-performing child, one child performing on an average level, one weaker student, and one child with German as a second language as well as two children with different special needs. This was done in order to receive feedback from a variety of students and to conduct their specific needs. These interviews were conducted directly after a participatory observation.

During the interview the following topics were covered: Evaluation of the movies, evaluation of explanations and language, Interesting aspects, ability to focus on the movie, evaluation of the protagonists, evaluation of the animations, evaluation of the learning effect and evaluation of the materials.

Group Discussion with Teachers

Design and reception of the movies	Total Evaluation, concentration / attention, reference to the lifeworld, learning effect/ increasing competences, activation of previous knowledge, clarity and reduction to the essential, imagery and image quality, evaluation of the protagonists, evaluation of animations total, evaluation of animations in relation to the learning contents, correlation movie + material, suggestions for improvement
Design and use of the material	Total evaluation, example solutions, structure, explanatory definitions, photo which are content related, meaningful application of pictograms, clarity, activation of previous knowledge, reference to the lifeworld, reduction to the essential, suggestions for improvement
Didactic	Useful information for teachers, feedback, design of the instruction, reference to curricula, differentiation of learning objectives
Methodology and teaching structure	Learning effect, independent selection of tasks, concentration/ attention, motivation, (informal) testing, conclusion at the end of the learning sequence, recurring structure, comprehensibility, mixed tasks, activity orientation, peer-based work, differentiation levels
Accessibility	Clear labeling of the files, reduction of stimuli visualization of contents
Access and comprehensibility of language and text	Language and text of the material, language in the movie, usability for students with German as a second language
Use of I-Pads (Additional category for I-Pad class)	

Fig. 1. Coding system with sub codes

In a final qualitative step, the quality of the movies and materials was discussed in a group discussion with teachers from all the schools involved. In addition, this was used to ensure that all aspects, which are relevant for the teachers, were covered.

The group discussion with teachers of all participating schools was based on an interview guideline, which covered the following topics: Experiences made while implementing the teaching unit "City, countryside, river, Evaluation of the teaching unit "City, countryside, river", Evaluation of the movies watched in this teaching unit, Evaluation of the materials offered by "Planet School", Assessment of the accessibility of the materials, especially text and language, Appropriateness of the methods and didactical advices, Suggestions for improvement for the accompanying materials, Evaluation of the learning effect due to this teaching unit.

Both, group interviews with students and group discussions with teachers were recorded and transcribed afterwards [12]. Next, using MaxQDA, the interviews and discussions were paraphrased and reduced. Finally, all interviews as well as the record of the participatory observation were analyzed using the qualitative content analysis by Mayring. In order to use the qualitative content analysis by Mayring, core categories were defined. This was done deductively, according to a prior theoretical analysis and inductively, using the conducted material.

This was done with the aim to reduce the material to its main contents, which are still presenting the basic material [13] (Fig. 1).

This procedure interlocks qualitative and quantitative analysis methods. Thus, we get findings going beyond those individual cases, but still considering the specifics of the respective source of data.

4   Results

The four existing movies and corresponding materials were tested by the eight participating classes.

Based on these tests, an understanding of the quality of the media was achieved. In addition, helpful didactic concepts, methods and learning conditions were devised. Because the analysis and interpretation of these complex data is not finished yet, first descriptive findings of the quantitative survey will be outlined. As far as possible those are linked to the group interviews, flash feedbacks and participatory observation. At the HCI in Vancouver the final results will be presented.

4.1   Perspectives of Students and Teachers

This study focused on the perspective of students. In total, three research tools were used to conduct their perspectives. In order to analyze the group discussion with teachers the same category system as for the analysis of the group interviews with students, flash feedbacks and participatory observation was used. First findings from the 95-minute group discussion with teachers supplement the perspective of the students. The further analysis will provide more detailed findings regarding the learning materials and methodical-didactical aspects. These will be presented at the HCI conference.

Evaluation of the Movies

Approximately 65% of the students grade the movies as very good or good. The first two movies were the highest-ranked ones. The reason might be, that these two movies were produced completely new for inclusive education, whereas for the production of the movies three and four also archive materials were used (Table 1).

Table 1. How did you like the movie? Grade the movie.

		Frequency	Percent	Valid percent
Valid	Very good	107	31,7	33,8
	Good	114	33,7	36,0
	Satisfying	55	16,3	17,4
	Sufficient	24	7,1	7,6
	Inadequate	9	2,7	2,8
	Unsatisfactory	8	2,4	2,5
	Total	317	93,8	100,0
Missing	0	21	6,2	
Total		338	100,0	

"I liked the movie that much, that I give a thumps-up, because such movies should be produced more often." (Group interview S)

"I think these movies are well done and should stay that way. They should not be more thrilling. Students are supposed to learn, instead of having nightmares." (Group interview KK)

The group interviews with students show the reasons for the positive valuation: The students characterize the movies as thrilling and funny. They are fun, interesting and are well produced. Also the flash feedbacks confirm this valuation. The analysis of the flash feedbacks confirm these findings. The majority of the valuation of the movies are positive. Many students were able to remember and to reproduce the contents of the movies. Many students think that the contents are explained well in the movie. "Fun and learning in combination" (Flash feedback, movie 3, class 5a).

First results of the group discussion with the teachers show a mainly positive evaluation, too. The teachers stress the demanding character of the movies and the good mixture between documentary and fiction. A typical statement from the teacher discussion was: "But altogether the materials were nice and I had fun." (Flash Feedback KK).

Accessibility of the Language

Overall, the students consider the comprehensibility of the language in the movies very positively. Also the question regarding the comprehensibility on the word-level was evaluated very positive. 78, 7% graded the comprehensibility of the words as very good or good. The results of the group interviews show: They were able to listen well. A comprehensible language with a good speech rate and clear pronunciation was used. The given explanations were described as good because they contributed to a better understanding. Despite the mostly positive valuation there are also negative valuations: speech too fast, hardly understandable, speech too loud, speech too quiet, outdated language, drafted language, too much speech, too many explanations, unknown words, difficult for students with German as a second language (Table 2).

Table 2. The spoken words were easy to understand. The spoken words were hard to understand.

		Frequency	Percent	Valid percent
Valid	Very good	204	600	61,6
	Good	62	18,3	18,7
	Satisfying	46	13,6	13,9
	Sufficient	10	3,0	3,0
	Inadequate	3	,9	,9
	Unsatisfactory	6	1,8	1,8
	Total	331	97,9	100,0
Missing	0	7	2,1	
Total		338	100,0	

In the categories "Access and comprehensibility of language and text" the teachers considered positive the appropriate language level, although for students with special needs partly too complex. They praised that due to the movie-related support the students were able to understand relations from context, a better understanding due to repeated everyday life conversations as well as few questions and positive feedbacks by the students.

Animation

Mainly, the animations were evaluated positively. However, these evaluations differ widely between the different classes. Only 37, 6% answered the question how well the animations helped them to understand the topic with good or very good. The results of the group discussion regarding the animations do not correlate to those of the quantitative survey. On the one hand, the students say that the animations were cool, funny, cute, exciting, should last longer, reproduce the content of the movie, extend the movie, diversifies the movies and highlight particular animations. On the other hand students

Table 3. The animations were interesting and funny. The animations were uninteresting and not funny.

		Frequency	Percent	Valid percent
Valid	Very good	108	32,0	43,9
	Good	48	14,2	19,5
	Satisfying	36	10,7	14,6
	Sufficient	16	4,7	6,5
	Inadequate	10	3,0	4,1
	Unsatisfactory	28	8,3	11,4
	Total	246	72,8	100,0
Missing	0	92	27,2	
Total		338	100,0	

express negative evaluations because of the following reasons: waste of time, too childish, inappropriate timing, disturb their concentration, are too long, because of they forgot some of the contents, distract, disturb, strange sounds, should be talking, are not related to the content/topic (Table 3).

In a purely quantitative analysis of the group interviews, the negative statements regarding the animations are predominate. Using the analysis of the flash feedback as an additional source of data, it becomes clear, that the movies with animations obtain a better evaluation as those without. But also in the flash feedbacks, the evaluation is not exclusively positive.

The evaluation of the use of animations by the teachers is rather different. It is considered very good. They emphasize the positive reactions of the students and that the students were able to remember the contents and identify themselves with the animations.

Overall, the animations are regarded ambivalent.

Manageable Number of Protagonists

The quantitative data shows, that the students can empathize with the respective protagonists. The data of the interviews with students stresses the mainly positive identification. Especially the protagonists and their acting performance was valuated as very good or good (Table 4).

Table 4.   I can well imagine the life of the adolescents. I could not imagine the life of the adolescents.

		Frequency	Percent	Valid percent
Valid	Very good	174	51,5	53,2
	Good	67	19,8	20,5
	Satisfying	57	16,9	17,4
	Sufficient	19	5,6	5,8
	Inadequate	1	,3	,3
	Unsatisfactory	9	2,7	2,8
	Total	327	96,7	100,0
Missing	0	11	3,3	
Total		338	100,0	

The teachers in accordance with the students highlighted positively the protagonists. In particular, the male protagonist of episode one was considered appealing because of his demeanor and attitude. He offered a high identification potential. His methods to guide through the movie raised the attention. The everyday communication of the protagonists are linked to the children's realities. The first movie included a lot of everyday conversations, while the fourth movie included long monologues, which is less exciting for the students.

5 Discussion and Conclusion

The starting point for this study was the question how movies and other blended learning materials are used for blended learning in inclusive classrooms and which conditions lead to successful learning and teaching. Additionally, data on effective learning [4] and findings of research on evidence-based design of learning materials for inclusive education, which hitherto focused on traditional teaching and learning materials [5, 14] build the frame for this research. In Wember's scholastic learning model, which is oriented towards prevention, he mentions four central conditions for the development of inclusive education. The first condition is deliberate and meaningful use of differential instructional materials [6]. The findings demonstrated that collaborative, lifeworld-related and product-oriented learning with media should be guiding principles for the design of movies and materials for inclusive classrooms [15]. Especially students with special needs can profit from the variability of digital teaching- and learning material. Within the scope of this research, we were able to identify what is important when implementing principles for designing inclusive digital teaching- and learning materials. Because of the triangulation we were able to conduct the needs of the students as well as of the teachers. In comparison to the first part of the project, the second part focusses more on the perspectives of the students.

It must, however, be critically stated that the participatory observation only provided a few additional findings. But it helped to understand and categorize the data generated with the other methods. Furthermore, this data cannot be generalized due to the small sample. Especially, for the type of school "Gymansium" no statements can be made, because despite intensive efforts we were not be able to win over a "Gymnasium" to participate in this study.

All things considered, it became apparent that movies are a suitable learning tool for all students and therefore, are also highly suitable for inclusive education. Not every movie is equally suitable (neither for all students). The criteria for the design of movies developed in the first phase of this research project (concentration on the essential and clear explanations, closeness to real life and motivating frame actions as well as no distracting elements - both formal- and content-related) were essentially confirmed. Blended Learning Platforms such as "Planet School" offer good foundations for inclusive learning and teaching:

- The multi-media platform offers different ways to absorb information,
- Multi-media complies with the media usage habits of students
- Movies are a central media in the life of students. Therefore, it is motivation for them, when movies are also used in schools.
- The media and materials allow the reduction of complexity
- Learning impulses for all students, regardless of their level of performance, due to suitable and vivid media
- The media internet provides good opportunities, to offer a variety of materials fully accessible

This example of inclusive teaching and learning with a blended learning platform show not only how media based education can enhance everybody's ability to learn, but also that special education can be a key driver in proliferating media related learning. In order to accomplish the educational goals, the ideal approach to teaching and learning is to find the right balance between giving students the choice to meet their needs and preferences whilst maintaining a structured educational framework. Yet much more remains to be done going forward. Pedagogic change and a greater personalization of learning are both essential components for student centered, self-regulated, independent and inclusive learning [16].

References

1. Müller, I.: Moviebildung in der Schule. Ein moviedidaktisches Konzept für den Unterricht und die Lehrerbildung. kopaed, München (2012)
2. Bos, W., et al.: ICILS 2013 – Computer- und informationsbezogene Kompetenzen von Schülerinnen und Schülern in der 8. Jahrgangsstufe im internationalen Vergleich. Münster, Waxmann (2014)
3. Bosse, I.K.: Criteria for designing blended learning materials for inclusive education: perspectives of teachers and producers. In: Antona, M., Stephanidis, C. (eds.) Proceedings of 9th International Conference on Universal Access in Human-Computer Interaction Access to Learning, Health and Well-Being, UAHCI 2015 Held as Part of HCI International 2015 Los Angeles, CA, USA, Part III, 2–7 August 2015, pp. 2–11 (2015)
4. Hatti, J.: Visible Learning: A Synthesis of Over 800 Meta-analyses Relating to Achievement. Routledge, New York (2009)
5. Wellenreuther, M.: Forschungsbasierte Schulpädagogik. Anleitungen zur Nutzung empirischer Forschung für die Schulpraxis. Baltmannsweiler, Schneider Verlag Hohengehren (2009)
6. Wember, F.: Herausforderung Inklusion: Ein präventiv orientiertes Modell schulischen Lernens und vier zentrale Bedingungen inklusiver Unterrichtsentwicklung. Zeitschrift für Heilpädagogik, H. **10**, 380–387 (2013)
7. Bosse, I.: Gestaltungsprinzipien für digitale Lernmittel im Gemeinsamen Unterricht. Eine explorative Studie am Beispiel der Lernplattform Planet Schule. In: Mayrberger, K. (Hrsg.) Digital und vernetzt: Lernen heute. Gestaltung von Lernumgebungen mit digitalen Medien unter entgrenzten Bedingungen. Jahrbuch Medienpädagogik 2016, pp. 132–148. Springer, Heidelberg (2016)
8. Flick, U., von Kardoff, E., Steinke, I.: Qualitative Sozialforschung. Ein Handbuch. Rowohlt, Hamburg (2005)
9. Flick, U., von Kardoff, E., Steinke, I.: Companion to Qualitative Research. Sage Publications, Thousand Oaks (2004)
10. Meyer, H.: Was ist guter Unterricht? Cornelsen Scriptor, Berlin (2016)
11. Blatchford, P., Basset, P., Brown, P.: Teachers' and pupils' behavior in large and small classes: a systematic observation study of pupils aged 10 and 11 years. J. Educ. Psychol. **97**(3), 454–467 (2005). doi:10.1037/0022-0663.97.3.4549
12. Kuckartz, U.: Qualitative Inhaltsanalyse. Methoden, Praxis, Computerunterstützung. Beltz Juventa (2014)
13. Kuckartz, U., Rädiker, S., Ebert, T., Schehl, J.: Statistik. Eine verständliche Einführung. VS Verlag, Wiesbaden (2010)
14. Hillenbrand, C.: Evidenzbasierte Gestaltung von Lernmitteln für Inklusive Bildung. Vortrag (2014). http://www.medienberatung.schulministerium.nrw.de/Medienberatung-NRW/Dokumentationen/2013/130517_DialogVA-inklusive_Lernmittel/profhillenbrandlernmittel.pdf

15. Giering, B.: Lern_IT und Inklusion – eine Win-Win-Situation. Anregungen zur Medienausstattung und –nutzung an inklusiven Schulen. Computer Unterricht **94**, 20–22 (2014)
16. Bosse, I.K., Armstrong, N., Schmeink, D.: Is cloud computing the silver lining for European schools? Int. J. Digit. Soc. (IJDS) **7**(2), 1171–1176 (2016). doi:10.20533/ijds. 2040.2570.2016.0143, http://infonomics-society.org/ijds/published-papers/volume-7-2016/

Considerations for Designing Educational Software for Different Technological Devices and Pedagogical Approaches

Paulo Alexandre Bressan[1](✉), Thiago Henrique dos Reis[1], Artur Justiniano Roberto Jr.[1], and Marcelo de Paiva Guimarães[2]

[1] Laboratory of Educational Technology, Federal University of Alfenas, Alfenas, Brazil
paulo.bressan@gmail.com, thiago.henri.reis@gmail.com, arturjustiniano@gmail.com
[2] Faccamp Master Program, Open University of Brazil (UAB/UNIFESP), São Paulo, Brazil
marcelodepaiva@gmail.com

Abstract. Educational app development enables didatic content to be widely known and enhances the access of professors and students to technological resources, mainly in economically disadvantaged communities. However, building educational applications demands perceptive understanding in the way of approaching desired concepts, so as not to convey wrong information, especially in applications where graphic interface design is essential. This article presents and discusses important factors for the design of graphic educational applications: low-cost technologies, graphic modeling and assessment importance. The considerations presented in this work are based on the design and development of some applications to physics subjects, however they can also be useful for application projects from other subjects.

Keywords: Educational software · Software requirements · Graphic modeling

1 Introduction

Although in developing countries, such as Brazil, especially in public schools, where in one hand teachers and learners have to make do with lower quality and availability of equipment, on the other hand technological evolution has popularized access to a variety of devices with different functions, like sound, image and movement. In other countries, governments continuously invest in hardware and this measure accounts for their education expenditures, which are nevertheless important, but when not linked to development of appropriate educational software, will not meet desired results [1]. In this sense, building applications for low-cost equipment improves access to didactic content in society as a whole, contributing to avoid social exclusion through technology [2, 3].

The main objective of this article is to present considerations for analysis and design of educational software with graphic processing that is a popularization of didactic contents, which are: technologies for educational applications, graphic modeling and importance of tests. These considerations were designed to the experience gained do not

© Springer International Publishing AG 2017
M. Antona and C. Stephanidis (Eds.): UAHCI 2017, Part III, LNCS 10279, pp. 143–154, 2017.
DOI: 10.1007/978-3-319-58700-4_13

have the development of several projects designed to popularize access to didactic content to public school students from a region lacking Brazil in the educational context and technology. This work follows a definition of universal access and inclusion in the project:

> "A commitment to universal access rises from the desire to meet the interaction needs of divergent user populations in the information society. Universal access has been characterized as the ability or right of all individuals, in spite of varying levels of ability, skill, preferences, and needs, to obtain equitable access and have effective interaction with information technologies..." (Jacko [4])

Nowadays popularization and diversity of technological devices increases equipment availability, not only via schools, but also via teachers and students themselves. This fact is even more important in developing countries and, that means that the software can also be used in environments other than merely during classes. It is known that the quantity of mobile devices, tablets and smartphones is increasing among the population, and that these devices are becoming better and better, such as image recognition, geolocalization, motion detection, among others. Moreover, video games have a lot of devices with different functions, such as motion sensors and stereoscopic glasses.

The relation among teacher, software and student needs to be considered in order to determine the role of each one in the teaching-learning process. Although the software can be used individually by a student, the role of a teacher as a task advisor can improve the interaction of students with the didactic content. So, the software becomes a tool to bring about topics for discussion, not to draw attention for itself.

Project testing phase consists of a well-established computing practice to determine the system's capabilities and efficiencies, yet a couple of considerations need to be taken about the educational software. The terms capacity and efficiency do not refer to memory and processing performance, but instead, they express the capacity to include didactic content and efficiency on representing involved concepts. In these tests, human factor influences the results significantly and causes the evaluation process to be hard in quantitative terms, since it is difficult to confirm the results with a new test or to compare the results among methods. Beside this, it is emphasized that usability tests must be performed several times during project development together with teachers and students.

2   Related Work

Software design demands effort when the situation involved manipulates well-defined data. Besides this, when the topic involves didactic content and teacher-student and student-student relationships, the application design requires a user-focused design, which takes into account the user's effective participation during the analysis and development step.

Software engineering literature is rich in presenting methodologies for the design and analysis of software development, and many of them are suitable for specific cases. Methodologies in software development have evolved from rigid documentation methods to flexible and adaptive methods. Thus, a structured analysis has a series of documents that analysts need to elaborate at the beginning of the project, such as diagrams of classes, data, entity-relationship, among others, [5]. While this allows for full process control, agile methodologies are better suited to modern projects because of team leaders' and users' greater proximity to development and follow-up is concerned [6, 7]. Especially in education, because of a very subjective model along with many variations, the methods are highly recommended for an interaction between developers, teachers and students [1].

In general, upon the development of educational software, there are additional factors to be observed. First, which educational content will be made available by the tool or the teacher, and how they will be presented to students – whether on websites, desktop applications, mobile applications, interactive media, or others. Moreover, many educational software programs converge on the mechanisms of communication between the teacher and the students, and also with the students' activities' evaluation process, particularly in distance learning courses [8].

In many of these softwares, the didactic content per se will be presented in the form of texts, videos, audios, questionnaires, forums, and other mechanisms, and so the teacher must use an existing material or build his own, a task which requires to be knowledgeable about publishing in popular software [9]. Much work has been done in this direction and the volume of generated content is huge, but the interactivity of this user is smaller when compared to applications that involve some graphic processing, which are the concern in this article.

The graphic representation of didactic contents allows a better understanding of the concepts under discussion. Neither casting aside the students' ability nor the stimuli that a teacher provides to be imagined as more diverse situations, a virtual environment that models an object of study allows a greater interaction between teachers and students. In addition, graphical environments stand themselves as quite interesting ways to capture and captivate people's attention, especially younger generations, as with games for example.

3   Educational App Technologies

In Brazil, and possibly in developing countries, private schools can afford the modernization of a school environment, and are able to fill their activities with didactic content adapted for all kinds of technological devices. Since technological advancement has popularized electronic devices, adapting didactic content templates for low-cost equipment make applications more accessible for society in general, also favoring public education, and this is a way to improve education technologically.

It is noteworthy that the acquisition of these devices does not depend on public investment, although it could be of some use, since these are being acquired individually by teachers and students. This way the technological evolution in education would be occurring effectively through teachers and students, and educational applications would help in this process.

Evolution occurs in most diverse gadgets, such as in motion sensors of the device itself (accelerometer, georeferencing and gyroscope), data capture (cameras and touch) and data reproduction (sounds and images), as well as processing and memory features.

This has also enabled the creation of virtual reality environments (3D glasses) and augmented reality, among others.

While the quality of these features makes it possible to create interesting, complete, and complex interface applications, one's should stick to the relationship between the primary purpose of the application and the intended learning content. This means that these resources should be used wisely, while keeping the attention of their users in the studies involved.

In the sub-sections below it is presented some sensors and their characteristics that enhance their application in educational softwares.

3.1 Motion Capture Sensors

The evolution of video-game peripherals brought along a more natural way of capturing users movements, increasing interactivity and immersion. For many of these peripherals, it is possible to connect them to personal computers directly or through small adapters, and use them in applications via libraries made available by manufacturers.

The use of these peripherals is quite common due to the large number of people who play video games. Many benefits have been observed by the use of these peripherals in health projects [10–12] and education [13–15]. However, there is a wide variety of peripherals in terms of shapes, functionalities and data capture mechanisms.

Some peripherals detect parts of the human body through some sensors that do not require to stay in close contact with the body, such as Kinect and Leap Motion. Others require the user to hold them, such as Wii Remote and Playstation Move. Finally, Wii Fit and steering wheels equipped with force feedback need to be pressed.

3.2 Mobile Device Sensors

Technologies applied to smartphones and tablets in recent years have also contributed to user interactivity with applications. Sensors that can be found on these devices include gyroscope, GPS, accelerometer, touch screen, camera, microphone, among others. These sensors pick up signals of some sort and transform them into digital data, which can be processed. In addition, they are being very well accepted by people for their ease of use, as can be observed with the touch screen.

In [16] the mobile device accelerometer was used to input data on variation of the acceleration during a quite small time interval to demonstrate the occurrence of impulsive forces. The Lablet [17] application, in turn, uses the accelerometer to record gravity acceleration and the microphone to pick up the beep, within a concept where the application is an experiment lab. In addition to this, MobTracker [18] and VidAnalisys [19] use the camera to capture movements of an object while the experiment occurs.

3.3 Graphic Processing Capacity

The quality of the images rendered by electronic equipment (TVs, monitors and mobile devices) strongly contribute to users immersion in the activity performed, so much so that the industries seek better definitions of colors and resolutions. The graphics processing capability also influences immersion because it renders more realistic images and in shorter times within 2D or 3D.

The quality of the latest generations of smartphones allows users to immerse users in applications with virtual and enhanced reality, the latter allied with the ability of câmera capture. Currently, several devices (3D glasses) are smartphone-friendly and are able to create virtual stereoscopic environments in which users really feel within the modeled environment. These resources are still little explored in education, considering that this an area with great potential to be explored.

4   Graphic Modeling and Its Implications

Not all didactic content needs to be modeled within an application, or modeled on graphics application. But there are many didactic contents where its graphic modeling is strongly recommended due to the difficulty and complexity of its representation. In many cases, a 2D or 3D virtual environment provides freedom and ease during the time of study. By "freedom", we mean the amount of interactions as possible with the graphic models, and by "ease", it is meant for the amount of different images that can be obtained in a short time interval.

A content is suitable for modeling when the amount of graphic elements to be represented is large enough to be demonstrated by other means, rendering the process way too long, difficult or unfeasible. In this analysis it is noteworthy to find graphic elements - colors, figures and movements - consistent with the information to be represented so that the modeled concept does not lead to misunderstanding or induces unreal behavior. A classic examples is the "double jumping" from action game characters where, after jumping from the ground and, still in the air, the character gets a boost to get even higher with no help from a foothold whatsoever.

The application should also deliver the user a modeled environment to interact with, by modifying the parameters of the modeled objects and their viewing angles, as well as adding a variety of options. In this way, the teacher can build classes with more autonomy and more interactive activities.

Types of software that use graphic modeling are presented in the sub-sections below: serious game, graphic simulator and data capture tool.

4.1   Serious Game

A serious game direct towards a playful way of interacting with the player (user) to keep their attention, and that is not necessarily fun, although desirable. Thus, usually a theme is chosen to introduce and intermediate the discussion whereas a well-known basic structure from gaming experiences may be applied, such as phasing to address sub-themes, punctuation for player engagement, personification and feedback for hits and misses situations [20].

The subject chosen must appropriately meet the didatic content to avoid addressing wrong concepts or in the wrong way. A good choice also avoids later adaptations and allows a good connection between what has been studied and reality.

CineFut [13, 14] software, Fig. 1, was created for the parabolic cinematic motion theme, a very important subject physics education area. Although this content is very much present in games, its objectives are not the teaching-learning process in itself and its adaptation to a study environment requires a great effort from the teachers, both to adjust the discussion and to maintain its focus. In addition, it is common to find conceptual physics mistakes in games, given that they are focused in entertainment, such as characters jumping far beyond their real capabilities or changing direction during jump when a joystick is used. At CineFut the models were came alive with proportionally real dimensions, where the dimensions of the character, the distance to the goal, the size of the barrier and the movement of the ball can all be checked, as part of the pedagogical activity.

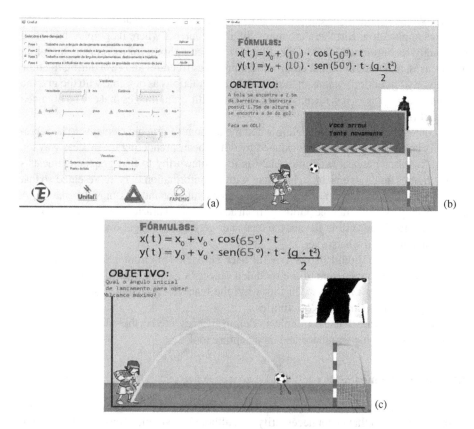

Fig. 1. (a) Select stage and options, (b) message of feedback, (c) graphic objects: parabola, speed vectors and coordinate system.

The CineFut features a character aiming to kick a ball to the goal, and to do that one's should set the angle and initial speed of the ball. Thus, the Kinect motion sensor was chosen as the motion capture equipment due to its conventional features and also because it also delivers a better user-player interaction. The very user adjusts the ball launch angle and kick speed [21]. The angle is determined by raising the right arm from the horizontal line of the body and the kick speed is discovered considering the gap of time between the right foot moving from backwards to forwards position. This way, an understanding of physical magnitudes is enhanced by the user's movements. By raising the left arm is possible to pause an animation at a desired point.

The CineFut was divided into 4 stages approaching 4 kinematics: maximum range, obstacle transposition, complementary angles and effects from gravity. A goal must be achieved by the students at each stage, which requires an understanding of a concept. Messages are displayed after every kick, as feedbacks for hits or misses. Unlikely most of the games, stages can be played in any order, so lesson plan is up to the teacher's will.

2D environment was adequate to approach the subjects of each stage, specially the animation created for the ball parabola, since the third axis would cause difficulty of visualization because it depends on the positioning of the 3D scene observer. This could be of some use to address the physical phenomena of dynamics and external forces upon it, such as ball rotation, altitude and resistance and air pressure.

4.2   Graphic Simulator

In turn, the graphical simulator models a problem to present its data in the most realistic way possible. Generally, the modeled data does not correspond to the real world and uses a graphical form that can be easily understood by its users, such as coordinate systems and vectors used in exact sciences. However it is imperative that the movements and animations produced are based on systems of equations provided by science, because the accuracy is elementary for a correct understanding of the concepts involved.

Astron 3D software [22] consists of a graphic simulator to render the apparent motion of the stars to any place on the globe and any time on the time scale. The apparent motion

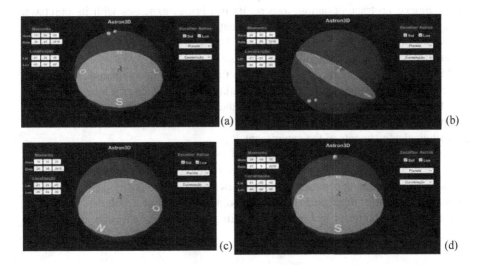

Fig. 2. (a) e (b) Screens with simulations of the moon and the sun during a new moon, from different points of view, (c) position of the sun on the day of the summer solstice and (d) representation of the position of the moon during the full moon [22].

is defined in astronomy as the movement of the perceived star in a half sphere above the observer, which is positioned at its center. Stellarium, Celestia and Cartes du Ciel softwares also render the stars with lots of information and have versions for mobile devices. Although they can be used in education, Astron 3D was designed specifically for this intent, and for that purpose it has a third person view of the celestial dome model, Fig. 2.

Astron 3D offers no challenges to be achieved nor sends feedback messages to users. For being a graphic simulator, the parameters, location, time and stars should be adjusted initially to render the models. The location will be adjusted to the length and latitude of a location, or a previously configured city. The time will be set in day, month, year, hour, minute and second. The stars can be selected from the sun, the moon, some planets to some stars.

The calculations in Astron 3D produces accurate images and avoid incorrect understanding of the physical phenomena involved. However, the focus of the application are the movements of celestial bodies and not their dimensions, because the representation of the stars in scale would reduce their sizes to some pixels of the screen causing difficulties of visualization. Thus, the construction of a model should focus on the simulator main objective, which, for education is favoring the teaching-learning process.

4.3 Data Capture Tool

In the data capture tool some device sensor obtains real-world information that is transformed into data that can easily be stored. In these tools the user defines the way to obtain the data, and can manage how the results will be made available, which, in most cases is done in tables, graphs and databases.

Physical experiments in school environments require capturing of data to understand the studied phenomena, which is usually performed with traditional instruments such as rulers, timers, protractors, among others. Its use brings expenses with its purchase, storage and maintenance, and the generated data is usually inaccurate and more time consuming to obtain. MobTracker software [18] can retrieve data from previously recorded videos or at the time of the experiment.

MobTracker does not recognize objects in the scene, it allows the user to mark the object at specific instants of the video, generating Cartesian data as a function of time. This form of interaction was designed so that the student participates in the data collection process, thus experiencing the behavior of the observed object, not worrying about the technical adjustments of the experiment.

Graphic elements are added on the video to reference the capture of the desired values, Fig. 3. First, the origin of the coordinate system is placed anywhere in the video and with any orientation of the axes. Second, two markers are positioned to determine a scale. After that it is determined how many points will be collected in the video, either by the number of points or by the interval of time between the collections, finally, data collection is performed manually.

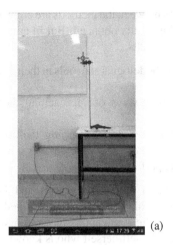 (a)  (b)

Fig. 3. (a) Two-dimensional graphic object from the coordinate system used to mark in the scene the origin of the system, (b) two-dimensional graphic objects used to point scales in the scene

This approach is already known from other papers, the Tracker software performs the same operations, but runs on personal computers [23, 24]. VidAnalysis [19] and Lablet [17] softwares work on mobile devices and use the graphical interface to support with data collection. Each of these applications performs the environment settings differently, but all use graphical interface to improve data collection and visualization.

Data capture tools streamline the process of obtaining data and optimize the time of class so that the teacher and students can focus on the results obtained, not only in the capture process, for a better understanding of physical concepts. The simplicity of these applications allows the leaner to conduct experiments outside the classroom environment, which contributes to the autonomy and independence of students with the concepts studied.

5   Testing Relevance

There are types, ways, and test styles that can be run during software development. In tests of usability, the aim are operation reactions, iconographic representations, sequences of operations, among others.

As "user" one must understand 2 different profiles, teacher and student, since each one has its way of interacting with the application. Thus the iconographic representation must be intuitive and compatible to the didactic content, mainly to avoid student's misinterpretations. The sequence of operations, in turn, can affect the autonomy of the teacher to create his own didactic sequence, for example, if the teacher adopts a serious game with well defined and linear phases, his didactic sequence will practically be defined by the phases.

In application tests, advances and disadvantages between the methods are compared, and statistical tools are widely used to validate the results obtained. But in education several factors hamper an objective analysis of the results:

- teacher training: each teacher adopts different methodologies and tools in their classes for different classes;
- didactic sequences: teachers can create numerous ways of approaching didactic content, for different classes or not;
- student profile: numerous and uncontrollable factors define learning facilities or difficulties of a student, and even more of a class of students, which makes it impossible to use statistical tools to compare the tests performed.

Thus, qualitative analysis is more recommended in applicability tests and better expresses comparisons between the methods studied. Although the results obtained with the students are crucial to determine the efficiency of the application, the opinion of the teachers is better prepared because it is the teacher himself/herself who is knowledged in the field of didactic sequences that can be used with the application.

6   Conclusion

For the aspects described in this article it is easy to observe that the development of educational software needs particular considerations when compared with software for other purposes. Even more so when graphic modeling is an essential element to address didactic content. This concern tends to gain ground as the quantity and quality of available technology resources is increasing and the focus on teaching content should not be lost.

The success of a didactic application depends on the appropriate choice of equipment, how the didactic content will be represented graphically and what results will be expected from the tests. This success contributes to the teaching-learning process and improves access to education through low-cost equipment, especially in underprivileged communities or in undeveloped countries, where there is no due attention by governments to education.

Acknowledgments. We would like to express our gratitude to FAPEMIG (Fundação de Amparo à Pesquisa do Estado de Minas Gerais) for all the financial support to this project.

References

1. Costa, A.P., da Costa, E.B.: Contributos para o Desenvolvimento de Software Educativo tendo por base Processos Centrados no Utilizador. Em Teial Revista de Educação Matemática e Tecnológica Iberoamericana, vol. 4, no. 2 (2013). ISSN 2177-9309
2. Abascal, J., Nicolle, C.: Moving towards inclusive design guidelines for socially and ethically aware HCI. Interact. Comput. **17**(5), 484–505 (2005). doi:10.1016/j.intcom.2005.03.002

3. Fitch, D.: Digital inclusion, social exclusion and retailing: an analysis of data from the 1999 Scottish household survey. In: Proceedings of IEEE 2002 International Symposium on Technology and Society (ISTAS 2002). Social Implications of Information and Communication Technology (n.d.). (Cat. No.02CH37293). doi:10.1109/istas.2002.1013831

4. Jacko, J.A., Hanson, V.L.: Universal access and inclusion in design. Univ. Access Inf. Soc. 2(1), 1–2 (2002). doi:10.1007/s10209-002-0030-x

5. Summerville, I.: Software Engineering (Update), 8th Edn. Pearson Education, New Delhi (2007). ISBN-13:978-0321313799, ISBN-10:0321313798

6. dos Santos Soares, M.: Metodologias ágeis extreme programming e scrum para o desenvolvimento de software. Revista Eletrônica de Sistemas de Informação 3(1) (2004). ISSN 1677-3071 doi:10.21529/RESI

7. Schwaber, K., Beedle, M.: Agile Software Development with Scrum, vol. 1. Prentice Hall, Upper Saddle River (2002)

8. Malheiros, A.P.S.: Educação matemática online: a elaboração de projetos de modelagem. 2008. 187 f. Tese (doutorado) - Universidade Estadual Paulista, Instituto de Geociências e Ciências Exatas. Disponível em (2008). http://hdl.handle.net/11449/102084

9. Oliveira, C.C., Oliveira, D.C., Oliveira, C.F., Cattelan, R.G., de Souza, J.N.: Árvore de Características de Software Educativo: Uma Proposta para Elicitação de Requisitos pelo Usuário. In: Brazilian Symposium on Computers in Education (Simpósio Brasileiro de Informática na Educação-SBIE), vol. 1, no. 1 (2010)

10. Sonnino, R., Matsumura, K.K., Bernardes, J.L., Nakamura, R., Tori, R.: Fusion4D: 4D unencumbered direct manipulation and visualization. In: 2013 XV Symposium on Virtual and Augmented Reality (2013). doi:10.1109/svr.2013.40

11. Shih, C.-H., Shih, C.-T., Chu, C.-L.: Assisting people with multiple disabilities actively correct abnormal standing posture with a Nintendo Wii balance board through controlling environmental stimulation. Res. Dev. Disabil. 31(4), 936–942 (2010). doi:10.1016/j.ridd. 2010.03.004

12. Goto, H., Mamorita, N., Takeuchi, A., Ikeda, N., Shirataka, M., Miyahara, H.: Diagnostic criterion of QT prolongation for healthy young Japanese men. J. Electrocardiol. 40(6), S82 (2007). doi:10.1016/j.jelectrocard.2007.08.027

13. Reis, T.H., Bichara, G.K., Bressan, P.A., Junior, A.J.R.: Ensinando Conceitos de Física com Sensores de Movimentos. In: SBC – Proceedings of SBGames 2014 (2014). ISSN 2179-2259

14. Barbosa Filho, M.A., Reis, T.H., Bressan, P.A., Junior, A.J.R.: Utilizando Sensor de Movimentos para o Ensino de Cinemática. In: XII Workshop de Realidade Virtual e Aumentada (2015). ISBN 978-85-7983-808-8

15. Abellán, F.J., Arenas, A., Núñez, M.J., Victoria, L.: The use of a Nintendo Wii remote control in physics experiments. Eur. J. Phys. 34(5), 1277–1286 (2013). doi: 10.1088/0143-0807/34/5/1277

16. de Jesus, V.L.B., Sasaki, D.G.G.: Uma visão diferenciada sobre o ensino de forças impulsivas usando um smartphone. Revista Brasileira de Ensino de Física 38(1) (2016). doi:10.1590/ s1806-11173812075

17. University of Auckland Label Team: Lablet – Physics Sensor Lab. Auckland, New Zealand (2016). http://lablet.auckland.ac.nz/ Accessed in em 03 Feb 2017

18. Reis, T.H., Bressan, P.A., Junior, A.J.R., Germinaro D.R.: Mobtracker: Um Aplicativo De Captura De Dados Para O Ensino De Física. In: XXII Simpósio Nacional de Ensino de Física – SNEF 2017 (2017)

19. Steele, G.: VidAnalysis...an app for physical analysis of motion in videos (2015). http:// vidanalysis.com/. Accessed 03 Feb 2017

20. Gee, J.P.: What Video Games Have to Teach Us About Learning and Literacy, 2nd Edn., Revised and Updated Edn. St. Martin's Press (2007). ISBN-13 978-1-4039-8453-1, ISBN-10 1-4039-8453-0

21. Moreira, M.A.: Teorias de aprendizagem, pp. 81–94, 1st Edn. EPU, São Paulo (1999). 195 p. ISBN 85-12-32140-7

22. Gonçalves, A.B., Silva, E.M., Botelho, R.B., Justiniano, A., Bressan, P.A.: Ensino De Astronomia Com Dispositivos Móveis Utilizando Ambiente Tridimensional. In: XXII Simpósio Nacional de Ensino de Física – SNEF 2017 (2017)

23. Bezerra Jr., A.G., de Oliveira, L.P., Lenz, J.A., Saavedra, N.: Videoanálise com o software livre Tracker no laboratório didático de Física: movimento parabólico e segunda lei de Newton. Caderno Brasileiro de Ensino de Física **29**, 469–490 (2012)

24. Lenz, J.A., Saavedra Filho, N.C., Bezerra Jr., A.G.: Utilização de TIC para o estudo do movimento: alguns experimentos didáticos com o software Tracker. Abakós **2**(2), 24–34 (2014). doi:10.5752/P.2316-9451.2014v2n2p24

Teaching Robot Programming Activities for Visually Impaired Students: A Systematic Review

Juliana Damasio Oliveira[✉], Márcia de Borba Campos,
Alexandre de Morais Amory, and Isabel Harb Manssour

Faculty of Informatics (FACIN), Pontifical Catholic University of Rio Grande
do Sul (PUCRS), Porto Alegre, Brazil
juliana.damasio@acad.pucrs.br, {marcia.campos,
alexandre.amory,isabel.manssour}@pucrs.br

Abstract. This paper presents a systematic review of studies concerning the use of robotics for the programming education of individuals with visual impairment. This study presents a thorough discussion and classification of the surveyed papers, including: different programming teaching methodologies based on robotics for people who are blind; the use of several robotics kits and programming environments; the evaluation procedure for each environment; and the challenges found during the teaching process. Based on these papers we created a guideline to prepare, conduct and evaluate a robot programming workshop for people who are visually impaired. These instructions include, for example, how to train instructors to work in workshops for people with visual disabilities, how to prepare concrete and digital support materials, suggestions of work dynamics for programming teaching, how to conduct collaborative activities, forms of feedback for the student to better understand the syntax and semantics of the language, recommendations for the development of a robotic environment concerning the hardware (robot) and software (programming language to operate the robot). These recommendations were validated with two users with visual impairment.

Keywords: Systematic review · Visual impairment · Teaching robot programming

1 Introduction

The first concepts of educational robotics have emerged with Solomon and Papert [1], with the establishment of the LOGO language which, through commands, allowed for the movement of a graphic turtle. The main idea of LOGO language was to encourage children to learn to program in a motivating and playful way [1].

Traditional teaching techniques mainly rely on visual models to help in the understanding of complex information, such as diagrams, flowcharts, tables, and images. Unfortunately, this type of teaching is not useful for visually impaired students [2]. Robots are being used to assist and to stimulate programming classes [3–5] and several robotics environments have been proposed to facilitate the teaching of programming.

© Springer International Publishing AG 2017
M. Antona and C. Stephanidis (Eds.): UAHCI 2017, Part III, LNCS 10279, pp. 155–167, 2017.
DOI: 10.1007/978-3-319-58700-4_14

However, according to [2, 13, 14], there are few initiatives to involve students who are visually impaired because many programming environments are based on graphical user interface, for instance, using drag and drop features, without satisfying the accessibility and usability criteria. Thus, those users that rely on software assistive technology such as, for example, screen readers or screen magnifiers, experience usability difficulties. Another challenge in the programming activity for people who are blind refers to the syntax of some programming languages. Some languages use unusual operators, commands, expressions, tab, punctuation marks, graphic symbols, characters in lowercase and uppercase, etc., which are not always intuitive for beginner programmers and cannot be read by users who are blind and use assistive technology.

Regarding robotics, some kits require participation from people who are not visually impaired to assemble the robot and sometimes set the scenario where it will move around. Other kits use stylized robots, hindering the recognition of these parts and the robot's front, sides and rear. These characteristics, although visually pleasing, may cause difficulties concerning the robot's recognition and their relation in the space when users make use of touch.

A blind individual needs additional support from non-visual stimuli to perceive the environment and build up mental maps. Also known as cognitive maps, they are defined by Long and Giudice [6] to describe the way people create and mentally remember images of the distances and directions to places beyond the reach of their perception. In this manner, receiving information of space through other senses, such as hearing and touch, collaborates to the creation of mind maps to represent the environment [7]. Multimodal interfaces must be included to increase the user's ability to orient and navigate the robot within an environment [8, 9]. The programming environment must use different sound clues to describe the movements, the location of the robot, and the objects around it. Still, the robot must be easy to handle such that the user who is blind can recognize parts and confirm the sound information through tactile feedback. Moreover, although this was not confirmed in the literature and this evaluation is not the focus of this paper, the authors believe that robotics could help to develop (or improve) orientation and mobility skills in blind users.

In this context, this paper presents a systematic review of works regarding the use of robotics for the programming education of individuals with visual impairment. This review may ease the work of educators, researchers and developers, helping in understanding the teaching methodologies, the robotics and programming kits, and how to prepare, lead and evaluate a programming workshop for people with visual disabilities.

2 Methodology

A systematic literature review (SLR) was performed, following to the protocol of Kitchenham [10]. The goal of the SLR was to identify and understand methodological procedures which make use of robotics as support to the teaching of programming to people who are visually impaired. Through this goal, the primary (1) and secondary (a, b, c, d) research questions were identified:

1. Which methodological procedures are being used in the teaching of programming with robots for people with visual disabilities?
   (a) Which are the methodologies for teaching robot programming to people with visual disabilities?
   (b) What are the characteristics of the programming environments used by people with visual disabilities?
   (c) What are the examples of good practices for teaching robot programming to people who are visually impaired?
   (d) Which were the difficulties/limitations in the use of robotics as support to the teaching of programming to people who are visually impaired?

The SLR was conducted in 4 digital libraries relevant to the area of Computer Science, namely: ACM Digital Library (http://dl.acm.org), ScienceDirect (http://www.sciencedirect.com/), Scopus (https://www.scopus.com/) and IEEE xplore (http://ieeexplore.ieee.org). Based on the research goal, a search expression (or search string) was constructed. First, the keywords related to the research topic were identified, as well as their alternative terms and synonyms. The search expression, which can be seen in Table 1, was adapted according to the search mechanism of each digital library, as to not alter its logical sense. The searches were performed in the abstract, title and keywords fields.

Table 1. Search expression

Keyword	Alternative terms and synonyms
Visual impairment	("blind" OR "visually impaired" OR "visual disability" OR "blindness" OR "student disability" OR "unsighted pupils" OR "visual impairments") **AND**
Programming	("programming" OR "program") **AND**
Robotic	("robot" OR "robotic" OR "robotics")

The articles found by this expression were included for full reading if the title, keyword or abstract met the inclusion criteria. The following inclusion and exclusion criteria were defined:

Inclusion Criteria

I1- The result must be written in the English language.
I2- The result must be fully available.
I3- The result must contain in its title, keywords or abstract some relation to this work's topic (people with visual disabilities, programming, robotics).

Exclusion Criteria

E1- In the case of similar or duplicated results, only the most recent will be considered.
E2- Results which explore topics on programming teaching in a broad manner, and not specifically towards people with visual disabilities.

E3- Results which explore topics on the use of robotics in a broad manner, and not specifically towards people with visual disabilities.

E4- The result is not in the areas of Computer Science or Engineering.

The papers with the "Accepted" status were fully read, as to verify if/how do they answered the research questions.

3   Results

The searches in the digital libraries yielded 125 articles. After application of the selection criteria, 9 articles remained for full reading. Table 2 informs the amount of articles found, duplicated and accepted in each digital library. Articles from the years 2008 to 2015 were identified, and Table 3 shows us the articles, the years and conferences in which they were published.

Table 2. Articles found in the search classified by digital library

Library	Amount of articles found	Amount of articles duplicated	Amount of articles selected
Scopus	66	3	8
ACM	19	4	0
IEEE xplore	7	5	1
ScienceDirect	33	0	0
Total	125	12	9

Table 3. Articles found in the search ordered by year

Reference	Year	Conference
[11]	2008	SIGCSE 2008 - Proceedings of the 39th ACM Technical Symposium on Computer Science Education
[12]	2010	ASSETS 2010 - Proceedings of the 12th International ACM SIGACCESS Conference on Computers and Accessibility
[13]	2011	ACM Transactions on Computing Education
[14]	2012	IEEE Transactions on Learning Technologies
[15]	2013	Proceedings - 2013 Conference on Technologies and Applications of Artificial Intelligence, TAAI 2013
[16]	2013	ASEE Annual Conference and Exposition, Conference Proceedings
[17]	2014	IEEE SSCI 2014: 2014 IEEE Symposium Series on Computational Intelligence - RiiSS 2014: 2014 IEEE Symposium on Robotic Intelligence in Informationally Structured Space, Proceedings
[18]	2014	ASSETS 2014 - Proceedings of the 16th International ACM SIGACCESS Conference on Computers and Accessibility
[19]	2015	IEEE International Workshop on Robot and Human Interactive Communication

The research questions are answered below.

1- Which methodological procedures are being used in the teaching of programming with robots for people with visual disabilities?
a. Which are the methodologies for teaching robot programming to people with visual disabilities?

Of the selected studies, 6 (six) presented the use of robotics workshops [11, 13, 14, 16–18] as the teaching methodology. Although articles [12, 19] present robotics and programming environments for people with visual impairment, the results include only activities with people who can see. In the study of Kakehashi et al. [15], sighted users were blindfolded. The relation between the amount of students, educational level and robotics programming knowledge [11, 13, 14, 16–18], which had participation from people with visual disabilities, are presented in Table 4. The workshop's duration varied between works, as well as the resources and amount of participants, as shown in Table 5.

Table 4. Students' profile

Reference	Educational level	Amount of users	Programming knowledge
[11]	Not cited	14	Not cited
[13]	Not cited	14	Not cited
[14]	Middle school	9	Not cited
[16]	Middle and high school	32	Some had programming experience
[17]	Junior and high school	7	No one had programming experience
[18]	Not cited	10	3 (three) did not have experience and 7 (seven) had some experience

Table 5. Number of workshops vs. duration vs. organization

Reference	Number of workshops	Duration	Organization
[11]	1	4 days	Teams
[13]	3	-	Teams (3 students)
[14]	-	2 weeks	Individual
[16]	-	4 h	Teams
[17]	1	90 min	Individual
[18]	-	4 days (with duration of 3 to 4 h per day)	Teams (2–3 students)

In the study of Kakehashi et al. [15], which was performed with blindfolded sighted people, two experiments were conducted, one to investigate the efficiency of the tactile information provided on the programming blocks, made of Japanese cedar and equipped with RFID readers, and another to verify if the P-CUBE was easier to program than using text programming with the Japanese Beauto Builder2[1] PC software. The first experiment was conducted with 16 participants between 20 and 38 years of age, which were blindfolded. The time necessary for each user to identify the concrete blocks and the accuracy were recorded. In the second experiment, there were 10 sighted users, and the work does not mention if they had prior programming knowledge or if they were blindfolded. The time necessary to complete the task in each programming environment was recorded. These experiments were not performed with people with visual disabilities, but show that the blocks are easily recognizable, just as the P-CUBE proved itself to be a resource that helps to understand how to program.

Some works [11, 13, 14, 16] cite the use of tutorials to present new programming concepts and language syntax, used in the respective studies. In general, the tutorials also contained the description of the activities to be performed. The tasks were designed in a way that each task was based on the knowledge obtained from the previous tasks, systematically increasing in difficulty and, as consequence, the necessary skills to their conclusion [14]. Also, during the tasks, the instructor would ask questions that required for the student to give a verbal answer [14]. According to Demo [20], the verbalization technique allows for an instructor to verify what and how the student is planning to solving a problem, and thus to verify the technical foundation occurring through a formulation which is particular to each student. In the work of Kakehashi et al. [17], the use of tutorials is not explicitly cited, but they describe an experimental programming class in which the participants with visual disability had to solve certain exercises, which included a solution with a sequential program, and then with a program with condition and repetition structures.

There are works that use scale models in different forms and with various materials. In the study of Kakehashi et al. [17], the participants with visual impairment controlled a robot through a course laid out in an E.V.A (Ethylene-vinyl Acetate) material, with a black line indicating the way the robot should follow (Fig. 1a). In the study of Ludi and Reichlmayr [11], a labyrinth was constructed for the robot to navigate (Fig. 1b), set on a table so that the participants could feel the path and the robot with touch, and understand the action performed by the robot through touch. In Park and Howard [16], the environment was modified according to the activity (Fig. 1c).

Fig. 1. (a) Trajectory with E.V.A (Source: [17]) (b) Labyrinth (Source: [11]) (c) Challenge (Source: [16])

b. Which are the characteristics of the programming environments used by people with visual disabilities?

Of the 9 (nine) works analyzed, 6 (six) used the LEGO mindstorm NXT [11–14, 16, 18] robotics kit. The others [15, 17, 19] created their own robots using the Arduino board. Figure 2a illustrates the robot used in the study of Ludi and Reichlmayr [13] and Fig. 2b depicts the robot used by Motoyoshi et al. [19].

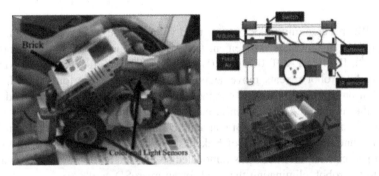

Fig. 2. (a) LEGO mindstorm NXT (Source: [13]) (b) robot with Arduino (Source: [19])

The studies of [11, 13] use the LEGO mindstorm NXT robotics kit composed by three motors (each mounted on a structure with a reduction box and a gyroscope/speed sensor) and touch, light, ultrasonic and sound sensors. The programming environment was developed by the open-source BricxCC[1]. The language used was the NXC[2], similar to the C language. According to the authors, this language was chosen for its syntax's simplicity, ease of learning and using and use with the screen reading software Jaws. The Windows operating system was used because the students were more familiar with it.

The studies of [12, 18] used the LEGO mindstorm NXT kit, switching from the BricxCC programming environment to the JBrick environment. JBrick's menu was simplified to 5 options, to minimize what is spoken by the screen reader, and in the article there is no mention of which options were left; BricxCC had 8 options. The language's commands were not cited.

The studies of [14, 16] used the LEGO mindstorm NXT kit composed by two motors with wheels and internal encoders for odometry calculations, two touch sensors to detect user input and collision events, a light sensor to detect landmarks on the floor, and an ultrasonic sensor to detect objects in front of the robot. The authors chose the BricxCC as the development environment. The commands for robot movement can be seen in Table 6. A Wii remote control (Wiimote) was used for haptic feedback. In the work of Howard et al. [14], the authors included a summarized feedback which was embedded in an intelligent agent called Robbie, which provides audio feedback to the student after his program is executed. Robbie was written in the C++ language.

The robot created by [15, 17, 19] is composed of an Arduino UNO microcontroller board, a microSD wireless card, a buzzer, two motors, a speed box and batteries.

Table 6. BricxCC's basic programming commands

Commands	Description
start_robot()	Switches the robot ON
move_up(X)	Moves the NXT robot forward an X number of times
turnleft(X)	Turns the NXT robot to the left an X number of times
turnright(X)	Turns the NXT robot to the right an X number of times
stop_robot()	Switches the robot OFF

The P-CUBE programming blocks were used (Fig. 3). The blocks used in this study had the following functions: Movement (forward, right, left, backwards), Timer (1st, 2nd, 3rd, 4th), IF (IF START IRsensor (L) END, IF START IRsensor (R) END) and LOOP (mobile robot repeats movements). The execution is performed as follows: information on the block's type is obtained through the block's RFID tag and transmitted to the computer. Then, this information is transmitted to the mobile robot using a microSD card. Thus, the user must manually connects the microSD card into robot to execute its functions. In the study of Kakehashi et al. [17], after testing with visually impaired participants, the robot was remodeled so that the RFID information was sent directly to the robot, eliminating the need for an microSD card.

Fig. 3. Programming blocks made of Japanese cedar (Source: [19])

c. Which are the examples of good practices for teaching robot programming to people with visual disabilities?

Thirty-four recommendations for good practices in the teaching of robot programming for visually impaired people were identified. These recommendations were grouped in the following categories, described as: workshop preparation (13), content and activities (12), work dynamics (4) and data acquisition and instruments (5).

Workshop Preparation (13)

- To provide a training section to people who will help in the workshop, so that they know the necessary strategies to work with people with visual impairment. [11]
- Ask previously how each participant would like to receive the tutorial. For example, the material in Braille or with enlarged fonts. [11, 13]

- Orientate the students in regards to the room, the objects' layout, type and location of the equipment. [11]
- Keep ample space for circulation, for example, between tables, chairs, etc., so that the visually impaired participants can move with more safety and autonomy. [11]
- Make screen reader and screen magnifier software available to the participants, which may be configured by them. [11]
- Control the noise level in the place where the activities are conducted. Use an ample room or several smaller rooms. [11]
- Orientate the participants with visual impairment to use headphones. [13]
- Use Braille tags to identify the robot's principal components. [11]
- Orientate the participants in regards to the robot's parts so they can become familiar with the robot, as well as with the download of programs, etc. [13]
- To have monitors (Computing or Engineering students, family members, etc.) to follow the participants' activities, so that they can encourage the active participation of everyone on their work groups. [11, 13]
- To place the labyrinth, or another area in which the robot will operate, in a height where the participants may interact. [13]
- To have tactile information so that the students may identify and recognize the scenario and robot path, for example, using E.V.A materials and tactile models. [17]
- To make available programming environments which can be seen/heard by the participants, such as the interfaces and source code. [13, 16]

Content and Activities (12)

- To provide tutorials with commented code examples. [13, 14]
- Create quick reference sheets for symbols or commands. This is especially useful for students with visual disabilities which have to learn many new commands and syntaxes. Take into consideration that the participants may write down their own notes, for example, using a text editor on the computer. [13]
- To provide a set of simple commands (library), which may be built in stages so that the students may learn more complex coding more easily. [16]
- Put comments on code, watching out for its length so that it does not impair reading when scrolling down the screen. [13]
- Break long lines as to not impair people with low vision which have to increase font size. [13]
- Make activities which can be performed autonomously by the participants, regardless of being blind or having low vision. [13]
- Suit the activities to age and fun. [13] It is possible to perform activities with games, music, geometric shapes drawing, kick-the-can, in which the user programs the robot to kick objects along the way. [16]
- Design activities in a way that participants can learn from their own mistakes and may rethink their solution strategies. [18]
- Design the tutorials and project challenges to facilitate a progression in the student's programming skills. [13]
- Present information through various ways: orally, written on the board for people with low vision and in booklet form, which may be printed in Braille and/or

downloaded into a computer for blind people. For students with low vision, a booklet may be provided with enlarged font, printed or in the computer. [13]
- To provide information through touch and audio. [15, 19]
- To provide multimodal feedback so that the students may easily test their robot and correct/update their codes. [16]

Work Dynamics (4)

- Ask the participants to alternate in programming the robot. The same goes for initiating and stopping the program on the robot itself. [13]
- Keep the participants active in the performance of the activities. In group tasks, allow everyone to have a part in the problem's solution. This diminishes the impact of a dominant personality and it avoids students from been isolated. [13]
- Allow that the participants are capable of interacting with the programming environment, turning the robot on and off, activate motors and sensors as well as executing the desired program. [13]
- Encourage the participants to relate with their own world the skills and challenges of the robot. For example, they may relate the sensors with their own paradigms of navigation. [13]

Data Acquisition and Instruments (5)

- Apply pre and post questionnaires. [11, 13, 14, 16]
- Collect feedback of the participants' family members. [11, 13]
- Perform semi structured interviews after the activities. [18]
- Collect comments from the participants on the workshop experience. [17]
- Use the number of attempts to complete each task as an evaluation measure. [14]

d. Which were the difficulties/limitations in the use of robotics as support to the teaching of programming to people with visual disabilities?

The limitations faced in the works [15, 19] were related to the process of transferring the program, as it was necessary to transfer the program to a microSD card and to connect it to the robot so it could execute the commands. During the activities, a sighted person would help in this task. The students commented that they would like to perform the robot's operations autonomously [17]. Another problem was for the people with visual disabilities to distinguish the start of blocks (IF, LOOP) and the end of blocks (IF, LOOP). The blocks' differences were not sufficiently clear to the users [17].

In the work [11, 13], the BricxCC software was not totally compatible with the screen reader software used, the JAWS. Thus, is was necessary to have the help of a sighted person to perform some activities, such as helping to find a certain line of code according to the compiler's error.

In the study of Howard et al. [14], there was incomprehension from the users regarding the robot's movement, more specifically to the feedback signals that distinguish between left and right turns.

Some difficulties were also reported by Ludi et al. [18]. There were problems regarding navigation in the code and, as future work, they proposed to perform a study with the use of different audios, such as pitch, earcons, to aid in programming. It was observed that the blind participants which sped up reading of the text (with the screen reader) at times would get lost in the code in terms of construction of IF/THEN and repetition blocks, especially when trying to correct mistakes. Another difficulty was that some participants were not familiar with the use of punctuation, such as brackets and braces, including their location on the keyboard. As for most participants, the possibility of working with a robot was something entirely new, and this may have influenced the study's results.

4   Discussion on the Review's Recommendations with Participants with Visual Disability

The recommendations for good practices were discussed with 2 participants, which have visual disabilities, one with low vision (P1) and another with congenital blindness (P2). P1 has 44 years and P2 has 23 years, both male. P1 and P2 were participating in a research project related to educational robotics, which has as objectives the development of a robot and of a robot programming language. P1 has intermediate knowledge on programming with C, C++, Python, Java, Pascal, Delphi and Logo, and P2 has basic knowledge in programming, having started with an experimental programming language based on Logo.

The discussions occurred individually with each participant. The different recommendation categories were explained and then the 29 recommendations were read and explained. The evaluator used an instrument to register the participants' feedback and to document disagreements and suggestions. It was chosen not to include recommendations related to the category of "Data acquisition and instruments".

As results, of the 29 presented recommendations, P1 and P2 disagreed on the recommendation to "Control the noise level in the place where the activities are conducted. Use an ample room or several smaller rooms. [11]", from the "Workshop preparation" category. The participants explained that the room's size may be irrelevant, if the students are using headphones. P1 also questioned the recommendation of "Use Braille tags to identify the robot's principal components. [11]", also from the "Workshop preparation" category, as he considers that it depends on the robot's size. P1 points out that the robot must be sufficiently large to be able to contain Braille information, when this is the chosen approach. Still, in the case of small robots, if it is important to identify the robot's parts through Braille tags, he suggests that a larger model of the robot be built.

5 Conclusion

In this work, we presented the protocol and results of the Systematic Review on the teaching of programming with the support of robotics for people with visual disabilities, which were published in events relevant to the Computer Science area. The search yielded 125 papers, in which 9 were read in full. The results aimed to answer which methodological procedures are being used in the teaching of programming with robots for people with visual disabilities. There was emphasis on the use of workshops and tutorials, the use of robotics kits such as the LEGO mindstorm NXT, along with the BricxCC programming environment. Good teaching practices were identified, which were categorized in: workshop preparation, contents and activities, work dynamics and data acquisition and instruments.

From a total of 34 recommendations, 29 were discussed with visually impaired participants, which agreed with most of them and proposed suggestions to 2 recommendations.

Acknowledgments. This work was supported by the CNPq/MCTIC/SECIS N° 20/2016, National Council for Scientific and Technological Development – CNPq. JDO is supported by CAPES/PROSUP scholarships.

References

1. Solomon, C.J., Papert, S.: A case study of a young child doing turtle graphics in LOGO. In: Proceedings of the National Computer Conference and Exposition, 7–10 June 1976, pp. 1049–1056. ACM, New York (1976)
2. Al-Ratta, N.M., Al-Khalifa, H.S.: Teaching programming for blinds: a review. In: Fourth International Conference on Information and Communication Technology and Accessibility (ICTA), pp. 1–5 (2013)
3. Benitti, F.B.V., Vahldick, A., Urban, D.L., Krueger, M.L., Halma, A.: Experimentação com Robótica Educativa no Ensino Médio: ambiente, atividades e resultados. In: An. Workshop Informática Na Esc. vol. 1, pp. 1811–1820 (2009)
4. Chetty, J.: LEGO© mindstorms: merely a toy or a powerful pedagogical tool for learning computer programming? In: 38th Australasian Computer Science Conference, vol. 159, pp. 111–118 (2015)
5. Norton, S.J., McRobbie, C.J., Ginns, I.S.: Problem solving in a middle school robotics design classroom. Res. Sci. Educ. **37**, 261–277 (2007)
6. Long, R.G., Giudice, N.A.: Establishing and maintaining orientation for orientation and mobility. In: Foundations of Orientation and Mobility, pp. 45–62. American Foundation for the Blind, New York (2010)
7. Lahav, O., Schloerb, D.W., Kumar, S., Srinivasan, M.A.: BlindAid: a learning environment for enabling people who are blind to explore and navigate through unknown real spaces. In: 2008 Virtual Rehabilitation, pp. 193–197 (2008)
8. Lahav, O., Mioduser, D.: Multisensory virtual environment for supporting blind persons' acquisition of spatial cognitive mapping, orientation and mobility skills. In: Proceedings of Third International Conference on Disability, Virtual Reality and Associated Technologies, ICDVRAT, pp. 53–58 (2000)

9. Yu, W., Kuber, R., Murphy, E., Strain, P., McAllister, G.: A novel multimodal interface for improving visually impaired people's web accessibility. Virtual Reality **9**, 133–148 (2005)
10. Brereton, P., Kitchenham, B.A., Budgen, D., Turner, M., Khalil, M.: Lessons from applying the systematic literature review process within the software engineering domain. J. Syst. Softw. **80**, 571–583 (2007)
11. Ludi, S., Reichlmayr, T.: Developing inclusive outreach activities for students with visual impairments. Presented at the SIGCSE 2008 - proceedings of the 39th ACM technical symposium on computer science education (2008)
12. Ludi, S., Abadi, M., Fujiki, Y., Herzberg, S., Sankaran, P.: JBrick: accessible LEGO mindstorm programming tool for users who are visually impaired. Presented at the ASSETS 2010 - proceedings of the 12th international ACM SIGACCESS conference on computers and accessibility (2010)
13. Ludi, S., Reichlmayr, T.: The use of robotics to promote computing to pre-college students with visual impairments. ACM Trans. Comput. Educ. **11**, 1–20 (2011)
14. Howard, A.M., Park, C.H., Remy, S.: Using haptic and auditory interaction tools to engage students with visual impairments in robot programming activities. IEEE Trans. Learn. Technol. **5**, 87–95 (2012)
15. Kakehashi, S., Motoyoshi, T., Koyanagi, K., Ohshima, T., Kawakami, H.: P-CUBE: block type programming tool for visual impairments. Presented at the proceedings of the conference on technologies and applications of artificial intelligence, TAAI (2013)
16. Park, C.H., Howard, A.M.: Engaging students with visual impairments in engineering and computer science through robotic game programming (research-to-practice). Presented at the ASEE annual conference and exposition, conference proceedings (2013)
17. Kakehashi, S., Motoyoshi, T., Koyanagi, K., Oshima, T., Masuta, H., Kawakami, H.: Improvement of P-CUBE: Algorithm education tool for visually impaired persons. Presented at the Robotic Intelligence In Informationally Structured Space (RiiSS), 2014 IEEE symposium on robotic intelligence in informationally structured space (2014)
18. Ludi, S., Ellis, L., Jordan, S.: An accessible robotics programming environment for visually impaired users. Presented at the ASSETS14 - proceedings of the 16th international ACM SIGACCESS conference on computers and accessibility (2014)
19. Motoyoshi, T., Kakehashi, S., Masuta, H., Koyanagi, K., Oshima, T., Kawakami, H.: The usefulness of P-CUBE as a programming education tool for programming beginners. Presented at the proceedings of the IEEE international workshop on robot and human interactive communication (2015)
20. Demo, P.: Educar pela pesquisa. Autores Associados LTDA, Campinas, SP (2011)

Participatory Design of Technology for Inclusive Education: A Case Study

Leonara de Medeiros Braz[1][(✉)], Eliane de Souza Ramos[2],
Maria Luisa Pozzebom Benedetti[3], and Heiko Hornung[1]

[1] Institute of Computing, University of Campinas (Unicamp),
Av. Albert Einstein, 1251, Campinas, SP, Brazil
leonarabraz@gmail.com, heiko@ic.unicamp.br
[2] School of Education, University of Campinas (Unicamp),
Rua Bertrand Russell, 801, Campinas, SP, Brazil
souzaramos80@gmail.com
[3] Municipal Department of Education - Amparo/São Paulo,
Rua Bernardino de Campos, 705, Amparo, SP, Brazil
mlpbenedetti@amparo.sp.gov.br

Abstract. Regular school must be for all, and technologies used in educational activities should match the learning and development potential of each student, as well as the possibilities of teachers to insert these technologies into educational activities. However, not all technologies promote inclusive learning and teaching. Tangible User Interfaces (TUIs) promote sensory engagement involving various senses. TUIs can provide more accessibility for users and thus be powerful tools to promote inclusive education. This paper investigates the hypothesis that Participatory Design with inclusive education teachers facilitates the creation of technology for inclusion in the classroom. We report on a series of Participatory Design activities, and illustrate and discuss how these resulted in the creation of a technology that is relevant in the situated context of inclusive schools in a Brazilian municipality. The design process can be described as a process of mutual learning, also contributing to continuous in-service training of the teachers. A preliminary prototype evaluation indicates that the created technology can be adopted by involved teachers and students.

Keywords: Inclusive education · Participatory design · Tangible user interfaces · Makey Makey®

1 Introduction

Regular school must be for all, and consequently, materials and technologies used in educational activities should match the learning and development potential of each student, as well as the possibilities teachers have to insert these resources in their daily activities. Materials such as paper notebooks, books, games, communication boards, pencil grips, magniers or switch inputs are well-known examples

© Springer International Publishing AG 2017
M. Antona and C. Stephanidis (Eds.): UAHCI 2017, Part III, LNCS 10279, pp. 168–187, 2017.
DOI: 10.1007/978-3-319-58700-4_15

of technologies that have been incorporated into school activities and that promote the participation of students who listen, see, move, think, act and bond in different ways. A look at scientific literature reveals ongoing research efforts for new technological artifacts to promote the development of the human condition and the construction of knowledge in the school.

A growing body of literature describes the development of new technologies that can be used by students with different cognitive, motor, sensor, psychological and social characteristics (e.g. [3,4,15]). Of the different technologies used in research within the context of education, Tangible User Interfaces (TUIs) stand out for two reasons. When inserted into the user's environment, TUIs promote sensory engagement involving various senses. According to Zuckerman et al. TUIs can provide more accessibility for users [17]. Thus, TUIs can be powerful tools to promote inclusive education.

However, not all technologies promote inclusive learning and teaching. Many technologies have been created for a specific special need or a specific activity, e.g., teaching traffic rules to students with visual or hearing impairment. Within the context of the classroom, it is not feasible to create artifacts for each combination of educational content and singular student characteristics. Furthermore, creating artifacts targeted at the needs of some might result in segregation of these students, since their activities in the classroom become individual and different from those of their classmates. Finally, teachers might feel reluctant to use unfamiliar technology they do not dominate completely.

In a context in which the teacher acts in a way that students feel challenged and continue to follow their different learning paths, the hypothesis of this paper is that the participation of inclusive education specialists during the process of design, development and evaluation facilitates the creation of differentiated and comprehensive materials and technologies that consider the individual characteristics of students, promoting their inclusion in the classroom.

To evaluate our hypothesis, we conducted a Participatory Design process to create a tangible technology that has the potential to promote inclusive education in regular schools, to the greatest possible extent, independent of cognitive, sensorial, physical or social characteristics of students. The tangible technology is based on Makey Makey[®1], a platform that permits creating TUIs without requiring advanced knowledge or skills in programming or making. The design process was conducted in a collaboration between researchers at the University of Campinas (Unicamp) and inclusive education professionals of the city of Amparo in São Paulo state, Brazil. In this paper, we present a case study of this design process.

The objective of this work is to evaluate how Participatory Design activities involving teachers, students and researchers can result in the creation of more accessible and relevant technologies that can be used by different students in regular school in a variety of different situations.

The remainder of this paper is structured as follows. Section 2 presents inclusive education in Brazil and in the municipality where this study was conducted.

---

[1] http://makeymakey.com/about/.

Section 3 presents related work. Sections 4 and 5 present the method used and the results obtained. Section 6 discusses our findings, Sect. 7 concludes.

2   Inclusive Education in Brazil and in the Municipality of Amparo

The Specialized Educational Service (SES; from the Brazilian-Portuguese "Atendimento Educacional Especializado (AEE), literally "specialized educational attendance") "identifies, elaborates and organizes pedagogic and accessibility resources that eliminate barriers to the full participation of students, considering their specific needs" ([1]; translation by the authors). The SES complements or supplements the formation of students, aiming at their autonomy in and outside of school, constituting a mandatory offering of the Brazilian school system. SES is different from school reinforcement, tutoring or other assistive services. It has particular functions of special education that are neither targeted at substituting regular classes nor at adapting curricula, activities or performance evaluations.

SES attends students that live situations of:

- **Disability:** students with long term impairments of a physical, intellectual or sensorial nature which might obstruct or impede full and effective participation in society due to barriers society imposes when these students interact in equal conditions with others [12].
- **Autism Spectrum Disorder:** students with alterations in neuropsychomotor development that affect social relationships or communication, or that result in repetitive, restricted patterns of behavior. This includes students with diagnoses of autism, Asperger syndrome, Rett syndrome, childhood disintegrative disorder and pervasive developmental disorder not otherwise specified [1].
- **Intellectual Giftedness:** these students must have the opportunity to participate in activities developed in collaborations between the students' schools and higher education institutions and institutes that develop and promote research, arts, sports, etc.

An SES teacher works to support the development of these students:

- providing teaching of languages and specific codes for communication and signing,
- offering contemporary technologies to promote accessibility,
- adapting and producing didactic materials, considering students' specific needs,
- facilitating curriculum enrichment for students living situations of intellectual giftedness.

This research was developed in collaboration with the municipality of Amparo, situated in the interior of the state of São Paulo, Brazil. Within the municipality, studies about inclusive education were initiated in 2001. In 2006, the program "Education has many faces – educating and learning in diversity" (from Brazilian Portuguese: "A Educação tem muitas faces – educando e aprendendo na diversidade"). The objective of this program is to guarantee to all students the right to high-quality access and permanency in public schools of the municipality. Since then, the professionals of the municipality strived to align their work with the Brazilian National Policy of Special Education within the Inclusive Perspective [1].

Over the years, four so-called "rooms with multifunctional resources" have been implanted. Four SES teachers attend the target audience of all schools within the municipality in these rooms equipped with pedagogic and accessible materials. The target audience includes students in preschool and primary school. To attend all students in their respective schools and thus provide a higher quality SES, with teachers able to more effectively articulate actions to promote accessibility and inclusion, the municipality plans to build these rooms in all schools, starting in 2018. More rooms with multifunctional resources enables the SES teachers to conduct more research and acquire, adapt or produce materials that promote accessibility. Although the municipality identified the need to expand the SES offering, all students in the program already have access to an SES close to what was proposed by the aforementioned special education policy [1].

3   Related Work

Technology is increasingly used to support teachers and students in the teaching and learning process. One of these technologies is the TUI, which has gained prominence in showing itself more and more present in the school environment, providing new means for acquiring knowledge and even for the inclusion of children and adolescents in the school environment.

As an example, Leong and Horn developed a TUI, called BEAM (Balancing Equations by Adapting Manipulatives), to assist primary school students in teaching mathematical concepts such as equality, multiplication and order of operation [8].

Another work using TUI in education consists of the Combinatorix application, created by Schneider et al., whose main objective was collaborative learning of probability and combinatorics by high school students. By using tangible tokens on an interactive table, the students could learn through presentation of effects and graphics on the table when making combinations between different tokens [14].

Cuendet et al. used a system based on a TUI, called TapaCarp to help train carpenter apprentices. In order to be integrated into the pedagogical practices of the school, TapaCarp was designed in a participatory way with carpentry teachers and apprentices [2].

Regarding inclusive education, Starcic et al. targeted students of a regular class including thoses with learning difficulties and low motor coordination.

The developed TUI helped these students to design geometric shapes. The students, through the manipulation of physical tokens on a table, could draw geometric shapes, which were identified and presented on a monitor [15].

Jafri et al. developed a TUI-based software solution for visually impaired children, to teach tactical shape perception and spatial awareness sub-concepts in small-scale space. The solution was comprised of 3D printed geometric objects used as tangible tokens, a tangible tracking system, and a spatial application. The spatial application was developed to enable the child to learn by manipulating the 3D printed objects [7].

Another example of an application in the context of inclusive education was presented by Hamidi et al. [4]. In this study the authors aimed at a group of students from a classroom who did not use or rarely used verbal communication. Thus, these authors developed a tangible communication board, to allow these students to communicate with their teachers by touching the board.

Lin and Chang showed how tangible interfaces can be used to motivate students to perform certain tasks [9]. The authors developed a system – using Makey Makey® as a base technology for their development – to increase the level of motivation of children with cerebral palsy in performing physical activities. In this work, students should challenge themselves to trigger a stick positioned in front of them, which then generated an animation on a TV.

Using the Sphero[2] as a tangible device, the researchers Oliveira et al. focused on creating games that use a ball as the main object of the game, such as football or bowling. Using a user-centered design approach, this study presented a game for people with cerebral palsy [11].

Analyzing these works, we realized that they were designed for a specific need and predefined activity, for example, to help children with cerebral palsy in the performance of a certain physical activity. This factor limits the use of such technologies in the inclusive school, because in this teaching context, teachers work with different pedagogical contents and in a process in which they must consider the development and learning possibilities of all students. This would require a considerable number of TUIs in the school environment.

Considering the principles of Design for All [16], and based on ergonomic principles, Goya et al. proposed the development of a gamepad with more accessible design that could be used by different people with diverse capabilities and limitations [3]. The authors developed a fixed device that was fixed to the user's legs, allowing people with different motor conditions to use the tool. Analyzing the work of Goya et al., a limitation regarding the device's use in games-related activities is its small number of commands.

In the scientific literature about the production of more accessible technologies to be used by different students in inclusive schools, the works where teachers participated in the process of creation and development of TUIs (e.g. [2]) did not make clear how this participation occurred. In an interview with the participants of our research, a teacher stated that *"often the technology may even be helping the student in his development, but the teacher does not have the knowledge*

---

[2] http://www.sphero.com/sphero.

or ability to use it, which causes its no-use". The consideration made by this teacher alerted us to the fact that the process of creating and developing a new technology to be used in the inclusive school can be facilitated if built on a Participatory Design dynamics [10] with teachers and researchers working together to design the technology, thus allowing stakeholders to know, understand, use and, above all, to appropriate the newly created technology.

4   Method

Based on the principles of Universal Design [16] and using methods and techniques of Participatory Design [10], we conducted a series of one to two-hour workshops, following an iterative design process consisting of the phases understand, study, design, build, and evaluate [6]. The eight workshop participants included two Human-Computer Interaction researchers of Unicamp, four inclusive education teachers, a coordinator of the inclusive education program of the city of Amparo, and a pedagogic advisor.

These eight participants participated in the process from its beginning including the design, construction and evaluation of the created technology. Furthermore, at the time of writing this paper, one student who participates in the SES program acted as the evaluator of a functional prototype. The participation of this student, as well as others in the future, is essential, since teachers and students, as part of the regular school, will make use of the constructed technology. Thus, the design of the technology needs to consider the challenging trajectories of students and the problems they face during each school day.

Participatory Design ideally gives a voice to all stakeholders impacted by a design and design decisions, and results in technologies that make sense to the stakeholders and are relevant to its users. In our case, this means that the created technology must contribute to the work teachers develop with students in regular schools. Furthermore, teachers should be able to appropriate the technology for their individual practices to provide a better teaching and learning quality.

Giving a voice to stakeholders in this work is manifested by its multi-authorship. Two authors are HCI researchers and two authors represent the stakeholders within the municipality of Amparo. This paper talks in multiple voices: each author contributed with text content besides commentary and suggestions, and we avoided to homogenize the writing style to make the multiple voices more explicit.

In the following, we describe the main stakeholders, the data collection and interpretation, as well as the design process.

4.1   Stakeholders

In the context of the SES, stakeholders comprise all people directly or indirectly involved in the development of a child as a student and citizen: the very student affected by the developed technology, SES teachers, teachers in the regular classroom, school faculty, parents, and relatives.

In this work, we involved two stakeholder groups: SES teachers and students who participate in the SES program. SES teachers are directly involved in the search and creation of technologies that highlight the abilities of a given student to permit this student to conduct scholarly activities. Students are directly affected by the technology use. Respecting the characteristics of each student, the participants of the design process decided together to include students only as evaluators in this stage of the design, potentially giving them less voice than a codesigner, but allowing them to participate in the process of improving the designed technology.

Teachers of regular classrooms participated as informants, discussing during interviews how the developed technology might be inserted into teaching and learning activities and what might be limitations. Furthermore, some teachers participated in a workshop during which we explained the concept of TUIs and elaborated with them practical examples of how to use TUIs in the regular classroom.

Parents did not directly participate. We explained the research project to the parents of the participating student and that it was approved by Unicamp's Ethics Committee; and they signed a consent form authorizing the participation of the student.

The levels of participation of each stakeholder group reflects the levels of participation already present in the SES program in the municipality of Amparo. Usually, SES teachers design (non-computerized) technologies, and evaluate them with students and teachers of regular classes.

4.2   Data Collection and Interpretation

Collected data were qualitative data, and included observations of workshop activities, interviews, informal conversations, and posters and other written material created during workshops. These data were captured by video recordings and manual annotations. Additional data included prototypes created during and between workshops. Videos were transcribed by one of the HCI researchers after each workshop. Some written material was created to facilitate data interpretation by promoting clarity and succinctness compared to sometimes parallel and imprecise oral communication.

The interpretation of video transcriptions and material created during the workshops was done by the HCI researcher for practical reasons: all participatory activities occurred during working hours of the education professionals, and it was thus deemed infeasible to schedule additional time for participatory interpretation. However, all interpretations were synthesized and then discussed among participants.

4.3   Design Process

We conducted a series of participatory one to two-hour workshops with the participants available at each time, and some activities between workshops. During the activities between workshops, only the HCI researchers participated. These activities included mostly follow-up and preparation of workshops, but also some design activities. The whole design process had a research objective, a practical objective, and an educational objective. The research objective, pursued by the HCI researchers, was to evaluate whether and how the Participatory Design activities might result in the creation of more accessible and relevant technologies. The practical objective, pursued by all participants, was to create a new technology that might be used within the context of SES or regular teaching and learning activities. The educational objective, pursued by the education professionals, was to contribute to the continuous in-service training of the participating teachers.

Before planning the design process, the HCI researchers made some exploratory visits to different schools in Amparo to better understand the SES program, how the SES teachers work, what activities they conduct and what materials and technologies they use. During these initial visits, all participants gained an initial understanding of each other's practices and objectives. These understandings evolved continuously throughout the process.

The scheduling of the workshops and other activities was mostly defined by the availability of the participating teachers. Activities that involved all eight primary participants occurred usually monthly, during one of the teachers fortnightly Friday encounters at one of the participating teachers' school. The workshops usually started after the coffee break that marked the end of the encounters among teachers, program coordinator and advisor. The content of the activities was planned by the two HCI researchers, to be better aligned with the research objectives and since the other participants had no experience in planning a Participatory Design process.

The sequence of activities followed an iterative process with the phases understand, study, design, build, and evaluate [6], whereas most iterations of the "study" and "build" phase and few iterations of the "design" phase were conducted by only the HCI researchers. Employed techniques included braindrawing, interviews, group discussions, scenario writing, storytelling, and the Wizard of Oz technique. Although the HCI researchers defined which methods to use, we tried to choose simple and accessible methods, often using materials that were already available at the respective school.

Explaining the Design Space. To explain to the participating education professionals what is a TUI, we initially conducted three encounters during which we explored three TUI prototypes created by one of the HCI researchers: the communication board, the tangible vest, and the "ludic carpet" (Fig. 1). These TUIs were inspired by activities and materials the researchers observed during the exploratory visits. The TUIs replicated or extended non-computational technologies already used by the SES teachers, and might be used during activities such as storytelling about daily routine.

During these three encounters, the SES teachers acted only as evaluators of the TUIs. Since they did not have any previous contact with TUIs, an objective of these encounters was to permit them to get familiar with this technology and get

Fig. 1. Low-fidelity prototypes presented during the first workshops.

a first impression of how it might be used for the SES. The HCI researchers tried to show diverse possibilities grounded in the teachers' existing practices, as well as to "break the ice" for future encounters. To this end, the prototypes were built with low-tech material such as cardboard, cloth, Velcro® and Styrofoam®. As hardware platform, we used Makey Makey®, and as software platform Scratch. A preoccupation of the HCI researchers was to create prototypes that did not focus on a disability but that were usable by students with diverse abilities.

We discussed the prototypes' potential to reduce barriers the students that frequent the SES program experienced in school. Although we conducted no formal evaluation, the HCI researchers tried to explore by guided questions to what extent the prototypes were accessible to students with different needs, and how the prototypes might be improved to better adapt to the teachers' practices and the students' needs.

Participatory Workshops for Designing a Tangible Technology. During the first encounters, some important aspects of design had already been uncovered and discussed. The technology should support the student in communication without negatively affecting other activities. It had become clear the high-level guiding ideals for design had to include:

- autonomy of the student, i.e. the student should be able to use the technology without requiring assistance of an additional intermediary between student and teacher; and
- conscious use of the environment, i.e. the technology should be able to be inserted into reality of the classroom with its furniture including tables that already contain other school supplies.

The following workshops initiated the creative process of thinking about and creating this technology. During the first workshop, the HCI researchers asked the participating teachers to "dream up" tangible technologies that considered the individual students each teacher worked with. In previous activities not reported in this paper we had perceived that during creative group techniques such as brainwriting, the teachers often put ideas on paper that already appeared previously. To get more diverse ideas, we thus opted to ask each teacher to individually create their ideas, either in writing or in drawing.

At the next workshop, we discussed the ideas presented during the previous workshop more formally, asking the SES teachers to prioritize strong and weak points regarding their application to inclusive education. Subsequently we created a joint proposal together with all participants and conducted a braindrawing session to materialize the ideas in graphic form.

One HCI researcher then created a non-functional cardboard prototype of a physical input device, and the HCI researchers and an SES teacher evaluated whether the prototype dimensions were compatible with the students' chairs and tables, and whether they could be easily adapted to be used ergonomically by different students. To this end, we visited preschool and elementary school classes during class-time attended by two different SES students and asked them to use the physical controls of the prototype.

During the following workshop, we evaluated how the technology might be inserted into teaching activities in the regular classroom. To this end, one HCI researcher created an architectural cardboard model of a classroom with movable pieces, and a miniature table, a computer screen, tablet, speaker boxes and a representation of the device to be designed. The SES teachers then discussed different configurations of the device, possible accessories, and how these could be used in the classroom, including the physical location as well as class dynamics.

In the subsequent workshop, we employed an enactment technique with a prototype of the physical input device and paper cutouts to discuss how the technology might be inserted into the classroom and to understand how a student might interact with it. For the enactment, we used mathematics as an example school subject and an activity adapted from an activity one of the SES teachers already conducted using pen and paper. One SES teacher acted as teacher, the other as student.

To gather more requirements for the accompanying application to create activities to be used with the physical device, we conducted another braindrawing session, in which in each iteration, each participant moved to the next table that contained an evolving drawing of an activity within the context of a specific school subject (mathematics, Portuguese, arts, music, history, geography, science and physical education). The objective of specifying school subjects was to cover different dynamics in class.

To evaluate whether the functional prototype could be employed during real activities in the classroom, we conducted an evaluation with one of the SES teachers and one of her students. The student was six years old, had cerebral palsy, was a wheelchair users with limited upper limb mobility, did not communicate orally, but could express herself with facial and body expressions. The informal evaluation consisted in two steps. First, teacher and student used the prototype in an activity that resembled an activity the two usually conducted using a desktop computer and a mouse switch (the student was not able to use the mouse, but could press a mouse switch; the mouse pointer was placed by the teacher). One HCI researcher acted as facilitator, the other as observer, and the activity took 15 min. Immediately after, the HCI researchers and the teacher discussed the activity.

5   Results

After the first activities during the exploratory visits, the SES teachers commented that *"the way the application was presented, it is only a different form of conducting the activity, not being any different [from the existing techniques] and not bringing any advantages"*. They also put forth the question of *"how could we improve [these applications] so that the children can use them?"* The pedagogic advisor asked the teachers *"What would you need to produce this material in accordance with [the needs of] your students? Thinking about producing an actual [functional] technology. If you would like to change the content of [the prototype], what would you have to do?"* (Fig. 2).

Fig. 2. Teachers and an HCI researcher discussing a TUI prototype.

We interpreted these manifestations as evidence that the participants understood the concept of TUIs and saw their potential for inclusive education. These and similar comments also marked the point of SES teachers beginning to effectively act as codesigners.

During the ideation activity, the SES teachers presented the following ideas: a table with physical buttons and a tablet, a pedalboard for interaction using the feet, a wall-mounted device with sensors to communicate with gaze and eye movement, and an application *"with animations, since the student feels more interested by activities that have animations"*. In a subsequent activity, the ideas were discussed and their main elements prioritized. The consensus of prioritizing ideas and elements was that the technology to be designed should involve a tabletop with buttons and a pedalboard below the table, to permit use by students with different abilities and preferences. Furthermore, applications controlled by these physical input devices should make use of animations. Based on these ideas we conducted a braindrawing session to externalize the participants' different ideas (Fig. 3).

Fig. 3. Different ideas for the tabletop and pedalboard, generated during a braindrawing session.

The subsequent activities with cardboard prototypes and architectural models clarified details about the physical and spatial configuration of the physical input devices and additional accessories. For example, ideas such as additional screens or tablets, a projector as well as speaker boxes, mounted in different locations in the classroom, were discussed with respect to aspects such as the possibility to facilitate the communication between the students using the technology and the rest of the classroom. The SES teachers participated differently in these activities: two involved themselves actively, interacting with the prototypes, the other two preferred to only contribute to the discussions. In the end, we decided to have a small number of buttons on the tabletop as well as the pedal board, a laptop on the table, since this is already used in the classroom, as well as a projector to share contents with teachers and students.

The first high-fidelity prototype had five buttons on the tabletop, and five on the pedalboard, following a suggestion of the teachers to be able to work with digits from zero to nine. A discussion revealed that five pedals would be difficult to use for many students, and that four pedals would be easier to use and sufficient for many activities. The physical design of the tabletop buttons was also revised to facilitate the use by students with less physical strength. Together with the physical prototype we discussed some initial ideas about the accompanying applications. Important points included the limited internet access in some schools, as well as general metaphors of an activity list, and whether this should be organized by school subject, by author, or by students' abilities.

The main result of the activity including the three teachers of inclusive classrooms was that the two groups could create a low-fidelity prototype of a TUI to be used in the classroom within only 30 min, after only having been exposed to the concept of a TUI for less than one hour. The two proposals used physical arrows to navigate within an application. This indicated to us, that technologies such as the one described in this paper make sense and are relevant in the classroom, and that teachers might be able to appropriate this kind of technology for their own teaching activities.

Although we tried to encourage some diversity in the braindrawing session for generating ideas for the application for creating and organizing activities by specifying different school subjects on each station, we observed that most participants only replicated their ideas when arriving at the next table. The main aspects of the application that emerged were the use of different media to be able to work in different contexts, i.e. videos in sign language, sounds for visually impaired students, and images. This result indicated, that although the SES teachers already could imagine how to use the designed technology, they still had difficulties imagining the creation of own content.

After activities and workshops spanning one year, the ideas had converged towards an "interactive table" with five buttons on the tabletop and a pedalboard with four pedals to be put under the table. Figure 4 shows an earlier version of the prototype, with a higher fidelity tabletop and a low-fidelity pedalboard, still with five pedals. In the prototype of the proposed technology, tabletop and pedalboard are connected to a laptop computer, which would be available at each school of the participating teachers. The reasoning behind designing a technology with buttons and pedals was that some of the students that frequent the SES program have limited or no mobility in the upper limbs while others have limited or no mobility in the lower limbs. For the teachers, it was important that the designed technology could support students in their development, providing challenges that stimulate the advance of abilities during school activities.

During the evaluation (Fig. 5), we used only the tabletop part of the prototype, since the student was a wheelchair user. In comparison to Fig. 4, the prototype had already evolved and included different buttons to be accessible to students with less strength and coordination in arms and hands. The activity consisted in matching animal drawings. In the center of a screen, the animal to be matched was presented, for example a lion. Below, two smaller drawings were presented, one of the matching animal and one of a different animal, in varying order.

Fig. 4. Iteration of the prototype of the proposed technology.

Fig. 5. Prototype evaluation with an SES teacher and one of her students.

The student was motivated, and despite her limited mobility and the fact that the prototype was configured to also use the buttons closest to her, she made efforts to reach the farthest ones. When the teacher explained that she could also use a closer button, she made clear that she wanted to use the farther button using an unmistakable facial expression. This and other behaviors that showed the efforts of the student and thus hinted at the potential of the technology promoting the development of the student, was commented by the teacher as very gratifying.

In the follow-up discussion with the teacher, the main positive point she mentioned was the autonomy the student gained in comparison to the similar activity were the teacher placed the mouse pointer and the student pressed the switch: "*She felt comfortable, acted alone. She had freedom. The autonomy and possibility of choice allowed [...] was rich*".

The teacher also contemplated the use of the prototype in the regular classroom, believing that "*it will make life easier in the classroom*". Besides the benefits for the student, the SES teacher recognized benefits for the teachers in the classroom: "*[The prototype] will give more options to the teacher, for example, she will be able to work with syllables, words, and others*".

6   Discussion

In this section, we discuss three main themes that are related to the three objectives of this work: we first discuss mutual learning along the process, which is related to the research objective (evaluate the Participatory Design process) and the educational objective (continuous in-service training), then reflect on the Participatory Design process, and finally on the design of the prototype.

For researchers and designers that do not have a profound knowledge about areas such as inclusive design and programs such as SES, Participatory Design is essential to understand the context in which research and design are inserted, and to design a product or service that is relevant to the target community. The same can be said about the participating teachers. At first, they had little knowledge about TUIs and processes of design. Participatory Design enabled the teachers to learn about these topics and to thus contribute effectively as codesigners within the project.

This mutual learning process was implicit and did not require formal training; it occurred along the process by sharing questions, doubts, preoccupations or proposals among equals, avoiding hierarchy, supervision or judgment that could stifle participation. In each subsequent activity, all participants felt more "in control". We consider mentioning this important, since when the researchers initially participated as facilitators and observers, the SES teachers felt more inhibited. To give an example, we quote one of the teachers: "*At the beginning, when you [the researchers] arrived, I didn't understand your language. I couldn't imagine anything [...]. But this process of construction was very good.*" Regarding the design process, mutual learning was probably facilitated by explicitly including moments for "understanding".

At some moment, the teachers might have had the preconception that their acts and ideas were being judged by the researchers. Another fact that might have contributed to feeling inhibited is that the researchers were experts in digital and tangible technology. The teachers might have believed that, by extension, the researchers were also experts in tangible technology *for inclusive education*. On the contrary, the researchers were experts only in digital and tangible technology, while the teachers were experts in inclusive education. The purpose of conducting Participatory Design was to join these different kinds of expertise.

The experience of creating a new technology together with researchers might also contribute to revise the existing processes of continuous in-service training of teachers, to avoid hierarchizing knowledge and practice. Our research provided evidence that some practices tend to inhibit teachers' creative processes, leading them to adopt a behavior that makes them ask their "*superiors*" what they should do when working with students, instead of creating and proposing collaborative and participatory actions.

These reflections show that, like the students, the teachers also require practices that are challenging and promote critical thinking to create and innovate their ways of teaching, abandoning practices that segregate and exclude.

In the previous paragraphs, we discussed mutual learning within the design process. In the following, we briefly discuss other dimensions that characterize this process [5]:

The SES teachers participated in the design process from its outset. Two exceptions are the choice of Makey Makey® as the base technology and the creation of some prototypes by an HCI researcher between participatory workshops. Since this was the first contact of the teachers with the design of a computerized technology, the researchers chose the base technology to start design activities without requiring an extensive pre-evaluation phase of alternatives. Now that the teachers have become more familiar with the possibilities of digital technology within the inclusive school, they should actively participate in the choice of future technologies. In fact, during some ideation activities, one teacher already suggested to investigate the web camera as a tool to increase accessibility to teaching and learning. Some prototypes were created between workshops by an HCI researcher, because the time of the teachers to participate in the project was limited by fortnightly one to two-hour meetings.

During the participatory activities, teachers acted as equals with the same power to influence and take decisions as the researchers. All critical decisions were discussed among the present participants. As described in the previous paragraphs, during some initial activities, the teachers were more guarded, partly possibly because they did not yet know the power they had at the outset of the project, and partly because during some initial activities the researchers participated more as facilitators and observers, thus possibly giving the impression of evaluating and judging the teachers.

Regarding the stance that "people play critical roles in design by being experts in their own lives" [5, p. 89], one could argue that students should have played a more active role in the design process, e.g. by participating as codesigners and not only as informants or testers. We opted for not including children or other stakeholders more actively into the process for the following reasons. The abilities, limits, preferences and needs of the students are so diverse that including a limited number of students would inevitably have missed important points, or put an unduly focus on specific special needs, which might have countered the ideals of Design for All. Furthermore, the participating teachers spent intensive time with different students and can thus be seen as deputy experts.

Finally, involving students only as testers and informants was more faithful to the process the SES teachers used to create materials and activities.

The focus of our work was not to develop a technology applicable in a general variety of educational contexts, but a technology that made sense and was relevant in the concrete context of the participating teachers' schools. To achieve this goal, we had to create a design process that considered the peculiarities of the situated context of SES in the municipality of Amparo. The different involvement of different stakeholders discussed in the previous paragraph is a consequence of these considerations. This was consistent with the teachers' current practice of creating low-tech materials for students they are intimately familiar with. Interestingly, the teachers' practices are well aligned with practices of Design for All in HCI. Hence, the technology was not created for specific "disabilities", but considering every student in the classroom should be able to use it. The new technology designed by the participants is not intended to replace any existing materials and practices, but might enrich the possibilities of access to what is taught and shared during class, supporting both teachers and students.

Although a common guideline for design is to use non-functional low-fidelity prototypes in early stages of design to promote the deconstruction of presented ideas and generation of more diverse new ideas, we believe the use of more functional prototypes in a mid-level fidelity was adequate for this design process, since it helped the participating SES teachers, who were accustomed to traditional desktop or mobile technology, to understand what a TUI-based device might be able to do. With the intention to making them feel more confident and encouraging them to engage in critique with the prototypes we reverted to lower fidelity prototypes during subsequent activities, using materials the SES teachers themselves used in their practices.

Based on the principle that a "disability" is no property of a student but of a technology that inhibits a student to grow, the participatory activities tried to explore how technology might support students in their development without focusing on their "impairments". The participating SES teachers contributed with specific individual knowledge, e.g. one was a specialist for SES with visually impaired students, another for deaf and hard of hearing students. The participatory activities promoted the sharing of these different kinds of knowledge and thus the creation of a technology that supports students' development lowering barriers of access. The development of the technology strived to enable students to leverage their abilities while enabling teachers to challenge students to develop additional abilities. For example, for students not communicating orally, the designed technology permits a different kind of communication, for students who cannot use the hands, the technology permits interaction with the feet.

7   Conclusion

The reports of the teachers and the involvement of the participants in the design, development and evaluation of a new technology showed that this participation benefits the process of inclusion in the classroom of the regular school, since it enables thinking about how to eliminate barriers that prevent students from access to knowledge, the school environment, and the people there.

Our work aimed at creating a technology that makes sense and is relevant within the context of the inclusive classroom. The participatory approach to design has shown its strength: the participating SES teachers knew their students and their needs very well and were thus able to better think about technologies that facilitate the development of students' abilities and learning possibilities. This knowledge promoted the incorporation of the new technology, and thus new practices, within the work of teachers in the regular classroom.

The knowledge construction of the teachers reminds us that, per Piaget [13], the process of knowledge acquisition is driven by imbalance, and occurs when the subject enters into contact with the object of knowledge, then encounters difficulties to assimilate and perform an action on this object, subsequently assimilates new information about the object and finally accommodates this information, thus returning to a state of balance. This process can be called adaptation. Hence we are continually changing, constructing ourselves with the relations between the individual and the environment.

Initially, the researchers explained the concept of TUIs to the other participants by means of different prototypes created based on and inspired by materials already used by the teachers. These prototypes were discussed with respect to their potential to eliminate learning barriers, stimulate inclusive practices, as well as possible limitations. During the subsequent workshops, we conducted Participatory Design activities using techniques such as braindrawing, semi-structured interviews, group discussions, as well as different prototyping techniques.

The technological artifact resulting from the workshops was a tabletop interface with five·buttons and a pedalboard with four foot pedals that can be used instead of or additionally to the tabletop interface. Based on the discussions during the workshops as well as on preliminary evaluations in an inclusive kindergarten, an inclusive elementary school class, and during an individual activity involving one student and one teacher, the prototypes have been iteratively refined.

The participants of the design process could gradually construct shared meanings of concepts related to HCI and inclusive education. This process was facilitated by the facts that the practice of creating low-tech material for inclusive education is similar to participatory and inclusive design in HCI, and that Makey Makey® as a platform permits to create physical prototypes and educational activities that have a technological complexity similar to what teachers are already used to.

The workshop and classroom activities showed that the design process resulted in prototypes that make sense in the educational contexts of the participating teachers, and that these prototypes can be used in a variety of different activities as well as by a variety of different students. For example, during an evaluation that replicated an activity in which a student with cerebral palsy previously had used a switch input device, the respective teacher found that the student gained more autonomy, and the teacher more flexibility.

The results of the work presented in this paper provide evidence that Participatory Design together with an adequate technological platform can produce technologies that can be used by a variety of different students in a variety of different situations. Our next steps involve the creation of an application for authoring educational activities to be used with the physical prototypes. Furthermore, it is necessary to investigate the use in different educational situations as well as to what extent teachers can create their own physical prototypes and respective educational activities.

Future work includes activities with students with different abilities who frequent the SES program. Another important question is how teachers in the classroom use the technology and whether they can include it in their existing activities in a relevant way. Since an important goal of the design project is to enable the teachers to use the physical prototype – and possibly other devices they create in the future – during their own scholarly activities, other future work involves the design of an application to create, manage and adapt activities to be executed with physical input devices such as the prototype presented in this paper. Some design goals and concrete requirements could already be elicited during the presented participatory activities, e.g. promoting the development of students' abilities and permitting the use of custom images, sound and videos. This application is instrumental for our long-term goal: facilitating the appropriation of technologies like the one presented in this paper by teachers during their individual daily practices in the inclusive school.

Acknowledgments. We thank the Department of Education of the municipality of Amparo for their support and all other participants for their time and effort. We also thank the LEPED and InterHAD research groups for insightful discussions. This work was partially funded by the Brazilian National Council for Scientific and Technological Development (CNPq, process 133797/2015-5).

References

1. Brasil: Ministério da Educação, Secretaria de Educação Especial. Política Nacional de Educação Especial na Perspectiva Inclusiva. MEC/SEESP, Brasília (2008)
2. Cuendet, S., Dehler-Zufferey, J., Ortoleva, G., Dillenbourg, P.: An integrated way of using a tangible user interface in a classroom. Int. J. Comput. Support. Collab. Learn. **10**(2), 183–208 (2015)
3. Goya, J., Bonm, G., Yonashiro, M., Paschoarelli, L.: Criação e desenvolvimento de um controlador de jogos eletrônicos: Um projeto inclusivo. XI SBGames (2012)
4. Hamidi, F., Baljko, M., Kunic, T., Feraday, R.: Do-It-Yourself (DIY) assistive technology: a communication board case study. In: Miesenberger, K., Fels, D., Archambault, D., Peňáz, P., Zagler, W. (eds.) ICCHP 2014. LNCS, vol. 8548, pp. 287–294. Springer, Cham (2014). doi:10.1007/978-3-319-08599-9_44
5. Halskov, K., Hansen, N.B.: The diversity of participatory design research practice at PDC 2002–2012. Int. J. Hum. Comput. Stud. **74**, 81–92 (2015)
6. Harper, R.H.: Being Human: Human-Computer Interaction in the Year 2020. Microsoft Research Limited, Cambridge (2008)

7. Jafri, R., Asmaa, M.A., Syed, A.A.: A tangible user interface-based application utilizing 3D-printed manipulatives for teaching tactual shape perception and spatial awareness sub-concepts to visually impaired children. Int. J. Child-Comput. Interact. **11**, 3–11 (2016)

8. Leong, Z.A., Horn, M.S.: The beam: a digitally enhanced balance beam for mathematics education. In: Proceedings of the 9th International Conference on Interaction Design and Children, pp. 290–292. ACM (2010)

9. Lin, C.-Y., Chang, Y.-M.: Increase in physical activities in kindergarten children with cerebral palsy by employing MaKey-MaKey-based task systems. Res. Dev. Disabil. **35**(9), 1963–1969 (2014)

10. Muller, M.J., Druin, A.: Participatory design: the third space in HCI. In: Jacko, J.A. (ed.) Human-Computer Interaction Handbook, Human Factors and Ergonomics, 3rd edn, pp. 1125–1154. CRC Press, Boca Raton (2012)

11. Oliveira, E., Sousa, G., Magalhães, I., Tavares, T.: The use of multisensory user interfaces for games centered in people with cerebral palsy. In: Antona, M., Stephanidis, C. (eds.) UAHCI 2015. LNCS, vol. 9177, pp. 514–524. Springer, Cham (2015). doi:10.1007/978-3-319-20684-4_50

12. Brasil: Secretaria de Direitos Humanos da Presidência da República. Convenção sobre os Direitos das Pessoas com Deficiência e seu Protocolo Facultativo: tem seu texto aprovado pelo Decreto Legislativo n 186, de 09 de julho de 2008 e tem sua entrada em vigor pelo Decreto n 6949, de 25 de agosto. Brasília (2010)

13. Piaget, J.: A equilibração das estruturas cognitivas. Zahar, Rio de Janeiro (1975)

14. Schneider, B., Blikstein, P., Mackay, W.: Combinatorix: a tangible user interface that supports collaborative learning of probabilities. In: Proceedings of the 2012 ACM International Conference on Interactive Tabletops and Surfaces, pp. 129–132. ACM (2012)

15. Starcic, A.I., Cotic, M., Zajc, M.: Designbased research on the use of a tangible user interface for geometry teaching in an inclusive classroom. Br. J. Educ. Technol. **44**(5), 729–744 (2013)

16. Stephanidis, C., Savidis, A.: Universal access in the information society: methods, tools, and interaction technologies. Univ. Access Inf. Soc. **1**(1), 40–55 (2001)

17. Zuckerman, O., Arida, S., Resnick, M.: Extending tangible interfaces for education: digital Montessori-inspired Manipulatives. In: Proceedings of the SIGCHI Conference on Human Factors in Computing Systems, pp. 859–868. ACM (2005)

QUIMIVOX MOBILE: Assistive Tool to Teach Mendeleev Table

Alex Santos de Oliveira[1], Bruno Merlin[1(✉)], Heleno Fülber[1],
João Elias Vidueira Ferreira[2], and Tatiana Nazaré de Carvalho Artur Barros[3]

[1] Universidade Federal do Pará (UFPA), Tucuruí, PA, Brazil
alex-tuc@hotmail.com, brunomerlin@gmail.com, fulber@gmail.com
[2] Instituto Federal do Pará (IFPA), Tucuruí, PA, Brazil
joao.elias@yahoo.com.br
[3] Universidade Federal do Pará (UFPA), Belém, PA, Brazil
tatiufpa@gmail.com

Abstract. Technical progress brings new educational tools implemented in mobile devices. However, this improvement rarely benefit to blind and visually impaired people because no software adaptation are made to attend visual impairment. Thus, researches are needed to make technological adaptations that will attend this public. To purchase this aim, this work presents a piece of software named Quimivox Mobile, implemented in *Android* OS. It enables to retrieve chemical information in periodic table toward voice synthesis and simple interactions. The software is designed to be accessible for every people, visually impaired users or notThe software has been evaluated toward experimental tests involving visually impaired users. The experiment highlight that the software is very pertinent and efficient to help visually impaired user in chemical study.

Keywords: Visual impairment · Accessibility mobile · Assistive technology

1 Introduction

"A good sketch is better than a long speech"… For sighted people. Graphics and sketches are power tools to organize and to communicate synthetically pieces of information and correlation between them. A good sketch appeals to the visual memory and helps to remember easily processes, relationships, comparative statistics, data evolutions, geographical data, sequences (timelines for instance), etc. Even if relief impressions may help blind people to explore a sketch by touch (D'Angiulli et al. 1998; Picard and Lebaz 2012; Picard et al. 2013), the tactilo-kinesthetic (haptic) perception and exploration does not enable an immediate and global understanding (D'Angiulli et al. 1998; Withagen et al. 2010). Understanding structured information through a haptic exploration may require a high cognitive effort and a complementary explanation of the figure may be required (Picard and Lebaz 2012; Van Doorn et al. 2012). Retrieving information into a sketch through haptic exploration is another challenging task (Lederman and Campbell 1983).

© Springer International Publishing AG 2017
M. Antona and C. Stephanidis (Eds.): UAHCI 2017, Part III, LNCS 10279, pp. 188–197, 2017.
DOI: 10.1007/978-3-319-58700-4_16

Sketches are commonly used in educational processes. However, this powerful communication and learning tool remains inaccessible for blind people the most part of the time. In Brazil, local of this study, where the integration politic aims at keeping impaired people into everyone school (SÁ 2006), the schools equipped with a relief printer are very few, the teachers really trained to deal with impairment are very few, and teachers have no other tools that may help them to adapt the teaching to impairments.

Smartphones are very widespread among adolescents. They also offer accessibility mode enabling basic uses for blind people (Frey et al. 2011; Romero et al. 2011). They would be a good vehicle to implant assistive educational tools completing the traditional school material. These tools would be a good way to translate, explain, or adapt visual contents to blind people. Moreover, they could reach the final users without a significant investment.

Chemistry is a discipline very rich in symbols and representations. They are very important in the understanding of chemical processes (Kozma et al. 2000). But, these representations are not easily turned accessible to blind people. Moreover without an adapted physical material that could be manipulated. Then, alternative lessons support would be useful to fulfill this lack. For this purpose, we are presenting here the assistive tool Quimivox Mobile, developed for smartphones, tackling some aspects of chemistry lessons: the Mendeleev periodic table and chemical properties of elements.

The rest of the article is divided into four section and a conclusion. The first section presents the social context and challenges of the research. The second section reviews the state of art. The third section explains Quimivox Mobile paradigms and interactions, and the last section describes the evaluation performed with final users. Then, the conclusion highlights the good acceptation of the tool and new evolution perspectives extracted during the evaluation process.

2   Social Context of the Study

In Brazil, local of this study, according to the IBGE (Brazilian Institute of Geography and Statistics), about 6,5 million peoples suffer of sever vision problems. Among them 582.000 are totally blind and 6 million suffer of low vision requiring accessible tools and structures (Isaude 2015). Sever vision problems are the most common impairments into Brazilian society.

With regard to chemistry learning, visual impaired students are confronted to two main problems: the limits of Brazilian impaired people integration politic and the specificity of chemistry discipline that have a rich symbolic language.

2.1   Limits of Impaired People Integration Politic in Brazil

Since the beginning of the last decade, Brazil initiated a politic in favor of impaired people integration. At first sight, these politic orientations seem to be ambitious. However, political discourses and law adoptions were not systematically sustained by the material and the human investments into the public sphere required to turn it effective.

Thus, in regard for visual impairment, blind children and students are integrated into normal schools like every other child (children with or without other impairment). From a social point of view, this inclusion is a good thing. However, the schools are very frequently not prepared to receipt them correctly: the structure is physically not prepared, the professors are not trained to lead with visual impairment (or any other kind of impairment), and basic material support such as braille printer or other numeric solution (braille keyboard, screen readers, etc.) are not provided to the schools. So, the responsibility is entirely in charge of headmaster and professors to improvise and adapt themselves to the situation without recommendations and orientations from specialists trained to lead with the specificity of the impairment.

As a consequence, a blind child is well socially integrated, but does not benefit of a specific teaching and learning environment required by his impairment and suffer difficulties to accompany the lessons.

2.2 Teaching Chemistry to Blind People

Chemistry discipline involves the understanding of several representation elaborated toward a high set of symbols (Kozma et al. 2000). These representations define a true visual language that ease drastically the understanding of the processes implicated into chemical reactions. Visuospacial perception and geometry are very important is the understanding (Wu and Shah 2004), that why many researchers work on improving representations in the education in chemistry field (Fjeld and Voegtli 2002; Linioua 2006). This visual language is difficult to adapt and translate for blind people. Teaching chemistry without the support of it is teaching another discipline and would require other lesson support and tools (and probably a specific professional formation too).

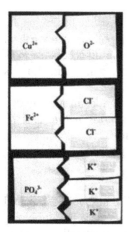

Fig. 1. Notched Braille cards illustrating ionic bonding between cations and anions (left). Tactile periodic trends' models made of clayns (middle) and plastic drinking straws (right) (Graybill et al. 2008)

Several recommendations exist to improve the teaching for blind and visually impaired students. The American Chemical Society Committee on Chemists with Disabilities (Miner et al. 2001) propose an instruction book to help the chemistry teacher to lead with every kind of impairment. Supalo (2005) published several orientation and among the how to elaborate relief material for blind people, how to write mathematical expression, perform quizzes and exams and how to turn laboratory safe. Graybill (2008) explained how to adapt a chemistry laboratory for blind people and present some strategies to perform measures, elaborate periodic table representation, ionic models, etc. (cf. Fig. 1).

3 State of Art

Quimivox mobile may help blind people to explore the Mendeleev periodic table using a Smartphone, so we oriented this state of art toward two aspects: (i) at first, we describes some accessibility tools and accessible application existing on Smartphone; (ii) and at last, the existing educational tool for chemistry learning.

3.1 Accessibility on Smartphone

Mobile devices, such as IOS or Android Smartphone, provide accessible tools for peoples with low vision and blind peoples. Sometimes, some graphical adaptations like zoom or increased fonts, color alteration and contrast increasing solve the accessibility problem for low vision. However, for blindness, the OS provides a complete adapted set of interactions. They provide feedbacks toward screen-readers and vibration. Navigation into the applications is performed by simple and double touch pressure (where simple touch serves as consultation of the interface components and double touch serves as input interaction), simple and multi-touch gestures and text input by voice recognition. Techniques such as BraillTouch (Frey et al. 2011; Romero et al. 2011), Fig. 2, also enables braille text inputs.

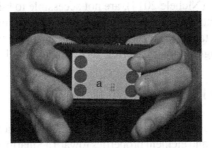

Fig. 2. BrailleTouch

However, there is not a systematical equivalency between sight and blind interaction modalities. Obviously, screen readers implanted on smartphone does not interpret the structure of the interface, or interface contents such as images or graphics in order to produce sense for blind people and then does not transcribe the visual organization of information (Shaik 2010). So, applications should take into account accessibility in their own design and sometimes specifically should be specifically redesigned for blindness like R-MAP (Shaik et al. 2010), or Sonic-Badminton (KIM 2016). It is unusual and many application remains inaccessible in spite of the native assistive tools.

3.2   Educational Tools in Chemistry on Smartphones

The principal scientific software oriented toward chemistry are helping to find probable chemical reaction into large databases of reactions. In regard to education, the computation is more exploited to produce pedagogic visual representation of the molecular structure and animated reaction behavior simulation. For instance, (Fjeld and Voegtli 2002) proposes an educational augmented workbench that enable to interact with atoms and molecules and CAVE (Linioua 2006) is an full immersive environment to observe 3D molecules.

These educational tools experiment how to improve the understanding toward a better visual representation and obviously are not reaching blind people. It is also the problem of the existing educational tools designed on smartphone in area of chemistry pointed by (Libman and Huang 2013) and the University of Chicago[1]. They are not targeting visual impaired users or are not accessible to them.

Some works (Linioua 2006, Fjeld and Voegtli 2002, Fjeld et al. 2007, Chen 2006) reproduce the manipulation of physical molecular models using haptic devices and augmented reality. We have no feedbacks from blind users about the experience of this systems. But, at first sight, we do not think that the 3D representation and haptic feedbacks would increase the haptic exploration by blind people in comparison with the manipulation of physical objects.

In regard to the periodic table more specifically, the tested applications such as Educalabs Periodic Table (a 3D periodic table providing information on element properties and their electronic organization), Xenubi Periodic table, or else Periodic Table Quiz (two applications helping to fix the knowledge after periodic table study), that are available for Portuguese (Nichele 2014), are not accessible to blind people.

In fact, the organizational information structure is very important in the understanding of Mendeleev table. So, it is a typical circumstance where we need a very specific application design in order to turn it accessible to blind people.

4   Quimivox Mobile

Quimivox Mobile enable blind users (and sight users too) to access Mendeleev table, electronic table structure and element properties toward a Smartphone with touch screen.

---

[1] http://guides.lib.uchicago.edu/c.php?g=297153&p=1983664 (accessed in 15/02/2017).

4.1 Main Paradigms

We designed Quimivox Mobile so as to benefit of existing accessible resources provided by Android operating system. We also reuse the standard interaction and navigation paradigms used for accessible applications on Smartphone.

Quimivox Mobile follows simple guidelines (cf. Fig. 2):

- Basic gesture to navigate into menus and into the periodic table (up, down, right and left, interacting with one or two fingers);
- Simple pressure to require a feedback about the selected item;
- Double pressure to enter into a menu or element;
- Vocal synthesis in redundancy with the graphical output.

However, the vocal synthesis is not only a text-to-speech screen lecture, whereas it brings other contextual information to help the user to understand the global structure of the table and orienting him to retrieve needed information. As well as the navigation into the periodic period, Quimivox Mobile offers alternatives strategy to help the users to access to element information. Among them, users can look into the element lists organized by atomic number or alphabetic order, with several interaction shortcuts to

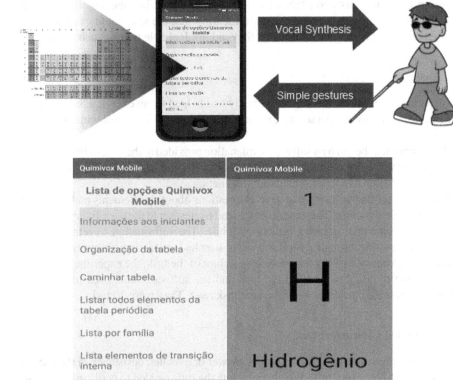

Fig. 3. Quimivox Mobile paradigms

improve the navigation. We are also implementing a vocal research in the current version of the software (it was not implemented yet for the first evaluation). At the start of the application, the software provide a description of interaction paradigms, software structure and content. The user may interrupt the description and may cancel it for the next application starts. The software is optimized for blind people, but it remains plainly accessible to everyone, what enable a discussion between sighted and blind people about the periodic table through the software (Fig. 3).

5   Experimental Evaluation Process

The Quimivox Mobile usability has been experimentally evaluated by final users: 10 blind peoples, toward qualitative aspects.

5.1   Users

The ten users were aged 19 to 44. They all completed high school, 6 were graduating, and two of them had completed graduation. Four of the users were blind since the birth and had no visual memory. The other turned blind after several years and conserved a visual memory. Some of the users had basic notions of the Mendeleev Table purpose: organization of elements into a table. However, at the beginning, the majority of them was reluctant to participate to the evaluation fearing that the test would evaluate their knowledge toward Mendeleev Table and they did not feel able to pass such a test.

5.2   Tasks

The experimentation was realized individually and helped by an experimenter member of the project. The users operate on a Smartphone Galaxy J5 equipped with Quimivox Mobile.

The experiment began by a software explanation provided at the start of the software. The explanation described the content of the software, the interaction and navigation paradigms, and how to access to element information.

Then, the user had to respond at several questions about the elements and about the Mendeleev table structure. The experimenter read a question to the user. Every response was accessible navigating into Quimivox Mobile. The information to retrieved was many time accessible through several ways. The user had to search the response by using the software. After evaluating the success or failure of the task, the experimenter registered the time required to perform the task and the software tools used to meet the information and the carried on with the next task read. They were 10 tasks.

5.3   Evaluated Characteristics

We evaluated the success or failure (wrong answer or eventual desistence of the user to achieve the task) for every task. We also evaluate the time needed to perform every task and the path used to reach the information. The task was timed by the experimenter.

At the end of the experiment, every user had access to an electronic questionnaire appreciating qualitative aspect of the tools accessibility, usability and utility (criteria evaluated between 0 – very bad to 10 – excellent). A last section of the questionnaire invited them to express open critics and improvement suggestion.

The experimenter was also present to observe and report any problem encountered by the user or any spontaneous reaction from him during the task realization.

5.4 Results

Every user completed every task successfully. The time required to perform the task and retrieve the information has been evaluated satisfactory by the users. Born blind users required more time to perform the tasks (between 14 and 16 min) than users that turned blind after several years and conserved a visual memory (between 9 and 12 min).

The users tend to select a tool and maintain the same research strategy to perform the different tasks. No user used every available tools.

The qualitative questioner highlighted a very good acceptability of the software. At first, the users reinforced the utility of the software and considered at unanimity that Quimivox Mobile could be a very useful tools to help chemistry teaching to visual impaired users.

They also highlighted the very good accessibility of the tools and observed that the navigation strategy are very coherent with the accessibility standard that turn the software very intuitive to learn.

At last, they underlined the importance of the software auto-explication at the start of the software that enable to have a first global idea about the services that the software provide, and how and where are organized the menu and tools.

The users proposed some interesting improvement too. The only real critic was the inexistence of a simple interaction enabling to interrupt the vocal synthesis. They explained that frequently, when they wanted to locate themselves into the software, they started a long and needless speech traducing the whole information of the pages. So, they suggested an interaction to interrupt the voice synthesis when desired.

Some of the users suggested another alternative to organize the elements: a menu with elements organized by alphabetic order. The alphabetic order is presented as a search criterion more natural when the user research information toward an element characteristic independently of the table structure.

In order to improve the interaction velocity, some users also suggested to provide some interaction shortcuts mainly to navigate in long lists.

At last, some users recommended a vocal research. This vocal research was ever in development but not available during the experimentation.

6   Conclusion

So, the project achieves its objectives and enable to provide a new tool helping visual impaired users in chemistry learning. The success of Quimivox Mobile is because it does not act only as a standard and generic assistive tool, such as screen reader, whereas it is completely designed to deal with visual impairment. Then, the chemistry contents are organized and explained for the blind users and the visual clues needed to understand the information structure and organization are translated for them.

The evaluation received very positive feedbacks and suggested several improvement. Soon we will propose a new version of Quimivox Mobile integrating these suggestions.

References

Chen, Y.-C.: A study of comparing the use of augmented reality and physical models in chemistry education. In: Proceedings of the 2006 ACM International Conference on Virtual Reality Continuum and its Applications, 14 June–17 April 2006, Hong Kong, China (2006)

D'Anguilli, A., Kennedy, J.M., Heller, M.A.: Blind children recognizing tactile pictures respond like sighted children given guidance in exploration. Scand. J. Psychol. **39**(3), 187–190 (1998)

Fjeld, M., Voegtli, B.M.: Augmented chemistry: an interactive educational workbench. In: Proceedings of the International Symposium on Mixed and Augmented Reality, pp. 259–321 (2002)

Fjeld, M., Frederikkson, J., Ejdestig, M., Duca, F., Bötschi, K., Voegtli, B., Juchli, P.: Tangible user interface for chemistry education: comparative evaluation and re-design. In: Proceedings of the SIGCHI Conference on Human Factors in Computing Systems, CHI 2007, pp. 805–808. ACM, New York (2007)

Frey, B., Southern, C., Romero, M.: BrailleTouch: mobile texting for the visually impaired. In: Stephanidis, C. (ed.) UAHCI 2011. LNCS, vol. 6767, pp. 19–25. Springer, Heidelberg (2011). doi:10.1007/978-3-642-21666-4_3

Graybill, C.M., Supalo, C.A., Mallouk, T.E., Amorosi, C., Rankel, L.: Low-cost laboratory adaptations for precollege students who are blind or visually impaired. J. Chem. Educ. **85**(2), 243 (2008)

https://pt.wikipedia.org/wiki/Ficheiro:Periodic_table_pt.svg

Isaude: Brasil-tem-65-milhoes-de-pessoas-com-deficiencia-visual-e-582-mil-cegos. Disponível em: <http://www.isaude.net/pt-BR/noticia/31410/foto-saude/brasil-tem-65-milhoesde-pessoas-com-deficiencia-visual-e-582-mil-cegos>. Accessed 2 Apr 2015

Kozma, R., Chin, E., Russel, J., Marx, N.: The roles of representations and tools in the chemistry laboratory and their implications for chemistry learning. J. Learn. Sci. **9**(2), 105–143 (2000)

Lederman, S.J., Campbell, J.I.: Tangible line graphs: an evaluation and some systematic strategies for exploration. J. Vis. Impairment Blindness **77**, 108–112 (1983)

Libman, D., Huang, L.: Chemistry on the go: review of chemistry apps on smartphones. J. Chem. Educ. **90**, 320–325 (2013)

Limnioua, M., Robert, D., Papadopoulos, N.: Full immersive virtual environment CAVETM in chemistry education. Comput. Educ. **51**(2), 584–593 (2008)

Miner, D.L., Nieman, R., Swanson, A.B., Woods, M.: Teaching Chemistry to Students with Disabilities: A Manual for High Schools, Colleges, and Graduate Programs, 4th edn. The American Chemical Society (2001). Editors Kelley Carpenter, Copy Editor American Chemical Society Committee on Chemists with Disabilities

Nichele, A.G.: Aplicativos para o ensino e aprendizagem de Química. CINTED (2014)

Picard, D., Lebaz, S.: Identifying raised-line drawings by touch: a hard but not impossible task. J. Vis. Impairment Blindness **106**(7), 427–431 (2012)

Picard, D., Albaret, J.-M., Mazella, A.: Haptic identification of raised-line drawings by children, adolescents and young adults: an age-related skill. Haptics-e **5**, 24–28 (2013)

Romero, M., Frey, B., Southern, C., Abowd, G.D.: BrailleTouch: designing a mobile eyes-free soft keyboard. In: Proceedings of the 13th International Conference on Human Computer Interaction with Mobile Devices and Services, 30 August–02 September 2011, Stockholm, Sweden (2011)

de Elizabet Dias, S.Á.: Atendimento Educacional Especializado. Brasília, DF, Brazil: s.n., 2006 (2006)

Shaik, A.S., Hossain, G., Yeasin, M.: Design, development and performance evaluation of reconfigured mobile Android phone for people who are blind or visually impaired. In: Proceedings of the 28th ACM International Conference on Design of Communication, SIGDOC 2010 (2010)

Supalo, C.: Techniques to enhance instructors' teaching effectiveness with chemistry students who are blind or visually impaired. J. Chem. Educ. **82**(10), 1513 (2005)

Van Doorn, G.H., Dubaj, V., Wuillemin, D.B., Richardson, B.L., Symonns, M.A.: Cognitive load can explain differences in active and passive touch. In: Isokoski, P., Springare, J. (eds.) Haptics: Perception, Devices, Mobility, and Communication, EuroHaptics 2012. LNCS, vol. 7282, pp. 91–102. Springer, Heidelberg (2012). doi:10.1007/978-3-642-31401-8_9

Withagen, A., Verloed, M.P.J., Janssen, N.M., Knoors, H., Verhoeven, L.: Tactile functioning in children who are blind: a clinical perspective. J. Vis. Impairment Blindness **1**, 43–54 (2010)

Wu, H.K., Shah, P.: Exploring visuospatial thinking in chemistry learning. Sci. Educ. **88**(3), 465–492 (2004)

The Use of Computational Artifacts to Support Deaf Learning: An Approach Based on the Direct Way Methodology

Marta Angélica Montiel Ferreira[1(✉)], Juliana Bueno[2],
Rodrigo Bonacin[1,3], and Laura Sánchez García[2]

[1] FACCAMP, Rua Guatemala, 167, Campo Limpo Paulista,
SP 13231-230, Brazil
zmontefer@gmail.com, rodrigo.bonacin@cti.gov.br
[2] Informatics Department, Federal University of Paraná, Centro Politécnico,
Jardim das Américas, Curitiba, PR, Brazil
{juliana,laura}@inf.ufpr.br
[3] Center for Information Technology Renato Archer,
Rodovia Dom Pedro I, Km 143,6, Campinas, SP 13069-901, Brazil

Abstract. Deaf users face various difficulties accessing the Web. These difficulties are frequently due to low skills on written language, which is a consequence of approaches that do not favor appropriate methods such as bilingual literacy. This method make use of sign language skills to teach a second written language. In this paper, we present studies with deaf students that explore the direct way methodology articulated with computational artifacts aiming to promote the bilingual literacy. This article presents 10 meetings where we performed learning activities with 3 teachers and 12 deaf students. The objective was to apply our approach to improve the reading and writing skills on Portuguese language, as a second language. The studies point out positive results, and the possibility of exploring this approach from the early years of child literacy.

Keywords: Web accessibility · Deaf accessibility · Deaf literacy · Direct way methodology

1 Introduction

Deaf literacy challenges and barriers have been addressed by various studies [2, 6, 8]. Such challenges and barriers are related to numerous issues, which occur even when the deaf students are immersed in a bilingual context (i.e., when the first language is a sign language – L1 and the second language is a written language – L2).

A key issue is the adoption of inappropriate bilingual education strategies, which are mostly guided by listeners teaching contexts (i.e., in alphabetization principles) [11]. Principles of alphabetization based on the phonetics are indeed not suitable for deaf learning, which must be based on their own literacy context [2, 5]. Although this is highly accepted, there are many open questions related to deaf literacy methods, such as: "Are there methods able to promote fully literacy skills on deaf student?" and "Could deaf students to become critical readers?"

M. Antona and C. Stephanidis (Eds.): UAHCI 2017, Part III, LNCS 10279, pp. 198–209, 2017.
DOI: 10.1007/978-3-319-58700-4_17

Our hypothesis is that the answers to these questions are "yes". Thus, we based our proposal on previous studies [2, 5], as well as the "direct way" literacy methodology. This methodology was proposed by the French Reading Association (AFL- *Association Française pour la Lecture*) aiming to educate *critical readers*. It has the objective of goes "from the message to the code" as argued by Foucambert[1]. This methodology has been applied on French schools for more than 40 years and it has proven results in acquisition of a second written language by foreign students [4, 11, 12].

Previous studies adapted and experienced the "direct way" methodology in the context of deaf literacy on L2 [3]. Thus, this article has two goals that complement existing studies: (1) to validate the application of the "direct way" methodology in the context of adult education, aiming improve their understanding on L2. In our case, the Portuguese language is learned by lessons explained using Brazilian Sign Language – Libras (L1); and (2) to explore the potentials of computational artifacts (e.g, Websites, portals, blogs and text editors) for boosting literacy activities using the direct way.

Aiming to achieve these goals, we conducted a qualitative and exploratory study with the participation of 12 deaf students aged from 12 to 29. This study was held during 8 meetings with students and 2 meetings with a teacher targeting to elicit and prepare the activities and artifacts used in the study. The students had various levels of education (from elementary to graduated), all of them use Libras as first language (L1) and Portuguese as second one (L1), 5 of which also oralized. Two bilingual teachers participated of the meetings, both with proficiency certification in Libras and large experience in teaching deaf. The practices were structured according to five principles proposed by the "direct way" methodology.

As a result, we systematized a set of literacy process issues grounded on the practices with the students. This process is described in the article and the perspectives of application of this process in a long term project are also discussed. We considered difficulties, limitations and challenges of applying this process in regular activities of the Deaf Service Center of Amapá state, Brazil.

The work is structured as follows: Sect. 2 presents the theoretical background and related work including the direct way methodology and web accessibility issues and methods; Sect. 3 describes the activities with deaf users, including the participants, artifacts and procedures; Sect. 4 presents the interpretation of the results, discussions and limitations; and, Sect. 5 concludes the paper.

2   Theoretical Background and Related Work

In this section, firstly, we present the importance of the Sign Language as a mediating tool for the acquisition and improvement of written language skills. With this objective, we investigated new perspectives for bilingual literacy aiming to amplify the reading and writing autonomy of the deaf. In order to achieve this objective, we explored the "direct way" methodology, which proved positive in previous studies [4, 10]. In this

---

[1] http://www.lecture.org/ressources/anglais/from_message.html.

sense, we argue that the direct way methodology can be explored with Web accessibility concepts and tools.

2.1 Direct Way Methodology

As mentioned before, the direct way literacy methodology was proposed by AFL with the objective of educate critical readers working on texts in a systematic way in order to "go from message to code". A code is classified as a graphic [9] or orthographic. The students have access to graphic resources of a book by understanding the written messages.

This methodology aims to explore the text in the following aspects:

- The organization of the text (*e.g.*, genre, articulations, structure, …), besides its relations with other texts (*e.g.*, references to others books, …);
- The grammatical structures (*e.g.*, organization of sentences, punctuation, grouping of words, expressions, order, …) and the effects produced by grammatical changes in the expressions;
- The words, including lexical fields, sonorities, meanings, functions, spelling, transformation, family, constructions and synonyms, to cite some [1].

This methodology purposes to deeply explore texts making the readers to acquire researcher' skills [1, 5]. Including, for instance, the abilities to develop hypotheses, to identity provisional rules, and to compare them with other texts to validate them [5].

Thus, in the direct way methodology, the reading process is considered as a model that supposes the permanent interaction between the reader' previous knowledge and information presented in the text (Fig. 1). Razet emphasize that "the objective, when

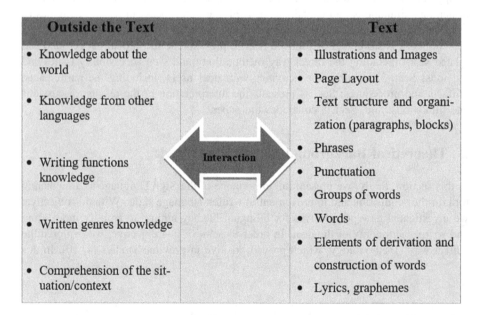

Fig. 1. Elements of interaction between outside and text zone (Based on [1])

presenting the text, is to make the students realize that there is, in the act of reading, a constant interaction between the information coming from the reader and the information contained in the text itself" [12:75].

Regarding the selection of texts to be worked on the learning activities, the AFL [1] stresses that they should not be produced to be a text for "learning to read", but rather, texts should be produced as writing work (in physical or virtual medium). These texts can have, for instance, content about the students' social context, news, among other contents that have a relation with all the areas the life of the students. The teacher should produce or select text that stimulate the contact with the everyday use of written language, for instance: personal letters, forms, tickets, news, culinary recipes, package inserts, comic books, shopping list, restaurant menu, e-mails, computer chats, virtual classes, among others.

2.2 Web Accessibility

In this work, literacy issues are articulated with web accessibility issue, we studied how the literacy can affect the accessibility, as well as how literacy can make the Web more comprehensible to deaf people [7, 10]. According to Shneiderman (2000), universal usability aims to allow access to information to the largest number of possible users on the Web. The interfaces should provide accessibility to different types of users, as a way to guarantee access to information and services available on the Web [13].

Accessibility on the Web means that people with disabilities in fact can perceive, understand, navigate and interact in addition to being able to contribute to the Web [7]. Consequently, with the objective of making the Web accessible, W3C's Web Accessibility Initiative (WAI)[2] published three guidelines as follows:

- Web Content Accessibility Guidelines (WCAG) that contains criteria to make Web content accessible to people with disabilities;
- Authoring Tool Accessibility Guidelines (ATAG) that focus on Web content authoring tools making they more accessible to authors with disabilities and supporting the production of more accessible Web content;
- User Agent Accessibility Guidelines (UAAG) that focus on how developers can design user agents that make web more accessible to people with disabilities.

The WCAG 2.0 specification includes four principles that provide the foundation for Web accessibility: 1. Perceivable – including 4 recommendations (text alternatives, time-based media, adaptable and distinguishable) on how to make content perceivable to all (it can't be invisible to all of their senses), 2. Operable – including 4 recommendations (keyboard accessible, enough time, seizures and navigable) on how to make components and navigation operable, 3. Understandable – including 3 recommendations (readable, predictable and input assistance) on how to make information and operation understandable, and, 4. Robust – including a recommendation

---

[2] http://www.w3.org/WAI.

(compatible) on how to make content robust enough that it can be interpreted reliably by a wide variety of user agents, including assistive technologies.

In the specific case of deafness, the W3C proposes solutions such as to have text equivalent to audio content. Other complex techniques, such as the use of avatars are also present in the literature. These type of recommendations and techniques are useful, however the deaf still faces difficulties in reading texts and interacting on the Web, demanding design from methodologies that make use of the existing solutions to fit their needs [7].

This work make use of the bilingual literacy philosophy by means of Direct Way methodology mediated by accessible computational artifacts. The long term objective is to propose a new method for providing a full learning of the Portuguese language, in order to make the deaf able to read and write fluently in a written language (L2) as well as to explore these abilities to access information and interact on the Web.

3   Studies with Deaf Users

We report 10 meetings with deaf users and teachers held at the the Deaf Service Center CAS (Centro de Atendimento ao Surdo) in the city of Macapá, state of Amapá, Brazil. The first two meetings were conducted only with the three teacher of the CAS. The first teacher is a listener, hold graduation degree in pedagogic, had 48 years old and is fluent in LIBRAS. The second teacher is deaf, hold graduation degree in pedagogy, had 43 years old and is fluent in LIBRAS and lip reading. The third teacher is deaf, hold graduation degree in pedagogy, had 51 years old and is fluent in LIBRAS and lip reading.

The center had 12 deaf students enrolled, being 6 students in the morning and 6 students in the afternoon. The students had between 12 and 29 years, being 4 female and 8 male. Considering their educational levels, two participants held university degrees, while the others are high school or elementary school students. All students have profound hearing loss (legally considered deaf) and are able to do lip reading. Sign language is used by all students.

The classes take place twice a week, the listener teacher give classes in both periods, one deaf teacher take turn in the morning and the other in the afternoon. So, there were always two teachers (a listener and a deaf) in a class of six students. For the research activities, the class was divided into groups of 3 students each, as they do activities with psychologists and speech therapists.

The objective of the two initial meetings were to plan the next teaching/learning meetings, making an evaluation of the context and preparing the artifacts to be explored in practical activities with the students (that took place from the third meetings). In the following paragraphs, we describe the scope of each meetings, including the planning meetings (1 and 2) and the meetings developed with students in sequence.

MEETING 1 (Planning Meeting)
Participants: 3 teacher and the researcher
Duration: 2 h
Objectives: The objective was to prepare an agenda for the next meetings and decide key themes to be work during the practical activities.

Developed Activities: After an initial group discussion, the participants investigated (using the Web and their own experiences) alternatives to define an activity and theme that is accessible to all students. Thus, in this meeting the participants decided that the theme to be explored would be "HEALTHY FOOD". They agreed that this is a broad theme, with easy access to Web content by teachers and students, and this was considered a topic of general interest.

It was also of common agreement that deaf students already had prior knowledge about this theme, and, consequently, this theme could be explored in various types of activities. It was decided that during the meetings that teachers could also emphasize the importance of creating healthier eating habits from the adolescence to have a healthy old age.

MEETING 2 (Planning Meeting)

Participants: 3 teacher and the researcher

Duration: 3 h

Objectives: Design of the practical activities.

Developed Activities: At this meeting, the participants divided the activities to be worked on in the following 8 meeting. For the participants (teachers and researcher), it was clear that the focus should be to provide collective learning opportunities, by means of an organized writing practices, exploring a vocabulary in Libras (L1) and Portuguese Language (L2) including texts and content Web. Therefore, making use of various artifacts related to the same theme, including various content sources such as blogs and websites. The participants decided that the students would use mobile devices to perform the proposed activities.

The group also decided that for a better efficiency of the activities, 3 students should participate in each activity at a time. The participants also defined the document set that should be explored in each activity. Each of the planned meetings should had the maximum duration of 30 min.

MEETING 3

Participants: 2 teachers (a deaf and a listener) and 3 deaf students

Duration: 30 min

Objectives: Practice reading and evaluating the use of unfamiliar words

Developed Activities: Firstly, the teacher read a text in Libras, while each student received a copy of the written text. This text was selected on the web, and synthesized, using a text editor, and then printed by the teachers. After, the students expressed their concerns about reading the text, consequently, the difficulty of the participating students with the written Portuguese language was made explicit in this meeting.

MEETING 4

Participants: 2 teachers (a deaf and a listener) and 3 deaf students

Duration: 30 min

Objectives: Explore other types of artifacts and content

Developed Activities: Firstly, each student should report what they normally eat in their houses using sign language. The teacher explained the need to have healthy meals. They stressed the necessity of eating various types of food. Then, the teachers wrote on the board the foods mentioned by the students, and they cut out the foods from

Fig. 2. Pictures of Meeting 4

textbooks (left side of Fig. 2) to make a poster (right side of Fig. 2). They also did web searches using their mobile apps.

MEETING 5

Participants: 2 teachers (a deaf and a listener) and 3 deaf students
Duration: 30 min
Objectives: Construct a glossary with the words of the presented texts
Developed Activities: Firstly, the teachers searched on the web text related to the theme, formed it in a text editor, and printed. Then, the teachers gave to the students another text about healthy eating and they were asked to mark the words they already knew. The idea was to build a glossary with them. The student should verify the words with highest occurrences in the text. In addition to exploring the text, the teacher also explained in Libras the importance of having a healthy and balanced diet. Each food mentioned by the students would be written on the board. Then, with the objective of creating a glossary in Libras and Portuguese, the students cut out the words form the text, and fixed them in their exercise books.

MEETING 6

Participants: 2 teachers (a deaf and a listener) and 3 deaf students
Duration: 30 min
Objectives: Verify the vocabulary extension (words about foods) of the deaf students knew in Portuguese and Libras
Developed Activities: This meeting focused on working the Food Groups (Cereals, Milk, Meat, Fruits and Vegetables). Each student should choose in a piece of paper with the name of a food and classify it in a group of food. In addition, to verify the students' vocabulary, this meeting also aimed to improve the awareness about the need of eating healthy foods. In sequence, the students did search on the Web in group, and then they synthesized the recovered content in a text editor, printed it and discussed with other students (Fig. 3).

Fig. 3. Teachers during the meeting 6

MEETING 7

Participants: 2 teachers (a deaf and a listener) and 3 deaf students

Duration: 30 min

Objectives: Explore the selection of foods for a meal, associating the food names (written) with meals types

Developed Activities: In this meeting the students had to set meals menu. The teachers had 4 meals options for the students: breakfast, snack, lunch and dinner. The student should choose the foods written in piece of papers and compose the foods to constitute a healthy meal, i.e., the students selected small number of foods for the meal from an extensive list. After that, using a text editor, they printed their meals and presented to the others. The teachers made videos of this meeting and sent to the students at the end.

MEETING 8

Participants: 2 teachers (a deaf and a listener) and 3 deaf students

Duration: 30 min

Objectives: Practice words learned from past activities

Fig. 4. Picture of the teacher explaining the activities of meeting 8

Developed Activities: This meeting (Fig. 4) initiated with reading another text about healthy eating. The text was selected on the web and printed. Each student had to explain what (s)he understood. The teachers did not aid the students to read, they focused on verify the words learned in the last meetings and the words that were not assimilated. At the end, the teachers explained to the students the unfamiliar words.

MEETING 9

Participants: 2 teachers (a deaf and a listener) and 3 deaf students
Duration: 30 min
Objectives: Check which words were learned from past activities
Developed Activities: The teacher prepared a set of foods written on pieces of paper and collected pictures of these foods from the Web. The students cut the names and pictures and placed them together. The teacher also presented Web images that could be explored by the students.

MEETING 10

Participants: 2 teachers (a deaf and a listener) and 3 deaf students
Duration: 30 min
Objectives: Explore the written form of the Portuguese language
Developed Activities: In meeting 8 the students received a homework, whose results were used during meeting 10. The teacher asked to the students to take note what they eaten in the main meals. The teacher digitalized the annotations (Fig. 5) and shared on a Web driver. They were also printed and distributed to the students during the meeting. After, each student presented the food that they eaten to their colleagues, explaining each kind of food they eaten, the groups of foods and whether the food is healthy or not.

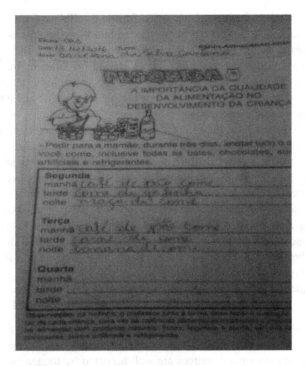

Fig. 5. Example of Students' meals annotations

4   Results, Discussions and Limitations

The analysis of the results pointed out that the major difficulty that the students faced on this study was their limited vocabulary in Portuguese and Libras. The teachers realized that the students do not know the various synonyms of a word. For example, during the meetings they frequently recognized a fruit, but they did not know how to writing the name and even the sign in Libras.

The main limitation of this study is the number of students, since today there are only 12 students enrolled in the center, divided in two classes, one in the morning and the other in the afternoon. However, the groups of 3 students each contributed to carry out the activities in a faster and efficient way. This small groups was also important to provide a closer relationship with the students. According to the teachers, in initial observation with groups of 6 students the students were agitated. The teachers had concerns that the activities with "many" students would be more time consuming. The limit of 30 min was also important to guarantee a good development of the activities, as they had other classes in the same day, and consequently long meetings could reduce the motivation and concentration of the students in the activities.

Some simple words such as "vitamin" were not recognized by the majority of the students. In this case they usually knew the some fruits has vitamin, but they were not aware of that our body needs vitamins. For instance, when the teacher questioned about the word vitamin in a text about the benefits of the vitamins, the student reposed:

"I make this at home sometimes, I put some fruit and milk" (referring to fresh fruit mixed drinks with milk). So, the teacher requested that they should search on the web (using their mobile) word "vitamin". They explored the results in the classroom, and only after this the teacher explained in Libras the need for vitamins for health.

The teachers do not reported difficulties in using technology devices. They use technological devices in their daily lives, for example all students had a mobile phone and used common mobile applications.

According to the teachers, the students had difficulties in memorize the meaning of a new written word: "When we teach a new word they can not memorize its meanings, and always forget it in a short period", this reinforce the need to practice in several forms the same word, including situations of their daily lives, as proposed by the direct way. For instance, the teachers noticed that the students could understand better the text during the 7th meeting. As mentioned before, they set meals menus based on healthy foods, avoiding industrialized products. This is contextualized in your daily experiences, for instance, a student said "I frequently eat sweet cookies at dinner, can I do this?", the teacher interacted with the student explaining "You can do this sometimes, but not every day, because this is not healthy".

Finally, at the end of the meetings, the researchers asked to the teachers stress five important points learned from the meetings, which can be synthesized as follows:

- Deaf students were interested in using technology in the classroom, they considered that technology resources make classes more productive and interesting;
- The use of computational resources are well accepted by the teachers too;
- The purpose of the texts explored in the activities were understood by all the participants;
- The methodology was applied in a productive way;
- The methodology needs to be explored on gradually and continuously way.

5 Conclusion and Future Work

Nowadays, the literature presents some useful Web accessibility alternatives for deaf users. However, they still find barriers related to difficulties with the written language (L2). In this article, we use the direct way methodology of literacy mediated by accessible computational artifacts, to support teaching L2 to deaf students. The objective is to improve reading skills and provide full autonomy in accessing information on the Web.

The practical activities with deaf students produced positive results. The general propose of the meetings were properly understood, and the deaf students also understood the importance of eating healthier (secondary objective). Teachers also stressed that the methodology is very productive, and it needs to be explored on gradually and continuously way. Thus, for more consistent results, it should be applied in a continuous learning process in a longer term program. As the next steps of this research, we propose to explore the approach to teach the syntactic and semantic structures of the Portuguese language (L2).

References

1. Association Française Pour La Lecture: Actes de lecture: les principes de la voie directe, n° 100 (2007). http://www.lecture.org/revues_livres/actes_lectures/AL/AL100/al100p049.pdf. Accessed Feb 2017
2. Bueno, J., García, L.S.: Pesquisa-ação na construção de insumos conceituais para um ambiente computacional de apoio ao letramento bilíngue de crianças surdas. In: XXVI Simpósio Brasileiro de Informática na Educação – SBIE, pp. 887–896 (2015)
3. Bueno, J., Sánchez García, L.: Action research to generate requirements for a computational environment supporting bilingual literacy of deaf children. In: Stephanidis, C., Antona, M. (eds.) UAHCI 2014. LNCS, vol. 8514, pp. 245–253. Springer, Cham (2014). doi:10.1007/978-3-319-07440-5_23
4. Bueno, J.: Pesquisa-ação na construção de insumos conceituais para um ambiente computacional de apoio ao letramento bilíngue de crianças surdas. Doctoral dissertation UFPR, Curitiba (2014)
5. Cherem, L.P., Rammé, V., Pedra, N.S., Olmo, F.C.: Dossiê Especial: Didática sem Fronteiras, vol. 2, pp. 93–110. Revista X, Curitiba (2014). http://revistas.ufpr.br/revistax/issue/view/1899. Accessed Feb 2017
6. Ferreira, M.A.M., Bueno, J., Bonacin, R.: Encouraging the learning of written language by deaf users: web recommendations and practices. In: Antona, M., Stephanidis, C. (eds.) UAHCI 2016. LNCS, vol. 9739, pp. 3–15. Springer, Cham (2016). doi:10.1007/978-3-319-40238-3_1
7. Ferreira, M.A.M.: Design inclusivo e participativo na web: incluindo pessoas surdas. Master Thesis Faccamp, Campo Limpo Paulista (2014)
8. García, L.S. et al.: HCI architecture for deaf communities cultural inclusion and citizenship. In: 15th International Conference on Enterprise Information Systems. Lisboa: ICEIS 2013, vol. 3, pp. 68–75 (2013)
9. Goody, J.: La raison graphique, p. 97. Les éditions de Minuit, Paris (1985)
10. Haiduski, A.S.L.: Ambiente de autoria web de apoio ao letramento infantil. Master Thesis UFPR, Curitiba (2016)
11. Ng'ethe, G.G., Blake, E.H., Glaser, M.: Supporting deaf adult learners training in computer literacy classes. In: Zvacek, S., Restivo, M.T., Uhomoibhi, J., Helfert, M. (eds.) CSEDU 2015. CCIS, vol. 583, pp. 598–617. Springer, Cham (2016). doi:10.1007/978-3-319-29585-5_34
12. Razet, C.: De la lecture d'une histoire à la lecture d'une écriture. In: GERFLINT (ed.). Synergies Brésil, pp. 59–74. Editora Humanitas, São Paulo (2012)
13. Shneiderman, B.: Universal usability. Commun. ACM **43**(5), 85–91 (2000)

Evaluation of an Automatic Essay Correction System Used as an Assessment Tool

Sergio A.A. Freitas[(✉)], Edna D. Canedo, Cristóvão L. Frinhani,
Maurício F. Vidotti, and Marcia C. Silva

University of Brasilia, Brasília, Brazil
{sergiofreitas,ednacanedo}@unb.br, cristovao.frinhani@gmail.com,
mauricio.vidotti@gmail.com, marciasillva@gmail.com

Abstract. In this paper, we evaluate an automatic correction essay system used as an assessment tool on a gamified course. The gamified course uses a question/answer battle as its main strategy to engage and empower students' learning. As educational methodology, it uses peer review strategy on flipped classrooms. In such context, it was developed an automatic essay correction system, called Milsa, to be used by students out off the classroom. Milsa is used to insert questions and template answers, to automatically correct the questions based on template answers, to show the students the question, the answer and the resulting grade and, finally, to learn from the users' feedback on the answer's evaluation. Milsa is used as an assessment tool to measure students' development at the gamified course. Then, we evaluate the contribution of Milsa to the students' learning process at the course. We conducted and analyzed tests based on data collected at classes and Milsa: individual flow aligned between the classes, the assessments and an Intrinsic Motivation Inventory (IMI) questionnaire. Finally, we discusses the advantages and disadvantages of the use of Milsa as a social network that helps students with disabilities.

Keywords: Active learning · Gamification · Usability and user experience · Automatic essay correction

1 Introduction

The gamification of activities other than games has become one of the main objectives of a new area of research. In the education area, the proposal could not be different: the new generations on the higher education has a lot of experience in the virtual information environment and games. So, nothing more natural than checking the adherence of gamification to teaching this new student profile. In this scenario, we gamified the Computer System Architecture discipline (CSA) of the Software Engineering course at University of Brasilia (Brazil) [1] and tested it for a year (two semesters). The gamification core is simple: a battle of knowledge in which the students studies at home (flipped classroom [2]) and comes to the classes to ask and answers questions to/from their

© Springer International Publishing AG 2017
M. Antona and C. Stephanidis (Eds.): UAHCI 2017, Part III, LNCS 10279, pp. 210–222, 2017.
DOI: 10.1007/978-3-319-58700-4_18

colleagues (peer review [3]). The classes are called "battles" and there are three assessments (called "missions") during the course. Each mission last a week and is "played" at a network system called Milsa [4]

The gamification course produce plenty of data: each battle is composed of duels between two parts. Each part could be a group, a student or half of the class. The information of each duel produces a large database: identification of student(s), division of the points (called "patacas"[1] or "bins"), the collaboration of the rest of the class, types of participation, types of the questions (Bloom's taxonomy [5, 6]) and so on. This huge database enables us to track, for example, an individual student path at the whole course: if she is collaborative or competitive, if she prefers to play together or not, the preferred type of question, the answers and so on.

By the end of the semester, we applied an IMI questionnaire [7] to evaluate the students' intrinsic motivation.

Using the collected data on the "battles", the IMI questionnaire and the Milsa itself, we used statistical tools to evaluate the similarities between the behaviors of students at classroom, their motivations and how they answered the assessments at Milsa. This enables us to evaluate if Milsa is contributing to the learning process.

Finally, considering that Milsa is a web application[2] design to automatically correct answers for a given question, it is easy to imaging a social network based on it. Such social network may both promote universal access and help students with disabilities.

The remainder of the paper is organized as follows: Sect. 2 presents the gamification, describing the used framework; Sect. 3 presents the description of the gamified course, its structure and instruments; Sect. 4 presents the Milsa system, its internal organization and usage; Sect. 5 presents the results and discussion; Sect. 6 presents a proposal on the use of Milsa as a social network, discussing advantages and disadvantages to students with disabilities and Sect. 7 presents conclusions and further research lines.

2   The Gamification Framework

Gamification is defined as the use of game elements in a non-game context [4]. It seems a natural choose to be used for educating newer generations. Gamification advocates the use of design elements and game principles to increase engagement, motivation and user pleasure in performing daily tasks [8, 9]. Although games are used in education since 1980 [10], only recently the difference between games and gamification are stablished [11, 12] and begins to be statistically tested in education [1, 13, 14].

Gamification may produce motivation and engagement on students. Some researchers found good results [1, 14] and others not [13]. Our work is based on the Octalysis framework proposed by Yu Kai-Chou [9]. He presents eight basic human motivations called Core Drivers:

---

[1]   In Portuguese, Pataca is the same name for both an old real coin and the currency used on uncle scrooge story (bin). Pataca is a great symbol for gamification, linking the real to the virtual.

[2]   Available at https://www.fabrica.fga.unb.br/milsa.

1. Epic Meaning & Calling – when the player believes that she is doing something greater, for a greater good or that she has been *chosen* to do something transcendental.
2. Development & Accomplishment - when the player observes their progress, skill development and, eventually, overcoming challenges.
3. Empowerment & Feedback - when the player is involved in a creative process where she repeatedly has to discover *things* and try different combinations.
4. Ownership & Possession - when the player is motivated because she has the sense of ownership of something.
5. Social Influence & Relatedness - when the player is motivated by social elements that influence people, including: orientation, acceptance, social responses, companionship, as well as competition and envy.
6. Scarcity & Impatience - when the player is motivated by the desire for something they cannot have or may take time to occur.
7. Unpredictability & Curiosity - when the player is motivated by wanting to figure out what will happen next.
8. Loss & Avoidance - when the player is motivated by the prevention of something negative that may occur.

At each of these motivations there are a set of game techniques that may induce and strengthen the associated core driver. Some examples are: Narrative, Beginner's Luck, Elitism, Points, and Badges among others.

We used Octalysis to model both the students' motivation profiles and to create a gamified project that implements the profiles. The result is a map for the students:

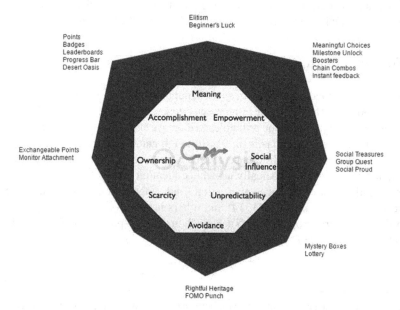

Fig. 1. The resulting gamification project for CSA in the Octalysis model (source: Octalysis group)

competition, collaboration, anxiety and so on, mapping a set of motivations. The resulting gamification project for CSA course is depicted in Fig. 1 on Octalysis layout.

The main motivations modelled for the students are: Empowerment, Accomplishment and Social Influence. Also Meaning, Ownership, Unpredictability and Avoidance have some influence on the students. The model is the used to produce an associated game to be used as the gamified CSA course.

We adopted McGonigal's [8] four characteristics for games: goal, rules, feedback and voluntary participation. The goal indicates the goal by which a player wishes to play the game. The voluntary participation is the freedom that the player has to try or not the game and involves the freedom to choose their own paths and strategies within the game. The gamified course is presented next.

3 A Funny Course

The gamified space was created from the model. In it the student sees the CSA course as if it is a game: the goal is to complete the course with exploitation, the rules are the directions, the teaching plan and the description of the game, the feedbacks are the answers to the questions of the game, interaction with other students and the victories achieved during the game.

The gamified space consists of the following elements: physical space (classroom), virtual space (Moodle environment), information sources (books, videos and internet), players (students, teacher and assistants), the (re)definition of nomenclature and the game.

3.1 Course Description

The Computer System Architecture (CSA) is a compulsory course of 60 h, offered in the 4th semester of the undergraduate Software Engineering course at University of Brasilia. The average number of students was 35 per semester.

The learning objective of CSA is to demonstrate for the students how a program is executed by the hardware (CPU). At the end of the course, students are expected to learn about the CPU organization, its components and how they interact to run a program.

The gamification process enables a daily student action track: his performance (in terms of earned patacas per class), their interaction, the questions and answers and, finally, how they interact with the colleagues. It's possible to track the learning path of each individual student. To be approved in the course, the students must earn a certain number of patacas.

3.2 The Classroom

The classroom is an important element in the gamification. The game will be played, in large part, in this space. Inside the classroom, each student has a free movements, free talk, and ways to expresses himself. No media projectors or computers are used. Also, access to the internet and use of smartphones are not allowed.

3.3 Virtual Space

Planning, control and communication of Gamification occur in virtual space, in this case, in the institutional Moodle. In this space is the class schedule, a list with topics of each class, materials available (videos), list of others activities, all the material produced in the game (aiming to give transparency to the results) and, lastly, players ranking.

3.4 Definition of the Nomenclature

For effective gamification, it is necessary create a virtual world in players mind, going way of from terms that links to real world. Thus traditional nomenclatures should be replaced. Terms like class, teachers, and exams must be banished from the course vocabulary, they became: Course = game, class = battle, student = player, teacher = oracle, monitor = pythoness, points = patacas (bins), in-class assessments = duel, assessments after class = challenges and, finally, tests/works = missions.

3.5 Assessments

The assessments are named "missions". The missions are archived outside the classroom environment. The idea is that each mission both integrate contents and provides online gaming. The missions are executed using the Milsa web interface. Milsa enables the processes of managing the questions and answers, and evaluating the questions and answers in a peer review manner.

3.6 And Now, Let's Play

The central element of the game is the knowledge duel between players (individual or group). The set of duels is called a battle. The subject of each battle is about one or more topic of the course and is previously available in Moodle. The battles set cover all the topics of the discipline. In order for the players to succeed in the duels, a preliminary preparation is necessary with study of the available sources.

After each battle, a set of challenges are available in the virtual environment that the player can perform and thus gain more bins. Each month, missions are available and are executed by the players during a week. All the activities of the game: duels, challenges and missions that are successfully performed generate bins. The goal of the game is accumulate bins. At the end of the game, each player maps their bins on a final grade.

A Duel

A duel consists of a question and answer dispute between players. A group (challenging) of players constructs a question pertaining to the battle theme for the other group (challenged) to respond. The oracle plays the role of referee and judges how much the question is worth. Possible values are one to three bins, depending on the complexity of the question. The total time for a duel is five minutes.

The challenged group wins as much as three bins by satisfactorily answering the question. The challenging group wins bins if the response is not satisfactory. The earned

Bins are divided among the members of the group. There is a limit of 6 bins per player for each battle.

The other players who are not participating in the duel can complement both the question and the answer. If a question has not been answered completely, any player outside the duel can supplement the answer and earn the additional score. If the challenged group does not respond satisfactorily, the players in the audience can supplement the response and win one bin. At the end of the duel, the challenger must respond correctly to the question under penalty of being invalidated. The formation of groups is defined by oracle at the beginning of each battle, both in relation to the number of members and the formation criteria, which may be random and by free association.

The Battles
The battles are meeting destined to carry out the duels. Each battle has a pre-defined theme previously available in the virtual environment. The player's absence on the day of the battle corresponds to the loss of the bins disputed on the respective day.

Local Helpers
Two local auxiliaries are assigned to manage the battle and to registry all the information necessary to the execution of the game in the classroom. The assistants are responsible for recording the duels (group members, earnings and audience collaboration) and controlling the time.

The Challenges
Beyond the battles' dynamics that induces players to study at home, it is posed fixation questions (multiple choice questions) named challenges. The challenges are available for four weeks in the virtual environment immediately after the corresponding battle. There are ten random questions on the topics of the battle and the answer of 6 or more questions leads to the gain of one pataca.

The Missions
Missions are activities that must be done individually and outside the classroom. They consist of research, production, answering and evaluation of questions for other players. For the execution of the missions a second virtual environment was created for this purpose - Milsa.

4 Milsa System

In Milsa, the players create open-ended questions (essays) that are answered by the other players and are automatically evaluated by the automatic correction system.

Milsa is compounded of two parts: the web interface and the correction algorithm core. The web interface enables CSA's students to play the missions for a period of time (normally a week), divided in four stages:

1. First, the students use the system to create a certain number of questions and answers. The answers are templates that will be used by the correction mechanism.

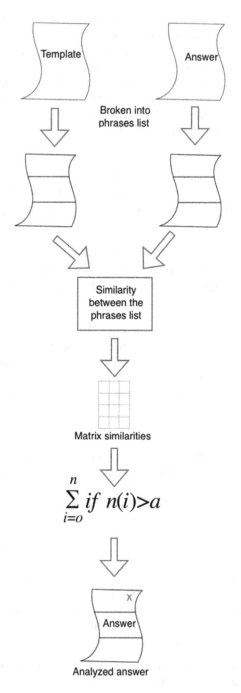

Fig. 2. Milsa core comparison workflow

2. At the second stage, the students enter the system to answer questions. The questions are the ones created they colleagues. They are randomly choose among others students questions.
3. At the third stage, Milsa automatically correct each answered based on the template for the question and calculates a grade. The grades range from 0 (zero) to 10 (ten).
4. Finally, the player who created the question must evaluate the response given by the other student, the grade automatically calculated by Milsa and writes a justification if he disagrees with the automatic system's evaluation.

The correction algorithm core [4] is based on similarity algorithms: LSA [15] and STATIS [16], and genetic algorithm [17, 18]. It compares two texts: the template and a given answer (Fig. 2).

The process begins with the template of question and response of question being broken into phrases list, to use the algorithms it was defined that the template of question and response of question would be divided by commas, for each piece of the template of question will be given a value that is used to calculate the final score of the answer.

The similarity between text answer and text template, is used to infer a value for the answer. The value ranges from 0 to 10.

5   Results and Discussion

Respectively, 37 and 42 students had taken the CSA course, in the first and second semesters of. It produces a plenty of data that are organized as the following data sources:

1. DS01 - A questionnaire of 17 questions, of which 8 questions are demographic and 9 questions are the students' sensation about their motivation and engagement at the gamified course. It was used a Likert scale of 5 values. The questionnaire was applied when 3/4 of the course had been completed in both semesters.
2. DS02 - An IMI questionnaire [19] of 27 question (Likert scale of 7 values) to evaluate the Intrinsic Motivation of the students during the course. The questions are categorized as: Interest/Enjoyment (7 questions), Perceived Competence (6 questions), Effort/Importance (5 questions), Pressure/Tension (5 questions) and Value/Usefulness (4 questions).
3. DS03 - A large database (spreadsheet) that reports each individual action of each student during every duel in the battles. It contains information such as the number of earned pataca at each duel, the number of the members of each group, the number and type of collaborations during the battles.

Those data sources are used to answer the following questions:

Q1: Are the students motivated to play the game and Milsa?
Q2: Does the use of Milsa produce Intrinsic Motivation?
Q3: Do the students have an aligned behavior between the battles and the execution of the missions in Milsa?

Following are the results and discussion for those questions.

5.1   Are the Students Motivated to Use Milsa?

In order to measure if the CSA course and Milsa are motivating the students we introduced in DS01 the following questions:

- (Q1.1) Do you see the CSA course as a game?
- (Q1.2) As a game, are you motivated to play it?
- (Q1.3) Do you consider CSA more engaging than other disciplines already done?
- (Q1.4) Do you consider CSA more laborious than other disciplines already done?
- (Q1.5) Do you consider that CSA induces more collaboration/cooperation than other disciplines already done?
- (Q1.6) Would you recommend to a colleague enrolling in the CSA discipline?

The questionnaire was applied on classes during 2016. There are 36 responses ($n = 36$) on 1st semester and 38 responses on 2nd semester ($n2 = 38$). The Cronbach's Alphas are, respectively: 0.736 and 0.807. The results are shown on Table 1.

Table 1.   Results for the engaging questionnaire

Item	1st semester		2nd semester	
	Mean	Sd	Mean	Sd
Q1.1	3.630	1.114	3.763	1.217
Q1.2	3.037	1.125	3.263	1.131
Q1.3	3.815	0.962	3.895	1.180
Q1.4	3.852	1.026	3.237	1.024
Q1.5	3.630	1.043	3.351	1.337
Q1.6	4.000	0.877	4.158	1.078

After analyzing the data, we point out:

- There is a high agreement among the students to recommend the game for a colleague (Q1.6).
- The discipline seems more engaging that other disciplines (Q1.3) and looks as a game (Q1.1).
- There is some indecision about seeing CSA more laborious than other disciplines. At first semester, they have a sensation of more work to do. At the second semester, this value decreased.

In conclusion, there is evidence that the CSA course and Milsa produce engagement and motivation. This is reinforced by the fact that the students highly recommend it to their colleagues. We constructed a gamification on the students' learning process that is implemented as a game. Not a game to be played as learning tool.

5.2   Does the Use of Milsa Produce Intrinsic Motivation?

In the gamified course, the intrinsic motivation is directed by enjoyment in the task of using Milsa, and must exists within the individual rather than relying on external pressures or a desire for consideration.

To analyze the IM for Milsa use at the CSA course, we applied an IMI questionnaire. The 7 questions of the Interest/Enjoyment part follow:

- (Q2.1) I enjoyed using Milsa very much.
- (Q2.2) Milsa was fun to do.
- (Q2.3) I thought Milsa was a boring task (R).
- (Q2.4) Milsa did not hold my attention at all (R).
- (Q2.5) I would describe Milsa as very interesting.
- (Q2.6) I thought Milsa was quite enjoyable.
- (Q2.7) While I was using Milsa, I was thinking about how much I enjoyed it.

The questionnaire was applied only on the second semester of 2016. There are 38 responses (n = 38). The Cronbach's Alpha for the whole questionnaire is 0.815 and 0.852 for the 7 questions of the Interest/Enjoyment category. The results are shown in Table 2.

Table 2. The Interest/Enjoyment category results

	Mean	Sd
Q2.1	4.865	1.669
Q2.2	5.459	1.483
Q2.3	2.027	1.481
Q2.4	1.622	1.114
Q2.5	5.162	1.500
Q2.6	4.514	1.643
Q2.7	4.568	1.692

The conclusions after analyzing the data are:

- The students found Milsa funny (Question 2) and very interesting (Question 5).
- As the value for Question 1 poses, they enjoyed using Milsa very much.

In conclusion, there are good evidences that the students enjoy playing Milsa, and have fun and interest in it, inducing intrinsic motivation.

5.3 Do the Students Have an Aligned Behavior Between the Battles and the Execution of the Missions in Milsa?

We used DS03 to analysis of the aligned between the students' behavior when either playing battle or Milsa is interesting because we can evaluate if the students are trying to cheat or not the gamification.

To analyze this indicator, we established a relation between the number of patacas actually earned and the possible number of patacas that could be obtained by the same player (IndBattle). This ratio is then compared with the number of patacas that the same player won on a given mission in relation to the maximum possible number of patacas for the same mission (IndMission). A thereabout 10% approach margin was used between IndBattle and IndMission, Table 3 depicts the results.

Table 3. IndBattle compared to IndMission

Item	1st semester	2nd semester
	# IndBattle x IndMission	# IndBattle x IndMission
Ind ≤ 0.1	30 students	27 students
Ind > 0.1	7 students	15 students
Total students	37	42
Aligned	81%	64%

Comparing the students of two semesters, the first one presents a higher aligned (81%) than the second semester. A mean of about 72% of the all students have a behavior aligned between classes and their answers at Milsa.

6   A Brief Study on Universal Access and Accessibility Using Milsa

Milsa could be extended as a social network of questions and answers where anyone could both exercises their knowledge on a set of already existent essays and producing essays for others. The essays can be organized by hierarchical subject areas (math, computer science, CSA among others), by difficult levels and by school grades.

Considering the experience of using Milsa in the CSA course, such social network will be very interesting because it may be used anonymously, by anyone, anywhere, anytime. This provides universal access to knowledge and benefits anyone with disabilities in a way similar to the Khan Academy proposal [20], specially to autism.

Next, we discuss some advantages and disadvantages of this network.

Advantages:

1. It could be used anonymously, so people would not worry on failures and be embarrassed on showing them to colleagues.
2. As the essays are produced by people to people that have the same knowledge level, the used language will be very similar and may produce a better learning impact [21].
3. It could be used from anywhere and anytime, providing freedom to the user to interact.
4. Categorization may provide an efficient manner to answer question of one's interests.

Disadvantages:

1. There must some concerns on the language used and translations. Although it is possible to create a categorization to separate languages as in Wikipedia.
2. Some cultural approach may be need, but if the creator of an essay is from the same culture, it would be minimal.
3. The system will heavily use internet.
4. Finally, there would be necessary some sort of moderation. Though this service can be provided by the same users.

Such considerations provide a theoretical reflection of how students with disabilities could have benefits from the use of the Milsa system, extending it as a social network.

7 Conclusion

We got evidences that Milsa are actually contributing to the students' learning process at the CSA gamified course. We conducted and analyzed tests based on data collected at classes and Milsa: individual flow aligned between the classes, the assessments and an Intrinsic Motivation Inventory (IMI) questionnaire.

The students look at Milsa as a continuation classroom. They enjoy the possibility of answering at home, but are also very critic about their questions, the correction of the system and the answers given by others.

We identified that about 72% of the students have a behavior aligned between classes and their answers at Milsa and the students have motivations aligned to their answers at Milsa.

Finally, we suggest the extension of Milsa as a social network and discuss some advantages and disadvantages of its uses, specially, its universal access and accessibility aspects.

Acknowledgments. We would like to thanks FAP/DF regarding financial support, the University of Brasilia – UnB by providing an excellent teaching environment.

References

1. Freitas, S.A.A., Lima, T., Canedo, E.D., Alves, L., Costa, R.L.: Gamificação e avaliação do engajamento dos estudantes em uma disciplina técnica de curso de graduação. In: XXVII Simpósio Brasileiro de Informática na Educação (SBIE) (Uberlândia - MG 2016). doi: 10.5753/cbie.sbie.2016.370
2. Bergmann, J., Sams, A.: Flip Your Classroom: Reach Every Student in Every Class Every Day. International Society for Technology in Education, Washington, DC. (2012). ISBN 1564843157
3. Bernstein, D., Burnett, A.N., Goodburn, A., Savory, P.: Making Teaching and Learning Visible: Course Portfolios and the Peer Review of Teaching. Jossey-Bass, Hoboken (2006)
4. Frinhani, C.L., Freitas, S.A.A., Fernandes, M.V., Canedo, E.D.: An automatic essay correction for an active learning environment. In Proceedings of the 13th ACS/IEEE International Conference on Computer Systems and Applications (Agadir, Morocco 2016). IEEE (2016)
5. Anderson, L.W., Krathwohl, D.R. (eds.): A Taxonomy for Learning, Teaching, and Assessing: A Revision of Bloom's Taxonomy of Educational Objectives. Longman, New York (2001)
6. Bloom, B.S. (ed.): Taxonomy of Educational Objectives, the Classification of Educational Goals – Handbook I: Cognitive Domain. McKay, New York (1956)
7. Entwistle, N., McCune, V.: The conceptual bases of study strategy inventories. Educ. Psychol. Rev. **16**, 325 (2004). doi:10.1007/s10648-004-0003-0
8. McGonigal, J.: Reality Is Broken: Why Games Make Us Better and How They Can Change the World. Penguin Books, London (2011)
9. Chou, Y.-K.: Actionable Gamification: Beyond Points, Badges, and Leaderboards. Leanpub, Victoria (2015)
10. Malone, T.W., Lepper, M.R.: Making learning fun: a taxonomy of intrinsic motivations for learning. In: Snow, R.E., Farr, M.J. (eds.) Aptitude, Learning and Instruction III: Conative and Affective Process Analyses. Erlbaum, Hillsdale (1987)

11. Deterding, S., Sicart, M., Nacke, L., O'Hara, K., Dixon, D.: Gamification: using game-design elements in non-gaming contexts. In: Proceedings of the 2011 Annual Conference on Human Factors in Computing Systems, pp. 2425–2428 (2011)
12. Zichermann, G., Cunningham, C.: Gamification by Design: Implementing Game Mechanics in Web and Mobile Apps. O'Reilly Media, Sebastopol (2011)
13. Hanus, M.D., Fox, J.: Assessing the effects of gamification in the classroom: a longitudinal study on intrinsic motivation, social comparison, satisfaction, effort, and academic performance. Comput. Educ. **80**, 152–161 (2015)
14. Hew, K.F., Huang, B., Chu, K.W.S., Chiu, D.K.W.: Engaging Asian students through game mechanics: findings from two experiment studies. Comput. Educ. **92-93**, 221–236 (2016)
15. Landauer, T.K., Foltz, P.W., Laham, D.: An introduction to latent semantic analysis. Discourse Process. **25**(2), 259–284 (1998)
16. Li, Y., Bandar, Z.A., Mclean, D.: An approach for measuring semantic similarity between words using multiple information sources. IEEE Trans. Knowl. Data Eng. **4**, 871–882 (2003)
17. Michalski, R.S., Bratko, I., Kubat, M.: Machine Learning and Data Mining: Methods and Applications. Wiley, Haboken (1998)
18. Guo, P., Wang, X., Han, Y. The enhanced genetic algorithms for the optimization design. In: 3rd International Conference on Biomedical Engineering and Informatics, pp. 2990–2994 (2010)
19. Ryan, R.M., Connell, J.P., Plant, R.W.: Emotions in non-directed text learning. Learn. Individ. Differ. **2**, 1–17 (1990)
20. Khan, S.: The One World Schoolhouse: Education Reimagined. Twelve (2013)
21. Freitas, S.A.A., Silva, W.C.M.P., Marsicano, G.: Using an active learning environment to increase students' engagement. In: 29th Conference on Software Engineering Education and Training (Dallas - TX 2016), pp. 232–236. IEEE (2016)

A Bridge to Cognition Through Intelligent Games

Carla V.M. Marques, Carlo E.T. Oliveira$^{(\boxtimes)}$, and Claudia L.R. Motta

Universidade Federal do Rio de Janeiro, Rio de Janeiro, Brazil
{carla.veronica, carlo, claudiam}@nce.ufrj.br

Abstract. Computational neuropedagogy applies neuroscience to the problem of learning, whilst learning is intrinsic to the process of understanding. An intelligent game is a neuropedagogical ludic instrument constructed through a scientific process to achieve introspection into cognitive aspects of human reasoning.

The postulate of universal access presupposes a universal cognition apparatus, and fortunately this is the case. Contrariwise, what is not the case is a presupposed uniformly developed apparatus, equally available in each individual. Understanding and accounting for the distinct configuration of each individual is a requirement of universal knowledge access. Intelligent games can cleverly access a non mediated view of the cognition machine.

This work presents an intelligent game calibrated to three developmental dimensions to collect vestiges from the internal cognition engine, revealing the innards of EICA. EICA is the Engine of Internal Cognitive Acquisition, universally installed in every human brain which is responsible for the main course of cognition process. Learning is accomplished by the EICA machine, consisting of eight recognized hierarchical states ranging from simple to high complexity.

The inference that cognition machinery is equally available to every person is the principle behind the proposition of an effective universal access to knowledge. Monitoring the EICA machine performance is a mean to assess and even adapt the process of learning. Under the universal access principle, this means that beyond all the differences that uniquely identify each individual, everyone can have access to knowledge through intelligent systems.

Keywords: Neuroscience · Neuropedagogy · Cognition · Games · Accessibility · Knowledge · Learning

1 Introduction

Computational neuropedagogy applies neuroscience to the problem of learning. In the intent to achieve this it produces instruments to assess and intervene in human learning. Intelligent games are examples of such instruments, being computer games developed through a elaborated scientific process. These games purport to achieve introspection into cognitive aspects of learning. They can tap into the unconscious process of learning and interchange information between computer and human cognition.

© Springer International Publishing AG 2017
M. Antona and C. Stephanidis (Eds.): UAHCI 2017, Part III, LNCS 10279, pp. 223–232, 2017.
DOI: 10.1007/978-3-319-58700-4_19

An intelligent game is piece of software designed to provide a direct interface to the human cognitive engine. The scientific process preceding the conception of such a game takes several steps to convey the theoretical statements into programmable code features. The construction of a dimensional model is the principle of a intelligent game fit to explore a given cognitive space. A cognition domain so defined is bound to activate the corresponding cognitive functions in the brain learning mechanism.

This model uses phylogenetic, ontogenetic and microgenetic dimensions [3] to synchronize with the internal cognitive machine and collect details about its functionality. Those dimensions constrain cognitive operations to the realm of learning procedures, together with the respective probing reactions. Amidst the many signals obtained from those reactions, some can be investigated in search of telltale vestiges of internal gears behind its performance. Those vestiges are detected and discriminated to correspond to what theory predicts about leaning. The aforementioned discriminating machine provides an unmediated channel into the mind, capable of monitoring the cognition innards.

Such direct interface into human cognition is useful in assessing individual competences and levels of understanding of episodic frames. Effective access to knowledge implies in a formal understanding and interconnection of the whole set of information acquired by sensory channels. Follows that, in this sense, universal access requires scaffolding beyond just viso-motor and audio-phonetic senses and interfaces. Evaluating the coalescence of cognition processes into terminal forms can provide assessment to the level of true understanding.

2   The Observability of Cognition

Cognition is an internal process mostly unaccessible from the conscious mind. As Penrose [1] remarks, consciousness is a process occurring as deep as quantum events in microtubules inside brains cells. Down below in brain functionality is the cognition process, even deeper away from consciousness, mostly pertaining to subconscious thought. The hermetic quality of those processes poses an apparent insurmountable obstacle to direct observation with available technology for years to come. At psychogenesis level, some testing can assess intellectual development, since it is a process taking place is a span of years. Microgenesis, evolving in the short span of minutes, leaves scarce traces of is whatabouts.

In the microgenetic dimension, several microprocesses concatenate to complete a chain of understanding that embodies the human reasoning. If any of these processes is broken, there is no real access to the information, since it has no meaning. There are several theories on how microgenetics works. Inhelder [6] draws the most acknowledged theory, solidly drawing from the extensive works of her colleague, Jean Piaget. Kienits [4] extends Inhelder view to more recent experiments.

Microgenetics defines a set of states and a procedure to walk through these states using an internal encoding and processing befit to brain innards. Microgenetic theory affirms that those states and processes must exist, notwithstanding the lack of access to the actual states or transactions of mind. In principle, all brains should feature the same structure and the same learning machine original installation. However, individual brain formation process and cultural interactions tend to reconfigure some areas to be prevalent and detrimental to others. Therefore, microgenesis theories implies in a sort of machine existing in each and every brain, capable of stepping through all these states to complete the cognitive process.

On the empirical side, waywardly to theory expectations, instead of a consistently staging of learning performances, what comes about is a large diversity of cognition abilities scattered among human population. Such diversity sources from the psychogenic formation and matching predisposition of brain abilities from phenotypical DNA expression.

3 Universal Access and Cognition Paradigms

Universal access presupposes a universal cognition apparatus. The universality of learning capabilities is a recurring theory in many fields, being Chomsky [2] one of its most regarded and influential scientist. Assuring universal access to information from the cognitive side requires monitoring the effectiveness of learning. The prevailing trend on the effort towards knowledge access is standardize the education system. The purpose is the implantation of a homogeneous cognition apparatus in each and very individual. Although seemingly a noble, even utopic errand, might not be totally beneficial or even attainable to the human race.

Acknowledging and accounting for the distinct installment of each individual cognition is a better proposal for universal knowledge accessibility. Preserving the natural variations on the individual cognitive machinery is a less intrusive approach. Diversity is a defensive asset for any species, catering for fluctuations of environmental conditions. Instead of attempting the elimination of differences, they must be accounted for and harmonized to bring about the required level of understanding acknowledgeable as universal access to cognition.

The utmost perspective of cognition assertion should consist of tapping into the brain machinery and observe the completion of the knowledge acquisition process. Yet, issuing from the complexity and encapsulation of its innards, cognition internal gears remains mostly unobservable whatsoever. Nevertheless, inspection of cognition machinery is still a feasible undertaking taking into consideration its products, particularly to its byproducts. Follows that cognition is the driving force behind most volitive reactions. Operating behind the scenes, cognition merges into its responses apparently unintentional artifacts. Considering those artifacts as inherent outcomes of cognition operations, they elicit as subtle clues of its mechanism.

Inferably, most volitive responses that encompass a motor activity originate ultimately from transitions inside the cognitive machinery. Transitions are convulsive physical events incurring in telltale evidence, namely high order harmonics, that may propagate unintentionally through the whole system and end up as an elusive signature of cognitive state shifting.

A cognition tracking machine can then log the acquisition process and mark the level of understanding attained. Postulating on the existence of a cognition machine, more precisely an automaton, cognitive processes evolves propositionally in a cascade of entangled and coordinated automata operations. More plainly stated, the full process of understanding develops inside the cognitive machinery as continuous flow of intercommunicating languages across the several automata engaged in the reasoning effort. Thereafter, the whole process of accessing and acquiring a knowledge transcribes to a collection of scripts in a language circumscribed to the mental realm, unrelated to any other human language. Capturing and interpreting the internal cognition language is the key to assess the score of understanding.

4   An Instrument to Investigate the Cognition Engine

Theory suggests cognition as a pipeline of languages (Seminerio [5]), cascading the refinement of understanding up to the higher levels of abstraction. A suitable model of language processing exerting the computation of meaning comprises of a collection of automata. Investigation of automata can be procured by exercising input states that steps the machine across a conspicuous walkthrough of its operation.

4.1   Development of a Research Mode

Given a theoretical model of the analyzed machine, ensues the protocol required to reverse engineer the language processing mechanism. Figure 1 depicts the original theoretical machine model, based in studies of human linguistics. Named states and proposed transitions presuppose a linear progression in the interpretation of meaning.

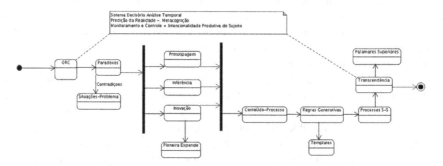

Fig. 1. Theoretical model of cognitive learning finite state machine

Since the study purposes the investigation of the learning process, a suitable dimensional space involves three views of temporal development spans. Those dimensions recur in the learning procedures and represent evolution in three scalar ranges, namely phylogenetic, ontogenetic and microgenetic. Figure 2 represents a fragment of the phylogenetic dimension. Learning is represented by the human achievements in mathematics, language and science in prehistoric periods.

A complete dimensional model was developed to infuse the required stimuli into the learning apparatus in order to capture the full transactional profile inherent to cognitive language processing. An intelligent game was designed and calibrated to

Scenario	Historical Context	Technological Artifact	Description	Linguistic Artifact	Description	Mathematical Concept	Description
	2000000 B.C. – Lower Paleolithic	Staff	It could be any piece of wood used for personal defense and exploitation.	Color differentiation	Part of the understanding of visual languages	Groups	Used for food group differentiation
	200000 B.C. – Middle Paleolithic	Fire	Essential for protection from cold and predators and for feeding	Signs	Used before the development of spoken languages	Food Counting	Necessary to ensure the feeding of the whole group
	30000 B.C. – Upper Paleolithic	Ink	In the cave paintings, blood, clay, latex, fat, egg white, iron oxide, etc. were used.	Cave paintings	Predecessors of any organized writing system	Cave paintings	Essential in a time when there were no numbering systems

Fig. 2. Phylogenetic dimension with historic marker of cognitive evolution

Fig. 3. The intelligent game for EICA

three developmental dimensions to collect vestiges from the internal cognition engine and unveil the minutia of the language processing automata.

The game (Fig. 3) takes the form of a scene where a paleolithic character try to make his way into the observation of the world in which he lives. Carefully designed assets conducts the caveman actions into the prospective realm of cognition, forcing advances an retrogresses in the reasoning process, coupled with the respective volitionary investigative reactions determined by the internal automata.

This automata, entitled to compile the incoming sensory information into cognitive knowledge have being identified in Marques [7] as the Engine of Internal Cognition Acquisition (EICA). EICA is a neurobiological computing apparatus installed ubiquitously in human brains which endows any individual with the cognition proceedings characteristic to the Homo Sapiens species. This machine is the evolutionary solution to achieve the high level of abstraction responsible for the outstanding human cognitive abilities.

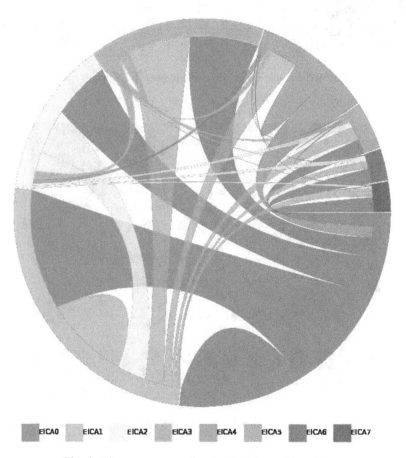

Fig. 4. Ideogram representing EICA states and transitions

4.2 Anatomy of the Cognitive Machinery

The instrumentation and observation of EICA requires a complex study and development process capable of exposing the subtle telltale traces of internal cognition machinery. The basis to the aforementioned intelligent game is the exertion of the learning process. Learning is accomplished by the EICA machine, consisting of eight recognized hierarchical states, ranging from simple to high complexity.

EICA is the essence of human learning machinery, consisting of a finite state machine in which each subsequent state correspond to a more complex cognitive achievement. Observed in EICA tracking experiments, eight recognizable states are the hallmark of the cognition automata, shown in Fig. 4.

Colored sections represent the states and colored arcs indicate the transitions between states. Cognitive acquisition cycles follows sensory information with volitive prospectives responses emanating from evolving or involving transitions in EICA states. The ideogram demonstrates that beyond the linear perspective of the theoretical model, transitions occurs to non adjacent states and in both forward an backward directions.

Ensuing transitive streams develop into concatenated expressions of meaning, imprinting the effectuated access to the given information as new linguistic nodes in the epistemic knowledge network. Although restrained to internal communication interchange among the internal cognitive structures those linguistic nodes can be observed to be the same across non related individuals. The reverse engineering necessary for that consists of inducing the volitionary response through the retrace of phylogenetic, ontogenetic and microgenetic path development. The prospecting instrument for cognitive unveillance guides the acquisition machinery into retracing the three dimensional

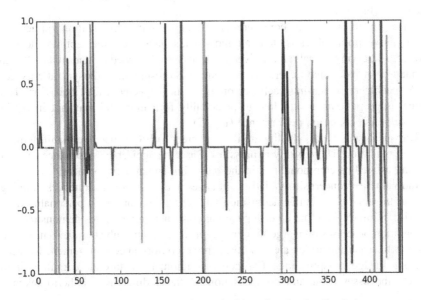

Fig. 5. Emerging pattern already marked in colors by the discriminator

ranges of thought development, namely the evolution of reasoning within the species, within the development of an individual and within the coalescence of an idea.

4.3   The Microgenetic-Paleopathic Resonance

The foremost feature of this intelligent game resides in exploiting the microgenetic-paleopathic resonance to expose the innards of the learning cognitive apparatus. Encompassing the whole stream of prospective reactions, emerges a common pattern, recognizable for every and each individual. The pattern features a rhythmical response interwoven with seemingly chaotic jitter, apparently disconnected of the given information. The microgenetic-paleopathic resonance or Resonance of Marques [7] consisting of coupling between the high energy nervous motricity impulses and the faint and undetectable occurrence of transitions within the cognition machinery. A precisely calibrated analog-digital discriminator can recognize and trace (Fig. 5) the disturbance in the output signal caused by the originating cognitive computation of meaning orchestrated by the EICA machinery. EICA state set is evenly distributed among even the smallest and heterogeneous population, notwithstanding the fact that it differs for each an every person, difference which must be circumvented to convey equality of understanding and universal access to information and learning.

4.4   Depicting the Cognitive Landscape

The EICA machine operation complies with a rather strict deterministic behavior which is the same in every individual observed in the available experiments. The temporal distribution of states and transitions are rather logic and regular across the sampled population (Fig. 6).

Equity in EICA machine configuration among the human population implies, from the cognitive point of view, that all individuals have the same aptitude to learn, therefore deserving equal and universal access to knowledge and understanding. Uniqueness in individual experience and education results in a idiosyncratic usage of EICA machinery, departing each person from the expected EICA behavior. Those unique usage patterns are kindred to personality formation and may not imply in a better or worse cognition performance (Fig. 7).

Universality and individuality are both inherent to EICA machine manifestation in human population. Universality express itself as a recognizable consonance of operation and as well as commonalities in the reasoning stream development.

Individuality concerns to variations in states and transitional sequences defining a peculiar traversal of cognitive acquisition landscape singularizing a personality driven behavior. Similarities in the diverse meaning construction narratives demonstrates that all cognition processes converge to a prototypical epistemic subject quiescent in every person whilst particularities alert to an adaptive conformance requirement for accessible knowledge outspreading. The personal idiomatic nature of cognition inflow requires the assessment and compensation of those differences hitherto taken for

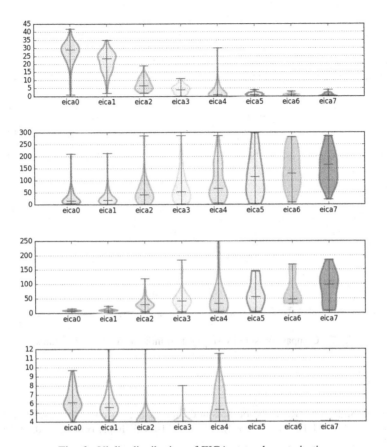

Fig. 6. Violin distribution of EICA state characterization

granted in education, eventually hindering the establishment of a universal access to knowledge.

4.5 Learning Process and Effective Accessibility

Understanding both the universality and nonuniversality of cognition process assures that learning is accessible to any human being at any level. The inference that cognition machinery is equally available to every person is the principle sustaining the proposition for an effective universal access. However, unique and personalized use case profile of EICA states provides both for essential diversity and complexity for effective and efficient learning. Monitoring EICA machine performance is a mean to assess and even adapt the process of learning.

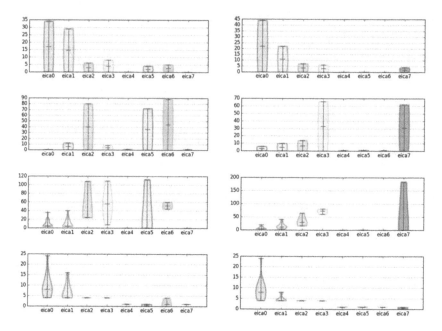

Fig. 7. Comparison side by side of two individual EICA signatures

References

1. Hameroff, S., Penrose, R.: Consciousness in the universe: a review of the 'Orch OR' theory. Phys. Life Rev. **11**(1), 39–78 (2014). ISSN 1571-0645. http://dx.doi.org/10.1016/j.plrev. 2013.08.002
2. Chomsky, N.: Aspects of the Theory of Syntax, vol. 11. MIT press, Cambridge (2014)
3. Langer, J.: Phylogenetic and ontogenetic origins of cognition: classification. In: Piaget, Evolution, and Development, pp. 33–54 (1998)
4. Lemos, M.K., Motta, C.L.R., Marques, C.V.M., Oliveira, C.E.T., Fróes, M., e Silva, J.O.P.: Fio Condutor Microgenético: uma metodologia para a mediação metacognitiva em jogos computacionais. Revista Brasileira de Informática na Educação **22**, 1–17 (2014)
5. Seminério, F.L.P.: Infra-estrutura da cognição: fatores ou linguagens? Rio de Janeiro: FGV; ISOP (1984)
6. Inhelder, B.: Le cheminement des découvertes de lénfant. Recherche sur les microgenèses cognitives. Delachaux et Niestlé, Paris (1992)
7. Marques, C.V.M.: Eica - Estruturas Internas Cognitivas Aprendentes: Um Modelo Neuro-Computacional Aplicado À Instância Psíquica Do Sistema Pessoa Em Espaços Dimensionais. [doctorate thesis], p. 195. Universidade Federal do Rio de Janeiro, Rio de Janeiro (RJ - Brazil) (2017)

Chatbot and Dialogue Demonstration with a Humanoid Robot in the Lecture Class

Shu Matsuura$^{(\boxtimes)}$ and Riki Ishimura

Faculty of Education, Tokyo Gakugei University,
4-1-1 Nukuikita, Koganei, Tokyo 184-8501, Japan
shumats0@gmail.com

Abstract. This paper describes ideas to extend the way of verbal lecture visually and verbally. Firstly, we conducted questionnaires to the first-year university students of the science education. As for the attention to the verbal and visual information, we noticed participants' worry about keeping following with the verbal lecturing. We also noticed the participants' preference for the visual presentation. These imply a potential necessity of visual presentation that supplements the lecturer's speech in a real time. On the other hand, the results showed a preference for the learning under familiar atmosphere. For the visualization of lecture talk, we created a chatbot on the platform of Api.ai to exhibit a brief explanation or a question of the words as the lecturer utters them. This text visualization provides the basis of the lecture in sync of lecturer's talk. We also used a humanoid robot for verbal presentation as a partner of the lecturer. The Topic Maps was introduced to build the dialogues for analogy and association. The analogy topic map was constructed based on a Japanese entertainment riddle. Robot dialogues were conducted by connecting an online learning system based on Topic Maps.

Keywords: Chatbot · Topic maps · Humanoid robot NAO · Online learning system

1 Introduction

For lecturers of higher education, the lecturing is a performance and interaction with the participants. Such a performance is an interface of knowledge and information for the participants. Also, it is an opportunity to think by themselves or with others on the related issues. The role of the lecturer is not simply transmitting the knowledge anymore as the information is becoming more and more ubiquitous for the people of any generation. Rather, the lecture has to inspire the participants to become positive in thinking, feeling, acting, and establishing the knowledge.

Skills of lecturing as a performing art have been studied elaborately [1]. Recently, more and more new technology has been applied to make the lecture interactive and experience rich based on the learning theories. Applications of the artificial intelligence and communication robot are two hot topics to explore the future learning. However, we should be aware of the demand of actual participants to the lecture room, and at the same time, how the technology can be unified with the lecturer's specific art of performing.

© Springer International Publishing AG 2017
M. Antona and C. Stephanidis (Eds.): UAHCI 2017, Part III, LNCS 10279, pp. 233–246, 2017.
DOI: 10.1007/978-3-319-58700-4_20

In this study, we conduct a questionnaire survey to clarify the classroom participants' tendencies. Then, we attempt to introduce a text visualization that supplements
the lecture's talk on sync. Further, we use a humanoid robot to introduce a dialogue that
stimulates participants' intuition within the lecture's logical talk. In this study, we
describe these attempts and the results of participants' attitude survey.

2   Method

To survey the tendency of students' preference for the visual and verbal presentation,
questionnaires with five ranks Likert scale were made and conducted to the 1st-grade
university students in a science education classroom. The total number of students
participated was 53. The questions were on the logical tendency and the preference for
expression and learning. The survey was carried out after a brief introductory practice
of the following terminology visualization and robot talk.

The terminology visualization we developed is a chatbot using the api.ai conver-
sational user experience platform [2]. The terminologies used in the lecture are registered for detection through voice recognition of a PC. For the response words of the
chatbot, we registered the short texts of the meaning, definitions, comments, or simple
questions on the terms. The chatbot service was developed and implemented on the api.
ai website. At the classroom, opening the chatbot page, the lecturer turns on the voice
recognition when to pronounce the registered words. Then the chatbot replies the texts
to explain the term. The texts shown in the chatbot page are displayed in the LCD
hanged from the roof.

For verbal communications, we used a humanoid robot NAO [3]. NAO has vision
and voice recognition and can talk with the human. NAO's emotional expression has
also been applied to the interactive teaching [4]. NAO can transmit URL requests
through Wi-Fi and receives XML or JSON data.

One of the authors has developed an online learning system, "Everyday Physics on
Web (EPW) [5]," based on Topic Maps, a standard of indexing technology (ISO/IEC
13250:2003). This website was meant for the support of introductory science and
science education lectures.

Topic Maps constitute of "*topic*," "*association*," and "*occurrence*," where a *topic*
represents an entity, an *association* links two topics, and *occurrence* links a *topic* to the
actual web materials on the *topic*. Various types of *associations* are defined so that the
topics and the *topic* instances are structured using various types of *associations*.

EPW has been developed on the basis of the Ontopia development and runtime
environment for Topic Maps [6, 7]. Ontopia Topic Maps remote access protocol
(TMRAP) enabled URL requests by the Topic Maps query language. EPW ontology
and the way to access EPW from NAO have already been described briefly in [8].

3 Result and Discussion

3.1 Questionnaire

Table 1 shows the list of the questions together with their shortened index phrases and the average values of the answers obtained. The index phrases are used to retrieve the questions from the figures in this section. Error values indicate the corrected sample standard deviations. These questions were delivered after a brief trial of the text visualization and the robot dialogue with an instructor. The list was arranged in the descending order of the mean value.

Table 1. Questions on learning and average values.

No.	Question	Shortened index of question	(average) ± (sample standard deviation)
Q1	Do you understand things better, when you feel familiar with them?	Familiarity Brings Understanding	4.3 ± 0.7
Q2	Do you obtain information mainly by vision?	Obtain Information By Vision	4.0 ± 0.9
Q3	Do you think the structured knowledge is most important to comprehend things?	Structured Knowledge Important	$3.9(8) \pm 0.9$
Q4	Do you memorize others' words well?	Memorize Others' Words	3.8 ± 1.0
Q5	Do you understand things better, when you are smiling?	Understanding While Smiling	3.8 ± 0.9
Q6	Do you understand things better, when your feel relaxed?	Understanding While Relaxing	3.7 ± 1.1
Q7	Do you think you mainly use words to think?	Think With Words	$3.6(9) \pm 1.2$
Q8	Do you like to be provided of inspiring expressions on the things you need to comprehend or attain?	Inspiring Information	$3.6(6) \pm 1.0$
Q9	Do you think a sense of unity between you and the things is most important before comprehending it with words?	Sense Of Unity	$3.6(0) \pm 1.1$
Q10	Do you prefer rational understanding?	Rational Understanding	$3.5(6) \pm 1.2$
Q11	Are you interested in the dialogue between two or more person rather than the monologue in speech?	Prefer Dialogue	$3.5(2) \pm 1.0$
Q12	Do you tend to understand things intuitively?	Intuitive Understanding	$3.4(5) \pm 1.1$

(continued)

Table 1. (*continued*)

No.	Question	Shortened index of question	(average) ± (sample standard deviation)
Q13	Do you feel the inspiration is most important to comprehend things?	Inspiration To Comprehend	3.3 ± 1.3
Q14	Do you remember a monologue better than dialogue?	Remember Monologue Better Than Dialogue	3.2(2) ± 1.2
Q15	Does the speech of one person rather than the dialogue between two or more persons attract you?	Speech Attracts Better Than Dialogue	3.2(0) ± 1.1
Q16	Can you keep concentration on lecturer's long talks?	Keep Concentration On Talk	3.0 ± 1.3
Q17	Do you understand things better, when you feel tense?	Understanding While Feeling Tense	2.9 ± 1.2
Q18	Do visual images added to the text distract you?	Image Distracts	2.5 ± 1.2

We found five underlying tendencies from Table 1 as described below.

Tendency 1: Q1, 5, 6, and 17 show that the participants feel they can understand things better under pleasant and relaxed state than when they feel tense.

Tendency 2: Q2, 4, and 18 show that the participants memorize things well from the verbal information, while many of them obtain information from visual symbols. However, the result of Q16 shows that many of them feel difficulty to keep their concentration on the instructor's long talks.

Tendency 3: Q3, 7, and 10 show that many of the participants infer rationally based on the established knowledge. This rationality might reflect that the participants belong to the science education division of the faculty of education, and most of them have strength in the subjects of sciences. They can make use of the established scientific concepts to consider the real problems.

Tendency 4: Q8, 9, 12, and 13 show that some of the participants have a tendency of comprehending intuitively. They might feel that inspiration is important.

Tendency 5: Q11, 14, and 15 indicate that a part of participants prefers a straight-forward explanation in a monologue style. Also, a part of participants feels interested in the dialogue better than monologue.

Figure 1 shows a histogram of participants' answers concerning the tendency 1. 32% of them agreed or strongly agreed that they understand well while feeling tense. As shown in Table 2, the correlation coefficient ρ between "Understanding While Feeling Tense" and "Understanding While Relaxing" indicates that they are negatively correlated. Thus, as a learning condition, some students may prefer relaxing atmosphere while others prefer tense. Furthermore, 85% of participants agreed or strongly agreed that they have a better understanding when they feel familiarity on the subject.

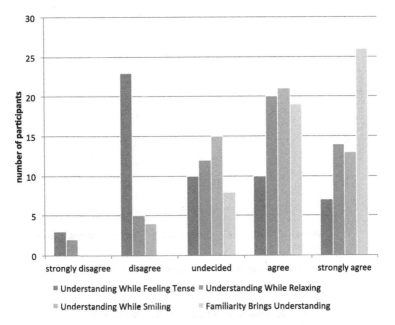

Fig. 1. Histogram of answers for tendency 1

Table 2. Correlation coefficients ρ for tendency 1

Indices of questions examined	ρ	p-value
"Understanding While Feeling Tense" vs. "Understanding While Relaxing"	-0.49	2.0×10^{-4}
"Familiarity Brings Understanding" vs. "Understanding While Relaxing"	0.51	1.0×10^{-4}

"Familiarity Brings Understanding" is also moderately correlated with "Understanding While Smiling" with the correlation coefficient of 0.51. This correlation implies that at least for a part of students, a moderate humor possibly makes their mind open for thinking and learning the subject.

Figure 2 shows the histogram of the answers on visual and verbal information gain indicated as tendency 2. 75% and 70% of participants agreed or strongly agreed that they obtain and memorize information visually and verbally, respectively. The answers for "Obtain Information By Vision" and "Memorize Others' Word" showed no correlation, with the coefficient of 0.09. However, to understand a lecturer's talk, one has to keep attention to the talk, thinking on the meaning of what they hear synchronously. 38% of participants disagreed or strongly disagreed with "Keep Concentration On Talk." This anxiety in keeping attention suggests participants' needs on the supplemental visual presentation. In many cases, the lecturer uses the blackboard or the presentation tools for summarizing or enrich the verbal explanation.

Figure 3 shows the histogram on the tendency 3 concerning the participants' understanding. 74% of participants agreed or strongly agreed on the importance of the

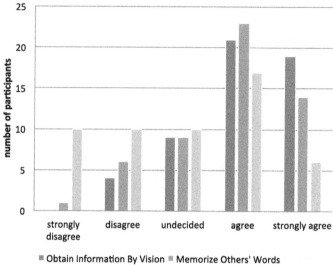

Fig. 2. Histogram of answers for tendency 2

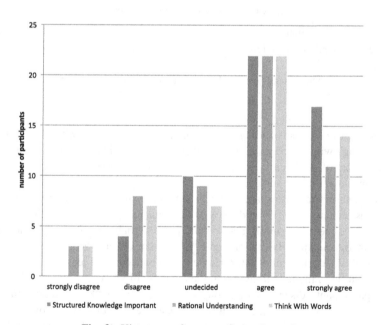

Fig. 3. Histogram of answers for tendency 3

Table 3. Correlation coefficients ρ for tendency 3

Indices of questions examined	ρ	p-value
"Rational Understanding" vs. "Think With Words"	0.53	4.7×10^{-5}
"Rational Understanding" vs. "Structured Knowledge Important"	0.45	7.0×10^{-4}

structured knowledge as the base of learning. The science-oriented students are particularly trained to consider things based on the established knowledge on nature or mathematics. The answers on "Rational Understanding" was found moderately correlated with "Think With Words" with the correlation coefficient of 0.53, as well as with "Structured Knowledge Important" with that of 0.45 as shown in Table 3. This implies the particular importance of the participants' use of words on scientific concepts for both thinking and learning. Therefore, it may be meaningful to reinforce the students' knowledge structure by providing such as the definition of terminology or the knowledge that supports the concepts that the lecturer uses.

On the other hand, inspiration and intuition are also essential factors for the scientific inference. Particularly, the heuristic consideration or abductive reasoning in the scientific exploration cannot be without inspiration and intuition. Figure 4 for the tendency 4 shows the histogram on these functions of the mind. 47% of participants agreed or strongly agreed with the both of the questions "Inspiration To Comprehend" and "Intuitive Understanding." As shown in Table 4, the moderate correlations are

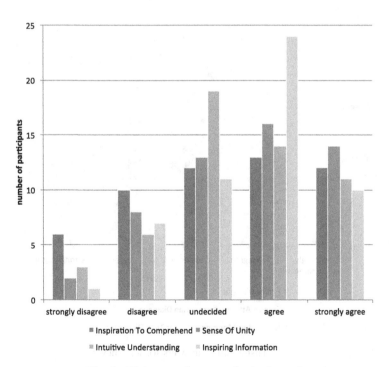

Fig. 4. Histogram of answers for tendency 4

Table 4. Correlation coefficients ρ for tendency 4

Indices of questions examined	ρ	p-value
"Inspiration To Comprehend" vs. "Sense Of Unity"	0.52	7.0×10^{-5}
"Sense Of Unity" vs. "Intuitive Understanding"	0.56	1.3×10^{-5}
"Intuitive Understanding" vs. "Inspiration To Comprehend"	0.63	5.1×10^{-7}

found among the results of the above items and "Sense Of Unity." On the other hand, 64% of participants agreed or strongly agreed with the expectation of "Inspiring Information." The last question showed no correlation with the former three questions. Thus, the students seem to require an inspiring component in the instruction, regardless of whether they have intuitive or rational tendency of reasoning.

Figure 5 shows the histogram on the tendency 5, which is about the participants' preference for the monologue and dialogue form of verbal presentations. In the traditional large classroom lecture on natural sciences, the lecturer makes a step-by-step explanation in the monologue form, using a blackboard. This style is efficient as an explanation of the theory construct, as far as the students can catch up with the talk. This will hold for 36% of the participants who agreed or strongly agreed with "Speech Attracts Better Than Dialogue," and will also be true for 45% of participants who agreed or strongly agreed with "Remember Monologue Better Than Dialogue."

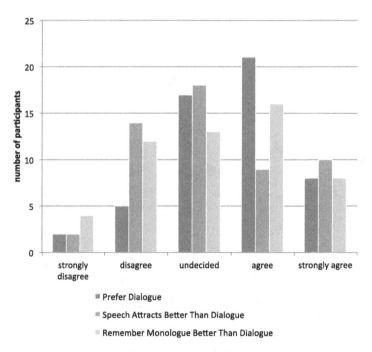

Fig. 5. Histogram of answers for tendency 5

Table 5. Correlation coefficients ρ for tendency 5

Indices of questions examined	ρ	p-value
"Remember Monologue Better Than Dialogue" vs. "Speech Attracts Better Than Dialogue"	0.53	4.7×10^{-15}
"Remember Monologue Better Than Dialogue" vs. "Prefer Dialogue"	-0.51	9.0×10^{-5}

However, on the other hand, 55% of participants agreed or strongly agreed with "Prefer Dialogue." This result indicates that the dialogue between two or more peoples stimulates the participants more than monologue by a single lecturer. Also, as seen in Table 5, "Prefer Dialogue" showed a negative correlation with "Remember Monologue Better Than Dialogue." Thus, in the classroom, a part of participants prefer dialogue form of presentation.

3.2 Visualization of Speech Contents

Terminology visualization chatbot was applied in three sessions of successive lectures. This lecture aimed at providing opportunities to the students to reconsider the roles and the issues of science education based on the human history and the tasks for the construction of future society. Therefore, sometimes the students need to review the meanings or definitions of the sociological terminology.

We provided brief explanations of a number of terms that the lecturer utters in the classroom, using the terminology visualization chatbot. The examples of the terms visualized are, "layer," "identity," "nation state," "1st, 2nd, 3rd, 4th industrial revolution," "capitalism," "frontier," "democracy," "big government," "small government," "neoliberalism," "state socialism, " "the world is flat," "fluidity of labor," etc. In case speaker's verbal input is not matched by any of the words defined, one of the phrases predetermined for simple response are replied, such as, "indeed," "well," "then?" etc. To display the terms, the lecturer started verbal recognition on PC just before speaking the term. The display of each terminology was not repeated many times. Rather the lecturer showed the visualization mostly once for each term in the introductory phase of the lecture.

Table 6 shows the summary of the participants' comments on the terminology visualization. These comments were collected at the end of second practice using the e-learning system. At this time, the participants were already so familiar with the display that some of them said they forgot to notice the display most of the lecture time. 48% of the participants commented positive effect of the display. The lecturer can display the terms at an appropriate timing according to his intent and can continue to talk recognizing that the participants notice the display.

However, 26% of participants feared about losing attention to the lecturer by noticing the display. Particularly, loss of concentration seemed to occur when one notice the miss-recognition of speech. Application of the machine learning of verbal recognition and adaptation to the lecture might improve the system.

Table 6. Summary of the comments on the terminology visualization

Content of comment	Percentage of participants [%]
By displaying explanations of the terms, it became possible to understand the content of the lecture smoothly	48
It will be of the assistance to students with hearing disabilities or inconvenience	26
The degree of concentration on the lecture will be reduced if we see the miss-display associated with miss-recognition of speech	26
Improvement of display or user interface is necessary	17
It may be particularly useful in certain situations, such as when conducting science experiments, practical training or large lecture meetings	13

13% of participants noted that this tool might help the students who have any inconvenience in the hearing. Normally, the lecturer prepares a visual presentation or the blackboard usage. Terminology visualization will supplement them effectively.

Besides, some participants pointed out the following problem. Although checking the uncertain terminology on time is quite smooth for following the lecture, it could be important that the learner review by him/herself the uncertain terms after the lecture. Some rearrangements might be necessary for the lecture design, to avoid making the learners passive on gaining knowledge.

3.3 Dialogue with Humanoid Robot

We made use of the humanoid robot NAO to provide verbal communication in the form of dialogue with the lecturer. In comparison with the terminology visualization, which supports the establishment of structured knowledge in the lecture, the dialogue with the humanoid robot rather contributes to building a humorous atmosphere. Also, we attempt to build a possible way to include intuitiveness or inspiration in the dialogue form. Particularly, we focus the analogy and the association in the following sections.

Analogy and *Nazokake*. The purpose of this dialogue is to use an analogy to make the scientific concept easier to understand. We connect scientific notions with daily life things that are imaginable for the learners of a wide range of the age.

Nazokake is a form of the riddle that is often done by the professional entertainer [9]. *Nazokake* connects two completely different entities with a common hidden feature. The homophony in the Japanese language is often used for this common feature. Also, conceptual similarity or equality is used as well. *Nazokake* is successful if the difference between the two entities is surprising and the finding of the hidden connection is amazing. Since the rule of *Nazokake* is clear, there are some attempts to generate *Nazokake* automatically using semantic relationships [10].

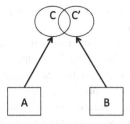

Fig. 6. Relationships of *Nazokake* elements

Figure 6 shows the relationships of *Nazokake* elements. A and B are two different entities. In the *Nazokake* play, the starting entity A is given as a question. After the player answers B to the question A, he is asked what is hidden behind them. Then he reveals C(C'), as the main part of the humor. In the figure, C is associated with A, and C' is associated with B. C and C' are homophonic words or they have the similar meanings. To answer *Nazokake*, one firstly finds several C's, and then finds the candidates of C' and B. Finally, the answerer selects the best combination of A and B.

Here, we consider the case that B is an analogy of A, and A is a scientific concept. Although A can be understood logically, learners might map the new notions to the already attained knowledge established in their minds to recognize the notion. That is, it is helpful to understand A by an analogy of B that is already familiar to the learner. To find the familiar topic B via our online learning system, we next apply the method of solving *Nazokake*.

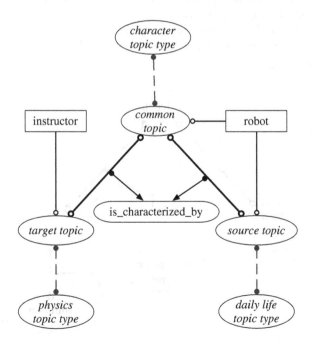

Fig. 7. Topic map ontology of analogy

Figure 7 shows a topic map ontology to find a *source topic* B from a *target topic* A. Let the *target topic* in question A is a *topic instance* of physics subject. Let A be "evaporation" for example. Assume the instructor intend to explain a temperature decrease caused by the evaporation. That is, evaporating molecules take away the kinetic energy from the liquid. The liquid molecules collide with each other transferring kinetic energy. As some molecules obtain enough kinetic energy to get out of the intermolecular force of liquid molecules, they evaporate, and their kinetic energy is taken away from the liquid. This situation may be named as "deprived of heat." An analogous situation in the *daily life topic* is for example "a debut of a fellow." A fellow in an amateur band group gets public fame. Then, he/she gets away to be professional, and, in turn, the band gets less active for a while. This amateur band *topic* B can be related with A in the context of "deprived of heat." We register a *topic* of "deprive of heat" as C. Now the *topic* C (in general partially) characterizes both A and B. Both A - C and B - C are associated by is_characterized_by *association* as shown in the figure. Finding an appropriate C in agreement with the intent of the instructor, the system can retrieve B as an analogy of A.

Association. Association also refers to the connection of two different entities that share some common natures or similarities. Association is thought to contribute to the construction of inspiration-oriented dialogue. In this study, we consider "speaking of" pattern introduction of a *topic*.

Figure 8 shows the topic map for generating the following simple dialogue.
Instructor: This is the year of Rooster. Speaking of the Rooster Zodiac?
NAO: Speaking of the Rooster Zodiac, I recall the chicken.
Instructor: Speaking of the chicken?
NAO: Speaking of the chicken, I recall the egg.
Instructor: Can you tell me an experiment on the egg?
NAO: Spinning egg.

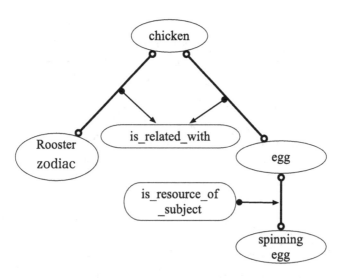

Fig. 8. Topic map for simple dialogue to find associated *topic*

The instructor can talk more in the intervals of these dialogue patterns. In the topic map, a neutral *association*, is_related_with, links "Rooster Zodiac," "chicken," and "egg" with each other. A specific *association*, is_resource_of_subject, links "egg" with a simple experiment demonstration "spinning egg."

The *topic* "chicken" may have relations with the subjects other than "egg" and "Rooster Zodiac." The robot reaches "egg" in the repetition of a fixed phrase "Speaking of?" Implementation of more targeted recalling is a future problem.

Participants' responses. Table 7 shows the questions on the humanoid robot demonstration and the average values of the results. Table 8 shows the values of the correlation coefficient between any two of the questions. Participants felt the humanoid robot and its dialogue enjoyable and showed a positive attitude towards the man-machine interactions. The answers were moderately correlated with each other, implying that participants' impressions on the communicative machine are consistent. In the participants' free descriptions, most of the impressions were about the friendly atmosphere brought by the robot and fun of its dialogue. In this sense, the dialogue with the robot is suitable for producing intuitiveness and entertainment.

Table 7. Questions on the humanoid robot demonstration and average values of answers.

Question	Shortened index of question	(average) $\pm$ (sample standard deviation)
Do you feel enjoyable if you have a communication robot close to you?	Enjoyable With Robot	3.6 $\pm$ 1.1
Can the communication robot be a partner of you?	Robot Partner	3.1 $\pm$ 1.3
Do you think more interaction will be required between man and machine?	More Man-Machine Interaction	3.4 $\pm$ 1.2

Table 8. Correlation coefficients ρ for answers on the robot.

Indices of questions examined	ρ	p-value
"Enjoyable With Robot" vs. "Robot Partner"	0.52	7.0×10^{-5}
"More Man Machine Interaction" vs. "Enjoyable With Robot"	0.56	1.3×10^{-5}
"More Man Machine Interaction" vs. "Robot Partner"	0.63	5.1×10^{-7}

4   Conclusion

A Likert scale survey question on the visual and verbal presentation and comprehension were conducted to students of university classroom to explore the tendency of students' preference. The results indicated that the students learn better under a relaxed situation rather than feeling tense. They obtain knowledge both from visual and verbal information. Although they can follow instructor's monologue, they feel difficulty to keep concentration on the long monologue, and a part of them feel interested in the more interactive dialogue style.

Based on the results of the survey, we developed a terminology visualization that provided the brief explanation of the terms using voice recognition and Api.ai chatbot. This chatbot supplements lecturer's verbal explanation with visual information in sync with the explanation. It was found from a survey that this terminology visualization was helpful to understand the lecture smoothly. However, loss of concentration occurs when miss-recognition and inappropriate display happen.

For dialogue presentation, we utilized the humanoid NAO that communicated with an online learning system constructed based on a topic map. Using dialogue form, analogy and association were implemented to create intuitive and relaxing part of the talk. From the result of the survey, it was found that the participants felt the dialogue between the humanoid robot and lecturer was enjoyable and brings about a friendly atmosphere in the lecture.

The visual and verbal presentations described in this study add new elements that are adaptable to the lecture. At the same time, it was pointed out that they could be distracting elements. The future task will be to refine them to become unified expressions with the lecturer.

Acknowledgement. This study was funded in part by a Grant-in-Aid for Scientific Research (C) 15K00912 from the Ministry of Education, Culture, Sports, Science and Technology, Japan.

References

1. Davis, J.: Dialogue, monologue and soliloquy in the large lecture class. Int. J. Teach. Learn. Higher Educ. **19**(2), 178–182 (2007)
2. api.ai. https://api.ai
3. SoftBank Robotics. https://www.ald.softbankrobotics.com/en
4. Anis, M., Elnaggar, A., Reichardt, D.: Exploring interactive teaching of a multi-modal emotional expression of a humanoid robot. In: 2016 Future Technologies Conference, pp. 908–915 (2016)
5. "Everyday Physics on Web," http://tm.u-gakugei.ac.jp/epw/
6. Matsuura, S.,: Development of a trans-field learning system based on multidimensional topic maps. In: Leipziger Beiträge zur Informatik: Band XIX, Linked Topic Maps, vol. 19, pp. 83–89. University of Leipzig (2009)
7. Ontopia. https://github.com/ontopia/ontopia
8. Matsuura, S., Naito, M.: Shaping dialogues with a humanoid robot based on an e-learning system. In: 2016 11th International Conference on Computer Science & Education (ICCSE), pp. 7–12 (2016)
9. Szirmai, M.: Raising multicultural awareness by teaching humour in foreign language classes. In: Alao, G., Plard, M.D., Suzuki, E., Roger, S.Y. (eds.) Didactique plurilingue et pluriculturelle: L'acteur en context modialisé, (Archives Contemporaires), pp. 193–202 (2012)
10. Uchimura, K., Nadamoto, A.: Automatic generation of NAZOKAKE by using web content. IPSJ SIG Technical Report, Vol. 2009-DBS-148, No. 25, pp. 1–6 (2009)

Universal Design to a Learning Environment-Object Adding Network as Condition and Data Visualization as Framework to Provide Universal Access

Izabel P. Meister[✉], Felipe Vieira Pacheco, Eduardo Eiji Ono,
Suelen Carolyne Polese de Magalhães, Tiago Paes de Lira,
Margeci Leal de Freitas Alves, Vanessa Itacaramby Pardim, João Luis Gaspar,
Marco Antonio Pinheiro Diógenes Júnior, Daniel Gongora,
Valéria Gomes Bastos, and Marcelo da Silva Franco

Universidade Federal de São Paulo, Rua Sena Madureira, 1500 4 andar,
São Paulo, SP 04021-001, Brazil
```
{i.meister,vieira.pacheco,eduardo.ono,suelen.magalhaes,tplira,
margeci.alves,joao.gaspar,marco.diogenes,daniel.gongora,vbastos,
marcelo.franco}@unifesp.br, vanessa.itacaramby@gmail.com
```

Abstract. This paper focus on grounding two elements articulated to design a Virtual-learning environment-object based in universal access and universal design. First, it proposes to understand a learning environment as a digital artifact itself. Secondly, it appropriates the principles of universal design to draw it. The investigation has the assumption to add the network as condition and data visualization as a framework to generate a universal design to learning space, modeling it in the online Educational Design course running by Universidade Federal de São Paulo (UNIFESP). The investigation is a qualitative research based in a combination of design, design thinking methods and netnographic. Expected result is a roll of conceptual and practical guidelines to multidisciplinary group to build a learning virtual environment-object based in universal design, networks and data visualization to provide universal access.

Keywords: Universal access · Universal design · Online education · Network · Data visualization

1 Introduction

The authors have a general understanding that Universal Design to learning is related with Educational Design (or Instructional Design) and Educational resources production to achieve the learning objectives of diverse profiles of students, boarding design centered in the user. The Educational Designer and multidisciplinary group responsible to prepare learning environments situated in different contexts should be aligning to build flexible material of learning. Diversity of languages, symbols, activities, challengers and understanding options, should giving choices to student to build his learning.

This paper has as assumption to understand a learning environment as a digital artifact itself once the object has the ubiquity principle as well:

© Springer International Publishing AG 2017
M. Antona and C. Stephanidis (Eds.): UAHCI 2017, Part III, LNCS 10279, pp. 247–258, 2017.
DOI: 10.1007/978-3-319-58700-4_21

- People, resources, and objects floating in a flux of learning into different education contexts, devices and scenarios.
- Mobility, autonomy to manipulate and learning from it.
- It appropriates the principles of universal design to draw it.

Universal Design has seven principles [1] developed in 1997 by architects, designers and design researches from North Carolina State university under Education department of National Institute of disability and rehabilitation Research financing (USA). The group aimed to find parameters to develop environments, products and communication in design for all without adaptation or specialized design to a segmented group. It emerged from barrier-free concepts, accessibility, adaptive and assistive movements blending aesthetics into this core of concepts and movements. They outlined the following parameters: equitable use, flexibility in use, simple and intuitive, perceptible information, tolerance for error, low physical effort, size and space for approach and use.

In a contemporary context, the universality of design in virtual environments produces a complex and contradictory scenario where the hardness of objects and builds meets malleable structures once it can adapt themselves in agreement with the device used; technology environment became part of agents and structures. Borrowing from Mario Costa and Fred Forest [2] their observations of artistic practical and their relations with technological environment, we understood technology as a base of social organization able to produce changes in physical environments as well as in our metal systems of representation. This context brings to designers new resources and tools to create. In addition, we are constantly reconsidering our perceptions as a condition to apprehend the world that we are living. Fluidity is the concept that emerges from these observations once formats and devices results in different settings or shapes. We can say that fluidity is a condition to permeability and aesthetics then follows a flow. "Flow of information from unfixed and often uncertain and unpredictable processes" [3, p. 10].

Thus, the pattern is the flow that brings together a dynamic set of driving forces that is in constantly update due to the exchange of experiences between the agents, structures and technologies themselves. Any proposal of universality that contends hardness could create barriers. An important issue emerges here: it is about how to break barriers to different disabilities in virtual learning spaces. The usual trend is to offer devices to attend each disability that browsers, operating systems and devices themselves barred. These study points the browser interface as a place to personalize the content. It is the first layer to be offer as a Design Universal. Browsers companies as Google, for example, provides functionality for each level of disability (visual, auditory, mobility, and mental) in the Chrome browser as a converted text reader for audio or a filter to improve color and contrast perception. To use them, you need to download the extension and configure it according to your need. This vision requires the project to have an open, collaborative and networked design to support students. Customization does not mean an opposition to universal design, it is part of holistic conception based in complexity and chaos theories that preconize contradictory, new relations between agents, structures methodologies and technologies.

The investigation has the assumption to add the network as condition and data visualization as a framework to generate a universal design to learning space. Thus, The Universal Design (UD) gets together with Universal Design for Learning (UDL). UDL is a setting of strategies, techniques and flexibles materials to help students to learn (with or without disables). It is a tripod formed by multiple means of representation, engagement, action and expression based.

Composed of the seven principles of universal design and complemented by two more: apprenticeship community – when educational environment promotes interaction and communication between students and between students and University; and the educational environment – where the instruction should be design to be welcoming and inclusive. UDL tells us about design of the curriculum as part of all design. It means have a collaborative work with professors and pedagogical group as well. Curriculum more universal means less adaptation needed. Research and innovation into practice is a base for providing guiding principles thinking to an entirely new system with flexibility at its core [3].

The design multidisciplinary group considered these concepts and principles during the planning of the Online Technological Undergraduate Course in Educational Design (TEDE), at Universidade Federal de São Paulo (UNIFESP).

2   The Online Educational Design Course

The online Educational Design course running by Open University of Brazil/UNIFESP Center (UAB) is a technological project-based course with five semesters. The Educational Design (DE) is a professional that works in educational spaces proposing methodologies and technologies that make feasible and potentiate the teaching and learning processes. In this sense, the undergraduate course of Technology in Educational Design privileges design-based methodologies in learning environments with digital mediations. It analyzes examples, models and educational platforms through experimentation and authoring productions about languages, methodologies, standards and digital formats in an active, integrating and transversal process. The student is also prompted to think about the innovation and impact of educational solutions in the social, economic and scientific spheres. The five semesters of the course contemplate practical actions and reflections in open and networked educational contexts (1o semester); Non-formal inclusive contexts (2o semester); Formal academic contexts (3o semester); Corporations contexts (4o semester); Students have to elaborate a short educational project during each semester and a complete educational design project as a course final work.

The design multidisciplinary team is a group formed by young people coming from diverse University online learning projects. They have different backgrounds, knowledge and experiences; and professors from The Open University of Brazil/UNIFESP Center. This group seeks to combine applied research, online learning experience and strategies, technology, communication and design creativity experience to the daily creation of virtual learning environments, didactic materials and resources. The challengers here are build a learning space to a course that the aims to prepare Educational Designers in their own field of action.

The first goal is inspiration. A clear interface was thought from the beginning to attend a Universal Design, where navigation, interactivity and accessibility would significantly facilitate communication, providing the student not only the experience of becoming a professional capable of thinking about UDL projects but gives them a good experience as a virtual student. The team believed that such experience and the perception of the work of the production team in the search for a dynamic and easily accessible environment would serve as inspiration in the formation of this future professional of the area.

The second goal is do not have barriers to understand the learning environment. Students should be able to have available all resources, information and applications to access, navigate and be immersive in the environment; to understand what means study online organizing time, space and activities. Before they access is possible contact help-desk to solve technical or academic problems, more than this, they will provide well-being to our students.

The third goal is make online students part of the university. The learning environment has links to connect them to different sites of the UNIFESP, telling then about student life, undergraduate information, places and activities to students and so on. Social nets, web TV, podcast are some of resources at hand. Course has between three and five face-to-face meetings in the university campus to each semester.

The fourth goal is to draw a learning space to a project-based curriculum where interactivity and collaboration are basilar as far is a course in process; it means an open educational design as a principle. The project proposes scaffold knowledge in the exchange of experiences, learning and teaching strategies, given immersive use of tools and resources to the future professional. Student is invited to reflect about diversity emerging and create his own perspective developing autonomy.

The fifth goal is reach simplicity through a Moodle interface avoiding not necessary resources, working fluidity and interactivity, appropriate methodologies, strategies, language, design, technology, communication to support relations between students, teachers and learning.

3   Method

The investigation is still in progress and this paper spots first conclusions. It is a qualitative research. As are multidisciplinary team of researchers, with no designers in it, a combination of design, design thinking and netnographic methods was the first research draw. It proposes to build the research in the own field, having collection, analyses and interpretation of data during the process; data, cultural behaviors and decisions can be taken from insights as Ethnography indicates because it is short time execution project. Design thinking translates and synthesizes to no-designers the main steps from design creating methods: immersion to understand the problem; analysis and syntheses of people, needs, scenarios, technologies, environments, activities. Brainstorming of ideas, creation of forms, models, experiences. Evaluations take place any times during the process to give feedback.

It is a research process motivated by the following questions:

- Would decentralizing nets provide equality, less effort and flexibility in use?
- Is data visualization able to build the simple and intuitive use?

- Is data visualization able to provide perceptible information about the environment and about the learning process?
- Both network and data visualization are able to tolerate an error?

A first draw of research has the follow steps:

1. Immersion, experience - diagnosis, data collect and analysis for comprehension and syntheses using PACT (people, activities, contexts and technologies to design the environment main necessities) and Universal Design.
2. Evaluation.
3. Creativity – ideas, concepts, technologies, prototype and interaction.
4. Evaluation.
5. Implementation.
6. Evaluation.

As part of immersion and experience, the lieder proposed that team works the course identity and communication. A first challenger was motivating future students that will attend selective process. The logo designed using the articulation of four pillars of the course indicates in the curriculum: education, technology, design and communication (Fig. 1).

Fig. 1. Logo, 2016.

Words like innovation, creativity, classic, and elegancy, dynamic and modern were guidelines as well team created persona that represent the future students based in people who brings some of these characteristics: David Garrett, Germany classical musician who mix classic and modern music. Sheldon Cooper, Big Bang theory series character who is a doctor in physics working with highlights technologies. This persona was the baseline to create the first advertising piece, the course website: http://tede.sites. unifesp.br (Fig. 2).

Fig. 2. Website model, 2016.

This concept generates others communication pieces articulated with a media plan running by DCI (institutional Communication department) and multidisciplinary team (Fig. 3).

Fig. 3. Banners to facebook

To complete information about the course the group posted a set of videos in the website (Fig. 4).

Fig. 4. Videos in the website, 2017

This immersion in the communication outlines the course design and languages conceptions. It is coherent with this first conception and with the process of universal design/universal design to learning, adding sketch illustrator technique. Communication plan helps comprehension by design team about form, design, language, conception to Learning environment.

Reception from the public resulted in 367 people attending the selective process that had 30 students' vacancies with only a month adverting. It was a first evaluation of the design process.

Creativity was explored from there given ideas, concepts, technologies, prototype and interaction to the learning environment as can be view below (Figs. 5 and 6).

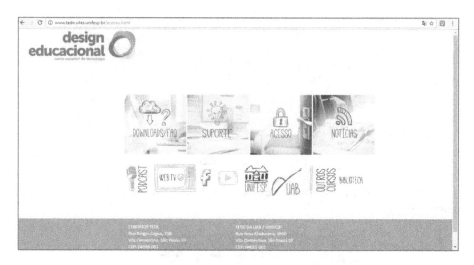

Fig. 5. Moodle interface access, 2017

Fig. 6. Moodle interface logged, 2017

In a typical qualitative research, analysis categories are emerged from the research field. In this case, it means a review and articulation of Universal Design and Universal Design for learning to produce a Learning Environments Guidelines to design.

4   First Version of Learning Environments Guidelines to Design

Relating Universal Design (UD) and Universal Design for learning (UDL) team works the environment using UD and UDL parameters interpretation and appropriation to build a first version of guidelines to learning environments.

Conceptual principles:

1. Learning virtual environment-object based in UD and UDL, networks and data visualization to provide universal access are fluid, permeable, flexible and not predictable at all.
2. Learning virtual environment design should foster networks, interactivity and collaboration to provide immersion, engagement, self-regulation and permanence.
3. Data visualization and data analytics are able to create options to representation, comprehension and perception.
4. Affectivity, recognition and learning strategy building engagement, representation, actions and expressions.
5. Communication channels providing support and relations.
6. Technologies able to enlacing learning.
7. Design of learning environment understanding as an open and continuous process.
8. Design focusing on people and being able to break effects of stigmas and stereotypes for students.
9. Design contributing to make learning more inviting and effective to students mitigating student evasion.
10. Design and curriculum should provide choices of learning and environment organization to student transforming his perspective of learning space in a personal and collaborative learning environment.
11. Design and curriculum do not have to create barriers to understand the learning environment.
12. Design is a structured learning and communicational environment; it should not to be overwriting or create conflict with information.
13. Design and curriculum are part of the same process needing to build a dialogue.
14. Design and curriculum should incorporate others considerations such as economic, engineering, cultural, gender concerns into their articulate process.

Design parameters:

1. Equitable use: diversity is design essence and approaches it from science. Providing same means for all users working between identical and equivalent, making the design appealing for all. "One size does not fit all" [4, p. 70].
2. Flexibility in use: design has principles and not rules. It exists to create trends, solutions and process to people, accommodating a wide range of individual needs, preferences and abilities. Feedback is essential to flexibility to provide choice, adaptability, accuracy and precision use.

3. Simple and intuitive use: less is more (Ludwig Mies van der Rohe[1]) is a mantra, but this paper suggest that less is more but should be effective; Complexity and chaos theories show us that is not possible reduce all to simple. In this context the investigation suggest change it to: clear and intuitive use, simple when possible. It means being consistent in importance to design information and be able to accommodate a wide range of literacy and language skills.

4. Perceptible information: design is not the main object, learning is. However, it cannot be transparent, should provide communicational elements to make easier, highlight or reinforce the understanding of information and support building knowledge. Using different modes for redundant presentation of information, promoting contrast between essential and not essential information, providing compatibility and legibility.

5. Tolerance for error: this element must be observes from two different perspectives. First, tolerance for error as a learning strategy reinforced by design and curriculum strategies to create different learning routes and feedbacks to transform error in learning experience. Secondly, tolerance for error as almost zero to navigation and interface bugs. A short research with two questions about hypotactic design environments developed by Tiago Paes de Lira, team designer, in 2016, highlights this perception. He asked around 30 people about how many times they will try to place a car in a car parking. A second question was about how many times they will click icons to find contact area in a site. Both answers told us about 70% will be frustrated at second try. Design should minimizes adverse consequences of accidental or unintended actions, in navigation and interface, material e resource, arranging elements, providing warnings of hazards and errors, fail safe features and avoiding unconscious action where vigilance is needed.

6. Low physical effort: provide comfort and less effort balancing body and operating forces, repetitive actions in addiction with curriculum for all, including access to disables.

7. Size and space for approach and use: providing an interface design can be understand as a composition of information and data, navigation, interaction and elements to support different learning needs, providing clear and intuitive use.

8. Learning apprentice's communities: the environment promotes interaction and communication between students and between students, teachers and university.

9. Educational environment: place where instruction is projects to be welcoming and inclusive (Fig. 7).

---

[1] German Architect.

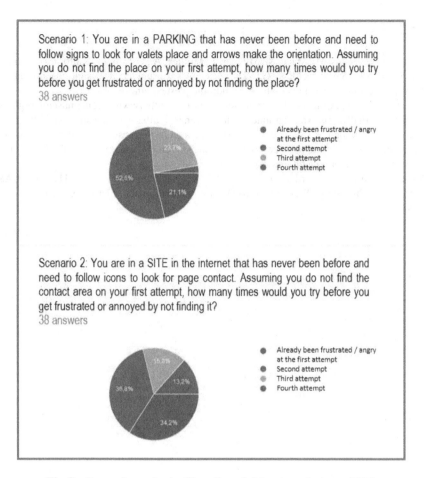

Scenario 1: You are in a PARKING that has never been before and need to follow signs to look for valets place and arrows make the orientation. Assuming you do not find the place on your first attempt, how many times would you try before you get frustrated or annoyed by not finding the place?
38 answers

● Already been frustrated / angry at the first attempt
● Second attempt
● Third attempt
● Fourth attempt

Scenario 2: You are in a SITE in the internet that has never been before and need to follow icons to look for page contact. Assuming you do not find the contact area on your first attempt, how many times would you try before you get frustrated or annoyed by not finding it?
38 answers

● Already been frustrated / angry at the first attempt
● Second attempt
● Third attempt
● Fourth attempt

Fig. 7. Research running by Tiago Paes de Lira, team designer, 2016.

5   Conclusions

The investigation applied in the design of learning environments results in a team engaged and able to create learning spaces and educational design. The result was a roll of conceptual and practical guidelines to help multidisciplinary team to create a learning virtual environment-object based in universal design, networks and data visualization to provide universal access. Future proceedings aim to organize the first environment evaluation by students, professors, and online support group. Documentation and guidelines design review are expected as well.

References

1. Connell, B.R., Jones, M., Mace, R., Mueller, J., Mullick, A., Ostroff, E., Sanford, J., Steinfeld, E., Story, M., Vanderheiden, G.: The principles of universal design (1997). https://www.ncsu.edu/ncsu/design/cud/about_ud/udprinciplestext.htm
2. Forest, F.: For an Aesthetics of Communication (1984). http://www.webnetmuseum.org/html/en/expo-retrfredforest/textes_critiques/textes_divers/4manifeste_esth_com_en.htm#text
3. Arantes, P.: Tudo que é sólido, derrete. Da estética da forma à estética do fluxo. Associação Nacional dos Programas de Pós-Graduação em Comunicação (2015). http://www.compos.org.br/data/biblioteca_233.pdf
4. Meyer, A., Rose, D.H., Gordon, D.: Universal Design for Learning: Theory and Practice. CAST Professional Publishing, Wakefield (2014). http://udltheorypractice.cast.org/login

Wearable Life: A Wrist-Worn Application to Assist Students in Special Education

Hui Zheng and Vivian Genaro Motti[✉]

Department of Information Sciences and Technology,
Volgenau School of Engineering, George Mason University,
Fairfax, VA 22030, USA
{hzheng5,vmotti}@gmu.edu

Abstract. Wrist-worn wearables hold promising potential in educational settings, specially as assistive technologies for students with intellectual and developmental disabilities (IDD). The possibility to integrate multiple sensors and actuators, summed with the close contact with end users, continuous and unobtrusive usage, accessible placement and conventional look enable wrist-worn applications to accommodate requirements from diverse domains. In special education, wrist-worn wearables have potential to support students in their everyday learning activities. The concrete opportunities in this domain are still unclear though. To explore the potential of wrist-worn applications in special education, we employ user-centered design techniques to elicit the application needs and system requirements. Then, we formally specified, developed and tested an assistive application. The Wearable Life app is a cross-platform solution that integrates a mobile and a wearable device to assist students with intellectual and developmental disabilities and as such enhance their educational experience.

Keywords: Wearable computing · Wrist-worn devices · Assistive technologies

1 Introduction

Wearable technologies are versatile, accommodating requirements from multiple domains [4]. In healthcare and fitness, wearables have been largely explored, in particular to track users' activities and monitor physiological signs in real time [13]. Despite the significant advances faced by wearable computing in the past decades, little is known about the potential of wrist-worn applications in educational settings [2], in special as assistive technologies to support students with intellectual and developmental disabilities.

To address this issue and leverage wearable technologies in special education, we employed a user-centered design approach and developed a cross-device application that integrates wrist-worn technologies with a mobile device to enhance the learning experiences of students with intellectual and developmental disabilities. We primarily elicited system requirements (functional and

© Springer International Publishing AG 2017
M. Antona and C. Stephanidis (Eds.): UAHCI 2017, Part III, LNCS 10279, pp. 259–276, 2017.
DOI: 10.1007/978-3-319-58700-4_22

non-functional) and assessed the application needs in terms of technology. Then, we conducted interviews and five focus group sessions with students and staff members (assistants in the special education program of the university). Using Hierarchical Task Analysis (HTA) and Unified Modeling Language (UML), we formally specified the design decisions for the assistive system proposed. To create, develop and test the application, an Android phone (Nexus 5x) with a Sony Smartwatch SWR50 were employed. To gather early feedback about the design, a pilot application was implemented using a Pebble Time smartwatch and a set of graphic user interface sketches (paper-based and digital designs) were created, evaluated and discussed within the research team.

The system proposed, named Wearable Life (WL), provides a computational solution that integrates a mobile and a wearable platform to assist students with intellectual and developmental disabilities (IDD). WL promotes independent living by supporting students in their everyday activities in class and on campus. The educational activities supported involve interpersonal communication, mood assessment, collaborative work, event planning, location and reminders.

This paper describes the development process of the application and a feasibility assessment, including key findings of five focus group sessions and interviews, the list of requirements elicited (functional and nonfunctional aspects), the system specification (formal models, design decisions for hardware, software, user interfaces and interaction), as well as the challenges faced and lessons learned in the development process. We also derive and discuss design implications for future work on wrist-worn applications as assistive technologies for students with intellectual and developmental disabilities in special education settings.

2   Wearable Technologies

Wearable technologies are characterized by body-worn devices equipped with sensors and actuators that provide computational solutions to support users in their daily lives [12]. The versatility of wearable computers due to their various form factors, sensors and actuators, enables applications in diverse fields [6], spanning across healthcare, education and user interaction [20,22,25,26]. Wearable technologies are able to continuously collect users' data, process it, and offer prompt notifications, supporting users' activities and providing services and information in (near) real time. The capability to inform and empower human users, augmenting and enhancing their senses, boost the potential of wearable solutions in numerous domains.

2.1   Wearables in Education

Wearables, thanks to their conventional look, small dimension and alternative placements for easy access, provide several opportunities for applications in teaching-learning environments [2]. Activities that can be potentially supported include student engagement, contextual learning, recording and sharing, evaluation and feedback, among others [4].

Existing applications of wearables in education include: the investigation of a wearable shirt to explore visualizations of body parts [17] and for teaching anatomy and physiology to children using e-textiles [16]. Head-mounted devices (such as Peer [19] and Google Glass [18]) have been studied to provide augmented reality experiences in classroom settings [1], for instance to teach physics to high school students [10].

Despite its large potential, the challenges related to the complexity of building wearable applications [6,14], limit the existing work in wearable learning to an exploratory stage [2].

2.2 Wearables as Assistive Technologies

Research on wearable technologies as assistive technologies started to gain increasing attention more recently. Head-mounted displays, such as Google Glass, have been explored to address the needs of special populations, including: older adults [9], users who are color-blind [23], children with autism [24], persons with Aphasia [28], upper body motor impairments [11], and hearing loss [7].

Wrist-worn devices have been explored to detect activity patterns and repetitive movements of children with autism [8] and to support users with visual impairments to recognize faces [15], and to communicate using Braille [5]. To the best of our knowledge, the closest research on the domain of wearables and special education focused on the design of an independent behavior management application to help children manage problem behaviors with minimal supervision [27].

Concerning the design approaches for technological solutions in special education, according to Kientz et al. (2007), the following design consideration is key: one must fully understand the domain through user-centric approaches, seeking to facilitate the adoption of technology with solutions that are unobtrusive, easy to use and to adopt [8].

Wearable technologies have significantly evolved in the past decades, still few works focus on their potential in special education, in particular as assistive technologies to support students with intellectual and developmental disabilities (such as deficit of attention, Down syndrome and bipolar disorder) in their everyday activities.

3   Methods

To better understand how wrist-worn wearables can serve as assistive technologies in special education, we adopted a user-centered design approach, combining user studies (focus groups and interviews) with iterative prototyping sessions (user interface sketches). For the technical development of the application proposed, we integrated a wearable device (Sony Smartwatch) with a mobile platform (Nexus 5x). The wrist-worn device employed in the study was a Sony SWR50, a smart watch commercially available, and as mobile phone, we used a Nexus 5x smartphone with Android as operating system.

This study was conducted in a suburban Fairfax, Virginia four-year inclusive higher education (IHE) setting. The IHE has a postsecondary education (PSE) program for college students with intellectual and developmental disabilities (CSWSIDD). The PSE Program provides specialized instructions in skill development for academic learning, employment, and social integration with support from matriculating undergraduate and graduate students attending the same IHE. As part of their academic learning and integration in college academics, the CSWIDD at this IHE also participate in regular college courses (Exploration courses) alongside diverse peers without disabilities. The overarching issue related to this site is the limited resources available to provide individualized support services for CSWIDD in their Exploration classes. Although academic support service personnel (ASSP) attend classes with the CSWIDD, they provide the services quietly and are not able to effectively assist the CSWIDD with developing independence in navigating the college academics learning thereby limiting their benefit from the experience.

Seeking to elicit the system requirements and identify the application needs, we conducted firstly two semi-structured interviews with three staff members of the program, and secondly five focus group sessions with the university staff (support staff who assist the students), program administrators and students. Both functional and nonfunctional requirements were identified through qualitative analysis of the study contents and the technology needs were identified based on the analysis of the requirements.

Once the requirements were elicited, the research team conducted a needs' assessment to select the devices and platforms that properly met the system requirements. The needs' assessment was followed by a design and discussion session, to define the graphic user interfaces for the system. This session was followed by prototyping, implementation and tests of the application proposed. The study protocol received IRB-approval prior to data collection.

The study participants were recruited using purposeful sampling selection criteria [21]. Participants are of diverse race and ethnicity (African American, Caucasians, and Middle Eastern), gender (male and female), and age. All students are English-speaking young adults, who have IDD, and are over 18 years of age (M = 19.5, SD = 11.7). The students' diagnosis, medical, and educational history were evaluated before admission to the Program and are determined as qualified participants for this study. All students have a modified high-school diploma and are non-matriculating students. They attend academic classes at the IHE from 9 a.m. to 3 p.m., Monday through Friday, with designated lunch period from 11:20 a.m. to 12 p.m. Within the 9 a.m. to 3 p.m. time frame, participants follow college-level (Exploration) courses in lieu of the special education classes. Each participant's Exploration course is different and has different accommodations, such as preferred seating or extended time for coursework completion. The participants selected through the purposeful sampling procedure have experiences participating in multiple Exploration courses at this targeted IHE, have competent understanding and command of expressive language, are technology savvy, can willingly accept or decline participation in the study, and have some independence in academic learning. Their familiarity with the type of technology application being explored, ability to read and answer the interview questions, and knowledge of difficulties associated with participation in their Exploration courses makes them perfect fit for the study.

The focus group sessions were documented with audio and video after getting the informed consent of all participants, and the multimedia contents were transcribed verbatim for qualitative text analysis.

3.1 User-Centered Design

The research team, composed by two developers (computer scientists), one designer, and one HCI expert, met initially with faculty of the PSE Program who have extensive experience in special education for university students with learning, intellectual and developmental disabilities. The initial semi-structured interviews were conducted to assess the application needs and better understand the study context. A pilot demonstration of the application was implemented using a Pebble Time and a Nexus 5x phone to gather initial feedback.

Five focus group sessions were conducted between June and December 2016. The three first sessions had 5 participants each, including 15 staff members (14 females, 1 male), assistants that support students in their daily activities. The two last focus group sessions were conducted with 9 students (3 females, 6 males), young adults with intellectual and developmental disabilities following a postsecondary education program in the university. All the sessions were documented in audio and video, and focused on eliciting requirements for the application, prioritizing those, anticipating potential concerns, and getting insights regarding technology acceptance. The sessions lasted around one hour each, were moderated by 2 researchers with Special Education and Human Computer Interaction background. The study protocol received IRB-approval and the multimedia contents (audio and video files) were transcribed verbatim for content analysis. Notes were taken during the focus groups and a summary of the key findings was generated immediately after the sessions were concluded. No incentives were provided for the study subjects to gather a more impartial perspective from potential users and as such prevent bias in the data collection.

The qualitative analysis of the contents aimed at defining the application scope, refining the list of requirements initially elicited, and listing the benefits and drawbacks of the application proposed, as described in the result section. Seeking to complete the requirements elicitation, the text contents were annotated, highlighting sentences according to their semantic association to requirement (functional and non-functional), relevance to the study, frequency, advantages and potential concerns.

3.2 Development

A set of graphic user interface sketches was initially generated, in a paper-based approach to gather initial feedback (pros and cons) about the application interfaces, icons, and layout. The development process followed an iterative incremental approach, in which high-priority requirements and functions were implemented and tested first. The platform chosen for implementing the app was Android Wear (version 1.5), and the Sony smart watch was connected with the Nexus 5x mobile phone using the Bluetooth protocol.

To start the prototype development, we focused on implementing the in-class subsystem requirements which include most of the interactions between the student and staff members. Initially, for pilot tests and demonstration, we used a Pebble Time smart watch along with a Nexus 5x Android phone. The key advantages of the Pebble Time watch included its affordable price (around US$70), long-lasting battery life (around one week) and waterproof feature. Due to the discontinuity of the production of the Pebble device announced in December 2016, and interruption in the warranty support, upgrades and maintenance, a new wearable platform had to be selected. To choose another smart watch to replace the Pebble watch, we carefully analyzed the application needs and list of requirements, considering the eventual costs (financial, development efforts, learning curve and training) and long-term benefits (including: platform stability, upgrades, maintenance, documentation and scalability). A needs assessment report was generated to document the analysis results.

In the focus group sessions conducted with the students and staff members, a demonstration application of the Pebble watch and Nexus phone was presented for feedback, showing a set of basic functions for the in-class activities, including: monitoring and moderating student attention levels and assisting student during question and answer sessions. This initial demo served as a pilot study, being relevant to communicate the design decisions for the application proposed (including graphic interfaces and interactive solutions) to the end users (students and staff), and as such get their feedback, advice and suggestions concerning the existing solution and additional requirements.

To select a novel wearable device, two main quality criteria were considered – the affordability of the device and the waterproof feature. Besides this, in the updated needs assessment, we also considered additional characteristics of the device, including: the battery life, embedded sensors, compatibility with mobile operating systems and flexibility for implementation according to key project requirements.

As the long-term goal of the project considers scaling the application for a larger number of students in the PSE program, we analyzed the financial costs of existing smartwatches. We immediately discarded watches that were too expensive (e.g. Apple Watch series 2 with the price of nearly 400 dollars). We also investigated other mainstream wearable solutions, selecting Android Wear to develop the wearable app. The Sony SmartWatch 3 was selected, given that its features meet the key requirements of the study. To specify, the price of Sony Smartwatch 3 (around 140 US dollars in February 2017) was reasonable among the other Android Wear watches analyzed. Besides this, the Sony Smartwatch 3 has battery life of two days, lasting longer than most Android Wear watches in general. The battery life was raised as a key concern during the focus group sessions, in which the staff members mentioned that a longer battery life could prevent students from forgetting to recharge their devices.

The waterproof feature of the Sony Smartwatch 3 is also convenient to the project needs, being emphasized as an important requirement by the staff in the focus group sessions. The GPS and Compass features of the Sony Smartwatch 3 were also pointed as relevant device features, being helpful to assist the students, especially freshman, in finding their location on campus (including: classrooms, library, dining rooms, sport center, etc.). Finally, for future releases of the application, the accelerometer and the gyroscope sensors combined with intelligent algorithms for pattern recognition could be explored to detect whether the student is sleepy in class by analyzing his/her movement and biosignals (as explored in [3]).

Concerning connectivity features, the smartwatch selected offers three options: Bluetooth, WiFi and NFC, which provides alternative connections to pair the watch with a phone or any other relevant device. On the aspect of the compatibility, the Sony Smartwatch 3 supports Android 4.3 and onwards as well as Android Wear 1.5. For display, the Sony Smartwatch 3 carries the 1.8″ transflective display with 320×320 resolution.

Currently, to provide continuous assistance in class for students with intellectual and developmental disabilities, a staff member sits near the student. To reduce stigma and be as unobtrusive as possible, in the focus group the staff members mentioned that it would be preferable if they could actually sit in the back of the classroom. To consider this preference in the implementation of the application, we use the notification feature of the smartwatch. In this scenario, the staff sitting in the back of the class can easily use the application installed on the mobile phone to send notifications with text and vibration to the student's smartwatch, remotely assisting them in class.

To develop the application, we used Android studio as a platform. For programming, we used the Android 7.0 Nougat along with Android Wear 1.5. On the phone side, the application provides the functions corresponding to the requirements, which represents the common routine of the staff while assisting the students. On the watch, the notifications are shown immediately to the student. The two devices used are paired via Bluetooth; with the maximum range reaching up to 100 m, the Bluetooth connection is sufficient for most regular classroom environments.

3.3 Design Decisions

The in-class functions implemented can be divided in two main categories according to their trigger events. The first ones are triggered by a clicking action of the staff (touch the phone screen to select a menu option) and the second ones are triggered by a logical condition, such as a given time or activity potentially detected (e.g. sleeping). To illustrate one example of application for the first category (action), if the staff observes that the student is talking too loud during a group discussion, the staff can select the "lower voice" button and immediately the phone will send a notification to the student watch with the following text message "Please lower your voice" or a corresponding graphic icon (e.g. silence sign). To call the student attention to check the message without being too obtrusive, the watch quickly vibrates and lightens itself up. For the second category (time-based events), in the case of the class break, the staff can set a countdown timer of 5 or 10 min, and when the time is over, the phone application automatically sends a notification to inform the student about the end of the break. Also, for the second category, to reduce the student anxiety due to a long class, a notification is sent to inform the student 10 or 15 min before the class is over. Once the time of the end of class is set, the reminder can be set to repeat according to the class schedule, using the alarm service of Android, and as such requiring less configuration efforts for the staff.

To define the notifications on the watch, most of them are set to be silent in order to avoid disturbing the instructor and other students in class. Noisy environments, such as a dance class scenario, could be handled exceptionally. Also, most notifications are just presenting the message sent by the staff without any specific requirements to get feedback from the student. In principle, the notification should be unobtrusive, avoiding too much explicit interaction of the student as this could distract the student in class. However, there are a few cases where the feedback from the student is needed. For instance, when the student receives the notification asking whether he/she feels sleepy, the student should confirm or deny, so that the staff knows the subjective feeling of the student. Thus, based on the staff's observation and student's feedback, the staff could make better decisions to help the student in class. This feedback feature of the notification is implemented by adding a specific action to the Android notification. Also, Android Wear provides features to separate the action of the watch notification from the action of the phone notification, so that we can develop different actions for the student and staff.

4   Results

The requirements elicited for the application focus on three phases of the student activities: before, during and after class. The 13 main requirements identified for the application proposed (functional requirements) are listed in Table 1.

Concerning non-functional requirements for the application, the three major features identified in the user studies were: (a) Ease of use: the solutions for user interfaces, interaction and navigation must be simple, light weighted, minimalistic, meaningful, and intuitive; (b) Sturdy: the device should resist shocks and humidity, as it is expected to be worn continuously in a daily basis; (c) Responsive: to provide meaningful feedback for users, in a timely and quickly fashion (in real time or near real time).

4.1   Requirement Elicitation

In the requirements elicitation, three major stages in the special education setting were identified regarding the potential for an assistive system to support. As

Table 1. List of key system requirements

Out-class	In-class
Before class	*During class*
Present class vocabulary flash cards and text	Mediate student mood (anxious, bored) and behavior (sleepy, agitated)
Send class reminder time, location, announcements, and required materials	Maintain student attention and alertness for focus and communication
Checklist for materials and actions switch off or set the mobile phone in silence or airplane mode	Coordinate a presentation moderation of a seminar
After class	Coordinate student collaboration in group for interpersonal communication
Send homework reminders assignments, quizzes, exercises	Present a countdown towards the end of class: snack break, question, lunch
Review vocabulary through flash cards	Moderate student questions: timing, relevancy, frequency
Support planning for next events shuttle, ride, lunch, meetings, etc.	Provide a reward, or incentive to reinforce a good behavior

Table 1 shows, the assistive system can support users *before, during* and *after* class. In the requirements elicitation, we also identified two main system perspectives – the assistant and the student view. The former, implemented as a mobile application, corresponds to the assistant view, so that he/she can mediate the communication with the student and his/her behavior. The later, the student view, corresponds to the wrist-worn application. The mobile app, developed for Android using a Nexus 5x device, combined with the wrist-worn application is in close contact with the student, providing prompt notifications and reminders whenever necessary.

The watch application was initially developed using a Pebble Time (for demonstration purposes in the pilot study) then an updated version was implemented and tested using a Sony Watch. The devices are connected via Bluetooth with a 100-meter range of reach, which is suitable for most classroom environments.

From the materials collected in the focus group sessions with the staff, four reference documents were employed to derive system requirements: (i) the checklist for courses and (ii) the checklist for skills are applied before class, (iii) the zones of regulation for mood assessment are applied during class, and (iv) the frame protocols are used after class. These documents are described as follows.

- **Course Checklist:** refers to the mediation of the students behavior right before class starts, verifying whether the student arrived on time, brought the necessary materials, switched off the phone (silence mode), sit down, and is ready to listen actively and take notes.

- **Skills Checklist:** refers to the activities that the student should master right
  before a new semester begins, including Blackboard and email access, basic
  computer usage, and Internet access.
- **Zones of Regulation:** refers to the ability of the students to self-regulate
  and control their emotions. It includes four actions to take, namely resting,
  proceeding, slowing down (calming down) and stopping (in case of inappropriate behavior or extreme emotional state).
- **Frame:** refers to the study guide prepared by the staff to help students to
  learn and/or memorize class contents. It generally includes four main ideas
  with four sub items (detailed information describing a main idea).

Once the requirements were elicited a set of formal models were generated to
specify the system requirements, and also a set of user interface prototypes were
built to discuss the system implementation, design decisions and assess those
according to their usefulness. A combination of graphic and haptic modality was
used to provide feedback for users and different layouts and graphics for the
contents were assessed (e.g. grid, tab, buttons-menu and icons).

4.2   Technical Implementation

Models. To formally specify the tasks involved in the assistive system, we created three diagrams for hierarchical task analysis (HTA), focusing on activities
that take place before, during and after class. Also, to capture the dynamic
behavior of the users and design the app, we used UML diagrams (use case and
sequence diagrams). The Use Case Diagrams were created to specify the system
requirements considering user behaviors of three specific actors – students, staff
and instructor.

Figure 1 illustrates the use case diagram for the in-class features. It provides
an overview of 12 functions related to in class scenarios, including the main
events and their relationship with the system. The behavior corresponding to
"Maintaining student's attention and alertness" is triggered by a staff input
event. This behavior includes "Send notification", an event which sends the
notification to the watch of student, corresponding for instance to the routine
when the staff observes the student noting he/she is absent-minded in class in
the traditional special education scenario. Also, for the "Coordinate student's
presentation" behavior, the staff helps the student to present a seminar in class,
reminding the student for instance to advance the slides, as well as informing the
student of the remaining time to the end of his/her presentation. This behavior
includes the "Send notification" and "Present countdown" events. The "Present
countdown" also sends notifications to the student temporally, including thus
a "Send notification" event too. As we mentioned in Sect. 3.2, once the ending
time of a class has been set, the behavior "Remind of the end of class" will
be repeated weekly using the "Set alarm" event which sends the notification to
the student 10 or 15 min before the end of the class in case they get impatient,
anxious or bored.

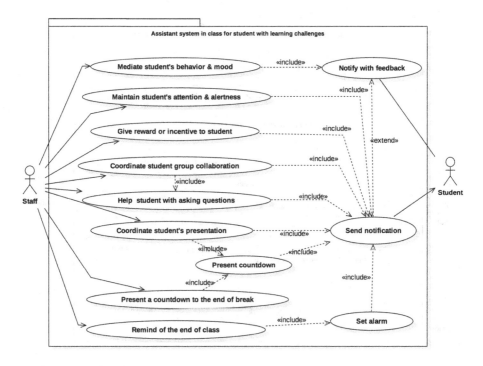

Fig. 1. Use case diagram of in-class assistive system

Figure 2 shows the use case diagram created to define the key events and features of the off-class application. It includes off-class system requirements, covering events that take place either before or after a class. Before class and after class requirements are integrated in the same system mainly because these features have overlapping functions (e.g. reminder and learning vocabulary through flash cards). Figure 2 shows time-based events related to reminders, such as "Remind of Class information" which includes the location of the classroom and required materials to bring to the class, and "Remind of silence phone mode" presented right before a class starts. Compared to the in-class system, we note less off-class interaction between actors. The main role of the Staff and/or Instructor consists in uploading the content of vocabulary with flash cards, listing assignments and so on. The role of student involves checking the list of necessary materials and be reminded at a certain time through a watch and/or a phone notification.

Architecture. To illustrate the interaction between the staff and the student of the in-class system, Fig. 3 shows the communication between the phone of the staff and the watch of student in class. The staff and the student interact with each other through notifications sent from the phone to the watch via Bluetooth connection, which implemented by using notification API provided by Android and Android Wear.

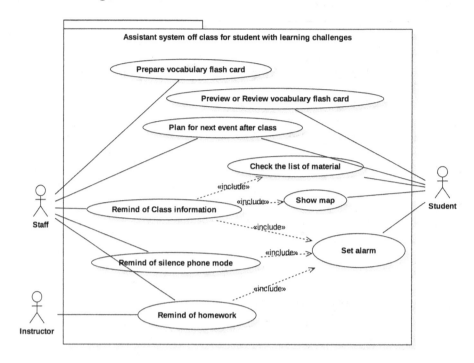

Fig. 2. Use case diagram of off-class assistive system for staff and students

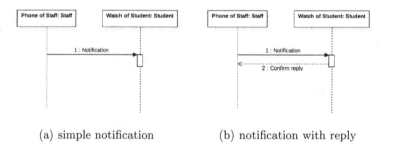

(a) simple notification   (b) notification with reply

Fig. 3. Communication between the Phone and Watch in Class via Notifications. (a) Shows the simple notification presenting the message and alert sent from the staff. And (b) shows the notification which also gets the feedback from the student besides sending the simple notification

As illustrated in the Fig. 3, two kinds of notifications are used for communication. One of them (Fig. 3a) is the notification which just presents to the student a message and an alert, and the other one (Fig. 3b) is the notification to which the student should reply. As mentioned in Sect. 3.2, to keep the student focused in the class rather than excessively interacting with the watch, most of the notifications sent by the staff to the student in class belong to the simple notification kind, except for those notifications with the goal of confirming the mood and emotional state of the student (such as: bored, anxious and sleepy), which belong to the second kind of notification (with a reply option). To specify, the notification with a reply option is sent when the staff observes the that student has a tendency to sleep and then the notification will be sent to verify whether the observation is valid. Hence, it will guide the staff to offer personalized interventions to the student (e.g. go for a walk, drink water, etc.). For the Android smartwatch, by sliding the notification horizontally (from right to left), the action button will appear on the entire screen of the watch enabling the student to send a reply message.

User Interfaces. Following an iterative and incremental life cycle, we designed and built a set of prototypes seeking to get the feedback and evaluation from the staff and the student since early development stages, and as such, being able to refine the design and adjust the resulting prototypes according to the feedback received. As previously mentioned, we developed the first prototype for the in-class scenario using a Pebble Time watch and a Nexus 5x phone with Android, to gather early feedback. Because Pebble services were discontinued, we continued the project development using Android and Android Wear platform, but developing the application for a novel device—the Sony Smartwatch 3 (still paired with a Nexus 5x Android phone).

Figure 4 shows a set of prototype interfaces, including two screen shots of the phone (top) and six pictures of the notifications received on the Sony Smartwatch (bottom and right column). The first column of the Fig. 4(a) illustrates a scenario of a group conversation in class, in which the staff thought the student engaged very well, so he/she clicked on the "Well Done" button (menu item) to encourage the student, as shown on the phone (screen shot in the upper part of the first column). Meanwhile, a notification with the applause and encouragement message is displayed on the student's smartwatch (bottom part of the first column).

Furthermore, with respect to the middle part of the Fig. 4(b), it illustrates the option of "reminding the student of the end of the class break" by using a countdown. The corresponding phone screen shots are shown on the upper part of the Fig. 4(b). Once the class break begins, the staff can input the number of minutes (for example 10 min) depending on how long the break was given by the instructor and a notification is then sent automatically to the student when the countdown is completed. A stop and notify button is provided in case the break ends earlier than expected. The staff can also use the notify button if they notice that the student has not come back to the classroom after the first call. The bottom part of the Fig. 4(b) shows the notification that the smartwatch receives at the end of the class break.

The third column of the Fig. 4(c) shows one example of the notifications with replies for behavior mediation. The first user interface (top) asks the students whether they feel tired or not, and the following screens show three reply options by sliding the interface from right to left (yes, no, maybe).

(a) Discussion   (b) Class break   (c) Behavior

Fig. 4. Eight screenshots illustrating the user interfaces of the mobile and the wearable application.

Specifically, these notifications on the watch exemplify a mood mediation scenario and can be sent by the staff for instance when they notice that the student is feeling tired. To confirm his/her observation, the staff can ask the student the corresponding question using a watch notification. Figure 4(c) asks whether the student feels tired, and the following three notifications provides the student with three default answers ("YES", "MAYBE" and "NO"). The bottom of each interface shows a list of dots, indicating that after the question is shown on the initial screen of the watch, the user can slide it right to see the reply choices on the following interfaces. At last, the answer of the student will show on the staff's phone in the form of Android "Toast" (a short notification message that is placed on top of the interface).

As Fig. 4 illustrates, we employ different background images according to the notification types. On the unlocked watch screen, the "Well Done" message is placed over a thumbs-up background, while the "end of the class break" one uses the background of a classroom, and the "behavior mediation for feeling tired" one uses the background of a tired character in class. To gather further insights on the background images, we are running iterative design sessions along with a survey, seeking to identify the specific preferences of the students and staff. With sketching drafts designed, we will continue to evaluate and create an icon set and a library of images exclusive for the Wearable Life application.

5 Discussion

This paper describes the development of an assistant application to help students with intellectual and developmental disabilities aimed at enhancing their learning experiences, promoting independence and reducing stigmas. The first version of the application demonstrates the technical feasibility of mediating the student-staff communication through a wrist-worn application. To implement the application requirements for the in-class scenario, two key challenges emerged. Firstly, the development of a dual-control watch app (which is more complex than just sending a notification to the watch from phone) because the watch and the phone normally belong to a single owner. In the use case scenarios for the study, we often have two users in control—the student and the staff member. Secondly, the notifications for in-class scenarios face a major trade-off: how to notify the student without disturbing the class dynamics, i.e. with minimal impact to the student attention in class, and no (or low) interference to the colleagues nearby.

Further assessments are needed to address these issues, as well as to identify additional benefits of facilitating the communication between staff and student with wearable computing solutions. We hypothesize that the wearable app has potential to be less obtrusive than the current approach in which the assistant calls the student attention and talks to him/her in class. The wrist-worn wearable, by being in close contact to the student, can provide him/her a quick and unobtrusive notification without distracting and disturbing other students located near the user. Besides conducting further evaluations to quantify and assess the impact of the solution concerning students' attention and interruptions, in the future, we also plan to observe, identify and model the specific events that trigger the interaction between staff and student, so that we can fully automate the mediation process based on information sensed from the users' contexts, such as: audio from the professor (through speech recognition combined with natural language processing solutions), time of the lecture towards the end or a break, or inappropriate behaviors of the student.

Although the initial results show that both students and staff are enthusiastic about using novel technologies in classroom settings and willing to accept the solution proposed, further efforts are needed to properly assess how the application performs when deployed in a larger scale.

6 Conclusion

Smart watch applications hold a promising potential as assistive technologies to support students with intellectual and developmental disabilities in educational settings, contributing to the students' autonomy and reducing potential stigmas associated to having a personal assistant to continuously follow, closely monitor and mediate the student activities. This paper presents the design and development of Wearable Life app, demonstrating the feasibility of employing a cross-platform solution that integrates a wrist-worn wearable (Sony smart watch) and a smart phone (Nexus 5x) to assist students with special needs in their learning activities. The application focuses primarily on mediating students' communication and moderating their behavior. Initial results indicate that students are enthusiastic to adopt novel technologies and demonstrate high acceptance levels to use emerging technologies as assistive solutions for education. Results also show that the student assistants find the application to be helpful, useful and relevant to support their work and daily activities. As future work, we will continue to design and evaluate alternative user interfaces, besides also conducting further assessments of the technologies to better explore how they can successfully contribute to assist students in a more automated and a larger scale approach.

Acknowledgment. We thank all study participants and the PSE program staff for facilitating this research project, in special Prof. Anna Evmenova, Prof. Heidi Graff and Kudirat Giwa-Lawal. We also thank George Mason University for the financial support and the Mason Oscar program for assisting in this project, in special the students Alaa Zabara for the user interface design sketches and Alejandro Rosado for preparing the needs assessment report.

References

1. Billinghurst, M.: Augmented Reality in Education, vol. 12. New Horizons for Learning, Seattle (2002)
2. Bower, M., Sturman, D.: What are the educational affordances of wearable technologies? Comput. Educ. **88**, 343–353 (2015)
3. Chen, Y., Hao, H.W., Hu, Y.X., Li, L.M.: Wireless wrist-wearable wake/sleep identification device for closed-loop deep brain stimulation. Electron. Lett. **49**(7), 452–453 (2013)
4. Demir, E.B.K., Demir, K.: Enhancing learning with wearable technologies in and out of educational settings. In: Digital Tools for Seamless Learning, vol. 119. IGI Global (2016)
5. Dot: Braille Smart Watch. https://dotincorp.com/
6. Graham, D., Zhou, G.: Prototyping wearables: a code-first approach to the design of embedded systems. IEEE Internet of Things J. **3**(5), 806–815 (2016)
7. Jain, D., Findlater, L., Gilkeson, J., Holland, B., Duraiswami, R., Zotkin, D., Vogler, C., Froehlich, J.E.: Head-mounted display visualizations to support sound awareness for the deaf and hard of hearing. In: Proceedings of the 33rd Annual ACM Conference on Human Factors in Computing Systems, pp. 241–250. ACM (2015)

8. Kientz, J., Hayes, G., Westeyn, T., Starner, T., Abowd, G.: Pervasive computing and autism: assisting caregivers of children with special needs. IEEE Pervasive Comput. **6**(1), 28–35 (2007)

9. Kunze, K., Henze, N., Kise, K.: Wearable computing for older adults: initial insights into head-mounted display usage. In: Proceedings of the ACM International Joint Conference on Pervasive and Ubiquitous Computing: Adjunct Publication, pp. 83–86. ACM, New York (2014). doi:10.1145/2638728.2638747

10. Lukowicz, P., Poxrucker, A., Weppner, J., Bischke, B., Kuhn, J., Hirth, M.: Glassphysics: using google glass to support high school physics experiments. In: Proceedings of the ACM International Symposium on Wearable Computers, pp. 151–154. ACM (2015)

11. Malu, M., Findlater, L.: Personalized, wearable control of a head-mounted display for users with upper body motor impairments. In: Proceedings of the 33rd Annual ACM Conference on Human Factors in Computing Systems, pp. 221–230. ACM (2015)

12. Mann, S.: Wearable computing: a first step toward personal imaging. Computer **30**(2), 25–32 (1997)

13. Motti, V.G., Caine, K.: An overview of wearable applications for healthcare: requirements and challenges. In: Adjunct Proceedings of the ACM International Joint Conference on Pervasive and Ubiquitous Computing and Proceedings of the ACM International Symposium on Wearable Computers (UbiComp/ISWC 2015 Adjunct), pp. 635–641. ACM, New York (2015)

14. Ngai, G., Chan, S.C., Cheung, J.C., Lau, W.W.: Deploying a wearable computing platform for computing education. IEEE Trans. Learn. Technol. **3**(1), 45–55 (2010)

15. Sousa Britto Neto, L., Maike, V.R.M.L., Koch, F.L., Baranauskas, M.C.C., Rezende Rocha, A., Goldenstein, S.K.: A wearable face recognition system built into a smartwatch and the blind and low vision users. In: Hammoudi, S., Maciaszek, L., Teniente, E., Camp, O., Cordeiro, J. (eds.) ICEIS 2015. LNBIP, vol. 241, pp. 515–528. Springer, Cham (2015). doi:10.1007/978-3-319-29133-8_25

16. Norooz, L., Froehlich, J.: Exploring early designs for teaching anatomy and physiology to children using wearable e-textiles. In: Proceedings of the 12th International Conference on Interaction Design and Children, pp. 577–580. ACM (2013)

17. Norooz, L., Mauriello, M.L., Jorgensen, A., McNally, B., Froehlich, J.E.: BodyVis: a new approach to body learning through wearable sensing and visualization. In: Proceedings of the 33rd Annual ACM Conference on Human Factors in Computing Systems, pp. 1025–1034. ACM (2015)

18. Parslow, G.R.: Commentary: Google glass: a head-up display to facilitate teaching and learning. Biochem. Mol. Biol. Educ. **42**(1), 91–92 (2014)

19. Peer: A Mixed Reality Educational Experience. http://itsdpark.com/peer/

20. Perrault, S.T., Lecolinet, E., J., Guiard, Y.: Watchit: simple gestures and eyes-free interaction for wristwatches and bracelets. In: Proceedings of SIGCHI Conference on Human Factors in Computing Systems, CHI 2013, pp. 1451–1460 (2013)

21. Reybold, L.E., Lammert, J.D., Stribling, S.M.: Participant selection as a conscious research method: thinking forward and the deliberation of 'Emergent' findings. Qual. Res. **13**(6), 699–716 (2013). doi:10.1177/1468794112465634

22. Russis, L.D., Bonino, D., Corno, F.: The smart home controller on your wrist. In: Proceedings of the ACM Conference on Pervasive and Ubiquitous Computing Adjunct Publication, UbiComp 2013 Adjunct, pp. 785–792 (2013)

23. Tanuwidjaja, E., Huynh, D., Koa, K., Nguyen, C., Shao, C., Torbett, P., Weibel, N.: Chroma: a wearable augmented-reality solution for color blindness. In: Proceedings of the ACM International Joint Conference on Pervasive and Ubiquitous Computing, pp. 799–810. ACM (2014)
24. Washington, P., Voss, C., Haber, N., Tanaka, S., Daniels, J., Feinstein, C., Wall, D.: A wearable social interaction aid for children with autism. In: Proceedings of the CHI Conference Extended Abstracts on Human Factors in Computing Systems, pp. 2348–2354. ACM (2016)
25. Xiao, R.: ViBand: high-fidelity bio-acoustic sensing using commodity smartwatch accelerometers. In: Proceedings of the 29th Annual Symposium on User Interface Software and Technology, UIST 2016, pp. 321–333 (2016)
26. Zhou, J., Zhang, Y., Laput, G., Harrison, C.: AuraSense: enabling expressive around - smartwatch interactions with electric field sensing. In: Proceedings of the 29th Annual Symposium on User Interface Software and Technology, UIST 2016, pp. 81–86 (2016)
27. Zakaria, C., Davis, R.C.: Demo: wearable application to manage problem behavior in children with neurodevelopmental disorders. In: Proceedings of the 14th Annual International Conference on Mobile Systems, Applications, and Services Companion, MobiSys 2016 Companion, pp. 127–127 (2016)
28. Williams, K., Moffatt, K., Hong, J., Faroqi-Shah, Y., Findlater, L.: The cost of turning heads: a comparison of a head-worn display to a smartphone for supporting persons with aphasia in conversation. In: Proceedings of the 18th International ACM SIGACCESS Conference on Computers and Accessibility, pp. 111–120. ACM (2016)

Universal Access to Mobility

Identifying Sound Cues of the Outdoor Environment by Blind People to Represent Landmarks on Audio-Tactile Maps

Nazatul Naquiah Abd Hamid[⊠], Wan Adilah Wan Adnan,
and Fariza Hanis Abdul Razak

Faculty of Computer and Mathematical Sciences,
Universiti Teknologi MARA (UiTM), Shah Alam, Selangor, Malaysia
nazatul84@gmail.com,
{adilah,fariza}@tmsk.uitm.edu.my

Abstract. Blind people often rely on sound cues to gather information about their surrounding whenever they are in an environment. Various sound cues produced by events encourage blind people to identify the source that produces the sound. Having the skill in identifying sound cues could facilitate blind people in wayfinding and increase their awareness of the environment. As the literature suggests, there are 2 dimensions (object and action) that are considered crucial when evaluating the identifiability of sound cues. We therefore conducted a study with blind participants at Malaysian Association for the Blind (MAB) to investigate their ability in identifying sound cues that represent landmarks of an outdoor environment. The objective of this study was to examine which sound cues that were suitable to represent landmarks in the outdoor environment based on the correct identification by the participants according to the 2 dimensions as mentioned above. The findings of this study showed that not all sound cues used in the evaluation could be correctly identified by the blind participants. Lack of auditory skills and dependent on peers when travelling in the outdoor environment were among the factors that contributed to the inability of some blind participants to identify the sound cues. However, blind participants who have exposure to the outdoor environment were able to identify majority of the sound cues correctly. As for the next phase, the sound cues that obtained high scores based on the object and action in the study; will be incorporated on audio-tactile maps for map exploration. This paper also concludes by discussing some recommendations on how to improve the use of sound cues according to blind people preferences.

Keywords: Sound cues · Landmarks · Audio-tactile maps · Blind people

1 Introduction

Human has the ability to listen to a wide range of sounds. Information perceived from sounds tells us about what is happening around us no matter near or distant. On the other hand, sounds can affect listener's emotions, behavior and actions. For example, the sound of train approaching gives us a hint whether we should run for it or not.

© Springer International Publishing AG 2017
M. Antona and C. Stephanidis (Eds.): UAHCI 2017, Part III, LNCS 10279, pp. 279–290, 2017.
DOI: 10.1007/978-3-319-58700-4_23

We learn to distinguish sounds that have particular importance based on the information carried by it. Active listeners such as blind people rely on sound cues in daily tasks (e.g. real world navigation) due to the absence of vision as the primary sense. While touch offers limited information, sounds can provide more information beyond the reach of a blind person. Therefore, in this study, we focused on evaluating the identifiability of sound cues (non-speech sound) of the outdoor environment by blind people.

2 Background

Apart from implementing speech on navigation systems, there are a range of related works that proposed the use of non-speech sound to present information to the end user. Ambient sounds are categorized as non-speech sounds that produce from real events (e.g. traffic noise, raining) and can consist of different meanings [1]. Ambient sounds are enriched with information that can simultaneously reach the listener without paying attention to a particular sound. The ability to carry complex information in a single sound enables user to identify the sound easily and relates it to the specific event [2]. For example, the tapping sound produces by a white cane changes when different ground textures are encountered. This provides information not only on the type of ground textures but also awareness to the user whether he or she has deviated from the correct path.

The characteristics displayed by ambient sounds make it an ideal solution to improve the method of presenting geographical information on auditory display. For example, ambient sounds have been used in virtual maps [3] to imitate the environment. In reality, ambient sounds are used as sound cues by blind people to guide their wayfinding. Koutsoklenis and Papadopoulos [4] investigate the use of sound cues by blind people in urban wayfinding. They discovered that each of the sound cues produced by events has different reasons and are associated with the sound sources and causes. These sound cues were used by blind participants in their study to identify landmarks in the environment. The sound cues also were used to help them to determine their orientation, to understand the type of environment and to maintain course towards the intended destination [5]. For instance, the sound of a car passing acknowledges the participants of the direction of the car.

2.1 The Implementation of Sound in Interactive Map Displays

Sounds have been implemented in interactive map displays to convey geographical information to the user. For example, speech is usually used to present information of a landmark or direction to places [5], using ambient sounds for city maps exploration [6, 7] and ambient sounds in tangible user interface [8].

Sounds are also implemented on auditory displays that are specifically designed to cater the needs of blind people to access information. Audio-tactile map is an example of auditory display that enables blind people to learn geographical maps using touch and hearing, which is based on multimodal approach. This is an attempt to improve the design of conventional tactile maps by replacing Braille labelling with auditory elements, for example [5, 9–13]. These studies consist of demonstration of synthesized speech use in relatively simple settings where instruction on where to start and description of the route names and certain landmarks were given. However, there is a lack of evaluations on the effectiveness of the speech use given in the previous studies. Also, less attention has been given so far to devising comprehensive and communication rich systems of audio-tactile maps in the literature. This leads to a concern on how auditory elements are intelligible enough to provide the basis for configurationally understanding of the environment of a place to blind people using audio-tactile maps (Fig. 1).

Fig. 1. A user was using an audio-tactile map to explore a map of a town [9]

Koutsoklenis [4] and Papadopoulos [14] points out that ambient sound has high potential that can be implemented on auditory display, for example audio-tactile maps to support blind people in learning maps of the real world. By integrating ambient sounds, it enables the user to perceive information of the environment that was not able to be conveyed through speech. Furthermore, the use of ambient sound may reduce the map exploration time. For example, user can obtain information of near and distal landmarks at a time when exploring a map. In contrast, speech is normally used to describe every object presented on a map which demands user's attention to focus on the content of the message. To alleviate this problem, ambient sounds can be implemented in auditory display by researchers as an alternative way to provide additional information to the user.

As mentioned, ambient sounds are able to present a variety of visual information in a simplified format and recognized way [15]. They are even can be easily located than speech because user can obtain the meaning directly from the produced sounds [16]. However, to produce a map where the information of the landmarks is presented using ambient sounds cannot be simply made, especially for blind user. Many ambient sounds are naturally conflict. For example, the sound of water fountain and raining can be mistaken for each other. Therefore, a careful design of ambient sound as the auditory icons on auditory interface such as audio-tactile map, is necessary because it is complicated to recognize events.

Mynatt [17] evaluated the auditory icons to represent icons on the Mercator interface for blind users. Her study showed that the blind users had problems to identify the auditory icons presented in the interface. Therefore, Mynatt proposed a methodology on how to identify and design auditory icons [17]. There were a few works which incorporated auditory icons on audio-tactile maps, for instance [18], however, none of these studies evaluated the identifiability of the auditory icons with blind users. As our research involves incorporating auditory icons on audio-tactile maps, therefore, we initially carried out this study to identify sound cues of the outdoor environment by adopting methodology proposed by Mynatt's [17].

3 Objective

The objective of this study is to evaluate the identifiability of the sound cues by blind people.

4 Methodology

To achieve our objective, we carried out a user study with a group of blind people at Malaysian Association for the Blind (MAB) complex.

4.1 Blind Participants

Ten (10) totally blind people (3 females and 7 males) from Malaysian Association for the Blind (MAB) volunteered to take part in the study. The participants have different level of experience in performing independent travelling in the outdoor environment and varied mobility skills. The mean age of the participants was 23 years.

4.2 Sound Cues

There were seven (7) type of sound cues used in this study which were derived from our previous study with blind participants at MAB [19]. Most of the sound cues listed in Table 1 can be used to represent the outdoor environment of MAB complex. For each sound cue, they were represented by 3 to 5 identical sound cues which made up a total number of 50 sound cues. Each sound cue was differed based on the object and action that produce the sound. The sound cues that were tested in this study were listed as in Table 1 next page.

Table 1. List of sound cues

No.	Type of sound cues	Sound cues
1	Vehicle	Car passing by
		Monorail passing by
2	Roadwork	Worker drilling
3	Street traffic	Vehicle passing by on a busy street
4	Ground textures	Concrete pavement
		Grass
		Gravel
		Wooden floor
5	White cane	Person walking using a white cane on concrete floor
		Person walking using a white cane on gravel
6	Water	Water flowing
7	Sound made by animals	Birds chirping

4.3 User Study

The evaluation was done individually in a room provided at MAB. Participants were first introduced to the audio-tactile map to ensure that they understood how the audio-tactile map generally worked. Later, they were asked to identify the sound cues and then would be acknowledged if their sound cues were chosen to be incorporated on audio-tactile map. Each blind participant was exposed to each sound for approximately 15 s. Before the sound cues were played, the participants were reminded that they could request to repeat the sound if they had trouble in identifying them. After listening to each sound cue, participants needed to describe the object and action that produced the sound cue. The activities done in this study were video recorded. Time was not recorded for this study. At the end of the study, participants were required to answer open-ended questions. Participants were compensated with light refreshments for their time and participation in the study.

5 Results

The sounds were analyzed based on the accuracy of participants' identification on the object and action that produced the sound. The percentage of participants who correctly identified each sound according to the action and object required to produce the sound are presented in Table 2.

From the table above, there were seven sound cues that obtained highest score on action and object. This means that most participants had no problem in identifying these sound cues regardless of the object and action. These sound cues are S1 for 'Worker drilling' (50% action, 70% object), S4 for 'Person walking on concrete pavement' (80% action, 90% object), S1 for 'Person walking on grass' (50% action, 80% object), S2 for 'Person walking on gravel' (80% action, 90% object), S1 for 'Person walking using white cane on gravel' (30% action, 70% object), S5 for 'Water flowing' (60% action, 80% object) and S2 for 'Birds chirping' (90% action, 90% object).

Table 2. Percentage of participants with correct action and object identification by sound

Type	Description	Sound	% correct by participants (action)	% correct by participants (object)
Vehicle passing	Car passes by	S1	50%	60%
		S2	80%	60%
		S3	80%	20%
		S4	70%	10%
		S5	10%	0%
	Monorail passes by	S1	80%	50%
		S2	80%	70%
		S3	40%	50%
		S4	20%	10%
		S5	90%	60%
Roadwork	Worker drilling	S1	50%	70%
		S2	0%	0%
		S3	10%	10%
		S4	30%	10%
		S5	10%	10%
Street traffic	Vehicle passes by on a busy street	S1	20%	10%
		S2	80%	10%
		S3	30%	20%
		S4	0%	0%
		S5	10%	10%
Ground textures	Person walking on concrete pavement	S1	70%	10%
		S2	50%	90%
		S3	50%	70%
		S4	80%	90%
		S5	20%	80%
	Person walking on grass	S1	50%	80%
		S2	10%	30%
		S3	10%	60%
		S4	0%	40%
	Person walking on gravel	S1	40%	90%
		S2	80%	90%
		S3	10%	60%
	Person walking on wooden floor	S1	60%	70%
		S2	20%	80%
		S3	30%	70%
		S4	20%	60%
		S5	10%	60%

(*continued*)

Table 2. (*continued*)

Type	Description	Sound	% correct by participants (action)	% correct by participants (object)
White cane	Person walking using white cane on concrete floor	S1	0%	70%
	Person walking using white cane on gravel	S1	30%	70%
		S2	20%	60%
Water	Water flowing	S1	20%	50%
		S2	10%	60%
		S3	30%	70%
		S4	10%	70%
		S5	60%	80%
Sound made by animals	Birds chirping	S1	10%	10%
		S2	90%	90%
		S3	60%	60%
		S4	60%	60%
		S5	80%	80%

The following four sound cues had inconsistencies in the percentage of correct identification by participants which made it difficult to identify which is the best sound cue to be selected. For 'Car passing', S1 and S2 obtained the highest percentage where 60% of the participants managed to identify the object of the sound cues. However, most participants managed to identify correctly for the action of S2 and S3. For 'Monorail passes by', 70% of the participants managed to identify S2 for the object dimension but 90% of the participants managed to identify correctly the action for S5. Similarly, for 'Vehicle passes by on a busy street', only 20% of the participants managed to identify the object correctly for S3 although it is the highest percentage among other sound cues of the same type. Surprisingly, 80% of the participants managed to identify correctly for action for S2. There is 80% of the participants who managed to correctly identified object of S2 for 'Person walking on wooden floor'. However, 60% of the participants managed to identify the action correctly for S1.

Overall, it can be seen that participants had problems in identifying the object or action for sound cues that representing vehicles as mentioned above.

Post-test interview

The following describes responses from participants on the open-ended questions:

- *Question 1 Suitability of the sound cues used*

All 10 participants agreed that the sound cues used in this study were suitable to represent landmarks and incorporated on audio-tactile maps.

- *Question 2 Sound cue characteristics*

Participants were asked about the characteristics of a sound cue that should have to represent landmarks on maps. Some of them suggested that a sound cue needs to be clear for the listener to recognize and can be repeated if they are not sure of the sounds, the length of the sounds played needs to be appropriate (not too short or too long) and the loudness should be appropriate (not too slow or too loud).

- *Question 3 Memorizing map layout*

All 10 participants thought that through the use of sound cues on maps can possibly help them to be able to memorize and recognize of a place.

- *Question 4 Comments or suggestions*

None of the participants provided any further comments or suggestions.

6 Discussion

There are many identical sounds that can represent a landmark, it can be a difficult task for a designer to choose the best sound because it cannot be based on the designer's intuition but on the user's preference. The main purpose to conduct the identifiability study is to avoid usability issues occurred among the end users, in this case, the blind people, at the end of the day.

From this study, results on the accuracy of participants' identification on the object and action that produced the sound have been gathered as presented in Table 2. The percentage of participants who correctly identified each sound according to the action and object was different. For certain sound cues, most participants were able to identify the object that produces the sound. Similar case goes to action. Although the sound cues that were used were from the same type of sound cues however, the characteristics of the object that produce the sound were different. For example, the sound of a car passing, although every sound cues that were used in this study to represent a car passing consists of same object (car) and action (passing), some participants were unable to identify the object or action correctly. Another example is the sound of a person walking using a white cane on a concrete pavement. The tapping sound made by the white cane seems was not familiar by some participants in this study. It was surprising because it was expected that the blind participants are already familiar with the sound of white cane however, it was the other way round. Based on observation, this could be due to only some blind students who frequently used white cane when travelling around MAB meanwhile others prefer to be free from using the white cane around the MAB area. Therefore, the familiarity of some blind participants with the tapping sound made by the white cane on concrete pavement can be reduced to certain extent since they are not exposed frequently to the sound. Another reason is, even if some of them have experienced listening to the sound cue, they are probably not aware of the importance of getting to know the sound. However, although some of the sound cues were unable to be identified correctly by some participants, there are still other sound cues from the same type that can be identified by most participants. The sound of roadwork was among the sound cues that is difficult to be identified by the participants.

This could be due to the lack of exposure to such sound cues when travelling in the outdoor environment. Roadwork can only be encountered by coincidence. In contrast, the sound of birds chirping was familiar by most participants and they managed to identify the object and action that produce the sounds very well. It can be concluded that sound of birds chirping is the easiest sound that can be identified by the participants compared to other sounds listed in Table 2.

6.1   Factors Contribute to the Results

The following discusses the factors that possibly contribute towards the results obtained on the accuracy of identifying object and action that produce the sound cues as listed in Table 2 by blind participants in this study.

- *Confused with other sounds*

Mynatt states that sounds are naturally conflict [17]. One sound can be mistakenly identified as another sound. Participants in this study also faced similar problem. For instance, the sound of train passing by was mistakenly identified as air conditioner or lorry by some participants. The sound cue used reminded them to different object that produce the sound. There are many different objects that produce nearly or the same sound. It has been expected that this factor would influence the result of this study. Therefore, only the most identifiable sound cue will be chosen to be used for future work.

- *Lack of exposure to outdoor environment*

Identifying sound cues based on the object and the action that produced the sound can be a difficult task not only for blind population but also for sighted population as well [20]. During the interview session, blind participants were asked about their frequency of travelling independently in the outdoor environment. The aim was to understand whether the frequency of travelling in the outdoor environment independently can increase the auditory skills among blind participants. Six (6) participants mentioned that they never travel alone in the outdoor environment and rely mostly on their friends help whenever they need to go out. Two (2) of the participants mentioned that they travel less than once a week and the other two (2) travel about a couple of times a week independently in the outdoor environment. From the answers given, it can be seen that majority of the participants have lack of exposure to outdoor environment. The six (6) participants never travel alone and preferred to be accompanied by friends. When they travel with others, they rely on their friends' help and this probably limits them to learn about their surrounding on their own. They possibly set in their mind on getting to the intended place safe and sound without encountering hassles as their main priority. When they have this in mind, they maybe forget about the importance of themselves creating awareness on important landmarks and sound cues that are available along the journey. This somehow restricts these participants' ability not only in auditory skills, but also their level of confidence. Participants who frequently travel independently have a good exposure on different kinds of sound which they hear throughout their journey. For example, they may gain new knowledge about sounds that they never encounter and these sounds can be additional perception to them. Participants who use public transport will familiar with the sounds of public transport that they usually ride. For instance, these participants may be able to identify the sound of a monorail approaching.

- *Lack of awareness about the importance of sound cues*

As mentioned above, some blind participants rely on their friends' help to travel within places in the outdoor environment. This factor reduces their awareness of the importance in identifying sound cues that are available around them. From listening to sound cues and being able to distinguish them, requires continuous learning. Questions like what produces this sound and where this sound comes from, should be asked in one's mind when one listening to certain sound cues. Sound cues carry rich information that can facilitate one to understand about his or her surroundings. Therefore, one should be taught to create the awareness within themselves about the importance of the information that sound cues try to convey. Otherwise, it would be difficult for them to develop at least a nearly accurate internal representation of a place.

- *Individual differences*

Age and experience in travelling. Ranging from children to adult, the increase of age and the frequency of exposure to sound cues in the environment can help people in developing their auditory skills. However, even with the increase of age does not guarantee for a person to be skilled in auditory if the frequency of exposure to sounds is lack. This has been proven by the findings obtained in this study. P1, P2, P6, P7, P8 and P9 have the same age however P2, P6, P7 and P9 never travel alone in an outdoor environment. There are several sound cues that were not able to be correctly identified by these participants on the action or the object dimension. It is yet true that when the age of a person increased, it is assumed that the person should acquire more experiences in identifying sounds since he or she has been exposed to travelling between places in the environment. Through age and increase experience exploring the environment may increase hearing sensitivity of blind people than those who have less experience [21].

Background. Participants in this study came from different backgrounds. Some of them came from rural areas. Growing up in different areas influences the way the participants identify the sound cues in this study. There exist conflicts of misidentifying sound cues such as mistaken sound cue A for B since the sound cues used in this study were representing the urban area of the outdoor environment outside of MAB complex. Participants from rural areas might have different assumptions of what they hear to participants from urban areas. For example, the sound of worker drilling into something usually takes place at the urban area where roadwork or building construction is done. For some participants from the rural areas mistakenly identify the sound cue as the sound of a motorbike, a car or a bus. Another example is the sound of a car passing might be different from person to person. This could be influenced by the occurrence of the person listening to the different type of car that usually passing by in their surroundings. The sound produce by a car may vary according to their fuel source, the age of the car, and the condition of the car.

Mobility training. One of the factors that may contribute to the results is the experience of each participant in mobility training. There were three (3) participants who never received mobility training in their entire life. Other participants received mobility training but the training that they received was at different frequency. P1 undergo training once a month, P3 only received basic mobility training in 2015, P4 undergo training once per two weeks, P5 received the training once a week, P7 received training if there is an activity, P9 received training at blind welfare once a week and twice a week at MAB, P10 received mobility training during primary school and secondary school around 2 to 3 times and once at MAB. Participants who received mobility training explained that they learned on how to use white cane for walking between places, going up and down the stairs and use of tactile paving. One participant (P5) mentioned that during her mobility training, she learned how to differentiate the surface area using white cane, use senses and perform road crossing. Most of the trainings involved inside the building or at the building compound. The training was emphasized more on the use of white cane instead. There was a lack of exposure on listening to different sounds in the outdoor environment. However, P5 learned to cross the road using white cane during the training and she had the opportunity to listen to sound of car passing and sound of street traffic.

7   Conclusion

This paper presents an initial study on identifying sound cues by blind people. The findings showed that there are various factors that influenced the results of this study. Apart from the nature of the sound which is naturally conflict, the lack of exposure and awareness to the importance of getting to know about sound cues among the participants also plays important roles. Added to that, individual differences also play an important role that contributes to the result. Based on these factors, it is important to carry a study to identify sound cues that before incorporating them on any auditory display. Therefore, the need for the involvement by the end user from the early phase is really important.

Acknowledgments. We would like to express our gratitude to Mrs. Sumitha Thavanendran, Mr. Mohd Fazli bin Kameri, Mr. Muhammad Amjad bin Mohd Ikrom and the blind participants for their constant assistance in data gathering at Malaysian Association for the Blind (MAB), Brickfields, Kuala Lumpur. Without their help, we would not have been able to understand and write this research paper. Any opinions, findings, recommendations and conclusions expressed in this paper were those of the authors and do not necessarily reflect the opinions of MAB. We also would like to record our sincere thanks to the Faculty of Computer and Mathematical Sciences, Universiti Teknologi MARA (UiTM) for their support and funding of this paper.

References

1. Vanderveer, N.J.: Ecological acoustics: human perception of environmental sounds. Ph.D. dissertation, Cornell University (1979)
2. Gaver, W.W.: How do we hear in the world? Explorations in ecological acoustics. Ecol. Psychol. **5**, 285–313 (1993)

3. Loeliger, E., Stockman, T.: Wayfinding without visual cues: evaluation of an interactive audio map system. Interact. Comput. **26**(5), 403–416 (2014)
4. Koutsoklenis, A., Papadopoulos, K.: Auditory cues used for wayfinding in urban environments by individuals with visual impairments. J. Visual Impairment Blindness **105** (10), 703–714 (2011)
5. Brock, A., Truillet, P., Oriola, B., Jouffrais, C.: Usage of multimodal maps for blind people: why and how. In: ACM International Conference on Interactive Tabletops and Surfaces, Saarbrücken, Germany (2010)
6. Heuten, W., et al.: Interactive 3D sonification for the exploration of city maps. In: Proceedings of the 4th Nordic Conference on Human-Computer Interaction: Changing Roles, Oslo, Norway (2006)
7. Heuten, W., et al.: Interactive exploration of city maps with auditory torches. In: CHI 2007 Extended Abstracts on Human factors in Computing Systems, San Jose, CA, USA (2007)
8. Pielot, M., et al.: Tangible user interface for the exploration of auditory city maps. In: Oakley, I., Brewster, S. (eds.) Haptic and Audio Interaction Design, vol. 4813, pp. 86–97. Springer, Heidelberg (2007)
9. Hamid, N.N.A., Edwards, A.D.N.: Facilitating route learning using interactive audio-tactile maps for blind and visually impaired people. In: Extended Abstracts CHI 2013, pp. 37–42. ACM Press (2013)
10. Minatani, K., et al.: Tactile Map Automated Creation System to Enhance the Mobility of Blind Persons - Its Design Concept and Evaluation through Experiment Computers Helping People with Special Needs, vol. 6180, pp. 534–540. Springer, Heidelberg (2010)
11. Paladugu, D.A., Wang, Z., Li, B.: On presenting audio-tactile maps to visually impaired users for getting directions. In: Proceedings of the 28th International Conference Extended Abstracts on Human Factors in Computing Systems, Atlanta, Georgia, USA (2010)
12. Miele, J.A., Landau, S., Gilden, D.: Talking TMAP: automated generation of audio-tactile maps using Smith-Kettlewell's TMAP software. Br. J. Visual Impairment **24**, 93–100 (2006)
13. Wang, Z., Li, B., Hedgpeth, T., Haven, T.: Instant tactile-audio map: enabling access to digital maps for people with visual impairment. In: Proceedings of the 11th International ACM SIGACCESS Conference on Computers and Accessibility, Pittsburgh, Pennsylvania, USA (2009)
14. Papadopoulos, K., Papadimitriou, K., Koutsoklenis, A.: The role of auditory cues in the spatial knowledge of blind individuals. Int. J. Spec. Educ. **27**(2), 169–180 (2012)
15. Blattner, M.M., et al.: Earcons and icons: their structure and common design principles. Hum. Comput. Interact. **4**, 11–44 (1989)
16. Hemenway, K.: Psychological issues in the use of icons in command menus. In: Conference on Human Factors in Computer Systems, New York (1982)
17. Mynatt, E.D.: Designing auditory icons. In: Proceeding of the International Conference on Auditory Display, Santa Fe, pp. 109–120 (1994)
18. Campin, B., et al.: SVG maps for people with visual impairment. In: Presented at the SVG OPEN Conference (2003)
19. Hamid, N.N.A., Adnan, W.A.W., Razak, F.H.A.: Case study: understanding the current learning techniques of wayfinding at Malaysian Association for the Blind (MAB). In: Proceeding of the International Conference on User Science and Engineering (2016, to appear)
20. Jacko, J.: The identifiability of auditory icons for use in education software for children. Interact. Comput. **8**(2), 121–133 (1996)
21. Thaler, L., Arnott, S.R., Goodale, M.A.: Neural correlates of natural human echolocation in early and late blind echolocation experts. PLoS ONE **6**(5), e20162 (2011)

Design of Geographic Information Systems to Promote Accessibility and Universal Access

Hugo Fernandes[1(✉)], Ricardo Teixeira[2], Bruno Daniel[2], Cristina Alves[2], Arsénio Reis[1],
Hugo Paredes[1], Vitor Filipe[1], and João Barroso[1]

[1] School of Science and Technology (ECT),
INESC TEC and University of Trás-os-Montes e Alto Douro,
Quinta de Prados, Apt.1013, 5001-801 Vila Real, Portugal
hugof@utad.pt
[2] School of Science and Technology (ECT), University of Trás-os-Montes e Alto Douro,
Quinta de Prados, Apt. 1013, 5001-801 Vila Real, Portugal

Abstract. Digital systems and solutions providing location based services for everyday activities are supported by geographic information systems that are typically problem-oriented. Although recently some approaches try to combine data from multiple sources to provide a better user experience, most often than not, these extra sources of input are not meaningful and act merely as an extension or augmentation of the user's physical context, providing extra data that not always adds extra value to the service. In this work, a geographic information system that provides valuable data for multiple audiences, with different restrictions and requirements, is presented. This work also presents the concept of 'awareness', implemented using a hierarchical layering system. Using lists of information layers, together with an appropriate categorization of user requirements, the proposed information system can feed different final applications with different data, for different types of users, promoting accessibility and universal access.

Keywords: Geographic information systems · Accessibility · Blind

1 Introduction

Although in recent years the number of digital systems and solutions providing location based services for everyday activities has been massively growing, accompanied by an increasingly wider spectrum of final applications from general tourism to specific sports, the design of the information systems that support them is still very much problem-oriented. In most cases, each application is supported by its own geographic information system. Lately there are some approaches that try to combine data from multiple sources to provide a better user experience. Most often than not, these extra sources of input are not meaningful and act merely as an extension or augmentation of the user's physical context, providing extra data that not always adds extra value to the service. Other recent approaches extend the services they provide by adding new services that when integrated, significantly enrich the user experience. One example of this is the inclusion of data from public transport systems into route calculation, which not only enriches the

© Springer International Publishing AG 2017
M. Antona and C. Stephanidis (Eds.): UAHCI 2017, Part III, LNCS 10279, pp. 291–299, 2017.
DOI: 10.1007/978-3-319-58700-4_24

service provided but also extends the target audience. Although very successful in their implementation, these approaches focus only on adding new value by adding new integrated services, as new services usually mean new audience. But they are still rigid internally, being designed with a very specific purpose in mind.

In this work, a new approach on the design of geographic information systems is presented which focus on reaching new audiences by adding versatility in terms of target users to its database internal design. This approach does not exclude the idea of adding and integrating new services as seen in similar works, but is focused on designing an information system capable of storing data in a way in which different sets of users may access different sets of information according to their needs, or limitations. Accessibility is one of the major examples of how adding new services not always leads to a greater audience, as new services are usually designed to reach new individuals of the same audience. As an example, visually impaired users are one type of users with disability that represent a target audience with different characteristics, needs and limitations than users with motor impairment. These two types of audience are also very different from users who use geographic information systems for tourism. These are three examples of audiences that would greatly benefit from one versatile geographic information system, which, by design, could be used to reach different audiences, using different client applications, but of course this concept may very well extend to other types of audience.

In this paper, Sect. 2 briefly describes the most common approaches for storing and delivering geographic information to 'domestic' users (non-professional). Section 3 describes the proposed design approach to enhance accessibility and universal access. This section describes the features intended, as well as the way the geographic information system is implemented to provide them. Finally, Sect. 4 presents some final remarks.

2   Related Work

Although some progress has been made in extending geographic information system technologies to include spatial analytic techniques, methods which involve relations and accessible connections between locations have rarely been developed [1]. The main cause for this is that the typical ways of data representation depends on representing all geographic information using simple points, lines and polygons, or some combination of them, and phenomena which builds relationships on top of these elements adds complexity to analysis which GIS vendors regard as being too specific to the wide range of applications. However, the extension of GIS systems to include analysis and modeling methods, which directly deal with these spatial interactions, is essential to achieve potential as a general-purpose tool [2]. In this sense, some works have been developed to include such considerations into GIS systems and data analysis [3]. Although some approaches have been created to simplify some of the techniques, typically these systems have some complexity.

Another consideration when designing a GIS for all, is the right for everyone to be able to use them, regardless of their physical limitations. In this sense, visually impaired users, or people with mobility limitations find themselves at big disadvantage, mainly due to the lack of information specifically directed to them assist them. In the last decades some approaches and guidelines have been suggested to create such systems [4]. These systems are, usually, very problem-oriented and use proprietary geographic information systems, as proposed by the models typically proposed in the field [5–8].

The idea that information can be stored in one place for different applications has generated the idea of creating information systems that use layers to store data with multi-purpose in mind [9]. However, the actual implementations of this concept usually try to combine data from multiple sources to provide a better user experience. Most often than not, these extra sources of input are not meaningful and act merely as an extension or augmentation of the user's physical context, providing extra data that not always adds extra value to the service [10, 11].

Using the experience and input from the concepts reviewed in this section, as well as continuing previous work [12] by the authors, in this work a web-based geographic information system that promotes accessibility and universal access is proposed.

3   The Proposed Geographic Information System

This work presents the design of a geographic information system that can be used to store points of interest beyond the scope of what is considered as traditional, like monuments, buildings, streets or touristic attractions. It is also intended to store special points of interest like zebra crossings, stairs or dangerous zones (areas). In fact, any point of interest, of any kind, may be added using the approach presented in this section. An awareness level is also an attribute of each point of interest as obviously a user with motor or visual impairment must be much more aware of some obstacles than of other spatial features. Route branch classification is another concept used in this work, as a user with motor impairment has different limitations and requirements than users with other mobility restrictions. Using the concepts of awareness and route classification, all the information can be grouped into lists of layers that have been stored with a specific audience in mind. Together with an appro-priate interface, client applications can use filtered data from the information system to provide customized experiences for different target users, according to their limitations, disability or general application purpose. The web interface designed to manage the all the information is also described in this section, showing practical examples of how a list of points of interest and special routes can be designed to feed the client application devel-oped for the CE4Blind project, helping blind users to navigate.

All the concepts described in this work can be used to extend the number of different audiences, showing how one single geographic information system can be designed with universal access in mind, allowing to reach different audiences, with distinct purposes.

3.1   System Architecture

The platform's implementation is based in three fundamental parts: the definition of a well-organized database structure where the information stored can be adequately managed; the development of an intuitive, user-friendly, back office where a system administrator can manage the information stored; and, a communication channel where the different mobile application (user side) can access the filtered information, according to the use case (Fig. 1).

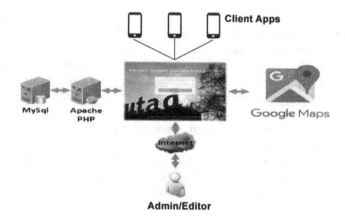

Fig. 1. System architecture.

The practical implementation of the system has been made using recent technologies directed to the development of web-based applications. On the server side, the programming language used was PHP (Hypertext Preprocessor) and the Laravel framework. On the client side, Bootstrap is used to provide for a user-friendly and responsive interface. Responsiveness allows for data visualization across many different devices. Being a web application, in addition to the technologies already enumerated, Javascript and jQuery are also used to add fluidity to the dynamic interface. The API Javascript Google Maps is used for geo-referencing purposes. All data is stored in a MySQL database.

3.2 Information Management – Back Office

The back office offers access to different types of users, with different access levels, or permissions. For the practical implementation, two types of users have been created: an 'administrator' type, with a very large set of permissions, and an 'editor' with less permissions. An authentication system was implemented to control the access, adding security to the platform, allowing only for registered users to make changes to the information. The administrator is allowed to manage users (editors). He also has at his service functionalities specially designed to introduce new geo-referenced data, edit it or remove it.

For the geo-referencing of POIs, as well as the geo-referencing of areas (polygons), the process is described as follows: to geo-reference a POI the user must select the option "Insert Tag/Object" to mark the position on the map. In the case of areas, the user must select the option "Insert Polygon", and draw the desired shape on the map. A polygon is defined by a set of points (coordinates) which, combined, draws any geometric shape (Fig. 2). Polygons can be used to represent areas like buildings or zebra crossings. To enrich the descriptions associated to a POI, it is common to draw an area using the polygon tool, and then associate the POIs with the area they are contained by.

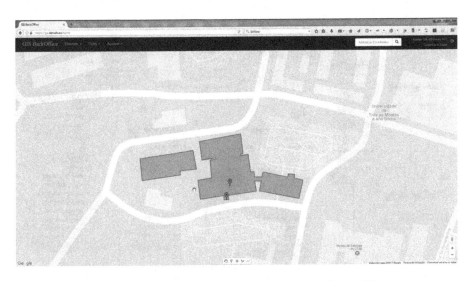

Fig. 2. Back office is used to see and manage geo-referenced items

A practical example of this is the geo-referencing of a zebra crossing. If a zebra crossing is stored using only a POI feature, only its coordinates are known. But if an area is drawn for storing the POI, the final user can be informed about the zebra crossing's location as well as the area it is contained by.

Together with the geo-referencing process, another functionality is implemented in the proposed system specifically oriented to promote accessibility and universal access. The concept is referred in this work as "awareness". It tries to mimic the way humans naturally interface with the real world while moving around, being more, or less, aware of their surroundings, by choice. For this purpose, a set of information layers are hierarchically defined to establish awareness levels and contain the corresponding information associated with each level. When a POI (or polygon) is georeferenced, the layers to which it is associated must be defined, and a separate description of the same POI is given to each of the selected layers. In a practical final application, while navigating, the user can define the current awareness level he desires, and receive the corresponding descriptions, filtered from the hierarchical layer description system. When a POI is associated with a polygon, this association may be also described (according to the awareness levels defined).

3.3 Overall Database Design

To address all the features proposed, the database needs to be designed in a way that it stores categorized data, according to the feature implemented. For example, storing a point of interest (POI) requires much more than just storing information about its geographic coordinates. Information like POI type, or the layer it refers to, must also be stored. The same applies to other features being stored, like areas (zones), layers, etc. Spanning this level of categorization to all the features intended creates the overall database design presented in Fig. 3.

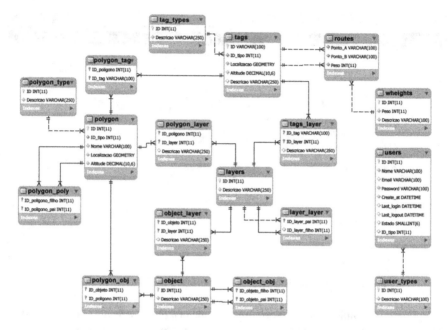

Fig. 3. Overall design of the database of the geographic information system.

Each feature implemented is supported by a set of database tables, and the different features, and corresponding sets of tables, have relations between them that provide for the overall functionality and flexibility in the delivery of the information. Some examples are described in the following subsections.

In the context of the proposed database for the geographic information system, points of interest are tagged by their location (Fig. 4). In this sense, a central table named "tags" store information about a POI's geographic coordinates, altitude and a set of general descriptions associated with the corresponding awareness levels (layering system, as described in Sect. 3.2).

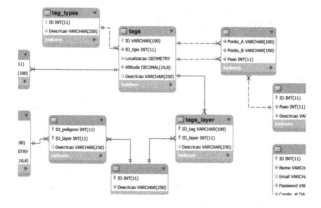

Fig. 4. Tables that store POI information (tags).

The concept used in the tagging of points of interest applies to the geo-referencing of areas (polygons), as well. Information about location, altitude, the relation to the hierarchical layering system and polygon categorization are stored in the tables marked in color in Fig. 5. According to the overall database scheme presented in Fig. 3, information about general objects present in and specific location can be stored using the same concept and methodology. Objects can relate to polygons and layers, and describe elements physically present in an environment that are not POI. These objects can store (e.g.) visual features for computer vision systems.

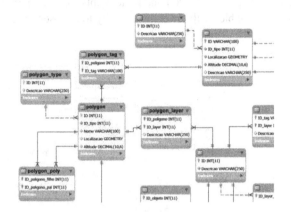

Fig. 5. Tables that store information about areas (polygons).

Figure 6 represents the data structure used to manage the hierarchical layering system. Each layer is linked above and below (father/son) to another layer. Each layer represents an awareness level and can be linked to tags, objects and polygons.

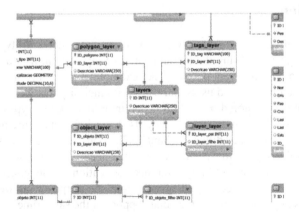

Fig. 6. Tables that store the hierarchical layering system.

Paths that a user can safely navigate are stored in the geographical information system as well. Paths connect points-of-interest. Naturally, humans can determine multiple paths to a destination based on their preferences and/or limitations. An example of this is the path that a user in wheelchair chooses to reach a destination. The routing system defined in this work uses weights to differentiate between how accessible a path between two consecutive points of interest is (Fig. 7). To create detailed routes between points of interest, a distinction must be made about general points of interest and points that compose a route. Intersections, curves, etc., are stored in the "tags" table. The distinction is that these points, used to connect points of interest, are "invisible" in the map and are used only as support the mechanisms of routing algorithms. This is the main reason why points of interest are not stored in a dedicated "poi" table. POI and route points share similar attributes and are stored in the same "tags" table, with different visibility to the user, using the hierarchical layering system.

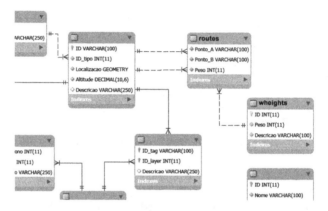

Fig. 7. Tables that store the routing information.

4   Conclusion

The main goal of this information system is to promote accessibility and universal access. For this purpose, using the hierarchical layering system, lists of layers can be used to export data for different purposes. An example of this is the application of this concept with visually impaired users and users with mobility restrictions. Some of the information that can be stored in the GIS is common to these two types of users (e.g., services, toilets, building entrances), but they also have different requirements. By using different lists of layers to feed different client applications, users can access filtered data from the geographic system that perfectly suits their needs, or restrictions. This concept can be used to promote accessibility. Another application of this concept is tourism. Lists of layers can be created specifically for touristic purposes, as well, promoting universal access and extending the financial support, at the same time.

The current implementation of this work is already under test at the campus of the University of Trás-os-Montes e Alto Douro, in Portugal. This geographic information system is the source of data for testing an application specifically designed for blind users, under the CE4BLIND project (UTAP-EXPL/EEI-SII/0043/2014). Results from these tests will be released in a follow-up publication.

For the purpose of touristic application, collaboration with the City of Porto, Portugal, has already been planned. The current implementation of this system has been designed in a way that geographic information is stored using different levels of detail ("awareness"). Different lists of layers can be created for different purposes (user profiles), so, different packages of information can be created from this one single pool of data for different final purposes, for groups of people with different requirements or physical limitations, assuring for the promotion of universal access, as proposed in the main goal of this work.

Acknowledgements. This work has been partially funded by the 2015 Digital Inclusion and Literacy Prize - Integrated System for Enhancing the Autonomy of the Blind, granted by the ICT and Society network, a special interest group created by the Portuguese national funding agency for science, research and technology (FCT).

References

1. Fischer, M., Scholten, H.J., Unwin, D. (eds.): Spatial Analytical Perspectives on GIS. Taylor and Francis, London (1996)
2. Goodchild, M.F., Haining, R., Wise, S.: Integrating GIS and spatial data analysis: problems and possibilities. Int. J. Geogr. Inf. Syst. **6**(5), 407–423 (1992)
3. Jiang, B., Claramunt, C., Batty, M.: Geometric accessibility and geographic information: extending desktop GIS to space syntax. Comput. Environ. Urban Syst. **23**(2), 127–146 (1999)
4. Loomis, J.M., Golledge, R.G., Klatzky, R.L.: Systems for the visually impaired. In: Fundamentals of Wearable Computers and Augmented Reality, p. 429. CRC Press, Boca Raton (2001)
5. Loomis, J.M., Golledge, R.G., Klatzky, R.L.: Navigation system for the blind: auditory display modes and guidance. Presence Teleoperators Virtual Environ. **7**(2), 193–203 (1998)
6. Huang, B., Liu, N.: Mobile navigation guide for the visually disabled. Transp. Res. Rec. J. Transp. Res. Board **1885**, 28–34 (2004)
7. Alesheikh, A.A., Helali, H., Behroz, H.A.: Web GIS: technologies and its applications. In: Symposium on Geospatial Theory, Processing and Applications, vol. 15, July 2002
8. Almeida, J., Fernandes, H., Filipe, V., Barroso, J.: Web platform architecture to support the geographic information system of the University of Trás-os-Montes and Alto Douro Campus. In: International Conference on New Trends in Information and Service Science, NISS 2009, pp. 1112–1117. IEEE, June 2009
9. Schütze, E., Vatterrott, I.H.R.: Current state of technology and potential of Smart Map Browsing in web browsers. Doctoral dissertation, thesis, University of Applied Sciences Bremen (2007). http://www.smartmapbrowsing.org/thesis_EmanuelSchuetze.pdf
10. Dempsey, C.: Make Your Own Maps with Google Maps Engine Lite ~ GIS Lounge, 27 March 2013. https://www.gislounge.com/make-your-own-small-maps-with-google-maps-engine-lite/. Accessed 01 Mar 2017
11. Gmap4 = Google Maps GIS Viewer Topo Maps USNG Grid Geolocation More (n.d.). https://mappingsupport.com/p/gmap4-arcgis-layers-on-google-maps.html. Accessed 01 Mar 2017
12. Fernandes, H., Conceição, N., Paredes, H., Pereira, A., Araújo, P., Barroso, J.: Providing accessibility to blind people using GIS. Univ. Access Inf. Soc. **11**(4), 399–407 (2012)

Assess User Needs for Time-Related Information to Design an Airport Guide System

Yilin Elaine Liu[✉] and Jon A. Sanford

Georgia Institute of Technology, Atlanta, USA
y.elaineliu@gatech.edu, jon.sanford@design.gatech.edu

Abstract. Airport activity planning and navigation are challenging because they involve planning for complex activities, including the mandatory activities for someone to get on a flight (e.g. check-in, security check), the discretionary activities (e.g. shopping, dining) and the travels connecting different activity areas. In order to successfully plan the activities and navigate at airports, time is a factor that most travelers would consider. In this paper, a survey investigating the utility of time information was presented. Travelers with different abilities were included in the survey in order to investigate the effect of abilities on the perceived utility of time information. It provided evidence for integrating time information into navigation aids to better facilitate travelers with different abilities. It also suggested that further investigation is needed to identify additional information needs of travelers in situations where time is not considered as important.

Keywords: Navigation · Air travel · Disability · Time-related information

1 Introduction

Airports are complex constructions that support a variety of activities. Navigation, as one fundamental activity that one has to perform in order to get to areas for other activities, gets more complicated than just getting from point A to point B. According to Hoogendoorn and Bovy [4] travelers at airports as pedestrians, plan and navigate at three different levels: Strategic level (i.e. deciding departure time and activity pattern), Tactical level (i.e. activity scheduling, activity area choice and route choice to reach activity areas), and Operational level (i.e. walking behavior). The decisions travelers make at each level will have influence on their decisions at other two levels that the three levels are interrelated to each other. Unfortunately, the challenges and user needs regarding airport navigation have never been examined from this perspective. They are usually examined separately from each other and for different purposes. Traditional airport navigation research has been focusing on the operational level that signage [3, 6], maps [5, 6], asking other people [6] and airport navigation systems on kiosks [8] or handheld devices [7] have been identified as solutions to support the walking behavior. Research focusing on assessing travelers' experience with airports and investigating service needs for airports have identified the information needs at the strategic level and

© Springer International Publishing AG 2017
M. Antona and C. Stephanidis (Eds.): UAHCI 2017, Part III, LNCS 10279, pp. 300–307, 2017.
DOI: 10.1007/978-3-319-58700-4_25

the tactical level. These needs include access of information regarding flight schedule, gate assignments/changes, and short waiting time [1, 2]. The separation of the three levels when examining the problems and user needs results in solutions and recommendations that address only a small piece of the challenge. For example, flight schedule and gate changes have a big impact on travelers planning of the activities. Travelers may have more time or less time for other activities at airport due to the schedule changes. Without the flight information (i.e. schedule and gate assignment), only knowing how to get to each gate by following the signage will lead travelers to nowhere. The integration of the information that supports each of the three levels is necessary for travelers to plan and navigate to different destinations effectively. A mobile guide application is developed to provide information to support all the three levels of pedestrian behaviors at airports. There were several important design research questions raised in the development of the application. These questions are: What time-related information travelers would consider to be useful? Are there any factors affecting its usefulness? In order to answer these questions, a survey was developed to investigate the utility of time information for travelers with different abilities and age under different situations.

2 Background

The existing navigation aids are usually focusing on how to aid someone to get from point A to point B without any planning facilitators for aiding travelers' decisions on their destinations. Unlike Hoogendoorn and Bovy [4] who examined navigation as a part of pedestrian's behaviors, the existing navigation aids do not consider navigation as a means for a traveler to get to a destination and achieve a higher-level goal at the destination (e.g. dining, shopping, check-in). The existing navigation systems, especially those designed for travelers with disabilities, usually only emphasize the communication of the directional information.

For travelers with mobility impairments, including those who have difficulties with mobility due to sensory impairments (e.g. visual impairments), navigation aids are developed to allow them to plan routes (to a pre-defined destination) and explore environments they are going to visit before the trip. Some navigation aids also incorporated ADA standards when suggesting routes to reduce the physical barriers travelers would encounter when navigation [9]. For travelers with visual impairments, some navigation aids utilize tactile feedback to communicate route information to travelers [10, 11], while others utilize auditory feedback to communicate those information [12, 13]. There are also navigation aids developed specifically for people with cognitive impairments. These applications are usually focusing on simplifying the provision of navigational information. Providing more direct and graphical navigation information is a common practice [14, 15].

Travelers with disabilities experience more difficulties about the environment when they try to plan their trips and navigate through the trips. They usually consider a set of environmental factors when planning trips. These environmental factors include barriers they want to avoid (e.g. stairs for wheelchair users) and facilitators they need (e.g. ramps). At airports, in addition to these environmental factors, time becomes a unique factor that the activity planning and navigation are all affected by it. Lacking of time information when planning and navigation may introduce more difficulties to travelers with disabilities than it does to those who without. Thus, there is a need for the investigation of the utility of time information, especially for travelers with disabilities. More importantly, the utility of time information should be investigated in the context of navigation, not only in the context of trip planning to ensure that its effectiveness could be investigated at all three levels of pedestrian behaviors to facilitate travelers at airports to achieve their high level goals (e.g. successful departure or arrival).

3 Method

An online survey was designed to collect the opinions of travelers with different abilities toward the utility of time information given by a mobile guide application when planning activities and routes at airports. The time information was specified as the combined time of the waiting time at the destination to start an activity (e.g. get security check) and the walking time to get to a destination. In the survey, two departure scenarios were introduced to the participants and two different tasks were described in each scenario. The factor that varied between scenarios was time pressure. The two tasks that were introduced in each scenario were: Task 1, mandatory activity, going to the security check point and Task 2, discretionary activity, finding a restaurant. These two tasks represented the two types of activities one would do at airports: mandatory activities and discretionary activities. In Scenario A, participants were asked to rate the helpfulness of the time information for the two tasks when they did not have much time before boarding. In Scenario B, participants were asked to rate the helpfulness of the time information for the two tasks when they had plenty of time before boarding. The demographic information such as age, travel experience, and disabilities were also collected.

There were three hypotheses made in this survey study:

- **H1:** The information about walking time (indicating physical effort) and waiting time is useful for travelers with various abilities when planning activities and routes at airports.
- **H2:** Different time pressures (varied in different scenarios) and different types of activities (represented by different tasks in each scenario) have impact on travelers' ratings for the helpfulness of time information.
- **H3:** The rating for the helpfulness of time information will vary with individual's abilities.

The inclusion criteria for this study is anyone aged over 18 years old and had at least traveled by air once in the past two years. The survey was sent to a local university and to a list of 193 older adults to collect responses. The responses were analyzed to test the above hypotheses and help researchers and designers to further understand the needs of users with different abilities (and age) for time at airports.

4 Results

There were in total of 42 participants responded to the survey and 36 of them completed all the questions. These completed responses were used in result analysis. Overall, participants rated very positively for the utility of the time information. Difference between the ratings for each scenario and each task were observed and the differences were tested for their significance level. There was only one paired comparison between scenarios and tasks (Scenario A-Task 1 vs. Scenario B-Task 1) had the difference that seemed to be significant with the p-value less than 0.1 (See Table 1 for "Pair 3" comparison). Participants were categorized into different groups based on their demographic information. The impact of group differences on the average rating for the utility of time information in all four conditions (i.e. two tasks in two scenarios) was tested. The detailed results are presented as below.

Table 1. Gender and age information of 36 participants

	Total	<65 y/o	>=65 y/o
Female	27	9	18
Male	9	3	6

4.1 Demographics

There were 9 males, 27 females responded to the survey. One third of the participants were younger adults who were younger than 65 years old and two thirds of the participants were older adults who aged 65 and older (see Table 2).

Table 2. Disability information of 36 participants. *Included participants with multiple disabilities (who were repeatedly counted). The numbers in the parentheses indicate the numbers of respondents with only one type of disabilities.

Total	None	Vision impairments	Hearing impairments	Mobility impairments
36	16	10 (7)*	9 (4)*	7 (4)*

Among the 36 participants, 16 of them did not have any disabilities. Ten of them identified themselves as having vision impairments, nine of them identified themselves as having hearing impairments, and seven of them identified themselves as having mobility impairments (see Table 3). In total there were **five** participants who had multiple disabilities. There was one participant (P38) had all three types of disabilities: Visual Impairments, Deaf in both ears, Serious difficulties walking without using a walking aid. Two participants (P18, P35) reported to have both hearing and mobility impairments. Two participants (P34, P41) reported to have both hearing and visual impairments.

Table 3. Travel experience information of 36 participants

	Less than or equal to 8 times	More than 8 times
<65 y/o	6	6
>=65 y/o	22	2
Total	28	8

Regarding the travel experience, there were 8 participants (which was less than one fourth of the participants) who had traveled more than 8 times in the past two years and they were considered as frequent air travelers in this survey.

4.2 Time Pressure Effect and Activity Type Effect (Within Participants)

Participants gave ratings for the helpfulness of time information in four conditions:

- Condition 1. Going to a security check point when time pressure is high (Scenario A, Task 1)
- Condition 2. Finding a restaurant (on the airside) when time pressure is high (Scenario A, Task 2)
- Condition 3. Going to a security check point when time pressure is low (Scenario B, Task 1)
- Condition 4. Finding a restaurant (on the airside) when time pressure is low (Scenario B, Task 2)

The ratings were on a five-point scale in which "1" was for "not helpful at all" and "5" was for "extremely helpful". Participants rated the time information to be the most helpful for condition one with a mean score of 4.25. They rated the time information to be the least helpful for condition four with a mean score of 3.94. The average ratings of four conditions (i.e. variable "Helpfulness_OverallAvg") were calculated by adding up the ratings in four conditions and divided by four. The mean of the average ratings of four conditions was 4.0694, which indicated the participants considered the time information to be very helpful overall (see Tables 4 and 5).

Table 4. Helpfulness ratings in four conditions and the average rating scores for all four conditions

Descriptive Statistics

	N	Range	Minimum	Maximum	Mean		Std. Deviation	Variance
	Statistic	Statistic	Statistic	Statistic	Statistic	Std. Error	Statistic	Statistic
Helpfulness_ScenarioAT ask1	36	4	1	5	4.25	.161	.967	.936
Helpfulness_ScenarioAT ask2	36	4	1	5	4.08	.175	1.052	1.107
Helpfulness_ScenarioBT ask1	36	4	1	5	4.00	.144	.862	.743
Helpfulness_ScenarioBT ask2	36	4	1	5	3.94	.173	1.040	1.083
Helpfulness_OverallAvg	36	4.00	1.00	5.00	4.0694	.14037	.84221	.709
Valid N (listwise)	36							

Table 5. Paired samples test of utility ratings for four conditions

Paired Samples Test

| | | Paired Differences | | | | | | | |
| | | | | | 95% Confidence Interval of the Difference | | | | |
		Mean	Std. Deviation	Std. Error Mean	Lower	Upper	t	df	Sig. (2-tailed)
Pair 1	Helpfulness_ScenarioAT ask1 - Helpfulness_ScenarioAT ask2	.167	.941	.157	-.152	.485	1.063	35	.295
Pair 2	Helpfulness_ScenarioBT ask1 - Helpfulness_ScenarioBT ask2	.056	.674	.112	-.172	.284	.495	35	.624
Pair 3	Helpfulness_ScenarioAT ask1 - Helpfulness_ScenarioBT ask1	.250	.841	.140	-.035	.535	1.784	35	.083
Pair 4	Helpfulness_ScenarioAT ask2 - Helpfulness_ScenarioBT ask2	.139	.762	.127	-.119	.397	1.094	35	.281

The within-participants differences between the ratings in four conditions were tested in paired comparisons for their significance. None of the comparisons had significant differences. There was one comparison between different time pressure for the same mandatory activity (Paired 3 in Table 1) turned out to have a trend for being significant ($p = 0.083$). This suggested that travelers may consider time information to be less helpful when they do not need to worry about time when planning for mandatory activities.

4.3   Group Comparisons (Between Participants)

Group differences were also tested for their significance. There were five between-participants comparisons being carried out to test their differences. The groups were categorized based on participants' abilities, age, and air travel experience. Detailed group descriptions can be found in Table 6.

The only significant group difference of the ratings was between the group of individuals with mobility impairments and those without. Participants with mobility impairments considered the time information to be less helpful compared to

Table 6. Group comparisons of the average ratings for the helpfulness of time information

| Variable | Value | | Significance level (p) |
	1	2	
Group_Mobility	None	Mobility impairments	0.032*
Group_Vision	None	Visual impairments	0.683
Group_Hearing	None	Hearing impairments	0.193
Group_Age	<65 y/o	>=65 y/o	0.583
Group_TravelExperience	1–8 times	More than 8 times	0.836

participants who without mobility impairments. There was no observed significant difference of the ratings between other groups.

5 Discussion

The results of this study indicated that the time information (i.e. walking time and waiting time) is helpful for travelers with different abilities to plan activities and routes at airports. Our first hypothesis was thus tested to be true. It is an important piece of information that could facilitate the overall navigation at airports. This information is currently not available to travelers and this could contribute to their navigational and planning difficulties. The existing ways of communicating time-related information are placing signs of estimated waiting time at destinations or putting signs about the estimated walking time to a specific location. They tend to be less effective than the way of providing time information that was presented in the survey (i.e. through a mobile application). For example, having the waiting time to be available at a desti- nation is not effective at all when someone is trying to plan for their destinations based on the waiting time. Regarding our hypothesis two, it was tested to be partially true because we only observed slightly significant difference between scenarios and tasks. It suggested that time pressure could be a factor affecting travelers' attitudes towards time information. In some situations, where the time pressure is low, travelers may consider other information to be more helpful than time. From a design perspective, it is worth further investigating about the type of information travelers would need in those sit- uations. Our third hypothesis about the difference of ratings caused by abilities, it was also tested to be partially true that we only observed travelers with mobility impair- ments having significant different ratings than others. For travelers with mobility impairments, the time information was found to be less important. This may suggest that for travelers with mobility impairments, they may consider other information such as accessibility to be more critical than waiting time and walking time when planning for activities and routes. It is possible and promising to integrate this information into the design of airport guide systems to aid travelers with different abilities to better plan activities and navigate at airports.

6 Future Work

Given the relatively small sample size, the data collection is still ongoing to collect more responses to further investigate traveler's needs and test the hypotheses. We hope to find strong evidence to support the design decision of integrating time information as a part of navigation aids for airports. This finding could be generalized to other indoor navigation scenarios when time is important, such as navigation in hospitals. This study emphasized the importance of planning in navigation, which is generally overlooked in existing navigation studies. The next step will be to collect more data and other information that travelers consider to be important. These findings will be used to design a context-aware guide system for air travelers.

References

1. Burdette, D., Hickman, M.: Investigation of information needs of departing air passengers. Transp. Res. Rec. J. Transp. Res. Board **1744**, 72–81 (2001)
2. Gupta, R., Venkaiah, V.: Airport passengers: their needs and satisfaction. SCMS J. Indian Manag. **12**(3), 46–58 (2015)
3. Dolliole, K.C.: Synthesis 51 Impacts of Aging Travelers on Airports (2014)
4. Hoogendoorn, S.P., Bovy, P.H.L.: Pedestrian route-choice and activity scheduling theory and models. Transp. Res. Part B Methodol. **38**(2), 169–190 (2004). http://doi.org/10.1016/S0191-2615(03)00007-9
5. Churchill, A., Dada, E., de Barros, A.G., Wirasinghe, S.C.: Quantifying and validating measures of airport terminal wayfinding. J. Air Transp. Manag. **14**(3), 151–158 (2008). http://doi.org/10.1016/j.jairtraman.2008.03.005
6. Fewings, R.: Wayfinding and airport terminal design. J. Navig. **54**(2), 177–185 (2001). http://doi.org/10.1017/S0373463301001369
7. Radaha, T.R., Johnson, M.E.: Mobile Indoor Navigation Application for Airport Transits (2013)
8. Horton, T.B.: SKINNI: The Smart Kiosk Information Navigation and Note-Posting Interface (2004)
9. Karimi, H.A., Ghafourian, M.: Indoor routing for individuals with special needs and preferences. Trans. GIS **14**(3), 299–329 (2010)
10. Pielot, M., Poppinga, B., Heuten, W., Boll, S.: A tactile compass for eyes-free pedestrian navigation. In: Campos, P., Graham, N., Jorge, J., Nunes, N., Palanque, P., Winckler, M. (eds.) INTERACT 2011. LNCS, vol. 6947, pp. 640–656. Springer, Heidelberg (2011). doi:10.1007/978-3-642-23771-3_47
11. Heuten, W., Henze, N., Boll, S., Pielot, M.: Tactile wayfinder: a non-visual support system for wayfinding. In: Proceedings of the 5th Nordic Conference on Human-Computer Interaction: Building Bridges, pp. 172–181. ACM, October 2008
12. Gedawy, H.K.: Designing an interface and path translator for a smart phone-based indoor navigation system for visually impaired users. Doctoral dissertation, Qatar Foundation (2011)
13. Walker, B.N., Lindsay, J.: Navigation performance with a virtual auditory display: effects of beacon sound, capture radius, and practice. Hum. Fact. J. Hum. Fact. Ergon. Soc. **48**(2), 265–278 (2006)
14. Chang, Y.J., Chu, Y.Y., Chen, C.N., Wang, T.Y.: Mobile computing for indoor wayfinding based on Bluetooth sensors for individuals with cognitive impairments. In: 3rd International Symposium on Wireless Pervasive Computing, ISWPC 2008, pp. 623–627. IEEE, May 2008
15. Liu, A.L., Hile, H., Borriello, G., Brown, P.A., Harniss, M., Kautz, H., Johnson, K.: Customizing directions in an automated wayfinding system for individuals with cognitive impairment. In: Proceedings of the 11th International ACM SIGACCESS Conference on Computers and Accessibility, pp. 27–34. ACM, October 2009

Lived Experiences and Technology in the Design of Urban Nature Parks for Accessibility

Tiiu Poldma[1,4(✉)], Hélène Carbonneau[2], Sylvie Miaux[2],
Barbara Mazer[3,5], Guylaine Le Dorze[1,6,7], Alexandra Gilbert[2],
Zakia Hammouni[1,6], and Abdulkader El-Khatib[1,6]

[1] École de design, Université de Montréal, Montréal, Canada
{Tiiu.poldma, Guylaine.le.dorze, Zakia.hammouni}
@umontreal.ca, Abdulkader.elkhatib@gmail.com
[2] Department of Leisure, Culture and Tourism Studies,
Université du Québec à Trois-Rivières, Trois-Rivières, Canada
{Helene.carbonneau, Sylvie.Miaux,
Alexandra.Gilbert}@uqtr.ca
[3] School of Physical and Occupational Therapy,
McGill University, Montreal, Canada
Barbara.mazer@mcgill.ca
[4] Centre for Interdisciplinary Research in Rehabilitation
of Greater Montreal - Centre de recherche IRGLM, Montréal, Canada
[5] Centre for Interdisciplinary Research in Rehabilitation
of Greater Montreal- Jewish, Rehabilitation Hospital, Laval, Canada
[6] Centre for Interdisciplinary Research in Rehabilitation of Greater Montreal,
Montréal, Canada
[7] School of Speech-Language Pathology and Audiology,
Université de Montréal, Montréal, Canada

Abstract. This exploratory research project explores the mobility challenges of outdoor navigation and way-finding, through the lens of the person with a disability. Obstacles in social participation and human interaction with technology within the urban environment are salient issues driving this research study about mobility and accessibility when navigating urban parks. People with disabilities, specifically those with mobility limitations, such as people in motorized wheelchairs, have particular needs that must be addressed to maximize social participation within in the urban environment and involvement in leisure activities. This study examines the physical environment and social activities that occur in a typical leisure filled day at the park, what obstacles hamper navigation, and what issues emerge from the perspective of the person with the disability. The study data collection proceeds from a constructivist perspective using a participatory approach (Living Lab), wherein researchers and participants collaborated together to create the activity and also to assess its success post activity. Data collection tools included walkabouts, recording conversation in real time, and discussions both before and after the research activity. The study is presented with examples, and the emergent issues help reveal opportunities for potential ways to both respond to mobility challenges and integrate way-finding, as a means for future development of mobility and

© Springer International Publishing AG 2017
M. Antona and C. Stephanidis (Eds.): UAHCI 2017, Part III, LNCS 10279, pp. 308–319, 2017.
DOI: 10.1007/978-3-319-58700-4_26

navigational tools for better accessibility and enjoyment of social activities within the urban park environment.

Keywords: Accessibility · Way-finding · Inclusive environments · Urban nature parks · Navigational tools · Living labs · User experiences

1 Introduction

This exploratory research project looks at the obstacles in social participation, and how human interaction with technology within the urban environment has an impact on mobility and accessibility when navigating urban parks. Social participation is the key in activities such as leisure and people with disabilities, in particular those with limitations requiring navigation such as people in motorized wheelchairs, have particular needs that must be addressed to have access in the urban environment. Leisure activities are vital to social participation and quality of life. Too often, in urban city centers, parks are provided for able-bodied use with limited technological aids for people of different abilities.

In this paper, we present a current, ongoing research study that constructs how people with disabilities use and navigate parks for social activities and leisure, the challenge they encounter in terms of mobility challenges, what Human Computer Interaction (HCI) issues arise when navigating urban parklands and what solutions might be possible to enhance navigation and access to the parks and their various services. From a universal perspective, people with disabilities can benefit from urban parks as much as other citizens who frequent parks such as families with children or the elderly who might want to go to the park for leisure activities. Parks provide diverse activities to enhance both engagement with nature, as well as encourage social activities with others, as a means of supporting a more active everyday lifestyle (Poldma et al. 2014; Shikako-Thomas et al. 2008). For persons with disabilities, parks can be challenging, as what might seem easy to navigate, actually is complex for people, depending on their relative ability to navigate the park and its various features. In this research study, we investigated how the "Human Development Model - Disability Creation Process (HDM-DCP)" is applied when people engage together in leisure activities, and how to integrate both practices and devices that emerge from the research conducted. This paper proposes understanding the human needs, and provides prospective ways that navigation systems might be integrated into the user experiences of leisure through HCI tools. We will present how leisure activities can be enhanced for persons with disabilities, how social participation contributes to a more active lifestyle and what technological means might enhance leisure activity. We then present the ongoing research with a case study showing how these ideas are applied in a participatory action research project in an urban city park.

2   Background: Social Participation, Leisure, Inclusive Outdoor Experiences, and Navigation and Technological Aids for Accessibility

We explore these issues from the following perspectives: Social participation and active leisure, inclusive outdoor activities, and issues of mobility and technological integration (HCI integration).

2.1   Social Participation and an Active Lifestyle

Social participation manifests itself in 5 ways (1) Maintaining social relations as an individual; (2) Maintaining social relations in the context of a group; (3) Participation in collective activities (leisure, courses, conferences), (4) Doing organized or unorganized volunteer work; and (5) Engaging in socio-political causes (Raymond et al. 2008). Leisure activities include diverse practices that align cultural activities with physical activities and sports.

The latter are important for people with disabilities as they contribute to a more active lifestyle, and in particular, outdoor activities contribute to physical and mental well-being. Contact with people in outdoor activities plays a major role to prevent sedentary tendencies in society in general, and that is even more salient with people living with disabilities (Badia et al. 2013; Buttimer et Tierney 2005; Shikako-Thomas et al. 2008; Anderson et Heyne 2010). Furthermore, social contact alleviates a sense of powerlessness brought on by perceptions of alienation that can occur when people do not perceive themselves as part of a social reality (Hall 1981).

2.2   Inclusive Outdoor Experiences

While outdoor activities are a vital means to develop good physical and mental health, certain groups of people consider themselves excluded from these types of activities (Williams et al. 2004). In particular, persons with disabilities have more difficulties accessing outdoor activities outside of those offered by specialized centers, such as adaptive skiing for people with special needs, and what programs are offered for inclusive outdoor activities (Carbonneau et al. 2017; Freudenberg and Arlinghaus 2010; McAvoy). The outdoor setting plays an important role factor in the success of the outdoor activities and how these provide benefits for persons with disabilities, by providing a sense of pride, accomplishment and freedom. For example, in a study conducted within 15 different places such as ski clubs, sailing clubs, and provincial parks, the determinants of outdoor leisure experience aligned with specific sports such as swimming, cycling, etc. in the natural settings such as mountains, lakes, and forests and with adapted assistance (Carbonneau et al. 2017).

Furthermore, research on urban and outdoor environments show that how settings are conceived and designed affect how socially inclusive the spaces are as they receive participants (Lawton 1974; Dogu and Erkip 2000). An important aspect of the ability to enjoy the outdoors, for example, is how the activities evoke passion and pleasure while in the activity for the person with a disability and their capacity to arrive and circulate socially. Furthermore, aside from the pleasure associated with being outdoors, the benefits of socialisation that accompany the activity reduce isolation (Sutherland and Stroot 2010) and enhance mental health (Wilson and Christensen 2012). Way-finding is a specific means to assist in grounding access and providing a means for such socialization, decrease disorientation and increase a sense of security (Dogu and Erkip 2000).

2.3 A Universal Design Approach and HCI Needs

A second issue is how easily an activity is accessible both physically and also in terms of the navigational aids available to the prospective leisure activity user. In this exploratory study we take a universal design approach that favors accessibility for all people in all types of situations (Mace 1997; Lidwell et al. 2003) and use HCI navigational tools. As disabilities vary in terms of scope and need, this has an impact on the nature of navigational aids and apps available for facilitating arrival and access to the leisure activities. People are able to navigate the urban park when their universal needs are met. When enhanced with HCI tools, this enhancement becomes positive (Lidwell et al. 2003). Studies show that when persons with disabilities are supported with universal accessible support in the form of navigational tools, whether physical or in the forms of apps, their capacity to positively enjoy the environment increases (Dogu and Erkip 2000). These issues have a direct impact on the capacity and persistence for the person with a disability in participating actively in the particular park or leisure activity. In this context, animation in terms of apps and adaptation, to aid in accessing the park, play a major role in providing optimal conditions for park access by the person with a disability.

3 Navigation and Technology Aides for Leisure Activities as a Means of Easing Way-Finding

There is a lack of literature and understanding about how the outdoor activity and its infrastructure affect the participation and the quality of the experience of the person with a disability, in terms of ease of navigation in urban parks. Way-finding is one way to facilitate how people navigate circulation paths and the various elements within the urban environment and offers a way to assist how a person makes decisions to go from one part of an environment to another. (Paul and Passini 2002; Lidwell et al. 2003). What way-finding markers assist in circulation and how navigational tools can provide clarity in how the way-finding occurs in an outdoor park are salient issues to be investigated. When way-finding is absent and cognitive mental maps are not available as part of the urban park experience, the very physical design of the urban park may hamper navigation and accessibility for persons with disabilities.

Issues such as the design of the park and the navigational tools provided in terms of access to the park with transport, access within the park and navigating the park using pathways and terrain that accommodates various needs are all factors to consider. It is thus vital to understand both the park and urban environment characteristics, the park layouts and how they are designed, and what specific facilities are provided both physical and in terms of HCI navigational tools. (National Park Service 2015; Burns et al. 2009).

Finally, transport to and from the activity, and the park, are also factors that affect the quality of the experience. In urban parks the relative proximity of transport drop-offs and parking are features of importance and there is little understanding of these more personal needs of the person with a disability and their capacity to arrive and navigate with the park. A necessary and pertinent issue to understand is the navigation to and from the park, and how to develop specific activities accessible within urban parks (Fullerton 2003).

3.1   Experiencing the Outdoors in an Urban Park and How Social Factors Are Impacted by Environmental Factors

The experience of accessible outdoor activities in urban parks is tantalizing for persons with disabilities when they can arrive at the park with adaptive municipal transport services. Social participation as a component of this experience enhances the quality of the experience of citizens with disabilities and has been demonstrated as a factor in well-being. (Swaine et al. 2014; Poldma et al. 2014).

Social participation has a significant effect on environmental factors (RIPPH 2017). Studies show that social participation enables and enhances the quality of life of users within the environments that they do activities (Labbé et al. 2017). Social participation is also enhanced when environmental factors are considered as salient to social access (Poldma et al. 2014; Swaine et al. 2014). A deeper understanding of how environmental factors in an urban park is also necessary to understand how to maximize social participation, what role HCI factors play, and how socialization can be enhanced when considering the physical aspects of the environment. Environmental factors include the characteristics of the physical space, as well as the social and individual attitude towards a particular environment (OMS 2001; Poldma et al. 2014). In an urban park, the physical environment includes climactic, geographic and natural elements of the surrounding environment and the man-made, artificial and constructed features of urban parks.

The individual attitude towards the environment refers to the individual attitudes and capacities to situate themselves in the immediate environment. For a person with disabilities this is a salient feature of their capacity to navigate the spaces of urban cities in general, and urban parks in particular. The societal environment includes abstract features such as politics, procedures and community services of the society or of the culture within which the individual participates. The desire to maximize the ideal accessibility conditions of the outdoor experience for the person with disabilities depends on providing complete and appropriate infrastructure features that support access and that are able to assist in the full integration of the person within the urban park. HCI and apps are a means to accomplish these objectives and understanding the participants' individual and personal experience is vital for this purpose.

4 Methodological Overview and Objectives

This research study unfolds with two phases: (1) Activities that are documented in the situation of a leisure day out in the urban park, and (2) the analysis of what emerges from the data collected. The methodological approach is predicated on a constructivist approach, the Living Lab, wherein the researchers and participants participate together in the situation that is being studied, and the reality constructed reveals new insights into the issues facing persons with disabilities. Researchers and participants co-construct the issues of accessing and navigating the park together, first in a preparatory meeting and then in a leisure activity held at the park, including a picnic lunch and walkabouts. All participants participate collectively in the leisure experiences, and the researchers prepare the participants for the leisure activity in advance of the activity. During the walkabout, user conversations and observations in real time are documented to glean the park experiences first – hand and to understand the issues within the park hampering full inclusive leisure participation.

Specific objectives were to:

(1) Understand the expectations and needs of the person with a disability regarding urban parks and outdoor activities;
(2) Understand the inclusive outdoor park experience;
(3) Identify the environmental factors that facilitate or limit the quality of the urban park outdoor experience;
(4) Determine the environmental factors that facilitate access to urban parks, within the context of a Living Lab with park partners;
(5) Document the actions that have effectively facilitated the accessibility to outdoor experiences in parks that assure an optimal outdoor experience for persons with disabilities.

A salient feature of these objectives is the ability of persons with disabilities to use HCI as a means to both access and use these urban park features.

4.1 Methodology

This research project is done within the framework of a participatory approach, within the Living Lab of the urban park. First, this qualitative approach is predicated on the «Living Lab» concept. Living labs are considered ideal mechanisms for studying in depth the persons' experience in real time. The Living Lab approach used here is done in an urban park, where participants and partner-collaborators collaborate with researchers in co-constructing the experiences. Leminen, Westerlund and Nyström (2012) define the approach as follows: *«Physical and other stakeholders, all collaborating for creation, protoyping, validating and testing of new technologies, services, products and systems in real life contexts»*. The physical environment of the urban park is the place where all participants collaborate together to create and validate the activities and wherein the living lab, the lived experiences are accounted for. The services that are produced in a context of this real time environment are also at the basis of studying what supports experiences promoting pleasure and participation to the

Fig. 1. Views of the urban park with participants (Photo: courtesy Z. Hammouni)

fullest degree possible. The knowledge gleaned is co-constructed as researchers accompany the participants in leisure activities within the park that are planned in advance. Here in Fig. 1 we see the participants in the park as we toured in one of the case studies and that is presented in this paper:

Data collection proceeded using two tools. First, the experiences in the park are documented using the «Mobils» method (Murray 2009; Miaux 2007; Miaux et al. 2010). Mobils method is used to document the walkabouts in the urban park, the participant experiences and the determinant components of how the itinerary is experienced by the participants in real time (Miaux 2007). This data then informs the qualities and obstacles of the environment where people navigate. There are three stages that include: (1) Meeting the participants to discuss their concerns, desires, apprehensions and specific needs; (2) A visit using video camera, photo, and recording devices to capture the experiences «in-vivo», in real time within the urban park; and (3) a meeting post visit to talk about the experience.

Second, the physical features and characteristics of the outdoor visual environment and how activities are integrated physically and socially were documented using the Environment Quality and Satisfaction Tool (EQST) (Poldma 2007; Poldma et al. 2014). The EQST documents the physical, visual and activity characteristics of the physical site and throughout the walkabouts, the obstacles and features of the site during these activities, and how way-finding occurs. Photos are taken and integrated into the subsequent analysis. The EQST is used to permit the evaluation of the physical environment; circulation and way-finding paths are documented and the analysis of the features allow researchers to consider how the urban park and its features compliment, or hinder, the quality of the experience. Finally, using both tools researchers also document the inter-relations of the person with others in the park and their use of HCI to facilitate their journey.

Finally, the two data collection results were transcribed and brought together for two analyses. First, an interpretive analysis to consider what emerges from the data. The analysis proceeded with a culling of the emergent, salient themes from the data. Second, a Visual Content Analysis (Rose 2001; Poldma et al. 2014) was conducted to evaluate the physical conditions of the site described in this study, as well as how circulation and way-finding occurred during the walk-about and leisure activities.

4.2   Sampling and Study Elements

This study was done in three locations; three different urban parks in various sized metropolitan centres. Both semi-urban and urban parks were selected in small, medium and larger metropolises. The sampling consisted of three urban park sites, with small participant numbers (n = 6 in small; n = 5 in medium and 6 in large parks) and included 2–4 research assistants and 3 of 4 co-investigators at each visit. The participants were people with disabilities of varying degrees and of different types, and this was done as a conscious choice, to provide the broadest cross-section possible of abilities and experiences. Characteristics of the participants included persons in motorized wheelchairs, persons with low vision or auditory impairments, persons with aphasia, and blind persons requiring guide dogs. In each case, the researchers accompanied the participants and were experts from rehabilitation or occupational therapy sciences. For the purposes of this paper, we present the emergent results of one of the case studies with visual and narrative examples.

5   Analysis of Preliminary Results: Constructing a Portrait of the Issues and Potential Solutions

In the analysis phase, initial results include several emergent issues and suggestions as offered by the participants. Given the constructive nature of the research, expression and discussion of ideas were encouraged as concerns arose. The analysis also included a visual content examination of the park's physical features and how the circulation and navigation occurred on site.

Participants spoke about having searched before the trip for information about the park, because they usually prepare a trip and identify the various accessibility features of the environment they will visit. However, participants had not found such information. During the park visit, participants identified the need for clear information on site, about the park's features in order to again plan and readjust the ongoing outing as needs arose (for example, location of toilets, of dog park, picnic area, etc.). Such information was not provided and affected their experience of the park. For example, the participant using an ordinary wheelchair had a long and tortuous journey, as well as difficulty navigating parts of the park that were not accessible in order to find the picnic area where other participants were having lunch. This anecdote was followed by many observations of the lack of way-finding sign posts to indicate pathways or directions. Clear visual maps and navigation tools for individuals with visual limitations in the form of apps provided both in advance or at the arrival of the park could facilitate navigation, exploration and satisfaction with the park experience.

Also noteworthy were difficulties in terms of physical accessibility, such as a complex system of fenced doors for entering and exiting the dog park, changes in the ground surface including rocks where cement sections ended, inclined sections on the walkway. Another type of issue occurred where a feature was apparently accessible but was not in practice. For example, because a picnic table was a level up from the grass on a cement platform, it thus became inaccessible. In another example, at the children's playground, what appeared to researchers as "accessible" with even pathways to the play area, was not, as the people mobilizing in wheelchairs sank into the sand and had to deal with the concrete floor that was uneven underneath.

Aesthetic features such as the pagoda are there to encourage people to admire views and interact socially, and yet this feature was only accessible by stairs. This created a social separation and stigma for those who arrived with a wheelchair or a dog guide, and could not access the pagoda. Another aesthetic feature such as the lake area included a semi-circle of benches immobilized in cement without a section of space where a wheelchair could have backed in thus preventing one from enjoying the landscape and conversing about one's experience of the site with another non-wheelchair user, contributing again to the potential sense of exclusion one could feel (Fig. 2).

Fig. 2. A feature of the park (Photo : courtesy T. Poldma)

6   Discussion

The walkabouts and data analysis reveal that participant views on appropriate and useful navigation systems are vital for the development of both the physical and social nature of the urban park. The meetings with participants to discuss their concerns, desires, apprehensions and specific needs framed the visit beforehand, and the post-visit meeting to discuss their perceptions and experiences after the activity, were vital for discovering the emergent issues.

Much of the discussion with participants about their views of issues and obstacles within the urban park experience centered around the lack of HCI integration to facilitate the navigation and accessibility features of the park. The addition of both apps and mobility navigation devices may enhance the park experience; however, without the integration of cognitive way-finding devices, such as maps, and social activities, such as having a picnic, the use of the apps and navigational devices is secondary. Of primary importance to the participants is the ability to pre-conceive their navigational pathways to and within the urban park, and then once there, use the navigational devices (HCI) and physical pathways and way-finding devices physically in place to move around and enjoy the park experience. However, with the features in the actual park such as the pagoda, eating areas and playgrounds, there is reason to believe that our participants' experience was not as pleasurable as it should have been. An app that could locate specific accessible spots for aesthetic experience and conversation could allow for the fulfillment of various needs that parks are assumed to satisfy.

Potential solutions are related to social participation, way-finding and navigational options and in particular, in terms of time and the overall visit experience. First, pre-visit participatory maps, apps and other assistive devices can facilitate the preparation for persons with disabilities. Second, way-finding apps and physical on-site way-finding benchmarks can be provided to facilitate the arrival and the activity itself. Finally, social participation can be enhanced with physical design elements that integrate activities for everyone, and by eliminating features in the urban park that create isolation and stigma. Hampering social participation are presumptions of solutions that are "accessible" and yet do not provide real access for the person with a disability, placing them into an uncomfortable situation of stigmatisation.

The documentation of both visual and verbal data in real time provided the researchers with rich and detailed data about the urban park walkabout and the outdoor activity experiences that were conducted on the three different sites. Each site had its particular characteristics and each group of participants had their particular needs. The analysis revealed how the physical features and characteristics of the outdoor visual environment provided either an obstacle or a support for certain social activities.

From the perspective of the participants, frustrations run high when (a) the access to information about an outdoor place is limited to only information provided to the general public; (b) when, upon arrival, way-finding and signage are unclear or absent in terms of providing cognitive navigational direction for the participant arriving on site, and when the physical conditions of the site hamper access, even with preparation and apps showing the way. For example, getting down a hill that was not part of the information provided, prevents people with wheelchairs accessing the social activity of a picnic as the hill was not part of the information that they received initially.

7 Conclusion

This exploratory study reveals the challenges of the people with disabilities when they attempt to navigate the outdoor environment and the mobility challenges that these produce. The results show that navigation systems and services would benefit from a closer integration of mobility apps, and how HCI offers a means to alleviate current mobility challenges and the information needed to access the urban park.

The urban Living Lab provided a rich experience for both participants and researchers to explore together issues of accessibility, what HCI solutions might be useful and how working together in experiencing a leisure activity forges new understanding about how to make the enjoyment of public parks easier for persons with disabilities and for everyone in an inclusive manner.

References

Anderson, L.S., Heyne, L.A.: Physical activity for children and adults with disabilities: an issue of "amplified" importance. Disabil. Health J. **3**, 71–73 (2010)

Badia, M., Orgaz, M.B., Verdugo, M.A., Ullàn, A.M.: Patterns and determinants of leisure participation of youth and adults with developmental disabilities. J. Intell. Disabil. Res. **57**(4), 319–332 (2013)

Burns, N., Paterson, K., Watson, N.: An inclusive outdoors? Disabled people's experiences of countryside leisure services. Leisure Stud. **28**(4), 403–417 (2009)

Buttimer, J., Tierney, E.: Patterns of leisure and participation among adolescents with a mild intellectual disability. J. Intell. Disabil. **9**(1), 1–18 (2005)

Carbonneau, H., Duquette, M.M., St-Onge, M. et Gilbert, A.: Pour une expérience de plein air accessible et sécuritaire pour les personnes ayant des incapacités: Final report, Laboratoire en loisir et vie communautaire, UQTR, Trois-Rivières (2017)

Dogu, U., Erkip, F.: Spatial factors affecting way-finding and orientation: a case study in a shopping mall. Environ. Behav. **32**(6), 731–755 (2000)

Freudenberg, P., Arlinghaus, R.: Benefits and constraints of outdoor recreation. Leisure Sci. **32**, 55–71 (2010)

Fullerton A.: Inclusive practices used by outdoor programs. In: Brannan, S. (ed.) Including Youth with Disabilities in Outdoor Programs: Best Practices, Outcomes and Resources, pp. 81–110, 241–246. Sagamore Publishing, Champaign (2003)

Hall, E.T.: Beyond Culture. Anchor Books, Garden City (1981)

Labbé, D., Poldma, T., Fichten, C., Havel, A., Kehayia, E., Mazer, B., McKinley, P., Rochette, A. Swaine, B.: Rehabilitation in the real life environment of the shopping mall. Disability and Rehabilitation, pp. 1–9, January 2017. http://dx.doi.org/10.1080/09638288.2016.1277394

Leminen, S., Westelund, M., Nyström, A.-G.:. Living Labs as Open – Innovation networks. In: Technology Innovation Management, pp. 5–10 (2012)

Mace, R.: Seven principles of Universal Design (1997). http://universaldesign.ie/What-is-Universal-Design/The-7-Principles/7-Principals-.pdf

McAvoy, L.: Outdoors for everyone: opportunities that include people with disabilities. Parks Recreation **36**(8), 24–36 (2001)

Miaux, S.: Chapitre 8: les marqueurs de l'itinéraire au service d'une approche opérationnelle des déplacements. Les indicateurs sociaux territoriaux, sous la direction de Gilles Sénécal, pp. 167–185. Presses de l'Université Laval, Québec (2007)

Miaux, S., Drouin, L., Morency, P., Paquin, S., Gauvin, L., Jacquemin, C.: Making the narrative walk-in-real-time methodology relevant for public health intervention: towards an integrative approach. Health Place **16**(6), 1166–1173 (2010)

Murray, L.: Looking at and looking back: visualization in mobile research. Qual. Res. **9**(4), 469–488 (2009)

National Park Service: All in, Accessibility in the National Park Service, 2015–2020. US Departament of the Interior (2014)

Organisation mondiale de la Santé: Classification international du fonctionnement et du handicap: CIF. Organisation mondiale de la Santé, Genève (2001)

Paul, A., Passini, R.: Wayfinding: People, Signs and Architecture. McGraw-Hill, New York (2002)

Poldma, T., Brack, D.: Lighting study at the Moe Levin Centre of the Douglas Hospital. Analysis report of the Phase I: Exploration study of the effects of light on behaviour and well-being of people with dementia in a specialized environment, p. 23. Douglas Hospital, Montreal, McGill University and Université de Montréal (2007)

Poldma, T., Desjardins, M., Mazurik, K., De Grosbois, E., Herbane, H., Artis, G.: Understanding people's needs in a community public space: about accessibility and lived experience. ALTER Eur. J. Disabil. Res. **8**(3), 206–216 (2014)

Lawton, M.P.: Being and the institutional building. In: Lang, J., Burnette, C., Moleski, W., Vachon, D. (eds.) Designing for Human Behaviour, pp. 60–72. Dowdon, Hutchinson & Ross, Inc., Stroudsburg (1974)

Lidwell, W., Holden, K., Butler, J.: Universal Principles of Design. Rockport Publishers, Gloucester (2003)

Raymond, É., Gagné, D., Sévigny, A., Tourigny, A.: La participation sociale des aînés dans une perspective de vieillissement en santé. Réflexion critique appuyée sur une analyse documentaire. DSP de l'Agence de la santé et des services sociaux de la Capitale-Nationale, INSPQ, CEVQ et IVPSA (2008)

RIPPH: What is social participation. Retrieved from RIPPH/International network on disability creation process (2017). http://ripph.qc.ca/en/hdm-dcp/what-social-participation. Accessed 30 Apr 2017

Rose, G.: Visual Methodologies. Sage, London (2001)

Shikako-Thomas, K., Majnemer, A., Law, M., Lach, L.: Determinants of participation in leisure activities in children and youth with cerebral palsy: systematic review. Phys. Occup. Ther. Pediatr. **28**(2), 155–169 (2008)

Sutherland, S., Stroot, S.: The impact of participation in an inclusive adventure education trip on group dynamics. J. Leisure Res. **42**(1), 153–176 (2010)

Swaine, B., Kehayia, E., Longo, C., Ahmed, S., Archambault, P., Kairy, D., Fung, J. Lamontagne, A., Le Dorze, G., Lefebvre, H., Overbury, O. Poldma, T.: Creating a rehabilitation living lab to optimize the social participation and inclusion for persons with disabilities. ALTER, Eur. J. Disabil., J. européen de recherche sur le handicap **8**(3) (2014)

Williams, R., Vogelsong, H., Green, G., Cordell, K.: Outdoor recreation participation of people with mobility disabilities survey of recreation and environment. J. Park Recreation Admin. **22**(2), 85–101 (2004)

Wilson, J.F., Christensen, K.M.: The relationship between outdoor recreation and depression among individuals with disabilities. J. Leisure Res. **44**(4), 486–506 (2012)

Outdoor Wayfinding and Navigation for People Who Are Blind: Accessing the Built Environment

Robert Wall Emerson[✉]

Department of Blindness and Low Vision Studies,
Western Michigan University, Kalamazoo, USA
robert.wall@wmich.edu

Abstract. People who are blind use a range of tools and training to optimize their travel in the built environment. However, changes in the built environment have brought new challenges for blind mobility. Developments in technology, whether used by the person who is blind or designed within the built environment offer ways to overcome mobility challenges. Technology used by a person who is blind includes GPS units, ultrasonic detectors, and smartphone applications that offer travel system information. Technology designed to increase accessibility to the built environment includes accessible pedestrian signals, smart paint, talking signs, autonomous vehicles, integrated travel systems, and devices that communicate between the pedestrian and the built environment.

Keywords: Blind · Visual impairment · Pedestrian · Built environment · Accessibility · Orientation · Mobility

1 Introduction

1.1 Incidence of Visual Impairment

A person with a visual impairment includes people with a mild visual impairment (visual acuity of about 20/60) to people who are classified as blind (visual acuity 20/200 or worse) [1]. A person who is classified as blind might have useful but blurry vision, clear vision but a severely limited field of view, have only light perception, or have no vision at all [1]. All of these situations will impact a person's ability to travel effectively. Globally, it is estimated that 39 million people are blind and 246 million have low vision [2]. In the United States, in 2013, 2.3% of the population (or 7,327,800 people) were estimated by the American Community Survey as having a visual impairment [3]. It is estimated that there are 480,000 Canadians who are blind or who have low vision [4]. The majority of people with a visual impairment travel through a range of environments and use a range of tools to do so. While some might rely heavily on a human guide or a dog guide, most travel independently using learned skills and some combination of tools. These skills and tools are employed for both mobility (allowing one's self to move effectively in an environment) and orientation (knowing where one is within an environment).

© Springer International Publishing AG 2017
M. Antona and C. Stephanidis (Eds.): UAHCI 2017, Part III, LNCS 10279, pp. 320–334, 2017.
DOI: 10.1007/978-3-319-58700-4_27

1.2 Mobility

Most tools used by people who are blind are used to detect objects in the environment and surfaces changes such as drop offs. The most commonly used mobility tool is a long cane or white cane. As the most commonly used mobility device, the long cane has seen little change in decades. When the modern long cane was developed in the 1940s, aluminum was chosen as the shaft material. More recently, canes are also made of carbon fiber and fiberglass. Canes can have solid shafts or be folded into 4 or 5 segments for easier carrying and storage when not in use. Current long cane users can also choose from a variety of cane tips. Some are designed for longer use, some for easier use in long grass or rough terrain, and others for easy use in snow. In general, however, the cane is only as effective as the person wielding it.

Since the primary goals of cane use are obstacle and drop off detection, recent research has delved more deeply than in the past into how cane and user characteristics impact these two outcomes. For drop off detection, younger users are better than older users [5], constant contact is better than two point touch [6], preferred cane technique does not make a difference [7], and cane length is not a factor unless approximately 10% longer than the prescribed length [8, 9]. Heaviness and flexibility of the cane shaft is a factor on drop off detection but is differentially impactful according to which common cane technique is being employed [10]. For obstacle detection, constant contact is better than two point touch [11], but a cane's length or the width with which it is swung is not a factor [12].

Beyond the white cane, there have been a range of technologically based devices developed over the years designed to improve the mobility of people who are blind. Many have used ultrasonic waves and provided auditory or vibrotactile feedback about objects in the environment [13]. Some of these devices were worn on a person's body, some attached to a cane, and some were held in a person's hand. Few of these have seen widespread adoption. Those still in production and limited use are the Sonic Pathfinder, the Hand Guide, the Miniguide, and the K Sonar [13].

1.3 Orientation

In order to optimally get from one place to another independently, a person who is blind needs to be able to locate him or herself within that environment. For many years the only way to accomplish this was to build up a repertoire of landmarks on a traveled route or within a defined area. More recently, GPS based devices have seen greater use. An early version linked a GPS unit with a braille based computer called a BrailleNote. Later devices incorporated the GPS and interaction unit into one for smaller and easier to use devices. Devices currently under widespread use include the Trekker Breeze, the Trekker Maestro, or a GPS unit within a smartphone. Depending on the accuracy of the GPS unit, travelers who are blind are now able to locate themselves according to streets, intersections, or addresses. Many people who are blind have used GPS devices to virtually explore the area around them, looking for specific locations, or to simply observe their environment as a person who is sighted might. Many GPS units allow for routes to be remembered and recalled or planned ahead of time to make travel more efficient.

But all of these devices used by a person who is blind, whether simple tools or technological marvels, place the onus of responsibility for travel on the traveler, with no adaptations of the built environment.

2 The Built Environment

People who are blind travel in all environments. They walk on sidewalks, cross streets, shop in malls, use buses, fly on airplanes, and generally travel as any other independent person does. By virtue of having limited or no sight, people with a visual impairment sometimes need a different way of getting information readily available to other pedestrian through vision. Historically, one of the main sources of useful information for a person relying on sound for navigation in an urban setting was the flow of traffic. Traffic flow can tell a person whether a street is one way or two way, how wide a street is, how close a person is to an intersection, and how close a person is to the street. All of these bits of information, combined with knowledge of how a city is laid out, allows a person to determine approximately where they are and perhaps even what direction they are walking. This process was used by people who were blind for decades and many skills taught by orientation and mobility (O&M) specialists were developed to take advantage of the usefulness of traffic flow information.

In the past 20 or so years, significant changes have been made to the typical environment in which a person who is blind will travel. Intersections have grown larger due to increased traffic flow, corners are more rounded to provide a greater turn radius for large vehicles, signals are increasingly linked to create platooning, intersections are more commonly actuated so that traffic signals react to the presence or lack of vehicles, and there are new and more complicated intersection geometries in use.

2.1 Impacts of Changes in the Built Environment on People Who Are Blind

One of the earlier changes to the built environment that impacted pedestrians who are blind was the creation of wheelchair ramps. These ramps were necessary to allow wheelchair users the ability to easily move between the sidewalk and street without having to deal with large level changes. However, once these ramps were becoming more prevalent, it was evident that pedestrians who were blind would often walk into the street without realizing it [14]. Detectable warnings in the form of truncated domes were developed to address this issue [15–18] (see Fig. 1). These surface treatments indicate the boundary between the walking surface and the road surface but do not provide any sort of alignment information. Countries other than the United States employ a secondary surface treatment that indicates where a crossing point exists and that provides some alignment information (see Fig. 2).

Fig. 1. Detectable warnings as commonly installed on a wheelchair ramp.

Fig. 2. Surface treatments used to guide pedestrians

When a pedestrian who is blind is at a legal crossing place, the traditional cue for determining when to begin crossing is the surge of traffic moving parallel with the pedestrian's intended line of travel. However, if no traffic is available, if the environment is noisy, or if the pedestrian has a problem perceiving the traffic, this cue might not be available. The solution for this issue of accessibility is the provision of accessible pedestrian signals (APS) [19]. This solution provides a pushbutton on each corner of an intersection that a pedestrian pushes when they wish to cross a street. At the appropriate time in the traffic cycle, which would be when the visual walk signal is lit for that pedestrian, an auditory signal is produced that indicates that the visual walk signal is lit. Many forms of APS also provide a vibrotactile signal so that a pedestrian who is deafblind can access the information. Note that the APS system does not indicate whether it is safe to cross, but only that the visual walk signal is lit: the same information available to a sighted pedestrian [20].

The need for additional guidance and access to information has become more necessary with the increase in actuated intersections. Before intersection actuation, intersections would cycle through regular intervals of one street and then the other street having a green traffic signal. As intersections have grown larger and traffic signal cycles have become more complex, keeping track of the cycle of traffic phases has become more difficult for pedestrians who are blind [21, 22]. At many larger urban intersections, both streets that meet at the intersection might have a traffic phase where vehicles proceed straight through the intersection, plus dedicated phases where traffic is only allowed to turn left, plus many other combinations of vehicular movement patterns. With the addition of traffic actuation, where the presence or length of a given traffic phase depends on what vehicles are queued in which lane, there might not be a regular pattern of traffic phases or lengths. If a pedestrian cannot visually perceive what the traffic is doing, the sequence of cycles may be difficult to ascertain. This is compounded by larger intersections where traffic that is turning from across the intersection might sound like it is proceeding straight, since those vehicles must move forward some distance before they begin their turn. In this situation, it is easy for a pedestrian who is blind to confuse a turning traffic movement with a parallel surge of traffic. The existence of an APS is designed to address this set of issues.

One of the latest developments in the built environment that is impacting the independent travel of pedestrians who are blind is the use of more complex intersection geometries. From the 1990s to the 2000s, this issue was focused on the increased building of roundabout intersections. Roundabouts present a particular problem to people who are blind because traffic does not have to stop and because walking paths

Fig. 3. A roundabout showing curved sidewalks and roadways with crossing facilities

and roadways are generally curved, often obscuring where crossing points are [23] (Fig. 3).

When crossing at a roundabout, a pedestrian who is blind must either determine that a large enough gap exists between vehicles to allow a crossing, cross in front of a stopped vehicle, or force a vehicle to stop. Determining that a large enough gap exists is easily done if traffic volume is light but if traffic is heavy, a pedestrian might not have a large enough gap for quite some time. In these cases, it has been shown that the longer a pedestrian is forced to wait, the more risk they are willing to assume in their crossing decisions [24].

If a pedestrian is not able to determine that a large enough gap exists between vehicles, the pedestrian needs to identify when a vehicle stops to allow the pedestrian to cross. However, a vehicle simply stopping does not provide the same amount of information to a pedestrian who is blind as it does to a pedestrian who is sighted. The driver might be looking at other traffic in the roundabout or be stopping for some reason unrelated to the pedestrian. If there are two lanes of traffic, a stopped vehicle in the first lane might auditorily mask the sound of an approaching vehicle in the second lane [25]. In cases where gaps are not easily identified and the pedestrian is unsure of yielding vehicles, there are some behaviors pedestrians can engage in that maximize yielding. The most effective behaviors are holding up a palm toward approaching vehicles or taking a single step into the roadway [26–28]. However, these strategies do not provide absolute safety and many pedestrians who are blind will not feel confident in using such strategies.

Some efforts that have been made to provide access to roundabouts for pedestrians who are blind include using tabled crossings that force vehicles to slow and, at roundabouts with higher traffic volumes, Pedestrian Hybrid Beacons (PHBs) that provide a red light for vehicles when a pedestrian pushes a pushbutton. These environmental modifications have been shown to increase yielding and access [29] but are not in widespread implementation. Nonetheless, even more complex geometries have already been developed that require new and different access innovations. Many newer intersection geometries such as a

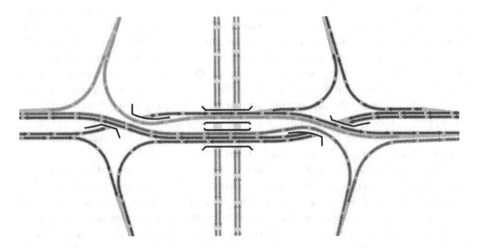

Fig. 4. Traffic paths through a double diamond interchange (Color figure online)

double diamond, the continuous flow intersection, a median U-turn, or a superstreet were designed to remove left turning traffic movements from where two streets crossed [30]. However, in doing so, some of these intersection geometries create extremely confusing paths and soundscapes for pedestrians who are blind. Some, like the diverging diamond, are solvable problems, given proper training and infrastructure (Fig. 4). Others, like the continuous flow intersection pose a greatly enhanced risk for pedestrians who are blind.

2.2 Developments in Using Technology to Create Smart Environments to Assist People Who Are Blind

Thus far, relatively low level innovations to the built environment have been used to try to solve accessibility issues for people who are blind. Audible beacons, raised cross-walks, and pedestrian channeling with fences can improve accessibility for pedestrians who are blind but these solutions tend to address specific issues at specific locations. In order to address systemic accessibility issues, more advanced technological solutions are being explored. These more technology based solutions also tend to be targeted at one element of transportation or mobility but are more able to be leveraged at a later date into something larger. There are three general classes into which current technologies can be placed: those that use technology to link blind pedestrians to intermediaries for help in navigating environments, those that attempt to enhance the amount of environmental information a blind pedestrian has access to, and those that create a platform in which the blind pedestrian interacts with the environment in a way that allows each to respond and adapt to the other.

An example of technology using intermediaries to help pedestrians who are blind to navigate environments is AIRA. In this system, a person who is blind wears a pair of eyeglasses outfitted with Google Glass or Vuzix. When the user requires information or assistance, they tap on the glasses to activate the system and a live, trained AIRA agent links in with the user. The agent is able to locate the user on their computer and also is able to see what is in the user's environment through a camera on the glasses. The user and agent converse and the agent gives the user necessary information which might include describing the environment, looking up transit information, plotting ideal routes to destinations, or even suggesting local restaurants. The agent stays on the line with the user as long as necessary until the user no longer needs the agent's services. Currently AIRA has 20 trained agents and has interacted with a select number of beta test individuals who are blind in cities across the United States. There are also other systems using a similar paradigm, such as a tele-guidance navigation system in Finland [31] and a remote guidance system developed at Brunel University in the UK [32]. Other similar systems use combinations of GPS, GIS, Digital Maps, Bluetooth, voice/video links through internet and GSM connections, digital web cams [33–36].

The development of smartphones, especially in combination with GPS, has allowed an explosion of apps designed to enhance environmental information available to pedestrians who are blind. Some, such as Tap Tap See and LookTel are not directly related to navigation but allow a person who is blind to be able to know more precisely what is in the environment around them. Tap Tap See takes a picture with the smartphone's camera, processes the picture, then speaks what is in the picture. Apps designed to enhance access to navigational information by people who are blind generally use some combination of Google maps, Apple maps, OpenStreetMaps, and GPS to provide location information. Different applications offer different options or user portals. Examples of these apps include:

- Blindsquare (uses data from Foursquare, OpenStreetMap, and Apple Maps to note current location, plan routes, link to transit apps, notes locations of interest, and explore maps),
- Sendero GPS Look Around (announces heading and cross streets, points of interest, voice over for Google maps),
- iMove (saves waypoints and links them to alerts and user recorded sounds),
- The Seeing Assistant Move (based on OpenStreetMaps, notes current location, plan routes, notes locations of interest, controlled by voice),
- Sendero Seeing Eye GPS (fully accessible turn by turn GPS app),
- City Lights (vibrates 3 times whenever near a traffic light),
- Smart Ride (transit directions, real time predications, and transportation routes),
- ViaOpta Nav (uses Apple Maps and Google Maps, GPS app that includes searches for accessibility information such as tactile paving and audible traffic signals),
- Ariadne GPS (notes current location, saves waypoints, explores maps),
- Microsoft soundscapes (provide 3D audio to traveler including turn by turn directions, and information about nearby items, points of interest, and obstacles).

There is also a range of standalone GPS based devices such as the Trekker Breeze, the Trekker Maestro, the Kapten, or the Braillenote GPS that are designed to provide travel information to people who are blind. While the Trekker series of GPS units enjoyed success within the blindness community, they are no longer being offered and even products still produced such as the Kapten, the Braillenote GPS, (see Fig. 5) are being replaced in user's life by smartphone based applications or other technologies that incorporate more features or link to other systems. Integrated systems such as Cydalion combine a smartphone, acoustic feedback, and vibrotactile feedback (through a vest for Cydalion) to provide warning of environmental obstacles.

The development of devices to aid people who are blind has a long history of devices not accepted by end users. However, the increasing precision of GPS technologies and the ease of having a range of digital tools on a smartphone has increased the chance that a person will have access to a tool that they find useful. The drawback in this recent plethora of applications and devices geared toward people who are blind is that it is difficult for even beneficial tools to draw the interest they deserve.

Finally, there are systems being developed to leverage a range of technologies embedded in the built environment to allow for interaction between the environment and the traveler. In 2016, 78 medium sized cities in the United States responded to the Department of Transportation's Smart City Challenge [37]. In this competition, cities developed proposals to create systems to make transportation safer, easier, and more reliable. Some common mobility challenges seen through the proposals include connecting underserved populations to transit from the first and last mile of their routes, coordinating systems, optimizing transport of goods, increasing parking and payment efficiency, limiting climate impact, and optimizing traffic flow [38]. The 7 finalists

Fig. 5. Images of the Braillenote GPS from Humanware and the Kapten from Kapsys

chosen to work with the Department of Transportation to further their ideas included Austin, Columbus, Denver, Kansas City, Pittsburgh, Portland, and San Francisco. In most cases, the proposed systems involve increased access to people with disabilities, with several specifically addressing needs of people with visual impairments. By ensuring that all city inhabitants have easy access to and use of the proposed systems, a city stands a better chance of developing a system that will be accepted and effective.

In Helsinki and the West Midlands, UK, the Mobility-as-a-service Initiative demonstrates how the internet of things and other trends in urban travel might be combined to create a new form of travel system [39]. The initiative is envisaging a time when there is no private car ownership but instead all inhabitants of the city will combine public transportation (bus, train, metro), on demand services (Uber, Lyft), and dedicated mini buses to plan and travel routes. As seen in Fig. 6, building the proper supports in the infrastructure allows a traveler to use one interface to access the full range of transport options linked in one system to plan and complete routes in an optimal manner.

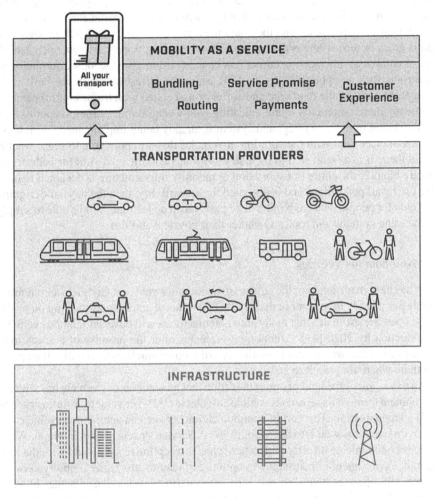

Fig. 6. Graphic of the mobility as a service system

Many proposals for developing smart city transportation include leveraging the internet of things, where the increasing number of elements in the built environment that have the ability to send and receive data allow for a broad network of digital connectedness. For example, there are several cities that are experimenting with some combination of beacons and smart signs so that any pedestrian, including those who are blind, can know when a bus or train will arrive, what route that bus or train is servicing, what the stops are when riding a transportation system, the layout of transit terminals, and a range of other useful pieces of travel information. As cities begin to put in place streetlights, garbage cans, and traffic lights that can all be connected in a digital web, it will be easier to create smartphone applications accessible to all pedestrians that allow for precise location information and interaction with a transportation system that is always in motion. If an urban system has smart garbage cans, buses, light poles, and traffic signals (among other things), a pedestrian who is blind that is employing an app linked to that system will be able to know not only where they are within the urban landscape but what smart items are around them and the status of those items (such as whether a light is green or red). There is even a project investigating smart paint where crosswalk lines or paint at an intersection corner can be accessed to give location information to pedestrians with an applicable device [40]. Since the infrastructure of the built environment, principally the hardware and software associated with traffic control devices, are already more commonly communicating with a central transportation control hub, the foundation of such an integrated system is already being implemented. With these systems in place, and with the addition of vehicles that are more able to sense what is around them, it is a small step to include pedestrians into the mix. And for pedestrians who are blind, if the entire transportation or mobility infrastructure is designed to optimize use by all pedestrians and is designed for accessibility, then the days of designing tools only for people who are blind will be past and all pedestrians will be able to simply use the same systems and tools, no matter their physical abilities.

2.3 Autonomous Vehicles

Much has been made lately of the advent of autonomous vehicles. Google's autonomous vehicle has already logged more than 1,000,000 miles of autonomous driving on public roads. There are estimates that many auto manufacturers will have autonomous vehicles in production by 2020 [41]. Autonomous vehicles offer the promise of a scenario in which a pedestrian who is blind can simply order up a vehicle, which will drive up and take them where they want to go.

An extension of the kind of communication that an autonomous vehicle has with the environment through its sensors is vehicle-to-vehicle (V2V) or vehicle-to-infrastructure (V2I) communication. This sort of communication between an autonomous vehicle and the environment fits well into the Mobility As A Service system shown in Fig. 6. When vehicles communicate directly with other vehicles to optimize safety and with the road and built environment infrastructure to optimize efficiency, the entire mobility network theoretically operates better. In this type of scenario, a pedestrian, whether blind or sighted, who has a device on their person that communicates their location to the built environment infrastructure, can access information about their location, the state of the surrounding infrastructure (construction, traffic light status, traffic volume, bus schedules, etc.) and vehicles approaching that pedestrian will be able to take any action required to avoid collisions.

While technologies previously discussed in this article were generally designed to assist people who are blind in navigating the built environment, autonomous vehicles are a trend in the transportation arena that do not target people who are blind. As such, it is important that advocates for people who are blind are part of the design process so that any wholesale modifications to the travel environment are made with the needs and abilities of people who are blind in mind. In this regard, interfaces through which a person communicates with an autonomous vehicle need to be accessible to people who are blind. When smartphones were first introduced, the touch screen interface posed an accessibility issue for people who are blind. However, with the development of voice over software for touch screens and other innovative overlays, people who are blind can now use touch screens adeptly for most applications. A similar interface solution will need to be designed into autonomous vehicle interactions since it is likely that people who are blind will be using autonomous vehicles regularly.

Five levels of automation have been adopted by the National Highway Transportation Safety Administration when referring to autonomous vehicles [42]. These levels are:

- Level 0: No automation (human driver in control of driving task)
- Level 1: Driver assistance (vehicle systems assist in either steering or acceleration/deceleration only in reaction to environmental information)
- Level 2: Partial automation (vehicle systems assist in both steering and acceleration/deceleration in reaction to environmental information)
- Level 3: Conditional automation (vehicle systems perform all aspects of driving task with human driver always ready to intervene)
- Level 4: High automation (vehicle systems perform all aspects of driving task even if human driver does not intervene when requested)
- Level 5: Full automation (vehicle systems perform all aspects of driving task full time) [42].

Theoretically, a large number of autonomous vehicles operating even at level 1 would eliminate a third of the annual crashes and fatalities on U.S. roadways [42]. Reductions in congestion, energy use, carbon emissions, and cost are also theorized [42].

Autonomous vehicles, especially at level 5, hold the promise of opening up travel possibilities for people who are blind more than any other development in recent memory. If the theoretical models hold true, a person who is blind will be able to use their smartphone to call up a vehicle that will meet them at their residence. The vehicle will not be subject to the schedule of a driver or other passengers and so will be on time more often. This is already a huge benefit since many people who are blind use paratransit services for longer routes in a city and many paratransit operations are notorious for being late and requiring at least 24 h scheduling ahead of time. Some sort of system will need to be incorporated into the autonomous use system to ensure that a person who is blind is able to know when the vehicle has arrived and which vehicle is the one they ordered. Once in the vehicle, the person who is blind will be able to take advantage of travel applications or devices such as those discussed previously to monitor their location or view nearby points of interest as they travel in the vehicle. Single person autonomous vehicles will be able to be linked to mass transit systems so that a person who is blind could take a single person vehicle to a metro stop or train station to begin a longer trip.

Whether a short inner city trip or a longer trip between cities, if autonomous vehicles are an integral part of the design of an overall mobility system, then a person who is blind will be able to access all levels and portions of the transport system the same as a person who is sighted. Of course, there will always be a place for personal mobility training and use of low tech devices such as the long cane. Any level of technological advancement will get a person only so close to a destination, the final leg of a journey will always be a person traveling with their own set of skills to locate a final destination.

References

1. Dandona, L., Dandona, R.: Revision of visual impairment definitions in the international statistical classification of diseases. BMC Med. **4** (2006). doi:10.1186/1741-7015-4-7
2. World Health Organization: Visual impairment and blindness. http://www.who.int/mediacentre/factsheets/fs282/en/
3. Erickson, W., Lee, C., von Schrader, S.: Disability Statistics from the 2013 American Community Survey (ACS). Cornell University Employment and Disability Institute (EDI), Ithaca (2015)
4. Canadian National Institute for the Blind: Fast facts about vision loss. http://www.cnib.ca/en/about/media/vision-loss/pages/default.aspx
5. Kim, D., Wall Emerson, R., Curtis, A.: Analysis of user characteristics related to drop-off detection with long cane. J. Rehab. Res. Dev. **47**, 233–242 (2010)
6. Kim, D., Wall Emerson, R., Curtis, A.: Drop-off detection with the long cane: effects of different cane techniques on performance. J. Vis. Imp. Blind. **103**, 519–530 (2009)
7. Kim, D., Wall Emerson, R., Curtis, A.: Interaction effects of the amount of practice, preferred cane technique, and type of cane technique used on drop-off detection performance. J. Vis. Imp. Blind. **104**, 453–463 (2010)
8. Kim, D., Wall Emerson, R.: Effect of cane length on drop-off detection performance. J. Vis. Imp. Blind. **106**, 31–35 (2012)
9. Rodgers, M., Wall Emerson, R.: Human factor analysis of long cane design: weight and length. J. Vis. Imp. Blind. **99**, 622–632 (2005)
10. Kim, D., Wall Emerson, R., Naghshineh, K., Auer, A.: Drop-off detection with the long cane: effect of cane shaft weight and rifidity on performance. Ergonomics (2016). doi: 10.1080/00140139.2016.1171403
11. Kim, D., Wall Emerson, R.: Effect of cane technique on obstacle detection performance. J. Vis. Imp. Blind. **108**, 335–340 (2014)
12. Kim, D., Wall Emerson, R., Naghshineh, K.: Effect of cane length and swing arc width on drop-off and obstacle detection with the long cane. Br. J. Vis. Imp. (submitted)
13. Smith, D.L., Penrod, W.M.: Adaptive technology for orientation and mobility. In: Wiener, W.R., Welsh, R.L., Blasch, B.B. (eds.) Foundations of Orientation and Mobility. History and Theory, vol. I, pp. 241–276. AFB Press, New York (2010)
14. Barlow, J., Bentzen, B.L.: Cues blind travelers use to detect streets. Final report. Department of Transportation, Federal Transit Administration, Volpe National Transportation Systems Center, Cambridge, MA (1994)
15. Hauger, J.S., Safewright, M.P., Rigby, J.C., McAuley, W.J.: Detectable warnings project: report of field tests and observations. Final report to U.S. Architectural and Transportation Barriers Compliance Board, Virginia Polytechnic Institute and State University, Blacksburg, VA (1994)
16. Bentzen, B.L., Nolin, T.L., Easton, R.D., Desmarais, L. Mitchell, P.A.: Detectable warning surfaces: detectability by individuals with visual impairments, and safety and negotiability for individuals with physical impairments. Final Report DOT-VNTSC-FTA-94-4 and FTA-MA-06-0201-94-2. U.S. Department of Transportation, Federal Transit Administration, Volpe National Transportation Systems Center, and Project ACTION, National Easter Seal Society (1994)

17. Hauger, J., Rigby, J., Safewright, M., McAuley, W.: Detectable warning surfaces at curb ramps. J. Vis. Imp. Blind. **90**, 512–525 (1996)
18. Bentzen, B.L., Barlow, J.M., Tabor, L.S.: Detectable Warnings: Synthesis of U.S. and International Practice. U.S. Access Board, Washington, D.C. (2000)
19. Harkey, D.L., Carter, D.L., Barlow, J.M., Bentzen, B.L., Myers, L., Scott, A.: Guidelines for accessible pedestrian signals. Final Report for NCHRP Project 3-62, NCHRP Web-only Document 117B (2007). http://onlinepubs.trb.org/onlinepubs/nchrp/nchrp_w117b.pdf
20. Harkey, D.L., Carter, D.L., Barlow, J.M., Bentzen B.L.: Accessible Pedestrian Signals: A Guide to Best Practice. NCHRP Web-only Document 117A (2007). http://onlinepubs.trb.org/onlinepubs/nchrp/nchrp_w117a.pdf
21. Barlow, J.M., Franck, L.: Crossroads: modern interactive intersections and accessible pedestrian signals. J. Vis. Imp. Blind. **99**, 599–610 (2005)
22. Barlow, J.M., Bentzen, B.L., Bond, T.: Blind pedestrians and the changing technology and geometry of signalized intersections: safety, orientation and independence. J. Vis. Imp. Blind. **99**, 587–598 (2005)
23. Guth, D.A., Ashmead, D.H., Long, R.G., Wall, R.S., Ponchillia, P.E.: Blind and sighted pedestrians at roundabouts. Hum. Fact. **47**, 314–331 (2005)
24. Ashmead, D.H., Guth, D.A., Wall, R., Long, R.G., Ponchillia, P.E.: Street crossing by sighted and blind pedestrians at a modern roundabout. J. Trans. Eng. **131**, 812–821 (2005)
25. Long, R.G., Guth, D.A., Ashmead, D.H., Wall Emerson, R., Ponchillia, P.E.: Modern roundabouts: access by pedestrians who are blind. J. Vis. Imp. Blind. **99**, 611–621 (2005)
26. Bourquin, E., Wall Emerson, R., Sauerburger, D.: Conditions that influence drivers' yielding behavior while crossing at uncontrolled intersections. J. Vis. Imp. Blind. **105**, 760–769 (2011)
27. Bourquin, E., Wall Emerson, R., Barlow, J., Sauerburger, D.: Conditions that influence drivers' yielding behavior in turning vehicles at intersections with traffic signal controls. J. Vis. Imp. Blind. **108**, 173–186 (2014)
28. Bourquin, E., Wall Emerson, R., Barlow, J., Sauerburger, D.: Conditions that influence drivers' behavior at a roundabout. J. Vis. Imp. Blind. **110** (in press)
29. Schroeder, B., Hughes, R., Rouphail, N., Cunningham, C., Salamati, K., Long, R., Guth, D., Wall Emerson, R., Kim, D., Barlow, J., Bentzen, B.L., Rodergerdts, L., Myers, E.: Crossing solutions at roundabouts and channelized turn lanes for pedestrians with vision disabilities. NCHRP Report 674, National Cooperative Highway Research Program, Transportation Research Board, Washington, D.C. (2011)
30. Hughes, W., Jagannathan, R., Sengupta, D., Hummer, J.: Alternative Intersections/Interchanges: Informational Report (AIIR). U.S. Department of Transportation, Federal Highway Administration Office of Safety, Washington, D.C. (2010)
31. Chaudary, B., Paajala, I., Keino, E., Pulli, P.: Tele-guidance based navigation system for the visually impaired and blind persons. In: Giokas, K., Bokor, L., Hopfgartner, F. (eds.) eHealth 360°. LNICSSITE, vol. 181, pp. 9–16. Springer, Cham (2017). doi:10.1007/978-3-319-49655-9_2
32. Garaj, V., Jirawimut, R., Ptasinski, P., Cecelja, F., Balachandran, W.: A system for remote sighted guidance of visually impaired pedestrians. Br. J. Vis. Impair. **21**, 55–63 (2003)
33. Baranksi, P., Polanczyk, M., Strumillo, P.: A remote guidance system for the blind. In: Proceedings of IEEE International Conference on e-Health Networking Applications and Services, pp. 386–390 (2010)
34. Bujacz, M., Baranski, P., Moranski, M., Strumillo, P., Materka, A.: Remote guidance for the blind – a proposed teleassistance system and navigation trials. In: Proceedings of International Conference on Human System Interaction, pp. 888–892 (2008)
35. Koley, S., Mishra, R.: Voice operated outdoor navigation system for visually impaired person. Int. J. Eng. Trends Technol. **3**(2), 153–157 (2012)

36. Hunaiti, Z., Garaj, V., Balachandran, W.: A remote vision guidance system for visually impaired pedestrians. Int. J. Navig. **59**(3), 497–504 (2006)
37. U.S. Department of Transportation: Smart city challenge. https://www.transportation.gov/smartcity
38. U.S. Department of Transportation: Smart city challenge lessons learned. https://www.transportation.gov/sites/dot.gov/files/docs/Smart%20City%20Challenge%20Lessons%20Learned.pdf
39. MAAS Global. www.maas.global/maas-as-a-concept
40. Lannutti, J.: Personal Communication. Ohio State University, Columbus (2017)
41. Anderson, J.M., Kalra, N., Stanley, K.D., Sorensen, P., Samaras, C., Oluwatola, O.A.: Autonomous Vehicle Technology: A Guide for Poliymakers. The RAND Corporation, Santa Monica (2016)
42. SAE International: U.S. Department of Transportation's new policy on automated vehicles adopts SAE international's levels of automation for defining driving automation in on-road motor vehicles (2016). https://www.sae.org/news/3544/

Inclusive Design Thinking for Accessible Signage in Urban Parks in Taiwan

Ko-Chiu Wu$^{(\boxtimes)}$ and Hsuan Wang

National Taipei University of Technology, Taipei, Taiwan (R.O.C.)
kochiuwu@mail.ntut.edu.tw, hsuanwang@ntut.edu.tw

Abstract. Taiwan is rapidly becoming an aged society, which has led to a focus on the changing needs of the public. One of these is the renovation of urban parks. To make these facilities more accessible, developers must reconsider wayfinding systems and signage design. A questionnaire was distributed among 347 participants to gauge opinions of the following dimensions of park signage systems: mind-map recognition, general needs & safety, sign layout & design, capabilities & perception. Statistical analysis was then conducted to discover how perspectives differ among age groups and people with differing disabilities. The results indicate that elderly and disabled groups were most concerned with the dimensions of general needs & safety and capabilities & perception. This evidence allows for the consideration of the nuanced needs of varying demographics, thereby satisfying user needs and removing constraints. This study serves to add to the body of work on inclusive design and identifies the union of sets where optimal solutions are found to meet user expectations.

Keywords: Inclusive design · Park planning · Aged society · Wayfinding · Barrier free · Autonomous access

1 Background

Lower fertility rates and increased life expectancies have resulted in a demographic shift in Taiwan. This has given rise to a cluster of social care issues associated with an aged society which have not yet received wide attention. An increasing number of senior citizens are being forced to adapt quickly to an independent lifestyle whether they are seriously failing in physical and mental capabilities or not. In 2016 Taiwan's population presented an even distribution among age groups: ages 0–19/19.5%, ages 20–34/21.3%, ages 35–49/24.1%, ages 50–64/22.0%, ages over 65/13.1% [1]. It is therefore important that we start to pay attention to inclusive design as opposed to designs specific to select groups of physically or mentally challenged individuals.

Aging trends have been reflected in urban planning policy in the government's emphasis on the optimization of public facilities. Between 2001 and 2010 urban park area increased from 2,635 to 4,428 hectares [2]. Policy has further reflected the needs of a diversifying population (in 2016 the disabled and elderly populations made up 4.94% and 13.13% respectively of the total population). Focus has been placed on altering standardized designs to cater to those with special needs. Figure 1 presents a schema for product design catering to users of different ages and capabilities.

© Springer International Publishing AG 2017
M. Antona and C. Stephanidis (Eds.): UAHCI 2017, Part III, LNCS 10279, pp. 335–347, 2017.
DOI: 10.1007/978-3-319-58700-4_28

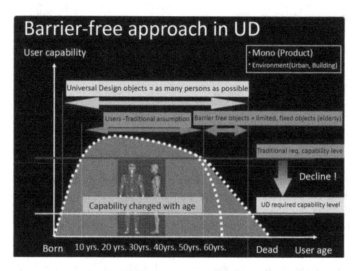

Fig. 1. Barrier-free approach in UD [3]

For example, barrier-free regulations have been promulgated to increase access for the disabled to public facilities. Inclusive design satisfies the needs of assorted user groups, including senior people. It requires an in-depth understanding of the specific needs of differing groups.

Kitchener et al. [4] pointed out that while older adults with physical disabilities made up 58% of Medicaid's HCBS waiver programs, this sector only benefited from 24% of total expenditures. Kane et al. [5] suggested that adults with similar degrees and types of disabilities but of different ages must be treated differently in terms of options for service and budget allocations, emphasizing that "fairness need not mean one size fits all" (p. 278). A one-size-fits-all approach hinders the development of more appropriate strategies to mediate the impact of disabilities in these various groups. This approach also lacks sufficient evidence related to the usefulness versus cost-effectiveness of different strategies. This highlights the subtleties involved in the design of universal public services that reasonably meet the specific needs of mixed groups.

In its campaign for healthy cities, with the aim of providing healthier, more comfortable human environments, the World Health Organization (WHO) sought out sufficient information and conducted extensive planning in order to ensure equity and fairness in its implementations and to optimize limited resources [6]. This model demonstrates the necessity of first identifying user needs. Ritsatakis [7] found cities in phase IV continue to focus on vulnerable groups rather than the full social gradient. More attention must be given to evaluating the effectiveness of actions aimed at enhancing local governance of health, and to improving the knowledge base for monitoring progress and avoiding health inequalities related to a greater part of the socioeconomic gradient. Taiwan is a member of the Healthy City Network in the West Pacific. It is necessary for the authorities in these cities to examine data related to the allocation and effectiveness of resources in order to ensure fair use of available budgets for the creation of an elderly- and disabled-friendly city.

A primary concern for age-friendly cities is autonomous access for all city-dwellers to urban parks. Davis and Weisbeck [8] pointed out that "the ability to find one's way, known as wayfinding, is essential for maintaining independence in the world" (p. S118). Carefully designed signage is therefore key to ensuring accessibility for people with different types of disabilities. The present study conducted a survey among a diversified group of visitors to urban parks. This research forms part of a greater effort to make Taiwan a senior-friendly country. It simultaneously improves the allocation of resources within public facilities through the formulation of policies regarding urban green spaces.

2 Objectives

2.1 Aging in Place and Accessibility to Open Space

Domestic settings have a significant effect on the wellbeing of the elderly [9]. The use and accessibility of urban facilities helps strengthen senior people's engagement in social activities, thereby helping them maintain an active lifestyle [10]. Satariano et al. [11] proffered that mobility disability affects senior people's daily activities such as shopping and walking, which in turn causes physical weakness. Sugiyama and Ward Thompson [12] investigated constraints associated with walking by the elderly. They found that walking for recreation is aided by the pleasantness of open space and lack of nuisances, whereas walking for transport is aided by good paths and good facilities. Rosenberg et al. [13] examined the requirements of middle-aged and older adults with mobility disabilities to identify the barriers affecting participants' access to outdoor environments. In terms of the interplay among mobility, built environments, and health, "studies that focus more broadly at relating built environment features to various types of mobility among older adults with mobility limitations are needed" (p. 277). Bosch and Gharaveis [14] reviewed literature focusing on the means by which older adults experiencing visual or cognitive decline recognize wayfinding signs, concluding that future efforts should center on technology-based solutions, facility planning and the design of strategies to improve navigation. de Paolis and Guerini [15] focused on the role of design in the fruition of territories and cultural development, with particular emphasis on accessibility and orientation in paths and places by people with different abilities. Thus, one of the objectives of this study is to investigate how people of different ages and disabilities navigate autonomously in urban parks.

2.2 Wayfinding by Elderly Park Users

Urban parks are shared spaces utilized by individuals wishing to engage in outdoor leisure activities. Several factors, such as age [16], accessibility [17], and mobility [18], have an impact on the use of urban parks. Identification of these factors positively impacts park design, construction, and development. Hashim and Said [19] investigated visitors' wayfinding behavior in a theme park, using the Rasch Measurement

Model to analyze tourists' wayfinding performance and their perception of the surroundings in four dimensions: space, spatial, color, and quality of experience. Dong and Siu [20] explored how visitors' predispositions affect their views of the rendition of services in a theme park. Variables comprised substantive staging of servicescape, communicative staging of servicescape, desire for active participation, fantastic imaginary orientation, service experience evaluation, experience intensification, and experience extension. Wu and Song [21] proposed that future research on inclusive design include the interrelated, multi-faceted needs of all users, and that each category of park design should have different loading values for motion, sensory, and cognitive capability. There exists an obvious gap in the literature in terms of research into the wayfinding behavior of mixed-age groups, and those with different types and degrees of disabilities in urban parks.

3   Methods

3.1   Concepts

The signage system of barrier-free facilities typically displays wayfinding information. This study categorizes individuals into young and old (by 55 years old), and able-bodied and disabled groups. Participants comprised people with visual impairments, hearing impairments, extremity disabilities, and multiple disabilities. Questionnaires were distributed at college gates, parks, medical clinics and hospitals, department stores, and juridical associations related to the physically or mentally disabled.

3.2   Survey

The major aim of this questionnaire was to determine if current signage systems meet the needs of both senior citizens and disabled people, specifically whether these designs provide sufficient information for users to smoothly navigate public spaces in a convenient, safe, effective way. The scale is a five-point Likert scale: totally agree (5) to totally disagree (1). The questionnaire covered four dimensions: mind-map recognition, general needs & safety, sign layout & design, capabilities & perception. There were 23 questions in total which were developed by investigating current park conditions (see Fig. 2) and revised by two expert meetings. Ten pretests were conducted in northern Taiwan on Sept. 17, 2016. Based on these results, we revised the questionnaire (see Table 1), and then distributed it in northern Taiwan during the period of Sept. 30 to Oct. 23, 2016.

3.3   Statistical Analysis

For statistical analysis, we used t-tests to discriminate users with different types of disabilities and their opinions of park facilities and signage planning. We used confirmatory factor analysis (CFA) to confirm these second-order factors (four dimensions)

1) Facility maps should provide sufficient information for users to form a mind-map of the area.

2) Difficult paths or routes should be clearly marked.

3) Signal words can be marked on the road for users with low vision.

4) The height & angle of the signboard should be user-friendly for people in wheelchairs.

5) International symbols of access should be used in regulatory signs for the convenience of people with hearing impairments.

6) Large graphics with sharp color contrasts on the outside walls of a restroom help people with weak eyesight.

7) Regulatory signs should convey basic information with simple, easy-to-understand wording.

8) A sign that indicates barrier-free parking should be erected near the entrance of a park or plaza, so other vehicles will not park in this area.

Fig. 2. Signs in urban parks in Taiwan

Table 1. Observed (OB)/Latent Variables and questionnaire

OB.	Questions
Latent Variable-Mind-map recognition (MR) – Attention (AU)	
au1	When I go to a park to exercise, I pay more attention to directional signs
au2	When I visit a park for recreational purposes, I pay more attention to eye-catching signs
au3	When I find myself strolling in a large park with complicated facilities, I feel a sense of uncertainty
Latent Variable-Mind-map recognition (MR) – Map (MP)	
mp1	When I find myself in an unfamiliar place, I check available maps
mp2	Facility maps should provide sufficient information for users to form a mind-map
Latent Variable-General needs & safety (NS) – Safety (SC)	
sc1	Regulatory signs should convey basic information with simple, easy-to-understand wording
sc2	I think recognizable signs, touch screens or sound technology should be set up at dangerous places so as to warn the disabled of the impending danger
sc3	A sign that indicates barrier-free parking should be erected near the entrance of a park or plaza, so other vehicles will not park in this area
Latent Variable-General needs & safety (NS) - Needs (NE)	
ne1	Signs that indicate barrier-free facilities should be set up to meet the needs of individuals with different capabilities
ne2	I think the signs in a park should clearly indicate the location of barrier-free facilities
Latent Variable-Sign layout & design (SD) – Layout (LO)	
lo1	The layout and size of words in a sign should vary according to frequency of use, direction and speed of reading among users
lo2	For senior people to comprehend instructions and access emergency buttons in a large park, relevant signs should be incorporated into park facilities
Latent Variable-Sign layout & design (SD) – Entrance (ER)	
er1	Difficult paths or routes (such as slope of ramps higher than 1/20) should be marked on a map representing the surrounding area of a park or plaza
er2	I think a tactile map is necessary at the entrance of any building for the convenience of the visually impaired
er3	A tactile map (with a touch-screen) should mark out exit, entrance, and positioning signs
Latent Variable-Capabilities & perception (CP) - Hearing-impaired (HI)	
hi1	International symbols of access should be used in regulatory signs for the convenience of people with hearing impairments
hi2	An easy-to-follow, unified signage system can help hearing-impaired people to quickly find their way
Latent Variable-Capabilities & perception (CP) - Visually-impaired (VI)	
vi1	Considering that the visually-impaired have a poor ability to discern colors, a single color or red/green hues should be avoided in signage systems
vi2	A barrier-free signage system should be put up in convenient locations and provide digital devices to help the visually-impaired in navigation

(*continued*)

Table 1. (*continued*)

OB.	Questions
vi3	It is better to use large graphics with sharp color contrasts on the outside wall of a restroom for the convenience of people with weak eyesight
Latent Variable-Capabilities & perception (CP) - Sign perception (SP)	
sp1	The height and angle of the signboard should be user-friendly for people in wheelchairs
sp2	Signal words can be marked on the road for users with low vision
sp3	If there is an information kiosk in a park, I try to find it to locate the facilities I am looking for

and first-order factors (attention, map, safety, needs, layout, entrance, hearing-impaired, visually-impaired, sign perception) and their weights. The 1st order CFA, 2nd order CFA and t-test were combined to describe the differing needs of users of different ages and types of disabilities.

4 Result

4.1 Participants

400 questionnaires were distributed, and we obtained 347 effective returned questionnaires, representing a return rate of 86.75%. There were 170 males and 177 females (see Table 2). Of the 347, 229 were individuals with mental or physical disabilities (Table 3).

Table 2. Crosstabs of sex and various educated participants

	Primary school/under	Junior high school	Senior high school	Undergraduate	Graduate school/above	Total
Male	10	7	26	93	34	170
	5.9%	4.1%	15.3%	54.7%	20.0%	100.0%
Female	19	8	19	98	33	177
	10.7%	4.5%	10.7%	55.4%	18.6%	100.0%
Sum	29	15	45	191	67	347
	8.4%	4.3%	13.0%	55.0%	19.3%	100.0%

4.2 Confirmatory Factor Analysis

Figure 3 shows the results of Second Order CFA, in which the t-value for all paths reached a level of significance. This confirms model aggregation, which can be further divided up into four 2nd order factors: mind-map recognition (MR), general needs & safety (NS), sign layout & design (SD), capabilities & perception (CP) and nine 1st order factors: AU, MP, SC, NE, LO, ER, HI, VI, and SP. RMSEA = 0.077, the model is acceptable.

Table 3. Crosstabs of aged and various disabled participants

	None	Physically disabled	Hearing-impaired	Vision-impaired	Cerebral palsied	Cognitive disorder	Multiple obstacles	Other disabled	Total
Under/&55ys.	78	36	31	20	12	6	20	35	238
	32.8%	15.1%	13.0%	8.4%	5.0%	2.5%	8.4%	14.7%	100.0%
Over 55ys.	40	47	7	5	1	1	5	3	109
	36.7%	43.1%	6.4%	4.6%	0.9%	0.9%	4.6%	2.8%	100.0%
Sum	118	83	38	25	13	7	25	38	347
	34.0%	23.9%	11.0%	7.2%	3.7%	2.0%	7.2%	11.0%	100.0%

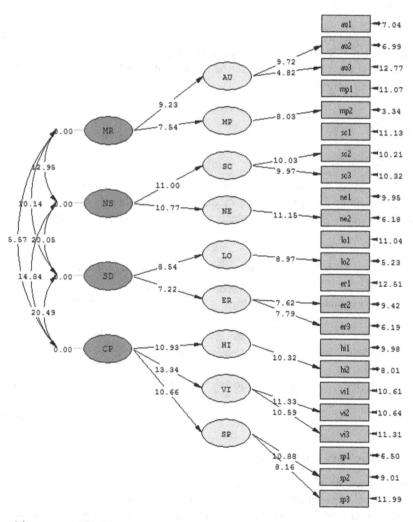

Chi-Square=661.77, df=215, P-value=0.00000, RMSEA=0.077

Fig. 3. Second Order CFA

A *t*-test was conducted to evaluate how users of different ages and with different types of disabilities view the 23 questions. Table 4 shows that significant differences occur in mp2, sc1, sc2, sc3, ne1, ne2, lo1, er3, vi1, vi2, hi1, hi2, sp1, sp3 among young people with disabilities (N = 188), elderly people with disabilities (N = 41), young able-bodied people (N = 93), and elderly able-bodied people (N = 25).

Table 4. *t*-test for different aged and disabled/able-bodied group

Variables	Group-Mean (SD)		*p(F*-test)	*p(t*-test)
mp2	Elderly disabled-4.12 (.714)	Young able-bodied-4.51 (.524)	.338	.001
	Young able-bodied-4.51 (.524)	Young disabled-4.22 (.801)	.010	.002
	Young able-bodied-4.51 (.524)	Elderly able-bodied-4.24 (.723)	.479	.041
sc1	Elderly disabled-4.37(.662)	Young able-bodied-4.68 (.514)	.005	.009
	Young able-bodied-4.68 (.514)	Young disabled-4.39 (.755)	.000	.000
	Young able-bodied-4.68 (.514)	Elderly able-bodied-4.44 (.507)	.395	.042
sc2	Young disabled-4.34 (.774)	Elderly disabled-4.05 (.669)	.329	.050
sc3	Elderly disabled-4.05 (.669)	Young able-bodied-4.44(.650)	.095	.002
	Young disabled-4.36 (.683)	Elderly disabled-4.12 (.678)	.023	.010
	Young able-bodied-4.44 (.650)	Elderly able-bodied-4.08 (.759)	.448	.019
ne1	Elderly disabled-4.12(.678)	Young able-bodied-4.41 (.576)	.898	.013
	Young disabled-4.39 (.606)	Elderly disabled-4.12 (.678)	.429	.013
ne2	Elderly disabled-4.20 (.782)	Young able-bodied-4.47(.563)	.007	.044
	Young disabled-4.39 (.649)	Elderly able-bodied-4.08 (.493)	.000	.008
	Young able-bodied-4.47 (.563)	Elderly able-bodied-4.08 (.493)	.000	.001
lo1	Elderly disabled-4.02 (.612)	Young able-bodied-4.34 (.759)	.002	.011
	Young disabled-4.31 (.711)	Elderly disabled-4.02 (.612)	.002	.010
er3	Elderly disabled-4.07(.721)	Young able-bodied-4.41 (.755)	.241	.018
hi1	Elderly disabled-4.05(.669)	Young able-bodied-4.47 (.618)	.100	.000
	Young disabled-4.45 (.640)	Elderly disabled-4.05 (.669)	.027	.001
	Young able-bodied-4.47 (.618)	Elderly able-bodied-4.12 (.600)	.027	.013
	Young disabled-4.45 (.640)	Elderly able-bodied-4.12 (.600)	.008	.015
hi2	Elderly disabled-3.98 (.758)	Young able-bodied-4.47 (.618)	.943	.000
	Young disabled-4.40 (.634)	Elderly disabled-3.98 (.758)	.935	.000
vi1	Elderly disabled-.380 (.558)	Young able-bodied-4.15(.884)	.001	.007
	Young disabled-4.29(.740)	Elderly able-bodied-3.96(.676)	.023	.032
	Young disabled-4.29 (.740)	Elderly disabled-3.80 (.558)	.001	.000
vi2	Young disabled-4.31 (.717)	Elderly disabled-3.95 (.705)	.076	.004
sp1	Young disabled-4.36 (.750)	Elderly disabled-4.05 (.705)	.017	.015
sp3	Elderly disabled-3.37 (1.318)	Young able-bodied-4.03(.994)	.007	.005
	Young disabled-3.89 (1.051)	Elderly disabled-3.37 (1.318)	.015	.021

The results produced from the 2nd order CFA and *t*-test were combined to illustrate the differing needs of users of different ages and types of disabilities (see Fig. 4). No discernable differences were shown in mind-map recognition, general needs & safety, sign layout & design, capabilities & perception. However, the young disabled and young able-bodied people held different views in mp2 and sc1, while the able-bodied young and elderly have divergent opinions in mp2, sc1, sc3, ne2, and hi1. These variables are clustered in the dimension of general needs & safety. Divergent views are held by the elderly disabled and young able-bodied people and in mp2, sc1, sc3, ne1, ne2, lo1, er3, hi1, hi2, vi1, sp3. Divergent views are held by the disabled young and elderly in sc2, sc3, ne1, lo1, hi1, hi2, vi1, vi2, sp1, sp3, which are manifested in two dimensions: general needs & safety and capabilities & perception.

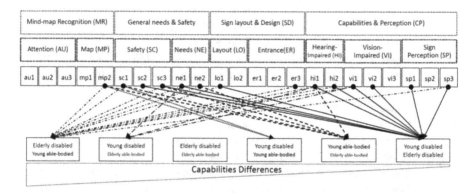

Fig. 4. Relationships among different capabilities users and signage settings at park

5   Discussion

There is a need to understand the complex relationships between mobility, the built environment, and health in an ageing society. Inclusive design mandates a close examination of mobility under different contexts. The following results were revealed: (1) Four dimensions of wayfinding behavior and users' application of the signage system are confirmed as follows: Mind-map Recognition, General needs & Safety, Sign layout & Design, Capabilities & Perception. (2) Significant differences exist in how people of differing ages and types of disabilities view the four dimensions of a signage system.

5.1   Dimensions of Wayfinding and Signage

Dong and Siu [20] investigated the needs of theme park visitors and discovered that desire for active participation and fantastic imaginary orientation affects their wayfinding experience. McCormack et al. [22] explored the use of urban parks from the perspective of users, pinpointing the attributes of safety, aesthetics, amenities, maintenance, and proximity as stimuli for visiting a park. We are convinced (by confirmatory factors analysis) that wayfinding behavior and sign planning help to facilitate the navigation process for park-goers. This study is divided into nine 1st order factors: attention, map, safety, general needs, layout, entrance, hearing-impaired, vision-impaired, and sign perception. The first four are relevant psychological factors associated with wayfinding behavior, whereas the latter five 1st order factors are sign-design factors important to users with differing types of disabilities. Our results show that Taiwan park-goers in urban areas do not stress pleasantness in the wayfinding process. Rather, they put high priority on safety of daily livings and the formulation of a useful mind-map.

5.2   Evaluations According to Age and Disability

We compared the opinions of users of different ages and types of disabilities in terms of wayfinding behavior and signage systems. Results show that among the following dissimilar groups very few differences were observed: elderly disabled vs. elderly able-bodied; young disabled vs. young able-bodied. In contrast, the following pairs of groups habited significantly different opinions in the dimension of general needs & safety: elderly disabled vs. young able-bodied; young able-bodied vs. elderly able-bodied and young disabled vs. elderly disabled. Similarly, the following pairs of groups habited significantly different opinions in the dimension of capabilities & perception: elderly disabled vs. young able-bodied; young disabled vs. elderly able-bodied and young disabled vs. elderly disabled.

With regard to the dimensions of mind-map recognition and sign layout & design, little disparity was observed among groups, whether they were highly heterogeneous or not. Clearly the majority of the participants were accepting of standardized design. However, groups with similar levels of capability (young able-bodied vs. elderly able-bodied, and young disabled vs. elderly disabled) and greatly varying levels of capability (young able-bodied vs. elderly disabled, and young disabled vs. elderly able-bodied) held differing opinions in the dimensions of general needs & safety and capabilities & perception in the design of urban parks (see Fig. 4). In Fig. 5, we see a U curve for the relationship between levels of difference in capability and variables counted (i.e. young disabled vs. elderly disabled groups had 10 significantly different perceptions). This shows that an optimal (inclusive) design requires efforts to address the various needs of each group.

Because researchers only obtain a partial result using traditional analysis of a single group of the disabled or senior citizens, in this study we made an effort to discriminate groups before exploring the applicability of inclusive design. The major contributions of this study lies in this discrimination of users with differing types of disabilities and their opinions of barrier-free facilities. These results serve as useful reference in the process of signage design. It promotes an aggregation model featuring segmented designs, allowing designers to become aware of slight differences. This enables compromise in design to allow for shared use of facilities and flexible constraints to suit the maximum range of clients. It is advised that future researchers employ different assistive devices for the disabled with differing ages and capabilities, and employ structural equation modelling (SEM) to develop causal models.

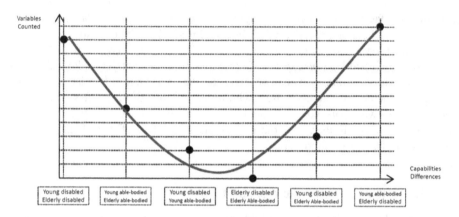

Fig. 5. U-curve of capabilities differences and variables counted

6 Conclusion

The rapidly aged society in Taiwan has prompted changes in the requirements for public facilities and positioning services. This paper conducted a survey among 347 park-goers in urban areas, and obtained the following results: (1) Four dimensions of wayfinding behavior and users' application of the signage system were confirmed as follows: mind-map recognition, general needs & safety, sign layout & design, capabilities & perception. (2) Significant differences exist in how people of similar groups view the four dimensions of a signage system.

This evidence indicates the necessity for consideration of the subtle differences among varying demographics. This study further elucidates the requirements for inclusive design, which aims to identify the union of sets where optimal solutions are found to meet user expectations.

References

1. Department of Household Registration, Ministry of Interior, R.O.C.: Statistics [Electronic data] (2016). http://www.ris.gov.tw/en/web/ris3-english/home. Accessed 21 Dec 2016
2. Directorate General of Budget, Accounting and Statistics, Executive Yuan, R.O.C.: National Statistics [Electronic data] (2016). http://www.stat.gov.tw/mp.asp?mp=4. Accessed 21 Dec 2016
3. Nitanai, S.: (似内志朗), Barrier-free approach in UD (ユーザーのためのグッドデザイン), Lecture at Hokkaido Universal Design Organization, (北海道ユニバーサルデザイン機構講演), 26 May 2004. http://www.jfma.or.jp/research/scm10/image/result10-04.pdf. Accessed 21 Dec 2016
4. Kitchener, M., Ng, T., Miller, N., Harrington, C.: Medicaid home and community-based services: national program trends. Health Aff. **24**(1), 206–212 (2005)

5. Kane, R.L., Priester, R., Neumann, D.: Does disparity in the way disabled older adults are treated imply ageism? Gerontologist **47**(3), 271–279 (2007). doi:10.1093/geront/47.3.271. [PubMed]
6. Webster, P., Lipp, A.: The evolution of the WHO city health profiles: a content review. Health Promot. Int. **24**(S1), i56–i63 (2009)
7. Ritsatakis, A.: Equity and the social determinants of health in European cities. J. Urban Health **90**(Suppl. 1), 92–104 (2013)
8. Davis, R.L., Weisbeck, C.: Search strategies used by older adults in a virtual reality place learning task. Gerontologist **55**(S1), S118–S127 (2015)
9. Wahl, H.W., Fange, A., Oswald, F., Gitlin, L.N., Iwarsson, S.: The home environment and disability-related outcomes in aging individuals: what is the empirical evidence? Gerontologist **49**(3), 355–367 (2009)
10. Vine, D., Buys, L., Aird, R.: Experiences of neighbourhood walkability among older Australians living in high density inner-city areas. Planning Theory Pract. **13**(3), 421–444 (2012). doi:10.1080/14649357.2012.696675
11. Satariano, W.A., Kealey, M., Hubbard, A., Kurtovich, E., Ivey, S.L., Bayles, C.M., Hunter, R.H., Prohaska, T.R.: Mobility disability in older adults: at the intersection of people and places. Gerontologist **56**(3), 525–534 (2016). doi:10.1093/geront/gnu094. [PubMed]
12. Sugiyama, T., Ward Thompson, C.: Associations between characteristics of neighbourhood open space and older people's walking. Urban Forest. Urban Greening **7**(1), 41–51 (2008). doi:10.1016/j.ufug.2007.12.002
13. Rosenberg, D.E., Huang, D.L., Simonovich, S.D., Belza, B.: Outdoor built environment barriers and facilitators to activity among midlife and older adults with mobility disabilities. Gerontologist **53**(2), 268–279 (2012). doi:10.1093/geront/gns119
14. Bosch, S.J., Gharaveis, A.: Flying solo: a review of the literature on wayfinding for older adults experiencing visual or cognitive decline. Appl. Ergon. **58**, 327–333 (2017)
15. de Paolis, R., Guerini, S.: Wayfinding design and accessibility. GSTF J. Eng. Technol. **3**(2), 72–79 (2015)
16. Brajša-Žganec, A.: Merkaš., M., Šverko, I.: Quality of life and leisure activities: how do leisure activities contribute to subjective well-being? Soc. Indic. Res. **102**(1), 81–91 (2010). doi:10.1007/s11205-010-9724-2
17. Kaczynski, A.T., Potwarka, L.R., Smale, B.J.A., Havitz, M.E.: Association of parkland proximity with neighborhood and park-based physical activity: variations by gender and age. Leis. Sci. Interdiscip. J. **31**(2), 174–191 (2009). doi:10.1080/01490400802686045
18. Schipperijn, J., Stigsdotter, U.K., Randrup, T.B., Troelsen, J.: Influences on the use of urban green space – a case study in Odense, Denmark. Urban Forest. Urban Greening **9**(1), 25–32 (2010). doi:10.1016/j.ufug.2009.09.002
19. Hashim, M.S., Said, I.: Effectiveness of wayfinding towards spatial space and human behavior in theme park. Procedia Soc. Behav. Sci. **85**, 282–295 (2013)
20. Dong, P., Siu, N.Y.-M.: Servicescape elements, customer predispositions and service experience: the case of theme park visitors. Tour. Manag. **36**, 541–551 (2013)
21. Wu, K.C., Song, L.Y.: A case for inclusive design: analyzing the needs of those who frequent Taiwan's urban parks. Appl. Ergon. **58**, 254–264 (2017)
22. McCormack, G.R., Rock, M., Toohey, A.M., Hignell, D.: Characteristics of urban parks associated with park use and physical activity: a review of qualitative research. Health Place **16**(4), 712–726 (2010). doi:10.1016/j.healthplace.2010.03.003

Accessible Tourism for Deaf People in Poland: The SITur and SITex Programs as Proposals for Accessible Urban Information

Alina Zajadacz[1]([⊠]) and Przemysław Szmal[2]

[1] Department of Tourism and Recreation, Faculty of Geographical
and Geological Sciences, Adam Mickiewicz University in Poznań,
ul. Dziegielowa 27, 61-680 Poznań, Poland
alina@amu.edu.pl
[2] Institute of Informatics, Silesian University of Technology,
ul. Akademicka 16, 44-100 Gliwice, Poland
przemyslaw.szmal@polsl.pl

Abstract. SITur and SITex are multimedia programs addressed to Deaf tourists, whose main communication means is Polish Sign Language (PJM). In this article we present the background and main assumptions for the development of the programs, conducted experiments and conclusions regarding further development directions. By assumption, creating programs was carried with the participation of their beneficiaries. Before programs development, the style of leisure and tourist destination of the Deaf in Poland were recognized using questionnaire interviews; for comparison, the same questions were asked to a control group of hearing. Besides texts, maps, pictures, pictograms, the programs include PJM animation module, borrowed from Thetos translation program. PJM users repeatedly tested the programs, i.a. on selected tourism routes. The PJM and the tourism industry experts also reviewed them. Feedback from the Deaf environment is currently used to improve programs – to complement vocabulary and animation expression (including facial expressions of avatar-translator).

Keywords: Disability · The Deaf · Hearing impairment · Accessible tourism · Accessible information · Tourist information system

1 Introduction

Both the elimination of physical barriers, as well as better adjustment of information system are of key importance in finding ways to increase the availability of open spaces for people with disabilities (PwD). The concept of 'Accessibility' in the context of the needs of PwD 'is defined as meaning that people with disabilities have access, on an equal basis with others, to the physical environment, transportation, information and communications technologies and systems (ICT), and other facilities and services. There are still major barriers in all of these areas. For example, on average in the EU-27, only 5% of public websites

© Springer International Publishing AG 2017
M. Antona and C. Stephanidis (Eds.): UAHCI 2017, Part III, LNCS 10279, pp. 348–359, 2017.
DOI: 10.1007/978-3-319-58700-4_29

comply fully with web accessibility standards, though more are partially accessible' (European Disability Strategy 2010–2020, p. 5).

A number of measures aimed at increasing accessibility were taken in recent years, also in the sphere of human life associated with high mobility in space, i.e. tourism. The idea of 'Accessible Tourism' is widely promoted (Buhalis and Darcy 2011; Buhalis et al. 2012; Gillovic and McIntosh 2015; Zajadacz 2015; World Tourism Organization 2013, 2015, 2016a,b,c). The concept of 'Accessible Tourism' refers to the adaptation of environments and of tourism products and services so as to enable access, use and enjoyment by all users, under the principles of Universal Design. 'This is a form of tourism that involves a collaborative process among stakeholders that enables people with access requirements, including mobility, vision, hearing and cognitive dimensions of access, to function independently and with equity and dignity through the delivery of universally designed tourism products, services and environments' (World Tourism Organization 2013, p. 4).

The implementation of these goals is possible through the development of 'communication through digital media. With new, mobile technologies, destinations and providers can reach wider audiences and provide tourists with access to larger amounts of information and also personalised content. This information is more agile and allows customers to compare different offers and services, thus providing them with greater autonomy in their decision-making' (World Tourism Organization 2016b, p. 4). The search for optimal solutions in the field of information technology addressed to people with a certain type of disability requires, in compliance with the principles of universal active design, the participation of beneficiaries, which corresponds to the assumptions of social IT science.

The article presents the results of research on the multimedia programs addressed to a selected group of tourists with disability – Deaf people, for whom the primary means of communication is sign language. The study focused on both social characteristics of the environment of the Deaf (style of tourist trips, needs for tourist information), as well as on the search for optimal solutions within the information and communication technology (ICT). The assumptions for two multimedia programs SITur and SITex, representing a proposal for automatic translation of texts into Polish Sign Language (PJM), are the outcome of the research. Program names refer to their function as useful tools in the System of Tourist Information: (1) SITur under field conditions (outdoor) and (2) Sitex for exposure indoors. Their implication is aimed at increasing the accessibility of tourism for the community of people who use PJM by eliminating language barriers - to facilitate: (1) access to tourist information for deaf people, as well as (2) passing information in PJM to people working in the service of tourist traffic. The proposed solutions are of innovative character because in Poland so far only solutions such as cooperation with a sign language interpreter or movies with an instructor of sign language were used in terms of facilities of the transmission of tourist information addressed to persons using PJM. They also stress the need to take into account the general problems of the Deaf in activities related to accessible tourism because such activities are often focused only on the physical accessibility (i.e. the needs of people with physical disabilities).

2   Background: Deaf Culture, Deafhood and Tourism of Deaf People

Despite the development of initiatives related to an increase in the availability of tourism for PwD, the tourism of the Deaf rarely was a separate subject of study. One gets the impression that people with hearing impairments or who are Deaf are a group that has been omitted from the tourism literature (Barnes et al. 2010). Tourism, however, is an integral part of social life, so a lot of relevant information to better understand the behavior of tourists who use sign language is also provided through the development of 'inside Deaf culture' (Padden and Humphries 1990, 2006; Goodstein 2006; Ladd 2007).

The term 'Deaf culture' was developed in the 1970s to give utterance to the belief that Deaf communities contained their own ways of life mediated through their sign languages' (Ladd 2007, p. xvii). People with impaired hearing and unable to receive speech through hearing are culturally considered to be Deaf. A characteristic feature of this group is the inability to master oral speech in a natural way, i.e. by imitation. Thus, their natural language is a sign language and, moreover, they share common life experiences (Szczepankowski 1999). For people who use sign language (with a smaller content of signs – 'words' in the dictionary and different grammatical structure than the audio language), the national language is largely a 'second language', often not quite fully understood (also in the form of text). The perception of Deaf people as those who lost their hearing and who live in 'a world of silence' is deeply untrue (Szczepankowski 1999). In fact, as for a hearing person it is normal to hear and speak, and the prospect of hearing loss seems to be a tragedy, for the Deaf from birth, 'to not hear' is a natural phenomenon. In their midst, communicating through sign language they are fully operational. What is more, memories of adults, the Deaf children of hearing parents, testify to the fact that at home, they did not perceive their parents as people with disabilities, this experience came only as a result of social relations (Fellinger et al. 2005).

The concept of 'Deafhood' in relation to the culture of the Deaf was introduced by Ladd (2007) in the 90s of 20th century. As he explains, 'Deafhood is not seen as a finite state but as a process by which Deaf individuals come to actualize their Deaf identity, positing that those individuals construct that identity around several differently ordered sets of priorities and principles, which are affected by various factors such as nation, era, and class' (Ladd 2007, p. xviii).

The definition of hearing impairment varies in different parts of the world but people with such impairments can be simply thought of as those who have experienced some form of hearing loss and have access needs that require hearing augmentation. Deaf capital D is used specifically as a signifier that this group regard themselves as a distinct cultural group who are unified by the use of sign language. Quite simply, people who are Deaf do not regard themselves as having a disability but as part of a separate cultural group ("Deaf" – see: Woodward 1972; Padden and Humphries 1990, 2006; Ladd 2007; Barnes et al. 2010; Rydberg 2010).

The quality and personalization of the services play the key role in guaranteeing the satisfaction of tourist trips. Creating optimal tourist offer addressed to the segment of the tourism market of Deaf people requires understanding of their needs' and expectations (i.e. the diagnosis of tourist demand). Information on style of tourist travel and recreation of the deaf were included in the studies devoted to the social characteristics of this group (including Prillwitz 1996). They were rarely a separate object of study (Zajadacz 2014; Zajadacz and Śniadek 2013). Behavior observed in their free time (i.e. remaining at their disposal) was treated as a kind of indicator of preferred activity. Prillwitz (1996) stated that the way of spending free time by Deaf people shows clearly that Deaf people look primarily for some contact with individuals like themselves. Problems in communication here are almost none, which guarantees comfort and opportunity to rest (Prillwitz 1996, p. 242). Staying in their own environment allows them to rest, especially from the problems arising from restricted communication with the hearing environment. 'Deaf people refer with great sentiment to meetings in their own environment, which can also be seen from the fact that they do not make similar contacts with the hearing, even when it would possible be on the basis of common interests and because of external circumstances (...) prefer to remain among their own group and freely talk to each other' (Prillwitz 1996, p. 242). Similarly, with regard to travel and holidays, the author states that Deaf people prefer to spend both weekends and holidays with the family, in the circle of other Deaf people. 'When they leave for holidays, they rarely come into closer contact with the hearing. (...) Here we have yet another proof of compactness of the community of the deaf, which is perceived as an oasis of respite – be with the deaf it means relax, to be with the hearing it means work!' (Prillwitz 1996, p. 245).

Satisfaction with the rest, as well as recreational activities in public places, taken by Deaf people, were the subject of research of Oliva (2006) and Atherton (2007). They referred at the same time to the theory of recreation as a personal experience of 'flow', 'flow feelings' (flow, flow feeling) – a feeling of comfort that is possible when the free choice of a variety of recreational activities is guaranteed, but also full engagement in leisure activities, not only in the role of participant, but also the organizer of recreational outdoor activities, is necessary. At the same time it was emphasized that the possibility of achieving comfort and satisfaction with the rest depends on both of services for the Deaf (e.g. the availability of a sign language interpreter), as well as largely on the individual attitude of the person (acceptance of deafness) – willingness to seek individual ways of development (Ladd 2007). Moreover, the more opportunities the Deaf have to preserve their identity, maintaining both deafness and the resulting language the essence of it, the more chances for comfort they have (Halleux and Poncelet 2001; Hauser et al. 2010). In the case of overcoming the language barrier, the attitude of hearing people who should first come out with the initiative of conversation is vital (Atherton 2007). From the perspective of the Deaf, the use of sign language by hearing people is a sign of respect and is a good base for social integration. Willingness to make conversation, manifested by hearing people is more important than the smooth handling of sign language (Young et al. 2000).

Studies on the tourist activity of disabled people helped to develop a number of treatment-related stays outdoors. For example, Berman and Davis-Berman (1995, pp. 1–7) presented the therapeutic relevance of trips for which people with disabilities were responsible and which were run by them. They emphasized the fact that the natural environment allows for broader treatment than it is possible in the clinic. Terry (1995, p. 26) also presented rehabilitation and therapeutic functions of tourism related to activity and contact with nature. In the case of open-air workshop participants, each victory over themselves, their own limitations raises the level of self-esteem. Furthermore, such activities allow to maintain a high level of involvement of participants in rehabilitation programs (Terry 1995, p. 26). For the organizers of tourism and leisure sets of principles and recommendations taking into account the needs of the Deaf were developed (UK Council on Deafness 2005; Access to the countryside by deaf visitors 2006).

Availability of the offer and customer satisfaction undoubtedly play a fundamental role for the development of tourism referred to as 'business of dreams' or 'business of happiness'. A review of studies concerning tourism and recreation of people using sign language indicates that access to tourist information providing free, independent choice of tourist offer or an individual organization of the trip are the main conditions in this respect. An effective system of tourist information (in terms of scope and content of its forms of communication) is an essential 'connecting channel' between creators and recipients of tourist offer. 'Private companies and public sector stakeholders in tourism must deliver accurate, relevant and timely information to their customers, prior to, during and even after the journey. Ensuring accessible information is without any doubt a key to successfully communicating with visitors in all of the stages of their journey' (World Tourism Organization 2016b, p. 4). For people who use sign language, communication in the natural language, as well as through texts and graphics, is essential.

3   Objectives and Methods

The main aim of this article is to present the assumptions used in the process of developing and degree of development of two multimedia programs: SITur and SITex, addressed to Deaf tourists, for whom the primary means of communication is PJM. The focus is also on the discussion of results related to the current development stage of programs and indication of further optimal directions of their expansion. The basic assumption of building of the program was the participation of its beneficiaries in the creation of the program.

The study consisted of two stages. The first stage included recognizing the style of leisure and tourist destination of the Deaf against a control group of hearing people in Poland. For the process of data collection (2005–2008) questionnaire interviews were used, which were conducted with the participation of a sign language interpreter [$n = 292$]. The studies were conducted in the branches of Polish Association of the Deaf, located in all regions in Poland. The study among hearing people was conducted at the same time [n = 1,780]; they answered the same questions. In both surveys the distribution of basic demographic characteristics had proportional representation (such as age, sex, place of residence). Comparative analysis of expression in both groups showed the specificity of tourism and recreation of the Deaf (i.a. Zajadacz 2010a, 2012). The results indicate that participation in tourism (taking into account the number of tourist trips per year) of Deaf does not differ in a statistically significant way from the studied control group of hearing. The more difficult financial situation of the Deaf, however, affects their travel style (search for cheaper tourist offer, selection of cheap means of transport, closer destinations, more frequent trips off the peak season). In addition, the preference to travel in a group of people with similar characteristics is observed (i.e. the environment of the Deaf), as well as the expectation of the availability of information in graphical form, subtitling and sign language (Zajadacz 2011). Styles of tourist trips were presented in the article 'Tourism Activities of Deaf Poles' (Zajadacz and Śniadek 2013) and two monographs (Zajadacz 2010a, 2012). The preferred sources of tourist information used by Deaf people (Zajadacz 2014), the needs in terms of its content and forms of communication were analyzed in detail (Table 1).

Table 1. Sources of information on opportunities for tourism during holidays. Applied abbreviations: [a] – statistical significance $p \leq 0.05$; 'D' – Deaf individuals; 'H' – Hearing individuals. Source: Zajadacz 2014: 10.

Source of information	D	H	p
	% indications		
Newspapers	19.16	15.26	0.1908[a]
Internet	34.73	54.67	0.0000[a]
Travel agencies	11.98	21.19	0.0051[a]
Tourist information centres	5.99	5.04	0.5996[a]
Opinions of family and friends	26.35	53.78	0.0000[a]
Institutions (church, school)	2.40	2.44	0.9689[a]
Travel guides	7.78	13.26	0.0447[a]
Other	2.40	0.89	0.0722[a]

The second stage (2008–2010) included the development of SITur and SITex programs, containing both texts, maps, pictures, pictograms and also PJM animation module, borrowed from Thetos translation program (Zajadacz 2010b). In all stages of the work people using the PJM were directly involved.

4   Results: SITur and SITex Programs Dedicated to Deaf Tourists

Deaf people using the Polish Sign Language (PJM) are featured users of SITur and SITex programs – the ability to read text is not required. However, the programs can also be used by people who are not familiar with the sign language. The programs provide users with a number of presentations. The content of each presentation is divided into chapters, each consisting of one or more slides. Appropriately selected illustrations and textual descriptions for them, and sign language messages equivalent to them in terms of the content, are shown on the slides. The sign content is presented by an avatar, a virtual animated character. Control of the programs (chapter selection, stop, resume of sign presentation and change of its pace etc.) is done by commands passed by a touch screen or using the mouse. The solutions used in the system Thetos (Szmal and Suszczańska 2001; Suszczańska et al. 2004; Romaniuk et al. 2014) [http://thetos.polsl.pl/], including its display and linguistic module, were applied to implement the programs (Szmal 2010).

To implement SITur and SITex, the solutions used in the Thetos system (Szmal and Suszczańska 2001; Suszczańska et al. 2004; Romaniuk et al. 2014) [http://thetos.polsl.pl/] were applied (Szmal 2010). A decisive factor for choosing it was the fact that, at the start of the research related to tourism of the Deaf in Poland (including its limitations and facilities necessary for its development), it was the most extensive system containing PJM translator. Other relevant facilities aimed at passing tourist information to people using PJM included movies with PJM instructor. Such solutions are legible and useful for the Deaf but do not allow automatic translation of the content (texts) into PJM which, in case of changes in the communicated information, creates the need for further recording. Hence, Thetos seemed to be the most promising tool that allows easy (through the introduction of the text) and fast way to transfer information in PJM. Now in a few words we will describe Thetos.

The system consists of two main modules: linguistic and display module. The linguistic module is a rule-based translator from Polish into an intermediate language, which is in fact a textual form of PJM sign language. The module consists of several sub-modules implementing the successive steps of processing the input text – morphological analysis, syntax and semantic analysis, and multistage generation of the output text. During generation, compatibility with the sign language rules is kept. The translator effectively converts a comprehensive set of Polish language structures. It uses extensive electronic dictionaries, including – among others – a morphological dictionary, covering about 90,000 items (words in basic form), and a syntactic-generative dictionary of over 12,000 items (verbs).

The task of the display module of Thetos is to control the movements of the avatar. The module receives the intermediary text which is a sequence of words representing individual signs of the sign language. The words are accompanied by symbols indicating the emotional content associated with specific signs and phrases. The module processes signs in the order they appear in the text.

The module uses a dictionary-library of signs; it has about 1500 signs. For known signs, the module plays back the corresponding "atomic" multimedia animations. For unknown signs, it displays their equivalent in the finger alphabet. While playing longer sign sequences, partial animations are seamlessly glued. As for the "atomic" animations, they are prepared by the animator manually (using special supporting tools) basing on actual, filmed signs; the animation takes into account the dynamics of movements.

Let us return to SITur and SITex programs. Unlike the original Thetos system, they do not require translation on-line. For this reason they only include the Thetos display module using the input text in the requested format. This text can be prepared by any technique.

Preparing text for the display module is a key issue. It starts from a text in the (Polish) spoken language; the text is provided by qualified tourist guides or museum curators – the latter if the presentations relate to museum exhibitions. The text is then translated into its textual sign equivalent. The translation could be entirely performed by hand, but this would be a quite tedious task. In order to partly mechanize it, we used the Thetos linguistic module. We employed it for the preparation of a raw version of the translation, which was then manually adjusted and smoothed by a person familiar with PJM. The SITur (Fig. 1) program is designed to bring the content closer in field conditions, tourist trails, and a pilot version includes two routes covering the oldest parts of the city of Poznan (Ostrow Tumski and the Old Market). In turn, the SITex program allows to present exhibition content in stationary conditions (e.g. in museums, galleries, tourist information points, infokiosks).

Both programs are based on the same resource of PJM dictionary of Thetos system. The difference between them lies only in choosing the content relevant

Fig. 1. The SITur program (sample slides)

to the character of the visited place. Information, in accordance with the suggestions of the deaf, were passed in graphic form: maps, photos, drawings, pictograms and as avatar – PJM translator (Fig. 1).

5   Discussion and Conclusions

Testing the SITur and SITex programs by Deaf people showed, above all, the need to supplement the vocabulary, including words related to tourism. In the pilot form of the programs, in the absence of a relevant sign in the PJM, ideographic signs (conceptual) were replaced by dactylographic signs (spelling words). Tourism is a phenomenon that is growing rapidly, accompanied by the development of new concepts, expressed also in PJM signs. It implies a continuous process of supplementing the dictionary database with PJM signs, on which both programs are based. The first dictionary of sign language in terms of tourist signs was established in Poland in 1981 and included 734 sign language ideographic signs. Until today, a large number of signs related to this subject have been created. The total amount of signs, evaluated 40 years ago at approx. 4000, is currently estimated at more than 7000. The signs are formed as the needs for communicating, acquiring knowledge and mastering new technologies arise. The rapid development of the sign vocabulary occurs in those areas where there is a need or inspiration to define new concepts and, consequently, the creation of new sign language signs. Tourism belongs to such areas today.

The second important issue that drew the attention of users of programs is the need to improve graphics animation, so that avatar's body language, especially facial expressions, would express the emotions that would be helpful to understand the context of the described contents. The programs therefore require further development in terms of PJM base and plasticizing of animation. In contrast, work on them, especially the testing process, has brought significant social effects.

The employees of the National Museum in Poznan, which was included in the descriptions of the suggested tourist routes, admitted that the project was important to them, primarily due to changes in current beliefs about sharing and popularizing museum exhibits. The way of describing the exhibition has not been determined, as it is usually the case, by the museum and scientific language, typical of the discipline to which collected in the museum exhibits belong. Visitors and their specific language of communication became the priority in this case. The descriptions were adapted to its character, conventions and vocabulary. For some regular visitors, as museum curators noticed, these descriptions seemed too simple and not corresponding to what they were used to. It was assumed, however, that communicating with a diverse group of visitors, including such specific visitors as Deaf people, requires the use of such means of communication that are understood by them. This positive change in attitude towards increasing the availability of museum collections for speakers of PJM encourages to visit the museum those who previously did not feel good in it, mainly because of the way used to communicate with the visitors. According to museum staff, the SITur and SITex programs are likely to become important tools that will bring art and museum closer to the Deaf. Its implementation in the National Museum in Poznan was a significant experience for both employees and visitors to the museum – sensibilizing to the needs of the Deaf.

Summing up the current effects work, it is clear that the series of studies (covering both social problems and IT tools), conducted with the participation of representatives of the people who use sign language, helped to establish the key needs (from their perspective) and desired solutions to increase the availability of tourism (including tourist information system). Moreover, the current level of advancement of the recommended SITur and Sitex programs is too low to make them operate as universal tools working on different routes and in different places or tourist areas. They require first and foremost the development of the system of sign language translation, both in terms of vocabulary and visual expression of the avatar. The selection of interesting sightseeing and hiking content requires continuous cooperation with the Deaf. In addition, proofreading texts in terms of their adaptation to the expectations of the users of sign language is necessary. These tasks are a challenge for the subsequent activities.

Acknowledgements. In the period 2008–2010 the research was conducted within the research project: "Tourism of the deaf and the possibility of its activation through the use of multimedia system of tourist information SIT" N N114 208,334. The research team included the following participants: Prof. Dr. Bogdan Szczepankowski Faculty of Humanities, Cardinal Stefan Wyszynski University in Warsaw; PhD. Przemysław Szmal, PhD. Nina Suszczańska, MSc. Tomasz Grudziński Software Department, Institute of Informatics, Faculty of Automatic Control, Electronics and Computer Science, Silesian University of Technology, and PhD. Alina Zajadacz, Department of Tourism and Recreation, A. Mickiewicz University in Poznań (manager of the grant).

References

Access to the countryside by deaf visitors: Scottish Natural Heritage, Commissioned Report No. 171, ROAME No. F03AB05 (2006)

Atherton, M.: Acquiring Social Capital through Shared Deafness. Sport, Leisure, Culture and Social Capital: Discourse and Practice. LSA Publication, no. 100, pp. 67–78 (2007)

Barnes, C., Mercer, G., Shakespeare, T.: Exploring Disability: A Sociological Introduction. Polity Press, Malden (2010)

Berman, D.S., Davis-Berman, J.: Adventure as psychotherapy: a mental health perspective. J. Leisurability **22**, 1–7 (1995)

Buhalis, D., Darcy, S. (eds.): Accessible Tourism, Concepts and Issues, Aspects of Tourism. Channel View Publications, Bristol (2011)

Buhalis, D., Darcy, S., Ambrose, I. (eds.): Best practice in accessible Tourism. Inclusion, Disability, Ageing Population and Tourism, Aspects of Tourism. Channel View Publications, Bristol (2012)

European Disability Strategy 2010–2020: A Renewed Commitment to a Barrier-Free Europe. Brussels, November 15 2010 COM (2010). 636 final. http://eur-lex.europa.eu/legal-content/EN/TXT/PDF/?uri=CELEX:52010DC0636&from=EN. Accessed Nov 3 2016

Fellinger, J., Holzinger, D., Schoberberger, R., Lenz, G.: Psychosoziale merkmale bei gehoerlosen. Daten aus einer Spezialambulanz fuer Gehoerlose, Nervenarzt **76**, 43–51 (2005)

Gillovic, B., McIntosh, A.: Stakeholder perspectives of the future of accessible tourism in New Zealand. J. Tourism Futures **1**(3), 223–239 (2015)

Goodstein, H. (ed.): The Deaf Way II Reader: Perspectives from the Second International Conference on Deaf Culture. Galaudet Univ Pr, Chicago (2006)

Halleux, C., Poncelet, F.: Not a disability. The Lancet, vol. 358, p. S16, December 2001. Supplement

Hauser, P., Oheran, A., Mckee, M., Steider, A., Thew, D.: Deaf epistemology: deafhood and deafness. Am. Ann. Deaf **154**(5), 486–492 (2010)

Ladd, P.: Understanding deaf culture. In: Search of Deafhood, University of Bristol, Cromwell Press (2007)

Oliva, G.A.: The deaf community, leisure, and public recreation. In: Goodstein, H. (ed.) The Deaf Way II Reader: Perspectives from the Second International Conference on Deaf Culture, pp. 305–311. Gallaudet University Press, Washington (2006)

Padden, C.A., Humphries, T.L.: Deaf in America: Voices from a Culture. Harvard University Press, Cambridge (1990)

Padden, C.A., Humphries, T.L.: Inside Deaf Culture. Harvard University Press, Cambridge (2006)

Prillwitz, S.: Jezyk, Komunikacja i Zdolności Poznawcze Niesłyszacych. WSP, Warszawa (1996)

Rydberg, E.: Deaf people and the Labour Market in Sweden: Education Employment Economy. Studies from the Swedish Institute for Disability Research, no. 32. Oerebro University, Oerebro (2010)

Romaniuk, J., Suszczańska, N., Szmal, P.: Thel, a language for utterance generation in the thetos system. In: Vetulani, Z., Mariani, J. (eds.) LTC 2011. LNCS, vol. 8387, pp. 129–140. Springer, Cham (2014). doi:10.1007/978-3-319-08958-4_11

Suszczańska, N., Szmal, P., Kulików, S.: Continuous text translation using text modeling in the thetos system. Int. J. Comput. Intell. **1**(4), 338–341 (2004)

Szczepankowski, B.: Niesłyszacy - Głusi - Głuchoniemi. Wyrównywanie Szans. WSiP, Warszawa (1999)

Szczepankowski, B.: Franciszek Ksawery Prek – pierwszy gluchoniemy literat. In: Lubińska-Kościółek, E., Plutecka, K. (eds.), Stymulowanie potencjalu twórczego osób z różnymi potrzebami edukacyjnymi, pp. 39–50. Impuls, Kraków (2011)

Szmal, P.: Programy SITex i SITur. In: Zajadacz A. (ed.) The SITex and SITur programs as tools designed to provide information to visitors and tourists using the Polish Sign Language, pp. 1–31. (+ CD) Wyd. Naukowe UAM, Poznan (2010)

Szmal, P., Suszczańska, N.: Selected problems of translation from the Polish written language to the sign language. Archiwum Informatyki Teoretycznej i Stosowanej **13**(1), 37–51 (2001)

Terry, T.: Universal adventure programming: opening our programs to people with physical disabilities. J. Leisurability **22**(2), 28–30 (1995)

UK Council on Deafness: Deaf Awareness Week: Examples of Good Practice (2005). http://www.deafcouncil.org.uk/daw/goodp.htm#at. Accessed Nov 3 2016

Woodward, J.: Implications for sociolinguistics research among the deaf. Sign Lang. Stud. **1**, 1–7 (1972)

World Tourism Organization: Recommendations on Accessible Tourism for All. UNWTO, Madrid (2013)

World Tourism Organization and Fundación ACS: Manual on Accessible Tourism for All - Public-Private Partnerships and Good Practices. UNWTO, Madrid (2015)

World Tourism Organization: Accessible Tourism for All: An Opportunity within Our Reach. UNWTO, Madrid (2016a)

World Tourism Organization: Recommendations on Accessible Information in Tourism. UNWTO, Madrid (2016b)

World Tourism Organization: World Tourism Day 2016 'Tourism for All - promoting universal accessibility' Good Practices in the Accessible Tourism Supply Chain. UNWTO, Madrid (2016c)

Young, A., Acerman, J., Kyle, J.: On creating a workable signing environment: deaf and hearing perspectives. J. Deaf Stud. Deaf Educ. 5(2), 186–195 (2000)

Zajadacz, A.: Czas wolny, turystyka i rekreacja osób niesłyszacych w Polsce. Zarys specyfiki problemu, Seria Turystyka i Rekreacja, Studia i Prace, T. 4, Wyd. Naukowe UAM, Poznań (2010a)

Zajadacz A. (ed.): The SITex and SITur programs as tools designed to provide information to visitors and tourists using the Polish Sign Language, pp. 1–31. (+ CD) Wyd. Naukowe UAM, Poznan (2010b)

Zajadacz, A.: Attitudes to social integration of deaf and hearing people during leisure time in Poland. In: Wyrzykowski, J., Marak, J. (eds.) Tourism Role in the Regional Economy. Social, Health-Related, Economic and Spatial Conditions of Disabled Peoples Tourism Development, pp. 310–326. Wyższa Szkoła Handlowa we Wrocławiu, Wrocław (2011)

Zajadacz, A.: Turystyka osób niesłyszacych - ujecie geograficzne. Bogucki Wydawnictwo Naukowe, Poznań (2012)

Zajadacz, A.: Sources of tourist information used by Deaf people. Case study: the Polish Deaf community. Curr. Issues Tourism 17(5), 434–454 (2014)

Zajadacz, A., Śniadek, J.: Tourism activities of deaf poles. Phys. Cult. Sport Stud. Res. 58(1), 17–32 (2013)

Zajadacz, A.: Evolution of models of disability as a basis for further policy changes in accessible tourism. J. Tourism Futures 1(3), 189–202 (2015)

Universal Access to Information and Media

Impact of Cognitive Learning Disorders on Accessing Online Resources

Alexander Cadzow[(⊠)]

C3L, Sawbrideworth, UK
alex@cadzow.com

Abstract. The present document assesses the impact of learning cognitive disorders on accessing online resources. This paper relates to Human Factor and Systems Interaction since it covers the wider social concerns leading to improved access to computers and system by currently disadvantaged groups in this paper focuses on people with cognitive learning disorders. This is a thought exercise study and examines how technology, represented by online resources, is made available without discriminating against those with learning cognitive disorders. The learning impact has been assessed by the Human Factors based methods of Soft Systems Methodology (SSM), Usability Engineering (UE) and Ontology Sketch Modelling (OSM). The major finding of the study is that whilst there are tools that make access to many resources more equitable, there is still limited understanding of how those with cognitive disorders assimilate information. In addressing this aspect, the present document has examined the wider role of semantic web technology that by introducing codification of context and pragmatics can improve the presentation of knowledge such that those with cognitive learning disorders can achieve non-discriminatory access to online resources. The aim of this paper is to consider how online resources are presented to ensure that irrespective of the level of cognitive impairment the semantic value of resources is conveyed equally to all users. From this study, a few key lessons were learned from examining the impact of learning cognitive disorder on accessing online resources. The impact can be minimal since guidelines and web standards if followed ensure sites and systems have adequate accessibility and usability design or built into the interfaces from the beginning. Also, it could be argued for greater built-in support to allow for less reliance on 3rd party aid tools since while that would give benefit to users with cognitive learning disorders it would also benefit all users since it is natural to take advantage of tools which can benefit the overall work process. Finally, a future study should cover a more in-depth assessment which could involve a blind test of tasks with a mixture of people with and without learning disabilities to ensure a more in-depth examination of the impact of learning cognitive disorders on accessing online resources.

Keywords: UX and usability · User experience

© Springer International Publishing AG 2017
M. Antona and C. Stephanidis (Eds.): UAHCI 2017, Part III, LNCS 10279, pp. 363–381, 2017.
DOI: 10.1007/978-3-319-58700-4_30

1 Introduction

The present document assesses the impact of learning cognitive disorders on accessing online resources. This is a thought exercise study and examines how technology, represented by online resources, is made available without discriminating against those with learning cognitive disorders. The learning impact has been assessed by the Human Factors based methods Soft Systems Methodology (SSM), Usability Engineering (UE) and Ontology Sketch Modelling (OSM). The major finding of the study is that whilst there are tools that make access to many resources more equitable, there is still limited understanding of how those with cognitive disorders assimilate information. In addressing this aspect, the present document has examined the wider role of semantic web technology that by introducing codification of context and pragmatics can improve the presentation of knowledge such that those with cognitive learning disorders can achieve non-discriminatory access to online resources.

2 Disclaimer

The author of this paper has the learning disorder dyslexia (word blindness) and has been diagnosed with mild Asperger's syndrome. Asperger's syndrome is one of a few recognised autism spectrum disorders (ASD) and has been on the "high functioning" end of the spectrum. Affected children and adults have difficulty with social interactions and exhibit a restricted range of interests and/or repetitive behaviours. In the author's case, this is best exhibited through uncoordinated motor movements (managed through a few physical therapies) and poor performance in non-verbal communication and reasoning leading to often an over-literal interpretation of information and instruction. It is generally considered that across the ASD that those with Asperger syndrome do not have significant delays or difficulties in language or cognitive development but may have difficulty in expressing their knowledge.

3 Aim

To consider how links are presented to ensure that irrespective of the level of cognitive impairment the semantic value of a link is conveyed.

4 Objectives

1. Assess Bournemouth University mySearch resource site against accessibility metrics as the main case study (http://eds.a.ebscohost.com/eds/search/advanced?sid=c1ab44a9-47c4-440a-bebf-4969354e6aa5%40sessionmgr4002&vid=0&hid=4111).
2. Define learning cognitive disorders within the context of using a simplified ontology.
3. Examine other case studies with similar a premise to make a comparative analysis of how many others have looked at this topic.

4. From the definitions gained from the conceptual model examine their impact.
5. Define the relevance of semantic web in relation to the topic.

5   Background Information

This project concerns accessibility of online resources which refers to the degree to which an interactive product, i.e. the online resource, is accessible by as large a proportion of the accessing population as possible. There is a need to strike a balance in the design of the online resource and the means to access it between usability and accessibility for all people regardless of whether they a disability or not. This often requires a need for a site or system to allow for assistive technologies (Preece et al. 2015, p. 18) The aides focus on reading, speaking and listening to enhance accessibility. Often these are third party tools which are applied to sites and systems instead of being built in. Since there needs to be a balance between usability and accessibility often these tools are not built into sites or systems so there are sometimes issues of compatibility (Preece et al. 2015, pp. 82–83). This project considers accessibility and usability when assessing the impact of learning cognitive disorder on accessing online resources.

Furthermore, as stated in the EU's Digital Single Market initiative: "Web accessibility is not just a question of technical standards and of web architecture and design. It is not a concern for web developers only, but also a question of political will and of moral obligation now enshrined in the United Nations Convention on the Rights of Persons with Disabilities (UNCRPD). Article 9 of the Convention requires that appropriate measures are taken to ensure access for persons with disabilities, on an equal basis with others, to inter alia information and communication technologies, including the Internet" (https://ec.europa.eu and www.un.org).

It can be asserted therefore that universal web access is not a "nice to have" but should be defined as an essential element of non-discriminatory behaviour. The concern addressed in the present document is how to address accessibility for cognitive as opposed to physical disability.

6   Definitions

Cognitive Disorder. A category of mental health disorders that primarily affect learning, memory, perception, and problem solving, and include amnesia, dementia, and delirium.

NOTE. For the present document only those cognitive disorders that impact learning is considered. Thus those cognitive disorders that impact an individual's ability to interpret or process what they see or hear. It is generally considered that the impact of learning cognitive disorders is that there is a gap between the patient's intelligence and ability to perform. Patients may have difficulties with spoken and written language, self-control, coordination, and/or attention. As a result, patients may have a hard time with schoolwork or performing tasks at work (Cognitive and learning disorders 2016). There is a sliding scale of learning cognitive disorders which can mean when assessing users can be difficult because often most people develop their own coping methods though often there are similar patterns in the coping methods.

Dyslexia. a learning difficulty that primarily affects the skills involved in accurate and fluent word reading and spelling.

NOTE. The impact of dyslexia is that sufferers generally, read and write very slowly and exhibit some or all of the following characteristics: (NHS Dyslexia 2016) Confuse the order of letters in words; Write letters the wrong way round – such as writing "b" instead of "d"; Have poor or inconsistent spelling; Understand information when told verbally, but have difficulty with information that's written down; Find it hard to carry out a sequence of directions; Struggle with planning and organisation. However, people with dyslexia often have good skills in other areas, such as creative thinking and problem-solving.

Dysgraphia. Neurological condition that impairs writing and memory processing (Dysgraphia.org.uk).

NOTE. Dysgraphia is sometimes considered to be a specific type of cognitive learning disability but is also viewed as a sub-set of dyslexia where dyslexia is considered the broadest cognitive learning disorder. In the present document, dysgraphia has been treated as a distinct learning disability.

Semantic Web. A set of formats and protocols for the interchange of data (where on the Web there is only an interchange of documents).

NOTE. Tim Berners-Lee et al. defined the semantic web in a paper published in 2001 as a vision for an extension of the World Wide Web that enables people to share content beyond the boundaries of applications and websites. It has been described in rather different ways: as a utopic vision, as a web of data, or merely as a natural paradigm shift in our daily use of the Web (semanticweb.org 2012). How it relates to this assessment is by how mySearch is a foundation of the semantic web since it can access different databases and knowledge centres.

Usability. (ISO 9241 definition) effectiveness, efficiency, and satisfaction with which specified users achieve specified goals under certain environments'.

Accessibility. Extent to which products, systems, services, environments and facilities can be used by people from a population with the widest range of characteristics and capabilities, to achieve a specified goal in a specified context of use (from ISO 26800).

7 Past Case Studies

Whilst the World Wide Web has been in existence since Tim Berners-Lee's first proposals and his subsequent invitation to collaborate on 6th August 1991 the question of accessibility has been many years in coming to "the web". Whilst there has been some work in the various standards groups, the W3C first published its own "Web Content Accessibility Guidelines" in May 1999 and subsequently updated to the current version 2 in 2008 there have been very few past case studies addressing accessibility for an audience of cognitively impaired users. Rather accessibility has been addressed to give assurance of the rendering of content across a range of devices, to assure that figures and labels are tagged where the tag data can be converted to speech. There are a small number of comparable past studies to the topic addressed in this exercise that use a similar basis and methods but which do not provide comparative results. These foregoing case studies have been used to establish a baseline in the present this study from which the issues discussed here can use.

Advancing the Semantic Web via Library Functions. The first case study used in establishing a baseline is "Advancing the Semantic Web via Library Functions" which explores the applicability of primary library functions (collection development, cataloguing, reference, and circulation) to the Semantic Web. This case study relates to the use of BU mySearch since it complements the physical library at BU by providing the ability to search large digital collections of journals, articles and books. It functions in a similar way to the physical library. The similarities between semantic web and libraries are that they are a response to collating bodies of information. It was concluded that library functions can translate to a Semantic Web function (Greenberg 2007). Since this exercise looks at the impact of learning cognitive disorder on accessing online resources we should consider the next step in ensuring that any conclusions can be applied to future ways of searching and accessing data.

Cognitive support for ontology modelling. The second case study is "Cognitive support for ontology modelling" the examined previous work in this domain and explaining the nature of cognitive support on the basis that knowledge engineering tools are becoming ever more complex, and therefore increased cognitive support will be necessary to leverage the potential of those tools. They define cognitive support as leveraging innate human abilities, such as visual information processing, to increase human understanding and cognition of challenging problems. This relates to this exercise since users with cognitive learning problems use tools to aid their ability to process information. They identified a lack of support for tools which aid cognitive support when accessing knowledge-based databases which what mySearch functions as (Ernst et al. 2005). The use of aid tools for learning cognitive disorders is important when accessing online resources so there is an expectation that they will work with sites and systems without trouble. Since through this exercise, an ontology sketch model will be examined the need to consider how tools can be implemented is necessary. Ontologies are used to visualise and show how domains and taxonomies relate and connect to each other and are tied into the development of the semantic web which

this exercise aims to show how tools that aid users with cognitive learning disorders fit into the development of the semantic web.

Knowledge networks in the age of the Semantic Web. The reason for the need to look at issues of accessibility and universal access is examined in the paper "Knowledge networks in the age of the Semantic Web" since the technologies of the Semantic Web are envisioned will hopefully foster innovation and greater understanding plus insight into collected knowledge. While that paper examines the Semantic Web from a medical and pharmaceutical viewpoint the overall conclusion that these knowledge networks are becoming more complex and necessary as they become the main depository of information, this holds true across most other disciplines (Neumann and Prusak 2007). While the paper does not examine issues of accessibility this lack of examination should be corrected which this exercise will attempt to achieve by looking at the overview of the need for people of all abilities should be able to use and understanding the knowledge when people with cognitive learning disorders access these networks.

The Impact of Cognitive Intervention Program and Music Therapy in Learning Disabilities. While this paper "The Impact of Cognitive Intervention Program and Music Therapy in Learning Disabilities" is not about sites or web semantics it illustrates the importance that aids, in this case, music therapy, can help people with learning disabilities. The study suggested that interconnection of "Music Therapy" with a "Cognitive Intervention Program" has enabled children with a learning disability to increase their performance in four problem areas namely: planning; attention; simultaneous (parallel) processing; and successive (sequential) processing. These are areas which 3rd party aid tools applied to sites and systems aim to improve this assignment is examining. Also, the case study found that since intervention in these areas improves these skills for people with learning disabilities they can aid weaknesses they may have (Skeja 2014). Even though this case study seems unrelated it illustrates the key point that the clear majority of people with learning cognitive disorder develop their own coping mechanisms when dealing with the problems they have. Here music helps as an aid while with using sites and systems the 3rd party tools are the help. So, when considering the approaches to examine the impact when accessing online resources, we must consider that each user will use the aids to their own advantage and that no user will likely to be alike when using the tools.

8 Approaches

8.1 Soft Systems Methodology

Systems-based methodology for tackling real-world problems in which known-to-be-desirable ends cannot be taken as given. Soft systems methodology is based upon a phenomenological stance (applying the philosophical study of the structures of experience and consciousness to problem-solving) (Checkland 2005, p. 318). When used to examine the impact cognitive learning disorders have when accessing online resources, it aims to show how users interact with the system being analysed and the rationales for decisions to use aids tools and how they are used themselves with the system.

Rich Picture is the expression of a problem situation compiled by an investigator, often by examining elements of structure, elements of the process, and the situation climate (Checkland 2005, p. 317). How people with learning cognitive disorders use mySearch and how it works (Fig. 1).

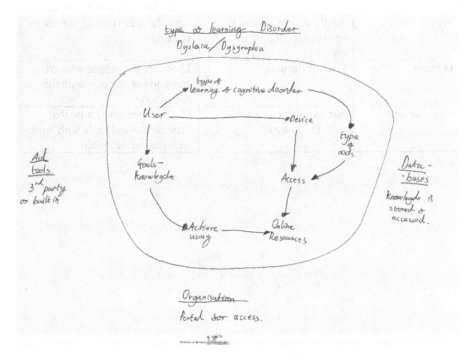

Fig. 1. Rich picture see Appendix 1 for larger

Root Definitions – Customer Actor Transformation Worldview Owners Environment. Aconcise, tightly constructed description of a human activity which states what the system is; what it does is then elaborated in a conceptual model which is built based on the definition (Checkland 2005, p. 317). The CATWOE method is used here to develop the root definitions and their conceptual models.

Conceptual models. They allow for a systemic account of a human activity system. These models presented here contain the minimum necessary activities for the system to be the one named in the root definition (Checkland 2005, p. 313). There are two root definitions paired with two conceptual models presented here in this paper looking at how a user with a cognitive learning disorder would use the site or system. The first root definition and conceptual model show the use of aid tools with a site and the second shows User-system interaction (Figs. 2 and 3).

Aid tools

Domain	Description	Justification
Customer	User with learning disorder	The User being described has the cognitive learning disorder.
Actor	Aid tools	The devices or software used by the user.
Transformation	Applying aids to a system	How improved understanding would be gained from the site.
Worldview	Apply aids to an article to read processing of an article	How the user is using the site or system.
Owners	User of the aids	These are the people who are going to use the aids with the site or system.
Environment	Are the aids compatible with the system?	The user needs to know that their chosen aid tools with work with the site or system

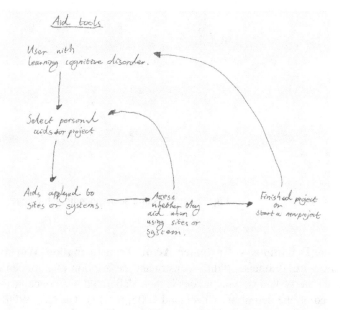

Fig. 2. Conceptual model of aid tools see appendix for larger

User-System interaction

Domain	Description	Justification
Customer	User accessing the site or system	How the task will start
Actor	System or site architecture	What the User will interact with
Transformation	Using aids to with the results	To gain a better understanding of the results
Worldview	People with cognitive learning disorders using aids with the site or systems	Interaction between the User and the System
Owners	System or site administration	Responsible for ensuring aids work with the site or system
Environment	Compatibility of aid tools	The application of the 3rd party aid tools to user interfaces of the site or system may not work as desired.

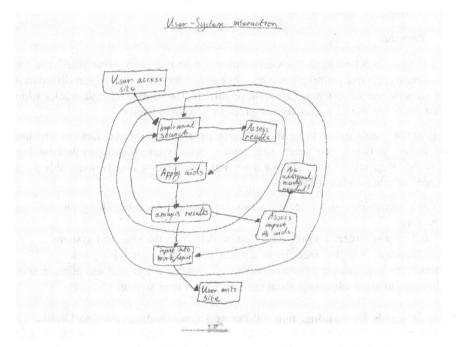

Fig. 3. Conceptual model of user-system interaction see appendix for larger

Comparison with the real world. The user-system interaction shown here are generalised overviews about how the users use the aids to better their processing of the articles their searches would find. Though there are problems with these generalised overviews is that people who have cognitive learning disorders or learning disabilities are that the people have different levels of them when diagnosed and each person develops their own unique coping mechanism.

The lessons learned from SSM here is though while there are difficulties with generalised models it shows the process would be the same for all people with learning difficulties as they use online resources. This means the decision process can be studied and analysed to show how they can be improved when users interact with the system or site.

The findings and work process of the first approach of SMM will be used to lead and to influence the second approach. This is to allow a consistent analysis of accessing the impact of cognitive learning disorders when accessing online resources.

Usability Engineering (Inspection/Evaluation). Usability engineering is an area of which inspects and evaluates human-computer interactions and human-computer interfaces (HCI). Here Personas paired with relevant cognitive walkthroughs will be used to inspect and evaluate the HCI.

8.2 Persona

Each Persona is a final year university students who is a twenty-one years' old who each have a cognitive learning disorder. They are undertaking a final year dissertation. This scenario was chosen since it would require the use of research and articles which would entail the use of university resources to find these sources.

Dysgraphia – aids for writing and memory processing. Persona Details: The final year student is twenty-one years' old, female, who is undertaking an anthropology course. She requires the aids in taking notes and observations. Finally, these aids would be used the write up her dissertation.

- Voice recognition software. To allow for natural voice searching on sites and systems.
- Mind map software. To pull and organise data from the sites and systems.
- Audio notes. A digital recorder or a smart phone or a digital program.
- Reference and citation software. Endnote. To ensure the correct use of referencing but also to allow clear organisation. Pulled from their source.

Dyslexia – aids for spelling, note taking and proofreading. Persona Details: The final year student is twenty-one years' old, male, who is undertaking a Forensic Science course. He uses the aides to double check his aids to double check his work and ensure it is grammatically correct. Also by using the screen reader aid in processing audibly and visually sources he uses and allows him to better proofread his own work.

- Dictionary, physical or digital.
- Note taker. Use of a programme such as OneNote, Evernote, Windows Journal and Google Keep. Enables thought and ideas to be easily tracked. Data can be pulled directly from sites or systems.
- Screen reader. To to be used one the accessed sites and systems. Also, can be used on articles and sources.
- Reference and citation software. Endnote. To ensure the correct use of referencing but also to allow clear organisation. Pulled from their source

Cognitive Walk-through. Acognitive walkthrough shows how a person with one of these learning disabilities would hypothetical use the system or site being accessed. The Persona will have a task list with the action sequence that details the specific task flow from beginning to end.

Dysgraphia Task list.

1. Access myBU online search resource mySearch.
   1.1. Enable 3rd party voice recognition software to facilitate natural voice searching.
2. Enter the Search term for a topic.
3. Go through the search results.
   3.1. Note any chosen articles or journals found into categories in the mind mapping software.
   3.2. Create audio notes for each chosen articles or journal.
   3.3. Use Endnote to create a list of references using the BU-Harvard referencing system.
4. Either enter a new search term or exit mySearch.

Dyslexia Task list.

1. Access myBU online search resource mySearch.
   1.1. Ensure the physical or digital dictionary is nearby or open to allow for unfamiliar words or terms to be looked-up.
2. Enter the search term for the chosen topic.
3. Go through the search results.
   3.1. Use the screen reader to go through the chosen journals or articles.
   3.2. Enter sections of note from these journals or articles into Notetaker software.
   3.3. Use Endnote to create a list of references using the BU-Harvard referencing system.
4. Either enter a new search term or exit mySearch.

The results of applying these tasks would be that each persona would have a selection of notes and their relevant references. These can then be inserted into the main body of their dissertation with minimal fuss.

The key lessons learned from working the process of Usability Engineering is the lack of built-in support in mySearch for Users with cognitive learning disorders to aid them when they are undertaking searches for information. The use of personas to inspect mySearch showed that is not a big step-up to enable aid tools for Users with cognitive learning disorders. Since the tools are not specific for people with learning disabilities though they are the users most likely to take advantage of them. From this evaluation, the 3rd party aid tools generally work well when using the mySearch and any future developing could suggest versions of these tools being built into mySearch.

The findings from the usability engineering will influence the direction and pattern when developing of the OSM. The process of task lists will help in direction of the pathways when developing the OSM.

8.3   Ontology Sketch Modelling (OSM)

OSM when paired with usability and accessibility testing, this will bring the concepts and links discussed in the previous approaches into a single structure and flow. The WAVE tool will provide a baseline from which to work with when undertaking the OSM (http://wave. webaim.org/). By using the MySearch page (http://eds.a.ebscohost.com/eds/search/advanced?sid=e1bdc0ef-1c70-4c60-96a3-dc54dfd65687%40sessionmgr4004&vid=0&h id=4211&preview=false) with the WAVE tool as a baseline can be determined in order to see problems with accessibility which is one of the concerns of this impact. See next page for the image showing the layout of the web page in question.

Aside mySearch is built on technology and services from EBSCO host and its Research Databases. It provides subscriptions and access to different publishers of journals, magazines and books. So, an organisation such as Bournemouth University can gain access through a single portal instead should have individual subscriptions from those publishers (Figs 4 and 5).

Fig. 4. mySearch screen capture

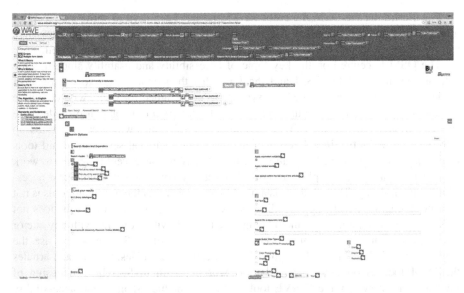

Fig. 5. mySearch after processing by WAVE tool

The previous page is a summary of what the WAVE tool detected the following: three Errors, three hundred and thirty-five Alerts, seventy-four Features, twenty-six Structural Elements, one-hundred and fifty HTML5 and ARIA and fourteen Contrast Errors. As can be seen from the figure these are in the end only minor issues which would easily be fixed and generally will not have a negative effect on a user with cognitive learning disabilities. It also illustrates that even though mySearch is powerful search engine tool it is still accessible to the widest possible range of users. It also helps to serve to illustrate when developing the OSM and the links between the semantic web how the options and data being pulled together into a single user interface (Fig. 6).

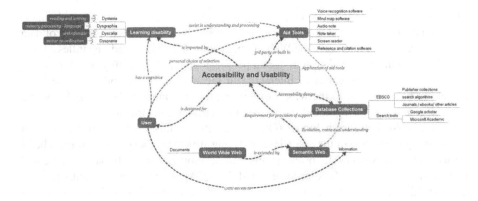

Fig. 6. OSM see appendix for larger

For illustrating the OSM the software XMind has been used to show a concept of how the links and connections of users with learning disabilities, access the knowledge and how the use of aid tools to improve accessibility and usability come together.

The OSM is centred on the key topic of accessibility and usability since this the natural conclusion of the SSM and the UE. This then comes back to the issue of guidelines and standards for sites and systems to be designed for Users with cognitive learning disorders. Though in the end, it is up to the organisations that provide these sites and systems to follow the Web standards and guidelines which can be tested up tools such as WAVE. Since Users will use their own personal selection of aid tools there is a need for seamless integration because largely people except programs to work straight away as plug and play are considered a key cornerstone of universal accessibility and usability. Though there is a need to remember that the use of aid tools is not specific to cognitive learning disabilities since anyone can use them but this does not undermine their importance in them being able to work without issues with any site or system. Since this assessment concerns the accessing of mySearch which use the services of EBSCO which collate published collections of articles, eBooks and articles the OSM focuses on the issues aid tools working with mySearch. The design of mySearch as shown by the WAVE tool has an acceptable usability and accessibility rating. So, the impact of cognitive learning disorders on accessing online resources through mySearch is minimal which leads then into what improvements could be applied which in the OSM is provided by the Semantic Web.

This in the future there could be developments which will hopefully see mySearch extended by the Semantic Web since it should be able to provide better contextual support when looking up information for topics which could mean better-personalised searches and more focused results. Also in theory, if the kind of aid tools discussed in this assignment in the future could be built into or more integrated into sites or systems such as mySearch as it should allow people with or without learning disabilities the option of greater accessibility by providing Users more options to process and access the desired information.

9 Discussion

The discussion will examine a wider role of semantic web technology on how humans understand and find or catalogue knowledge. The semantic web concerns a Web of data while the traditional internet is the Web of documents. There is a need, regardless of the complexity of the back-end system, for all people no matter their ability or any possible impairment (physical/mental) to interact with the user interface and the underlying content to be accessible to the widest extent and for all content to be accessible to the same degree (no content should be inaccessible through impairment).

The Ontological Sketch Model (OSM) presented in this paper is structured as an informal representation of the essential underlying structure of a system forming a basis for usability assessment. The primary aim is to develop an approach that is usable and that yields useful results. Studies have found that OSM allows a way of thinking about the usability of a system, including capturing important cognitive dimensions (Blandford and Green 1997). This relates to the relationship shown in the OSM presented earlier aims to the actions of a user and those accessing sites or systems of a domain. The OSM shows in the future the need for semantic web support which could potentially evolve the services such as EBSCO, Google Scholar and Microsoft Academic into better knowledge engineering tools. A published paper has shown that cognitive support tools can be used to leverage human abilities to increase human understanding and cognition of challenging problems (Ernst et al. 2005). This line of thinking could be applied to our OSM since the application of cognitive support tools also have the potential to improve universal accessibility and usability.

The nearly exponential growth in the availability of published digital information creates issues of how it can be usefully accessed. Conventional data-centric models such as those using in Relational Database modelling require complex normalisation and indexing to be accessed quickly. The underlying problem is that the information is not structured and cannot be readily indexed to allow for search. Adding keywords extends the data and if content creators do not take the time to provide keywords or phrases there is no guarantee that existing search engines will catalogue web pages. Furthermore, where search engines such as those from Google work it is based on page based keyword analysis and link indexing, furthermore indexing results can be skewed by buying index words and adding things like Analytics meta-data. Search results using existing models are not reliable or realistic given the commercial imperatives for site indexing. Solutions have been proposed in similar situations using concepts of a formal ontology paired with semantic process modelling. They concluded that formalisation of the semantics in conjunction with the use of inference engines allows the improvement of query functionalities (Thomas and Fellmann 2009). These possible solutions could allow for better search methods. This connects to a case study which looked at digital libraries in the knowledge era. The purpose was to show the expression and the exploitation of humanity's collective knowledge. They found that Semantic Web technologies and knowledge management technologies expand the frontiers of knowledge representation and sharing (Lytras et al. 2005). Though these solutions are about the underlying architecture that facilitates the ability to search for topics. Though ideally people should see no difference in the user interface while experience more accurate and precise results. It relates back to the issue of the impact of learning cognitive disorder on accessing online resources which any future improvements would also need to consider of accessibility and usability which should remain consistent regardless how improved the underlying search architecture is.

10 Appraisal of Objectives

Due to the nature of the learning cognitive disorders of dyscalculia and dysgraphia which are to do with arithmetic they were left out of the personas' since they are not relevant to articles and journal which are largely literature based. Also, the aid tools cover a broad range of learning disabilities so there would be little difference in help for the arithmetic type of learning disabilities.

There were few accessibilities issues with the mySearch website which lessened the impact of cognitive learning disorders on accessing resources through it. Though there is still room for future improvements such as at building the type of aid tools talked about directly into the site itself.

A problem is a lack of study on this specific issue since accessibility tools often get built into many sites so there is not an incentive to carry out a study into the impact of learning cognitive disorders into accessing online resources. This was shown through the lack of past relevant case studies which even though there is potential for learning cognitive disorders studies to cover a wide range of topics.

11 Conclusion

From this thought exercise, there are a few key lessons learned from examining the impact of learning cognitive disorder on accessing online resources. The impact can be minimal since guidelines and web standards if followed ensure sites and systems have adequate accessibility and usability design or built into the interfaces from the beginning. Also, it could be argued for greater built-in support to allow for less reliance on 3rd aid tools since while that would give benefit to users with cognitive learning disorders it would also benefit all users since it is natural to take advantage of tools which can benefit the overall work process. Finally, a future study should cover a more in-depth assessment which could involve a blind test of tasks with a mixture of people with and without learning disabilities to ensure a more in-depth examination of the impact of learning cognitive disorders on accessing online resources.

Appendix 1

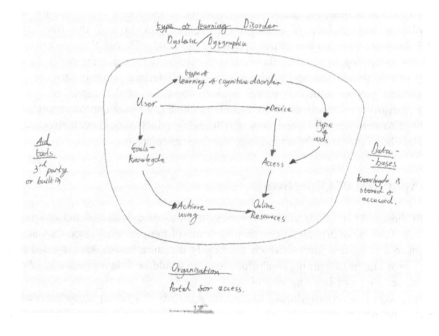

Appendix 2

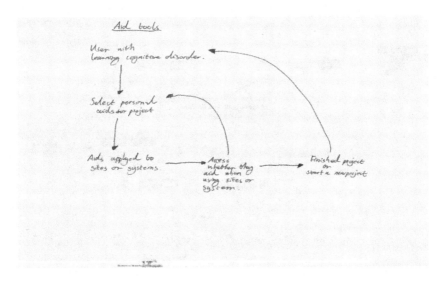

Appendix 3

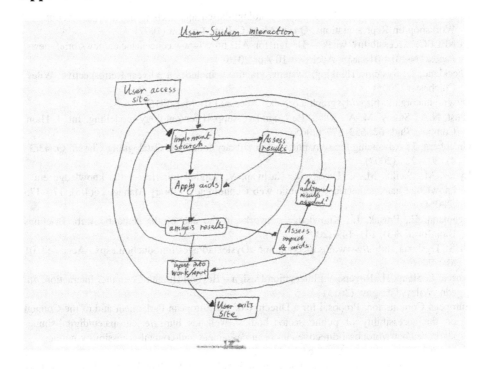

Appendix 4

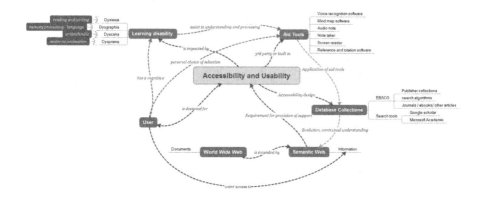

References

Blandford, A., Green, T.R.G.: OSM: an ontology-based approach to usability evaluation. In: Workshop on Representations, Queen Mary College London (1997)

CENELEC: Accessibility week – Design for All. http://www.cencenelec.eu/news/brief_news/Pages/TN-2014-018.aspx Accessed 10 Apr 2016

Checkland, P.: Systems Thinking, Systems Practice – Includes a 30-year Retrospective. Wiley, Chichester (2005)

Dysgraphia.org.uk. http://dysgraphia.org.uk/. Accessed 01 Mar 2016

Ernst, N.A., Storey, M.-A., Allen, P.: Cognitive support for ontology modelling. Int. J. Hum. Comput. Stud. **62**, 553–577 (2005)

Greenberg, J.: Advancing the semantic web via library functions. Cataloguing Classif. Q. **43**(3–4), 203–225 (2007)

Lytras, M., Sicilia, M.-A., Davies, J., Kashyap, V.: Digital libraries in the knowledge era – knowledge management and semantic web technologies. Library Manag. **26**(4/5), 170–175 (2005)

Neumann, E., Prusak, L.: Knowledge networks in the age of the semantic web. Briefings Bioinform. **8**(3), 141–149 (2007)

NHS: Dyslexia. http://www.nhs.uk/conditions/Dyslexia/Pages/Introduction.aspx. Accessed 01 Mar 2016

Preece, J., Sharp, H., Rogers, Y.: Interaction Design – Beyond Human-Computer Interaction, 4th edn. Wiley, Glasgow (2015)

European Commission: Proposal for a Directive of the European Parliament and of the Council on the accessibility of public sector bodies' websites https://ec.europa.eu/digital-single-market/en/news/proposal-directive-european-parliament-and-council-accessibility-public-sector-bodies-websites. Accessed 05 Mar 2016

Semanticweb.org.edu: Main Page. http://semanticweb.org/wiki/Main_Page.html. Accessed 04 Mar 2016

Skeja, E.: The impact of cognitive intervention program and music therapy in learning disabilities. Procedia Soc. Behav. Sci. **159**, 605–609 (2014)

Thomas, O., Fellmann, M.: Semantic process modelling – design and implementation of an ontology-based representation of business processes. Bus. Inf. Syst. Eng. **1**, 438 (2009)

United Nations: Convention on the Rights of Persons with Disabilities. http://www.un.org/disabilities/convention/conventionfull.shtml. Accessed 05 Mar 2016

Wellness: Cognitive and Learning Disorder. http://www.wellness.com/reference/conditions/cognitive-and-learning-disorders. Accessed 01 Mar 2016

W3: Usability – ISO 9241 Definition. https://www.w3.org/2002/Talks/0104-usabilityprocess/slide3-0.html. Accessed 10 Apr 2016

Young Female Consumers' Perceptions and Purchase Intentions Towards Character Economy

Cheih-Ying Chen[✉]

Department of Product Innovation and Entrepreneurship,
National Taipei University of Business, Taipei City, Taiwan, R.O.C.
c.y.chen@ntub.edu.tw

Abstract. A lovely cartoon character after being authorized can be used in a variety of products. Character economy influences young consumer' preferences, choices, and purchase intention. The purpose of this research was to investigate the impact of lovely cartoon characters on purchase intentions and brand preference among young female consumers of Taiwan. Structured questionnaire was used to collect data through survey research method and data was collected from 35 young female consumers. ANOVA was used as statistical techniques to test the research. Result showed that lovely characters have significant impact on young female consumers' purchase intentions and brand preference.

Keywords: Lovely characters · Character economy · Purchase intention · Digital development · Perception

1 Introduction

Authorizing is the process in character economy to apply for trademarks and copyright for these products and services. These authorized assets can usually be a name, a logo, an image, a sentence, a signature, or even a role/character. A lovely cartoon character after being authorized can be used in a variety of commodities; the economic benefits earned by these products, such as Hello Kitty, Mickey Mouse, Angry Birds and so on, are called character economy.

Concept of lovely cartoon characters evolved in last few decades and it has strengthened its roots. Character economy influences female young consumer' preferences, choices, and purchase intention. Young female consumers may logically be a major force in the character brand market, because they are economy shoppers, often demonstrate senses of high fashion, trend involvement, and the desire to find unique funny product offerings. From designers' perspective, a character design line is an extension of cultural and creative industry existing brand.

Most of the well-known characters like Hello Kitty, Mickey Mouse, One Piece, Spider-Man and Batman are derived from the traditional cartoon and wildly spread over the world through the comic film and television. However, because of the current network development, many roles are animated from blogs, FACEBOOK or LINE.

© Springer International Publishing AG 2017
M. Antona and C. Stephanidis (Eds.): UAHCI 2017, Part III, LNCS 10279, pp. 382–392, 2017.
DOI: 10.1007/978-3-319-58700-4_31

The greater the consumers' are digitally involved, the more likely they were to purchase digital character design product. Based on this rationale, it is researched that:

1: Young female consumers' attitudes towards character design product are positively and significantly related to their purchase intentions.
2: Digital development involvement will be positively and significantly related to young female consumers' purchase intentions towards character design product.

The main purpose in this study is to evaluate purchase intention and preference of young female consumers in a series of lovely characters products in Taiwan. In order to research the purchase intention and preference of the characters products and attain effective results, this study includes a questionnaire, and adopts the fixed random sampling for investigation.

2 Literature Review

2.1 Creative Industry and Characters Products

Creative industries are becoming increasingly important components of modern post-industrial knowledge-based economies. Not only are they thought to account for higher than average growth and job creation, they are also vehicles of cultural identity that play an important role in fostering cultural diversity [1]. In 2010, Taiwan's culture ministry incorporated animation, cartoon, character and educational entertainment into cultural and creative industry. They think that combining characters with animation, from general characters to 3D figures, will increase beneficial result of economy and ethnicity. For instance, Special liveries of EVA airline with Hello Kitty make a significant impact on consumer's emotion, thinking, association, action and senses. Those authorized characters and related products have caused a great stir, promoting character's culture and industry.

As far as creative product is concerned, applying design elements precisely such as shape, color, texture or material, will make user feel the visual or tactile pleasure. A designer should take different cultural, social customs or human behavior factors into consideration and put it into design concept, convey the true meaning of cultural symbols correctly by psychological comprehension. Understanding the user interaction with the needs of the product can make designers to combine different consumer perspectives easily, the design results can achieve a balanced appearance of aesthetics, as well as emotional expression around the user's mind.

The essence of the culture creative product is "user-oriented"; its value must be introduced into real life, turning design content into human and culture's emotional, putting the change of people's feelings into the product design so as to form user interaction with the product. While cultural objects can be incorporated into cultural design, three design features are identified as follows: (1) the inner level containing special content such as stories, emotion, and cultural features, (2) the mid-level containing function, operational concerns, usability, and safety, and (3) the outer level dealing with colors, texture, form, decoration, surface pattern, lines quality, and details [2].

Using the character in the story or scenario to introduction the digital information to consumers, and through the activity characters, digital scenarios and interactive mode, consumers feel the abstract implicit tension of the character products and digital content. Therefore, "character authorized commodity" is the use of the product under the empathy derived from stimulating the user's imagination, to make consumers fixated in the situation and left them feeling intoxicated by the actual experience.

2.2   The Cultural Symbols of Character Brands

Brand recognition is a combination of brand positioning and brand personality, order to establish a unique character the product or service in the minds of consumers. The brand recognition system that Aaker purposed [3] analyzes the brand with a strategic way, pointing out that the brand value of the enterprise through brand recognition, so that consumers can trust the brand. The most important element of brand identity is invariance of the market or product's "core identity". In addition, the development of core recognition needs to examine the four elements of brand identity system: 1. Product: characteristics, quality, type, use, users. 2. Organization: organizational trait, localization vs. globalization. 3. Personality: brand personality, customer and brand relationship. 4. Symbols: visual image, symbol, brand heritage [4]. Kotler [5] shows that brand builders often use some tools to enhance the brand image, a strong brand is usually present with a noun, a slogan, a color or a set of stories.

There are quite a few brand cases of animation or digital content derivative products. For the purpose of creating business opportunities and satisfying the consumer market, most popular cartoons or cartoons develop digital content and derivative products, such as Japan's Sanrio Hello Kitty, Hayao Miyazaki animation series, One Piece animation and so on. These animations create a market of their derivative products, such as stationery, pendant, daily necessities and dolls, and they even lead to a craze of collecting.

By the rise of the technology, there's also a big change in education, reading, leisure and entertainment in our daily life. People receive information from digital platforms, media and publishers start to release new products like E-books, electronic catalogs, online comics and online games on these platforms which can be downloaded and applied on app store anywhere. In recent years, because of the popularity of new technology and digital products, there are already a considerable number of authorized derivative products in the market, such as the mobile phone game Angry Birds. The network environment has had a significant impact on the character market. The communication of social network plays a very important role in the process. Take Kumamoto bear, for example, continue to become popular these years, it is social network that keeps setting off the wave. Besides, there are some characters rising from LINE Creators Market, too. From now on, character economy produce many characters by CGM (consumer generated media) and open the era of characters' market.

From June 2011 Line officially launched and just in less than five years, it has already reached over 200 million users in 230 countries, while Taiwan has 5th place for its 17 million users. Character e-stickers have a role to play in LINE's rapid growth. In January 2015, Line Friends' original characters won the Asian Licensing Awards

(ALA) and the "LIMA Asian Licensing Awards" to bring the role of Line Friends to the most representative role in Asia Champion throne, has launched more than 3,300 kinds of peripheral commodities items. In addition to content and functionality, the application of digital information interface design elements is also an attraction to consumers [6]. To shape a successful character, the key lies in a good design, an attractive design deals a good business.

Since the smartphone getting popularized, character brands will be reshuffled, character economy's market will no longer be held by those big companies. Today, it is a very suitable time to run the characters can be created by amateur designers and make fans through the network platform, some of them can even get some product's endorsement from other famous international roles. As the rising of digital economy, we can indicate the need of future.

2.3 Purchasing Intention

Purchasing intention can be seen as the subjective tendency of a consumer product, which includes consumer attitudes and external factors to a product or brand, and serves as an important indicator of future behavior. Dodds, Monroe and Grewal [7] consistent discussed that the purchase intention is the consumer is willing to buy the possibility of a product. When consumers evaluate the product brand and generate trust, coupled with external stimuli, they will have the intention to buy. Secara and Meghisan's [8] consumption is part of our earthly daily goals, and the successful brands are present in the film productions, architecture, music, books and cartoons, urban planning and even our body esthetic (cosmetic surgery and piercing). That's way we have to understand our emotions and our reactions to the environmental challenges.

Xieand Heung [9] pointed out that the quality of brand relationship, while measuring the strength and depth of the characteristics of the "relationship process" as the spindle, is richer than the brand loyalty. A good brand relationship quality will enhance product purchase intention and reduce brand conversion. The research also mentioned that if the brand has a unique and exciting brand personality, consumers will be partners with high strength of brand recognition and their purchase intention also increases.

Increase of the character design and expansion of the character's story with digital information dissemination can drive brand up to increase consumer purchasing intention. The brand relationship with characters builds brand personality to connect consumers' emotions for exciting their purchase intention. Heiser, Sierra and Torres [10] addressed the study reveal that compared with a human spokesperson in the same advertisement, the creative use of cartoon spokespeople in print ads leads to more positive consumer advertising outcomes, including attitude toward the ad, attitude toward the brand, and purchase intention of the advertised brand. Haroon, Haq and Najmonnisa [11] stated that role model has significant impact on young adults' purchase intentions, brand loyalty and positive word of mouth.

The key to the development of digital content and derivative products is to establish brand positioning and to meet the spirit of the brand, regardless of the stage in which the core brand is operated and the core value of the brand is determined. In addition, how to constantly innovate in product and hold the rate of consumer return is the focus of brand management. The character will have a life cycle, when the market expanded to a certain extent, if not to open up a new stage, the market will reach the ceiling. While the characters are more popular with promotional activities accessing to overseas markets or new media in social network, new supporters will increase. As digital networks increase in ubiquity, businesses that do a better job of harnessing the power of the character economy will win.

In this paper, we will discuss the relationship between the characters of brand and character economy, the extension of characters and the application of consumer goods. Investigates and analyzes the young female consumers in Taiwan, explores their association factor to consumers' willingness, and explore the cute images of consumers for the characters.

3   Methods

3.1   Questionnaire

The main purpose in this study is to evaluate purchase intention and preference of young female consumers for a series of lovely characters products in Taiwan. In order to explore the purchase intention and preference of the characters products and attain effective results, this study designed a questionnaire (Table 1), and adopted the fixed random sampling for investigation near to large department stores. The analysis of lovely characters is researched through questionnaire and ANOVA analysis to examine lovely characters and consumer preference.

Table 1. Ten questionnaire items of purchase intention and preference

Item	Question
Q_1	I think that Hello Kitty/Mickey/Line Moon/Angry Bird is fashionable
Q_2	I am willing to purchase Hello Kitty/Mickey/Line Moon/Angry Bird's product
Q_3	I will recommend other people to buy Hello Kitty/Mickey/Line Moon/Angry Bird's product
Q_4	I will buy Hello Kitty/Mickey/Line Moon/Angry Bird's product as a gift for friend
Q_5	I have a series of Hello Kitty/Mickey/Line Moon/Angry Bird's product
Q_6	I will complete convenient store's loyalty card in order to exchange Hello Kitty/Mickey/Line Moon/Angry Bird's product
Q_7	I will buy Hello Kitty/Mickey/Line Moon/Angry Bird's product because of its story
Q_8	When I used Hello Kitty/Mickey/Line Moon/Angry Bird's product, I had an inexplicable satisfaction

Note: agree or disagree five-level Likert

3.2   Subjects

A total of 35 subjects live in Taiwan participated in this experiment, all females with ages ranging from 18 to 25; all have considerable familiarity of lovely characters.

In this study young female consumers are focused, because they are more love to buy cute cultural & creative products. The greater the young female consumers' are digitally involved, the more likely they were to purchase digital character design product. Based on this rationale, it is researched that:

1. Young female consumers' attitudes towards character design product are positively and significantly related to their purchase intentions.
2. Digital development involvement will be positively and significantly related to young female consumers' purchase intentions towards character design product.

3.3 Procedure

Before the formal survey, subjects were informed of the research purpose, and then the subjects were asked to evaluate purchase intention and preference for a series of lovely characters products. There are four lovely characters (Hello Kitty/Mickey/Line Moon/Angry Bird) in this investigation. The four lovely characters to be evaluated randomly presented for the subjects. Additionally, subjects were asked to make ticks on agree or disagree five-level Likert in accordance to their evaluation of the 8 evaluation items of the questionnaire. At the ending of the experiment, data collected on the reaction of participants was further statistically analyzed.

4 Results

4.1 Average Evaluation of the Lovely Characters

In this study, results of the average evaluation of the four lovely characters were shown in Table 2.

Table 2. The average evaluation of the four lovely characters

Item	A series of lovely characters image							
	Hello Kitty		Mickey		Line Moon		Angry Bird	
	Mean	S.D.	Mean	S.D.	Mean	S.D.	Mean	S.D.
Q_1	3.37	0.69	3.77	0.65	3.11	0.83	3.00	0.77
Q_2	3.14	0.77	3.43	0.85	3.26	1.04	2.43	0.66
Q_3	2.80	0.68	3.40	0.81	3.00	0.94	2.69	0.80
Q_4	3.34	0.91	3.66	1.03	3.14	0.97	2.57	0.74
Q_5	2.89	0.93	3.29	1.07	3.06	1.08	2.60	1.12
Q_6	2.69	0.80	3.49	1.10	2.94	1.08	2.57	0.88
Q_7	3.20	0.93	3.86	0.91	2.97	1.01	2.74	0.82
Q_8	3.03	1.07	3.09	0.78	2.74	0.70	2.34	0.68

Young female consumers' attitudes towards character design product are positively and significantly related to their purchase intentions. They think character design products with some sense of fashion design by the average evaluation of Q1 above 3.

Form the average evaluation list of Q2, Q3, and Q4 above 3, young female consumer purchase character design products ordinarily and they buy Mickey, Hello Kitty and Line Moon's product as a gift for friend.

Form the average evaluation list of Q7, and Q8 above 3, the traditional cartoon characters (Mickey and Hello Kitty) have more stories with books and movies, then the individuality and traits of the traditional cartoon characters make people feel nice and happy.

4.2   ANOVA Evaluation of the Lovely Characters

Analysis of variance (ANOVA, Table 3) showed that there was significant difference among different lovely characters products to the eight questionnaire items. Therefore, this study further conducted a pair-wise comparison test by using Scheffé Test.

Table 3. The ANOVA of the questionnaire item for the four lovely characters

	Questionnaire item							
	Q_1	Q_2	Q_3	Q_4	Q_5	Q_6	Q_7	Q_8
F	7.538	9.578	5.236	8.664	2.634	6.124	9.515	5.951
P	0.000	0.000	0.002	0.000	0.052	0.001	0.000	0.001

Table 4. Scheffé Test on Q1 with the four lovely characters

	Hello Kitty (3.37)	Mickey (3.77)	Line Moon (3.11)	Angry Bird (3.00)
Hello Kitty		0.166	0.548	0.222
Mickey	0.166		0.004	0.000*
Line Moon	0.548	0.004		0.936
Angry Bird	0.222	0.000*	0.936	

( ): average involvement degree for the four lovely characters;
*: $p < 0.05$

The analytic results in Table 4 showed that Mickey is more fashionable than other Angry Bird. Mickey is 92 years old and Angry Bird is 6 years old, but there is no age difference among the lovely characters. Age does not exist in lovely characters and they may always be fashionable and loved.

The analytic results in Table 5 showed that Mickey and Line Moon are more popular than Angry Bird, then consumers willing to purchase Mickey and Line Moon's products more than Angry Bird's products.

Table 5. Scheffé Test on Q2 with the four lovely characters

	Hello Kitty (3.14)	Mickey (3.43)	Line Moon (3.26)	Angry Bird (2.43)
Hello Kitty		0.570	0.955	0.007
Mickey	0.570		0.866	0.000*
Line Moon	0.955	0.929		0.001*
Angry Bird	0.007	0.000*	0.001*	

( ): average involvement degree for the four lovely characters;
*: $p < 0.05$

Table 6. Scheffé Test on Q3 with the four lovely characters

	Hello Kitty (2.80)	Mickey (3.40)	Line Moon (3.00)	Angry Bird (2.69)
Hello Kitty		0.026	0.786	0.951
Mickey	0.026		0.240	0.005*
Line Moon	0.786	0.240		0.456
Angry Bird	0.951	0.005*	0.456	

( ): average involvement degree for the four lovely characters;
*: $p < 0.05$

The analytic results in Table 6 showed that Mickey is more popular than Angry Bird, then consumers recommend other people to buy Mickey's products more than Angry Bird's products.

Table 7. Scheffé Test on Q4 with the four lovely characters

	Hello Kitty (3.20)	Mickey (3.66)	Line Moon (3.14)	Angry Bird (2.57)
Hello Kitty		0.564	0.842	0.008*
Mickey	0.564		0.145	0.000*
Line Moon	0.842	0.145		0.084
Angry Bird	0.008*	0.000*	0.084	

( ): average involvement degree for the four lovely characters;
*: $p < 0.05$

The analytic results in Table 7 showed that Mickey and Hello Kitty is more cute than Angry Bird, then consumers willing to purchase Mickey and Hello Kitty's products product as a gift for friend more than Angry Bird's products.

Table 8. Scheffé Test on Q5 with the four lovely characters

	Hello Kitty (2.89)	Mickey (3.29)	Line Moon (3.06)	Angry Bird (2.60)
Hello Kitty		0.474	0.927	0.733
Mickey	0.474		0.844	0.065
Line Moon	0.927	0.844		0.352
Angry Bird	0.733	0.065	0.352	

( ): average involvement degree for the four lovely characters;
*: $p < 0.05$

The analytic results in Table 8 showed that there is no significant difference in the number of consumers who have the four lovely characters' products.

Table 9. Scheffé Test on Q6 with the four lovely characters

	Hello Kitty (2.69)	Mickey (3.49)	Line Moon (2.94)	Angry Bird (2.57)
Hello Kitty		0.010*	0.748	0.971
Mickey	0.010*		0.147	0.002*
Line Moon	0.748	0.147		0.469
Angry Bird	0.971	0.002*	0.469	

( ): average involvement degree for the four lovely characters;
*: $p < 0.05$

The analytic results in Table 9 showed that Mickey is more loved than other three lovely characters. Consumer is willing to complete convenient store's loyalty card in order to exchange Mickey's product.

Table 10. Scheffé Test on Q7 with the four lovely characters

	Hello Kitty (3.20)	Mickey (3.86)	Line Moon (2.97)	Angry Bird (2.74)
Hello Kitty		0.034 *	0.783	0.235
Mickey	0.034 *		0.002*	0.000*
Line Moon	0.783	0.002*		0.783
Angry Bird	0.235	0.000*	0.783	

( ): average involvement degree for the four lovely characters;
*: $p < 0.05$

The analytic results in Table 10 showed that Mickey has more stories than other three lovely characters. It can be deduced that Mickey creates more stories and easily associate with funny and lovely image.

Table 11. Scheffé Test on Q8 with the four lovely characters

	Hello Kitty (3.03)	Mickey (3.09)	Line Moon (2.74)	Angry Bird (2.34)
Hello Kitty		0.994	0.553	0.009*
Mickey	0.994		0.390	0.004*
Line Moon	0.553	0.390		0.253
Angry Bird	0.009*	0.004*	0.253	

(): average involvement degree for the four lovely characters; *: $p < 0.05$

The analytic results in Table 11 showed that consumers are more satisfied with Mickey and Hello Kitty than Angry Bird. It can be deduced that Mickey and Hello Kitty's product create more joyous and warm-hearted feeling.

5 Conclusion

This study mainly evaluated two issues:

First, we find young female consumer purchase character design products commonly, and they also think character design products with some sense of fashion design. They will buy character design product as a gift for friend. Young female consumers' attitudes towards character design product are positively related to their purchase intentions, especially the traditional cartoon character merchandise.

Second, we find young female consumers more like Mickey's products than Angry Bird's products. They like both Hello Kitty and Line Moon's merchandise no significant difference. Young female consumers consider that Mickey has more funny stories and Hello Kitty create more joyous and warm-hearted feeling to lead to the sale of products. The stories and individuality of character let historic cartoon brands are popular and fashionable. The character of digital development is positively related to female young consumers' purchase intentions, like Line moon. But the character of digital development must create some event to keep the character lifetime, avoid exit from the popular market, like Angry Bird.

Acknowledgments. The author would like to thank Ministry of Science and Technology of the Republic of China for financially supporting this research under Contract No. NSC 103-2410-H-141-008.

References

1. UNESCO (2016). http://portal.unesco.org/culture/es/files/30297/11942616973cultural_stat_EN.pdf/cultural_stat_EN.pdf
2. Leong, D., Clark, H.: Culture -based knowledge towards new design thinking and practice - a dialogue. Des. Issues **19**(3), 48–58 (2003)

3. Aaker, D.A.: Building Strong Brands. The Free Press, New York (1996)
4. Aaker, D.A., Joachimsthaler, E.: Brand Leadership: The Next Level of the Brand Revolution. Free Press, New York (2000)
5. Kotler, P.: Marketing management, 10th edn. Prentice-Hall, New Jersey (2000)
6. Line (2015). https://linecorp.com/zh-hant/
7. Dodds, W.B., Monroe, K.B., Grewal, D.: Effects of price, brand, and store information on buyers' product evaluations. J. Mark. Res. 307–319 (1991)
8. Secara, C., Meghisan, F.: Sensory systems and consumer behavior. Rev. Manag. Econ. Eng. 11(4), 33–41 (2012)
9. Xie, D., Heung, V.C.: The effects of brand relationship quality on responses to service failure of hotel consumers. Int. J. Hospitality Manag. 31(3), 735–744 (2012)
10. Heiser, R.S., Sierra, J.J., Torres, I.M.: Creativity via cartoon spokespeople in print Ads. J. Advertising 37(4), 75–84 (2008)
11. Haroon, M.Z., Haq, M.A., Najmonnisa: Impact of role model on behavioral and purchase intentions among youngsters: empirical evidence from Karachi, Pakistan. J. Manag. Sci. 2 (2), 243–255 (2015)

A Software to Capture Mental Models

Hashim Iqbal Chunpir[1,2(✉)] and Thomas Ludwig[1,2]

[1] Faculty of Informatics, University of Hamburg, Vogt-Kölln-str. 30, Hamburg, Germany
{ludwig,chunpir}@informatik.uni-hamburg.de
[2] German Climate Computing Centre (DKRZ), Bundesstraße 45a, Hamburg, Germany

Abstract. Research shows that people construct mental models of concepts, situations and things, thus the theory of mental models is a well-established phenomenon in science. While people are given a particular task, they also construct a mental model to solve that task, for instance; a task to draw spatial objects e.g. two polygons intersecting each other in a two-dimensional environment. Yet, there are merely fewer studies that point at a scientific software that helps to capture preferred and alternative mental models of people during tasks of drawing spatial objects. The major contribution of this work is foundation of an experimental environment as a software application that can recognise mental models of people during drawing spatial objects based on the spatial relations of the drawn objects. The software serves as an experimental environment to find out the preferred mental models based on spatial relations amongst drawn objects i.e. the preferred way of performing tasks to draw spatial objects. Regional Connectivity Calculus is used as an underlying spatial scheme to extract preferred mental models of people who draw drawings using the software. The time to perform each task, including the time to draw and the time to think to understand the drawing tasks is also determined by the software.

Keywords: Mental models · Mental Model Theory (MMT) · Preferred Mental Models (PMM) · Alternative mental models · Regional Connectivity Calculus (RCC) · Spatial relations · Drawing tasks · Polygons · Temporal tasks · Topological spatial relations

1 Introduction

Carrying out a study to confirm that whether preferred mental models exist amongst the people while they draw spatial objects in a two dimensional environment is an interesting problem. The purpose of this paper is to demonstrate a two dimensional spatial drawing environment, using that if experiments are conducted; one can possibly capture the mental models of human subjects and especially the repeating mental models also called preferred mental models of people, who interact with the drawing environment. The structure and function of the software is given in Sect. 5. Moreover, using this software, multiple and diverse studies can be conducted about the research into underlying mental models created by participants after they read tasks to draw objects of spatial nature. The software environment has already been tested and it is user friendly; for details see Sect. 7.

© Springer International Publishing AG 2017
M. Antona and C. Stephanidis (Eds.): UAHCI 2017, Part III, LNCS 10279, pp. 393–409, 2017.
DOI: 10.1007/978-3-319-58700-4_32

An illustration of our experimental study design to be conducted using this software is provided is Sect. 3. Moreover, in this section an overview of some of the examples of hypotheses that are aimed to be tested by using the software as well as a sample of the proposed assigned tasks to the participants is given. Nonetheless, experiments can also be designed as per requirements of other researchers who want to use this software as an experimental environment and their requirements can be easily incorporated into the software due to its modular structure. Successively, researchers can benefit from this software, as the software facilitates providing any sort of task descriptions to the participants pertaining to their experiment design. The technical architecture of the software is described in Sect. 8. Furthermore, the software also helps in analysis of data of the recorded experiments. Subsequently, it helps in capturing and examination of preferred mental models as well as alternative mental models, if found amongst the participants of an experiment, that might be formed after reading tasks to draw spatial objects, along with the time recording features provided by the software.

A mental model is a user's idea (perception) about the situation and is thought to be the basic structure of cognition, as Johnson-Laird proposes. Mental models are professed as internal representations in thinking processes. Mental models are the basis for all reasoning processes as suggested by Holland et al. [1]. The role of mental models is very important in acquiring expertise in a task domain [2]. The existence of preferred mental models is claimed by [3]. These are the models that repeat themselves over and over. That means that these models have the highest frequency of repeating themselves and that they are the common models [3–5]. Preferred mental models have the higher probability to appear [3]. Further information about the background on mental models and its associated concepts such as alternative and preferred mental models, qualitative reasoning, spatial relations and Regional Connectivity Calculus (RCC) is given in Sect. 2: Background and State of the Art.

These mental models have been examined in the one dimensional case by [4]. However, there is hardly a study that investigates the phenomenon of occurrence of preferred mental models in two-dimensional spatial environment. This software helps to answer an interesting research question amongst others that whether people possess preferred mental models that repeat quite often while they draw drawings as professed by Johnson-Laird and as also claimed by Markus Knauff. The future planned steps to be conducted in our experiments are briefly described in Sect. 4. Spatial relations formalise everyday notions such as being near to something or being a part of something. Furthermore, this software environment facilitates the investigation of spatial relations in two dimensional spaces by analysing the topological spatial relations between drawings automatically using RCC based spatial detection leading to a proposed future work and the conclusion is given in Sects. 9 and 10 respectively.

2   Background and State of the Art

2.1   Mental Models

The term "mental model" describes an abstraction of human thought and perception. The mind constructs "small-scale models" of reality that it uses to anticipate events

[6, 7]. A mental model can be a theoretical/imaginary picture of the real picture. Mental models are representations of reality that people use to understand specific phenomena. A mental model can be a perceived structure about a structure. A mental model can be a map of a map. It can be a concept about a concept, even a thought about a thought. It is a shadow of the real object. But this shadow is caricatured: It depends on the mental light which is thrown onto the object to be perceived.

2.2 Preferred and Alternative Mental Models

There are several experiments conducted by Rauh et al. [5] to find the different types of mental models that human brain constructs. The first experiment was conducted using material free of ambiguities, also free of interpretation problem trap. Allen's 13 intervals which are based on the temporal logic for representation of the spatial objects with respect to time, were used and served the basis of experiment. Spatial objects are prone to temporal changes [8]. According to the first experiment conducted, it was evident that the participants of the experiment prefer certain mental models over the others while solving the reasoning problems with multiple possible solutions. The second experiment shows that preferred mental models are easier to construct than valid alternative mental models constructed by the participants. This means that alternative mental models are the result of alternate inferences and are not preferred inferences [5]. The reasoning problem is thought to be as harder or difficult as many solutions it does support. The third and fourth experiments showed that there is a model revision process. Model revision process begins with constructing preferred mental models (PMM) and then goes on to alternative mental models. The mental models which are not easy to construct, have the highest possibility that they might be ignored.

Another interesting indication about preferred mental models (PMM) was found out by [3]. In this study, 13 Allen's temporal relations are used as the basis for experiments. The reason for using these temporal relations in spatial reasoning was based on the work done or at least the transferring trend set by Guesgen (1989), Mukerjee and Joe (1990), Hernandez (1994), as according to [3, 9]. Conferring to Freksa, Allen's theory is claimed to be cognitively adequate [10]. However, Knauff et al. conducted further investigation in this domain and brought the new concepts of inferential cognitive adequacy and conceptual cognitive adequacy to lime light [11].

The term cognitive adequacy was brought by the research in Geo-Spatial Information Systems (GIS) and Qualitative Spatial Reasoning (QSR) rather than the psychological research. Anything which is a model of human cognition is thought to be cognitively adequate in the strong sense [11]. Strube proposed to range cognitive adequacy from strong to weak, conforming to ergonomic standards. Cognitive adequacy is thought to be strong when a formal approach is claimed adequate model of human knowledge and reasoning mechanisms. Cognitive adequacy is thought to be weak when an assumption of formal approach can be characterised and user friendly [11].

Inferential cognitive adequacy is claimed if reasoning mechanism of calculus is structurally similar to the way people reason. *Conceptual* cognitive adequacy can be claimed if empirical evidence supports the assumption that a system of relations is a model of people conceptual knowledge of spatial relationships [11]. Knauff et al.

conducted an experiment with thirty-three participants, all students at University of Freiburg, age ranging from 20 to 42 years. The computer-aided experiment was set up that comprised of three main phases: a definition, a learning and an inference phase. The definition phase made the participants aware of descriptions and natural language expressions. The learning phase gave them a chance to conduct some trial to guarantee learning the relational concepts as specified in natural language.

The inference phase was the main part of experiment and subjects had to solve 144 spatial three-term series problems as given by Allen's 13 relations [3]. The outcome revealed the presence of Preferred Mental Models (PMM) for spatial inferences with Allen's Calculus. It must be very interesting to identify here that as already mentioned by Johnson Laird and Byrne the construction of mental models in Mental Model Theory (MMT) is a process consisting of three blocks or states [3, 5]:

I. A Comprehension State or model construction, that means reasoning of human mind depends on representational format. Construction of spatial mental models based on descriptions.
II. Description State or model inspection, that is ordering spatial information.
III. Validation phase or model variation i.e. deducing and making alternative models.

2.3 Qualitative Reasoning

The research in qualitative reasoning had been initiated and motivated not only in the domain of robotics, semantics of languages, architecture and navigation but also in other physical systems. The information from surroundings in human beings is perceived through various channels, such as sense of touch, vision, hearing, smell etc. The knowledge of space differs from other domains of knowledge. Physical space is one of the important topic in cognition. Events take place in this domain at a certain time frame. It is a useful reference domain for non-spatial concepts.

Spatial reasoning is a field dealing with the reasoning or the cognition about space. It is concerned about the spatial and temporal representations. The spatial representations are topology, orientation, distance, size and shape. The process of spatial reasoning can be told in three steps; one preparatory step and two qualitative abstraction steps. These steps focus on significant distinctions and liberate the unnecessary details. In our study, we focus on topological spatial relations. The preparatory step is to fix reasoning task by specifying a configuration space. In the second step, set of qualitative relation along with the (spatial) inference rules are described. The last step defines the conceptual neighbourhood [12].

2.4 Qualitative Relations

There has been quite much research done on spatial relations expressed in thought and in language. The researchers have divided the qualitative reasoning into spatial and temporal relations. Qualitative relations are divided into two as:

- Spatial relations
- Temporal relations

In this study we focus solely on spatial relations amongst the drawn objects.

Spatial Relations. Spatial relation is a relation of an object in space with certain other object. Commonly used spatial relations are the distance and directional relations. In directional relations there are internal directional relations and external directional relations. Spatial relations give information about the spatial structure of an object (normally in terms of distance, orientation and topology) regardless of the geometrical composition of an object. For instance a pentagon is present on the chair, so the details are given about the pentagon on the chair irrespective of the geometrical structure of pentagon or chair [13]. The spatial relations: topology, distance and orientation are given as under: The term "topology" stems from Mathematics. Topology is a branch of mathematics dealing continuity. Topology is the term for certain maths structure [14]. But also digital media deals with the subject. For the "Qualitative Spatial Relations," the topology is the basis [14]. In this case qualitative differences from objects can be known. One can acquire the orientation of the object from the spatial independence of distances angle.

The relational algebra is the basis for topological relations, it represents the algebraic manipulation of symbols. There are different methods in which we could describe the topological relations between two objects. Let us consider the topological relation between two objects, for instance object A and object B. There are two or more models to show the relations amongst two objects. One is Egenhofer's 9 Intersection Model (E9IM) and the other is Regional Connectivity Calculus (RCC).

Regional Connectivity Calculus (RCC). Mereotopology deals with parts and boundaries of objects. RCC is a mereotopological calculus between two objects and describes a mereotopological relation between two objects. It has further different variants, two well-known variants are RCC-5 and RCC-8. The RCC family allows reasoning about connection and part-of relationships about simple regions in the plane. Different other domains and regions such as three dimensional (3D), non-simple regions in the plane can also be dealt by RCC. In RCC-8, the different eight combinations are possible:

- DC (Disconnected)
- EC (Externally Connected)
- EQ (Equal)
- PO (Partially Overlapping)
- TPP (Tangentially Proper Part)
- TPPI (Tangentially Proper Part Inverse)
- NTPP (Non-Tangentially Proper Part)
- NTPPI (Non-Tangentially Proper Part Inverse)

RCC-5 is an epigrammatic version of RCC-8. The RCC-8 relations DC and EC are combined into one relation called DR. Similarly, NTTP and TTP are combined into PP and NTTPI and TTPI into PPI [15].

- DR (discrete from),
- PO (partially overlapping),
- EQ (equal),
- PP (proper part),

- PPI (proper part inverse).

3   Purpose of the Software

The software is designed to conduct experiments to find out preferred and alternative mental models among participants of experiments, who draw spatial objects following task instructions. Finding out preferred and alternative mental models amongst participants of the experiment are two research aspects formulated in the form of hypotheses among other set of hypotheses needed to be investigated using the software. It is already planned to conduct set of experiments using the software with the group of participants, who have adequate education and are also computer literate. However, the participants must be unaware of the aims of experiments and they must not possess the knowledge of topological relations i.e. RCC model amongst objects, at least explicitly. The course of action during the experiments is that the participants will be instructed to draw objects i.e. polygons as according to the task instructions, already included in the software. Thirty tasks of different complexity level are included in the software i.e. there is a mix of simple and complex tasks. Examples of tasks underlying topological relations i.e. RCC knowledge are as follows:

- *Draw two polygons: Polygon A is contained completely in polygon B.*
- *Draw two polygons: Polygon A is contained in polygon B and touches the boundary of polygon B from inside.*
- *Draw two polygons: Interior of polygon A intersects both the boundary and the interior of polygon B.*
- *Draw three polygons: Polygon A overlaps polygon B; polygon C is disjoint from polygon A.*

The examples of some of the hypotheses that will be tested using this software are as follows:

- *Preferred Mental Models (PMM) can be found in the drawings of participants.*
- *The human mind retains a mental model only for a limited time.*
- *Tasks which are ambiguous to a higher degree take more time for solution.*
- *As the tasks get more complex, the subjects increasingly start to think while they draw.*

4   Next Steps with the Software

Empirical data from the experiments will be collected and examined. The mental models from the drawn spatial objects i.e. polygons will be extracted out of these experiments based on RCC. All hypotheses will be tested and conclusions will be presented in the report. Observations will be made about the drawing behaviour of the participants while drawing. The mental behaviour of following the instructions will be observed. Interesting observations may be taken between the subjects with higher qualification and others with lower qualification. The extracted data to test the hypotheses will be transformed into information with the help of graphics such as bar charts, pie charts etc. The statistical analysis about the data samples is planned and other statistical formulae will be applied to check not only the reliability of data but also to record and extract further information that can be relevant and useful as an evidence to support or disqualify the hypotheses in future.

5   Sequence of Activities that the Software Facilitates While Conducting an Experiment

It is important to know the sequence of activities whilst conducting the experiments. The experiment starts with getting the information about the subject, i.e. the participant of the experiment. Before the participant starts drawing spatial objects after reading the task descriptions, she or he enters some attributes about personal details such as name,

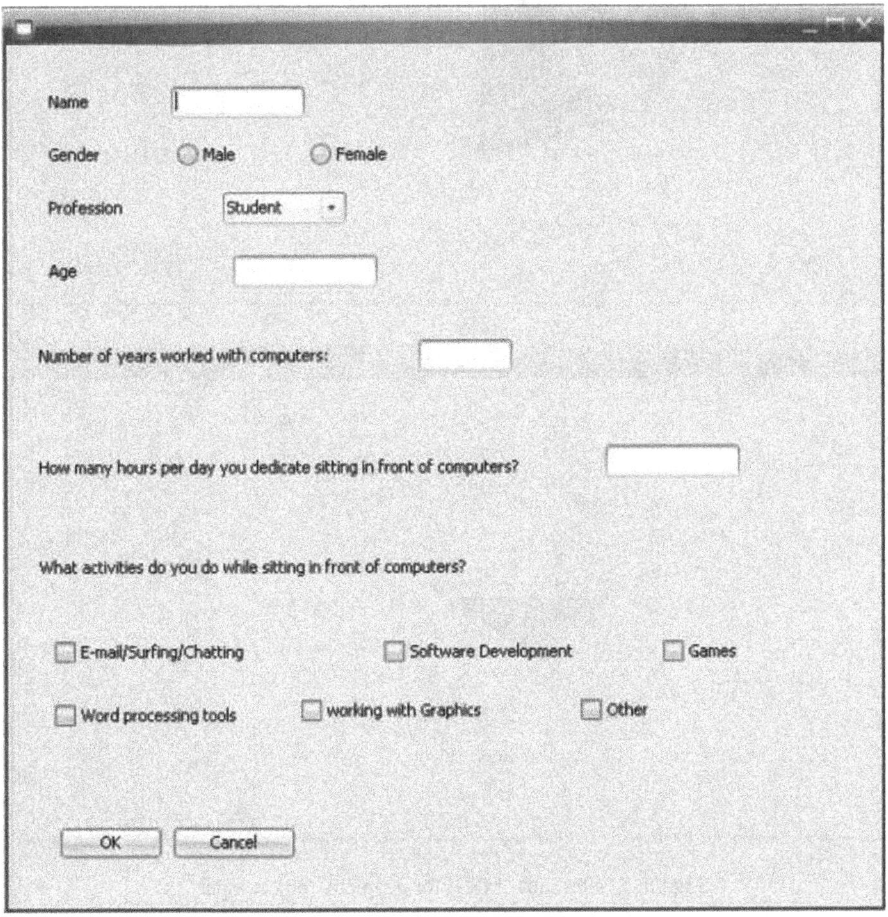

Fig. 1.   Screen-shot of GUI for subject's data input

gender, age and time that the participant dedicates in front of computer and others, see Fig. 1.

Then the subjects are required to follow the tasks. An example of the task description: *Draw two polygons: Polygon A is contained completely in polygon B.* While they read the task descriptions they are directed, in the descriptions, to draw objects in the form of polygons with some topological relation between the objects, as according to the task descriptions provided within the software, see Fig. 2.

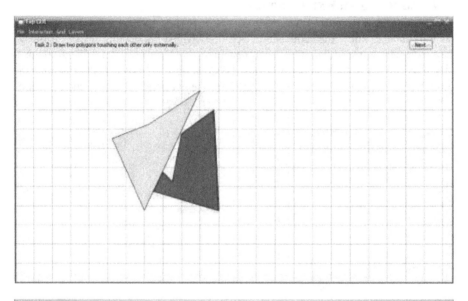

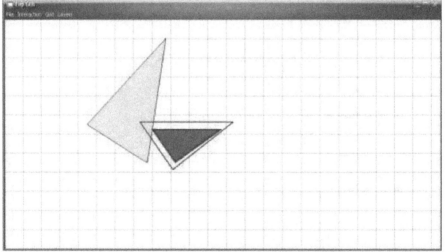

Fig. 2. Screen shot of GUI for geometric object input

The polygons are used in the software application because they can approximate any regular geometry. In order to display these instructions in the form of tasks and in order to record the data, a user friendly interface is provided for interaction to display the respective tasks and to allow the participants to draw polygons.

6 Structure and Capabilities of the Software

This computer based experimental software environment is designed to conduct the experiments to find out whether preferred and alternative mental models exist amongst the subjects, following a set of other hypotheses that can also tested using this software. The software allows the subjects to draw polygons based on the instructions provided to the subjects in the form of tasks. Moreover, software automatically detects the spatial relationships amongst the drawn objects using Java Topological Suite (JTS), an open source java library. The data is recorded as individual files. The software has three main components:

- A Front End interface
- A Back End evaluation
- An interface between the above

The requirements to design and develop the software in this project kept changing, based on the changes made in the experimental strategy to test the validity of hypotheses. Due to this reason the iterative design methodology was applied for prototyping, design, development and testing of the software.

6.1 Capturing Input from a Participant

Input from the subjects is taken in the form of drawings via the software's front end. The way a person draws on a piece of paper, in a similar manner an interface is provided to express the ideas in the form of drawings. For providing this functionality, a Graphical User Interface (GUI) environment, is designed. Different interfaces e.g. Tangible User Interface (TUI), Pen-based User Interface (PUI) etc. were considered, however, it was decided to use GUI because it is the most suitable one in our case [16]. Command-Line Interface (CLI) does not allow graphical representation and that's why this choice is not considered. TUI, tactile/touch interfaces are also not suitable. The GUI of the software facilitates subjects to be able to:

- provide their personal information
- draw polygons on the drawing area

The software is able to:

- record time to think to draw a task (tt)
- record time to draw a task (td)
- record total time to perform a task ($tp = tt + td$)

The tests with the software show that the subject are able to draw and place the objects freely in the space of the drawing area (panel or canvas).

6.2   Gathering Input

As the subjects draw polygons following one task and moving on to the next one, the data of each task is required to be stored. In this small or medium scale software which is designed for experiments, it is not necessary to use data bases which is required for storage and manipulation of large data. The information about the subjects' personal attributes such as their name, age, gender, their educational background, experience with computers etc., are saved in a file, separately for each subject. The two types of information stored in the file is about: the personal data provided by the subjects prior to the start of actual experimentation and the data of drawings drawn during experimentation, respectively.

The drawings captured from the subjects are also saved as an eXtensible Mark-up Language (XML) file with the coordinates of each polygon being drawn are also saved in files. The files contain the information about:

- the sequence in which the polygons are drawn
- total number of objects and their coordinates
- the time stamps for mechanical drawing (td) for each task
- the time stamps for performing (tp) each tasks

Files serve as an intermediate interface between the front end i.e. the GUI that interact with the subjects in order to capture input and the back end part. The back end part of the software is able to process and analyse all raw data to generate meaningful information for scientific interpretation. From this information, the conclusion can be made for the validity of hypotheses.

6.3   The Back End Evaluation

The back end evaluation process of software analyses all the recorded inputs captured in the XML files that contain the drawings and other attributes about the subjects. The drawings are analysed based on various RCC-8 spatial relationships that exist in between the drawn objects e.g. polygons. The data files about the participants and the drawings serve as an input to this back end evaluation process. The back end software programme has the capabilities to:

1. Detect whether the drawing for each task by each subject is correct or incorrect.
2. If the drawing for each task is correct then checking which valid solution (i.e. case) does it falls into. This is done only in a case where there can be more than one possible solutions.
3. The correct solutions and the valid cases (in case if there are more than one solutions possible) are found out in order to collect the preferred mental models, so the back end evaluation helps in finding out that whether the preferred and alternative mental models exist among the participants or not.
4. The invalid cases are collected to check if the invalid preferred models exist or not. However, topics concerning incorrect solutions and invalid mental models are out of scope in this study and will be dealt with in further studies, extending this study.

With the current back end process this can be achieved as well, even though it is planned to be dealt in future.

5. The timings can be noted e.g. the total time to perform each task *(tp)*, time to read a task and understand i.e. time to create mental model *(tt)* and time to draw it as well as time required to read and perform the task *(td)* in order to give information about timings.

6. The data from all the tasks including the tasks of repetitive nature are compared and if there is a repetition of the tasks i.e. repetitive tasks with different instructions, where ever it is required to check whether the task is repeated or not. Repetitive tasks are the tasks with a same solution but the task description are repeated.

7. The hypotheses made that are needed to be tested with the results of the experiments are evaluated after processing of files (based on the XML) which are recorded while drawing i.e. from the front end software activity.

In this way the back end part of the software, that is the evaluation process, processes experimental data, to testify that whether the hypotheses are supported. From the designed experimental strategies, the evaluation software evaluates the drawings of the subjects and produce clear results accordingly. This leads to the decision about the validity of the hypotheses.

The possible solutions to these tasks are already known and stored in a file. In order to testify, that whether drawings made by the subjects, match the correct solution, the back end evaluation must be done to determine and generate the results.

7   Implementation and Testing

The specification requirements for the software environment went on changing with the changes in hypotheses, in affect the changes in the strategies to test hypothesis were made, and finally the changes in task order and wording of the tasks. So, development of the software was an ongoing iterative process, because of the ever-changing require-ments. The complete implementation was not done at once rather in phases or steps. The testing and de-bugging was done several times during implementation and after the implementation. There are several types of testing that might be applied such as unit testing, integration testing, black box testing, white box testing, stress testing, usability testing, functional testing etc. to check the parts and the overall function of software. The software has not a big scope and is not a commercial application, that's why testing was done manually. The software is quite modular in structure plus in its function and the bugs were caught right away during programming, so there was no need of formal testing methodologies to be applied.

The user testing was done right after implementation, making sure that the software performs its function appropriately. However, during the process of development, some abnormal behaviours and some errors were found, but they were fixed immediately. Four software testers were assigned to check the usability and functionality of system. Different test data was fed into the software system to check whether the outcome is same as expected. The software ran completely successful as according to the predicted behavior and five people took part in experiments as subjects. The subjects have also commented about the usability of the system and approved that the software is easy to use and suitable for performing drawing tasks following the instructions.

8   Architecture of Software

In this section the overall architecture of this software is explained especially for the readers who are interested in the technical details of this software. The main technologies and programming languages used for the development are discussed here. The programming or the software development is done mainly in the Java language. It is not only chosen on the basis that no doubt, it is a popular programming language with an object-oriented approach and also supporting web based systems development. But the major reason for its choice was that while going through research of programming libraries or application programming interfaces (API), a very useful API, Java Topology Suite (JTS) was found. Another reason for using Java is that the current application can be extended to a web-based platform and experiments can be recorded on-line.

8.1   Graphical User Interface

The GUI was started with Abstract Windowing Toolkit (AWT) technology as an applet but was replaced after a while with Swing using J frames and panels. Reasons for this replacement was the advantages that Swing technology brings with. It is advanced and much richer than AWT. It is 100% Java based. It has much more graphical components such as progress bar etc. The most important feature of Swing that makes it distinguishable and better than AWT, is that it does not depend on host GUI peer controls, which makes it runnable in any platform. Host GUI controls are machine specific native controls. In AWT, each component depends on host GUI controls [17]. Therefore, with AWT the problem of Write Once Test Everywhere (WOTE) is not satisfactory due to its peer-based nature [18]. Further, if the bug exists in Swing it is the same as in the other platforms too, however with the AWT that is not the case [18]. Swing components has further advantages of customization of look and feel whilst AWT has only native interface.

With the help of Model-View-Controller (MVC) paradigm, much more flexible UI can be achieved. Swing also offers extra components such as icons, decorative borders and tool-tips for components. Swing components offer built-in double buffering and are light weight too (i.e. less resource intensive than AWT). One can also develop own components as Swing provides paint debugging support. The reason why Swing technology has become much flexible is because it is continuously developed and enhanced through the community process and the work done at Sun under the Java Desktop Network Components (JDNC) project [19]. Since we are not using client-server or web architecture and it is required to run the application on different machines, Swing is pretty much suitable here. For the client desktop, the standard way to develop Java applications is by using Swing. Java Server Faces (JSF) and Asynchronous JavaScript and XML (AJAX).

In the GUI of this software, Java2D: the API for drawing two-dimensional graphics in Java is used. The API helps in basic two-dimensional drawing operations. These operations can ultimately be treated as filling a shape, using paint and compositing a result on a screen. In Standard Edition (SE 6) version of the Java programming language, Java2D and Java OpenGL (JOGL) have become inter-operable. For instance, the features of JOGL can be used to draw animated 3D (three-dimensional) graphics instead of icons on a button. It also provides overlaying swing components on top of OpenGL rendering.

8.2 XML-Based File Structures

XML is being used to provide the basic structure of reading or writing data files stored in XML format (files containing list of tasks, task description, task solutions etc.). It functions as a container of the data present in the form of files, so that the front-end and back-end programs can be able to process, extract, exchange and add the information within the system for our experiments. Standard Generalised Markup Language (SGML) could have been another option. But it is a complex alternative to use, as XML is much simpler and easier to use. XML has almost all capabilities of SGML. It provides a robust and durable format for information storage and transmission [20]. Robust because it is based on a proven standard and durable because it uses plain-text file formats. It has wide variety of other advantages as well. The documents with the same type and consistence can be created without any structural errors. This is due to the reason that XML has a standardised mechanism of describing, controlling, or allowing or disallowing particular types of document structure. It is important to note that the structure has absolutely nothing whatever to do with formatting, appearance, or the actual text content of documents.

In order to exchange information amongst applications, each messaging system used to have its own format and all formats were different, which made inter-system messaging unnecessarily messy, complex and expensive. Now because of XML there is a common syntax for messaging which makes writing these systems much faster and more reliable. It distinguishes form from content. However, both are combined at output time to apply the required formatting to text or data identified by its structure such as location, position, rank, order etc. This is because XML file has all document information (text, data) and identifies its structure. The formatting and other processing needs are identified separately in a style-sheet or processing system [20].

It is possible to manipulate XML information programmatically (i.e. machine control). In this way documents can be converted into almost any other format with no loss of information; even can be pieced together from disparate sources, or taken apart and re-used in different ways [21].

8.3 XML Parsing

The XML files must be parsed to process the data. In this system, Document Object Model (DOM) is being used. However, for parsing XML files, in Java, another API; Simple API for XML (SAX) can also do the job. Thus both APIs can parse an XML file, however, there are some differences in the way that they perform this process of parsing. DOM is a tree-based API, whereas SAX is an event-based API [22]. SAX has handlers much like GUI handlers to report events. It reports parsing events such as the start and end of elements directly to the application through callbacks whereas DOM compiles an XML document into an internal tree structure, then allows an application to navigate that tree [22]. The record of parsing events is not required in this case and DOM is easy to handle and implement. That is why it is used in parsing the XML files.

8.4   Evaluator

Evaluator is a piece of software that reads all of the tasks done by each subjects. The tasks are in the form of XML files. Evaluator then checks the validity of every task against the validation file known as the task list i.e. also in XML format. It then checks for every participant that whether a task is valid or not. If a task is valid then it also specifies the valid case, if applicable. The evaluation of all subjects are written as an output to a text file.

The API known as Java Topology Suite (JTS), is responsible for getting the topological relation amongst the polygons, polygons are specified in the form of coordinates in a task XML file. The API is a Java code (version 1.2 and above). The API is developed by Vivid solutions (Vivid Solutions Website) and is a part of the Java Unified Mapping Platform project (JUMP) [23]. JUMP is a GUI-based application, that can view and process spatial data. It provides a highly extensible framework for the development and execution of custom spatial data processing applications. It includes many functions common to other popular Geographical Information Systems (GIS) products for analysis and manipulation of Geo-spatial data. The JUMP also provides a highly extensible framework for the development and execution of custom spatial data processing applications. Actually it uses classes from the JTS to provide a spatial object model compliant as specified by the Open GIS Consortium and other fundamental geometric operations [23].

JTS provides fundamental geometric functions and spatial object model. It has also the capability to support building further spatial applications, such as viewers, spatial query processors and tools for performing data validation, cleaning and integration [23]. It also supports a user-definable precision model and contains code for robust geometric computation. JTS also contain classes for spatial indexing. Geometries in JTS possess an interior, a boundary, and an exterior [23]. It offers following functions:

- spatial predicates based on the DE-9IM model
- overlay functions e.g. intersection, difference, union, symmetric difference
- buffer
- convex hull
- area, distance functions, and
- topological validity checking

The spatial data types provided by JTS are:

- Point
- Multi-Point
- Line-String

- Linear-Ring
- Multi-Line-String
- Polygon
- Multi-Polygon
- Geometry-Collection.

9 Conclusion

This work contributes to communities such as computer science, particularly; HCI, cognitive systems, cognitive science, architecture, psychological and other communities interested in examination of Mental Model Theory (MMT) together with spatial reasoning concepts, by presenting a software artefact that is an experimental two-dimensional drawing environment of spatial objects e.g. polygons. The software has an inbuilt reasoning engine based on Regional Connectivity Calculus (RCC-8), RCC is based on qualitative spatial reasoning and representation. This scientific software has capability to detect the topological relationships between two or more spatial objects e.g. polygons drawn on the canvas using GUI. Based on the topological relationships between two or more objects, the software can find out mental models of the participants i.e. human subjects. Besides, the software can also record time details such as time to draw (td) the spatial objects as well as time to think or understand the displayed drawing tasks on the GUI (tt) and of course the total time taken by the participant of an experiment to complete the task (tp). Software has been thoroughly tested and it offers appropriate user experience as well as usability to conduct experiments and to evaluate the results. Various hypotheses such as existence of preferred mental models or alternative mental models in two-dimensional spatial environment can be tested using the software. Consequently, this software can be used as an experimental environment to test hypotheses related to mental models and qualitative spatial relations amongst drawn spatial objects.

10 Further Extension of the Work

At the moment, only polygons can be drawn, however the software can be extended to incorporate other spatial objects such as poly lines, circles etc. A web based experimental environment can also be developed as an extension to this computer based application, if needed. This will allow more participants to take the experiments. However, in future, we plan to conduct experiments using this computer based software. The outcome from this work can be applied towards other practical applications. In the long run, diverse hypotheses can be tested using this software in various experimental studies from inter-disciplinary fields such as psychology, cognitive science, architecture and others. An example of a study is to find out whether difference exists between the mental models constructed by male or female participants during drawing experiments, for instance: in the domain of gender studies. Similarly, difference between mental models of people belonging to different culture, race, etc. can also be found. An extension from two dimensional (2D) to three dimension (3D) environment can also be made. Other qualitative spatial relations such as distance, directions as well as temporal relations can also be included in the software to develop a spatial-temporal reasoning engine in future. UI of the software can be extended to incorporate pen-based interface or others as according to the needs of a particular experiment design.

References

1. Holland, J.H., Holyoak, K.J., Nisbett, R.E., Thagard, P.R.: Induction: Processes of Inference, Learning, and Discovery. MIT Press, Cambridge (1986)
2. Schumacher, R.M., Czerwinski, M.P.: Mental models and the acquisition of expert knowledge. In: Hoffman, R.R. (ed.) The Psychology of Expertise, pp. 61–79. Springer, New York (1992)
3. Knauff, M., Rauh, R., Schlieder, C.: Preferred mental models in qualitative spatial reasoning: a cognitive assessment of Allen's calculus. In: Proceedings of the Seventeenth Annual Conference of the Cognitive Science Society, pp. 200–205 (1995)
4. Jahn, G., Johnson-Laird, P.N., Knauff, M.: Reasoning about consistency with spatial mental models: hidden and obvious indeterminacy in spatial descriptions. In: Freksa, C., Knauff, M., Krieg-Brückner, B., Nebel, B., Barkowsky, T. (eds.) Spatial Cognition 2004. LNCS, vol. 3343, pp. 165–180. Springer, Heidelberg (2005). doi:10.1007/978-3-540-32255-9_10
5. Rauh, R., Hagen, C., Knauff, M., Kußlig, T., Schlieder, C.: From preferred to alternative mental models in spatial reasoning. Spat. Cogn. Comput. 5, 239–269 (2005)
6. Craik, K.J.W.: The nature of explanation, vol. 445. CUP Archive (1967)
7. Gregory, R.L.: Forty years on: Kenneth Craik's the nature of explanation (1943). Perception 12(3), 233–237 (1983)
8. Allen, J.F.: Maintaining knowledge about temporal intervals. Commun. ACM 26(11), 832–843 (1983)
9. Freksa, C.: Qualitative spatial reasoning. In: Mark, D.M., Frank, A. (eds.) Cognitive and Linguistic Aspects of Geographic Space. Kluwer, Dordrecht (1991)
10. Freksa, C., Röhrig, R.: Dimensions of qualitative spatial reasoning. In: Cognitive and Linguistic Aspects of Geographic Space, pp. 361–372 (1993)
11. Knauff, M., Rauh, R., Renz, J.: A cognitive assessment of topological spatial relations: results from an empirical investigation. In: Hirtle, Stephen C., Frank, Andrew U. (eds.) COSIT 1997. LNCS, vol. 1329, pp. 193–206. Springer, Heidelberg (1997). doi:10.1007/3-540-63623-4_51
12. Schlieder, C.: Qualitative shape representation. Geogr. Objects Indeterminate Bound. 2, 123–140 (1996)
13. Egenhofer, M., Herring, J.: Categorizing Binary Topological Relationships Between Regions, Lines, and Points in Geographic Databases. Department of Surveying Engineering, University of Maine, Orono, ME (1991)
14. Cohn, A.G., Bennett, B., Gooday, J., Gotts, N.M.: Qualitative spatial representation and reasoning with the region connection calculus. Geoinformatica 1(3), 275–316 (1997)
15. Randell, D.A., Cui, Z., Cohn, A.: A spatial logic based on regions and connection. In: Nebel, B., Rich, C., Swartout, W. (eds.) Proceedings of the Third International Conference on Principles of Knowledge Representation and Reasoning, KR 1992, pp. 165–176. Morgan Kaufmann, San Mateo (1992)
16. Tuck, M.: The real history of the GUI. https://www.sitepoint.com/real-history-gui/. Accessed 25 Mar 2017
17. Feigenbaum, B., Nichols, S.: Accessibility design and coding guidelines for Java Swing and SWT GUI development (2008)
18. Zukowski, J.: The Definitive Guide to Java Swing. Apress, Berkeley (2005)

19. Nimphius, F., Mills, D.: Swing or JavaServer faces: which to choose? Oracle Technology Network (OTN). http://www.oracle.com/technetwork/articles/nimphius-mills-swing-jsf-092891.html. Accessed 26 Mar 2017
20. Morrison, M.: Teach Yourself XML in 24 Hours. Pearson International Education, New York (2003)
21. Fynn, P.: The XML FAQ (2017). http://xml.silmaril.ie/. Accessed 20 Feb 2017
22. Eckel, B.: Thinking in Java. Professional Technical Reference, 3rd edn. Prentice Hall (2002)
23. Davis, M.: Secrets of Java Topological Suite (JTS) (2007). http://2007.foss4g.org/presentations/view.php/115.html. Accessed 24 Mar 2017

Rethinking Audio Visualizations: Towards Better Visual Search in Audio Editing Interfaces

Evelyn Eika[1(✉)] and Frode E. Sandnes[1,2]

[1] Oslo and Akershus University College of Applied Sciences, Oslo, Norway
{Evelyn.Eika,frodes}@hioa.no
[2] Westerdals Oslo School of Art, Communication and Technology, Oslo, Norway

Abstract. QueryWaveform visualization is a key tool in audio editing. However, the visualization of audio waveforms has changed little since the emergence of the first software systems for audio editing several decades ago. This paper explores how audio is visualized. This paper shows that the commonly used time-domain representation exhibits redundant information that occupies valuable display real-estate in most audio editing software. An alternative waveform visualization approach is proposed that exploits elements from the existing visualization conventions while enhancing features that are important in visual search through digital audio. Alternatively, the method is a means for making more efficient use of the display real-estate. The proposed method is discussed in terms of its suitability for various visualization situations.

Keywords: Audio data · Waveforms · Visualization · Audio editing · Music software · Spectrogram

1 Introduction

Audio editing is used in many domains such as academic acoustical phonetic research [1], music production and recording [2], live performances [3], DJ'ing [4, 5], radio production, and more recently in podcasting [6]. Various forms of audio editors exist and are easily available such as the open source Audacity audio editor [7]. Common to most audio editors is that audio is represented directly as the audio waveform, that is, the audio signal in the audio domain. The audio waveform has become an iconic representation with the appearance of a diverse mountain range mirrored across a lake (see Fig. 1). Users will immediately recognize an audio visualization as audio due to the visual signature of the visualization without needing an explanation.

There have been very few developments in audio visualization since the first emergence of the digital audio-visual editing software more than three decades ago. One noteworthy exception is the use of color-to-code frequency characteristics in the time-domain signal. In other words, audio segments with different frequency signatures or transients are represented using different colors or intensities also known as EQ color coding. Such coding is used in several pieces of state-of-the-art DJ'ing software such as Serato [8] and Traktor [9] to help the DJs more easily locate cue points.

© Springer International Publishing AG 2017
M. Antona and C. Stephanidis (Eds.): UAHCI 2017, Part III, LNCS 10279, pp. 410–418, 2017.
DOI: 10.1007/978-3-319-58700-4_33

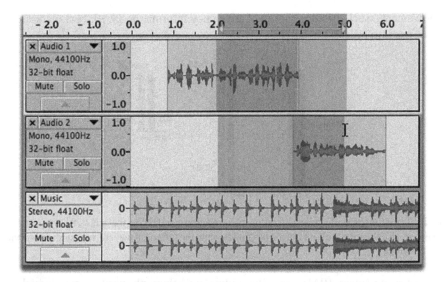

Fig. 1. Screenshot from the audacity audio editor (reproduced from the user manual, GNU General Public License). Multiple audio tracks are easily recognizable by their "mirrored mountain ranges". Potential cue points are recognizable as peaks in the signal.

One advantage of the color coding representation is that it is secondary to the time domain representation [10] that can help the user more quickly visually locate what they are looking for [11].

The visualizations of real-world audio appear as sequences of peaks and valleys mirrored above and below the timeline. We hypothesize herein that it is this mirroring effects that probably is the key feature that triggers the recognition of the visualization as an audio representation. Although this recognizable feature is a benefit, we argue that the mirroring of the signal above and below the time-line in most situations is redundant. Moreover, there is a limit to how many tracks that can be displayed simultaneously on a screen. We thus propose an audio visualization technique based on only displaying one side of the waveform. Special cases, in particular, DC information, are handled explicitly.

2   Background

The goal of the visualization field is to find the most effective ways to display data, being it numbers [12], texts [13], or volumes [14], and to facilitate user tasks. In the audio domain, VU-meters (volume unit meters) were used to visualize the signal level in early analogue recording equipment, and these analogue instrument meters were later replaced by LED-based VU-meters that are simple time-varying bar graphs.

The emergence of audio editing software allowed the recorded signals to be displayed as a function of time, namely, the waveform. This representation has survived with minor changes for several decades. In addition to the already mentioned improvements, such as color-coding of frequency information [8, 9], beat mark annotations has also been explored [15].

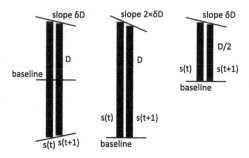

Fig. 2. Traditional waveform visualization mirrored above and below the axis (left), the proposed waveform visualization without mirroring (middle) and the proposed waveform visualization with half the width.

Root mean square (RMS) amplitude plots are commonly used in speech analysis software such as Praat [16], which can show the intensity of the signal as a trend as the absolute signal intensity is averaged over a moving window. The method proposed herein has similarities to RMS amplitude plots, but the proposed approach does not mask rapid changes in the audio signal. Moreover, the proposed method is capable of showing DC offsets which information is lost with the RMS calculation.

Oscilloscopes are often used to visualize signals in the time-domain, and oscilloscopes have allowed waveforms to be inspected before graphical user interfaces were commonly available [17]. Still, they have been less used by individuals working with audio, probably due to the fact that audio equipment was not built with oscilloscopes.

Spectrum analyzers were also used with early specialized audio equipment, and used to show the intensity of the various frequency bands as snapshots in time. Visual audio software allowed these spectrograms to be plotted as a two-dimensional image where the frequency bands are plotted as a function of time. Saliency maximization of two-dimensional audio spectrograms [18] was proposed to improve the visualizations. Frequency time-series have also been visualized in three dimensions [19]. More sophisticated domain-specific visualization techniques exist such as tone plots [20], fundamental frequency plots, and formant plots, as used in phonetic research [1].

Mel-scale spectrums, chromagrams, periodograms [21], phase space plots [22], and self-similarity plots, used for discovering repeating patterns [23], are examples of other types of audio visualizations. DiskPlay [24], a system where an overhead projector is used to project an image onto a white time-coded vinyl record, can be classified as utilizing a context-specific audio visualization. Various colors are used to indicate parts of a track that is already played, areas to be played, unused time-codes, cue points, etc.

In a slight variation on the same theme, the audio waveform is projected directly only to the white vinyl disk [25]. The waveform projection allows the user to access the audio directly via the turntable. The method proposed herein could be used to enhance such visualizations.

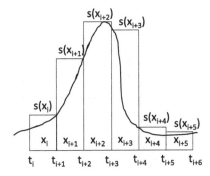

Fig. 3. Converting a signal from time-domain to pixel-domain by selecting the maximum value within each time window as a representative value for the audio signal.

With increasing amounts of unannotated audio and video material, visualization is one valuable tool, in addition to query by humming [26], to help a user navigate large audio contents without the time-consuming task of going through hours, or even days, of audio material. There are several initiatives to make visualization tools for this problem domain [27]. Researchers have also explored domain-specific visual tools for manually transcription of music [28] and speech [29]. Another avenue of research includes large display audio visualization [30].

3 The Proposed Method

The audio visualization proposed herein assumes that the audio is viewed as a waveform, that is, the amplitude of the audio signal is plotted as a function of time. Moreover, it is assumed that the audio signal is not viewed at sample level or micro level but at macro level (in seconds). The resulting view is thus an aggregated form of the waveform that appears as the energy, or loudness, of the signal. It is this assumption of aggregated view that forms the basis for the proposed method since the detailed information at waveform level is lost when viewed at a more course time scale. At the more coarse-grained time scale, the energy signature appears mirrored above and below the time axis.

We thus argue for only showing one side of the waveform, effectively the absolute value, namely

$$w'(t) = |w(t)| \tag{1}$$

where $w(t)$ is the signal amplitude at time t. Obvious benefits to this representation are that the differences between consecutive samples are doubled, and hence become more noticeable for the viewer (see Fig. 2 middle as opposed to Fig. 2 left). This difference enhancement is likely to contribute to better visual search in the waveform. Also, the proposed visualization requires just half the display real-estate compared to the traditional waveform with the same level of differences between consecutive samples since only half the height is needed when starting the sample at the axis, or half the width if the waveforms are displayed along the vertical direction. Yet, the proposed visual

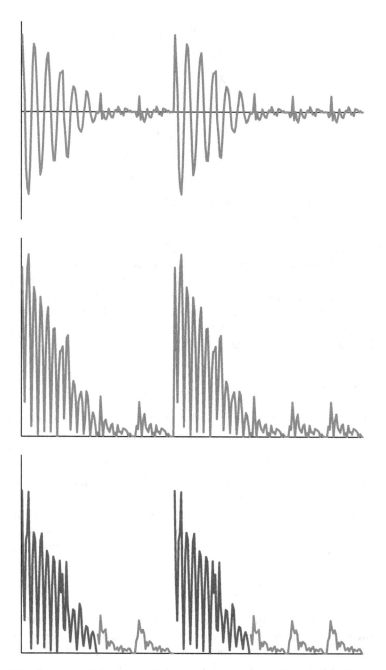

Fig. 4. The original waveform (top), absolute waveform plot (middle) and absolute waveform plot with colors denoting frequency (bottom). Red denotes a low frequency and blue denotes a high frequency. (Color figure online)

representation easily communicates the high and low intensity points in a signal. Thus, the simplified visualization facilitates simple search for particular feature points in the audio in a similar manner to traditional waveforms.

Further, to reflect the fact that we are looking at a waveform at a coarse-grained time scale, we convert the waveform w in the time domain t to the signal s in the pixel domain x as follows.

$$s(x) = \max(w(t)), t \in [t_1, t_2] \tag{2}$$

Here t_1 and t_2 represent the start time and end time respectively, corresponding to a given display pixel along the time domain. The max function achieves a type of simple anti-aliasing effect. Figure 3 illustrates the mapping.

Figure 4 illustrates the proposed visualization in practice. Figure 4 (top) shows a traditional waveform depicting an audio sample with a sequence regularly spaced hi-hats and two bass drums. Clearly, the hi-hats are a bit harder to spot than the two bass drums because of their different intensities. Figure 4 (middle) shows the same waveform with the proposed visualization approach. We argue that this waveform makes the differences between the peaks and valleys more visible than the traditional waveform representation. The bottom plot in Fig. 4 shows the same waveform with frequency color coding. Here, red represents a low (warm) frequency and blue represents a high (cold) frequency.

3.1 DC Offsets

One benefit of the traditional waveform display is that it allows DC, or direct current, signals to be easily spotted by the viewer such that they can be corrected and the sound quality improved. However, it is assumed that for most audio editing applications the audio is already DC-corrected, especially when working with third-party audio such as music in DJ software. Also, DC offset problems are probably less of a challenge with modern digital audio recording pipelines compared to analogue recording configurations.

Nevertheless, DC occurs naturally with certain sounds such as fuzz-guitars sounds. If working with audio that contains DC offsets, it is important to be aware of the DC levels especially when combining several sounds. We therefore propose to shift the signal according to the DC offset, namely

$$s'(x) = |s(x)| + DC(x) \tag{3}$$

where $DC(x)$ can simply be computed as a windowed average around the selected sample point, namely

$$DC(x) = \frac{1}{w} \sum_{i=-w/2}^{w/2} s(x+i) \tag{4}$$

Where w is the width of the averaging window. In other words, for each audio segment, the signal starts at the DC offset and ends at the peak. This concept is illustrated in Fig. 5.

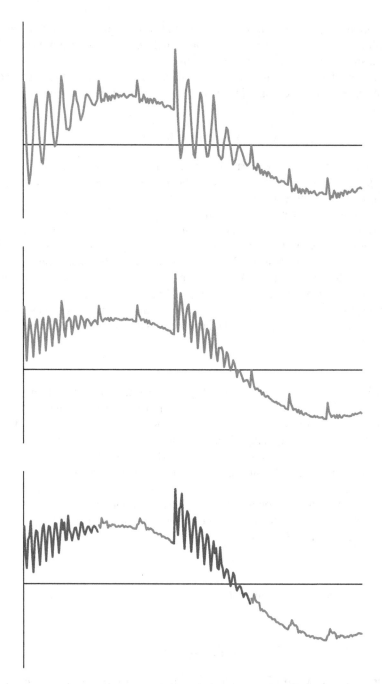

Fig. 5. The original waveform with DC-offset (top), absolute waveform plot with DC-offset (middle) and absolute waveform plot with DC-offset and colors denoting frequency (bottom). Red denotes a low frequency and blue denotes a high frequency. (Color figure online)

The top plot in Fig. 5 shows the original waveform from Fig. 3 top offset with a sinusoidal time-varying DC as a traditional waveform. Figure 5 middle shows the same signal using the proposed method. The shape of the DC offset is clearly seen from the bottom of the plot, and the peaks and valleys are visible on the top of the plot. Figure 5 bottom shows the proposed method with frequency coding.

4   Conclusions

This paper has argued for an alternative, yet simple method for visualizing audio waveforms. The technique involves displaying the absolute value of the waveform in the simplest case. This magnifies the variations in the signal making it easier for users to search for particular cue points. Alternatively, the real-estate consumed by the traditional waveform plots can be halved without reducing the quality and magnitude of the audio signature. This is particularly useful for current digital audio processing software where the users may work with a large number of parallel audio tracks. The proposed technique is intended for working with coarse-grained time scales. If working at finer-grained time scales, it may be beneficial and more suitable to switch to the traditional waveform visualization. Such mode changes can easily be done automatically in an editor according to the selected time scale. In future work it would be interesting to explore the use of graph embellishments [31] to improve the communicative effectiveness of audio visualizations.

References

1. Jian, H.-L.: On the tonal inventory of the Taiwanese language: a perceptual study. J. Taiwanese Vernacular **2**, 28–50 (2010)
2. Hracs, B.J.: A creative industry in transition: the rise of digitally driven independent music production. Growth Change **43**, 442–461 (2012)
3. Roma, G., Xambó, A.: A tabletop waveform editor for live performance. In: Proceedings of NIME, pp. 249–252 (2008)
4. Lopes, P.A., Ferreira, A., Pereira, J.A.: Multitouch interactive DJing surface. In: Proceedings of the 7th International Conference on Advances in Computer Entertainment Technology, pp. 28–31. ACM (2010)
5. Hansen, K.F., Bresin, R.: The skipproof virtual turntable for high-level control of scratching. Comput. Music J. **34**, 39–50 (2010)
6. Copley, J.: Audio and video podcasts of lectures for campus-based students: production and evaluation of student use. Innovations Educ. Teach. Int. **44**, 387–399 (2007)
7. Mazzoni, D., Brubeck, M., Haberman, J.: Audacity: free audio editor and recorder (2005). http://audacity.sourceforge.net
8. Serato: Serato DJ 1.9.4 Software manual (2016). https://serato.com/downloads/files/145095/Serato+DJ+1.9.4+Software+Manual+-+English.pdf
9. Native Instruments: TRAKTOR manual (2016). https://www.native-instruments.com/fileadmin/ni_media/downloads/manuals/TRAKTOR_PRO_2_9_Manual_Englisch_2015_08.pdf
10. Luder, C.B., Barber, P.J.: Redundant color coding on airborne CRT displays. Hum. Factors J. Hum. Factors Ergon. Soc. **26**, 19–32 (1984)

11. Green, B.F., Anderson, L.K.: Color coding in a visual search task. J. Exp. Psychol. **51**, 19–24 (1956)
12. Sandnes, F.E.: On the truthfulness of petal graphs for visualisation of data. In: Proceedings of NIK 2012, pp. 225–235 (2012). Tapir Academic Publishers
13. Eika, E., Sandnes, F.E.: Authoring WCAG2.0-compliant texts for the web through text readability visualization. In: Antona, M., Stephanidis, C. (eds.) UAHCI 2016. LNCS, vol. 9737, pp. 49–58. Springer, Cham (2016). doi:10.1007/978-3-319-40250-5_5
14. Sandnes, F.E.: Understanding WCAG2.0 color contrast requirements through 3D color space visualization. Stud. Health Technol. Inf. **229**, 366–375 (2016)
15. Andersen, T.H.: In the Mixxx: novel digital DJ interfaces. In: Proceedings of CHI 2005 Extended Abstracts on Human Factors in Computing Systems, pp. 1136–1137. ACM (2005)
16. Boersma, P.: Praat, a system for doing phonetics by computer. Glot int. **5**, 341–345 (2002)
17. Beckett, R.L.: Pitch perturbation as a function of subjective vocal construction. Folia Phoniatr. Logop. **21**, 416–425 (1969)
18. Lin, K.H., Zhuang, X., Goudeseune, C., King, S., Hasegawa-Johnson, M., Huang, T.S.: Improving faster-than-real-time human acoustic event detection by saliency-maximized audio visualization. In: 2012 IEEE International Conference on Acoustics, Speech and Signal Processing (ICASSP), pp. 2277–2280. IEEE (2012)
19. Misra, A., Wang, G., Cook, P.R.: SndTools: real-time audio DSP and 3D visualization. In: Proceedings of the International Computer Music Conference, International Computer Music Association (2005)
20. Gómez, E., Bonada, J.: Tonality visualization of polyphonic audio. In: Proceedings of International Computer Music Conference (2005)
21. Lartillot, O., Toiviainen, P.: A matlab toolbox for musical feature extraction from audio. In: International Conference on Digital Audio Effects, pp. 237–244 (2007)
22. Gerhard, D.: Audio visualization in phase space. In: Bridges: Mathematical Connections in Art, Music and Science, pp. 137–144 (1999)
23. Foote, J.: Visualizing music and audio using self-similarity. In: Proceedings of the Seventh ACM International Conference on Multimedia, Part 1, pp. 77–80. ACM (1999)
24. Heller, F., Borchers, J.: DiskPlay: in-track navigation on turntables. In: Proceedings of the SIGCHI Conference on Human Factors in Computing Systems, pp. 1829–1832. ACM (2012)
25. Heller, F., Borchers, J.O.: Visualizing song structure on timecode Vinyls. In: Proceedings of NIME, vol. 14, pp. 66–69 (2014)
26. Huang, Y.P., Lai, S.L., Sandnes, F.E.: A repeating pattern based query-by-humming fuzzy system for polyphonic melody retrieval. Appl. Soft. Comput. **33**, 197–206 (2015)
27. Kubat, R., DeCamp, P., Roy, B., Roy, D.: Totalrecall: visualization and semi-automatic annotation of very large audio-visual Corpora. ICMI **7**, 208–215 (2007)
28. Cannam, C., Landone, C., Sandler, M.: Sonic visualiser: an open source application for viewing, analysing, and annotating music audio files. In: Proceedings of the 18th ACM International Conference on Multimedia, pp. 1467–1468. ACM (2010)
29. Barras, C., Geoffrois, E., Wu, Z., Liberman, M.: Transcriber: a free tool for segmenting, labeling and transcribing speech. In: First International Conference on Language Resources and Evaluation (LREC), pp. 1373–1376 (1998)
30. Tzanetakis, G., Cook, P.: Marsyas3D: a prototype audio browser-editor using a large scale immersive visual and audio display. In: Proceedings of the 2001 International Conference on Auditory Display, pp, 250–254 (2001)
31. Sandnes, F.E., Dyrgrav, K.: Effects of graph embellishments on the perception of system states in mobile monitoring tasks. In: Luo, Y. (ed.) CDVE 2014. LNCS, vol. 8683, pp. 9–18. Springer, Cham (2014). doi:10.1007/978-3-319-10831-5_2

Media Use of Persons with Disabilities

Anne Haage[⊠] and Ingo K. Bosse

School of Rehabilitation Sciences, Dortmund University of Technologies,
Dortmund, Germany
{annegret.haage,ingo.bosse}@tu-dortmund.de

Abstract. The study "Media use of Persons with Disabilities" (MMB16 [1]) provides data on disabled people's access to and personal use of media and the limitations in the use of such media. Nowadays, full and effective participation in society [2] is not possible without full and effective participation in media and communication. To date, there is no valid data about media usage by the disabled in Germany.

This survey consists of interviews with 610 individuals with visual, hearing or physical impairments, or learning difficulties. Expert interviews and focus groups complete the study. The findings of this study show that impairment comes with specific limitations as regards media access and usage. In general, people with impairments and in particular those with learning difficulties, access connected devices more rarely than the general population. They go on the internet less often and use it less for communication and information. Many blind people are offliners, in particular if they acquired the impairment in adulthood. Age is an important personal factor determining media usage. The interaction of age, impairment and other context factors in particular, leads to the extremely rare use of digital media by older people. The disabled are heterogeneous. Full and equal participation in media and communication depends on the context factors which influence the participation level: age, housing, employment, obstacles and barriers to access, technical and personal support.

Keywords: Participation in media and communication · Disability · Digital divide · Media usage · Online and broadcast television · Accessibility · Assistive technologies

1 Introduction

The study "Media use of Persons with Disabilities" [1] contains data acquired from investigations conducted for the first time all over Germany on how much disabled people access and use media personally and the limitations of the media. This research was conducted by the Technical University of Dortmund, Faculty of Rehabilitation Research and the Hans-Bredow-Institute for Media Research in Hamburg.

Nowadays, full and effective participation in society [2] is not possible without full and effective participation in media and communication. The United Nations Convention on the Rights of Persons with Disabilities (UNCRPD) cites media as a key factor for access to information and communication on an equal level and social inclusion [3]. States Parties shall take appropriate measures to ensure that people with

© Springer International Publishing AG 2017
M. Antona and C. Stephanidis (Eds.): UAHCI 2017, Part III, LNCS 10279, pp. 419–435, 2017.
DOI: 10.1007/978-3-319-58700-4_34

disabilities have access, on an equal basis with others, to information and communications, including information and communications technologies and systems [2]. This
includes the mandate to collect a valid data base, statistical and research data, to enable
them to formulate and implement policies to give effect to the present "Convention"
[2]. There is very little basic data regarding the media-related needs of people with
disabilities and the corresponding barriers to accessing media. In Germany, there are no
binding obligations to avoid creating new barriers or eliminate existing barriers relating
to the accessibility of private media. Since 2013 the public broadcasters have been
legally obliged to offer accessible media, in particular they are required to produce
subtitling (captions) and audio descriptions. But there are no targets or quotas for the
provision of access to services as there are in Great Britain [4]. Due to the federal
system in Germany it is the responsibility of the federal states to legislate whether the
public broadcasting services have to meet the same standards of accessibility as government institutions the public administration. In the concluding observations in the
initial report on Germany the UN-Committee on the Rights of Persons with Disabilities
criticized the lack of binding obligations and made recommendations to "encourage
public and private broadcasting bodies to evaluate their work comprehensively
regarding the implementation of the right to accessibility" [5].

In their annual reports the public broadcasting services publish data on how
accessible their services are. The media authorities[1] monitor the accessibility of private
television channels and check the accessibility provided by the two main media groups
with the biggest television audience share.

This is the first study in Germany to examine the use of media and the needs of a
disabled audience. The few existing studies that deal explicitly with media and the
disabled are limited to a selection of media or to particular groups. (e.g., [6–11]). As the
previously mentioned MMB16 study was funded by the media authorities and the
welfare organization "Aktion Mensch", the main focus was on the use of television and
audio-visual content on the internet. The test persons were asked about their personal
use of the internet, radio and newspapers and access to services and devices in their
households. The study therefore also provides some basic data about the use of digital
media and what factors affect its access and use.

2 Research Design

In line with the "International Classification of Functioning, Disability and Health" by
The World Health Organization (WHO, [12]), this study is based on the understanding
that a disability is multidimensional and results from a number of interactions. How
much opportunity an individual has to participate depends on the prevailing environmental, contextual and personal factors.

Disability is linked to situations. This also applies to the use of media. The deaf face
limitations of accessibility to media and communication, because in Germany, not all of

---

[1] The 14 media authorities are in charge of licensing and controlling as well as structuring and
promoting commercial radio and television in Germany.

the television programmes have subtitles or use sign language. Their socio-economic situation affects their use of media, since disabled people who cannot afford to buy the latest generation of smartphone or hybrid broadcast broadband TV (Hbb TV), cannot benefit from advanced accessibility features. People living in residential homes may also be restricted in their use of media because they have limited access to computers and no support when using one [13]. Therefore, this study takes contextual and personal factors into account, such as type of residence, age, gender, employment and education.

Henceforth, the term 'disability' is used when media access and usage is impeded by limitations brought about by the interaction of individuals and environmental factors. The term 'impairment' is used to mean limitations caused by limited body functions and structures.

As regards impairment, four subgroups facing different limitations in the use of devices and media have been identified:

- Persons with visual impairment
- Persons with hearing impairment
- Persons with physical and motor impairments
- Persons with learning difficulties

The four subgroups are heterogeneous. People who are born deaf, deal with media in a different way than people who became hard of hearing during adulthood. The blind face different obstacles and need different accessibility features than the partially-sighted. Literacy problems also influence media usage [14]. For each subgroup, a sample was created showing a variance in the context factors relevant for media use. The first step of the study was to examine which context factors were particularly relevant for the media usage of each subgroup. Besides desk research, expert interviews were conducted with 13 experts for the four subgroups and three experts for the media usage of people with impairments in general. In all the subgroups, there were experts with and without impairments. The findings helped to design the sample for the second part of the study: standardized questioning of people with impairments.

The study sought to achieve a high variance when it came to characteristics such as age, gender and education. Other factors differed depending on the subgroup:

- visual impairment (n = 154): quota for blindness and partially sighted, time of occurrence of the impairment (birth, childhood/youth, adulthood)
- hearing impairment (n = 161): quota for hard of hearing, deafened and deaf
- physical and motor impairments (n = 148): quota for time of occurrence of the impairment (birth, childhood/youth, adulthood), type of residence (private households or residential homes), variance regarding employment (regular labour market, special labour market such as sheltered workshops, and economically inactive)
- learning difficulties (n = 147): quota for reading skills[2], type of residence (private households and residential homes) and variance regarding employment

---

[2] The study took up the concept of "advanced reading skills". The concept distinguishes between four levels of literacy: iconic, logographic, alphabetical and orthographical reading [15]. Alphabetical and orthographical reading are included under "reading skill" for the purposes of our study of media usage.

(regular labour market, special labour market such as sheltered workshops, and economically inactive)

It was important for each subgroup to be represented sufficiently, such that the number of cases provide meaningful results. The study aims to represent as realistic a regional distribution as possible with regard to the German federal states with a varying media landscape. This aim was met for all four subgroups.

The following Tables 1 and 2 document the types of residence and the employment situations of the sample and the subgroups.

Table 1. Composition of the sample: type of residence

	Private household		Residential home, sheltered housing groups	
	Number (n)	Share (%)	Number (n)	Share (%)
SG visual impairment	141	92	13	8
SG hearing impairment	157	98	4	2
SG physical impairment	99	67	49	33
SG learning difficulties	59	40	88	60
Total	456	75	154	25

Source: Media Use of Persons with Disability 2016 (MMB16), [1]
Assessment by the interviewer: Respondent lives in…

We chose a disproportional representation for the quantitative survey to represent the heterogeneity of the target group with their different needs for accessibility of media and devices.

The sample includes people with impairments from the age of 14, who live in Germany and use one medium at least occasionally. In June and July 2016, 610 people were questioned by experienced and trained interviewers from the IPSOS marketing research institute. Collaboration with IPSOS meant that every interview could be conducted face-to-face using additional tools, as necessary. The questionnaire was translated into easy-to-read text. Furthermore, videos were made by a certified deaf sign language interpreter. For a better understanding, a partly illustrated booklet was designed. 23 pretests were conducted with all the target groups. By collaborating with a large institute it was possible to make suitable allowances for regional variations. The use of 101 interviewers with experience of sensitive target groups shortened the time spent on field research.

Topics covered by the questionnaire:

- Subjective perception of impairment
- Media use in general
- TV use in particular
- Specific TV-related barriers and support

Table 2. Composition of the sample: labour market

	Regular labour market		Sheltered workshops	
	Number (n)	Share (%)	Number (n)	Share (%)
SG visual impairment	42	67	20	33
SG hearing impairment	63	72	24	27
SG physical impairment	29	39	24	27
SG learning difficulties	25	22	91	78
Total	159	26	178	29

Question: Do you work … on the regular labour market, in a sheltered workshop, in an outsourced workplace from a sheltered workshop, at a day activity center, on another basis? All respondents in employment (n = 341)

The questions used about media and TV were derived from the ARD/ZDF study "Mass Communication" [16, 17] to allow comparisons with the media usage of the general population in Germany. "Mass Communication" is a long-term study using a representative sample of 4,300 people aged 14 and over that has been carried out every 5 years since 1964 [18]. The questionnaire can be found in the annex to the final report of MMB 16 Bosse & Hasebrink 2016 (in German).

The third stage of the study dealt with focus groups with sensory impairments, their need for television, its limitations and the quality of access to German TV services. Measures were taken to ensure that all aspects relevant to the target group had been taken into account.

Studies on four focus groups with participants with different impairments were conducted:

- Blind and visually impaired people.
- Hard of hearing, deaf or deafened people, who communicate in spoken language (with speech-to-text interpretation).
- Deaf or deafened people, who communicate in sign language. The discussion was moderated by a deaf scientist.
- people with hearing and visual impairments, including deaf-blind people. The discussion was conducted in spoken language with speech-to-text interpretation.

3   Results/Findings

The main findings of the survey are presented in the following. The results of the expert interviews and focus groups are interspersed to explain or broaden the findings.

3.1   Access to Media and Devices

An important precondition for equal participation in media and communication is access to devices. New generations of digital devices like mobile media or digital television offer potentially greater possibilities of accessibility for different kinds of impairments.

The findings of the MMB16 study indicate that access to media and communication devices is lower among people with impairments than among the general population in Germany. Compared to the results of the study "Mass Communication" there are fewer devices with access to the internet in the households of the subjects interviewed with impairments than in households in Germany in general.

There are television sets in nearly all households and no difference can be seen from German households in general. However, the TVs are devices without access to the internet. Only 12% of the households have smart TVs with access to media libraries and other online usage options. This is a remarkable fact because some of the public service broadcasters' services in Germany are only accessible in media libraries on the internet. In particular, programmes with sign language can almost only be seen in internet media libraries. Only two news magazines with sign language are transmitted on linear television. Some special accessibility features such as adapting subtitles to individual needs (subtitle font size, position and background) are only available with Hbb TV (hybrid broadcast broadband TV)[3]. Such features are especially helpful to people with visual and hearing impairments.

Two thirds of the respondents own desktop computers or laptops; this is very similar to the general population. According to the "Mass Communication" study, 58% of the households possess a desktop computer and 64% a laptop [16]. There are major differences in mobile device possession. Far fewer people with impairments have access to mobile devices in their households than the general population. 45% of people with impairments own smartphones in the household and 18% own tablets. According to the "Mass Communication" study, 61% of the general public have access to smartphones in their households and 35% have access to tablets.

As shown in Table 3, age in particular, correlates with access to mobile devices. Almost double the number of respondents with impairments who were younger than 50, have access to smartphones than respondents aged 50+: 27% of the younger respondents own tablets in the household and 9% of the older respondents. The difference in relation to smart TVs is 9% points (17% to 8%). However, the younger respondents also have less access to mobile devices compared to the younger age group in the "Mass Communication" study. Comparing only respondents under the age of 30, 98% of the respondents in the "Mass Communication" study have access to smartphones but only 76% of the respondents in the MMB16 study in the same age group can access smartphones (a difference of 22% points). With regard to tablets, the difference is 23% points (54% in "Mass Communication" study and 31% MMB16). However, the low number of respondents between the ages of 14 and 29 in the MMB16 study (only 78) should be taken into account.

Differences in access to media are also shown by the type of residence (Table 3) but the difference is lower by age group. Devices with internet access are more likely in

---

[3] Since June 2016 the Berlin and Brandenburg public broadcasting service (rbb) has offered the option of personalizing subtitles with Hbb TV. This access feature was developed as part of the EU project DTV4All [19].

Table 3. Access to media in households (age groups and type of residence)

	14–49 years (n = 294)	50+ (n = 316)	Private household (n = 456)	Residential home (n = 154)
TV (without internet access)	80	90	83	92
Radio (without internet access)	71	85	78	79
Computer/Laptop	72	54	66	53
Smartphone	61	30	49	33
Mobile phone (with internet access)	30	47	38	42
Tablet	27	9	22	7
Smart TV (with internet access)	17	8	14	8
Radio (with internet access)	9	3	6	5

Question: Do you have access in your household to the following devices?

private households than in residential homes (smartphone: 49% vs. 33%; tablet: 29% vs. 7%; desktop computer/laptop: 66% vs. 53%).

Looking closer at the subgroups of impairments, it is striking that people with learning disabilities have significantly less access to media devices than the other three subgroups (Table 4). This applies to all devices except TV without internet access. Only half of the respondents with learning difficulties have a desktop computer in the household, a third own a smartphone and one in ten owns a tablet. People with learning difficulties living in private households are slightly more likely to have access to digital media, the same applies to people younger than 50.

Access to digital devices is greatest in the subgroup with hearing impairments. Almost two thirds have access to a desktop computer or laptop and 55% to smartphones. However, compared to the general population access to digital devices is less. The respondents who are hard of hearing were on average older and are less likely to have access to digital devices than the deaf and deafened respondents.

Differences are also apparent within the subgroup of visual impairment. More blind respondents have access to audio media, i.e. radio and MP3 players, whereas partially sighted respondents more often have access to digital devices. The difference is 19% points for tablets, 15 for smart TV, 12 for desktop computer and 9 for smartphones.

Within the subgroup with physical impairments the same correlation can be seen as in the total sample. Younger respondents and respondents who live in private households are more likely to have access to digital devices than older respondents and those who live in residential homes.

Similar findings were shown in the Ofcom study "Disabled consumers' use of communications services" in the UK, a consumers' experience survey with 4,004 consumers with disabilities aged 15 or over and 15,859 non-disabled consumers [20]. Also in the UK "the access to communication devices and services in the home was

Table 4. Access to media in households (subgroups of impairments)

	SG visual impairment (n = 154)	SG hearing impairment (n = 161)	SG physical impairment (n = 148)	SG learning difficulties (n = 154)
TV (without internet access)	81	82	85	93
Radio (without internet access)	86	67	86	75
Computer/Laptop	61	74	68	47
Smartphone	46	55	45	34
Mobile phone (with internet access)	44	44	42	40
Tablet	21	22	17	10
Smart TV (with internet access)	14	14	15	5
Radio (with internet access)	8	8	6	3

Question: Do you have access in your household to the following devices?

generally lower among consumers with disabilities than among those without" [20]. The results showed a correlation between age, socio-economic situation and access to connected devices, both for non-disabled and disabled consumers. But access to these devices was lower among disabled consumers in the same socio-economic group than among non-disabled consumers. The gap widened further among the consumers with a lower income and among older consumers [20].

The Ofcom study also showed the impact of employment. There were very few differences in the level of access to media devices between disabled and non-disabled consumers in employment [20]. The German study MMB16 produced a similar result. People who are employed and in education or training are more likely to have access to a computer, smartphone or tablet (desktop computer: 68% in education, 72% employed, 50% economically inactive; smartphone: 79% in education, 54% employed, 25% economically inactive). However, there is a correlation between age and employment, education or being economical inactive. A further distinction was made between the regular labour market and the special labour market, such as sheltered workshops. Significantly more respondents who work in the regular labour market (n = 159) have access to connected devices, than respondents who work in sheltered workshops (n = 178): desktop computer: 79% regular labour market, 65% sheltered workshops; smartphone: 74% regular labour market, 37% sheltered workshops; tablet: 33% regular labour market, 8% sheltered workshops; smart TV: 22% regular labour market, 6% sheltered workshops.

3.2   Use of Daily Media in General

Television is by far the most used daily medium and this is the case for all age groups and all groups of impairments (Table 5). In all subgroups, the respondents watch TV more frequently than the general population (88% at least several times a week). This is particularly the case for the older respondents 50+ as well as people with learning difficulties and those with physical impairments. The lowest percentage of regular television viewers are the blind (79%) and the deaf respondents (77%). This may be due to the comparatively low number of programmes with audio description or sign language on German television.

There is above-average radio usage by respondents in the subgroups with visual and physical impairment. In these subgroups, more respondents regularly listen to the radio than the population in general. For obvious reasons the percentage of radio listeners is low in the subgroup with hearing impairments. Nevertheless, 80% of the respondents who are hard of hearing regularly listen to the radio.

Fewer people with impairments read newspapers at least several times a week than among the general population in Germany. Older respondents are more likely to read newspapers than younger respondents. There is a big difference between people working in the regular labour market or in sheltered workshops. 65% of the respondents in the regular labour market and 29% of the respondents in sheltered workshops read newspapers regularly. There are more newspaper readers among the respondents with hearing impairments than among the general population (most of the older people who are hard of hearing). Also, disproportionately more older people with physical impairments read newspapers regularly. Not even half of the respondents with visual impairments read newspapers regularly. Almost half of the blind respondents never read newspapers. A reason for the low level of newspaper readers may be that there is a low supply of accessible newspapers for blind people. In Germany, digital editions of daily newspapers are mainly not accessible to the disabled, according to the experts.

Only one of five respondents with learning difficulties reads a newspaper at least several times a week. As expected, reading skills influence newspaper use. A third of the respondents of this subgroup with reading skills read the newspaper regularly. There are also correlations between the newspaper use and the type of residence, employment and age. People with learning difficulties are more likely to read newspapers when they live in private households or work in the regular labour market. The correlation between age and reading newspapers is the opposite of other subgroups. More young respondents with learning difficulties regularly read newspapers than older respondents (50+). This result is linked to reading skills, because only a third of the older respondents with learning difficulties have reading skills, compared to 70% of the younger respondents.

The Internet

Internet usage is strongly influenced by age. Fewer older participants use the internet regularly than younger participants. 52% of the respondents who are 50 and older, and 77% of the respondents under 50 use the internet at least several times a week.

Table 5. Personal use of media at least once a week (data in percent)

	Mass communication 2015*	MMB16 total sample		SG visual impairment		SG hearing impairment		SG physical impairment		SG learning difficulties	
	14+ (n = 4300)	14–49 (n = 294)	50+ (n = 316)	14–49 (n = 66)	50+ (n = 88)	14–49 (n = 79)	50+ (n = 82)	14–49 (n = 73)	50+ (n = 75)	14–49 (n = 76)	50+ (n = 71)
Radio	82	65	81	91	92	18	65	85	88	74	79
TV	88	90	94	82	88	86	94	99	97	93	99
Newspaper	60	45	57	42	52	71	90	40	67	24	15
Internet	71	77	52	80	48	95	61	81	52	51	45

Question: With regard to the radio, TV, newspapers and the internet: Regardless of the time you spend using each, I would like to know how often you use the different media: several times a day, once a day, 2 to 3 times a week, once a week, 2 to 3 times a month, once a month, less or never.
*Data of the long-term study Mass Communication [16].

The type of impairment also influences internet usage. In particular, fewer people with learning difficulties and blind people access the internet regularly. Fewer than every second respondent with learning difficulties goes on the internet at least several times a week. Reading skills and working conditions have an impact on the internet usage of this group. More participants with learning difficulties use the internet when working in the regular labour market and if they possess reading skills. People with learning difficulties differ from the other groups also in the variety and type of the internet activities. There are only five activities which more than 50% of the participants with learning difficulties carry out. First of all, they use video portals like YouTube followed by search engines, surfing, radio/music and online communities. Only one in three respondents looks for news on the internet. In the other groups, more people communicate via internet and social media, look for news or shop online. Only 16% of the respondents with learning difficulties use the internet for online shopping.

Two thirds of the respondents with visual impairments regularly use the internet and the other third never uses the internet. Many blind people in particular are offliners. 43% never go on the internet (Table 6). The time when the visual impairment first occurred influences internet usage. People born with a visual impairment use the internet more often and follow a broader range of activities than people who acquired the impairment in adulthood. (But the small number of cases sampled should be taken into account.) Nearly half of the visually impaired who acquired the impairment in adulthood are offliners (Table 6). Regarding the variety and type of activities on the internet, the respondents with visual impairments act in a more limited way than other groups. Search engines are only used by 77%, followed by news (54%), online shopping (52%) and surfing (50%). Only 42% communicate via internet and social media. This is the lowest percentage of all groups. Looking only at the blind respondents the share drops to 27%.

Inaccessible websites and apps are not the only barriers to internet use for the visually impaired and the blind in particular, as the experts state. Obstacles and barriers make it difficult to surf the internet and require a certain degree of technical understanding. Due to the rapid development of online applications, screen readers can hardly keep up with the development and users need to always have the latest version, otherwise blind users are excluded from many pages and applications. The rapid growth of audio-visual content on the internet, especially in social media, excludes visually impaired users, at least temporarily, from internet applications. These difficulties and barriers may be deterrents in particular for people who acquire the impairment in adulthood and have to learn new techniques and strategies at an advanced age.

The majority of the visually impaired respondents use a desktop computer for the internet, only 39% use a smartphone (32% in the case of the blind) and 20% tablets (12% of the blind). The relatively low percentage for mobile devices may be surprising, because they have advanced functions for easier usage. The earlier the respondents acquired the impairment the more they use mobile devices to access the internet. The experts found differences in the use of mobile devices with universal design features and computers with assisted technologies for the blind. Which device and technology a person chooses may be a question of age but also of technical expertise. Our findings give a clear picture. The majority of blind respondents use computers and only one in three uses mobile devices (68% vs. 32%). This may change with time but younger blind respondents under 50 also use a desktop computer more often (65%) than smartphones (41%) or tablets (12%).

Table 6. Percentage of Offliners who never use the internet

	Offliners* (%)
Sample (n = 610)	27
Age 14–14 years (n = 294)	14
Age 50 and older (n = 316)	39
All respondents with visual impairments (blind/visual impairment) (n = 154)	33
– Only blind respondents (n = 61)	43
– Born with visual impairments (n = 29)	10
– Acquired visual impairments in adulthood (n = 81)	49
All respondents with hearing impairments (n = 161)	19
All respondents with physical impairments (n = 148)	27
All respondents with learning difficulties (n = 147)	29
– Learning difficulties with reading skills (n = 75)	25
– Learning difficulties without reading skills (n = 72)	33

Question: With regard to the radio, TV, newspapers and the internet: Regardless of the time you spend on the internet, I would like to know how often you use the different media: several times a day, once a day, 2 to 3 times a week, once a week, 2 to 3 times a month, once a month, less or never
*Offliners = respondents who never use the internet

People with hearing impairments have an above-average use of the internet. 95% of the respondents younger than 50 years and 61% of the older respondents use the internet regularly. The differences between the deaf, deafened and the hard of hearing are related to age difference. The hard of hearing participants are much older than the deaf and deafened. The variety of activities is broader than in the other groups and the participants use more different devices to access the internet. Nearly three quarters of the respondents with hearing impairments search for daily news on the internet and use online communities, e-mail or instant messaging to communicate with others (88% younger respondents; 60% older). These findings reinforce the statements of the experts, who consider the internet to be a "revolution" for communication and information options for people with hearing impairment, especially the deaf and deafened.

69% of the respondents with physical impairments use the internet regularly; much younger than older participants. There is also a difference between people who live in private households or in residential homes. 74% of those living in private households and 60% of those in residential homes use the internet at least several times a week. It is to be noted that fewer people with learning difficulties living in care homes (48%) use the internet than people with physical impairments. (But the small sample should be taken into account, i.e. 49 people with physical impairments and 88 people with learning difficulties living in residential homes.) The variety of activities is broader than in the groups with visual impairments or with learning difficulties. More than 70% use search engines, online communities, e-mail or instant messaging, news sites or surf on the internet. About half of the respondents with physical impairments use a desktop computer, laptop or smartphones to access the internet and 21% use tablets.

Television – Preferences, Needs and Barriers

The focus of the study was on television, the usage and limitations on the usage. Television is the most widespread and the most used medium across all subgroups of impairments and age. There is only one exception, i.e. more blind respondents use radio more regularly than television. The percentage of regular users is slightly lower among blind and deaf persons than in other subgroups, i.e. 79% of the blind and 77% of the deaf respondents watch television at least several times a week. 18% of the blind and 13% of the deaf never watch TV. This points to another finding of the study, i.e. that blind and deaf people face greater limitations to their use of television than other subgroups.

Further evidence of the importance of television for media users with disabilities in Germany is shown by the motives they give for watching television. Pleasure, information and relaxation are the most frequent motives, followed by *"getting useful information for daily life"*, watching television by habit and *"having a say in things"*. In comparison to the general population, more respondents with impairments agree with these different motives. It would therefore seem that television has a higher functional significance for people with impairments than for the general population [1].

These findings mainly apply to linear television watched on "conventional" TVs without internet access. Online television is relatively insignificant. As indicated above, the respondents rarely have access to internet TVs in their households and only 11%–12% watch television on their desktop computers or laptops. Less than a third of the respondents use these devices to watch videos or television online. Of the younger participants under the age of 50, 38% watch videos or television online [1]. In comparison, 53% of the general population in Germany watch videos on the internet at least once a week [17]. These findings emphasize the necessity of incorporating accessibility features in German linear television. If subtitles, audio descriptions and sign language are only provided online, the majority of disabled media users will not be able to use them. Online television usage may rise in years to come but the lack of suitable digital devices and media habits should not be underestimated. The Ofcom study "Disabled consumers' use of communications service" in Great Britain in 2015 showed similar results, i.e. the disabled consumers were more likely to have access to free-to-air TV than non-disabled consumers and less likely to have access to Pay TV. "Access to devices and services was generally lower among those with disabilities than among non-disabled consumers" [20].

The results of the sensory impairment focus groups underlined the findings. The participants urgently requested accessible programmes on linear TV. It would seem that for a great majority of the respondents equal media participation means having accessible programmes on linear TV.

A large number of those sampled use assistive technologies or means when watching TV at least sometimes. Assistive technologies and means include audio descriptions, subtitles, sign language, easy-to-read captions, FM systems, sound processors or personal support. 58% of the younger respondents and 51% of the older respondents use at least one of these means at least sometimes to watch TV. Whether a television programme is accessible or not influences the programme choices of two thirds of the sample.

Of course, the needs and barriers depend on the impairments but over all groups, many respondents have problems with poor speech quality. Ambient noise, loud music or slurred speech limit many respondents in their use of television. Clean audio could be a solution for this problem. Remote control handling is also a frequent problem, not only for people with physical impairment but also for people with visual impairment, in particular the blind persons and those with learning difficulties. Bigger and easy-to-feel buttons on the remote control, voice output and a longer time slot to select the channels are the most wanted improvements.

These are the findings regarding the needs and barriers for the different impairments:

Vision: Most respondents requested more audio descriptions and better speech intelligibility. More blind respondents reported problems with speech intelligibility than partially sighted respondents. Partially sighted participants of the focus groups mentioned the lack of textual information on the screen as a limitation. Inserts and graphics with written information often appear on the screen without being read out. The respondents required audio descriptions for more broadcasting formats, such as live broadcasts of sporting events or shows, feature films, television magazines, documentaries and news. A quarter of the respondents have problems using the remote control, which is the highest proportion of all subgroups.

Hearing: For the impaired hearing subgroup, television accessibility means better speech intelligibility and sound quality, subtitles and more sign language on linear television. The enormous importance of accessibility is clearly shown by the fact that for nearly 90% of the respondents (n = 84) programme accessibility is a decision-making criterion as to what to watch on TV. More respondents than in other subgroups reported problems following TV programmes due to lack of accessibility. The most disabled subgroup is the deafened. Subtitles are equally important for the hard of hearing, deafened and deaf and subtitles should be available for 100% of broadcasting but German television, in particular the private broadcasting channels, are far from this state. Sign language is used by 94% of the deaf and 85% of the deafened respondents. They ask for a wider range of broadcasting formats with sign language, above all news programmes, documentaries, entertainment shows and sport. The focus groups stressed the need for sign language in children's programmes. Sign language should not be "hidden" in media libraries on the internet but provided in "conventional" linear programmes.

Dexterity: Limitations mainly occur with the remote control. Bigger, easy-to-feel buttons on the remote control and a longer time slot to select the channels would help. Respondents who sometimes have problems following programmes report that better speech intelligibility and easy-to-read captions would be helpful.

Learning difficulties: As expected, improved accessibility of audio-visual content by using sign language, subtitles and audio descriptions is less important for this subgroup. Easy-to-read and better speech intelligibility would be useful. The biggest problem is remote control handling. Except for the blind respondents, no other group had more respondents experiencing problems using the remote control. The respondents require easy-to-feel buttons on the remote control, voice output and suitable applications for smartphones and tablets.

3.3   A Growing Group: People with Visual and Hearing Problems

Thanks to the expert interviews, we were able to carry out a special statistical analysis of people with both visual and hearing problems. For this reason, we added two questions regarding visual and hearing problems[4] to identify respondents with both impairments. Every sixth respondent reported visual and hearing problems. Older persons especially, have visual and hearing problems additional to their main impairment. Two thirds of the respondents over 60 reported problems with both senses (Table 7).

This group faces special limitations in media usage. Compared to all respondents older than 60, this subgroup rarely reads newspapers but uses the internet slightly more frequently. Depending on the specific form of impairment, they have different needs regarding the accessibility of audio-visual content. Better speech intelligibility and easy-to-read captions are very important to the majority of the respondents. The focus group reported that slurred speech, people speaking simultaneously, ambient noise and loud music were the main problems. As regards subtitles, the focus groups participants referred to the legibility of subtitles, the frequent problems being poor background contrast and not enough time to read the subtitles [1].

---

[4] The questions were taken from the study "Gesundheit in Deutschland aktuell" (GEDA), a representative survey about the state of health in Germany [21].

Table 7. Respondents with visual and hearing problems

	Number (n)	Share (%)
Women	55	56
Men	43	44
14 to 39	8	8
40 to 59	26	27
60 and older	64	65
SG Visual impairments	24	25
SG Hearing impairments	30	31
SG Physical impairments	24	25
SG Learning difficulties	20	20

Source: Media Use of Persons with Disability 2016 (MMB16) [1].
Questions: Are you able to recognize a person's face from a distance of 4 m, e.g. on the other side of the road? Are you able to follow a conversation with several people? Answers: Yes, with no difficulty; Yes, with a little difficulty; No, with great difficulty; No, not at all.
Basis: Respondents with visual and hearing impairment (n = 98), who answered both questions yes, with a little difficulty or no, with great difficulties or no, not at all)

4 Conclusion

The MMB16 study is a first step towards collecting data on the participation and inclusion of people with disabilities in media and communication in Germany. It shows that impairment is accompanied by specific limitations to media access and usage. People with disability are as heterogeneous as the subgroups themselves and full and equal participation in media and communication depends on the context factors which influence the level and degree of participation, i.e. age, housing, employment, obstacles and barriers to access, technical and personal support. Considering this diversity, the approach chosen to describe different subgroups does not completely meet the many different forms of individual media use.

Age is an important personal factor shaping media usage and is also shown by general media usage studies. It would seem that the interaction of age, impairment and other context factors leads to the particularly rare use of digital media by older people with impairments.

Living and working in care homes and workshops for persons with disabilities does not mean that the individuals there are given any particular help accessing digital media. Indeed, the findings of the MMB16 study indicate a negative correlation between living in residential homes or working in sheltered workshops and digital media access and usage. Welfare associations should pay closer attention to digital participation.

The internet plays a major role in equal participation in media and communication. In general, people with impairments, but in particular those with intellectual impairments, are less likely to have access to connected devices than the general population, use the internet more infrequently and use it less for communication and information. The MMB16 study confirms the results of other studies in other countries [14]. Many blind people are offliners, even more so if they acquired the impairment in adulthood. Obstacles and barriers to access and the rapid growth of audio-visual content are further limitations to internet access.

Television plays a major role in the media resources of persons with impairments. More persons with a disability regularly watch TV compared to the general population in Germany. Therefore access service obligations are important for an equal participation in media. "Digital and online television could potentially offer greater access for persons with disabilities, particularly those with vision, hearing and physical impairments (Ellis 2012; Robare 2011; Slater, et al. 2010); however, this is far from automatic" [22]. Broadcasters must be obliged to provide accessibility options. In Germany, there are only loose agreements with public and non-public broadcasters. Furthermore, the findings of our study point to the problem that new technological solutions to improve accessibility require persons with disabilities to buy the latest generation of devices themselves. Due to different factors such as age, low income or unfavourable living conditions they often have no little or no access to the latest technology.

References

1. Bosse, I., Hasebrink, U.: Mediennutzung von Menschen mit Behinderungen. Forschungsbericht, Berlin (2016)
2. United Nations: Convention on the Rights of Persons with Disabilities. New York (2006)
3. Bosse, I.: Teilhabe in einer digitalen Gesellschaft – Wie Medien Inklusionsprozesse befördern können (2016). http://www.bpb.de/gesellschaft/medien/medienpolitik/172759/medien-und-inklusion
4. Ofcom: Television access services report 2015, London (2015). https://www.ofcom.org.uk/__data/assets/pdf_file/0029/71669/access-report-2015.pdf
5. Committee on the Rights of Persons with Disabilities: Concluding observations on the initial report of Germany (2015)
6. Berger, A., Caspers, T., et al.: Web 2.0/barrierefrei. Eine Studie zur Nutzung von Web 2.0 Anwendungen durch Menschen mit Behinderung, Bonn (2010)
7. Funke, G.: Wie Sonderschüler fernsehen. Das Fernsehen im Alltag von lernbehinderten Jugendlichen und Schülern mit Erziehungsschwierigkeiten; eine repräsentative Studie für NRW, 1. Aufl. Tectum, Marburg (2007)
8. Haferkamp, N.: Physische und psychische Einschränkungen. In: Wünsch, C., Schramm, H., Gehrau, V., et al. (eds.) Handbuch Medienrezeption, 1. Auflage. Nomos-Verl.-Ges. (2014)
9. Institut für Rundfunktechnik (IRT), Rundfunk Berlin-Brandenburg: Online-Umfrage zur Sprachverständlichkeit von TV-Produktionen für Hörgeschädigte, Berlin (2015)
10. Zaynel, N.: Wie Kinder und Jugendliche mit Down-Syndrom fernsehen. Medien+Erziehung 57(4), 50–55 (2013)

11. Zaynel, N.: Be independent, go online! How German children and adolescents with Down's Syndrome use the internet (2016). http://blogs.lse.ac.uk/parenting4digitalfuture/2016/02/17/be-independent-go-online-how-german-children-and-adolescents-with-downs-syndrome-use-the-internet/

12. World Health Organization (WHO): Internationale Klassifikation der Funktionsfähigkeit, Behinderung und Gesundheit (ICF), Genf (2005)

13. Mayerle, M.: "Woher hat er die Idee?". Selbstbestimmte Teilhabe von Menschen mit Lernschwierigkeiten durch Mediennutzung. Abschlussbericht der Begleitforschung im PIKSL-Labor. ZPE-Schriftenreihe, vol 40. Universität Gesamthochschule Siegen Zentrum f. Planung u. Evaluation Sozialer Dienste, Siegen (2014)

14. Caton, S., Chapman, M.: The use of social media and persons with intellectual disability. A systematic review and thematic analysis. J. Intellect. Dev. Disabil. **41**(2), 125–139 (2016). doi:10.3109/13668250.2016.1153052

15. Kuhl, J., Euker, N., Koch, A.: Evaluation eines Diagnoseverfahrens zur Erfassung der Lesekompetenz im weiteren und engeren Sinne von Menschen mit geistiger Behinderung. Heilpädagogische Forschung **39**(4), 183–198 (2013)

16. Engel, B., Breunig, C.: Massenkommunikation 2015: Mediennutzung im Intermediavergleich. Ergebnisse der ARD/ZDF-Langzeitstudie. Media-Perspektiven **7–8**, 310–322 (2015)

17. Media Perspektiven: Daten zur Mediensituation in Deutschland, Frankfurt am Main (2015)

18. Krupp, M.: Massenkommunikation IX. Eine Langzeitstudie zur Mediennutzung und Medienbewertung 1964–2015. Schriftenreihe Media-Perspektiven, vol 22. Nomos, Baden-Baden (2016)

19. RBB   Fernsehen.   http://www.rbb-online.de/fernsehen/untertitel_angebot/themen/personalisierbare-UT-in-HbbTV.html Accessed. 10 Feb 2017

20. Ofcom: Disabled consumers' use of communications service. A consumer Experience report, London (2015)

21. Robert Koch-Institut: Daten und Fakten: Ergebnisse der Studie "Gesundheit in Deutschland aktuell 2012", Berlin (2014)

22. Ellis, K., Kent, M.: Accessible television: the new frontier in disability media studies brings together industry innovation, government legislation and online activism. First Monday **20**(9), 3 (2015)

Now You See It, Now You Don't: Understanding User Interface Visibility

Ian Michael Hosking[✉] and P. John Clarkson

University of Cambridge, Cambridge, UK
{imh29,pjc10}@cam.ac.uk

Abstract. We live in a post-WIMP world. The traditional Windows, Icons, Menus and Pointers of the PC graphical user interface are no longer present in many hand-held devices. There has been a dramatic rise in the use of smart phones in particular, with Apple selling their billionth iPhone in 2016. This trend in devices and the shift to touch interfaces has caused concern with regards to usability and has been described by some as a "usability crisis". This alleged crisis is born out of a proliferation of product features combined with a trend towards minimalisation in user interface style. This means that user interface functions are potentially becoming less visible. The challenge is to try and quantify and understand what is happening with regards to UI visibility, which is deemed to be a critical component creating a usable interface. This paper demonstrates an approach to determining a "visibility score" for a product's user interface. The approach is applied to the home screen of an iPhone. This produces a visibility score of less than 10% in other words over 90% of the functions available are not visible at the top level. Such a score needs to be treated with caution but can help inform the general debate as well as creating useful insights for the designers of products.

Keywords: Usability · Visibility · WIMP · User interfaces · User experience

1 Introduction

We live in, what has been described as, a post-WIMP (Windows, Icons, Menu, Pointer) era [1–4], due to the growth of touch based devices in particular. Apple announced at the beginning of 2016 that they have 1 Billion active users on their non-WIMP products [5]. However, concerns have been raised about the usability of post-WIMP devices. Nielsen and Norman describe the situation as a "usability crisis" [6]. One of the key issues raised is the lack of visibility of user interface elements, which is deemed to be a critical and fundamental component of an effective user interface [6–8]. As Norman puts it, "The important design rule of a GUI is visibility" [8].

This alleged "crisis" is exacerbated by products that are suffering from a proliferation of features. For example, in Microsoft Word the number of commands in Word 1.0 was about 100 but by Word 2003 it had exceeded 1500. When Microsoft asked users what they wanted in the next version of Office, 9 out of 10 asked for features they already had in their current version [9]. Not only is not finding the required function a problem, but

© Springer International Publishing AG 2017
M. Antona and C. Stephanidis (Eds.): UAHCI 2017, Part III, LNCS 10279, pp. 436–445, 2017.
DOI: 10.1007/978-3-319-58700-4_35

the opposite problem of accidentally activating an undesired function is a issue too. For example, Apple's iOS has a delete mode for apps that is activated by a 'touch and hold' on an app icon [10]. This can lead to accidental deletion of an app and its data or simply confusing the user.

What we see is the combination of a proliferation of features with interfaces that lack visibility as they move to a minimalist design style. This is understandable as many post-WIMP devices must work within the constraints of smaller form factors such as those of smart phones. It is nonetheless a concern. The graphical user interface represented a major advance in user interface design from the command line interface style [11, 12]. "Seeing and pointing" replaced "remembering and typing" [13–15]. But as we see a shift to touch interfaces are we potentially taking a retrograde step from "see and point" to "remember and swipe" or with non-touch gestural interfaces to "remember and wave".

This paper shows an approach to quantifying how many features are available and how many are visible directly to the user. Effectively this creates a simple "visibility score" for a user interface. This approach is applied to the home screen of Apple iOS on an iPhone smart phone. The pros and cons of such an approach are then discussed and recommendations made about how the approach can be applied and developed further.

2   Method

The Apple mobile and tablet operating system, iOS was chosen because it is widely used [5] and mature, being in its tenth version [10]. The device chosen was an iPhone7 (see Fig. 1), as the latest in a series of iPhones, which over a billion of have been made [16]. The multitude and diversity of factory installed and user chosen apps led to selecting "app launching and management", that is performed via home screens (see Figs. 2 and 3), as the target area for analysis. Note that Apple calls each subsequent 'screen' of apps an "additional home screen" (see Fig. 3), hence the use of the plural term [10]. Out of the box there are two home screens. In addition to the ability to launch and manage apps, the home screens provide shortcuts to various actions for example turning the torch on or launching the camera. The iPhone 7 also has "3D Touch" interaction that enables users to access even more shortcuts by pressing the screen with higher force.

The configuration was based on the 'out of box' set of applications with the device configured as part of the set-up process. This configuration will vary from user to user but will not make a substantive difference to the common functions available. Although in reality a user would download apps that they want and reconfigure their layout it seems an acceptable compromise to create a benchmark configuration based on the 'out of box' app set. The task sequence explores all the functions available starting from the first home screen with the device awake and unlocked.

Interaction is broken down into the different modalities as follows:

- Buttons.
- Touch.
- Movement of the device.
- Voice.

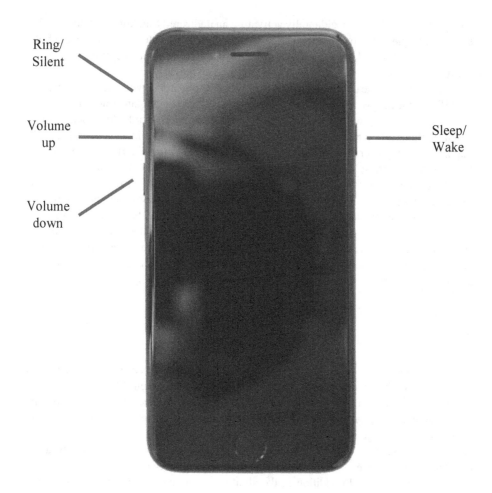

Fig. 1. iPhone 7 showing location of buttons

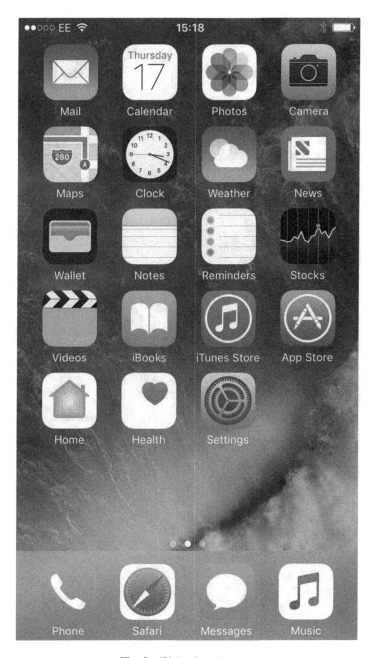

Fig. 2. iPhone home screen

Fig. 3. Additional home screen

There are several aspects that require definitions:

- State is the configuration of the phone at a point in time.
- Initial state is the starting point for the analysis. In this case the phone is awake, unlocked and on the first home screen.
- Level refers to the number of states from the initial state that the user navigates through. It is equivalent to the levels in a traditional menu system. Accordingly, the initial state represents the top level or level one.
- Function is defined broadly as an action presented to the user, that either presents a further range of actions or is an action in its own right, such as opening an app or a direct shortcut to an action within an app (e.g. creating a new message). To use the vernacular, a function is "a thing that a user can do". Such a broad definition is used to see how many of the "things a user can do" are visible. Such a definition is in contrast to more rigorous one, such as Gero's function-behaviour-state [17], which would have potentially over complicated an already detailed analysis.
- Unique refers to whether the function only appears once within the functions that are considered, in this case functions available from the home screens. Therefore, it is possible that the function may appear elsewhere within iOS and the apps that it supports.
- Visible is defined as any graphical element that is there to indicate the presence of a function.

Where appropriate the terminology, describing the user interface, is based on the iPhone User Guide [10], however terms are changed where greater clarity is required. For example, the difference between a light touch and a more forceful one on the home button is not distinguished completely in the Guide. In this case a double light press is described as a 'touch' of the home button which activates the reachability mode as opposed to a double press with greater force which is described as 'press', which activates the application switcher.

The analysis was recorded in a spreadsheet showing the functions that are available and the level they are at [18]. This is logically equivalent to a standard WIMP menu hierarchy. A handful of functions are available at all levels and this is noted accordingly. In practice the process was iterative to find the best structure and grouping within the spreadsheet. This was done in conjunction with 'live' testing on an iPhone which also revealed further functionality appropriate for analysis.

The analysis should be seen as comprehensive but not exhaustive. This is due in part to the fact any specific configuration does not allow for all options to be available. Also, a full state transition diagram covering every operational situation (e.g. receiving a call when navigating the home screen or the variation in quick action menus depending on previous app usage) would add significant complication. However, for the purposes of this analysis it is was deemed that the analysis was sufficiently comprehensive to highlight the issues around visibility.

3   Results

The approach resulted in 622 functions being analysed. As such they are too numerous to display them within the paper but the spreadsheet has been made available [18]. A

Table 1. An extract from the analysis spreadsheet

	Touch Screen				Action	Function Description	Function	Unique	Visible
	L1	L2	L3	L4					
108	Mail								
109	App icon				Press	Launch App	Y	Y	Y
110	App icon				Touch & hold →	App Configuration	Y	N	N
111		→ Configure App			Press 'cross'	Delete App	Y	N	N
112		→ Configure App			Drag to new location	Move App	Y	N	N
113		→ Configure App			Drag onto another app	Create Folder	Y	N	N
114		→ Configure App			Drag onto a folder	Add App to Folder	Y	N	N
115		→ Configure App			Drag to dock	Add to dock	Y	N	N
116		→ Configure App			Drag right	Create New Home Screen	Y	N	N
117	App icon				3D press →	Quick Actions Menu	Y	N	N
118		→ Quick Action			Press	New Message	Y	Y	N
119		→ Quick Action			Press	Search	Y	Y	N
120		→ Quick Action			Press	All VIP emails	Y	Y	N
121		→ Quick Action			Press	All inboxes folder	Y	Y	N
122		→ Quick Action			Press	VIP 1 emails	Y	Y	N
123		→ Quick Action			Press	VIP 2 emails	Y	Y	N
124		→ Quick Action			Press	VIP 3 emails	Y	Y	N
125		→ Quick Action			Press	VIP 4 emails	Y	Y	N

snapshot example is shown in Table 1 below. This is the analysis of the Mail app. It shows the functions available, which are at level one and two in the hierarchy of functions. The action required to activate the function is recorded as well as a description of the function. The final 3 columns then record if the line item is a function, if the function is unique with the boundary of the home screens function set and if the function is visible at the top level. These columns are then used to count the respective numbers. It should be a noted that a function may become visible at a lower level but in terms of discoverability at the top level it is invisible.

Table 2 provides a numerical summary of the entire analysis for the 4 different modalities considered. A percentage of the functions that are visible is calculated. In addition, a percentage of the visibility of unique functions is calculated separately. This is done because it considers each repeated function, e.g. deleting an app, as a single instance on the basis that if you cannot see app deletion for one app you cannot see it for all the apps. Conversely if you do 'know' it is there it reduces the impact of the lack of visibility of for all instances. It is a debatable point if this is useful, but if used it should be done so in conjunction with the other visibility number that includes repeated functions.

Table 2. A numerical summary of the functions analysed and their visibility

Modality	Number of functions	Number that are unique	Number that are visible	% that are visible	% of unique that are visible
Buttons	23	17	5	22%	29%
Touch	597	266	43	7%	16%
Movement	1	1	0	0%	0%
Microphone	1	1	0	0%	0%
Total	622	285	48	8%	17%

4   Discussion

The bare numbers present what appears to be a stark situation with regards to the high number of functions (622) and the low number of these that are visible (8%) even if repeated functions are removed the visibility figure only rises to 17%. The situation, with regard to the total number of functions, would be increased further as users download additional apps. If one was also to include all the in-app functions, then clearly the number would increase dramatically.

However, the situation is far more nuanced than the bare numbers. The issues around these are as follows:

- The relevance of each functions is not weighted in any way, for example with regard to their importance and frequency of use. As it stands the home screens appropriately prioritise the frequent and important task of launching apps. Secondary functions such as moving or deleting an app are made 'visible' by the 'touch and hold' of the app. This has the big advantage of reducing visual clutter. Indeed, it would be unrealistic to make all the functions visible.
- The numerical analysis does not consider prior knowledge of the users. In other words, their experience of using gestures on a touch device.
- In addition, there is a commercial imperative of offering new features to maintain sales. The needs of different users need to be balanced, in other words there is a function versus complexity trade-off.

Therefore, it can be argued that iOS strikes an appropriate balance between offering a rich set of functions and reducing visual clutter with a focus on the high priority and high frequency functions. However, the Microsoft Word example cited earlier is a cautionary tale and there is a real concern for novice or older users in particular that these user interfaces become overwhelming. The numerical analysis should not be used as a simple 'good to bad' scoring system but instead it should be used to highlight the overall status of the visibility of a system and to review whether the trade-offs that have been made are appropriate. In addition, support for novice or older users can be looked at, for example providing a simple mode or on screen prompts.

A logical extension of the work is to see if how visibility scores vary across products and how they change over time. Also, it is possible to test if the visibility score is a proxy for overall usability of a product or application. As stated above this simple score does not deal with the nuances of a particular user interface and therefore it is possible that it will not reliably correlate with usability.

5   Limitations

As it stands, the visibility scoring system has only been applied to one operating system and is further limited to the functionality surrounding the home screens. Therefore, without comparing it to other user interfaces and how it may correlate to usability it is not appropriate to cite a score as a good or bad rating for a particular user interface. As it stands the score should be used to inform an evaluation of a user interface and as such is a starting point rather than the end point of an evaluation.

6   Conclusion

The "usability crisis" description has merit, but the situation is nuanced and it is important to look beyond headline statements. There is reason to be concerned that modern post-WIMP interfaces represent a retrograde step with regards to usability. It is reminiscent of the era of the command line "remember and type", but with touch interfaces it is "remember and swipe". It would be a very large stretch to say things are in anyway as difficult as a command line interface but with the increasing reliance on technology it is something that needs to be monitored. Therefore, the ability to methodically assess what is happening with the visibility of user interface functions is important.

The ability to determine a "visibility score" is a contribution to this situation. As it stands the approach has only been applied to one aspect of one product. However, if used appropriately it can help inform both the overall debate and designers who are looking to understand the nature of their design. Further research is merited to compare visibility scores of different elements within products, across products and the evolution of these products over time.

References

1. Nielsen, J.: Noncommand user interfaces. Commun. ACM **36**, 83–99 (1993). doi: 10.1145/255950.153582
2. Gentner, D., Nielsen, J.: The Anti-Mac interface. Commun. ACM **39**, 70–82 (1996). doi: 10.1145/232014.232032
3. van Dam, A.: Post-WIMP user interfaces. Commun. ACM **40**, 63–67 (1997). doi: 10.1145/253671.253708
4. van Dam, A.: User interfaces: disappearing, dissolving, and evolving. Commun. ACM **44**, 50–52 (2001). doi:10.1145/365181.365192
5. Apple Inc.: Q1'16 Earnings Supplemental Material. Apple Inc. (2016)
6. Norman, D.A., Nielsen, J.: Gestural interfaces: a step backward in usability. Interactions **17**, 46–49 (2010). doi:10.1145/1836216.1836228
7. Shneiderman, B.: Direct manipulation: a step beyond programming languages. Computer **16**, 57–69 (1983). doi:10.1145/238218.238281

8. Norman, D.A.: Natural user interfaces are not natural. Interactions **17**, 6–10 (2010). doi: 10.1145/1744161.1744163

9. Caposella, C.: PDC 2005 keynote with Bill Gates. Presented at the Professional Developers Conference, Los Angeles, 13 September 13 2005

10. Apple Inc.: iPhone User Guide for iOS 10.2 (2016)

11. English, W.K., Engelbart, D.C., Berman, M.L.: Display-selection techniques for text manipulation. IEEE Trans. Hum. Factors Electron., 5–15 (1967). doi:10.1109/THFE. 1967.232994

12. Myers, B.A.: A brief history of human-computer interaction technology. Interactions **5**, 44–54 (1998). doi:10.1145/274430.274436

13. Irby, C., Bergsteinsson, L., Moran, T., Newman, W., Tesler, L.: A Methodology for User Interface Design. Xerox Corporation (1977)

14. Smith, D.C., Irby, C., Kimball, R., Verblank, B., Harslem, E.: Designing the star user interface. Byte **7**, 242–282 (1982)

15. Johnson, J.A., Roberts, T.L., Verplank, W., Smith, D.C., Irby, C.H., Beard, M., Mackey, K.: The xerox star: a retrospective. Computer **22**, 11–29 (1989). doi:10.1109/2.35211

16. Apple celebrates one billion iPhones (2016). http://www.apple.com/newsroom/2016/07/apple-celebrates-one-billion-iphones.html

17. Gero, J.S.: Design prototypes: a knowledge representation schema for design. AI Mag. **11**, 26 (1990)

18. Hosking, I.: iPhone visibility analysis R1 (2017). doi:10.17863/CAM.7616

Impressive Picture Selection from Wearable Camera Toward Pleasurable Recall of Group Activities

Eriko Kinoshita and Kaori Fujinami[✉]

Department of Computer and Information Sciences, Tokyo University of Agricalture and Technology, 2-24-16 Naka-cho, Koganei, Tokyo 184-8588, Japan
asa.kinoko0216@gmail.com, fujinami@cc.tuat.jp

Abstract. Wearable cameras allow us to capture large amount of video or still images in an automatic and implicit manner. However, the only necessary images should be filtered out from the captured data that contains meaningless and/or redundant information. In this paper, we propose a method to identify a set of still images by audio and video data, which is intended to let users feel pleasurable when they watch the images later.

Keywords: Wearable camera · Life logging · Image and audio analysis

1 Introduction

Wearable cameras such as SenseCam [6], GoPro [3] and A1H [8] enables automatic and implicit life-logging. A user would be aroused a particular emotion when he/she reviews the recorded data by recalling what happened at that moment. However, in such passive life-logging, particular moments should be identified from huge amount of data, e.g., video and still images, to reduce cognitive burden of the user, and summarization techniques have been proposed [1]. The main purpose of existing image summarization techniques is to improve the usability of life log browsing, in which the user's satisfaction in recording and reviewing memories is not fully considered.

We design the image summarization system by taking into account the effect of browsing. More specifically, we aim at detecting a moment in which a group of people feel pleasurable when they review the logged data, which we call *post-pleasurable*. Based on a preliminary user survey with 50 people, we identified two types of post-pleasurable moments obtained from an automatic recording device: (1) the same group members of the photo-taker talking with each other and (2) partying during a group activity. By contrast, beautiful and rare scenes were found to be less meaningful for automatic post-pleasurable scene selection because people explicitly take photos by themselves in such cases. In addition to the two moments, we added (3) "having interests in something" to the target moments because something that attracts a user should make him/her recall special emotions later.

M. Antona and C. Stephanidis (Eds.): UAHCI 2017, Part III, LNCS 10279, pp. 446–456, 2017.
DOI: 10.1007/978-3-319-58700-4_36

In this paper, we propose a method to identify scenes (2) and (3) using audio and visual data from first-person view camera. The rest of the paper is organized as follows. Section 2 examines related work to validate the approach of automatic photo taking and to state our approach in video summarization techniques. In Sect. 3, the system design and implementation is presented. A user study to understand the emotional effects by the proposed system in Sect. 4, followed by discussion in Sect. 5. Finally, we conclude the paper in Sect. 6.

2 Related Work

In the field of life-logging, research focusing on first-person viewpoint using body mounted camera is presented, which is called "visual life-logging" [1]. Sellen, et al. conducted experiments on memory recall using SenseCam [6] as a verification on the effectiveness of memory support of life-logging [10], in which photos taken automatically by a wearable camera is suggested that it is easier to recall past memories than photos taken voluntarily by a still camera. So, the usefulness of automatic shooting in our approach seems to be supported.

Summarization, keyframe selection in other words, techniques from video stream have been proposed to specify particular moments, which are used to reduce cognitive burden of the user to find appropriate ones from huge amount of data [1,2,5,7,9]. Image-based keyframe selection employs visual features such as contrast, color variance, sharpness, noise and saliency to identify non-redundant yet meaningful frame [2,7]. We consider that these visual features are basic ones and that they are not so effective in recalling pleasurable moments. Emotional features are effective in identifying more specific moments that relate to emotions of humans, e.g., enjoyment, fear, surprise, anger, etc. StartleCam [5] is a pioneering work in visual life-logging that leverages electrodermal activity (EDA) sensor, a.k.a. galvanic skin response (GSR) sensor, to extract frightening moments from photo stream, in which the sensor is attached on fingers or foot. Ratsamee, et al. proposed a keyframe selection method based on excitement measured from EDA sensor attached around the wrist, in cooperation with visual features from a smartphone's video camera hanging from the neck [9]. Although their study shares the motivation of keyframe selection from an emotional aspect with ours, we utilize only a video camera to reduce the physical load. Furthermore, we aim at selecting pictures for an entire group members even who do not wear recording devices.

3 System Design and Implementation

3.1 Overview

The proposed system assumes that a user attaches a camera on his/her head, e.g., eye glasses and headphones, and that the judgment process is carried out in an offline manner by providing a movie file. Figure 1 illustrates the processing flow; major components are "partying estimator" and "interest estimator" that

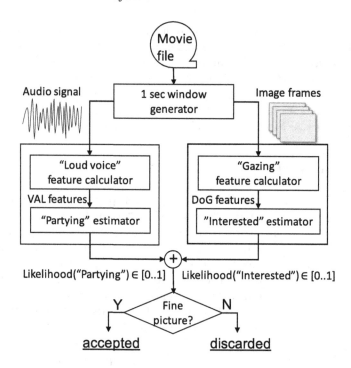

Fig. 1. Processing flow.

corresponds to the moment (2) and (3), respectively. The two estimators consist of binary classifiers that generate the recognition results on whether a particular period of time includes these moments (positive) or not (negative) with accompanying likelihood of *positive* ranging from 0 to 1. The two scores are merged, which is called "fine picture score", and the final decision is made on the score to obtain an output still image.

3.2 Features that Characterize Pleasurable Moments

Voice Audio Level: The "partying" moment is defined as what loud voice turns up, which is estimated every 1 s from audio signals. Voice audio level (VAL) features are represented by absolute audio levels and relative ones.

An absolute voice audio level (A-VAL) is calculated as follows. Firstly, maximum absolute amplitude ($maxAbsAmp$) is found in a sub-window of w ms. Secondly, the moving averages ($aveMaxAbsAmps$) are calculated against m samples of $maxAbsAmps$ with 1 sample sliding for 1 s. Finally, the sum of ($aveMaxAbsAmps$) is obtained as an A-VAL. Here, A-VAL$_{w,m}$ represents the value of A-VAL for sub-window of w ms and moving average of m samples. In addition to the absolute value, the difference of consecutive A-VAL$_{w,m}$ is utilized as relative voice audio level (R-VAL$_{w,m}$). By changing the length of sub-window (w), i.e., 100, 500, and 1000 ms, and the number of moving average samples (m), i.e., 7 and 9, a total of 12 features are defined.

Degree of Gazing: The moment of "interested" is defined as a moment in which the wearer of a camera is gazing at something, e.g., people, objects, landscape. We consider that people who have interests in something tend to keep their body still to fix their eyes and thus blurring is reduced.

Similar to VAL features, the degree of gazing (DoG) is defined by two aspects: absolute value and relative one, which are represented A-DoG and R-DoG, respectively. A-DoG is calculated by the sum of inter-frame histogram differences within one second, which means that smaller value indicates less movement and thus more interested. Here, gray-scale images are utilized. The difference of consecutive DoG values are used to obtain R-DoG values. By changing the time difference between frames, i.e., 250 ms and 500 ms, and gray-levels, i.e., 8, 64, and 256, a total of 12 features are calculated.

3.3   Implementation

Data Collection: Two estimators are built using supervised machine learning technique, which requires labeled datasets. We collected datasets of five events from two to six persons including the wearer of the video camera. The summed duration of the events is about 160 min. Table 1 summarizes the datasets. The audio and video is captured by Panasonic A1H [8] at 60 fps, and analyzed using OpenCV, in which an audio channel is separated. The audio channel was originally sampled at 48 kHz; however, the collected data were later down-sampled at 8 kHz to reduce the amount of data.

Table 1. Events in data collection

Event	Number of participants	Duration [min]
Playing darts	2	50
Playing in an amusement park	6	10
Playing a table game	4	40
Singing in a karaoke room	2	30
Drinking in a bar	3	30

Data Labeling: The labels for "partying" were added for each event by the participants of the event including the wearer of the camera every one second. The label "partying" was assigned if at least one person agreed, and the remaining part of the data was labeled as "others". By contrast, only the wearer labeled for "interested" because the state was wearer-dependent one. Similarly, other periods of time except for "interested" was assigned to "others". In total, 9580 time frames were provided for "partying" estimator, in which 324 time frames were labeled as "partying" and the rest of the dataset (9182) were "others". Regarding "interested" estimator, 292 time frames were labeled as "interested", while "9288" were "others". Due to the large unbalance in each dataset, we reduced the number of data of "others" to the same number as "partying" or "interested" with random sampling.

Feature Selection and Basic Estimator Performance: In Sect. 3.2, we specified the candidates of estimation features, in which 12 features were defined for both "partying" and "interested" estimators. However, the candidates may include redundant ones that can degrade the classification performance and over-consume processing power. So, we applied correlation-based feature subset evaluation method [4] for each feature groups, i.e., VAL and DoG, in combination with greedy stepwise forward selection of best feature subset. As a result, 11 features were selected from VAL features, while 7 were from DoG features. Table 2 shows the selected features. The results of 10 fold cross validation using RandomForest classifier were 0.810 and 0.731 in F-measures for "partying" and "interested" classification, respectively. Meanwhile, the F-measures of all (12) features were 0.805 and 0.731, respectively. So, the performance of "partying" estimator was slightly improved by selected features. However, the performance of "interested" estimator was not improved, and only one feature was removed.

Table 2. Selected features

For "partying" estimator (11 features)	For "interested" estimator (7 features)
$VAL_{100,5}$, $VAL_{500,5}$, $VAL_{1000,5}$, $VAL_{100,7}$, $VAL_{500,7}$, $VAL_{1000,7}$, R-$VAL_{100,5}$, $VAL_{500,5}$, $VAL_{1000,5}$, R-$VAL_{100,7}$, $VAL_{500,7}$	$DoG_{8,250}$, $DoG_{64,250}$, $DoG_{256,250}$ $DoG_{8,500}$, $DoG_{64,500}$, $DoG_{256,500}$ R-$DoG_{8,250}$

Integrating the Results of Two Estimators: The two binary classifiers judge if a given period of time represents the moments that make people who participated in the event feel pleasurable when they watch the images afterwards. A likelihood is obtained from the output of the binary classifier; we simply define the ratio of trees in RandomForest classifier that voted to "positive" class, i.e., "partying" and "interested", to the total number of trees as likelihood in the prototype implementation.

A single score, i.e., fine picture score (FPS), is obtained by weighted averaging. Here, the scores from the two classifiers are equally weighted as defined by Formula (1). To select output images, the system judges if the given moment should be accepted or rejected by applying a specific threshold against the fine picture score. In this paper, we do not apply thresholding. Instead, we investigate the relationship between subjects' ratings and the fine picture scores in next section.

$$FPS = 0.5 \times likelihood("partying") + 0.5 \times likelihood("interested") \quad (1)$$

4 Experiment

To understand the emotional effects by the system generated images, a user study was carried out.

4.1 Methodology

Three groups of three students participated to three different types of activities (Table 3). The group members know each other. One subject for each group wore the device and shot the video of the event, and another person became a wearer in another events. One event takes 15 to 20 mins.

One week after shooting, an interview session was held, where the participants rated 90 images (30 images × 3 events) from 1 (do not want to put it to their album at all) to 5 (definitely want to put it to their albums). The system calculated fine picture scores. In rating, pictures with various "fine picture score" were randomly selected and presented to the subjects in a random order. Note that the subjects did not know the fine picture scores that they were rating. Additionally, each wearer was asked to label the movie to either "partying", "interested", and "others" every one second to evaluate the accuracies of the two estimators.

Table 3. Different events performed in user study

Event	Characteristics
Walking	May not be watching conversation partner in talking
	Frequent and unstable gaze movement
	Shooting outdoors
Conversation at a table	My be watching conversation partner in talking
	Infrequent and unstable gaze movement
	Shooting indoors
Playing a table game	May not be watching conversation partner in talking
	Infrequent and periodic gaze movement
	Shooting indoors

4.2 Result

Impression on Pictures with Various Fine Picture Scores: Figure 2 shows the examples of pictures that have different levels of fine picture scores and user ratings. The pictures around the diagonal line from (0.0, 0.0) to (1.0, 1.0) indicate that the system's judgements are close to the subjects' feelings. Pictures B, E, and F have high subjects' ratings as supported by the subjects who argued that people in these pictures looked enjoying, although fine picture score of B is 0.00. By contrast, D and G have low user ratings because G was taken

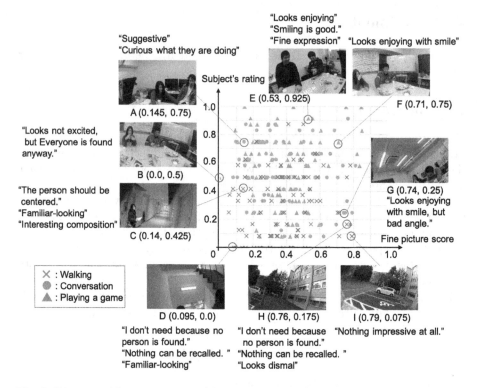

Fig. 2. Pictures with various pairs of fine picture score (the first element in the parentheses) and user rating (the second element). The subjects' comments are shown near each picture.

at too-much upper angle (bad angle) and no person is found (not impressive at all) in D although G has high system score (0.74).

Average correlation coefficients between system's judgements and subjects ratings per event are summarized in Table 4, which are calculated against the likelihood value of "partying" classification, "interested" classification, and fine picture score. The correlation coefficient of fine picture score does not show high correlation, i.e., the value for "walking" event (0.105) is the highest, and negative correlation exists in "conversation" event (−0.088). Regarding the likelihood of "partying" classifier, the value of "conversation" shows the highest (0.197), but negative correlation exists in "walking". Meanwhile, positive correlation is found only in "walking" (0.161) in the likelihood of "interested".

Figure 3 shows the breakdown of subjects' ratings per event category. One-way ANOVA shows that significant difference exists in the event types ($F(2, 267) = 3.03$, $p < 0.05$). The figure indicates that about half of the pictures in the "walking" category got negative impression of rating 1 or 2, while almost half of pictures in "gaming" had positive impression of rating 4 or 5. Opinions against pictures that all the subjects rated highest score "5" are "interesting moment was shot", "I can imagine their pleasurable moment as well as what they were doing", "I can understand the serious situation." By contrast, the pictures that had lowest score "1" were said that "none appears", "very blurred picture", "nothing impressive at all". Other comments from the subjects and the pairs of fine picture score and the subjects' ratings are mapped in Fig. 2.

Table 4. Correlation of system's judgements and subjects' ratings

	Walking	Conversation	Gaming
Likelihood of "Partying"	−0.023	0.197	0.167
Likelihood of "Interested"	0.161	−0.149	−0.097
Fine picture score	0.105	−0.088	0.077

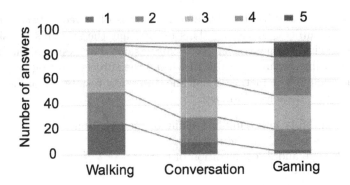

Fig. 3. The breakdown of subjects' ratings per event category. Rating 1 means that a subject does not want to keep the picture into his/her album, while he/she definitely do so in case of rating 5.

Accuracies of Two Estimators: Figure 4 shows box plots that show the difference in likelihood depending on the presence of labels from the subjects. In the figure, "Labeled" indicates that the subjects considered that the period of time was about (a) "partying" and (b) "interested", respectively. By contrast, "Not Labeled" means that no label was put by the subjects. Note that a period of time was labeled "partying" or "interested" if at least one subject agreed on. T-tests show that significant differences exist between "Labeled" and "Non Labeled" in the average of likelihood ($t(391) = 1.26 \times 10^{-76}$, $p < 0.05$ for "partying" and $t(7944) = 2.01 \times 10^{-4}$, $p < 0.05$ for "interested"). As shown in (a), there is a large difference depending on the presence of the label of "partying", which suggests that the system's estimation on the moment of "partying" is closer to the subjects' decision criteria than that of "interested".

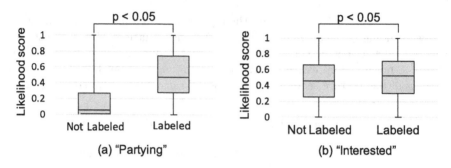

Fig. 4. Box plots of likelihood from user labeling.

5   Discussion

5.1   Factors that Affect Subjects' Rating of Pleasurable Moment

As shown in Fig. 2 and Table 4, little correlation is observed between fine shot scores and the subjects' decisions. This means that the system's decisions are not always consistent with the subjects' impressions. For example, picture G in Fig. 2 has high fine picture score (0.74), while the subject's rating is low (0.25) because the angle of the picture is not fine. Interview results reveal factors that degrades subjects' ratings as follows:

– High predictability and familiar-looking of the situation
– Small number of clues in the pictures
– Awkward angle and ill-composition of pictures
– Blurring pictures
– Small number of person in the picture
– Negative facial expression
– Duplication of pictures that are already presented

Subjects rated high score on the pictures that remind the subjects of the situations where a person who rarely tells a joke happened to do so and a weak game player accidentally won a game. This is because the situation is not predictable. By contrast, mundane situations failed in reminding the subjects of any special emotion and thus had low ratings (C, D). In addition to predictability, the number of clues in the picture may affect rating. Pictures H and I had opinions that they were not recallable and impressive, while a subject insisted that the deal in picture B reminded him of an exciting moment even though they were not smiling. These factors are content-dependent, which might be realized by image and audio understanding and person profiling based on big-data analysis.

As content-independent factors, awkward angle of pictures (G), ill-composed (C) and blurring pictures had low ratings. Duplication of pictures should also be avoided; actually, only the first pictures gained high ratings even though similar pictures existed. To remove such irrelevant pictures, blurry image detection [2] as well as keyframe selection [2,9] should be applied. Subjects liked pictures with more friends and fine facial expressions (B, E, F), rather than scenes without persons (D, H), which means the number of people and their facial expressions are important factors.

5.2   Difference in the Type of Engaged Events

As shown in Sect. 4.2, there is significant difference in the type of events. The "walking" category had lowest average rating. We consider that this comes from misidentification of "interested" moment. The periods of walking as his/her faces forward and standing still for a break might be judged as "interested" because the moment is determined based on the stability of frames in a video and very few camera fluctuation is observed during the period. Therefore, extra features that filter out such situation, i.e., the camera is stable but the user is not interested in anything, should be investigated. Other reasons could be because walking on the same old way did not provide any extraordinary scene and seeing friends from behind did not remind the subjects of any special emotion.

The event "gaming" obtained the highest average rating, which suggests that the subjects did not only remember pleasurable moments from the smiles in the picture, e.g., pictures E, F, and G in Fig. 2, but also the number of clues in the picture to recall the situation may affect rating as discussed in Sect. 5.1.

5.3   Integrating Fine Picture Scores of Two Aspects

Table 4 implies that an aspect of "interested" reflects the subjects' feelings in a situation with motion, e.g., "waling" although the correlation was very small. By contrast, an aspect of "partying" seems to fit the subjects' feelings in a situation with limited motion such as "conversation". We consider that this is because the gaze detected at a scene where it is always moving is more important than gaze detected at a scene with less motion. In addition, the degree of gaze in "conversation" or "gaming" tends to be always large, which makes it difficult to detect the moment that people are truly gazing with interest. Therefore, it is suggested that the influence of the aspect of "interested" becomes large in a situation where camera wearers move a lot, and that of "partying" increases in a situation with little movement. In this paper, the fine picture score is calculated with equally-weighted average of likelihood of these two aspects (see Formula (1)); however, the final score will be improved by changing the weight depending on the situations.

6   Conclusion

We proposed a system to extract still images from a first-person viewpoint video taken during a group activities to allow the members to recall pleasurable moments. The audio and video features that characterize the states of "partying" and "interested" are defined. Through a preliminary user study, we found content-independent factors that affect the likeability of the output images, as well as factors that need deep-understanding of the events in the picture and person profiling.

We are planning to enhance the system by dealing with content-independent factors such as the number of people, facial expression, angle, composition, and uniqueness of the moment.

Acknowledgment. This work was partially supported by a JSPS Grant-in-Aid for Scientific Research: 15K-00265.

References

1. Bolanos, M., Dimiccoli, M., Radeva, P.: Toward storytelling from visual lifelogging: an overview. IEEE Trans. Hum. Mach. Syst., 1–14 (2017). http://ieeexplore.ieee.org/document/7723826/
2. Chowdhury, S., McParlane, P.J., Ferdous, M.S., Jose, J.: "My day in review": visually summarising noisy lifelog data. In: Proceedings of the 5th ACM on International Conference on Multimedia Retrieval, ICMR 2015, pp. 607–610. ACM, New York (2015). http://doi.acm.org/10.1145/2671188.2749393
3. GoPro. Inc.: GoPro. http://gopro.com
4. Hall, M.A.: Correlation-based feature selection for machine learning. Ph.D. thesis, The University of Waikato (1999)
5. Healey, J., Picard, W., R.: StartleCam: a cybernetic wearable camera. In: Proceedings of the 2nd IEEE International Symposium on Wearable Computers, ISWC 1998, pp. 42–49 (1998)
6. Hodges, S., et al.: SenseCam: a retrospective memory aid. In: Dourish, P., Friday, A. (eds.) UbiComp 2006. LNCS, vol. 4206, pp. 177–193. Springer, Heidelberg (2006). http://link.springer.com/10.1007/11853565_11
7. Jinda-Apiraksa, A., Machajdik, J., Sablatnig, R.: A keyframe selection of lifelog image sequences. In: Proceedings of IAPR International Conference on Machine Vision Applications, Kyoto, pp. 33–36 (2013). http://www.mva-org.jp/Proceedings/2013USB/papers/03-04.pdf
8. Panasonic Corp.: A1H wearable camera. http://panasonic.jp/wearable/a1h/
9. Ratsamee, P., Mae, Y., Jinda-apiraksa, A., Horade, M., Kamiyama, K., Kojima, M., Arai, T.: Keyframe selection framework based on visual and excitement features for lifelog image sequences. Int. J. Soc. Robot. **7**(5), 859–874 (2015)
10. Sellen, A.J., Fogg, A., Aitken, M., Hodges, S., Rother, C., Wood, K.: Do life-logging technologies support memory for the past?: an experimental study using sensecam. In: Proceedings of the SIGCHI Conference on Human Factors in Computing Systems, CHI 2007, pp. 81–90 (2007). http://dl.acm.org/citation.cfm?id=1240636

Analytics Solution for Omni-Channel Merchandising

Chieh-Yu Liao, Chia-Chi Wu, Yu-Ling Hsu, and Yi-Chun Chen[(✉)]

Data Analytics Technology and Applications Research Institute,
Institute for Information Industry, Taipei City, Taiwan
{judyliao,arthurwu,ylhsu,divienchen}@iii.org.tw

Abstract. With the development of e-commerce, the business competition has risen significantly. Moreover, the channel of retail in Taiwan has evolved from single channel to multiple channels. Nowadays, customers' loyalties are not easy to retain due to a large number of choices of chain stores, warehouses, and e-commerce in the market. When a desired product is not available in one place, customers can still easily obtain it or choose the substitution by visiting other physical locations or the Internet, which results in loss of customer loyalty for a business. Therefore, as customer can easily change his mind in the multiple channels, how to rapidly understand customer needs is very important. This paper focuses on a development of omni-channel analytics solution platform using the field in cosmetics business as a demonstration. The platform provides business solutions to help corporations better understand their own brands and products sensibility in different merchandised channels, what customers really see and how they react. We provide a spectrum of techniques including data matching, aspect sentiment analysis, an integration and analysis of online auctions, online forums and social networks and other sources of data, such as real-time detection of sales trends or customers' evaluation and response of the goods. With these valuable information, an advantage of understanding market trends in order to immediately develop market strategies and advanced knowledge of various events influenced by positive and negative effects can all be expected to help the industries prevail against competitors and win public opinions.

Keywords: Omni-Channel merchandising · Data matching · Opinion mining

1 Introduction

If marketing has one goal, it's to reach the moments that's most influential to consumers' decisions. Every day, impressions of brands awareness developed from physical and digital touch points such as TV radio advertisements, social media, and conversations with friends and family (word of mouth), etc. These accumulated impressions then shape into initial consideration, which becomes a potential auction. Along with interested products in mind, consumers turn to social media for more researches or visiting in-store to have a clear visualization. In modern society, social network websites have become one of the major conduit for people to communicate, comment and interact with each other; potential buyers can share or learn about consumer products through platforms

© Springer International Publishing AG 2017
M. Antona and C. Stephanidis (Eds.): UAHCI 2017, Part III, LNCS 10279, pp. 457–470, 2017.
DOI: 10.1007/978-3-319-58700-4_37

and online reviews. After acquisition, consumers then share experiences and opinions toward the product as a reference for other future potential consumers.

Within the path of consumer journey (Fig. 1), consumers have enlarged its contact point of brands through different advertisement, yet a possibility loss in brand loyalty from competition might occurred. When a big interest hits a specific product, some channels faced an inventory shortage, which results in a possibility of consumers buying alternative products. For example, some portion of customers turn to Panasonic EH-NA65-K hair dryer when its competitor, Dyson Supersonic, was out of stock. Besides the issues of inventory shortage, competitive pricing also plays a big role in possible loss of brand loyalty. Due to uncertain market trends and easy access to various channels, brands have difficulty in pricing control and sales condition; therefore, some services have been proposed to help solve this challenge. For instant, Google Shopping [1] provides buyers a commodity parity analysis, but lack in sales and competitive analysis; 生意參謀 [2], a Chinese business analysis platform developed by Alibaba, provides business solution of sales, competitive products, and sentiment analysis for a single channel, yet information of multi-channel is missing. Therefore, So Fashion [3], an omni-channel commerce solution is developed to aids corporations enhance their sensibility towards the features of different merchandised channel in the market. It collects various retail channel transactions and consumers' reviews from multiple e-commerce platforms. Because dealing with inter-access road between the various commodity names are inconsistent, a proposal of data matching method is developed to help solving this problem.

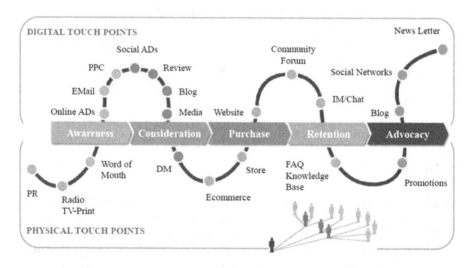

Fig. 1. An example of Path of consumer journey

Given that millions of products are sold, reviewed, and discussed on the internet, social media and shopping websites are important sources to collect sales information and user opinion. However, an issue of same item with different names sold by different merchants within different websites rise. Furthermore, such data is mostly not well structured and often contains missing or wrong values. For integrating and utilizing this kind of information on the internet, matching entities from heterogeneous data sources is an importance task. There are many studies aimed to overcome the entity matching challenge, such as Kannan et al. [5], Li et al. [8], and Zhang et al. [9]. There are also surveys of entity matching methods, such as Elmagarmid et al. [4], Köpcke and Rahm [6], and Köpcke et al. [7]. The difficulty of entity matching is varied among different types of entity. The difficulty levels of matching different entities evaluated according to related works and our experience are shown in Fig. 2.

Fig. 2. Difficulty levels of matching different entities

The rest of the paper is organized as follows: Sect. 2 defines the overall architecture of omni-channel merchandising analytics solution and Sect. 3 proposes So Fashion, a big data analytics solution for Omni-Channel Merchandising, using the field in cosmetics business as a demonstration. Concluding remarks are given in Sect. 4.

2   Proposed Framework

In this chapter, we describe our omni-channel merchandising analytics solution. Figure 3 shows the overall architecture of this solution. The solution is decomposed into three parts: data gathering, data matching method and analytics as a service. First, by using crawler technique, we implement our solution on real datasets in cleansers domain containing data from three auctions platform, i.e., Yahoo! Auction, Ruten Auction, and Taobao Auction and one forum, i.e., Urcosme. Second, we utilize data matching technique to deal with the product names inconsistencies problem on different channels. Then, by using some analysis methods, i.e., regression, principal component analysis, data mining, sentiment analysis etc., we provide three analytics as a service. We will describe data matching technique in detail in the following paragraphs.

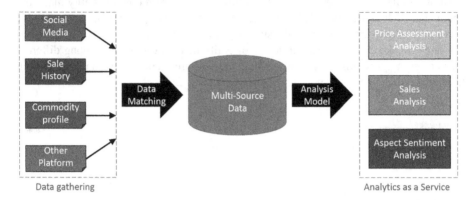

Fig. 3. Overall architecture for omni-channel merchandising analytics solution

Data matching, also called entity resolution, entity matching, duplicate identification, record linkage, or reference reconciliation, is the technique identifying different manifestations of the same real world object from different data source. The example of framework matching beauty products among auction sites in this paper is shown in Fig. 4. In this framework, we first generate a duplicate-free standard product list with a reference beauty website. For each offer in the auction sites, we estimated the total similarity between this offer and each product in the standard product list. We first match an offer to the most similar product in the standard product list, and then verify this matching with a classifier.

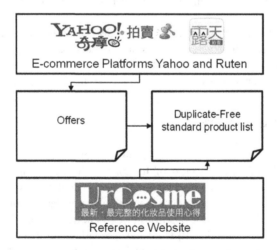

Fig. 4. The example of framework of data matching

There is an example of the standard product list in Fig. 5. We choose Urcosme (www.urcosme.com), a beauty product review website in Taiwan, as our reference website. For each beauty product in Urcosme, we collected the category, brand, and product name to generate a standard product list.

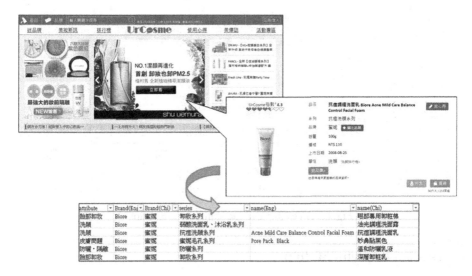

Fig. 5. An example of standard product list

Assume o_i is the ith offer in the auction sites, and sp_j is the jth product in the standard product list. $TS(o_i, sp_j)$, the similarity between o_i and sp_j, is estimated by:

$$TS(o_i, sp_j) = max(EBS(o_i, sp_j), CBS(o_i, sp_j)) \\ + max(EPS(o_i, sp_j), CPS(o_i, sp_j)),$$

where $EBS(o_i, sp_j)$, $CBS(o_i, sp_j)$, $EPS(o_i, sp_j)$, and $CPS(o_i, sp_j)$ are similarities of English brand, Chinese brand, English product, and Chinese product between o_i and sp_j, respectively which can be calculated by edit distance approaches. Different from traditional data matching tasks, the corresponding brand and product name of an offer in an auction website reside in an unstructured text and does not have attribute values with these offers. We used sliding windows to segment the title for each offer. An example is shown in Fig. 6. In this example, The Chinese brand of sp_{4236} is "蜜妮", and the title of o_{9566} is "Biore 蜜妮 抗痘調理洗面乳 100 g". To evaluate $CBS(o_{9566}, sp_{4236})$, the similarity of Chinese brand between sp_{4236} and o_{9566}, a sliding window with window size two is applied on the title, and generated segments "io", "or", "re", …, and "0 g". The similarity between each segment and "蜜妮" is calculated respectively, and the biggest one is the value of $CBS(o_{9566}, sp_{4236})$. The value of $EBS(o_i, sp_j)$, $EPS(o_i, sp_j)$, and $CPS(o_i, sp_j)$ are calculated likewise.

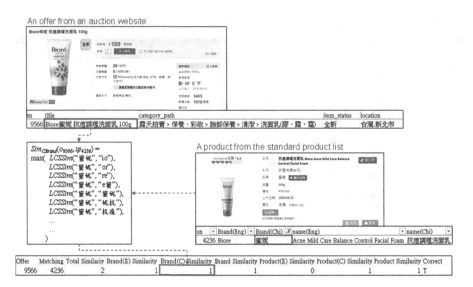

Fig. 6. An example of the similarity estimation

3   System Implementation

In this paper, we proposed So Fashion, a big data analytics solution for Omni-Channel Merchandising, using the field in cosmetics business as a demonstration. So Fashion collected various retail channel transactions and consumers' reviews from multiple e-commerce platforms and social networks. Through data analysis technique, So Fashion aids brand corporations enhance their sensibility towards the features of different merchandised channel in the market, supply and demand of the goods, as well as the competitions from the market. In this platform, it provides five analysis modules to help corporations better understand their own brands and products sensibility in different merchandised channels, what customers really see and how they react. Next, we introduce these analysis modules, respectively.

- Sales Ranking: Through integration and analysis of cross-border trading platform, this analytic service helps the business immediately manipulates the sale transactions, based on brand and category, of different channel. Figure 7 shows the variety of sales ranking. Moreover, an issue of different volume size of a same product can impact significantly in sales ranking. Therefore, we utilize a conduct of parser enable to separate and calculate the sales according to its volume, which provide the information about consumers purchasing trend in different trading platform. In the example of Fig. 7, due to selling 93 pieces of product samples, "全效活膚潔面乳" receives its second place in this week's ranking. In addition, we realize that product samples are most popular within C2C trading platform.

Fig. 7. An example of sales ranking

- Competitor Analysis: Based on consumer evaluation of commodity, this module explores the representative characteristics of products or brand competition. The competitor analysis module consists of two parts, Aspects of Competitor Comparison and Perceptual Bubble Chart. Certain types of documents, such as customer feedback or reviews, may contain fine-grained sentiment about different aspects of the entities (e.g. a product or brand) that are mentioned in the document. For instance, a review about a facial cleanser may contain opinionated sentences about its cleansing, moisturizing, price, ingredients, odor and other functionalities. This information can be highly valuable for understanding customers' opinion about a particular brand or product. Using the comparison of Aspect-based Sentiment Analysis, industry can better monitor their reputation, understand the needs of the market and comprehend the competitive advantage. Figure 8 shows the example of Aspects of Competitor Comparison. The radar chart shows evaluated aspects scores of each brand or product. The donut chart shows the percentage of particular aspect from different sources. In the Fig. 9, each of three colored bubbles represents three different competitors, and the grey bubbles means the representative characteristics of a brand or a product. There are three different connections within these bubbles. First, the closer concentration between colored and grey bubbles indicates the characteristics of each user's comments which are frequently discussed. The distance relationships between grey bubbles represents the correlation of numbers of time that are mentioned in comments. Last, the closer the colored circles are, the stronger associates and characteristics they have in common.

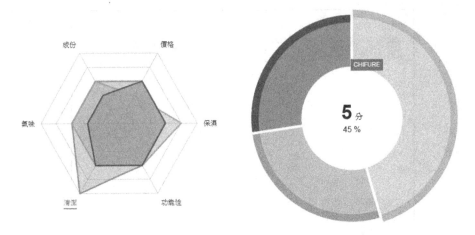

Fig. 8. An example of aspects of competitor comparison

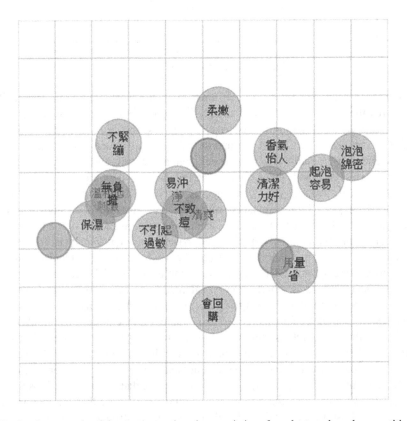

Fig. 9. An example of the representative characteristics of products or brand competition

- Sales Overview: In this analysis module, it provides the different level of transactions from brand, category to commodity and understands business position in various time interval by integrating and analyzing the cross-border large-scale e-commerce platform information. The information of brand's or commodity's historical sales and sales prediction is shown in Figs. 10 and 11, respectively. Figure 12 shows the association analysis of commodities, outer circle lists of commodities indicate what consumers also discussed along with acquisition. Figure 13 presents socio-demographic information about reviewers along with the reviews. It provides three types of reviewers' statistical information, i.e., age, skin and sign, for specific brand or merchandise.

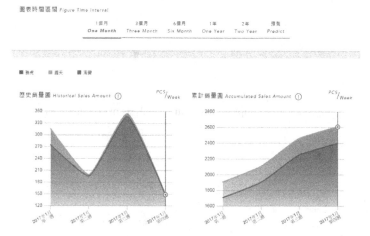

Fig. 10. An example of the information of brand's or commodity's historical sales

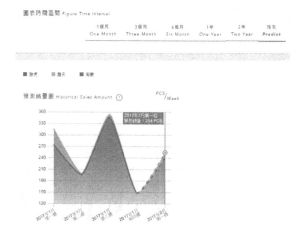

Fig. 11. An example of the information of brand's or commodity's sales prediction

Fig. 12. An example of association analysis of commodities

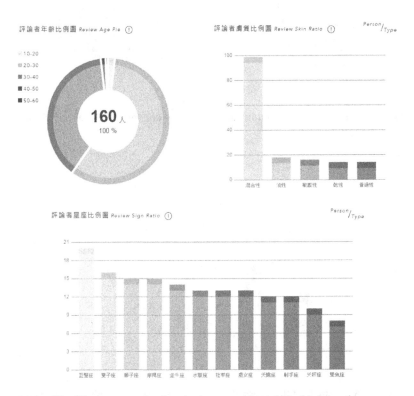

Fig. 13. An example of socio-demographic statistical information

- Price Comparison Analysis: In this analysis service, it provides users to search for products on online shopping websites and compare prices between different vendors. The example of price comparison result is shown in Fig. 14. Figure 15 presents the distributions of stores and sales by integrating the price information of commodity.

Fig. 14. An example of price comparison

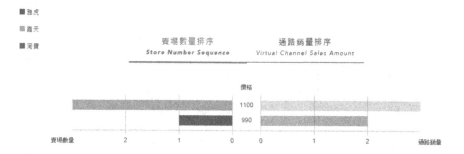

Fig. 15. An example of distributions of stores and sales

- Opinion Mining: Mining and summarizing opinions from users' reviews about specific brands or products and their aspects- can help brand industry decide what to businesses to better monitor their reputation and understand the needs of the market. Therefore, in this service, it provides three analysis results, product keywords, product aspect radar chart and the frequencies of commodity discussion. Tag clouds visualization application (Fig. 16) is the text-based visual representations of a set of tags shows the product keywords based on consumer experience posts/reviews from social network. Figure 17, product aspect radar chart, shows evaluated aspects scores of each brand or product. Moreover, it can list three positive and negative polarity representative sentences, respectively. Figure 18 shows the product discussion trend based on different time interval.

Fig. 16. An example of product keywords

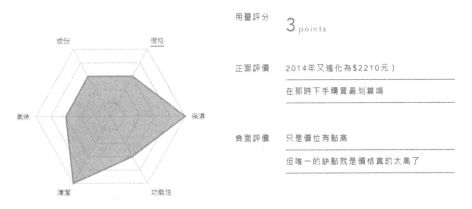

Fig. 17. An example of product aspects analysis

Fig. 18. An example of product discussion trend

4 Conclusions

In conclusion, the paper summarizes some important highlights. Our omni-channel merchandising solutions provide a better way for brand industries to maximize sales and shopper loyalty. In order to solve the problem of product names inconsistencies, we utilize data matching technique to identify different manifestations of the same real world object from different data source. Therefore, we propose a development of omni-channel analytics solution platform using the field in cosmetics business as a demonstration.

References

1. Google shopping. https://www.google.com/shopping
2. 生意參謀. http://sycm.taobao.com/portal/index.htm
3. So Fashion. http://sofashion.com.tw/cosmetic/login.html
4. Elmagarmid, A.K., Ipeirotis, P.G., Verykios, V.S.: Duplicate record detection: a survey. IEEE Trans. Knowl. Data Eng. **19**(1), 1–16 (2007)
5. Kannan, A., Givoni, I.E., Agrawal, R., Fuxman, A.: Matching Unstructured Product Offers to Structured Product Specifications (2011)
6. Köpcke, H., Rahm, E.: Frameworks for entity matching: a comparison. Data Knowl. Eng. **69**, 197–210 (2010)
7. Köpcke, H., Thor, A., Rahm, E.: Evaluation of entity resolution approaches on real-world match problems. Proc. VLDB Endowment **3**(1), 484–493 (2010)

8. Li, L., Li, J., Gao, H.: Rule-based method for entity resolution. IEEE Trans. Knowl. Data Eng. **27**(1), 250–263 (2015)
9. Zhang, D., Rubinstein, B.I.P., Gemmell, J.: Principled graph matching algorithms for integrating multiple data sources. IEEE Trans. Knowl. Data Eng. **27**(10), 2784–2796 (2015)

Temporal Evolution in Potential Functions While Peripheral Viewing Video Clips with/without Backgrounds

Masaru Miyao[1], Hiroki Takada[2(✉)], Akihiro Sugiura[3],
Fumiya Kinoshita[4], Masumi Takada[5], and Hiromu Ishio[6]

[1] Department of Information Engineering, Graduate School of Information
Science, Nagoya University, Furo-cho, Chikusa-Ku, Nagoya 464-8601, Japan
miyao@nagoya-u.jp
[2] Department of Human and Artificial Intelligent Systems, Graduate School
of Engineering, University of Fukui, 3-9-1 Bunkyo, Fukui 910-8507, Japan
takada@u-fukui.ac.jp
[3] Department of Radiology, Gifu University of Medical Science,
Seki 501-3892, Japan
[4] Institute of Innovation for Future Society, Nagoya University,
Nagoya 464-8601, Japan
[5] Faculty of Nursing and Rehabilitation Department, Chubu Gakuin University,
Seki 501-3993, Japan
[6] Fukuyama City University, Fukuyama 721-0964, Japan

Abstract. In daily life, stereoscopic image technology, such as 3D TV and movies, has become used in various places. Images, not limited to stereoscopic images, may exhibit unfavorable biological effects depending on the viewing and physical conditions, age, and individual differences. In our previous study, an increase was indicated in the sway values that were observed while/after peripheral viewing a stereoscopic video clip. Backgrounds are considered to affect our balance function. We examine the effect of the exposure to stereoscopic video clips without the background on our equilibrium function paper, and fifteen healthy young males voluntarily participated in the present study. Their stabilograms were recorded during monocular vision or binocular parallax vision using semipermeable smart glasses, where the subjects maintained the Romberg posture in stabilometry. We also measured the body sway with the subjects' eyes closed 0–3 min after the exposure to the video clips. We herein compare the temporal averaged potential functions to control the standing posture during the exposure to 2D/3D video clips with those after the exposure.

Keywords: Visually-Induced Motion Sickness (VIMS) · Stabilometry · Stereoscopic video clips · Background (BG) · Stochastic Differential Equation (SDE) · Temporally Averaged Potential Function (TAPF)

© Springer International Publishing AG 2017
M. Antona and C. Stephanidis (Eds.): UAHCI 2017, Part III, LNCS 10279, pp. 471–482, 2017.
DOI: 10.1007/978-3-319-58700-4_38

1 Introduction

In daily life, stereoscopic image technology, such as 3D TV and movies, has become used in various places. Binocular stereoscopic imaging methods markedly improved after 2009, and viewing of 3D contents for a prolonged period at home became common along with the sale of 3DTV, LCD, 3DPC, and game machines, in addition to 3D movies at movie theaters and theme parks. Stereoscopic imaging techniques have also become used for not only amusement but also in the industrial, medical care, and educational fields. In the industrial field, the techniques were introduced into 3DCAD, CAM, and CAE, and improved productivity and markedly shortened the development period. In the medical care field, stereoscopic images are useful to 3-dimensionally identify affected regions and lesions, improving the diagnostic accuracy and safety of surgery and reducing the stress of physicians, and are applied to medical 3DLCD and 3D endoscopic surgery support systems. However, images, not limited to stereoscopic images, may exhibit unfavorable biological effects depending on the viewing and physical conditions, age, and individual differences.

A body equilibrium function test, stabilometry, is considered useful to evaluate the equilibrium function. Stabilometry is generally performed on standing in Romberg's posture in which the feet are together and the eyes open and closed, and for 60 s each, sways of the center of pressure (CoP) are measured, which is regarded as a projection of the center of gravity. To increase the diagnostic value of stabilometry, measurement methods and analytical indices of stabilograms have been proposed such as area of sway, total locus length, total locus length per unit area, defined in Suzuki et al. [1]. The analytical indices include the total length of body sway and locus length per unit area. The latter is considered to represent micro changes in postural control and serve as a scale of proprioceptive postural control. Romberg's posture is an upright posture with the feet placed together. It is an unstable standing posture because the base of support is narrow, and so body sway becomes marked, and a reduced equilibrium function is likely to appear in stabilograms.

The methods to measure the influence of visually-induced motion sickness on the body include subjective psychological methods and physiological methods concerning autonomic nerve activity. Stereoscopic videos utilizing binocular stereoscopic vision often cause unpleasant symptoms of asthenopia, such as a headache and vomiting, depending on the audiovisual condition [2]. Simulator Sickness Questionnaire (SSQ) is the best known psychological measurement method to assess visually-induced motion sickness. This is comprised of 16 effective subjective items to assess simulator motion sickness extracted from 1,119 paired data on Motion Sickness Questionnaire (MSQ) measured before and after experiencing a simulator by factor analysis [3]. Visually-induced motion sickness (VIMS) is also assessed by physiological measurement methods using electrocardiography, blood pressure, respiratory rate, the number of eye blinks, electrogastrography, body sway, the resistance value of the skin, and perspiration [4–7]. It has been reported that the SSQ score was significantly increased from the pre-resting score by setting the interval between the bilateral heels at 17 cm in the group complaining of vibration load-induced motion sickness [7].

Although the mechanism of the symptoms does not have been elucidated and been unclear, our previous study showed an increase in sway values that were observed during peripheral viewing [8]. This result was supported by our subjective evaluation [9]. Especially in the background (BG), there is a large difference between human binocular image and artificial stereoscopic image to which our convergence corresponding to depth cues is not accommodated. That is why equilibrium function affects from peripheral viewing. In this study, we examine the effect of the exposure to stereoscopic video clips without the background on our equilibrium function.

2 Mathematical Models of Body Sway

To begin with, upright postures is considered to be instable. When humans maintain an upright posture, the body always sways. To ensure the posture, it is necessary to control the feet along a spatial perpendicular line from the center of gravity within the narrow base of support [10]. In the Romberg posture, the base supporting the body is the narrowest. The authors are investigating the instability of the systems to control upright posture which could become more instable on a tilting table [11].

Motion sickness symptoms can be identified by the stabilometry, and quantitation of the severity is being investigated. Stabilometry performed as a body balance function test is useful to diagnose and evaluate the stability of standing posture and its control system and balance disorders due to central diseases, as such it is useful to comprehensively investigate the balance function [1, 12]. In stabilometry, recording starts when the standing position stabilizes, and it is a simple 60-second test. To increase the diagnostic value of body sway, indices of stabilogram analysis were proposed including total length of the body sway and locus length per unit area [1, 12]. In addition to these, we proposed an index of stabilogram pattern analysis termed sparse density in consideration of the non-linearity of the posture control system [13], and apply it to quantitation of motion sickness [13–15].

Stabilograms represent a process accompanied by irregular swing components. Sways in the lateral and anteroposterior directions in stabilograms can be independently handled as recorded time-series [16]. Stochastic Differential Equation (SDE) is used as a mathematical model to describe body sway [17–20].

$$\frac{\partial x}{\partial t} = -\frac{\partial}{\partial x} U_x(x) + w_x(t), \tag{1}$$

$$\frac{\partial y}{\partial t} = -\frac{\partial}{\partial y} U_y(y) + w_y(t), \tag{2}$$

The time-series to be described is regarded as being produced by the Markov process, and when no abnormal diffusion is observed, the following formula is applied to the distribution in each measurement direction, G_z, and potential of the time-average, U_z, constituting SDE (z = x, y).

$$U_z(z) = -\frac{1}{2}\ln G_z(z) + const. \tag{3}$$

SDE (1) is capable of producing locally stable movement in the vicinity of the minimum of its potential surface, and a high density of measurement point, z, in the vicinity of the minimum is expected. This is considered dependent on the locus length per unit area, but the sparse density includes more local information in the measurement. In our analysis of stabilogram patterns, time and its hierarchy characteristic to the posture control system, which is difficult to theoretically elucidate can also be discussed by paying attention to microstructures observed in the time-average potential of the posture control system and numerical analysis by SDE. Nonlinearity of the right side first term has been discussed by us [20]. The stiffness control hypothesis [10] has begun to be reconsidered as in [21].

This new stabilogram pattern analysis method has already been applied to quantitate motion sickness induced by the blur of liquid crystal and stereoscopic viewing [8, 22–24]. Takada et al. discussed that peripheral vision contributed to an increase in the sway value [8], in which the period with an increase in sway was prolonged in resting with closed eyes after viewing corresponding to the duration of viewing [24].

3   Materials and Methods

Fifteen healthy young males (age, 21–24 years), who do not have had any otorhinolaryngologic or neurological diseases in the past, voluntary participated in this study. The experiment was sufficiently explained to the subjects, following which written consent was obtained from them.

In this experiment, the body sway was measured while viewing 2D/3D video clips with the use of semipermeable smart glasses that displayed content in the Sky Crystal (Olympus Memory Works Ltd. Co., Tokyo), which was modified with permission from the company and was used as the visual stimulus in this experiment. The stimulus includes spheres fixed in four corners, which supplies perspective. A sphere complexly ambulated in a video clip. The subjects stood on the detection stand of a stabilometer GS3000 (Anima Co. Ltd., Tokyo), without moving, with their feet together in the Romberg posture, for 30 s before the sway was recorded. Each sway of the CoP was then recorded at a sampling frequency of 20 Hz. The subjects were instructed to maintain the Romberg posture during the trials. For the first 60 s, the subjects were asked to do the following:

I. Gaze at a static circle with a diameter of 3 cm (Control).
II. Peripherally viewing video clips without pursuing the sphere.
III. Peripherally viewing video clips as same in II without the backgrounds (Fig. 1a)

The sphere of the video clip II ambulated in backgrounds with clues for visual depth (Fig. 1b).

We also measured body sway with eyes closed 0–3 min after the exposure to them, and the Post-stabilogram were composed every 1 min. We calculated sway values that

(a)

(b)

Fig. 1. One cut of the video clips without backgrounds (a) and with backgrounds (b) [24]

were obtained from stabilograms during/after exposure to video clips with/without the background (i.e. clouds in the sky/plain gray background).

The circle (I) was placed before the subjects, 2 m away, at their eye level. Stereoscopic video clips (II)/(III) and their monocular (2D) vision were shown to subjects on the binocular parallax 3D display. We measured the body sway and the subjective evaluation for each vision (I) Control, (II)-2D, (II)-3D, (III)-2D, and (III)-3D situation randomly, according to the abovementioned protocol.

We conducted the stabilometry with eyes open/closed. The experimental periods with eyes open and closed was designed in our experimental protocol to evaluate the severity of the VIMS during and after viewing the video clips. In stabilometry, the CoP on an x-y plane was recorded at each time step where x and y directions were defined as the right and the anterior axes on their faces, respectively. We herein examine whether the metamorphism is observed in the TAPF (2) by the motion sickness induced by peripherally viewing 3D video clips.

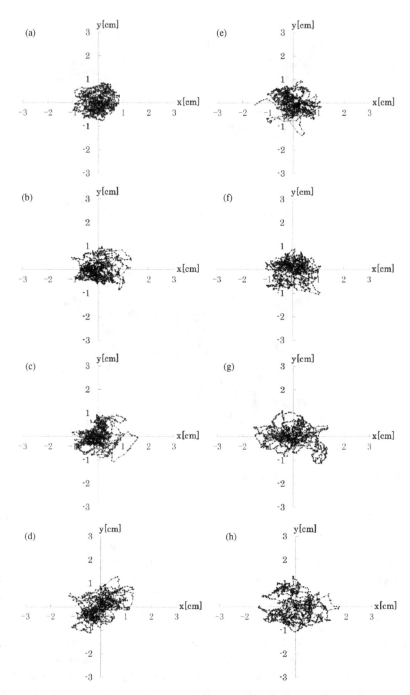

Fig. 2. Typical stabilograms while/after viewing 3D video clips with the backgrounds (a)–(d) and without the backgrounds (e)–(f): stabilograms with subjects' eyes' open (a), (e); stabilograms 0–1 after viewing a 3D video clip (b), (f); stabilograms 1–2 after viewing a 3D video clip (c), (g); stabilograms 2–3 after viewing a 3D video clip (d), (h)

4   Results

Stabilograms as in Fig. 2 were obtained for each experimental period from the time series of their CoP. Most stabilograms observed 0–2 min after viewing a 3D video clip with the background (II)-3D were dispersed compared with the control stabilograms. In contrast, no persistent tendency was observed in the stabilograms measured 2–3 min after the cutoff of the visual stimulus. However, most stabilograms observed 0–2 min after exposure to video clips without the background (III)-2D/3D were not dispersed compared with the control stabilograms. The stabilograms were dispersed three minutes after the cutoff of the visual stimulus.

Based on Eq. (3), the TAPFs have been estimated from distributions for all subjects (Fig. 3). Nonlinearity is often seen in the TAPFs as a mathematical expression of the equilibrium function [20]. However, we herein fit the parabolic functions to the TAPFs of x direction (Fig. 3a–d) and those of y direction (Fig. 3e–h) because the individual characteristics were not seen in this study. The graphs of the TAPFs obtained from stabilograms while viewing video clips (Fig. 3a, e) can be compared with those after viewing (Fig. 3b–d, f–h). A coefficient in higher degree was larger while viewing the 3D video clip with backgrounds than the others. This property disappeared 2–3 min after the exposure to the video clips.

5   Discussion

In the second last conference, we have reported the calculation results of the new index sparse density (SPD) and the previously stated sway values such as total locus length, area of sway, total locus length per unit area. These indices were calculated from each stabilogram recorded with the eyes open/closed. Any two of the following were assumed to be potentially important influencing factors: the solidity of the subjects' vision (2D/3D), existence of the backgrounds in the video clips, and persistence of the visual stimulus [24]. Regarding the description of body sway in the exposure to stereoscopic video clips, the mathematical model (1) was herein investigated, and we could observe temporal evolution in the potential function for the x-component after peripheral viewing the stereoscopic video clips (Fig. 3b–d). Specially, the nonlinearity could be also seen in the potential function for the y-component while peripheral viewing the video clips (Fig. 3e).

The complexity or the changes from control level could not be found in the potential function for the y-component while peripheral viewing the stereoscopic video clip with backgrounds (Fig. 3e). Our system to control upright posture might not be affect by the purtubation of backgrounds while viewing the 3D video clip on the surface and accumulate the influence of the purtubation on the equilibrium function. The nonlinearity could be also seen in the potential function for the y-component after peripheral viewing the 3D video clip with backgrounds (Fig. 3f).

In [24], a two-way analysis of variance (ANOVA) was conducted 15 times on these factors. In addition, the influence of the exposure to the video clips on our equilibrium system was investigated in comparison with the control data (I). The two-way ANOVA on the sway values did not reveal an interaction between any pair of two factors. According to the two-way ANOVA whose factors were set as the solidity and the

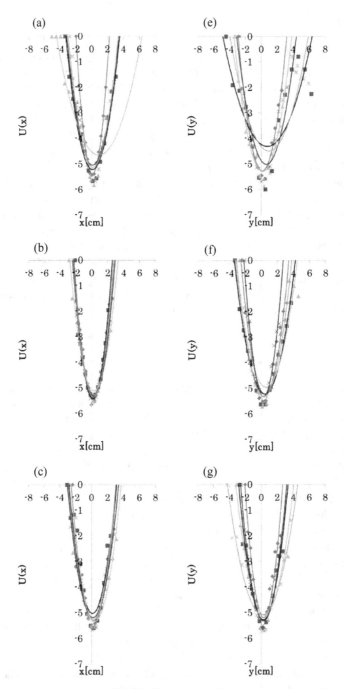

Fig. 3. TAPFs for *x*-component while/after viewing 2D/3D video clips (a)–(d) and for *y*-component (e)–(f): TAPFs were estimated from the stabilograms with subjects' eyes' open (a), (e); stabilograms 0–1 after viewing video clips (b), (f); stabilograms 1–2 after viewing video clips (c), (g); stabilograms 2–3 after viewing video clips (d), (h)

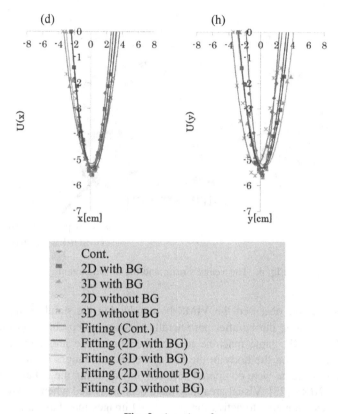

Fig. 3. (*continued*)

persistency, the former primary effect was observed from the total locus length per unit area during/after viewing the video clips with the background. Furthermore, the main effect of the background presence was observed from the total locus length per unit area during/after exposure to a 2D video clip in accordance with two-way ANOVA, whose factors were set to be the presence of the background and the persistency of the visual stimulus. We also found the same main effect while calculating the SPD S_3 during/after exposure to a 3D video clip, in accordance with two-way ANOVA.

The sway values, 0–2 min after the cutoff of the visual stimulus, also revealed that our equilibrium system was affected by the video clips with the background [24]. The sway values 2–3 min after the cutoff of the visual stimulus suggested that our equilibrium system was affected by the video clips with/without the background. The persistency of the upright posture might deteriorate in our equilibrium function. Conversely, the effect of the exposure to the video clips on our equilibrium function can be continued for 0–2 min. In contrast, the sway values 0–2 min after the cutoff of the visual stimulus suggested that our equilibrium system was not affected by the video clips without the background. Subjects tracked the sphere in the video clips owing to the absence of a background, and the VIMS did not occur by visual pursuit. Peripheral viewing could induce motion sickness, as our previous studies suggested.

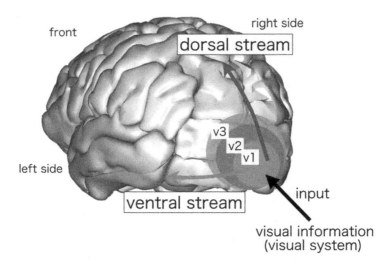

Fig. 4. The vental stream and the dorsal stream

In this study, we observed the VIMS by conducting the stabilometry. The sway values were evaluated during/after peripherally viewing video clips. On the contrast, we focused on a 3D game machine to increase knowledge about the influence of stereoscopic images on the body in the last conference. Changes in brain blood flow while playing the game were compared between playing using the 2D and 3D displays by measuring NIRS [25]. Visual area may have been activated when playing the game with 3D images compared to activation by 2D. 3D images may have a large influence on the left temporal lobe because thinking is required while playing the game.

It is known that there are two different cortial streams (vental and dorsal) as shown in Fig. 4. This division of visual information is traditionally separated into an object and spatial vision [26] or color/form and motion vision [27]. The later proceeds in an unconscious state, which may be corresponding to the 3D sickness induced by peripherally viewing. We will examine whether the exposure to sufficient loadings of 3D video clips affects the brain activity in the dorsal stream in the next step.

Acknowledgements. This work was supported in part by the Japan Society for the Promotion of Science, Grant-in-Aid for Scientific Research (B) Number 24300046 and (C) Number 26350004.

References

1. Suzuki, J., Matsunaga, T., Tokumatsu, K., Taguchi, K., Watanabe, I.: Q & A and a manual in stabilometry. Equipment Res. **55**, 64–77 (1996). (in Japanese)
2. Ukai, K., Howarth, P.A.: Visual fatigue caused by viewing stereoscopic motion images. Displays **29**, 106–116 (2008)
3. Kennedy, R.S., Lane, N.E., Berbaum, K.S., Lilienthal, M.G.: Simulator sickness questionnaire: an enhanced method for quantifying simulator sickness. Int. J. Aviat. Psychol. **3**, 203–220 (1993)

4. Himi, N., Koga, T., Nakamura, E., Kobashi, M., Yamane, M., Tsujioka, K.: Differences in autonomic responses between subjects with and without nausea while watching an irregularly oscillating video. Auton. Neurosci. Basic Clin. **116**, 46–53 (2004)
5. Holomes, S.R., Griffin, M.J.: Correlation between heart rate and the severity of motion sickness caused by optokinetic stimulation. J. Psychophysiol. **15**, 35–42 (2001)
6. Yokota, Y., Aoki, M., Mizuta, K.: Motion sickness susceptibility associated with visually induced postural instability and cardiac autonomic responses in healthy subjects. Acta Otolaryngol. **125**, 280–285 (2005)
7. Scibora, L.M., Villard, S., Bardy, B., Stoffregen, T.A.: Wider stance reduces body sway and motion sickness. In: Proceedings of VIMS 2007, pp. 18–23 (2007)
8. Takada, M., Fukui, Y., Matsuura, Y., Sato, M., Takada, H.: Peripheral viewing during exposure to a 2D/3D video clip: effects on the human body. Env. Health Prev. Med. **20**(2), 79–89 (2015)
9. Takada, M., Miyao, M., Takada, H.: Subjective evaluation of peripheral viewing during exposure to a 2D/3D video clip. In: Proceedings of IEEE VR 2015, pp. 291–292 (2015)
10. Winter, D.A., Patla, A.E., Prince, F., Ishac, M.: Stiffness control of balance in quiet standing. J. Neurophysiol. **80**, 1211–1221 (1998)
11. Fukui, Y., Mori, Y., Kinoshita, F., Takada, H.: A study of body sway on slopes with tilt angles of 10° and 20°. IEICE Technical rep., vol. 114, no. 361, pp. 7–10 (2014)
12. Okawa, T., Tokita, T., Shibata, Y., Ogawa, T., Miyata, H.: Stabilometry: significance of Locus Length Per Unit Area (L/A). Equipment Res. **54**(3), 283–293 (1995)
13. Takada, H., Kitaoka, Y., Ichikawa, M., Miyao, M.: Physical meaning on geometrical index for stabilometry. Equipment Res. **62**, 168–180 (2003)
14. Shimizu, Y., Takada, H., Kitaoka, Y., Nakayama, M.: Degrees of deterministic of sway of center-of-gravity with alcoholic intake. Equipment Res. **66**(1), 1–8 (2007)
15. Takada, H., Kitaoka, Y., Miyao, M., Matsuura, Y.: To set up standards for new indices in stabilometry. In: Proceedings of the 5th International Workshop on Biosignal Interpretation, pp. 203–206 (2005)
16. Goldie, P.A., Bach, T.M., Evans, O.M.: Force platform measures for evaluating postural control: reliability and validity. Arch. Phys. Med. Rehabil. **70**, 510–517 (1986)
17. Collins, J.J., De Luca, C.J.: Open-loop and closed-loop control of posture: a random-walk analysis of center of pressure trajectories. Exp. Brain Res. **95**, 308–318 (1993)
18. Newell, K.M., Slobounov, S.M., Slobounova, E.S., Molenaar, P.C.: Stochastic processes in postural center of pressure profiles. Exp. Brain Res. **113**, 158–164 (1997)
19. Emmerrik, R.E.A., Van Sprague, R.L., Newell, K.M.: Assessment of sway dynamics in tardive dyskinesia and developmental disability: sway profile orientation and stereotypy. Mov. Disord. **8**, 305–314 (1993)
20. Takada, H., Kitaoka, Y., Shimizu, Y.: Mathematicha index and model in stabilometry. Forma **16**, 17–46 (2001)
21. Asai, Y., Tasaka, Y., Nomura, K., Nomura, T., Casadio, M., Morasso, P.: A model of postural control in quiet standing: robust compensation of delay-induced instability using intermittent activation of feedback control. PLoS ONE **4**(7) (2009). Article no. e6169
22. Takada, H., Fujikake, K., Omori, M., Hasegawa, S., Watanabe, T., Miyao, M.: Reduction of body sway can be evaluated by sparse density during exposure to movies on liquid crystal displays. In: Proceedings of International Federation for Medical and Biological Engineering (IFMBE), vol. 23, pp. 987–991 (2008)
23. Takada, H., Miyao, M.: Visual fatigue and motion sickness induced by 3D video clip. Forma **27**, S67–S76 (2012)

24. Takada, H., Mori, Y., Miyakoshi, T.: Effect of background viewing on equilibrium systems. In: Antona, M., Stephanidis, C. (eds.) UAHCI 2015. LNCS, vol. 9176, pp. 255–263. Springer, Cham (2015). doi:10.1007/978-3-319-20681-3_24
25. Takada, M., Mori, Y., Kinoshita, F., Takada, H.: Changes in brain blood flow by the use of 2D/3D games. In: Antona, M., Stephanidis, C. (eds.) UAHCI 2016. LNCS, vol. 9739, pp. 516–523. Springer, Cham (2016). doi:10.1007/978-3-319-40238-3_49
26. Ungerleider, L.G., Mishkin, M.: Two cortical visual systems. In: Ingle, D.J., Mansfield, R.J.W., Goodale, M.A. (eds.) The Analysis of Visual Behavior, pp. 549–586. MIT Press, Cambridge (1982)
27. Van Essen, D.C., Maunsell, J.H.R.: Hierarchical organization and functional streams in the visual cortex. Trends Neurosci. 6, 370–375 (1983)

Camera Canvas: Photo Editing and Sharing App for People with Disabilities

Trung Ngo[1], Christopher Kwan[2], and John Magee[1(✉)]

[1] Department of Math and Computer Science, Clark University, 950 Main Street,
Worcester, MA 01610, USA
{trngo,jmagee}@clarku.edu,
[2] Department of Computer Science, Boston University,
111 Cummington Mall, Boston, MA 02215, USA
ckwan@cs.bu.edu

Abstract. We are motivated to make the interaction between a computer and people with disabilities better with more flexible interactions in their activities. Camera Canvas, the existing photo drawing and editing desktop software for motor-impaired individuals to operate a computer mouse, has been integrated well in the mouse-replacement interface, Camera Mouse. Therefore, our approach is to optimize Camera Canvas for the sake of helping gain a better experience in tailoring local photos/images. With more image filtering designed in computer vision techniques, Camera Canvas enhances better user experience. We conducted user studies with a few users without disabilities, who didn't operate or operated Camera Canvas with Camera Mouse. We have initiated features of social media sharing in the software, and evaluation of social media integration is planned for future work. Our ongoing work includes conducting additional user studies and optimizing the software based on feedback or survey.

Keywords: Assistive technology · Mouse-replacement interfaces · Accessible interfaces · Photo editing · Image filtering · Social media sharing

1 Introduction

The individuals who cannot speak or use their hands to operate a computer mouse are extremely limited in their means of communication. Our goal is to design the image-editing software that contributes to this group of users for their sakes of communication and emotional expression. The process of developing Camera Canvas helps us gain knowledge about user interface design for the people with motor impairments [1, 2].

Integrating Camera Canvas with the camera-based mouse-replacement interfaces, especially the Camera Mouse input system [3], would gain a significant impact for the people with disabilities, by enabling them to control the mouse pointer by other facial movements such as moving their eyes, nose in front of a camera. A click is registered when the user keeps the mouse pointer within a small radius of the item to be selected, for a certain amount of time, one second. It's known that Camera Canvas can be also used with other camera-based mouse-replacement interfaces [4, 5]. There have been

© Springer International Publishing AG 2017
M. Antona and C. Stephanidis (Eds.): UAHCI 2017, Part III, LNCS 10279, pp. 483–491, 2017.
DOI: 10.1007/978-3-319-58700-4_39

other kinds of apps designed for use with Camera Mouse, where apps have been developed to enable the motor-impaired to create drawings: EaglePaint [1] is a program designed to draw freeform lines, EyeDraw is a one designed with an infrared eye tracker, and VoiceDraw is a drawing program, which makes drawing lines created from different sounds of users. Customizable [6] and automated [7] user interfaces have also been made for people with motor impairments.

Our approach was to develop a program that gives users photo-editing, filtering and sharing capabilities and that an interface would be customized extensively for further advanced tasks [1]. In fact, some users have better control of their movements along the axes [8], but some users only maneuver their movement well within a certain range. Therefore, we took into account that our program needs to be highly configured for a wide range of user groups.

The first version of Camera Canvas was designed to such a level that many users could participate in various tasks—drawing, editing, configuring the toolbar, and even playing simple games that could be highly interesting when being integrated with other mouse-replacement interfaces, especially Camera Mouse. However, we found the photo-editing task more potentially extensible. In fact, we proposed more image-filtering tasks that could be functioned for editing the local or self-drawing photos. And, we introduced color inversion, color rotation, corner detection and a few other techniques involved in this second version. Furthermore, given that Camera Canvas is a configurable desktop app, which could utilize the built-in computer system device like a webcam, we implemented the camera capture that runs a facial detection after a capturing the users' face.

2 Software Overview and Methods

2.1 Configuration and Toolbar

Camera Canvas has three configurable settings in the Settings menu: toolbar placement, button size, and toolbar sliding speed [1]. An example main menu is shown in Fig. 1. The placement and orientation of the toolbar are adjusted from horizontally top to

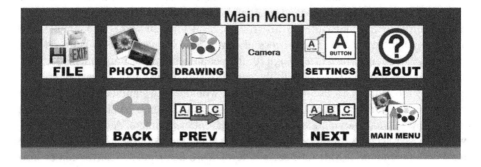

Fig. 1. Camera Canvas in default settings main menu with a horizontal top layout and smaller buttons. The below set of prev and next buttons indicates that there are more buttons off-screen.

vertically right (Fig. 2). Each setting constrains the mouse movement primarily along a single axis and in a single area of the screen so that users could gain more flexibility in controlling the setting toolbar in different areas of the screen [1]. Furthermore, we have added the Camera button as the main additional feature in the default Settings toolbar.

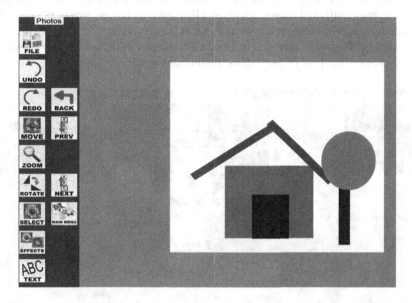

Fig. 2. User interface of Camera Canvas in photo-editing mode with the vertical left-sided photo settings toolbar.

2.2 Photo-Editing Tools

The originating version of Camera Canvas makes the drawing straight lines and geometric shapes plausible and creative for the people with disabilities thanks to the inspiration of drawing in EyeDraw [9]. For the Photo-editing mode, the originating version of Camera Canvas features several interaction techniques to make common photo-editing tasks possible. In specific, the Rotate tool uses a customized user interface component in Visual Studio, the IDE for our software suite, called a Choice Form, and it is equivalent to components such as sliders or small increment arrows, which are usually challenging for users controlling the mouse pointer.

There were several interaction techniques available in the first version of Camera Canvas, which common photo-editing tasks such as the rotation. For example, the Rotate tool uses a custom user interface component called a Choice Form that is easier for the motor-impaired having difficulties controlling the traditional mouse pointer. The middle of the Choice Form contains a preview of the titrated image, so the user could preview its effect before commenting the task.

2.3 Image Filtering

The updated version of Camera Canvas focuses more on introducing new features related to the image-filtering, photo-effect techniques (Fig. 3). Ranged from the simple task to more complex, intriguing ones, the new features include grayscale conversion, color inversion, color shift, and corner detection. Here, each technique was implemented in the same user interface design choice as those in the original version. In specific, each of these image filtering features has its Choice Form under the Effects button's directory with the preview mode of displaying the preliminary result of change.

Fig. 3. A grayscale-transformed image shown within our editing interface. The previous version of our interface also provided an interactive contrast control mechanism.

The first feature is grayscale transform, which turns the color image into a light intensity image. The human visual system is more attuned to intensity changes than color changes, therefore this mode may be beneficial for individuals with minor visual impairments in addition to possible motor impairments of our intended users. The ability to interactively adjust the contrast allows the user to manipulate the image in a way that they can explore details that might not be readily visible to them in the original color images. Figure 3 shows the straightforward result for the imported color image of a flower after using the grayscale feature combined with the contrast adjustment in the Preview mode.

The second feature, color inversion, is the task to transform each color components of the RGB (red-green-blue) values in the edited photo to its inverted values correspondingly. This technique creates a negative image, like what one would see on a physical film negative. In each color spectrum, dark areas become light, and light areas become dark. The negative technique may further be used to explore areas of the photograph that are not readily visible to the user in the original image. This approach may also be used by users for artistic effect. Figure 4 displays an inverted image alongside its original.

Fig. 4. The picture of a cat hanging on the tree branch in the original view (right) and after the color inversion process (left). (Color figure online)

The color shift also manipulates the RGB color values in the current. For example, Fig. 4 has many areas with a high amount of green color, which could be transformed more blueish after being processed by the blue color shift. We implemented three subtasks for the color rotation task since we want to examine all three color shift operations: red, green and blue. Like the previous features, this technique could be used for visual effect or to allow a user to explore details within the image. Figure 5 shows an image that has been manipulated by color shift and rotated.

Corner detection is also designed as a photo-effect feature (Fig. 6). This effect uses Canny Edge Detector to find the gradient edges and threshold these gradient values at zero. So, any pixel points which are not actually on the object edges would be set to zero, as to detect the outer line in the output using the Canny operator. Therefore, the effect creates a "sketch" of user's physical outer edges in white pixels on a black background. This effect was included to demonstrate a possible dramatic artistic style element as well as provide a way to explore the important edges in an image.

Fig. 5. The result of a self-made picture after being processed by color shift integrated with rotation of 180°.

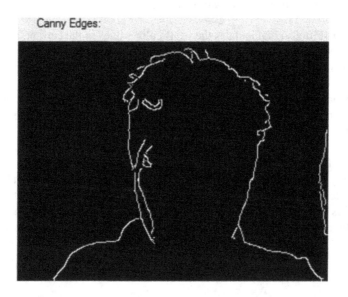

Fig. 6. The screenshot of our face run through the Camera Capture window application with the selected Canny Edge Detector

2.4 Camera Capture

We thought about the idea of getting interactions between the native software like Camera Canvas, and any mouse-replacement systems such as the compatible Camera Mouse. Their relation could produce the preliminary implementation of the additional feature called Camera Capture, which makes the use of the built-in webcam in the computer system.

Camera Capture starts with a task button in the Photo-editing setting toolbar with its similar name. When the user selected the button, he/she allows the computer to authorize the use of a webcam in the system. Camera Capture's user interface is designed more as a standalone program, which has its own Windows application, and Camera Capture consists of a few different Windows forms, most importantly the video capture form built in by the open-source library of C# for computer vision—Emgu. Camera Capture applies the famous feature classifier for object detection, the HAAR Cascading, which is used to distinguish the positive and foreground images with the negative ones by integrating it with Canny Edge detection in the given input. Canny Edge detection is also an alternative technique of corner detection, and basically it detects the outer edges of the foreground image alone and blacken the rest of the portrait.

2.5 Social Media Sharing

After completing a few important feature for enhancing more interactions in the photo-editing toolkit, we aimed at adding an advanced feature involving the tasks of social media sharing. In fact, the implementation for social media sharing feature is still under the construction for a few tasks for different social media platforms. We already registered the application on Facebook and Twitter platforms, so that Camera Canvas would hopefully connect more participants to each other, especially the group of people with disability but needs some attachment or connection under certain means. We are working to finish the photo-uploading and sharing tasks and test them on these platforms. Therefore, Camera Canvas featuring the social media interaction will be introduced soon.

3 Experimental Evaluation

We performed an informal observational evaluation of our new features in the Camera Canvas with seven participants.

The participants of our experiment in general found the program easy to use without prior experience using the Camera Mouse with other apps nor their background in understanding these image filtering techniques. The users expressed their interests in seeing how the edge background or give the benign feedback on the possible improvement for the visual look of the user interface.

We divided the subject roughly into two groups for software testing: a group for direct use of Camera Canvas and another one for integration of other mouse-replacement systems like Camera Mouse. For the tracking configuration in Camera Mouse, we set the feature tracking on each user's nose because it is large enough to stabilize the tracking movement throughout the testing.

The first group which consists of 4 users was assigned just to evaluate the Camera Canvas tended to feel a little easier to maneuver these tasks than the latter thanks to the traditional use of a mouse pointer when the first can operate the mouse manually. However, the latter, which consists of 3 users, found integrating with Camera Mouse more interacting and more flexible to complete some tasks in Camera Canvas. They all were allowed to run different tasks in Camera Canvas. Most of them liked the image filtering set of tasks because of its variability. The first two subjects enjoyed playing around with the feature of corner detection, where they were able to see through their facial shape in the interesting background of black and white theme. However, the last subject found the Color Rotation feature insignificant because the output image wasn't lucid enough in some cases for he to grasp the difference. But he tried playing around a lot on the feature of Camera Capture, and he enjoys adjusting different variables appeared in the separate Window form.

4 Ongoing Work

Our added features have been performed well for most of the users since the tasks are straightforward and quite simple. However, these, especially Camera Captures needs to get additional user studies of the group of people with disabilities as well as more amount of tests. We also plan to evaluate Camera Canvas with additional mouse-replacement interfaces. With more involvement of people with disabilities, we can modify or optimize the software to extend its accessibility to a higher, larger group of people.

We are also taking the designation of the operating system into consideration. Since Camera Canvas have only available in Windows and only as the desktop app, our motivation is to refactor the program, so it would be compatible, ready for installation, and deployed in Mac OS, Linux as well as in potentially mobile phones.

Acknowledgements. We would like to thank our participants for their valuable feedback and Wenxin Feng for her assistance during user studies.

References

1. Kwan, C., Betke, M.: Camera canvas: image editing software for people with disabilities. In: Proceedings of the 14th International Conference on Human-Computer Interaction (HCI International 2011), Orlando, Florida (2011)
2. Kwan, C., Paquette, I., Magee, J., Betke, M.: Adaptive sliding menubars make existing software more accessible to people with severe motion impairments. Univ. Access Inf. Soc. **13**(1), 5–22 (2014)
3. Betke, M., Gips, J., Fleming, P.: The camera mouse: visual tracking of body features to provide computer access for people with severe disabilities. IEEE Trans. Neural Syst. Rehabil. Eng. **10**(1), 1–10 (2002)
4. Gorodnichy, D., Dubrosky, E., Ali, M.: Working with computer hands-free using Nouse perceptual vision interface. In: Proceedings of the International CRB Workshop on Video Processing and Recognition, (VideoRec 2007). NRC, Montreal (2007)

5. Manresa-Yee, C., Varona, J., Perales, F.J., Negre, F., Muntaner, J.J.: Experiences hands-free interface. In: Proceedings of the 10th International ACM SIGACESS Conference on Computers and Accessibility, pp. 261–262. ACM, New York (2008)

6. Gajos, K.Z., Weld, D.S., Wobbrock, J.O.: Automatically generating personalized user interfaces with supple. Artif. Intell. **174**(12–13), 910–950 (2010)

7. Magee, J., Betke, M.: HAIL: hierarchical adaptive interface layout. In: Miesenberger, K., Klaus, J., Zagler, W., Karshmer, A. (eds.) ICCHP 2010. LNCS, vol. 6179, pp. 139–146. Springer, Heidelberg (2010). doi:10.1007/978-3-642-14097-6_24

8. Connor, C., Yu, E., Magee, J., Cansizoglu, E., Epstein, S., Betke, M.: Movement and recovery analysis of a mouse-replacement interface for users with severe disabilities. In: 13th International Conference on Human-Computer Interaction (HCI International 2009), San Diego, CA (2009)

9. Hornof, A.J., Cavender, A.: EyeDraw: enabling children with severe motor impairments to draw with their eyes. In: Proceedings of ACM CHI 205: Conference on Human Factors in Computing System, pp. 161–170. ACM, New York (2005)

Evaluation of Cerebral Blood Flow While Viewing 3D Video Clips

Masumi Takada[1], Keisuke Tateyama[2], Fumiya Kinoshita[3],
and Hiroki Takada[2(✉)]

[1] Faculty of Nursing and Rehabilitation Department, Chubu Gakuin University,
Seki 501-3993, Japan
[2] Department of Human and Artificial Intelligent Systems, Graduate School
of Engineering, University of Fukui, 3-9-1 Bunkyo, Fukui 910-8507, Japan
takada@u-fukui.ac.jp
[3] Institute of Innovation for Future Society,
Nagoya University, Nagoya 464-8601, Japan

Abstract. The technology provides an enhanced visual experience with realistic scene portrayal, but is known to cause motion sickness when stereoscopic video clips of rotating or blurred images are viewed. Viewers complain of symptoms such as eye fatigue, nausea, and dizziness. The underlying cause of these symptoms has not been identified; therefore, an investigation to determine the mechanism for the motion sickness is necessary. Previous stabilometry studies have reported that 3D sickness is induced by a peripheral viewing of stereoscopic video clips as opposed to the visual pursuit. In this study, the author investigated the influence of 3D recognition on brain activity. Functional near-infrared imaging (fNIRS) was used to determine if either peripheral viewing or visual pursuit changes brain activity. Stabilograms and eye movement were simultaneously recorded while the subject viewed video clips to confirm that the actual visual recognition method in use corresponded to our instructions. Using the fNIRS technique, cerebral blood flow was measured while the subject viewed stereoscopic video clips with and without a background. Following a preliminary test with the subject's eyes closed (baseline), changes in the concentration of oxygenated hemoglobin were measured. This test was performed for 70 s, with and without backgrounds, while the subject peripherally viewed a moving sphere. Compared to the baseline test, the concentration of oxygenated hemoglobin in the occipital lobe increased significantly during a viewing for both background cases. The result is consistent with both visual recognition methods. Furthermore, for both background cases, the concentration in the upper occipital lobe significantly increased during peripheral viewing versus visual pursuit. Peripheral viewing might enhance the activity in the dorsal stream, which could serve as an indication to the mechanism causing 3D sickness.

Keywords: Functional near-infrared imaging (fNIRS) · Stabilograms · Eye movement · Peripheral viewing · Visual pursuit

© Springer International Publishing AG 2017
M. Antona and C. Stephanidis (Eds.): UAHCI 2017, Part III, LNCS 10279, pp. 492–503, 2017.
DOI: 10.1007/978-3-319-58700-4_40

1 Introduction

When viewing images in film, television, mobile game consoles, etc., symptoms of motion sickness such as eye fatigue, nausea, and dizziness may occur. Though the mechanism for symptoms of such visually induced motion sickness is unknown, shaking images and recognizing rotation are said to be the causes. In recent years, it is possible to view three-dimensional (3D) images not only in 3D films at movie theaters and attractions in amusement parks, but also at home through 3D television, mobile game consoles, and head mounted displays. Compared to the past, when 3D images could only be viewed in limited locations, the technology has become more common, and opportunities to view 3D images have increased. 3D sickness is being reported as 3D images that enhance virtual reality have become more prevalent. Investigating causes and countermeasures is increasingly urgent from a public health point of view.

Sensory conflict theory is a well-known explanation for the cause of visually induced motion sickness. The theory describes a discrepancy between visual cues and cognition of vestibular/somatosensory sensations that triggers sickness [1] (as when visual information indicates motion while the body is actually stationary. There are other theories such as vergence-accommodation mismatch and poison theory, but these fail to elucidate the cause in sufficient detail. At present, studies on the impact 3D images have on the body are insufficient. Therefore, further accumulation of empirical studies is essential.

It has been confirmed in a stabilometry that compared to tracking a target while viewing 3D images, using peripheral vision for the entire screen triggers 3D sickness more readily [2]. Therefore, in this study, to elucidate the cause for 3D sickness, we examined the impact of viewing 3D images on brain activities and used functional near-infrared spectroscopy (fNIRS) to measure potential changes in brain activities during tracking and using peripheral vision for comparison. Also, we measured eye movements to confirm whether subjects were tracking or using peripheral vision while viewing images.

2 fNIRS

fNIRS uses a property of hemoglobin in which near-infrared light is absorbed, and can measure the rate of blood flow in a body noninvasively. When fNIRS is applied to the brain, it is able to measure changes in cerebral blood from within 2–3 cm from the scalp and identify activated sites. In other words, fNIRS is a test that can capture temporal changes in activation reaction of cerebral cortex accompanied with biological activities in a comprehensive and noninvasive manner [3–9].

Visible light with a wavelength of 400–700 nm has a high absorption of hemoglobin and other biological constituents, and since wavelength longer than near-infrared light absorbs more water, infrared light cannot move directly through the body. However, the absorption rate of hemoglobin in near-infrared light with a wavelength of 700–900 nm is higher than that of water. In this range of wavelength, extinction coefficients of oxygenated hemoglobin and deoxygenated hemoglobin are different, and the isosbestic point is near 805 nm. fNIRS uses multiple wavelengths for spectroscopic measurement and calculates concentrations of oxygenated hemoglobin and deoxygenated hemoglobin in blood [mg/L], and the total hemoglobin, which is the sum of the two [8].

3   Experimental Methods

3.1   fNIRS Measurements

We performed our experiment on 14 healthy males and females whose age ranged between 20 to 26 (mean ± standard deviation: 21.0 ± 1.8). The 3D image used for the experiment was recreated based on Sky Crystal (Olympus Memory Works Corp, Tokyo) with permission (Fig. 1). For fNIRS measurements, we used LABNIRS (Shimadzu Corporation, Kyoto). Images were displayed using 3D Display 55UF8500 (LG, Seoul). Measurements were taken in a darkroom, and subjects were seated for the experiment (Fig. 2). Subjects wore a head holder with transmission and reception probes. We used ch 1–ch 48 so that channels were arranged across the entire cerebral surface (Fig. 3). Following the 70-s test with eyes closed (Pre), subjects tracked 3D images for 70 s and used peripheral vision for another 70 s. These series were continued in five sets, and changes in cerebral blood flow were measured at 55 Hz. Two types of 3D images (with and without background) were used. A low-pass filter of 0.15 Hz was applied to the concentration of oxygenated hemoglobin obtained in the experiment to smooth the high-frequency component to calculate the integral value.

(a)   (b)

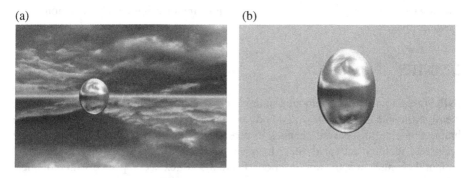

Fig. 1. Visual Stimulus; an image with background (a), an image without background (b)

Fig. 2. The visual distance was set to be 1.86 m.

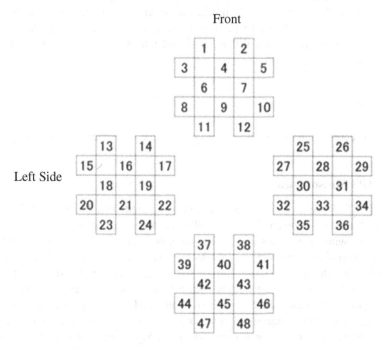

Fig. 3. Channel arrangement in fNIRS measurement

Integral values of oxygenated hemoglobin concentration for Pre, tracking, and peripheral vision for each channel were compared using Wilcoxon signed-rank test. The significance level is 0.05.

3.2 Measurement of Eye Movement

We performed our experiment on six healthy males with ages ranging from 23–24 (mean ± standard deviation: 23.3 ± 0.5). Images used for the experiment were recreated based on Sky Crystal (Olympus Memory Works Corp, Tokyo) with permission. For measurements, we used an eye mark recorder, EMR-9 (Nac Image Technology, Tokyo). Images were displayed with Display 55UF8500 (LG, Seoul). Measurements were taken in a darkroom, and subjects were seated for the experiment. Following the 60-s test with eyes closed (Pre), subjects tracked 2D images for 60 s and used peripheral vision for another 60 s. Two types of 2D images (with and without backgrounds) were used.

Tracking and peripheral vision eye movements were recorded with the sampling frequency of 60 Hz and resampled at 20 Hz. The position of the viewpoint for each sampling time during viewing—x-y coordinate [pix]—was measured and each index was recorded. Data were divided into x-direction (the right to the LCD screen is positive) and y-direction (vertically upward is positive), and are converted to a time series. Total locus length, outer peripheral area, and unit area locus length were evaluated. Also, we performed Wilcoxon signed rank test for each analytical index. The significance level is 0.05.

4 Results

We herein report results of the brain activity and eye movements in this study.

4.1 fNIRS Measurements

Figures 4 and 5 show channels, which were compared with Pre through Wilcoxon signed rank test and showed significant difference/trends, in color.

When viewing images without background, compared to Pre, oxygenated hemoglobin concentration in the occipital lobe increased regardless of the method of viewing ($p < 0.05$). The change was more notable when using peripheral vision compared to tracking. Similarly for viewing images with the background, oxygenated hemoglobin concentration in the occipital lobe increased. Compared to Pre, a greater increase in the oxygenated hemoglobin concentration was observed in the upper occipital lobe when using peripheral vision than when tracking (Fig. 5). Increase in oxygenated hemoglobin concentration in the frontal lobe compared to Pre was only confirmed when using peripheral vision for images without background.

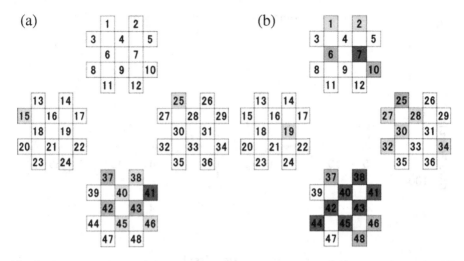

Fig. 4. Chs for which statistical increase in oxygenated hemoglobin was observed while viewing images without background: (a) tracking, (b) using peripheral vision (■: $p < 0.01$, ■: $p < 0.05$, ■: $p < 0.10$). (Color figure online)

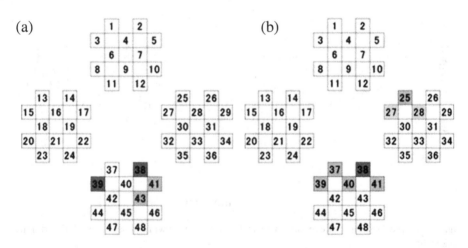

Fig. 5. Chs for which statistical increase in oxygenated hemoglobin as observed while viewing images with background: (a) tracking, (b) using peripheral vision (■: $p < 0.01$, ■: $p < 0.05$, ■: $p < 0.10$). (Color figure online)

(a)

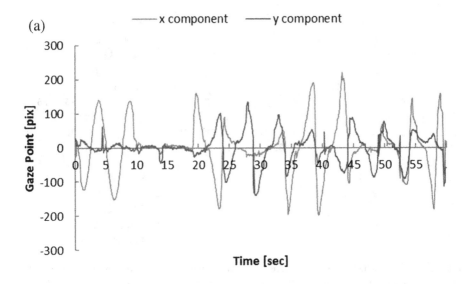

(b)

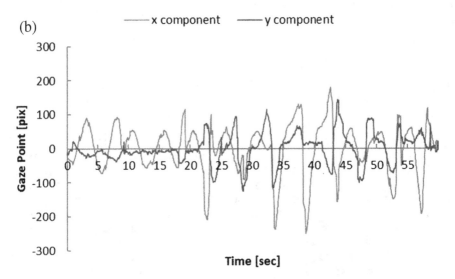

Fig. 6. A typical example of eye movements while tracking (a) without background, (b) with the backgrounds.

4.2   Eye Movement Measurements

Figure 6 shows temporal changes in eye movement when tracking. For the peak interval of x-axial components (periodic structure), the difference between subjects is small and there was in-phase variation. Figure 7 shows a typical example of a scatter

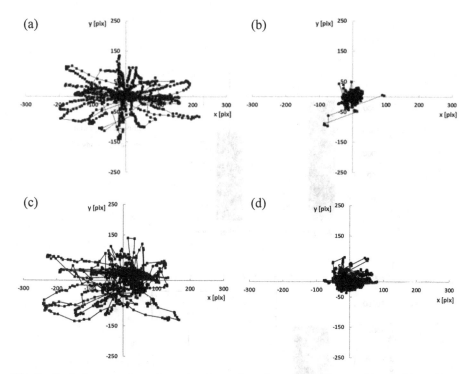

Fig. 7. Typical example of a scatter plot for viewpoint position: (a) without background/tracking, (b) without background/using peripheral vision, (c) with background/tracking, and (d) with background/using peripheral vision.

plot for viewpoint position obtained from measurements. Regardless of the background for the image, when tracking and using peripheral vision are compared, there was a clear difference in eye movement. On the other hand, when the scatter plot for viewpoint position for peripheral vision is compared, there was no difference with the background (Fig. 7b and d). However, when the scatter plot of the viewpoint position for tracking is compared, the viewpoint is focused at the center when there is no background (Fig. 7a and c).

We compared each analytical index calculated from scatter plots for viewpoints between viewing methods (Fig. 8). For the total locus length, there was no significant difference (Fig. 8a). For the outer peripheral area (Fig. 8b), regardless of the background, values while tracking were statistically higher compared to those measuring the use of peripheral vision. For the unit area locus length (Fig. 8c), values measuring the use of peripheral vision for images without background were statistically higher than those for tracking. Also, values measuring the use of peripheral vision for images with background were significantly higher than those for tracking.

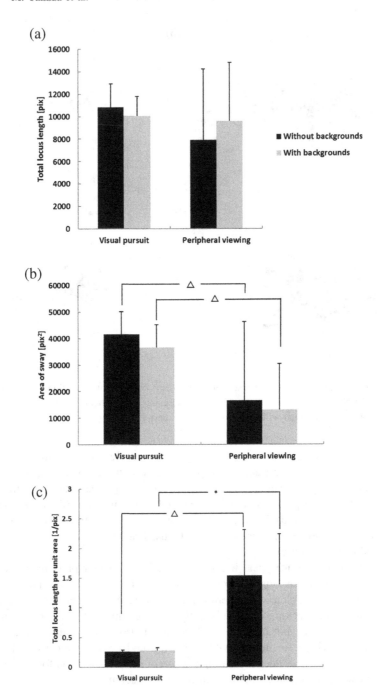

Fig. 8. Comparison of the sway values: total locus length (a), area of sway (b), and total locus length per unit area (c).

5 Discussions

In the last conference, we focused on a 3D game machine to increase knowledge about the influence of stereoscopic images on the body. Changes in brain blood flow while playing the game were compared between playing using the 2D and 3D displays by measuring NIRS [10]. Since the visual area responsible for vision is present in the occipital lobe [11–13], it may have been strongly influenced when 2D was switched to 3D.

A marked increase in brain blood flow was noted in the frontal, occipital, and left temporal lobes. In the frontal lobe, brain blood flow consistently increased from early 2D to late 2D at many channels. Since the frontal lobe controls psychogenesis, such as emotion, attention, thinking, and voluntary movement, brain blood flow may have continued to increase due to thinking and concentration on the game operation. In the occipital and left temporal lobes, brain blood flow increased from early 2D to 3D, and no significant difference was noted between 3D and late 2D. Various sensory areas are present in the left temporal lobe, and, in contrast to the right temporal lobe which memorizes sounds and shapes, the left temporal lobe memorizes and understands speech [10–13]. Since TETRiS® is a game requiring thinking, 3D images may have a large influence on the left temporal lobe.

The visual area responsible for vision is present in the occipital lobe, and various sensory areas are present in the left temporal lobe. Thus, sensory areas, such as the visual area, may have been activated when playing the game with 3D images compared to activation by 2D.

5.1 fNIRS Measurements

When there was no background, compared to Pre, values of oxygenated hemoglobin concentration showed more fluctuations when using peripheral vision compared to tracking. However, with the background, there was no significant fluctuation. For images with the background, information from the screen was increased, and subjects became distracted by images other than the target. Regardless of background, when compared with Pre, oxygenated hemoglobin concentration in the upper occipital lobe increased more for peripheral vision than for tracking. If we assume Neuro-Vascular-Coupling (NVC), when using peripheral vision, brain activities in the upper occipital lobe were accelerated. This is because brain activity on the dorsal visual pathway was promoted, which may be useful in examining the mechanism of 3D sickness [14]. Also, increase in oxygenated hemoglobin concentration in the frontal lobe compared to Pre was only observed when using peripheral vision for images without background. The frontal lobe is used for cognition. Since there is no information in this image other than the movement of the target, when using peripheral vision, it especially requires cognition that is associated with spatial recognition to grasp perspective. On the other hand, when tracking movements of the target, information on perspective was input to the frontal lobe through the ventral visual pathway. As discussed above, when using peripheral vision, brain activity in the dorsal visual pathway that controls spatial recognition is promoted, but with the lack of information on the background perspective, subjects supplemented spatial recognition in the frontal lobe through cognition, which increased the oxygenated hemoglobin concentration in the frontal lobe.

5.2 Eye Movement Measurements

In the x-axis components on eye movement, in-phase temporal fluctuations were observed in all subjects (Fig. 6). As such, homogeneous tracking of the visual target could be confirmed.

From the scatter plot of viewpoint location, we were able to confirm viewing methods. When backgrounds were compared for peripheral vision, there was no difference in the scatter plot related to viewpoint position (Fig. 7b and d). However, when backgrounds were compared for tracking, viewpoint position was focused at the center when there was no background in the image (Fig. 7a and c), and eye movement was stable. When using peripheral vision, movement of the visual target at the center of the field of vision did not have an impact.

In the outer peripheral area (Fig. 8b), regardless of background, compared to when using peripheral vision, values were statistically higher for tracking. For unit area locus length (Fig. 8c), when using peripheral vision for images without background, values were statistically higher compared to when tracking, confirming the findings of stable eye movement. Even when information on the background perspective is missing, conditions of peripheral vision do not change; and thus, there is insufficient data for spatial recognition. However, since these data have large scatter, we need to increase the number of subjects for further examination.

Acknowledgements. This work was supported in part by the Japan Society for the Promotion of Science, Grant-in-Aid for Research Activity Start-up Number 15H06711, Grant-in-Aid for Young Scientists (B) Number 16K16105, and that for Scientific Research (C) Number 17K00715.

References

1. Suzuki, J., Matsunaga, T., Tokumatsu, K., Taguchi, K., Watanabe, Y.: Q & A and a manual in stabilometry. Equilibr. Res. **55**(1), 64–77 (1996)
2. Takada, M., Fukui, Y., Matsuura, Y., Sato, M., Takada, H.: Peripheral viewing during exposure to a 2D/3D video clip: effects on the human body. Env. Health Prev. Med. **20**(2), 79–89 (2015)
3. Elwell, C.E., Cooper, C.E., Cope, M., Delpy, D.T.: Performance comparison of several published tissue near-infrared spectroscopy algorithms. Anal. Biochem. **227**, 54–68 (1995)
4. Fukuda, M., Mikuni, M.: A study of near-infrared spectroscopy in depression. J. Clin. Exp. Med. **219**, 1057–1062 (2006)
5. Hazeki, O., Tamura, M.: Quantitative analysis of hemoglobin oxygenation state of rat brain in situ by near-infrared spectroscopy. J. Appl. Physiol. **64**, 796–802 (1988)
6. Hoshi, Y., Tamura, M.: Detection of dynamic changes in cerebral oxygenation coupled to neural function during mental work in man. Neurosci. Lett. **150**, 5–8 (1993)

7. Kato, T., Kamei, A., Takashima, S., Ozaki, T.: Human visual cortical function during photic stimulation monitoring by means of near-infared spectroscopy. J. Cereb. Blood Flow Metab. **13**, 516–520 (1993)

8. Wray, S., Cope, M., Delpy, D.T., Wyatt, J.S., Reynolds, E.O.: Characterization of the near infrared absorption spectra of cytochrome aa3 and hemoglobin for the non-invasive monitoring of cerebral oxygenation. Biochemica et Biophysica A **933**, 184–192 (1988)

9. Zardecki, A.: Multiple scattering corrections to the Beer-Lambert law. In: Proceedings of the SPIE, pp. 103–110 (1983)

10. Takada, M., Mori, Y., Kinoshita, F., Takada, H.: Changes in brain blood flow by the use of 2D/3D games. In: Antona, M., Stephanidis, C. (eds.) UAHCI 2016. LNCS, vol. 9739, pp. 516–523. Springer, Cham (2016). doi:10.1007/978-3-319-40238-3_49

11. Sugihara, I.: Audition and equilibrium. In: Sakai, T., Kawahara, K. (eds.) Normal Structure and Function of Human Body. Nervous System 2, vol. 9, pp. 66–77. Nihon-Ijishinpo, Tokyo (2005)

12. Netter, F.H.: Netter Atlas of Human Anatomy, 6th edn. Saunders Elsevier, Philadelphia (2014)

13. Dox, I.G., Melloni, B.J., Eisner, G.M., Melloni, J.: Illustrated Medical Dictionary, 4th edn. Collins Reference, Glasgow (2001)

14. Ungerleider, L.G., Mishkin, M.: Two cortical visual systems. In: Ingle, D.J., et al. (eds.) Analysis of Visual Behavior. MIT Press, Cambridge (1982)

Design for Quality of Life Technologies

Low Cost Smart Homes for Elders

Gabriel Ferreira[1], Paulo Penicheiro[1], Ruben Bernardo[1], Luís Mendes[4,5],
João Barroso[3], and António Pereira[1,2(✉)]

[1] School of Technology and Management,
Computer Science and Communication Research Center,
Polytechnic Institute of Leiria, 2411-901 Leiria, Portugal
{2131218,2130628,2130664}@my.ipleiria.pt, apereira@ipleiria.pt
[2] Information and Communications Technologies Unit,
INOV INESC Innovation, Delegation Office at Leiria, Leiria, Portugal
[3] INESC TEC and University of Trás-os-Montes e Alto Douro, Quinta de Prados,
5000-801 Vila Real, Portugal
jbarroso@utad.pt
[4] Instituto de Telecomunicações, Lisbon, Portugal
lmendes@ipleiria.pt
[5] School of Technology and Management, Polytechnic Institute of Leiria,
2411-901 Leiria, Portugal

Abstract. The increase in life expectancy and the consequent aging of the general population pose, nowadays, major challenges to modern societies. Most elderly people have the usual problems related to old age, like health chronic problems and sensory and cognitive impairments. Besides that, in today's modern societies, where families have less and less time to look after for their old relatives, the isolation of the elderly is a real concern and a very current problem, which is enhanced if the elders live alone. To solve or, at least, mitigate that problem, it was developed a smart home for elders that is presented and described in this paper. The developed assistive home system, which is based on available technology, can ensure the quality of life, safety and well-being of all older adults that want or desire to live in the comfort of their home, near to their friends and in their neighborhood, instead of living in elder care centers. The proposed solution can record and analyze the elders' daily routines in order to alert (e.g., e-mails or text messages) the family members and/or social agents (e.g., doctors and caregivers) whenever an unusual situation occurs or when the elder is in danger, provide real-time audio and video when necessary and some comfort features, such as, automatic lighting and temperature control. The relevant events are recorded and maintained in a cloud database, which can be accessed through a dedicated website or by an Internet of Things (IoT) Application Programming Interface (API). Although this type of solution/service is focused in the elderly population, anybody can use it. The developed solution provides comfort and safety to elders and, at the same time, an easier way of monitoring all important events.

Keywords: Ambient assisted living · Internet of Things (IoT) · Anytime anywhere · Elderlies

© Springer International Publishing AG 2017
M. Antona and C. Stephanidis (Eds.): UAHCI 2017, Part III, LNCS 10279, pp. 507–517, 2017.
DOI: 10.1007/978-3-319-58700-4_41

1 Introduction

The term Internet of Things (IoT) was firstly used years ago by industry researchers, but only recently emerged into the mainstream public eye [1]. This new concept is used to describe the capacity of network connected equipments and devices to sense and collect different types of data and then share that information across the Internet in order to be processed and used in several applications. It is usual to find the term industrial Internet interchangeably with IoT [2], which is not the most correct since it refers primarily to commercial applications of the IoT technology in the manufacturing field, whereas the IoT covers a much wider range of applications and therefore not limited to industrial ones. Some claim that in the next decades IoT will have a paramount impact on how the society will evolve. The facts show that IoT is growing fast, gaining a vast attention from a wide range of industries, and it will be one of the most important areas of future technology [1].

A smart home is a house, apartment or other type of dwelling that uses home automation (also known as domotics) technology to monitor and control remotely and/or automatically the state of all electronic features installed in it. For example, in this type of houses, the home lighting, heating, ventilation, air conditioning, security and camera systems are all interconnected and can be controlled from any room in the home or remotely from any location in the world by using telecommunications systems and computers, tablets or smartphones. Thus, a smart home filled with connected devices (IoT devices) make the owners lives easier, more convenient and with improved comfort, security and energy efficiency [3]. In a near future, all the home comfort equipments (e.g. lighting, heating, ventilation and air conditioning), appliances (e.g. refrigerators, washers and dryers) and security and safety systems (e.g. sensors, monitors, cameras and alarm systems) will be all available remotely (through the Internet). The possibilities for smart home IoT devices are immense and can, in fact, contribute to improve immensely the quality of life of all citizens, above all the elderly.

The modern societies are facing a fast growing of aging population. Improved health and social care over recent years has increased life expectancy worldwide. Nearly 7% of the world's population is now over 65 years of age and the predictions show that older people will rise to approximately 20% by 2050 worldwide [4]. An important part of that population has health chronic conditions or diseases and lives alone, which raise concerns to the family members and respective caregivers [4]. One way to improve their comfort, security and provide a prompt help response in case of an emergency is to merge the traditional smart home with elderly assistive systems [5]. A smart home for elders besides incorporating the standard comfort equipments, smart appliances and security and safety systems should have health monitoring systems, such as, pulse, blood pressure, heart rate, fall detection devices and panic buttons. Some of these devices should be wearable in order to monitor in real-time the health status of the elderly. These devices must have versatile functions and be user-friendly in order to allow elders to perform tasks with minor intrusion and disturbance, pain, inconvenience or movement restrictions.

The type of environment provided by the smart homes for elders is based on a new paradigm of technology where people are assisted by an ambient intelligence, that is supported by a high range of data collecting and computing devices [6]. The environment collects all the necessary information about the context and presence of people and it is able to adapt to home occupants needs, habits, movements and emotions. Thus, this technology has the potential to enable people to live in their own home rather than being hospitalized or institutionalized [7]. The smart home for elders proposed in this paper presents a low cost solution of an in-home assistive system merged with a home automation system. The purpose of that is to provide to elders a pleasant way of live without the need to leave the comfort of their homes.

The rest of the paper is organized as follows. Section 2 presents some works related to the assistive home systems. The general architecture of the proposed smart home for elders is described in Sect. 3. In Sect. 4, the implementation of a functional scaled model of a smart home for elders is presented and in Sect. 5 the performance of the developed prototype is evaluated. Also, in this section, the performance of the developed prototype is evaluated. Finally, in Sect. 6, the conclusions are drawn and some ideas for future work are presented.

2 Background

The work presented by Costa et al. [6] states that ambient intelligence can transform current spaces into electronic environments that are responsive, assistive and sensitive to the human presence. Those electronic environments will be fully populated with dozens, hundreds or even thousands of connected devices that can share information and thus become intelligent. The massive deployment of electronic devices will invade everyday objects, turning them into smart entities, keeping their native features and characteristics while seamlessly promoting them to a new class of thinking and reasoning everyday objects [6].

The smart home for elderly care presented in [8], which is based on a wireless sensor network, demonstrates that ZigBee is well suited for smart homes and automation systems. ZigBee is a low cost, low power and low complexity wireless standard [8].

In [9], a smart elderly home monitoring system was designed and developed. In it, an Android-based smartphone with 3-axial accelerometer was used to detect falls of the carriers. Also, a remote panic button has implemented in the same Android-based smartphone. In this system, the smartphone uses Wi-Fi to connect to the TCP/IP network in order to access to the monitoring system. The developed system allows elderly and chronically ill patients to stay independently in their own homes knowing that they are being monitored.

The work presented by Gaddam et al. [10] uses intelligent sensors with cognitive ability to implement a home monitoring system for elder care application. These used sensors can detect the usage of electrical devices, bed usage patterns and flow of water. Besides that, the system also incorporates a panic button. The cognitive sensors provide information that can be used to monitor the elderly status by detecting any abnormal pattern in their daily home activities.

The work presented by Chan et al. [11] reviews how elderly and disabled can be monitored with numerous intelligent devices. Their article presents an international selection of leading smart home projects, as well as the associated technologies of wearable/implantable monitoring systems and assistive robotics. The latter are often designed as components of the larger smart home environment.

The qualitative study presented by Courtney [12] analyzes the relationship between privacy, living environment and willingness of older adults that live in residential care facilities to adopt smart home information technologies (IT). His work was based on the data obtained through focus groups and individual interviews. The study findings indicate that privacy can be a barrier for older adults' adoption of smart home IT, however, their own perception of their need for the technology may override their privacy concerns. Privacy concerns, as a barrier to technology adoption, can be influenced by both individual and community factors.

The works presented above are significant in the area of the smart homes for elders, and the concepts reported on those works are very useful and can be used as a base reference to the characteristics definition of low cost solutions, as the one proposed and described in this paper.

3   System Architecture

The system architecture of a low cost smart home for elders must be flexible and scalable and, through the use of several technologies, should provide, at any time, the right support to the elder. The flexibility of the system architecture is important to make it easy and inexpensive to deploy the elder in-home assistive system in any type of dwelling. After a home assistive system starts to operate at a given site, the scalability of the system architecture is also important to maintain the costs at lower levels. The scalability prevents the installation of new physical infrastructures (e.g., cables and equipments) each time that is necessary to add new functionalities or to provide the assistive services to new clients located in the same site. In vertical buildings or in apartment complexes, which usually have a great number of apartments and, consequently, with many potential clients, the assistive system should cover all the common areas since, at the end, the final costs will certainly be reduced. The services provided to authorize users should be always available in each house or apartment and in the common areas of the condominiums (if applicable). Therefore, the system architecture should be thought and developed always taking into account the type of housing complex. The services that a home automation and assistive system should provide constitute another important input to the system architecture definition since different services require different technologies. The system proposed in this paper was thought to provide home automation and in-home assistive features like comfort features, such as, automatic lighting and temperature control; security and surveillance services like intrusion detection, access control, video and audio recording; detection of harmful or dangerous situations (e.g., smoke, fire, flood and toxic-gases); elder real-time monitoring (e.g. heart rate, pulse, stress level and oxygenation); emergency calls (through the use of a panic button); and other home amenities, such as, automatic irrigation (when applied). The above-mentioned services are very important to the comfort and security of elders.

The system architecture is illustrated in Fig. 1 where the network structure and its constituent parts are highlighted. The control and monitoring of the clients' residences are performed remotely through the use of the internet services. The events and alerts are all recorded in the cloud servers located in the cloud datacenter and when an emergency situation emerges the right support is immediately triggered. The system online platform will have a common managing area for the condominium and a private managing area for each home or apartment. Since important data is saved and maintained in the servers, the users can access to it through the system online platform. The clients can obtain various informations related to the solution adopted and all their configurations and data.

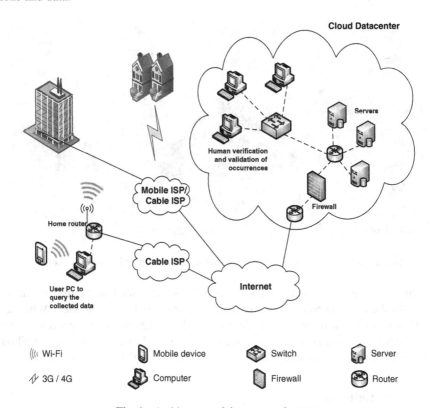

Fig. 1. Architecture of the proposed system.

Telecommunication networks are crucial to the system operation. At the house complexes, and whenever possible, communications should be performed wirelessly, using the IEEE 802.11n technology. In the situation where wireless communications are not viable, the areas should be served by copper cabling (CAT6). Common areas of the house complexes will accommodate racks with the network equipments. To connect the system deployed in the house complexes with the servers an internet service provider can be used.

Figure 2 shows the solution applied to a single-family detached home. As it can be seen, there are several sensors and actuators that are all connected to the house network. To monitor the elder in real-time, he must always use a sensory bracelet that is capable of measuring some health parameters and signals (e.g. heart rate, pulse, stress level and blood oxygen concentration) and transmit the acquired data to the platform servers if one or more health indicator suffers a significant change from the normal values. When this situation occurs an alarm is generated and the right emergency service is activated. The assistive system also supports the usage of a panic button that can be placed in a given place (e.g. near the bed) or accompany the elder. The panic button can be configured to directly call an emergency line or to establish a call to a relative of the elderly.

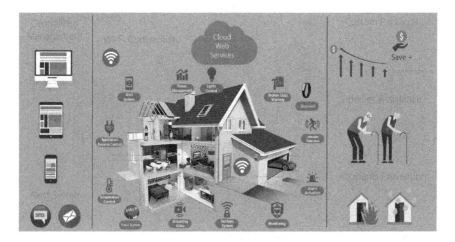

Fig. 2. Diagram of a full-integrated in-home automation and assistive system.

The home automation sensors and the assistive sensors send all the relevant information to the cloud servers to be managed and processed, as mentioned. When an abnormal situation occurs the system detects it and activates the right support services. The presented solution is the one that should be provided to elderlies that live all by themselves since it give them a better quality of life with real comfort and security.

4   Implementation

This section presents and describes the development and implementation of a functional prototype in order to demonstrate the technical and economic feasibility of the proposed home automation assistive system.

Figure 3 shows the architecture of the implemented system. In this prototype some of the functionalities presented in Sect. 3 were implemented. As it can be seen, the prototype can be divided in 3 distinct modules, namely, the comfort module, security module and the communication module. All these sub-systems are relevant to the well-being and sense of security of the elders.

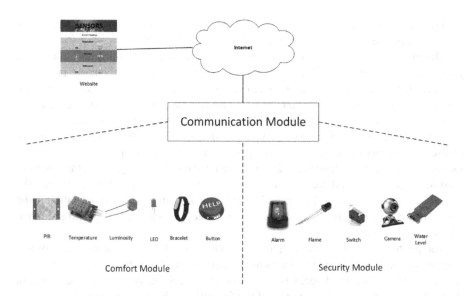

Fig. 3. Block diagram of the implemented prototype.

The implemented functions of the comfort module are the automatic lighting and the monitoring of the interior temperature and air humidity. The automatic lighting sub-system measures (light sensors) continuously the interior natural light in order to control the artificial light actuators. This system uses two thresholds of ambient light to define the light levels that must be activated. When the level one is reached, part of the illumination is activated (here simulated by LEDs) corresponding to a low artificial intensity light. When the interior natural light is really low, the second threshold is attained, and, consequently, the system activates all the available lights. The activation of the lights is also dependent of the presence of people at home.

The second feature of the comfort module is the monitoring of the temperature and humidity levels. As in the automatic lighting sub-system, the temperature and humidity are continuously monitored. The thresholds of the automatic lighting system and the levels of the interior temperature and humidity can be viewed and defined in the home managing console (tactile LCD display) or by using the web platform.

The goal of the security module is to provide the house protection and security of the home occupants. For that, it incorporates several types of sensors and, consequently, several sub-systems. To present house floods, a water level monitor sub-system, which is very useful in kitchens, bathrooms and laundries, was implemented. This sub-systems monitors the water level and when it reaches a given value, the solution activates an alarm and sends a warning to the web platform. Another security feature is the fire detection sub-system. The smart home uses a sensor that detects any kind of fire and triggers an alert and a warning to the web platform. The last security feature implemented in the prototype is the intrusion detection. Here, simple switches that simulate the magnetic doors and windows sensors were used. Every time each switch is activated, simulating an intrusion, the home control board (Raspberry Pi3 [13]) takes a picture of the place where the intrusion is taking place and send it to the web platform along with the corresponding warning. The house alarm is also turned on.

The communications module is responsible to send in real-time the information gathered by the house sensors to the web platform so that it can be managed, processed and recorded. The maintenance of the data in web servers allows the user to access it any time and everywhere. The management and control of every aspect of the system features by the client is always performed through the communications module.

In the implemented solution prototype, the main devices responsible to manage the comfort and security features are the Raspberry Pi3 [13] and the Yun [14]. To manage the security features the Raspberry Pi3 was used. Python [15] scripts with threads were used to process and send the pictures files to the web server. On the other hand, the Arduino was used to gather the sensors' information and update their information in the web platform so the users could access and visualize it. The Arduino was programmed with C language [16].

The platform website is one of the places where the clients can access and manage their information and collected data, as mentioned before. The website is structured into four main areas: Landing Page, Check Sensors, Check Security and Elderlies Care. In the website it can be found general useful informations, the procedures to monitor and control a smart home, the contacts of the service provider, emergency numbers and all the collected values of the home sensors. Since data is acquired in real-time the client can always check if something abnormal is happening. The entire site was developed using the languages HTML5 and CSS for composition and structure of the site; Java-Script and J-Query for the animations and some validations; and PHP was used to develop the scripts that gather data from sensors and the photographs, posting them to the respective areas of the website.

A photo of the implemented prototype is presented in Fig. 4. This photo shows some of the used electronic and communication boards and some sensors and actuators.

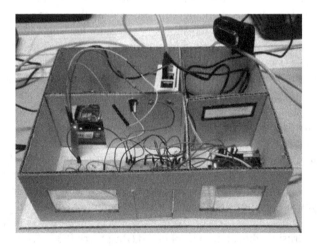

Fig. 4. Photo of the developed prototype.

Figure 5 shows the Sensor Check area of the website. As it can be seen, the sensor values are available to each client.

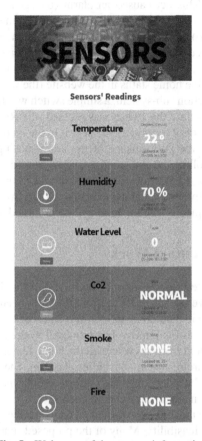

Fig. 5. Web page of the sensors information.

5   Tests Conducted to Analyze the Solution's Behavior

To assess the performance of all electronic parts (hardware and firmware) several tests were conducted. The used methodology is the following one. First, each sensor or actuator was tested independently of all the others. The information gathered by each sensor was displayed on the LCD screen. In this way, the performance was inferred by the operating status of the respective sensor. After the operation validation of all the sensors, the alarm associated to each sensor was tested. For that, abnormal situations were imposed to verify if the alarm is triggered. To simulate the alarm operation a buzzer was used. After confirming the right operation of each sensor and respective alarm, the communication with the server was evaluated.

To test the temperature and humidity monitoring sub-system, the sensors were submitted to abnormal conditions, which activate the alarm, sending its values to the

LCD display and to the website and generating a buzzer sound at the same time. For the fire detection assessment, a small flame (lighter) was approximated to the sensor to force an abnormal condition. This act caused an alarm (buzzer sound), an update of the contents of the home LCD display and the sending of an emergency message (word "FIRE") to the website. To test the flood detection sub-system, a cup of water was used. The sensor was submerged below the limit defined in the configuration script, forcing an abnormal value, which caused an alarm (buzzer sound), a new notice in the LCD display and an update of the home status in the website (the word "FLOOD" was sent). To test the intrusion detection sub-system, a simple switch was used (simulates the door or window sensor). Each time the switch was pressed, the Raspberry Pi3 [13] took a picture (through the control of a camera) and sent it to the website, also generating the respective alert. Finally, the performance of the automatic lighting sub-system was assessed simply by controlling the ambient light. The system acted accordingly with the specifications. Part of the LEDs (they simulate the real illumination) were activated when the ambient light level was maintained between the two defined thresholds and when the light were completely cut the lighting system turned all LEDs on.

6   Conclusion and Future Work

The paper proposes and describes a smart home for elders that integrate home automation systems with assistive ones in order to fulfill the elder needs. The system provides to the elder that live alone in their home the comfort and security he requires and, simultaneously, the tranquility to his family. The proposed system architecture allows the users to control anytime and from anywhere all the home features using the system app on any mobile device or through the system online platform. The elder's relatives (family members responsible for the elder) are always informed of his health and status situation and receive an alarm when abnormal situation occurs.

An operational scaled model is also presented and described in the paper in order to demonstrate the solution feasibility. Many of the proposed functionalities were implemented in the mockup house. The scaled model uses an Arduino Yun and a Raspberry Pi to control all the deployed sensors, to acquire all the sensors' data and to send it to the system cloud servers. Several functional tests that replicate daily situations were performed to assess the system. The obtained results show that the proposed solution is functional.

An important limitation of the implemented prototype is related to the cabled infrastructure. Thus, in a close future, and in order to improve the system flexibility and functionality, all the cabled parts of the infrastructure will be replaced by a wireless one. Other major feature that it will be developed and implemented in the proposed system is an ambient assisted living capable of detecting abnormal or unusual elder's behavior patterns and health problems, generating warnings or alarms to the care givers and elders' relatives. The ambient assisted living will be based on the behavior analysis algorithms that have the ability to process all the data collected from each sensor (deployed in the home and wearable).

Acknowledgements. This work was supported by Project "NanoSTIMA: Macro-to-Nano Human Sensing: Towards Integrated Multimodal Health Monitoring and Analytics/NORTE-01-0145-FEDER-000016" financed by the North Portugal Regional Operational Programme (NORTE 2020), under the PORTUGAL 2020 Partnership Agreement, and through the European Regional Development Fund (ERDF).

References

1. Lee, I., Lee, K.: The Internet of Things (IoT): applications, investments, and challenges for enterprises. Bus. Horiz. **58**(4), 431–440 (2015)
2. Gilchrist, A.: IIoT reference architecture. In: Gilchrist, A. (ed.) Industry 4.0, pp. 65–86. Apress, New York (2016)
3. Barlow, J., Venables, T.: Will technological innovation create the true lifetime home? Hous. Stud. **19**, 795–810 (2004). No. 907688161
4. OECD: Organisation for Economic Co-operation and Development, p. 55. OECD, Paris (2011)
5. Ni, Q., Hernando, A.B.G., de la Cruz, I.P.: The elderly's independent living in smart homes: a characterization of activities and sensing infrastructure survey to facilitate services development. Sensors (Basel) **15**(5), 11312–11362 (2015)
6. Costa, N., Domingues, P., Fdez-Riverola, F., Pereira, A.: A mobile virtual butler to bridge the gap between users and ambient assisted living: a smart home case study. Sensors (Basel) **14**(8), 14302–14329 (2014)
7. Menschner, P., et al.: Reaching into patients' homes–participatory designed AAL services. Electron. Mark. **21**(1), 63–76 (2011)
8. Ransing, R.S., Rajput, M.: Smart home for elderly care, based on wireless sensor network. In: 2015 International Conference on Nascent Technologies in the Engineering Field, pp. 1–5 (2015)
9. Lee, J.V., Chuah, Y.D., Chieng, K.T.H.: Smart elderly home monitoring system with an Android phone. Int. J. Smart Home **7**(3), 17–32 (2013)
10. Gaddam, A., Mukhopadhyay, S.C., Sen Gupta, G.: Elder care based on cognitive sensor network. IEEE Sens. J. **11**(3), 574–581 (2011)
11. Chan, M., Estève, D., Escriba, C., Campo, E.: A review of smart homes- present state and future challenges. Comput. Methods Programs Biomed. **91**(1), 55–81 (2008)
12. Courtney, K.L.: Privacy and senior willingness to adopt smart home information technology in residential care facilities. Methods Inf. Med. **47**(1), 76–81 (2008)
13. Raspberry Pi3. https://www.raspberrypi.org/products/raspberry-pi-3-model-b/. Accessed 05 Feb 2017
14. Arduino Yun. https://www.arduino.cc/en/Main/ArduinoBoardYun. Accessed 05 Feb 2017
15. Python. https://www.python.org/. Accessed 05 Feb 2017
16. Arduino Programming. https://www.arduino.cc/en/Reference/HomePage. Accessed 05 Feb 2017

Fire Warning System by Using GPS Monitoring and Quadcopters

Jei-Chen Hsieh[✉]

Department of Industrial Design, Tunghai University, Taichung, Taiwan
jeichen@thu.edu.tw

Abstract. Fire disasters are the most accidents that ordinary people meets. It always creates big losses. The research attempts to propose an interface planning that will make the users to react and judge more efficiently and correctly. By the warning systems implemented, according to the interior fire types it passes the messenger to owner and neighbors. It links with the geography information system and creates the records of the process to improve and update just in time. By implementing this new interface design to the disaster situation, the fire departments may judge disaster situation, make the correct dispatch, and decrease the casualties.

Keywords: Fire field · GPS · Sensors · Quadcopter

1 Introduction

From the 2015 statistics by National Fire Agency [1, 2], it shows: In 2015 the number of fire occurred 1,704 times, compared with 2014, 1,417 times, an increase of 287 times, an increase of 20.3%. In 2015 the fire of all kinds of buildings was the highest in 1,242 times, accounting for 72.9%. Compared with 2014 years, (Increase by 16.6%); the number of vehicles fire 234 times second, accounting for 13.7%, increase 53 times (by 29.3%). In 2015 Building fire to independent residential fire 530 times the first, accounting for all building fires of 42.7%.

The second residential fire occurred 228 times, accounting for 18.4%. Factory fire 186 times ranked No. 3, accounting for 15.0%. Fire place, the bedroom 257 times accounted for first, Accounting for 15.1%. Increase of 25 times over to compared with 2014. Roadside 172 second place, Accounting for 10.1%. An increase of 36 times Warehouse 145 times ranked No. 3, Accounting for 8.5%, an increase of 44 times.

The cause of fire to electrical equipment 582 times accounted for first, accounting for 34.2%. Increased 131 times; Artificial arson 268 second, accounting for 15.7%. Increased 55 times; Cigarette butts 147 times the third, accounting for 8.6%. Increase 1 times. The death toll was 117 (78 for males and 39 for females), a decrease of 5.6% compared to 124 in 2014.

The loss on property was NT $530.56 million, an increase of 94.428 million or 21.7% as compared with 436.13 million in 2014.

© Springer International Publishing AG 2017
M. Antona and C. Stephanidis (Eds.): UAHCI 2017, Part III, LNCS 10279, pp. 518–526, 2017.
DOI: 10.1007/978-3-319-58700-4_42

The data make the research focuses on the building, room, electric accidents and big losses. How to increase alarm attention in the first time and evoke people and owner notice to response is major topics.

2   Literature Review

Contemporary technologies, Quadcopter or Six-axis aircraft, and intelligence applications and the fire disasters cases are the major fields in literature review.

2.1   Contemporary Technologies

The wireless sensors detect the sources of the fire then send the signals to the owner's mobile phone on the remote site is the original idea. The global positioning system (GPS) techniques are used to identify the geographic position of settle targets as tanks, forests, and seashores etc. [1, 3–6].

For Quadcopter or Six-axis aircraft etc. are popular to supervise landscape, record the disaster on site, and take pictures from aerial view in related fields [7–9] (Fig. 1).

Fig. 1. Quadcopter monitors terrain.

Fig. 2. GPS locates road at the terminal site

All researches are focus on the pollution, laws, hardware establish, supply problem, green education, recycle and system impacts [1, 3–5, 7–11]. None of previous researches focus on the real time warning related with the victims and neighbors. The research tries to involve the intelligence technology to face the problems (Fig. 2).

2.2 Accidents in Fire Field

The accidents of fire field are always reported on newspapers [10, 11]. Figures 3, 4 and 5 show the status as following.

Fig. 3. Outside of the fire field.

Fig. 4. Short circuit loss of electrical appliances in case of fire

Fig. 5. Location of fire alarm in the fire field

3 Methodology

Cases studies and experts interview are used to know the real situation of the fire fields and the causes. Interview the victims to catch their daily life to see what accidents inside might help to handle the need of future design.

4 Implementation

By interviewing six fire fighters and 106 cases studies, the electric wire accidents are the major cause. Government sets the rule to help peoples to locates smoking alarms on roof. Still people could not know fire is happened at the first time. It always make disaster and can not reduce loss after all. To solve this problem four infrastructures by the flowcharts as Figs. 7, 8, 9 and 10 are implemented to pass the fire messages in the first emergency time. The owners warning system could handle the ordinary house status and fire status. It helps to watch the wire pipes are old to change or not. It also helps to know any fire accidents happens at the first time. The extinguishing system is set up by Fault Tolerance design. It works when two sensors or two alarms are turn on. It avoids the wrong motions to squander the extinguishers. Above system are supported by ZigBee NXP JN5168 solution as Fig. 6. The Quadcopters warning system will make high frequency sounds and fly around the neighbors. It hopes that people around pay attention to notice the disaster and do something.

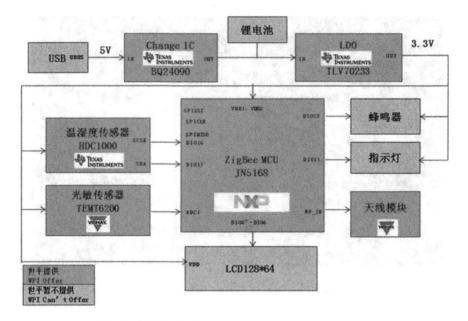

Fig. 6. NXP JN5168 Zigbee smart sensor solutions [12]

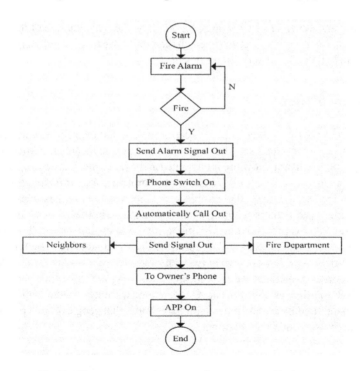

Fig. 7. The owner warning system in emergency (fire) status

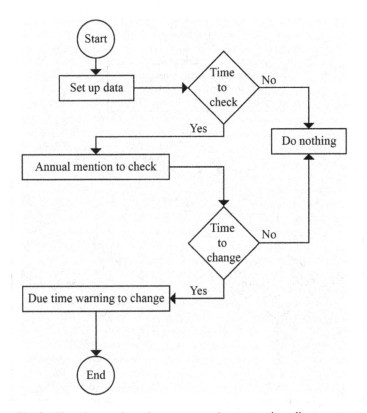

Fig. 8. Flowchart to show the owner warning system in ordinary status

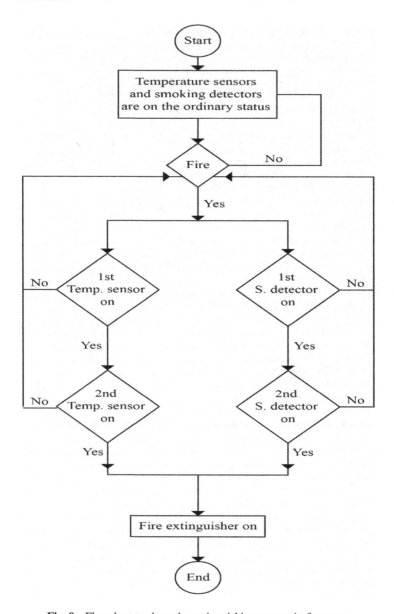

Fig. 9. Flowchart to show the extinguishing system in fire status

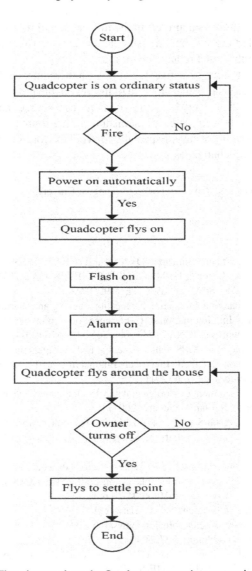

Fig. 10. Flowchart to show the Quadcopters warning system in fire status

5 Conclusion

Quickly in an emergency situation proposed design will send out distress signal. Reducing the fire disaster is the most important topic of research, by using contemporary wireless transmission technology as the construction to general home the design architecture is implemented here.

The application of universal aircraft in the fire status will receive signals automatically then lift and alert the surrounding personnel attention. This design is intended to help care of the neighbors and reduce the loss.

In the long-term timing of active viewing system requires a lot of government resources to complete. Such as the structure of the year in the premises whether the line material reaches the end of safety life and so on requires resources and long-term monitoring. Another issue is how to ensure extinguishing the fire source to reduce combustion and isolation of oxygen is not easy. Especially to avoid the forms of flashover and back draft are also the future challenges.

Acknowledgment. The research is supported by Tunghai University.

References

1. http://www.nfa.gov.tw/main/Unit.aspx?ID=&MenuID=378&ListID=129
2. http://www.nfa.gov.tw/Uploads/1/104%E5%B9%B4%E7%81%AB%E7%81%BD%E7%B5%B1%E8%A8%88%E5%88%86%E6%9E%90.pdf
3. Chandra, A.: GPS locator an application for location tracking and sharing using GPS for Java enabled handhelds. In: International Conference on Computational Intelligence and Communication Networks (CICN), 7–9 October, pp. 406–410 (2011)
4. Almomani, I.M.: Ubiquitous GPS vehicle tracking and management system. In: 2011 IEEE Jordan Conference on Applied Electrical Engineering and Computing Technologies (AEECT), 6–8 December, pp. 1–6 (2011)
5. Chen, C.Z.: Risk management of storage tanks in Taichung area: the application of GIS and GPS, Master Thesis, Fung Jar University (2001)
6. Guo, J.L.: Civil-NET e GPS precision positioning technology for unmanned vehicle axis system, Southern Taiwan University of Science and Technology, Electronic Engineering Department, Thesis (2013)
7. Omurlu, E., et al.: Nonlinear state-space representations of a quadrotor through bond-graph technique. In: 24th Chinese Control and Decision Conference (CCDC), pp. 620–627 (2012)
8. http://www.wfu.edu.tw/~wwwee/m10/06/04-20.pdf
9. https://www.youtube.com/watch?v=DYqg1nwkckI
10. http://m.ltn.com.tw/news/society/breakingnews/1655031
11. http://blog.yam.com/kiss486/article/72504035
12. http://www.wpgholdings.com/hotchannel/program_detail/zhtw/security/WPI-SMART-HOME-NXP-ZIGBEE-SMARTHOME-SENSOR

Robotic Assistants for Universal Access

Simeon Keates[(⊠)] and Peter Kyberd

University of Greenwich, Chatham Maritime, Kent ME4 4TB, UK
{s.keates,p.j.kyberd}@gre.ac.uk

Abstract. Much research is now focusing on how technology is moving away from the traditional computer to a range of smart devices in smart environments, the so-called Internet of Things. With this increase in computing power and decrease in form factor, we are approaching the possibility of a new generation of robotic assistants able to perform a range of tasks and activities to support all kinds of users. However, history shows that unless care is taken early in the design process, the users who may stand to benefit the most from such assistance may inadvertently be excluded from it. This paper examines some of those historical missteps and examines possible ways forward to ensure that the next generation robots support the principles of universal access.

Keywords: Robotic assistants · HCI · Inclusive design · Universal access · Assistive technology

1   Introduction

Technology is moving on apace. Computers have shrunk from being the size of a truck to a credit card in the form of the Raspberry Pi. Computing power has increased simultaneously, following the famous Moore's Law up until very recently [1]. At the same time, available communication bandwidth has increased substantially with the advent of new communication channels, such as 3G and 4G, offering new opportunities for assistive and/or healthcare applications [2, 3].

Historically, new technologies follow a typical path of development. In the early stages, the focus is on developing the new technology, overcoming the engineering challenges to make something that works [4]. The aim is to develop something that offers an increased level of functionality or something innovative. Users typically get overlooked in this early stage of development [5]. The usual outcome is a product that works best for users who are most like the designer. Those who are notably different, such as those who would benefit most from a universal access-based approach, usually do not fare so well.

Even where products have been developed specifically for users with significant functional impairments, there is no guarantee of a successful outcome. For example, in the 1990s, the EU funded a number of programmes through its TIDE (Telematics for the Integration of Disabled and Elderly people) initiative. Approximately $150 m was invested in this space, looking at the development of solutions from office workstations to wheelchair-mounted robots [6]. However, the success of those robots and others developed under similar initiatives was far from satisfactory [7]. Only the Handy

© Springer International Publishing AG 2017
M. Antona and C. Stephanidis (Eds.): UAHCI 2017, Part III, LNCS 10279, pp. 527–538, 2017.
DOI: 10.1007/978-3-319-58700-4_43

1 robot arm [8] and MANUS wheelchair-mounted robot [9] achieved any degree of successful take-up.

2   A Historical Example: The RAID Office Workstation

One example development under the TIDE initiative was the RAID office workstation, shown in Fig. 1. The robot was developed as a project between partners in the UK, Sweden and France.

Fig. 1. The RAID office workstation consisting of an RTX robot arm mounted on a gantry in a purpose-built office.

The robot consisted of a standard RTX robot arm mounted on a gantry so it could move around a specially prepared office space. A user could approach the desk on the left of the picture to control the robot using the Cambridge University Robotics Language (CURL), software developed specifically for such a purpose [10]. The design assumption was made that the user would want to access books and papers stored on the shelving, so would use the CURL interface to move the robot arm to pick up the Perspex containers holding them and bring the containers to the desk. The arm would then be used to pick up the contents and put them on the page-turner mounted next to the computer. The user would control the arm through the computer to turn each page so he or she could read the document.

Only 9 units of the robot were produced and went to each of the research partners. No units were sold commercially. There were several reasons for the lack of commercial success of this workstation. First, it was expensive, costing at least $55,000 just for the workstation and the robot. Second, it needed a dedicated office and for the office to be pre-adapted to support the workstation, for example with the shelving. Third, the interface was quite clunky and not easy to tailor or customize. Finally, and this was the biggest weakness, technology moved on. CDs and the Internet became commonplace, reducing the need for pieces of paper to be moved around. Other office workstations developed at the same time, such as DeVar and the Arlyn Arm Workstation did not fare any better [7].

The Handy 1 and MANUS robots did perform respectably well. Handy 1 was created by a small British start-up company with a view to being launched as a commercial product. It consisted of a robot arm mounted on a mobile base. Attached to the arm was a simple spoon. The user's food was placed in 5 segregated sections of a tray and through a straightforward interface, the user could feed themselves. This robot allowed many users to feed themselves independently for the first time in their lives. Thus a real need had been identified and a reasonably cheap solution (c. $6000) developed. A second variant was introduced allowing users to apply make-up. Approximately 150 units had been sold by 1997 [7].

The MANUS robot was developed in the Netherlands. It was fundamentally a robot arm mounted on the side of a wheelchair. As such, the robot was inherently mobile, albeit with the disadvantage of making the wheelchair notably wider in certain configurations. The cost was significantly more than the Handy 1 ($35,000), but sales were helped by an agreement between the development team and the Netherlands government, which was the largest buyer.

3   A User-Centered Approach to Rehabilitation Robotics

It is not just in the field of robotics where the introduction of new technology has stumbled because of lack of consideration of the needs and capabilities of the users. Early attempts at gesture recognition, for example, focused on the development of the technology rather than evaluating whether the technology actually offered a genuine benefit to the users [11].

There are numerous user-centered design approaches available in the literature. One such approach is the 7-level model, developed from a rehabilitation robotics project called IRVIS – the Interactive Robotic Visual Inspection System. The 7-level model was developed by expanding on a typical engineering design process, such as the following [12]:

- Stage 1 – define the problem – ensure there is a clear understanding of the requirements the product or system needs to meet – for universal access this will include a statement of who the users are and their needs, wants and aspirations
- Stage 2 – develop a solution – follow a user-centered design approach to create concepts and prototypes – for universal access this will include consideration of the full range of users, their knowledge, skills and capabilities

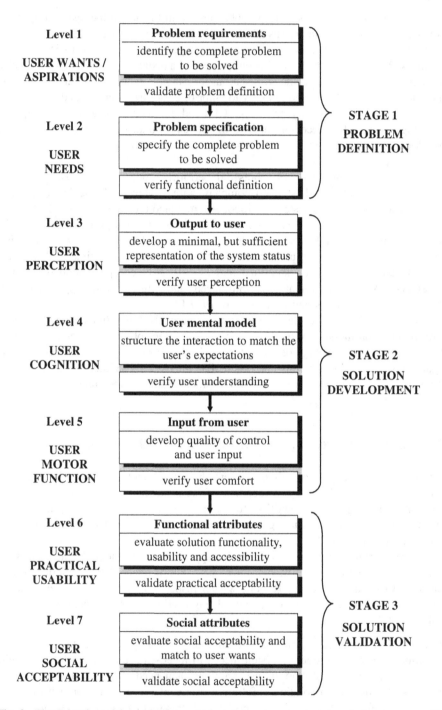

Fig. 2. The 7-level model, combining a typical three stage engineering design process with usability heuristics [15]

- Stage 3 – evaluate the solution – ensure that the finished design meets the specified requirements – for universal access this will include checking to ensure that the finished solution meets the wants, needs and aspirations for all users

To produce a successful universal access design, it is necessary to adopt strongly user-centered design practices. It is important to be able to modify and refine the device and its interface iteratively, combining both the above design steps with usability and accessibility evaluations. These evaluations typically involve measurement against known performance criteria, such as Jakob Nielsen's heuristic evaluation [13].

Developing a usable product or service interface for a wider range of user capabilities involves understanding the fundamental nature of the interaction. Typical interaction with an interface consists of the user perceiving an output from the product, deciding a course of action and then implementing the response. These steps can be explicitly identified as perception, cognition and motor actions [14] and relate directly to the user's sensory, cognitive and motor capabilities respectively. Three of Nielsen's heuristics explicitly address these functions:

- Visibility of system status – the user must be given sufficient feedback to gain a clear understanding of the current state of the complete system;
- Match between system and real world – the system must accurately follow the user's intentions;
- User control and freedom – the user must be given suitably intuitive and versatile controls for clear and succinct communication of intent.

Each of these heuristics effectively addresses the perceptual, cognitive and motor functions of the user. Building on these heuristics, the 7-level approach, shown in Fig. 2, addresses each of the system acceptability goals identified by Nielsen [15].

4 The 7-Level Model and IRVIS

IRVIS (Interactive Robotic Visual Inspection System) was developed to assist in the visual inspection of hybrid microcircuits during manufacture. Such circuits typically undergo up to 50 manual visual inspections to detect faults during manufacture. Each time a circuit is picked up, there is a finite chance of damage being done to the circuit through the action of manually picking it up and manipulating it under a microscope. IRVIS was developed to see if it was possible to inspect the circuits by effectively moving the microscope around the circuits rather than moving the circuits around the microscope. Furthermore, it was considered that as inspecting the circuits was a fundamentally visual task, someone with unimpaired vision, but perhaps a motor impairment may be able to undertake the task. Hence, one of the system requirements was that the robot should be accessible to a user with a motor impairment.

A prototype system was developed, as shown in Fig. 3. It consisted of a high power CCD camera mounted on a gantry. The tray of microcircuits could be mounted on the robot and the tray and camera could be moved through five degrees-of-freedom without the circuits needing to be picked up or handled.

Fig. 3. The prototype IRVIS robot [15]

The original interface, shown in Fig. 4, used a variant of the CURL interface developed for the RAID and EPI-RAID workstations. An initial user trial was undertaken, but significant problems were identified and a re-design was required [16]. The account of the re-design is detailed elsewhere [15], so a brief account will be provided here.

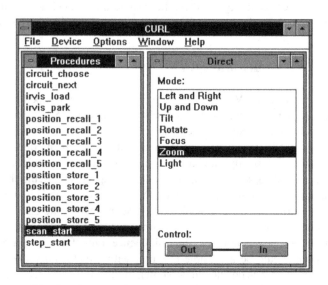

Fig. 4. The original IRVIS interface, using CURL [16]

4.1   Level 1 – Problem Requirements

The original design requirements were considered satisfactory, i.e. the basic functionality to be provided, but initially it was thought that the original user trials failed because the robot was too under-powered and too slow. A counter-position was that the interface was the source of the issues as the original design team had focused too much on developing the robot and not on the UI. The original UI required the users to select each motor in turn to complete an action and enter a numerical value for how far it should rotate. It was felt that this was a very inefficient control method.

4.2   Level 2 – Problem Specification

To resolve the dilemma whether it was the robot or the interface, a series of user observation sessions were undertaken of the manual inspection process. These sessions identified a number of key steps common to each manual visual inspection, such as rotation about a point, tilting, translation, zooming and focusing. Under the original interface, each of these actions took multiple steps to complete in a piece-wise fashion. Consequently, it was decided to forego a costly rebuild of the robot and focus on a more user-centered interface design.

4.3   Level 3 – Output to the User

To support the user, a virtual model of the robot was developed. A number of views and combination of views were provided and evaluated to ensure that the users could recognize where they were on a range of circuit layouts and what they were looking at.

4.4   Level 4 – User Mental Model

Having developed an interface layout that afforded sufficient visual feedback to the user, the next step was to add the full functionality of the IRVIS robot to the simulation. The user trials for this stage of the re-design were to ensure that the simulated robot response to user input was consistent with that of the actual hardware. The robot was connected to the computer and the users were initially asked to repeat the same procedure as for Level 3, only this time predicting what the robot would do in response to their actions. Once the users were comfortable controlling the robot, new functionality was added to the interface that replicated the five basic actions that had been seen from the manual inspectors: translation, rotation and so on.

4.5   Level 5 – Input from the User

The final stage of the re-design concentrated on assessing the ease of interaction between the user and the robot, identifying particular aspects of the interface that required modification. The task in the user trials changed from "What will the robot do

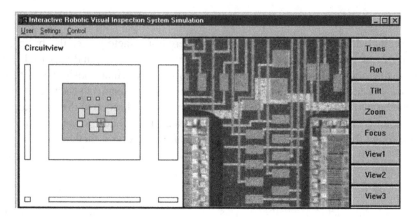

Fig. 5. The final IRVIS interface [15]

now?" to "Can you accomplish this goal?" As a result of this level, the final interface design was as shown in Fig. 5.

4.6   Level 6 – Functional Attributes

A series of user evaluation sessions were undertaken with users with a range of moderate to severe motor impairments. All of the users were able to navigate around the circuit tray without difficulty and within the time limit allowed. Likewise, all of the users were able to perform all of the other tasks seen in the manual inspection processes, such as tilting, rotating about a point, etc.

4.7   Level 7 – Social Attributes

Qualitative feedback from all the users was extremely favorable. Each user found the new interface easy and intuitive to use and all completed the tasks with a minimum of guidance. No user complained of the speed of response of IRVIS being too slow. This was an important result, because it had been previously thought that IRVIS was mechanically under-specified. A simple analysis showed why this was so. The original interface only allowed the use of one motor at a time. The new interface allowed potentially all five motors to be used simultaneously. The increased power available to the user significantly improved the overall speed of response.

5   Next Generation Robots

The examples given so far in this paper have focused on historical experiences. It is worth looking at how such robotic assistants may develop in the future and what roles they may play, especially in a universal access context. What is clear from the assistive robotic systems from the 1990s is that those designed with a clear purpose and benefit for the users in mind had the most successful take-up, especially the Handy 1. Similarly, the comparatively few examples of commercially successful robots for the home are focused on particular laborious tasks, such as vacuuming or mowing the lawn [17].

Consequently, it is clearly important to consider tasks that are important to users and especially those that support independent living or self-empowerment. Typical areas of life endeavor to consider include [18]:

- Lifelong learning and education
- Workplace
- Real world (i.e. extended activities of daily living)
- Entertainment
- Socialising

It is also important to consider the widest possible range of users [19] and impairment types. A somewhat stereotypical concept of an assistive robot is a robot guide dog for users with visual impairments [20]. However, robots can assist in a range of other impairments, such as cognitive [21] or communication impairments. Notable progress has been made in the use of robots to develop communication skills in children with autism, for example [22]. Robotic dogs have also been converted into conversation partners through the use of chatbots [23], see Fig. 6.

Fig. 6. A K9 shell converted into a chatbot as an exhibit at the Dundee Science Centre

Advances in artificial intelligence and natural language processing also offer opportunities for making such robotic systems into genuine communication partners [24]. Furthermore, advances in robotics are helping create a new generation of robots that are very much more anthropomorphic in their appearance and behaviors. One such development is the RoboThespian, shown in Fig. 7 [25, 26].

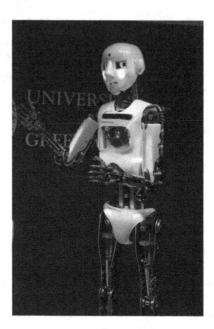

Fig. 7. A RoboThespian

RoboThespians are capable of simulating human movements from the waist up. They have been designed to emote and come pre-loaded with sample orations from Shakespeare to Terminator. The University of Greenwich has two RoboThespians and use them for outreach purposes. Their appearance and movement typically evokes a range of responses from curiosity and amusement to indications of fear and trepidation. We are currently exploring why different people respond to the robot in these ways.

6 Conclusions

Robotic assistants offer a fantastic opportunity to improve the lives of many people, especially those who are getting older or have functional impairments. However, to truly benefit from these opportunities, designers of such robots need to adopt user-centered inclusive design processes to ensure that they meet the needs, wants and aspirations of the users while not putting demands on them that exceed their skills, knowledge and capabilities.

Furthermore, designers of such robots will increase their chances of successful take-up of their products if they focus on supporting tasks that enable the users to accomplish tasks or activities that support independent living, such as with the Handy 1 and eating.

References

1. Bright, P.: Moore's Law really is dead this time. Ars Technica (2016). https://arstechnica. com/information-technology/2016/02/moores-law-really-is-dead-this-time/
2. Acharya, D., Kumar, V., Han, H.J.: Performance evaluation of data intensive mobile healthcare test-bed in a 4G environment. In: Proceedings of the 2nd ACM International Workshop on Pervasive Wireless Healthcare (MobileHealth 2012), pp. 21–26. ACM, New York (2012). doi:10.1145/2248341.2248353
3. Ball, L., Szymkowiak, A., Keates, S., Bradley, D., Brownsell, S.: eHealth and the internet of things. In: Proceedings of the 3rd International Conference on Pervasive Embedded Computing and Communication Systems, pp. 139–142. SCITEPRESS, Barcelona (2013). doi:10.5220/0004336701390142
4. Keates, S.: A pedagogical example of teaching Universal Access. Int. J. Univ. Access Inf. Soc. **14**(1), 97–110 (2015). doi:10.1007/s10209-014-0398-4. Springer
5. Cooper, A.: The Inmates are Running the Asylum. SAMS Publishing, Indianapolis (1999)
6. Buhler, C.: Robotics for rehabilitation – A European(?) perspective. In: Proceedings of the 5th International Conference on Rehabilitation Robotics (ICORR 1997), Bath, UK, pp. 5–11 (1997)
7. Mahoney, R.: Robotic products for rehabilitation: status and strategy. In: Proceedings of the 5th International Conference on Rehabilitation Robotics (ICORR 1997), Bath, UK. pp. 12–17 (1997)
8. Topping, M.J., Smith, J.K.: The development of handy 1. A robotic system to assist the severely disabled. Technol. Disabil. **10**(2), 95–105 (1999)
9. Tijsma, H.A., Liefhebber, F., Herder, J.L.: Evaluation of new user interface features for the manus robot arm. In: 9th International Conference on Rehabilitation Robotics, ICORR 2005, pp. 258–263. IEEE (2005). doi:10.1109/ICORR.2005.1501097
10. Dallaway, J.L., Mahoney, R.M., Jackson, R.D., Gosine, R.G.: An interactive robot control environment for rehabilitation applications. Robotica **11**(6), 541–551 (1993). doi:10.1017/S0263574700019391
11. Keates, S., Robinson, P.: Gestures and multimodal input. Behav. Inf. Technol. **18**(1), 36–44 (1999). doi:10.1080/014492999119237. Taylor and Francis Ltd.
12. Blessing, L.T.M., Chakrabati, A., Wallace, K.: A design research methodology. In: Proceedings of International Conference on Engineering Design 1995, Prague, Czech Republic, vol. 1, pp. 50–55 (1995)
13. Nielsen, J.: Usability Engineering. Morgan Kaufman Publishers, San Francisco (1993)
14. Card, S.K., Moran, T.P., Newell, A.: The Psychology of Human-Computer Interaction. Lawrence Erlbaum Associates, Hillsdale (1983)
15. Keates, S.: Designing for Accessibility: A Business Guide to Countering Design Exclusion. Lawrence Erlbaum Associates/CRC Press, Mahwah (2006)
16. Keates, S., Clarkson, P.J., Robinson, P.: Designing a usable interface for an interactive robot. In: Proceedings of the 6th International Conference on Rehabilitation Robotics (ICORR 1999), Stanford, CA, pp. 156–162 (1999)
17. Jodi Forlizzi, J., DiSalvo, C.: Service robots in the domestic environment: a study of the roomba vacuum in the home. In: Proceedings of the 1st ACM SIGCHI/SIGART Conference on Human-Robot Interaction (HRI 2006), pp. 258–265. ACM, New York (2006). doi:10.1145/1121241.1121286
18. Keates, S., Kozloski, J., Varker, P.: Cognitive impairments, HCI and daily living. In: Stephanidis, C. (ed.) UAHCI 2009. LNCS, vol. 5614, pp. 366–374. Springer, Heidelberg (2009). doi:10.1007/978-3-642-02707-9_42

19. Keates, S.: Engineering design for mechatronics—a pedagogical perspective. In: Hehenberger, P., Bradley, D. (eds.) Mechatronic Futures, pp. 221–238. Springer, Cham (2016). doi:10.1007/978-3-319-32156-1_14

20. Galatas, G., McMurrough, C., Mariottini, G.L., Makedon, F.: eyeDog: an assistive-guide robot for the visually impaired. In: Proceedings of the 4th International Conference on PErvasive Technologies Related to Assistive Environments (PETRA 2011). ACM, New York (2011) doi:10.1145/2141622.2141691

21. Keates, S., Adams, R., Bodine, C., Czaja, S., Gordon, W., Gregor, P., Hacker, E., Hanson, V., Kemp, J., Laff, M., Lewis, C., Pieper, M., Richards, J., Rose, D., Savidis, A., Schultz, G., Snayd, P., Trewin, S., Varker, P.: Cognitive and learning difficulties and how they affect access to IT systems. Int. J. Univ. Access Inf. Soc. 5(4), 329–339 (2007). doi:10.1007/s10209-006-0058-4. Springer

22. Robins, B., Dautenhahn, K., Te Boekhorst, R., Billard, A.: Robotic assistants in therapy and education of children with autism: can a small humanoid robot help encourage social interaction skills? Int. J. Univ. Access Inf. Soc. 4(2), 105–120 (2005). doi:10.1007/s10209-005-0116-3. Springer

23. Keates, S., Bradley, D., Sapeluk, A.: The future of universal access? Merging computing, design and engineering. In: Stephanidis, C., Antona, M. (eds.) UAHCI 2013. LNCS, vol. 8011, pp. 54–63. Springer, Heidelberg (2013). doi:10.1007/978-3-642-39194-1_7

24. Keates, S., Varker, P., Spowart, F.: Human-machine design considerations in advanced machine-learning systems. IEEE/IBM J. Res. Dev. 55(5), 4:1–4:10 (2011). doi:10.1147/JRD.2011.2163274. IEEE

25. Hashimoto, T., Kobayashi, H., Polishuk, A., Verner, I.: Elementary science lesson delivered by robot. In: Proceedings of the 8th ACM/IEEE International Conference on Human-Robot Interaction (HRI 2013), pp. 133–134. IEEE Press, Piscataway (2013)

26. Engineered Arts. RobotThespian. https://www.engineeredarts.co.uk/robothespian/

Study on the Application of Computer Simulation to Foldable Wheelchairs

Yu-Ting Lin[1(✉)], Fong-Gong Wu[1], and I-Jen Sung[2]

[1] Department of Industrial Design, National Cheng Kung University,
Tainan, Taiwan
yuting8312@gmail.com, fonggong@mail.ncku.edu.tw
[2] Department of Innovation Design, National Kaohsiung First University
of Science and Technology, Kaohsiung, Taiwan
jourdan@nkfust.edu.tw

Abstract. The traditional rental wheelchairs for households, or for use on public occasions (for instance, hospitals, entertainment parks, and department stores), are folded from both left and right sides. Nevertheless, the wheelchairs require a lot of space after being folded. In the current market, while there is a specially-designed wheelchair for air transportation, which becomes smaller and lighter after being folded, the folding is so complicated that it is not convenient for the elderly to use this wheelchair at home or outdoors. This study involves a series of designs, such as focus group interviews, design patent analysis, draft concept designs, and detailed designs. This study designs a more foldable, portable wheelchair for people who are able to walk, but unable to bear constant load due to aging, and thus, require assistance. The features of the product are, as follows: (1) faster folding: unlike a traditional wheelchair that is folded from both sides, the wheelchair of this study is equipped with four parallel, connecting poles, and it will fold providing the fixed latches are loosened and the back of the wheelchair is pulled backwards, which requires some preparation; (2) smaller size: its folded form is 40–50% less than that of a traditional wheelchair, and it can be stored in the small boot of 1,300 c.c.; (3) it is light-weight and labor- and time-saving: it is lighter than a traditional wheelchair, and can be pulled like a suitcase with four wheels after it is folded. With the aim of promoting social development through a more humanized wheelchair, this study develops a wheelchair with an innovative structure, which can greatly reduce the complicated folding steps and size of current wheelchairs; moreover, it can lighten the burden of caregivers and inspire relevant designers to make a wheelchair that better satisfies the needs of the elderly.

Keywords: Computer-assisted design · Elderly · Structure featuring fast folding · Wheelchair design

1 Introduction

Since its establishment as an aging society, Taiwan has witnessed a growing proportion of the elderly aged over 65. Compared with the US, South Korea, Singapore, Mainland China, Malaysia, and the Philippines, Taiwan has a significantly higher index of aging.

© Springer International Publishing AG 2017
M. Antona and C. Stephanidis (Eds.): UAHCI 2017, Part III, LNCS 10279, pp. 539–548, 2017.
DOI: 10.1007/978-3-319-58700-4_44

According to many experts and scholars worldwide, by 2018, the aged will account for 14.0% of the total population in Taiwan, and Taiwan will have become an over-aged society by 2026. This information indicates that, while people have a longer life span on average, their health is not as good as that in their youth due to the physical deterioration caused by aging. As there is a soaring demand for medical care and maintenance, there will be a corresponding greater need for action-supporting tools. In Taiwan, the number of potential users that require action-supporting tools due to physical problems is 1.4 million, which is about 6% of the total population of Taiwan. Therefore, how to use safe and appropriate action-supporting tools has become an essential issue for the future development of the action-supporting tool industry.

2 Literature Review

2.1 The Importance of Foldable Wheelchairs for the Elderly

The wheelchair is a common and important action-supporting tool for the elderly. Rental wheelchairs for use in households or on public occasions (for instance, hospitals, entertainment parks, and department stores) can only be folded by lifting the clothed mat; however, folding does not change the width, total length, or total height of the wheelchair, thus, the size remains large, which leads to the following problems:

(1) It will be impossible to store the wheelchair in the boot of a private car if the wheelchair remains large when folded. In this case, caregivers will face problem of failing to place the wheelchair in the boot without pushing the backseat forward.
(2) If the wheelchair is placed in the boot of a large vehicle, the large and heavy tool will increase the physical burden of female caregivers, and may result in physical harm.
(3) It is difficult to store an oversized folded wheelchair.

At present, there is a wheelchair for air transportation available on the market. While this wheelchair is smaller after it is folded, the folding procedure is very complicated and the structure is too simple; consequently, it is not suitable for use by the elderly at home. Most supporting tools in Taiwan are constructed to be highly operational and functional, as only the structural rationality and effects on rehabilitation are considered, meaning the form of products and the feelings of patients are often neglected. As a result, supporting tools can be as intimidating as instruments of torture. Therefore, the focus of this study is to design an attractive, convenient, and humanized wheelchair, which meets the demands of users, increases the value of products, and absorbs the professionalism of medical rehabilitation units; moreover, the wheelchair can be swiftly folded and its components can be replaced through modularization.

2.2 Evaluation and Application of Computer Simulation

Computer Simulation technology has been applied by manufacturers to evaluate the anticipated benefits of products for the confirmation and verification of development.

Currently, the multiple application method of Computer Simulation has become the standard for the development designs of industries. From this point of view, the awareness of Computer Simulation has been rising, thus, relevant software prices are constantly decreasing; moreover, the application interface is easily learned and operated. Operators can properly adjust products according to market demands without the need for innovation and change [1].

Computer-aided design conducts product design evaluations and the manufacturing processes through computer effects, etc., meaning its function lies in design computing and drafting. Design computing uses computers to conduct mechanical designs and the regular computing of engineering science. When designing the inner structure of a product, the application of technology optimization allows the optimal parameters of product functions and goals to be achieved. Computer graphics uses a graphics processing system to complete a design; in such a system, operators enter the desired shapes, sizes, and positions into a computer, which will automatically complete the graphic design [2].

According to the book entitled Good design! Touch people around the world, which was the first book for comprehensive understanding of product design/Drawing on a computer [3], in the process of designing, computer graphics can lead designers to their destination and enable them to create actual products suitable for manufacturing. Traditionally, designers adopt models made of Expanded Polyethylene, clay, and cardboard to cope with complicated forms. Although planar graphs, three-dimensional graphs, sectional graphs, and isometric graphs can be transformed into a 3D model, the transformation cannot offer the necessary data for manufacturing. Instead, the "models and drawings" of designers are interpreted by skillful cartographers and metallers, who put the design into production as a "co-designer". Wu [4] explored the application of computer simulation to artificial evaluation, and mentioned that environment, users' experience, the device, and the cost of raw materials were considered in product design; hence, computer simulation was adopted to develop and evaluate products, and used for modeling and production. The advantages of the computer simulation are, as follows:

(1) Computers can substitute for people during potentially harmful testing, avoid safety problems, examine hazards during operation, and estimate improvement of facilities.
(2) Computer simulation can save the time and funds required for experimentation (the layout of the experiment facilities and the funds for the subjects)
(3) Computer simulation takes less space and can facilitate artificial experiment evaluation.

3   Method

3.1   Expert Interview

Interview Survey is one of the most common ways of doing qualitative research. Amongst all, in-depth interview is most widely used. Interview Survey, an idea exchange activity between interviewers and interviewees by interaction and oral conversation. The opinions of the interviewees will then be generalised and analysed. Some practical practices are personal interviews, working group interviews, management interviews… etc. By collecting data from interview surveys, interviewers and interviewees are able to communicate in person, which makes the whole survey process more flexible and adaptable. In addition, interview surveys are easy, therefore, interviewees can simply answer the questions verbally even if they have any reading or writing disorders. To sum up, Interview Survey is a survey program that is widely applicable [5, 6].

The benefits of computer simulation are discussed through literature review, and the product development experiences of 10 professionals are collected during the interviews. The average of the ten experts is 15 years working experience; 6 for men (60%), and 4 for women (40%), respectively.

According to the interview results, computer simulation also plays an essential role in the field. In most cases, computer simulation is adopted to confirm the locations of structures and components, simulate product functions, and quickly browse and modify product form and modular design. As computer simulation renders the overall development faster and more efficient, the experts agree that the most important issue is to increase efficiency, followed by saving costs, reducing errors, previewing finished products, and increasing precision. Additionally, this technology is applied to create components with special specifications and equip products with imaginary situations.

3.2   Design Factors of the Customized Wheelchair

Observations of foldable wheelchairs sold on the market shows that they have the following problems:

(1) Wheelchairs can be folded by lifting the clothed mat in the middle. While the method is simple, as far as the form is concerned, the width, total length, and total height of the wheelchairs remain unchanged when folded. Consequently, a folded wheelchair remains so large that it cannot be stored in the boot of a car, which forces the caregiver to push the backseat forward to create room.

(2) Even if a folded wheelchair can be placed in the boot, its large size and weight (about 10 kg) still impose a tremendous physical challenge, especially on female caregivers.

(3) Even when wheelchairs are left unused, folded chairs are still too large for placement.

(4) In the current market, there is a specially-designed wheelchair for air transportation, which becomes smaller and lighter after being folded; however, the folding action is very complicated, and the structure is so simple that it is not convenient for the elderly to use this type of wheelchair at home.

In this study, the functions of foldable wheelchairs are analyzed and compared, and the analysis results and comparison are shown in the Table 1.

Table 1. Market analysis of foldable wheelchairs

Item \ Brand		Being Developed	KANG YANG	KANG ER FU
Size	Before folding	78.5×64.5×93.5 = 473,413.8 cm^3	100×68×87 = 591,600 cm^3	96×36×90 = 311,040 cm^3
	After folding	95.5×64.5×25.0 = 153,993.75 cm^3	100×31×87 = 269,700 cm^3	70×19×57 = 75,810 cm^3
Load capacity		100 kg	100 kg	100 kg
Way of folding		Folded from front and back	Folded from left and right sides	Folded first from left and rights sides and then from front and back
Difficulty of folding		Simple	Simple	Difficult
Time for folding		5 sec	5 sec	60 sec
Suggested price		NTD 4,980	NTD 5,800	NTD 4,980

According to the Table 1 data, the focus group method is adopted for a discussion among 10 professionals (industrial designers, product developers, and mechanical engineers). The design factors of a new foldable wheelchair are shown in the following Table 2.

Table 2. Design factors of the new foldable wheelchair

Item	Design factor	Description
1	Attractive	Physical features, material, and surface processing
2	Colorful	Overall color collocation
3	Light	Selected materials, the number of components, and overall structure
4	Comfortable	Surface materials, such as mat, back, and armrests
5	Detachable	Overall folding
6	Adjustable	Partial functions, such as armrests and pedal
7	Operable	Intuitive operation
8	Endurable	The adaptability of the selected materials, the complexity of the structure, and the problems caused by repetitious use
9	Portable	Easy folding, and the portability of a folded form
10	Simple	Singular function, without additional functions

According to the above design factors, the features of the new foldable wheelchair are, as follows:

(1) Faster folding: unlike a traditional wheelchair, which is folded from both sides, the wheelchair designed by this study is equipped with four paralleled, connected poles, which can be easily folded providing the fixed latches are loosened and the back of the wheelchair is pulled backwards, thus, requiring little preparation.
(2) Smaller size: its folded form is 40–50% less than that of a traditional wheelchair, and it can be stored in the small boot of 1,300 c.c.
(3) Lightweight (labor- and time-saving): it is lighter than a traditional wheelchair as a whole, and can be pulled like a suitcase with four wheels after it is folded.

4   Results

According to the above design factors and features, this study designs a new foldable wheelchair and demonstrates the functions through computer simulation.

4.1   Computer Drawing Model

First, 3D computer software (Ideas NX series) is applied for drawing, then, Solidworks 2015 is adopted to simulate the holes and combinations (Figs. 1 and 2) in order to confirm the intervention, product functions, and rationality of the overall structural adjustment.

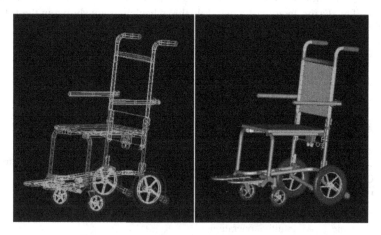

Fig. 1. Appearance of the computer simulated wheelchair (Graphs of the Computer Simulation of This Study)

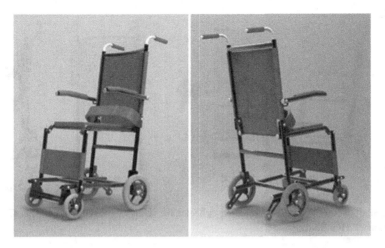

Fig. 2. Appearance of the computer simulated wheelchair (Graphs of the Computer Simulation of This Study)

According to the above design factors, the features of the new foldable wheelchair are, as follows:

(1) Faster folding: unlike a traditional wheelchair, which is folded from both sides, the wheelchair designed by this study is equipped with four paralleled, connected poles, which can be easily folded providing the fixed latches are loosened and the back of the wheelchair is pulled backwards, thus, requiring little preparation (Fig. 3).

Fig. 3. Function of the computer simulated wheelchair (Graphs of the Computer Simulation of This Study)

(2) Smaller size: its folded form is 40–50% less than that of a traditional wheelchair, and it can be stored in the small boot of 1,300 c.c (Fig. 4).

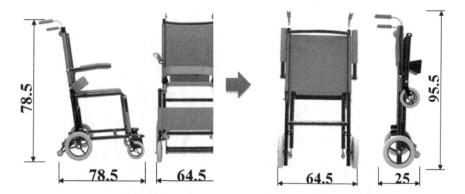

Fig. 4. Size of the computer simulated wheelchair (Unit: cm) (Graphs of the Computer Simulation of This Study)

(3) Lightweight (labor- and time-saving): it is lighter than a traditional wheelchair as a whole, and can be pulled like a suitcase with four wheels after it is folded.

4.2 Sample-Making Test

An ATOM 2.0 3D printer is used to make the wheelchair pipes, in a ratio (1:1), and the accessories are those of the existing wheelchairs available on the market. If some components are not sold on the market, the 3D printer is applied for fabrication (Fig. 5). A 3D printer is employed to conduct innovative testing before sample making.

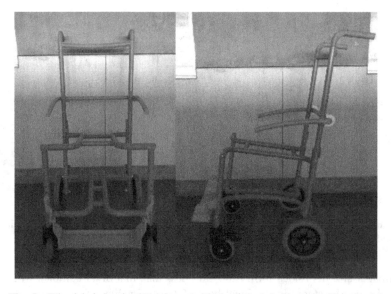

Fig. 5. Wheelchair by the 3D printer (with the ratio 1:1, Photo by This Study)

The feasibility of the structure is confirmed, and information regarding the structure and use of wheelchairs sold on the market is collected, and then, the problems in the portability of wheelchairs are solved for the re-design. The whole wheelchair is operated in a mechanical manner. After simulation, as based on the computer drawing, a model with the same ratio is created for the trial experiment; if it failed, the model would be further improved; if a success, mass production would be negotiated.

4.3   Interaction and Visual Design

The selected components are used to assemble the sample wheelchair and the functions are tested. The results of the test are, as Figs. 6 and 7.

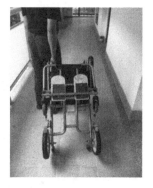

Fig. 6. Test on the actual functions of the wheelchair (Photo by This Study)

Fig. 7. The folded wheelchair is placed in the boot of a car of 1,300 c.c (Photo by This Study)

5   Conclusion

This study developed a wheelchair that is folded in an innovative manner; its folded form is 40–50% less than that of a traditional wheelchair; moreover, it is more labor-saving and time-saving. In addition to greatly reducing the workload of caregivers, it enhances consumers' intention to purchase. From the perspectives of users and artificial design, this new product is free from the problems of traditional wheelchairs, and users' needs are considered in the experiments, interviews, and observations during product design. The improvements and innovative design of this wheelchair will be patented. It is intended that a more humanized, convenient wheelchair with an innovative structure can greatly reduce the complicated steps of folding, as well as reduce the size of wheelchairs currently available on the market. Moreover, it can lighten the burden of caregivers and contribute to a more colorful life for the elderly.

References

1. Siemens Product Lifecycle Management Software Inc. (2017). https://www.plm.automation. siemens.com/zh_tw/plm/design-simulation.shtml
2. 2006–2017 MBAlib.com http://wiki.mbalib.com/zh-tw
3. Rodgers, P., Milton, A., trans. by Yang, J.Y.: Product design (Portfolio), pp. 112–114 (2012)
4. Wu, H.J., Chang, F.C.: Ergonomic evaluation of computer desks and chairs for children-based on computer simulation. J. Ergon. Study **13**(1), 41–51 (2011)
5. 2017 MBAlib.com http://wiki.mbalib.com/zh-tw
6. Introduction to Qualitative Research Methods: A Guidebook and Resource, 4th edn. (2015). http://as.wiley.com/WileyCDA/WileyTitle/productCd-1118767217,subjectCd-EV00.html

Mindfulness and Asynchronous Neurofeedback: Coping with Mind Wandering

Alessandro Marcengo[✉], Emanuela Sabena, and Angelo Crea

BeMindful, Turin, Italy
{alessandro.marcengo,emanuela.sabena,angelo.crea}@bemindful.it

Abstract. Mindfulness has taken over the past 25 years a status of autonomous paradigm in some medical and psychotherapeutic disciplines that have generated a pervasive interest about its clinical applications and the nourishment of the individual well-being. This tendency coexists with a technological direction that in recent years has enabled the development of personal and portable devices for EEG neurofeedback (already used to support the treatment of ADHD, DOC, autism, depression, anxiety disorders, etc.) easily usable in real life situations by the individual. We will discuss the pros and cons about the convergence between these two trends through the results of an 11 month autoetnographic study and the analysis of the data gathered during the long period usage of a personal meditation neurofeedback device.

Keywords: Mindfulness · MBSR · Neurofeedback · EEG · Quantified Self

1 Introduction

Technological advances in wearable and ubiquitous technologies have recently opened new opportunities for Quantified Self (QS). These systems aim to leverage sensors and mobile devices for collecting personal information in order to trigger self-reflection and enhance self-knowledge.

To this aim, we carried out an 11 month autoethnography, monitoring the daily session of meditation and the "quality" of this session in relationship with different intervening variables. The results of the study are somehow interesting: asynchronous neurofeedback could be considered a facilitator to overcome the notorious difficult start and continuity in mindfulness meditation and represent a valuable tool. The paper is structured as follow. Section 2 describe the present status of mindfulness in clinical and non clinical setting. Section 3 present the basic functioning and application of Neurofeedback. Section 4 describe the relationship between mindfulness, EEG and Mind Wandering. Section 5 presents the most relevant related work in relation of mindfulness and EEG/Neurofeedback. Section 6 describes the setting of our research while provides a picture of the practice of autoethnography both in anthropology and in Human-Computer Interaction. Section 7 describes results and future directions of the work. Section 8 draw some conclusions.

© Springer International Publishing AG 2017
M. Antona and C. Stephanidis (Eds.): UAHCI 2017, Part III, LNCS 10279, pp. 549–561, 2017.
DOI: 10.1007/978-3-319-58700-4_45

2 Mindfulness Today

The term Mindfulness is the English translation of the word "Sati" in Pali language, which means "mindfulness" or "bare attention." According to the definition of Jon Kabat-Zinn, Mindfulness means "paying attention in a particular way: on purpose, in the present moment and in a non-judgmental way." It is a question of voluntarily directing attention to what is occurring in your body and around ourself, moment by moment, listening more accurately to our personal experience, and observing it for what it is, not evaluating or criticizing it. The practice of this particular "attitude of mind", that can also be defined "awareness", is derived from the Theravada Buddhism, one of the two main currents of Buddhist thought, spread from 2500 years in South Asia and Southeast Europe, especially in Burma, Cambodia, Laos, Sri Lanka and Thailand, both in the monastic and secular ambience. The use, by the western medicine, of the Mindfulness for the promotion of health is a relatively recent acquisition, which began in the 70s in the United States. The Mindfulness is a form of meditation, so it requires time, energy, determination, firmness and discipline. From the point of view of involved mental processes it is embodied in paying attention, into the present moment, to four factors: the body, the sensory perceptions (physiological, physical and psychological belonging to the large domains of the pleasant, unpleasant, mixed and neutral), the mental formations (eg. anger, sorrow or compassion) and the objects of mind (every mental formation has an object, being angry with someone and for something, etc …). The observation of these elements of subjective experience takes place in a state of genuine non-reactive calm, in which you accept what is seen for what it is, allowing change to happen naturally, without obstruct or promote them and avoiding the usual resistance or the usual judgment that cause further suffering. The primary applications have been and still remain in the clinic area: the pioneering work of Jon Kabat-Zinn, professor of medicine at the University of Massachusetts had a very wide following both in the field of medicine and in the field of psychotherapy. The backbone of the applications is based on in the liberating power of awareness. More recently, however, these applications have been extended to the field of education and organizational domain as a proposal of a real healthier and aware lifestyle. One of the most important aspects of the Mindfulness practice is to devote himself with a constant and regular commitment over time. The suggestion that is given in all of Mindfulness training is to practice, if possible, every day, even if only for ten minutes. An indication that may sound rigid and restrictive, but whose meaning is to be found in the trust about the utility of the practice: awareness is a quality potentially present in each of us that can be reinforced through constant training; the more we exercise to be present, the more awareness grows over time. And the experience itself is the strongest confirmation of this simple mechanism. However, just the constancy of practice become from the beginning of the training one of the most difficult obstacles to overcome for almost all the practitioners; a rock which often recurs over and over again, cyclically, also over the years, even in the most experienced meditators. We collect a lot of evidence of this difficulty in our courses, and our own experience is punctuated occasionally by moments when the commitment vacillate. A strong base of the mindfulness approach is the close and organic connection with the scientific thought and the research: it is born indeed from personalities who are scientists, researchers, clinicians, and from the beginning has developed both from the field of practical experimentation, as from rigorous scientific research seeking to verify the actual effectiveness and operational mechanisms. Today, research on various issues related to the perspective of mindfulness are expanding exponentially, with several hundred research papers published each year in leading scientific journals.

3   Neurofeedback

Neurons of our brain constantly generate electrical activity recordable through electrodes placed on the scalp. The types of brain waves measured at a given time depends on the state in which the brain is. This can range from numbness and drowsiness up to a state of extreme focus and concentration. When we are involved in different activities, the electrical activity change. We mainly refers to 5 rhythms (or waves) brain: Delta, Theta, Alpha, Beta and Gamma. These rhythms differ in several aspects: the amplitude or voltage (measured in microvolt) and the frequency, defined as the number of cycles per second, measured in Hertz (Hz). Depending on their frequency we can have "slow" waves and " fast" waves. In particular the prevalence of certain brain waves show some types of mental states:

- Delta 1–4 Hz: sleep, intuition, unconscious thought
- Theta 4–8 Hz: sub-conscious thought, insight, meditative
- Alpha 8–12 Hz: neutral, peaceful, relaxed state
- Beta 15–21 Hz: being present, sustained attention, focusing,
- Gamma 33–64 Hz: integrative thinking, creativity, learning.

The nervous system works best when it is able to be flexible and change functioning even during a single activity, passing from moments of concentration to moments of thoughtfulness or creativity. However sometimes some imbalances are generated causing the preponderance of one rhythm limiting so the flexibility of CNS functioning. Therefore, as for the car gears, each band has a function and is not in itself positive or negative.

Neurofeedback is a tool through which an individual learns to change the amplitude, frequency and consistency of the electrophysiological aspects of his brain. Through neurofeedback, which allows real-time display on the monitor of a computer, of its own electroencephalographic activity, the brain is trained to produce brain waves into specific widths and in specific locations: providing immediate feedback to the brain about their operation, he becomes able to re-educate himself, until reaching the desired activity pattern. The purpose of the neurofeedback training is to teach the individual how to feel specific states of cortical activation and how to achieve these states voluntarily. Through neurofeedback training, in fact, the individual becomes aware of the different EEG states (EEG is a well-established, non-invasive, harmless method of recording the electrical activity of groups of brain cells) and becomes able to produce them when required. Many studies and research on neurofeedback have attested its effectiveness in the treatment of many clinical conditions, such as ADHD, epilepsy, anxiety, depression, chronic fatigue syndrome, fibromyalgia, sleep disturbance, Tourette's syndrome, obsessive-compulsive disorder. The neurofeedback was also used to increase cognitive performance, in the music domain, with athletes, with business executives, and for the cognitive improvement and increase of memory in normal college students.

The practice of mindfulness was associated with a neurophysiological mechanism involving the alpha rhythm and that would be connected to our attentional capacity.

Alpha waves have moderate amplitude and average "speed". Their presence, evident especially in the back of the brain, is associated with the closing of the eyes (Alpha Blocking) and state of calm, relaxation, daydreaming (even in full wakefulness). It is interesting to note that those who pray or meditate, instinctively close their eyes, as if unconsciously wanted to achieve an "Alpha state".

3.1 Muse

Novice meditators usually struggle with two issues: knowing whether they are "doing it right," and staying motivated. Muse addresses these issues by providing real-time "state of mind" feedback, providing an engaging motivational framework. Muse is based on electroencephalography (EEG) technology and could be considered a technological advance over earlier versions of EEG neurofeedback technologies. Muse is at present the most versatile and easy-to-use EEG system available for individual use. It is designed as a personal meditation assistant. It can pair with any tablet or smartphone and operate with the Muse application, which trains the user in meditation exercises and records EEG data. Muse is also used in hospitals, clinics, and universities as a research tool. Institutions currently using Muse in research include Harvard, Stanford, MIT, Mayo Clinic, NYU, McMaster University, University of Toronto, University College London, and many others. This device uses two channels on the left and two on the right, so it is ideal for exploring hemispheric asymmetries. Muse has two micro-USB ports on the back of the ear pods where two auxiliary electrodes can be attached. These electrodes can be used to measure EMG, ECG, or EEG on other areas of the head or body. It has been tested against industry standard EEG systems including the Brain Vision acti-CHamp system and the g.Tec g.USBamp system. Muse achieves comparable performance in voltage trace comparisons and in patterns of total and hemispheric power. The product is also an open platform: anyone can record raw data and anyone can build their own application. EEG data can be also recorded with MuseLab, MusePlayer, or via the third-party mobile application MuseMonitor (for Android and iOS).

4   Mind Wandering

Mind wandering is our daily and ordinary being distract from what we are doing: the daydreaming, the fantasies about the future, trying to anticipate something that we are going to do, the reliving of past scenes, the interior monologue, the imaginary conversation with someone. Mind wandering is therefore our mental life, the "movie" that flows in the head when we are not focused with our senses in a task which fully engages our attention. According to recent studies, nearly half of our mental life when we are awake is spent in a state of mind wandering, which involves the brain regions of the Default Mode Network (DMN), composed of some very large brain nodes, as such as the medial prefrontal cortex, posterior cingulate cortex and the inferior parietal and temporal cortices. Understanding the cognitive mechanisms and the neural basis of mind wandering can also help us understand how mindfulness work, because the mental training that takes place during the practice is basically a method to decrease the mind wandering. In people who are more mindful, and which are either for personal attitude or because they train through the techniques of mindfulness meditation, we experience less brain activity in the Default Mode Network (DMN). That's why understanding the mind wandering helps to better understand mindfulness: one is the opposite of the other. Mindfulness is the tendency to focus while mind wandering is the tendency to get distracted. Neuroscience in recent years have given a valuable contribution to the understanding of the neural mechanisms involved in the mind wandering and the role of the Default Mode Network (DMN). Its specificity and its relationship with the mind wandering allowed to identify the DMN as separate from the other, both functionally and structurally.

5   Related Work

Quantified Self applications aim at increasing individuals' self-knowledge by collecting a variety of personal data [1, 2]. Recently, the range of information detectable by such applications has widely increased [3, 4]. Moreover, new techniques for collecting data needing self-reporting [5], mining and structuring information [6, 7], as well as displaying it in meaningful visualizations [8–10] have been experimented to get "naive" users closer to the activity of self-monitoring [11, 12], as well as lead to new opportunities for designing self-tracking devices [13, 14]. Finally, new design techniques to allow a serendipitous navigation through data [15], as well as gamification methods [16–19] have been employed to increase users' intrinsic motivation [20], or drive individuals toward a change in their behavior [21], foreseeing the use of game elements in self-tracking domain [22].

Among these recent advancements in the Quantified Self context, an important element is represented by the possibility of tracking aspects related to the human cognition [23], such as attention [24], reading activities [25], and memories [26]. Progress in the development of wearables is now allowing to detect and track also more complex mind-related states, like meditative states, and more precisely mindfulness states. For such states, changes in the central system have been found as the most reliable indicator [27]: these changes can be commonly tracked in lab environment with EEG using electrodes placed on the scalp.

Different studies correlated neural activities with mindfulness states [28, 29], showing, for example, an EEG lowering (lowering the alpha rhythms and appearing of theta waves) during meditation [30–35]. For example, studies with mediation masters pointed that they experience a series of EEG changes during meditation, from appearance of alpha waves, their increase in amplitude, and then decrease of their frequency, to the appearance of theta waves [28]. The lowering of the alpha rhythm has been linked to increase in internal attention, and the increase in the theta band to relaxation, indicating that EEG measures correlates with the subjective experience of mindfulness [27].

Now, less obtrusive EEGs allow to monitor such states also outside the laboratory context. Self-monitoring one's attention is a key ability for mindfulness meditation: tracking and feeding information back about brain waves can support meditative states. This form of training is precisely provided by neurofeedback. It has been highlighted that neurofeedback can be effective in attention deficit disorder [30], epilepsy [36], learning disabilities [37] and autism spectrum disorders [38], and precisely meditation [28].

Different research successfully experimented neurofeedback as a support to mediation and mindfulness. Sensorium [39] is a neurofeedback environment that enable individuals to experience their brain waves and heart rate in the form of sounds and light effects. MeditAid [27] uses an aural neurofeedback to help users in mindfulness practices, by feeding brain activity data back through binaural bits: a user study showing that users were able to achieve a deeper level of meditation by using the system. Finally, RelaWorld [40] is a neuroadaptive virtual reality meditation system that combines virtual reality with neurofeedback to provide a tool for supporting meditation.

6   Study Outline

In our research, we recorded through a Muse device 9900 min (165 h) of meditation divided into 220 meditation sessions of 45 min over a period of 11 months. The practice of meditation adopted has always been the same: a sequence of Seated Meditation with attention to Breath, Body, Sounds, and Thoughts.

The aim was to understand how a neurofeedback device might improve adherence to daily practice or not considering the resistance that every meditator meets in the effort to keep the practice consistent over time, and if some sort of synchronous (during practice) or asynchronous (after practice) feedback could have an effect on the practice in terms of quantity or quality.

The measurements were made all by the same subject, an instructor of Mindful Based Interventionts (MBI's) with 10 years of practice. It was therefore chosen an approach based on Autoethnographic Method.

6.1   The Autoethnographic Method

Autoethnography requires that we observe ourselves observing, that we interrogate what we think and believe, and that we challenge our own assumptions, asking over and over if we have penetrated as many layers of our own defenses, fears, and insecurities as our project requires. Good autoethnography completely dissolves any idea of distance, doesn't produce 'findings', isn't generalizable, and only has credibility when is self-reflexive.

When it is done well, we can learn previously unspoken, unknown things. Autoethnography has been employed in HCI for evaluating technologies and gaining empathy with users of various types of devices [40]. It has been used in autobiographical design as a design research method that "drawing on extensive, genuine usage by those creating or building the system" allows designers "to uncover detailed, subtle understandings that they likely wouldn't have found with other user-centered design techniques because they might seem unremarkable". The recent popularity of this kind of self-study has to be retraced to the need of finding less-demanding techniques than traditional ethnographic methods, which are very expensive in terms of time and costs. Typically, ethnography will take place over a period of several months with at least the same amount of time spent in analysis and interpretations of the observations. So they can be inscribed in those approaches called as "rapid ethnography", which aims to understand users and their environments in a shortened timeframe. By using this method we tried to overcome the difficulties in observing users in private setting, such as during meditation, gathering a variety of data that would have been impossible to collect otherwise.

6.2 Ethnographic Setting

In the light of the aspects identified above and the chosen autoethnography methodology, we choose for a 11 month period of self-observation wearing the Muse Device during each seated meditation.

The considered measures has been:

- Length and percentage of estimated (from the meditator) concentrative time on each session
- Length and percentage of concentrative time of each session measured by Muse device
- Number of attention drop (mind wandering activation) counted by Muse device
- Notation by the meditator through self report for each session of thoughts, body sensation, pleasant/unpleasant quality of the experience
- Notation by the meditator through self report for each session of the subjective perception of time
- Time of day in which the meditation was made
- Notation of the amount of sleep each day.

7   Results

The first result that shall be highlighted is that there was an almost immediate abandonment of the synchronous feedback deemed distracting instead of easing. This is probably due to the advanced level of the practitioner. Advancing in the meditation practice, there is less and less need to have a guiding voice that appeals to notice any form mind wandering. The feedback of Muse does just that, it signals the loss of focus in a way that however is itself a disruptive stimulus. Very useful appears instead to the expert meditator the presence of the asynchronous feedback, meaning the tracking of the session available after each session.

Another interesting finding relates to the estimate by the meditator of concentrative capacity during the session. This estimate is pretty accurate but suffers from a kind of *recency* effect. In particular, if we consider only the last 15 min of the EEG registration (about one third of the session) the accuracy of the estimate has an error that varies around ±5%. If we consider the whole session the error compared to the value recorded by Muse varies around ±16%. Another aspect of estimation particularly interesting and logged during sessions regards the perception of perceived length of the session. All sessions last 45 min but at the same time the perception of time is highly variable. This is a well known phenomenon to all meditators, some sessions can "fly" while others seems to "never end". In our meditations we asked to sign the practice as "normal", "short" or "long" and what has been highlighted is that there is a close correlation between perception of time and concentrative capacity within the session. So practices that have achieved a high score in terms of maintaining the attentional focus were also the ones most often signed as "short" on the contrary those who have recorded more distractions and therefore a lower quality on attentional capacity are those that were signed more as "long." This data tells us that with the growth of the attention decreases the sense of boredom, so we can infer that the sense of boredom, a feeling often very unpleasant, is heavily based on scarce attentional capacity.

Finally we should highlight two more evidences. The first one is that the "quality" of the meditation measured through the attentional capacity (not activation of the mind wandering) strongly dependent on the amount of sleep in the previous night. The focus of activity requires a certain amount of energy. It is common that meditators especially in early stages feel very tired after meditation practices. This energy must be available. When the amount of sleep in not sufficient the energy deficit is immediately evidenced by a decreased attentional ability, from increased distractibility and a consequent feeling that the practice is more difficult and more boring. Less clear is rather the relationship with the time of day. The data in this study tell us that there are two times of the day in which the attentional capacity is systematically better: it is late morning (around 11:00) and late afternoon (around 17.00). The data have been recorded on a large number of sessions but only on one meditator so this result is obviously not generalizable. We can however suppose some causes for this. The first could be related to the distance from the meal times, particularly breakfast and lunch. It's possible that during digestion the ability to mobilize energies (also mental energies) is compromised and as such the attentional capacity would be reduced. Or it could be a simple cyclical trend linked to the personal metabolism of the meditator. Finally could be considered some aspects of greater complexity linked to changes in blood glucose or fat metabolism throughout the day. The "worst" sessions with less attentional capacity were those measured on the evening. Likely this is due to the contemporary occurrence of two conditions: the fatigue due to the day activities and the condition of digestion in place after dinner.

We were not able to highlight any aspect or any correlation between the content emerged during the sessions, both physical (pain, tension, etc.), both of mental type (thoughts, images, etc.) and the quality of the session as measured by Muse. One hypothesis could have build about a possible correlation between unpleasant feelings and content and a high score in terms of attention drop. Indeed, the data analysis did not produce such evidence.

7.1 Discussion and Further Research

The appearance of non-acceptance of the synchronous feedback from the practitioner is not generalizable, although noting the activation of mind wandering is an autonomous capacity that develops with practice and which therefore does not require in advanced phases any external feedback. To develop this autonomous capacity is actually the essence of the practice. However, to make this a generalizable insight, synchronous feedback should be tested with a sample of different meditators with different experience levels to assess if indeed there is an inverse correlation between level of experience and appreciation of the synchronous feedback.

Also about the ability to estimate the quality of the session the result does not appear generalizable. It is not possible to say how much this accuracy in estimating is a personal expression of a good awareness of the meditator involved or dependent on the experience level of the same. Again should be necessary to repeat the study with a larger sample that includes different practitioners with different levels of experience.

About the "short" perception of time in direct correlation with the degree of attentional capacity expressed in the session this only confirms a phenomenon known and widely documented in the literature. What future research could instead target is on one side, which are the unpleasant mental states connected in a large sample with the length of the session perception (boredom, restlessness, irritation, etc.) and on the other, in what amount these states may be present in clinical situations where there is a fundamental attention deficit. It is on the other hand known how this kind of unpleasant sensations are present in syndromes involving attention deficit such as ADHD (attention deficit hyperactivity disorder). Also the ability to focus as element strongly dependent from the mental energy represents a confirmation of a wel known fact in the literature. More interesting seems the relationship with the hour of the day but it was not possible to determine the origin. It is possible that aspects related to the digestion process are interfering with the mobilization of energy necessary to feed up the attentional capacity. However this is only an hypothesis that requires a thorough study on the relationship between attention and specific components of the meal (sugars, fats, proteins, etc.) in a sample on which assess the attention capacity in a laboratory setting.

Finally, our study did not reveal anything significant about the relationship between emerging content during sessions (or at least pleasant/unpleasant feeling) and the number of attention drop and mind wandering activation. A research of particular interest in this regard would require evidence from large numbers and big data from a worldwide network. Some experiments have been attempted to do so by platforms such as Dreamboard on dreams, an interesting variation would bring this same logic of distributed collection on the domain of meditative content.

8 Conclusions

The suggestion that is given in all Mindfulness training is to practice, if possible, every day, even if only for ten minutes. An indication that may sound rigid and restrictive, but whose meaning is to be found in the trust about the utility of the practice: awareness is a quality potentially present in each of us that can be reinforced through constant training; the more we exercise to be present, the more awareness grows over time. And the experience itself is the strongest confirmation of this simple mechanism. However, just the constancy of practice become from the beginning of the training one of the most difficult obstacles to overcome for almost all the practitioners; a rock which often recurs over and over again, cyclically, also over the years, even in the most experienced meditators.

These difficulties take the form of resistances. We can talk about internal resistance when they come by the individual himself (*I can not stand the boredom, I am not able, I feel pain, I can not sit still, I do not experience the benefits*). We can talk about external resistances if the individual attributes his difficulties with practice to external causes (*not enough time, I do not have a suitable space, I don't have a place to be alone, there are too many distractions*). The role of the asynchronous neurofeedback helps to overcome at least in part this resistance, especially on the meditator in the early stages of practice, when the value of repeatability and consistency has not yet grasped. This is similar with what happens using a fitness tracker: the neurofeedaback provides personal data relating to the practice which allow to derive some personal evidence. For example it is difficult to meditate after a big meal or it is easier when you are rested. This allows to make the sessions more concentrative, making the duration perceptually faster, experiencing less boredom or restlessness or other unpleasant sensations creating that wealth meditation amount that at some point will become a critical mass capable of perpetuating itself even in difficult times, which necessarily will come. We can consider neurofeedback a facilitator to overcome the initial obstacle of practice continuity and as such has a big impact for beginners. However, there is a risk: to transform the mediation practice into a performance, in a target score to reach or to improve. This approach would lead away from the deep intention inborn with mindfulness meditation and as such should always avoided carefully.

References

1. Marcengo, A., Rapp, A.: Visualization of human behavior data: the Quantified Self. In: Huang, L.H., Huang, W. (eds.) Innovative Approaches of Data Visualization and Visual Analytics, pp. 236–265. IGI Global, Hershey (2013). doi:10.4018/978-1-4666-4309-3
2. Rapp, A., Tirassa, M.: Know thyself: a theory of the self for personal informatics. Hum. Comput. Interact. (2017). doi:10.1080/07370024.2017.1285704
3. Rapp, A., Cena, F., Kay, J., Kummerfeld, B., Hopfgartner. F., Plumbaum, T., Larsen, J. E.: New frontiers of Quantified Self: finding new ways for engaging users in collecting and using personal data. In: Adjunct Proceedings of the 2015 ACM International Joint Conference on Pervasive and Ubiquitous Computing and Proceedings of the 2015 ACM International Symposium on Wearable Computers (UbiComp/ISWC 2015 Adjunct), pp. 969–972. ACM, New York (2015). doi:10.1145/2800835.2807947
4. Rapp, A., Cena, F., Kay, J., Kummerfeld, B., Hopfgartner, F., Plumbaum, T., Larsen, J.E., Epstein, D.A., Gouveia, R.: New frontiers of Quantified Self 2: going beyond numbers. In: Proceedings of the 2016 ACM International Joint Conference on Pervasive and Ubiquitous Computing: Adjunct (UbiComp 2016), pp. 506–509. ACM, New York (2016). doi: 10.1145/2968219.2968331

5. Sarzotti, F., Lombardi, I., Rapp, A., Marcengo, A., Cena, F.: Engaging users in self-reporting their data: a tangible interface for Quantified Self. In: Antona, M., Stephanidis, C. (eds.) UAHCI 2015. LNCS, vol. 9176, pp. 518–527. Springer, Cham (2015). doi: 10.1007/978-3-319-20681-3_49

6. Banaee, H., Ahmed, M.U., Loutfi, A.: Data mining for wearable sensors in health monitoring systems: a review of recent trends and challenges. Sensors **13**, 17472–17550 (2013)

7. Cena, F., Likavec, S., Rapp, A., Marcengo, A.: An ontology for Quantified Self: capturing the concepts behind the numbers. In: Proceedings of the 2016 ACM International Joint Conference on Pervasive and Ubiquitous Computing: Adjunct (UbiComp 2016), pp. 602–604. ACM, New York (2016). doi:10.1145/2968219.2968329

8. Nafus, D., Denman, P., Durham, L., Florez, O., Nachman, L., Sahay, S., Savage, E., Sharma, S., Strawn, D., Wouhaybi, R.H.: As simple as possible but no simpler: creating flexibility in personal informatics. In: CHI 2016 Extended Abstracts. ACM, New York (2016)

9. Hilviu, D., Rapp, A.: Narrating the Quantified Self. In: Adjunct Proceedings of the 2015 ACM International Joint Conference on Pervasive and Ubiquitous Computing and Proceedings of the 2015 ACM International Symposium on Wearable Computers (UbiComp/ISWC 2015 Adjunct), pp. 1051–1056. ACM, New York (2015). doi:10.1145/2800835.2800959

10. Epstein, D.A., Cordeiro, F., Bales, E., Fogarty, J., Munson, S.: Taming data complexity in lifelogs: exploring visual cuts of personal informatics data. In: Proceedings of the DIS 2014 Conference on Designing Interactive Systems. ACM, New York (2014)

11. Rapp, A., Cena, F.: Self-monitoring and technology: challenges and open issues in personal informatics. In: Stephanidis, C., Antona, M. (eds.) UAHCI 2014. LNCS, vol. 8516, pp. 613–622. Springer, Cham (2014). doi:10.1007/978-3-319-07509-9_58

12. Rapp, A., Cena, F.: Personal informatics for everyday life: how users without prior self-tracking experience engage with personal data. Int. J. Hum Comput Stud. **94**, 1–17 (2016). doi:10.1016/j.ijhcs.2016.05.006

13. Rapp, A., Cena, F.: Affordances for self-tracking wearable devices. In: Proceedings of International Symposium on Wearable Computers (ISWC 2015), pp. 141–142. ACM, New York (2015). doi:10.1145/2802083.2802090

14. Rapp, A., Cena, F., Hilviu, D., Tirassa, M.: Human body and smart objects. In: Adjunct Proceedings of the 2015 ACM International Joint Conference on Pervasive and Ubiquitous Computing and Proceedings of the 2015 ACM International Symposium on Wearable Computers (UbiComp/ISWC 2015 Adjunct), pp. 939–943. ACM, New York (2015). doi: 10.1145/2800835.2806204

15. Cardillo, D., Rapp, A., Benini, S., Console, L., Simeoni, R., Guercio, E., Leonardi, R.: The art of video MashUp: supporting creative users with an innovative and smart application. Multimedia Tools Appl. **53**(11), 1–23 (2011). doi:10.1007/s11042-009-0449-7

16. Rapp, A.: A qualitative investigation of gamification: motivational factors in online gamified services and applications. Int. J. Technol. Hum. Interact. **11**(1), 67–82 (2015). doi:10.4018/ijthi.2015010105

17. Deterding, S., Dixon, D., Khaled, R., Nacke, L.: From game design elements to gamefulness: defining "gamification". In: Proceedings of the 15th International Academic MindTrek Conference: Envisioning Future Media Environments (MindTrek 2011), pp. 9–15 (2011)

18. Rapp, A., Marcengo, M., Console, L., Simeoni, R.: Playing in the wild: enhancing user engagement in field evaluation methods. In: Proceeding of the 16th International Academic MindTrek Conference (MindTrek 2012), pp. 227–228. ACM, New York (2012). doi: 10.1145/2393132.2393180

19. Rapp, A., Cena, F., Gena, C., Marcengo, A., Console, L.: Using game mechanics for field evaluation of prototype social applications: a novel methodology. Behav. Inf. Technol. **35**(3), 184–195 (2016). doi:10.1080/0144929X.2015.1046931

20. Rapp, A.: Designing interactive systems through a game lens: an ethnographic approach. Comput. Hum. Behav. (2015). doi:10.1016/j.chb.2015.02.048

21. Rapp. A.: Drawing inspiration from world of warcraft: gamification design elements for behavior change technologies. Interact. Comput. (2017). doi:10.1093/iwc/iwx001

22. Rapp, A.: Meaningful game elements for personal informatics. In: Proceedings of the 2014 ACM International Symposium on Wearable Computers: Adjunct Program (ISWC 2014 Adjunct), pp. 125–130. ACM, New York (2014). doi:10.1145/2641248.2642734

23. Cena, F., Likavec, S., Rapp, A.: Quantified Self and modeling of human cognition. In: Adjunct Proceedings of the 2015 ACM International Joint Conference on Pervasive and Ubiquitous Computing and Proceedings of the 2015 ACM International Symposium on Wearable Computers (UbiComp/ISWC 2015 Adjunct), pp. 1021–1026. ACM, New York (2015). doi: 10.1145/2800835.2800954

24. Vidal, M., Nguyen, D.H., Lyons, K.: Looking at or through?: using eye tracking to infer attention location for wearable transparent displays. In: Proceedings of the 2014 ACM International Symposium on Wearable Computers (ISWC 2014), pp. 87–90. ACM, New York (2014)

25. Ishimaru, S., Dingler, T., Kunze, K., Kise, K., Dengel, A.: Reading interventions: tracking reading state and designing interventions. In: Proceedings of the 2016 ACM International Joint Conference on Pervasive and Ubiquitous Computing: Adjunct (UbiComp 2016), pp. 1759–1764. ACM, New York (2016)

26. Matassa, A., Rapp, A., Simeoni, R.: Wearable accessories for cycling: tracking memories in urban spaces. In: Proceedings of the 2013 ACM Conference on Pervasive and Ubiquitous Computing Adjunct Publication (UbiComp 2013 Adjunct), pp. 415–424. ACM, New York (2013). doi:10.1145/2494091.2495973

27. Sas, C., Chopra, R.: Meditaid: a wearable adaptive neurofeedback-based system for training mindfulness state. Pers. Ubiquit. Comput. **19**(7), 1169–1182 (2015)

28. Kasamatsu, A., Hirai, T.: An electroencephalographic study on the Zen meditation (Zazen). Psychiatry Clin. Neurosci. **20**(4), 315–336 (1966)

29. Lutz, A., Greischar, L.L., Rawlings, N.B., Ricard, M., Davidson, R.J.: Long-term meditators self-induce high-amplitude gamma synchrony during mental practice. Proc. Nat. Acad. Sci. USA **101**(46), 16369–16373 (2004)

30. Butnik, S.M.: Neurofeedback in adolescents and adults with attention deficit hyperactivity disorder. J. Clin. Psychol. **61**(5), 621–625 (2005)

31. Dooley, C.: The impact of meditative practices on physiology and neurology: a review of the literature. Sci. Discipulorium **4**, 35–59 (2009)

32. Cahn, B.R., Polich, J.: Meditation states and traits: EEG, ERP, and neuroimaging studies. Psychol. Bull. **132**(2), 180–211 (2006)

33. Fell, J., Axmacher, N., Haupt, S.: From alpha to gamma: electrophysiological correlates of meditation-related states of consciousness. Med. Hypotheses **75**(2), 218–224 (2010)

34. Stinson, B., Arthur, D.: A novel EEG for alpha brain state training, neurobiofeedback and behavior change. Complement. Ther. Clin. Pract. **19**(3), 114–118 (2013)

35. Travis, F.: Autonomic and EEG patterns distinguish transcending from other experiences during transcendental meditation practice. Int. J. Psychophysiol. **42**, 1–9 (2001)

36. Sterman, M., Egner, T.: Foundation and practice of neurofeedback for the treatment of epilepsy. Appl. Psychophysiol. Biofeedback **31**(1), 21–35 (2006)

37. Fernández, T., Herrera, W., Harmony, T., Díaz-Comas, L., Santiago, E., Sánchez, L., Bosch, J., Fernández-Bouzas, A., Otero, G., Ricardo-Garcell, J., Barraza, C., Aubert, E., Galán, L., Valdés, P.: Eeg and behavioral changes following neurofeedback treatment in learning disabled children. Clin. EEG Neurosci. **34**(3), 145–152 (2003)

38. Kouijzer, M.E., de Moor, J.M., Gerrits, B.J., Buitelaar, J.K., van Schie, H.T.: Long-term effects of neurofeedback treatment in autism. Res. Autism Spectr. Disord. **3**(2), 496–501 (2009)

39. Thilo, H.: The sensorium: a multimodal neurofeedback environment. Adv. Hum. Comput. Interact. 10 pages (2011). Article 3

40. Marcengo, A., Rapp, A., Cena, F., Geymonat, M.: The falsified self: complexities in personal data collection. In: Antona, M., Stephanidis, C. (eds.) UAHCI 2016. LNCS, vol. 9737, pp. 351–358. Springer, Cham (2016). doi:10.1007/978-3-319-40250-5_34

Data Design for Wellness and Sustainability

Flavio Montagner[1(✉)], Barbara Stabellini[1], Andrea Di Salvo[1], Paolo Marco Tamborrini[1], Alessandro Marcengo[2], and Marina Geymonat[2]

[1] DAD Department of Architecture and Design, Politecnico di Torino, Turin, Italy
{flavio.montagner,barbara.stabellini,andrea.disalvo,
paolo.tamborrini}@polito.it
[2] TIM, Turin, Italy
{alessandro.marcengo,marina.geymonat}@telecomitalia.it

Abstract. The paper describes the design-centered methodology and the design guidelines that guided the research and the development phase within the collaboration between the Architecture and Design Department of the Polytechnic of Turin and the Research Lab of TIM. The research wants to investigate how to expand boundaries of the wearable devices through the work of an interdisciplinary team and following the systemic design approach, a methodology that focuses on relations. Starting from an holistic diagnosis and the analysis of trends, the team define six personas, useful to write down essential guidelines and the two new concept. According to behaviours, habits and requirements, these concepts put human at the center of the whole process and the design gives a particular attention to the sustainability. In this perspective sustainability is defined as the creation of positive relations among people, able to generate and encourage the development of well-being conditions with results on the community as a whole.

Keywords: Design for quality of life technologies · Emotional and affective interaction for universal access · Sustainability

1 Introduction

The research entitled "Wellness and sustainability. Design of a system for monitoring a sustainable well-being" has the goal to design a system able to collect, interpret and return data coming from personal sphere and the surrounding context in an interactive way. The interpretation of data, some already traced and others still under development, will enable to track behaviors related to well-being and sustainability. The project is connected to the Specch.io platform. In particular, the multidisciplinary team followed the systemic design approach [1]; this approach is essential also in application areas that are different from those usually addressed. In fact, the designer adopts a holistic vision that includes verticalizations of the project unless they are integrated in the complex reference system. The strong points of the methodology are the relations that are designed among the various actors of the system. Designing in a systemic way implies, in fact, to exceed the limited boundaries of the single problem, to define as primary goal to build and feed virtuous relations.

© Springer International Publishing AG 2017
M. Antona and C. Stephanidis (Eds.): UAHCI 2017, Part III, LNCS 10279, pp. 562–578, 2017.
DOI: 10.1007/978-3-319-58700-4_46

In order to reach this important goal, the designer should consider the human as the center of the entire process [2]. A human who constantly generates communicative and therefore interactive outputs that immediately become inputs and keystones of other nodes, especially when they are generated and returned by digital devices [3]. Tools such as the holistic diagnosis and the construction of complex scenarios enable to read the big picture from the qualitative point of view, identifying critical issues and at the same time the intervention fields which, in some cases, can lead to the complete redesign of the system and its relations.

The concept of self-care in this way becomes part of this process because, in order to reach the well-being, design should, in the first instance, face needs, small daily actions, difficulties, good practices that are difficult to learn. In this way the systemic design is an approach able to relate and therefore to include, generating consequences on the social [4] and from the sustainability point of view [5].

Wearable devices are usually categorized into not univocal way, they are primarily used by quantified-selfer and self-tracker. Their main uses include: the simple collection of information, with the purpose of remembering and recording aspects of their lives; to satisfy curiosity to discover particular behaviors; adopt specific approaches to improve their health, their physical fitness, their emotional well-being, their social relations or their productivity at work [6].

The first part of the work has been dedicated to the creation of categories that: account for the complexity of the phenomenon; demonstrate the simplistic approach whereby these devices are usually considered; verify if and how they deal with environmental sustainability.

In addition to this, and more specifically, the team analyzed the difficulty in the interpretation of data. There is a huge number of available apps, developed by wearables producers or not, that show collected personal data; however the visualization is usually a general overview of the datum variation inside an activity, but this datum is not related in any way with the reference context, nor with other additional information that the individual collects separately.

These data are therefore always treated as separate components bringing out the absence of relations as a crucial point. In addition, with this interaction modality with the data, the user is often not able to understand, manage and interact with the complexity (e.g. physiological data). The data can be just read, preventing the higher level of interaction that would allow the user to reflect and decide to act differently for the future. The research team came to the identification of six personas to research and identify more clearly new categories of possible users, examining needs, environment, habits, etc. This distinctive approach is included within the systemic design approach as a fundamental part of interaction design.

This phase has allowed to include in the project a broad category of people interested in personal well-being and sustainability. The paper concludes with a set of guidelines and design notes for design: a new wearable that will tracks unexplored data related to behaviors and proxemics and will return them in an innovative way within the Specch.io platform; a domestic object that can collect and display, depending on the users, the data of the house system, parameters derived from appliances and home automation elements, but also by the behavior of those who live in the house.

2 Methodology

Wearable devices are usually used by individual person in order to check and collect private data. People certainly could decide to share some or all the data for example with specialists, speaking of health data, or with a selected community provided by the app itself, rather than with all the contacts on a social network, but this aspect seems to be just an appendix to the main private use. The connections are of course useful, the competition created on a social network can create more engagement between friends if the tracked data are about sport. However the research team found very few applications able to analyse relations between people or projects whereby the object can be the activator of an interaction. In this way the actual platforms seems to be designed following an user-centered designed based on a limited brief. The UCD methodology is indeed a good way to face the project but in order to explore new opportunities, with the clear goal of taking into account all the sustainable aspects of the project, the research team decided to follow the systemic design approach. One of the main concepts of the approach states that every output of a production must become an hight quality input of another production. This implies that a very large net, called system, of aware actors must be created in order to completely avoid any waste and to generate value in every single stage of the production process. Systemic design approach has been applied in many fields and today the food production can provide good examples. Applying the systemic approach to digital products or services means to consider inputs and outputs as part of a complex communication system in which every exchanged data can be communicative and therefore interactive in order to immediately become keystones of other nodes. This is the key of the creation of virtuous relations and connections between data, people, social communities. Looking for someone (or something if nodes are devices) interested in one quality output is, in fact, a way to design new innovative systems in which the projected relations could feed and generate different kind of data, combine existing data trying to give them a sustainable vision, stimulate a disruptive approach to the problem or the existing state of the art.

The whole process is based on multiple steps: an holistic diagnosis that expands the boundaries of the research in order to to take into account all the possible aspects that are often forgotten or not considered; it differs from the common benchmarking because the outlined connections includes transversal fields that could be connected. In this way the approach avoids too strict and vertical researches. After the creation of this map the designer analyses the actors involved or that can be involved creating profiles called personas. The focus during this phase is centred on behaviours, habits, requirements, hidden desiderata. The next phase consists in writing down a list of guidelines, useful for defining the concept. After that, the next phase is called concept and aims to give a vision about the future using creativity and transversality. Finally there is the executive phase that has to transform all the research into performances of a service or product. Next sections describe the phases of the research.

3 Holistic Diagnosis

The phase called holistic diagnosis can be compared to the scenario in the design-centred process rather than the description of the state of the art. The main differences consist of the hands on collection of data and the identification of the existing relations between the actors of the systems. In this case the research group produced a qualitative analysis of both the commercial wearable devices and the experimental ones that are reachable in literature. The goal is to find unexplored relations and opportunities.

The range and the variety of self-tracking technologies that are now available, particularly new devices and software, are vast. The Quantified Self website (the reference website of self-trackers) lists over 500 self-tracking tools; in addition to geolocalization, these include health, fitness, weight, sleep, diet and mood or emotion-tracking apps. Services and devices that refer to social interactions usually track emails, networks and social media status updates and comments [7]. Other tools noted there allow users to track: their meditation practices, television watching, computer use and driving habits, financial expenses, time use and work productivity, local environmental conditions, progress towards learning or the achievement of personal goals [8].

Interest in the Quantified Self has spread from being a proper noun, that specifically referred to the official Quantified Self website and community, to being now used as a common noun, a general term for self-tracking practices. Description such as "the quantified organization", "the quantified patient", "the quantified home", "the quantified baby", "the quantified patient", "the quantified doctor", "the quantified mind", "the quantified sex" and "the quantified pet" appeared in popular cultural artefacts such as blog posts and news items, demonstrating the taking up of the term Quantified Self and its application to more specific topic.

As there is a huge quantity of different applications, the research team divided wearable devices and software platforms into categories according to the market segment they belong to. In this way there are five distinct categories: Healthcare & Wellness, Sport & Fitness, Gaming, Lifestyle & Fashion e Security & Prevention [9].

- Healthcare & Wellness, all the devices that allow the user to earn more freedom, in this case users suffer from illnesses or need constant visits. This is done by maintaining an active and constant monitoring on biometric values, not only by the user, but also by the attending specialist (or whoever takes his place). This is made possible by accessing on demand analysis with the ability to analyse an accurate history of recorded past values. Among the possible variations we include not only those belonging to the physical sphere, but also to the psychological one. With the rising cost of health care and an increasing number of diseases (especially chronic ones), the sector linked to the welfare and health demonstrates great interest and huge development potential. The remote patient monitoring, but also the control of its parameters by the individual allows a considerable reduction in the costs of health services and in the time for medical visits, increasing the awareness of a healthier life to the patient. This market segment has a very high growth potential with almost endless opportunities for new technological solutions. The wearable technologies applied to the healthcare sector give patients more independence and freedom to move, aiming to meet the physical and emotional well-being [10, 11].

- Sports & Fitness, the devices acquire data useful to monitor and evaluate athletic performances. Taking advantage of the position, often in close contact with the body, the device can record not only exogenous data such as speed, repetitions, geolocation, etc., but also endogenous biometric data such as pulse rate, oxygenation, etc. It becomes increasingly important for professional athletes, but also for amateur, to get input and information on vital data during workouts and wearable technologies are the key for reaching such measurements. While GPS, heart rate and pedometer detectors are already widely used, the research on the development of ever newer and improved devices to monitor and display data quickly and securely is trying to reduce the time to market [12, 13].

- Gaming, is a category connected only to recreational field. The number of wearable devices belonging to this sector is rapidly dwindling. However, even this category has undergone tremendous changes and the devices that are now being used are more discreet than ever, allowing the user to try gaming and entertainment experiences ever more immersive. In such devices category are also included all the tools people use to manage household devices and everything related to communication and playing music and video [14, 15].

- Lifestyle & Fashion, this category includes devices intended to more heterogeneous use, from reading to entertainment notifications, through the management of personal commitments and the simple web browsing. It is a category that considers as the center of development the aesthetic-expressive aspect, often at the expense of functionality or innovation. Functions are often simple and limited, but thanks to a less technological appeal they can also capture its own market segment. The use of this kind of objects can be compared to the way people relate to smartphones [16, 17].

- Security & Prevention, from smart-lights to special equipment, all devices are developed to ensure greater safety both in the industrial and sports. Devices are mostly related to the prosumer market with ergonomic and mostly-functional features, at the expense of visual-appeal. In this case, the functions should be very specific and the reliability is the key feature. Compared to the previous category that aims to attract as many consumers as possible, in this case wearable devices are configured as actual working tools [18, 19].

The categories described above appear in scientific literature but they are often mixed and not detailed. However the research team identified a cross category that called self expressing. This category can track every data but its main goal is to show data in a reinterpreted and unconventional way. Smart textiles for artistic installations rather than devices with feedback made of moving lights can be, for example, part of this category. This group of wearables could be judged as less scientific and analytic from the point of view of the management of data, but they draw attention to a key factor: the relation between human, wearable and context. If it is true that the dropout rate in the use of wearable seems to be linked to poor variability of the data, once it reaches a threshold that identifies the routine, the analysed examples show that relations and interactions with the surrounding context are extremely undervalued, preventing both the expansion of the analysis of other connected data and the interaction with data that come from other devices that are not strictly personal. Aggregators' platforms are good answers to this problem, merging lots of data in order to obtain a holistic overview, but the risk of having a poor interaction based on feedback that last without variations during a long period remains the same.

Each type of device collects a certain type of data and communicates almost exclusively with its own app or with a small number of applications and users (such as doctors) that are based on the display of the individual data collected by the device. From a systemic point of view, these data are outputs that are not valued. Nodes that do not connect to each other. In this way the image that is returned will never be truly comprehensive and truthful: whether we speak of a sports performance, or medical values. As we will see in the paragraph relating to the concept, the systemic design approach leads the research team to consider the connections that exist between the data in our possession, highlighting any gap that may instead be filled to complete the overall picture.

4   Trends and Personas

Seeking for a comprehensive picture of wearable technology, it could be useful to understand what direction, from the commercial point of view, is moving the world of wearables and what are the biggest issues.

In the period between 2013 and 2015, the world of wearable technology has radically changed. In the first instance, the five (plus one) categories identified above have deeply changed in terms of percentage spread. Areas such as sports & fitness and lifestyle & fashion had a sharp increase in the percentage, rising from 28.6 to 40.8% for the first category, and from 23.7 to 37.9% for the second; even the security & prevention sector has increased significantly, jumping from 3.6 to 5.7%. Healthcare and Wellness sectors, instead, spread down from 16 to 7.8%; the gaming category underwent the biggest change, falling to 7.8% from the starting 28.1%.

But the most surprising factor is the decrease of the presented typologies of device. In 2013 the market was characterised by a huge presence of jacket and sweatshirt devices with the 16% in terms of diffusion, while all the other device typologies (about 21) had to carve up more or less consistent slices of the same market. After two years the picture radically changed with an overabundance of smartwatch (35%) and jewelery (primarily bracelets, with 29.1%) and only 9 other competitor devices to compete for a space in the graph. It can be then observed that ergonomics switched from considering almost entirety the human body to focus just on the wrists (at the bust) (Fig. 1). It should also be noted a big change in gender market's orientation: from the starting trend for unisex devices (74.4%) in two years the wearable technology became mainly aimed at a female audience (66%) [9].

Another study carried out in the period between 2014 and 2016 [20] shows that the diffusion rate is more than doubled, from 21 to 49%, 39% of which came to own more than one device. This indicates on the one hand greater confidence in a technology that is now well known, on the other hand a growing interest in the self-monitoring and a general passion (57% of respondents) for the possibilities offered by wearables.

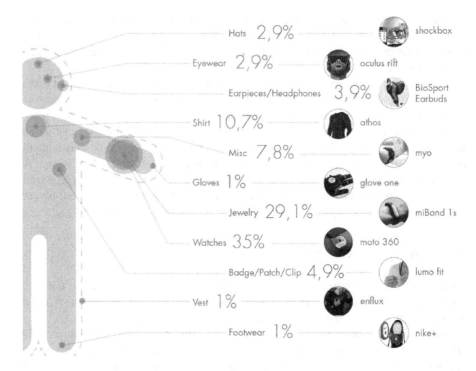

Hats 2,9% — shockbox

Eyewear 2,9% — oculus rift

Earpieces/Headphones 3,9% — BioSport Earbuds

Shirt 10,7% — athos

Misc 7,8% — myo

Gloves 1% — glove one

Jewelry 29,1% — miBand 1s

Watches 35% — moto 360

Badge/Patch/Clip 4,9% — lumo fit

Vest 1% — enflux

Footwear 1% — nike+

Fig. 1. Ergonomic analysis of wearables devices based on markets [9]

This trust in wearable technologies led consumers, companies and designers to imagine the possible developments and future scenarios related to greater interdependence between man and worn technology, whether it is in the medical field (with bracelets able to alleviate chronic pain conditions), whether in personal or social sphere (with devices capable of analyzing our mood and change the music we listen to rejoice), or able to remind the users the name of someone they met years earlier and allow them to greet him in a proper way and without embarrassment.

These new scenarios necessarily go beyond the technical - technological aspect (e.g. the battery life, UI, etc.) and lead users, indeed forces users, to look at people relations with these resources more broadly. Perhaps avoiding to consider them as means but as extensions of ourselves. From this stem new affordances that encourage people to reconsider the concept of wearability too [21] and our body as a dynamic interface [22].

This greater intimacy, leads consequently to identify different ways in which the device will silently collect data, will try to positively influence users' habits and then will return collected data [23].

From this principle springs, almost in parallel, a new attention to the world of jewelry, which goes beyond the cuff format (but which demonstrates its effectiveness in principle). Although not characterized by any kind of smart element, the jewel, is ancestrally a category of wearables toward which people are unconsciously more connected and already use, in some way, to relate with others and with ourselves. Using them people feel good and communicate to the outside a mood, status, etc. enabling it to proactively interact through the acquisition of data and the return of feedback of different nature, people may be able to amplify these inherent communicative characteristics. This happens therefore moving far from the now superfluous presence of a display [24]. But the spread of Quantified Self is not merit only of the new technologies, although increasingly smaller and more efficient. It is, in fact, possible to identify three other elements: the integration of these technologies in the constantly connected computing devices, such as smartphones; the widespread of social media which has normalized the practice of sharing information, and the emergence of cloud storage and computing that allows the access to a huge amount of data in order to map a collective intelligence [25].

An interesting element is users' expectation linked to an improvement in lifestyle based on elements that go beyond the simple physical activity. They talk about of increasing their productivity at work, safety of their children or loved ones and stress reduction; not only as an additional screen for our smartphones [26]. Wearable devices of this kind (though present in the market in rather small number) are expected not to isolate people, but rather help to better connect them with the surrounding world, including of course the people.

Despite this, it should be specified that by now this kind of technology does not always get through the turnaround test, i.e. the incentive to go back once left the house, for taking the device users forgave. Often people continue their day without it, more or less consciously convinced that the gap in the data collected does not affect so much the overall picture. Maybe people don't care enough about the picture or the added value is not as strong as they expected. Maybe, designer never faced the design's problems in the right ways.

Usually the declared trends in the field of technology products follow both an incremental vision regarding the future increasing performances of the products or the commercial diffusion of prototypes. From the design research point of view, this is important to evaluate disruptive opportunities at least in the approach to the research. In order to have an overview that could provide also a prevision of the needs of interested people, the research team designed eight personas based on data harvested in many heterogeneous articles and reports found both on literature and magazines.

Persona is a technique that employs fictitious users to guide decision making regarding features, interactions, and aesthetics; it is well known in user-centred design and interaction design methodology. This technique involves the creation of profiles with information derived from user and stakeholder interviews, reviews of market research and customer feedback, and statistics about how a product is used when available. Each persona is typically represented with photograph, name, description, and details about specific interests and relevant behaviors. This clarifies user needs and behaviors and is an effective means of creating empathy for the user perspective, making the target audience more real to designers and engineers [27].

4.1 The Six Personas

The creation of Personas was based in part on analysis of the six types of consumers related to wearable devices: the Curious, the Controller, the Self-Medic, the Finish line Fanatic, the Ubiquitous Future and the Quantified selfer. Each of them has characteristics, demographic age and goals, relations and different expectations from technology and wearable [28]. Drawing in part on data taken from market research of international institutions [29, 30] combined with national and regional ones [31] that allowed the team to modify and adapt certain features of the 6 types above-described. This approach was dictated by the need to get a picture as natural as possible of the natural habits of analyzed people. They have been created in this way: the balanced adult, the wealthy in the form, the young rampant, the elder bright, the sustainable excited and the responsible parent.

Below there is a brief description of one persona, the young rampant. She is a woman, she is 35 years old, without children, single, she obtained a master's degree with honors and taken a job contract that does not fully satisfy her. She is a girl who cares about her physical appearance and care mainly through the use of clothing and accessories, a passion that shares with her circle of friends. She is undoubtedly a tenacious young woman and full of ambitious goals, although the lifestyle that she leads is both stressful and very busy, she is discouraged, and makes every effort to achieve them. She is very sensitive to the environment, environmental issues and tries to do everything is possible to safeguard it, also renouncing to the use of private vehicles in favor of car and bike sharing. Despite this, she can not afford to spend much time for cooking, so prefers pre-cooked or frozen foods. At the technological level she has no equal, she uses perfectly any type of device with various purposes: leisure, work and physical activity.

Using personas as a reference for design purpose, the research team was able to obtain sufficient data and information that can guide the team in the creation of guidelines for our future project.

5   Guidelines

The holistic diagnosis previously carried out allowed the research team to define some guidelines useful for the following concept definition and the design phase. Speaking of which, it is interesting to mention a study of 2013 whereby Buenaflor e Kim highlighted which are the human factors that define the acceptance of wearable devices [32]. This study supported the definition of the adopted guidelines listed below:

- consider the fundamental needs, with regard to the social aspects: the wearable that appear to be more bought and more used fulfill the basic functions that are at the base of the Maslow's pyramid of needs: the physiological ones. These needs also refer to the quality of the environment in which people live (air, water, etc.). Nevertheless, bringing attention to a mainly social sphere, we can reconsider the fundamental needs including different data, for example by inserting the communication of a stress level as basic as communication and interaction with people around us;
- designing a sustainable device: the sustainability results a huge argument and it should not be seen as an add-on or a final touch to make the device simply green. Design should take into account all of the three aspects of the sustainability (environmental, economic and social), create positive relations between people and their environment, by generating and encouraging the development of wellness conditions with consequences not only on the individual but on the community as a whole;

- respect the personal privacy: the market of wearable shows that people tend to be wary of sharing personal information, especially if these may damage them in any way in social terms; for this reason the display tend to show always less information or only on-demand by user, not only therefore for an issue of consuming and energy-saving of the device. Design has to take into account this aspect, considering an interaction that is both communicative, but not invasive;
- guarantee ease of use of the device: the device must request the user a very low mental and physical effort in its use; in fact, when a technology is intuitive, the greater the confidence that the individual will have with it and then the higher will be the degree of acceptance; from the interaction point of view the device should work in a silent mode, avoiding undesired interferences, providing feedback to establish a dialogue and an interaction with the subject, the other connected users, the context;
- satisfy mobility needs, comfort and physical security: being a wearable device, it must be carefully considered all of those requirements that define the size, shape, weight, materials, etc., because they will be precisely those elements, previously determined by the definition of the requirements arising from the analysis that will determine the relation with the final subject.

6 Specch.io

The described system is thought to be embedded in Specch.io, a platform developed by the Telco with which our group collaborates. The system exploits the current availability of many applications aimed at providing individuals' with self-knowledge by collecting a variety of personal data [33, 34]. As we have seen, not only the range of information detectable by such applications has recently increased [35, 36], but also new methods for collecting and structuring data [37], as well as involving users through gameful elements [38–41], have been explored to engage also people that do not have any previous experience with self-tracking devices [42–44]. Specch.io aims at integrating different personal data, feeding them back to the users and allowing their exploration, favoring the individual wellness from a bio-psychosocial perspective.

The project integrates the concept of physical well-being with a greater theoretical and technological point of view, taking into account also the psychological and social sphere. The changes stimulated on individual or society level can take many forms and may have different levels of depth, both in terms of impact on the structure of the person, but also on the duration. The behavioral changes generally have an impact on the surface and do not last long time. The Specch.io project aims to build a platform to allow access to an integrated and complete view of the person, with the goal to improve the knowledge of his lifestyles, increasing his global awareness through the emergence of causal or space-time patterns and connections aiming to facilitate the change keeping in mind the goal of a greater personal well-being. At present, the system is represented by a flexible platform that is able to connect different devices at the same time. It is composed by two different interactive ways of displaying personal data: the first one allows the analytical exploration of information through quantitative graphs, enabling the thorough investigation and confrontation of all the collected data; the second one, instead is aimed at providing a snapshot of a single collected parameter (e.g. the sleep) by providing an impressionistic image of the user, where colors and shapes perceptually show some important information about the psycho-physiological state of the user.

7 Concept

From the definition of the personas it is possible to observe that the improvement of own lifestyle is of common interest to all wearables' users, improvement that today they mainly tend to pursue through the intervention in everyday aspects more quantifiable as nutrition and fitness. On the other hand there is also a rising attention to some factors less evident which are the elements that cause the increase of the negative stress in our lives, stress also called distress [45]. The goal is to learn to recognize them and know how to handle without erasing the positive aspects linked to the eustress [46].

The combination of these three components (physical, psychological and nutritional) defines the wellness: a philosophy of life that puts own well-being in the focus of attention of everyday goals.

Despite the factors involved are the three shortly described above, it is essential to take into account the context around the subject, considering therefore the relations that he establishes with it. For this reason, the concept defined is configured as "analyze and encourage attitudes by creating relations" and it should take into account the relations below described:

- relations between person and person: these relations have an high level of complexity and there is not always quantifiable because of their connection with personal representation or expression, but also mood, emotions, ecc. Elements as proxemics, individual reactions, education and non-verbal communication have a big influence on the quality of the relations established;
- relations between person and environment: these are the relations that are quantifiable in a more easy way, but also in this case, the subject influence this relation in a strong way. Environmental psychology, for example, has been working for years to study the relationships between people and the environment; environmental characteristics, place evaluation and creation, in fact, defines the quality of established connection;
- relations between person and object: relations of this type have characteristics resulting both from those related to the environment and from those related to relationships with other people. Features such as appearance and usability are some of the basic characteristics to establish a positive relationship with an object, while they become determinants proxemic values, anthropometric and organoleptic ones.

The strong relations' component suggests us that the design of only one device it can not be enough to satisfy guidelines and the concept exposed. For this reason, it becomes interesting to design a wearable device supporting by a domestic device, thus extending on one side data collection and on the other side sharing and return of these data, in a way integrating with the environment around.

In the paragraphs below will be described a new concept of wearable and a new concept of domestic device.

7.1   Wearable Device

The new concept of wearable device (Fig. 2) is an object that first of all tracks posture, gestures and proxemics in order to obtain qualitative data about wellness, in the second instance it tracks two important specific biometric data such as heart rate and galvanic skin response. These data are at the same time personal, contextual and relational because they vary depending on: the context in which the subject is operating, the people the subject is speaking with, people that are around him. Therefore obtaining data about the kind of walk, the gestures and the posture for example during a conversation can provide: a completely different vision, as it integrate communicative output-input of the subject; a relational map whence subject can recreate his activity merging other data like galvanic skin response.

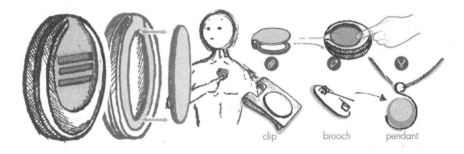

Fig. 2. New concept for wearable device

The new kind of data is tracked not only by an accelerometer and a gyroscope, as regards the upper body, but also by a component that has be able to mainly monitor the movements of the arms including the hands. The technology that can provide this datum is called Google Project Soli [47], it uses a doppler radar and it is still in the experimental stage. Using the same principle, but with different frequencies, heart rate can be monitored [48]; while in order to obtain GSR a mathematical process called SVM (Support Vector Machine) can be used matching ECG and HRV, avoiding a direct measuring [49] (Fig. 3). The appropriate position of the wearable from the functional and ergonomic point of view is on the breastbone. The wearable can therefore be formally designed according to gender, clothing habits and other personal needs in order to realise devices that can be hidden under the clothes (attached to a bra or to an undergarment), rather than shown like pendants and brooches. Furthermore the wearable can provide a kind of public feedback that communicates the subject's state, integrating the suggestions of the self-expressing transversal category discussed in the holistic diagnosis part.

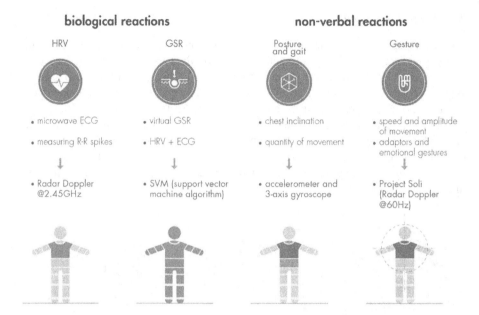

Fig. 3. Sensoral components included in wearable device

7.2 Domestic Device

The new concept of the domestic device (Fig. 4) is an object that diverges from usual smart home system objects or Internet of Things devices. It is, in fact, a tool with which people that live in the home can relate and interact among them in a dynamic way, both family components and roommates.

The spherical shape inspires different purposes and communicates a dynamism that is not a characteristic of tools or displays usually hung on a wall o used as common smartphones. The communication with the device is based on interaction. It collects both data from the domestic context and from the environment around the home, but also data from people that live in the home space. Starting from these data and relying to the gained experience, the device can visualize the information collected and modify domestic parameters (e.g. infotainment or temperature), reacting to subjects' input as vocal signals, tactile inputs or motion ones.

Therefore, the use can be playful, informative, functional or, in case of negative mood, just quiet.

Fig. 4. New concept of domestic device

8 Conclusions

The project has the ambition to innovate the field of wearable devices, the generation and data visualization, creating new modalities of use, different interactions and relations. From the design point of view, the research highlighted how it is possible to track not only new data, using technologies that now are adopted for other purposes, but also that there are wide margins so far unexplored. Despite at the moment there is not a functioning prototype, the first goal of the research has been faced and obtained using a different approach, the systemic design one, identifying guidelines and two new concept. The systemic design approach applied to digital-technological project demonstrated to be innovative because it allows to design new relations among actors, components, data and visualizations. According to the collected data and related researches guidelines appear to be solid and applicable because they refer to: real and hidden needs, the sustainability and privacy paradigm, the usability. From a methodological point of view, the process has been correctly followed and it has provided interesting directions also in a different field of application, uncommon for the approach.

9 Future Works

The research work is currently arrived to identify all technological elements and useful characteristics to truly realize the two objects and, therefore, validate the concepts that are declared in this paper. Future work consists in programming and connecting all the components in order to really track the behaviours and to return usable data. Despite this process can be far from the design skill, it will be managed and coordinated by the research team in order to: guarantee the identity of the project, highlight possibilities of the components not yet investigated, improve errors observed during the devices' use, but moreover create a truly usable and engaging interface among the actors of the system. Based on the first data obtained, it will be possible to understand how enlarge the boundaries of the system with the goal of collecting new kind of data and return them.

Acknowledgements. Specch.io project is based on the work of Alessandro Marcengo, Luca Buriano e Marina Geymonat.

Chapters 1 to 5 and 7 to 9 have been written by Flavio Montagner, Barbara Stabellini, Andrea Di Salvo, Paolo Marco Tamborrini;

Chapter 6 has been written by Alessandro Marcengo e Marina Geymonat.

References

1. Bistagnino, L.: Design sistemico: progettare la sostenibilità produttiva e ambientale. Slow Food, Bra (2011)
2. Germak, C.: Uomo al Centro del Progetto: Design per un Nuovo Umanesimo. Allemandi & C, Torino (2008)
3. Di Salvo, A., Tamborrini, P.M.: Interaction design tools for autism. In: Poppe, R., Meyer, J.-J., Veltkamp, R., Dastani, M. (eds.) INTETAIN 2016 2016. LNICSSITE, vol. 178, pp. 243–253. Springer, Cham (2017). doi:10.1007/978-3-319-49616-0_23
4. Celaschi, F., De Moraes, D.: Future, well-being, interdependence: key-words for contemporaneous design. Cadernos de Estudos Avançados em Design: Humanismo. Editora da Universidade do Estado de Minas Gerais, Belo Horizonte (2013)
5. Tamborrini, P.M.: Design sostenibile. Oggetti, sistemi e comportamenti. Mondadori Electa, Milano (2009)
6. Lupton, D.: The quantified self. Polity, Cambridge (2016)
7. Quantified Self. http://quantifiedself.com
8. Personal Informatics. http://www.personalinformatics.org/tools/
9. Berglund, M.E., Duvall, J., Dunne, L.E.: A survey of the historical scope and current trends of wearable technology applications. In: Proceedings of the 2016 ACM International Symposium on Wearable Computers, pp. 40–43. ACM (2016)
10. Preventice. http://www.preventicesolutions.com
11. QMedic. https://www.qmedichealth.com/
12. Whoop. http://whoop.com/
13. VivoSmart HR. https://buy.garmin.com/en-US/US/p/531166
14. Moff Band. http://www.moff.mobi/
15. HTC Vive. https://www.vive.com/eu/
16. Moto 360. https://www.motorola.com/us/products/moto-360
17. Samsung Charm. http://www.samsung.com/us/mobile/mobile-accessories/smartwatches/samsung-charm-black-ei-an920bbegus/
18. ShockBox. http://www.theshockbox.com/
19. Heads Up. https://www.headsupsafe.com
20. The Wearable Life 2.0. Connected living in a wearable world. http://pwc.com/CISwearables
21. Liu, X., Vega, K., Maes, P., Paradiso, J.A.: Wearability factors for skin interfaces. In: Proceedings of the 7th Augmented Human International Conference 2016, p. 21. ACM (2016)
22. Ryan, S.E.: Social fabrics: wearable+media+interconnectivity. Leonardo **42**(2), 114–116 (2009)

23. Sanches, P., Höök, K., Vaara, E., Weymann, C., Bylund, M., Ferreira, P., Peira, N., Sjölinder, M.: Mind the body!: designing a mobile stress management application encouraging personal reflection. In: Proceedings of the 8th ACM Conference on Designing Interactive Systems, pp. 47–56. ACM (2010)

24. Ju, A.L., Spasojevic, M.:. Smart jewelry: the future of mobile user interfaces. In: Proceedings of the 2015 Workshop on Future Mobile User Interfaces, pp. 13–15. ACM (2015)

25. Lévy, P.: L'intelligenza collettiva. Per un'antropologia del cyberspazio. Feltrinelli Editore, Milano (1996)

26. Schirra, S., Bentley, F.R.: It's kind of like an extra screen for my phone: understanding everyday uses of consumer smart watches. In: Proceedings of the 33rd Annual ACM Conference Extended Abstracts on Human Factors in Computing Systems, pp. 2151–2156. ACM (2015)

27. Butler, J., Holden, K., Lidwell, W.: Universal Principles of Design, Revised and Updated: 125 Ways to Enhance Usability, Influence Perception, Increase Appeal, Make Better Design Decisions, and Teach through Design. Rockport, Beverly (2010)

28. Rackspace Report 2013. The human cloud, wearable technology from novelty to production. http://www.rackspace.com/

29. Nielsen. http://www.nielsen.com/it/it.html

30. Experian. http://www.experian.com/

31. Istat. http://www.istat.it/

32. Buenaflor, C., Kim, H.C.: Six human factors to acceptability of wearable computers (2013)

33. Marcengo, A., Rapp, A.: Visualization of human behavior data: the quantified self. In: Huang, L.H., Huang, W. (eds.) Innovative approaches of data visualization and visual analytics, pp. 236–265. IGI Global, Hershey (2013). doi:10.4018/978-1-4666-4309-3

34. Rapp, A., Tirassa, M.: Know thyself: a theory of the self for personal informatics. Hum. Comput. Interact. (2017). doi:10.1080/07370024.2017.1285704

35. Rapp, A., Cena, F., Kay, J., Kummerfeld, B., Hopfgartner, F., Plumbaum, T., Larsen, J.E. Epstein, D.A., Gouveia, R.: New frontiers of quantified self 2: going beyond numbers. In: Proceedings of the 2016 ACM International Joint Conference on Pervasive and Ubiquitous Computing: Adjunct (UbiComp 2016), pp. 506–509. ACM, New York (2016). doi: 10.1145/2968219.2968331

36. Sarzotti, F., Lombardi, I., Rapp, A., Marcengo, A., Cena, F.: Engaging users in self-reporting their data: a tangible interface for quantified self. In: Antona, M., Stephanidis, C. (eds.) UAHCI 2015. LNCS, vol. 9176, pp. 518–527. Springer, Cham (2015). doi: 10.1007/978-3-319-20681-3_49

37. Hilviu, D., Rapp, A.: Narrating the Quantified Self. In: Adjunct Proceedings of the 2015 ACM International Joint Conference on Pervasive and Ubiquitous Computing and Proceedings of the 2015 ACM International Symposium on Wearable Computers (UbiComp/ISWC 2015 Adjunct), pp. 1051–1056. ACM, New York (2015). doi:10.1145/2800835.2800959

38. Rapp, A.: A Qualitative investigation of gamification: motivational factors in online gamified services and applications. Int. J. Technol. Hum. Interact. 11(1), 67–82 (2015). doi:10.4018/ijthi.2015010105

39. Rapp, A., Marcengo, M., Console, L., Simeoni, R.: Playing in the wild: enhancing user engagement in field evaluation methods. In: Proceeding of the 16th International Academic MindTrek Conference (MindTrek 2012), pp. 227–228. ACM, New York (2012). doi: 10.1145/2393132.2393180

40. Rapp, A., Cena, F., Gena, C., Marcengo, A., Console, L.: Using game mechanics for field evaluation of prototype social applications: a novel methodology. Behav. Inf. Technol. 35(3), 184–195 (2016). doi:10.1080/0144929X.2015.1046931

41. Rapp, A.: Designing interactive systems through a game lens: an ethnographic approach. Comput. Hum. Behav. (2015). doi:10.1016/j.chb.2015.02.048

42. Rapp, A., Cena, F.: Self-monitoring and technology: challenges and open issues in personal informatics. In: Stephanidis, C., Antona, M. (eds.) UAHCI 2014. LNCS, vol. 8516, pp. 613–622. Springer, Cham (2014). doi:10.1007/978-3-319-07509-9_58

43. Rapp, A., Cena, F.: Personal informatics for everyday life: how users without prior self-tracking experience engage with personal data. Int. J. Hum Comput Stud. **94**, 1–17 (2016). doi:10.1016/j.ijhcs.2016.05.006

44. Rapp A., Cena F.: Affordances for self-tracking wearable devices. In: Proceedings of International Symposium on Wearable Computers (ISWC 2015), pp. 141–142. ACM, New York (2015). doi:10.1145/2802083.2802090

45. Selye, H.: From Dream to Discovery: On Being a Scientist. Mcgraw Hill, New York (1964)

46. Selye, H.: Stress Without Distress. Lippincott Williams & Wilkins, Philadelphia (1975)

47. Project Soli. https://atap.google.com/soli/

48. Fletcher, R.R., Kulkarni, S.: Clip-on wireless wearable microwave sensor for ambulatory cardiac monitoring. In: 2010 Annual International Conference of the IEEE Engineering in Medicine and Biology Society (EMBC), pp. 365–369. IEEE (2010)

49. Liu, D., Ulrich, M.: Listen to Your Heart: Stress Prediction Using Consumer Heart Rate Sensors (2014)

Introducing Wearables in the Kitchen: An Assessment of User Acceptance in Younger and Older Adults

Valeria Orso[1](✉), Giovanni Nascimben[1], Francesca Gullà[2],
Roberto Menghi[2], Silvia Ceccacci[2], Lorenzo Cavalieri[2],
Michele Germani[2], Anna Spagnolli[1], and Luciano Gamberini[1]

[1] Padua University, Padua, Italy
{valeria.orso, anna.spagnolli, luciano.gamberini}
@unipd.it, giovanni.nascimben@studenti.unipd.it
[2] Università Politecnica delle Marche, Ancona, Italy
{f.gulla, r.menghi, s.ceccacci, lorenzo.cavalieri,
m.germani}@univpm.it

Abstract. Wearable computers allow users to record and access information at any time. The adoption and use of such devices is largely dependent on the users' acceptance of the technology. Previous studies investigated technology acceptance of wearables without having end-users directly trying the technology. The present paper aims at assessing the user acceptance of a wearable device to support cooking related activities, together with aspects of usability and experience of use. To this end, we developed a kitchen apron with embedded commands for navigating through the contents of a digital cookbook and asked a group of younger ($N = 15$, mean age 23.9 $SD = 2.5$) and older users ($N = 15$, mean age 30.3 $SD = 7.6$) to deploy it while preparing a recipe. Respondents' opinions were collected using questionnaires after they had accomplished the cooking task required. Overall, the kitchen apron was well received by both younger and older adults. Findings suggest that the perceived usefulness of the device and the compatibility of it with users' common activities accounted for the intention to adopt and use a wearable device in the kitchen.

Keywords: Technology acceptance · Wearable computers

1 Introduction

Wearable computers are fully functional and self-contained technological devices that can be worn or attached to user's body and that allow him/her to access information at any moment [23]. Given these characteristics, wearable devices are an ideal component for unobtrusively recording the users' state and for providing him/her constant access to commands and information, and they have been in fact extensively experimented in the healthcare domain and to support healthy lifestyles [5, 21]. Despite the advantages brought about by wearables in terms of continuous data recording, availability of

© Springer International Publishing AG 2017
M. Antona and C. Stephanidis (Eds.): UAHCI 2017, Part III, LNCS 10279, pp. 579–592, 2017.
DOI: 10.1007/978-3-319-58700-4_47

information and networking possibilities, the users' willingness to adopt and use such devices is highly affected by the user acceptance of the technology itself [1, 23, 32].

User acceptance of technology has been investigated in different context of use, and a number of factors affecting the acceptance have been identified, e.g., age, gender, technology expertise and environment of use [10, 22, 31]. However, previous studies have mainly assessed technology acceptance without having users directly experience a functioning device before making their judgments, rather the presentation of scenarios has been preferred [e.g., 25].

In the present study we aimed at assessing the user acceptance of a wearable device to support cooking-related activities in younger and older adults. To this end a kitchen apron with embedded commands for navigating through the contents of a digital cookbook was developed and was used by participants to complete a realistic cooking task before assessing users' technology acceptance. The system considered in the present paper consists of a common kitchen accessory, i.e., a kitchen apron, and a simple keyboard for inputting commands. We thus hypothesize no differences pertaining the overall technology acceptance in younger and older adults. In addition, given the low level of complexity of the interface, no differences regarding system usability and the experience of use are expected between the two groups. We hypothesize a difference in the propensity of using technology, favoring younger adults.

The remainder of the paper is structured as follows. First, the concept of technology acceptance is introduced with reference to wearable computers. Then, the methods for assessing technology acceptance, usability and experience of use are presented. The experiment is then reported, including details regarding the materials devised, the equipment used, the experimental setting and procedure and the participants. The data analysis and the results are then described, and are discussed. Finally, concluding remarks are presented.

2 Background

Generally speaking, technology acceptance refers to a conscious intention by the user to adopt and use a technological device. However, the interaction with wearable devices entail peculiar characteristics as compared to traditional computers, e.g., the location of use [1]. A refined definition of technology acceptance is thus provided below, followed by the methods that are usually employed to investigate users' attitudes.

2.1 Technology Acceptance of Wearables

Considering the users' perspective is crucial for determining whether the interaction with a wearable device is efficient and satisfactory [16]. However, usability and user experience are not the only factors accounting for technology adoption. Highly technological features alone are in fact not determinant for the user to adopt the device and it is well-known that a poor acceptance of the technology is associated with the deny of adopting and using the device, regardless of the potential benefits [4, 17].

According to the Technology Acceptance Model (TAM) [7] and the Unified Theory of Acceptance and Use of Technology (UTAUT) [26], user acceptance is defined along two central factors: the perceived ease of use, that is the impression that operating the device is effortless, and the perceived usefulness of the technology, that is the impression that the technology can benefit the user supporting him/her in the unfolding of the task. A number of factors, including the technological features of the device and the characteristic of the user, have been identified as affecting the technology acceptance in a number of different application domain (e.g., the workplace [4], hedonic information systems [11], and mobile devices [13]).

The context of use was found to play a relevant role in affecting technology acceptance of wearables, e.g., [31]. In particular, the healthcare scenario is in general associated to high acceptance rates among respondents [8] and was also found to be determinant in the acceptance of wearables, meaning that users would be willing to adopt the given technology for healthcare purposes but not for others, e.g., demanding job [23]. Regarding the domestic environment, the usage of wearables seems to be favored in the bedroom and living room, as compared to the kitchen [10, 31].

A number of demographic factors seem to play a role in the acceptance of technology, however results are mixed in this respect. Previous technology expertise seems to favor the adoption of wearable device [5, 22, 23, 25]. However, [10] showed that self-confidence in the use of technology does not affect respondents' judgments. Age seems not to affect the intention of use, even though older respondents were more concerned about the complexity of wearables than their younger counterparts [31]. In general, respondents' gender does not appear to affect their acceptance of technology [10, 31, 32]. The pressure made by friends and family members seems to the play a role, especially for older users [14].

Finally, the design and the appearance of the device plays also a determinant role: the wearable device should be comfortable and at the same time discreet [25, 28].

2.2 Assessing the Intention of Use of Wearables

To assess the willingness to adopt and use wearable devices, participants are usually asked to self-report their impressions and opinions regarding a device through a questionnaire. In the majority of the cases the completion of the questionnaire follows the presentation of a scenario, in which the respondents are illustrated the typical situations of use of the wearable device under examination [22, 25, 30]. Some studies had a more general aim to assess users' general attitude toward wearable technologies and a questionnaire alone was administered [10, 30, 31].

A more qualitative approach was also proposed. [3] investigated medical staff's attitude toward a wearable hand sanitizer system monitoring how much the user was effectively disinfecting his/her hands, by making participants first try a prototype in a laboratory setting and them let them discuss their impression in a focus group. Similarly, [24] investigated older adults' impressions of a wearable network of sensors by presenting them a prototype during a focus group session. Finally, [2] asked participants to try on two different wearable accessories, i.e., a backpack and an armband, which served different purposes according to the scenario presented to them. After, participants had made a series of movements following the experimenter's instructions, they were asked to complete a questionnaire.

3 Materials and Methods

In the present experiment, a total of three questionnaires were administered. A first questionnaire was devised to collect background information (name, age, gender and education) and aimed at assessing participants' habits in the kitchen and their cooking expertise. In particular, they were asked how often and for how many people they usually cooked and also if they were in the habit of consulting cookbooks and of which kind (i.e., paper book, digital cookbook via PC, tablet or smartphone). Regarding their cooking expertise, they were asked to indicate which recipe they would be able to prepare without consulting a cookbook. Participants could choose among six preparations of increasing difficulty: two options were easy to prepare, and were assigned a score of 1; two options were of intermediate difficulty, and were assigned a score of 2; and finally, two options were difficult to prepare without a cookbook and were assigned a score of 3. The higher the score gained by the user, the higher was assumed his/her expertise, and constituted a proxy of his/her cooking abilities.

The questionnaire investigating the user's acceptance of wearable devices validated by [23] was administered. It consists of 26 items in total, assessing 10 factors. A first factor measured the respondent's overall reaction toward technology, namely Attitude Toward Technologies (ATT) [27]. A second factor pertained the feelings of apprehension when using a technological device (3 items), i.e., Technology Anxiety (TA) [26]. Three items assessed the extent to which the user had the impression that using the device is compatible with his/her current habits and with the tools at his/her disposal, i.e., Facilitating Conditions (FC) [27]. The fourth factor pertained the respondent's impression that the device could enhance his/her performance, namely Perceived Usefulness (PU) [7]. Four items assessed the extent to which respondents perceived that using the device would be effortless, i.e. Effort Expectancy [26]. Behavioral Intention, i.e., the degree to which the respondent is able to formulate conscious plans to deploy the device for carrying out certain actions, was assessed by four items (BI) [7]. Two items assessed the extent to which users would be willing to use the technology as a consequence of social influence, namely Psychological Attachment (PA) [15]. Two items referred to the extent to which the user perceived that the information collected by the system would be safely stored and handled, i.e., Perceived Privacy (PP) [20]. Perceived Enjoyment (4 items) assessed the degree to which the respondent perceived that using the system would be pleasant, regardless of the consequences of the usage [26]. Finally, three items assessed the Perceived Comfort (PC) [12] of wearing the wearable system. Participants were asked to indicate their level of agreement on a 6-point Likert scale.

An additional questionnaire was devised to assess the experience of use with the system and to investigate aspects related to the usability of the system. Such post-experience questionnaire consisted of 20 items, to which the respondent was asked to mark his/her level of agreement on a 6-point Likert scale. In order to evaluate to which extent the system was perceived helpful in the unfolding of ordinary cooking activities, namely Usefulness [9], 4 items were included. The Ease of Use of the system, that is the degree to which users found the wearable simple to use, was assessed by 3 items [9]. A total of 5 items investigated the extent to which respondents had the impression that it was easy to navigate through the system, namely Navigability [9]. The Satisfaction of use, that is the extent to which users were happy of their interactions with the system, was assessed by a single item [9]. Again, a single item investigated the effort associated in learning how to operate the system, that is called Learnability [9]. The quality of the experience, namely Pleasantness, was investigated by 4 items [29]. Finally, 3 items evaluated to which extent the user had the impression that the system would interfere with the user's established practices [23].

3.1   Equipment

A kitchen apron with embedded commands was purposefully created for the study. On the left side of the apron was attached a plastic plaque holding five buttons. To simplify the interaction, only three of them were used in the present study to navigate through the pages of a digital cookbook: the one on the right side served to proceed to the next page, the one on the left side allowed to go back to previous page and the central one had an enter function (Fig. 1).

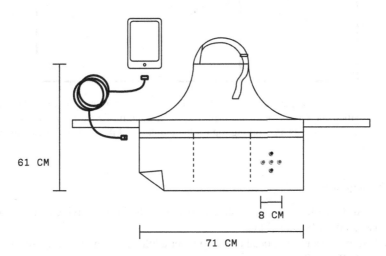

Fig. 1. A schematic representation of the kitchen apron connected through a USB cable with the tablet. The buttons used in the present experiment are highlighted in red. (Color figure online)

The digital cookbook was presented on a Microsoft Surface Pro 2 tablet (10.6"). The buttons on the apron were connected to a hardware schedule using Arduino IDE (Makey Makey 1.2). The schedule was connected to the tablet through an USB cable that was arranged in order not to interfere with users' actions.

3.2 Experimental Setting

The experiment took place in the kitchen of the lab facilities that was properly arranged to serve research purposes. A large table was placed in the middle of the room and served as the main working top. On the table participants found the utensils and the ingredients needed to prepare the requested recipe. Participants were asked to use the oven, which was placed closed to the main working top. Next to the oven, there was a secondary working top that participants could use. The setting was maintained the same for all participants (Fig. 2).

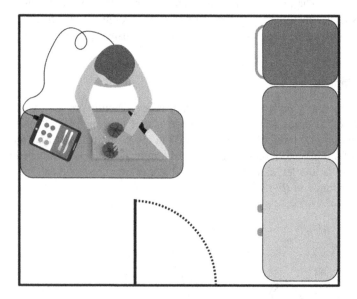

Fig. 2. A sketch of the experimental setting. On the left side, there was the main working top used by the participant. On the right side there was the kitchen furniture, that is the oven (on the top right corner), the secondary working top (in the middle) and the refrigerator (on the bottom right corner).

3.3 Participants

We recruited 30 participants in total. The overall sample was divided into two subgroups based on participants' age.

The first group was composed of 15 younger adults (7 women), with a mean age of 23.9 years old ($SD = 2.5$). The group of younger adults received on average 16 years of education ($SD = 1.3$). Regarding their habits in the kitchen, 8 participants out of 15 declared to cook once a day, 6 reported to cook more than once a day and only 1 was in the habit of cooking more than once a week but not on a daily basis. When cooking, 9 participants out of 15 reported to cook for more than one person. The expertise level in cooking was assessed by asking participants which recipes they would be able to cook without consulting a cookbook. A score ranging from 0 (no expertise at all) to 12 (high expertise) was assigned, according to the complexity of the recipes indicated by participants. We found that 5 participants had a low level of expertise, 7 had an intermediate level and 3 had a high expertise level in cooking. Regarding the use of cookbooks, only seven participants reported to use it while cooking, among those only one consulted paper cookbook, the others reported to consult recipes on the PC or on the smartphone. About their habits of using technologies, all younger participants affirmed to use the smartphone every day, 10 out 15 reported to also use the PC on a daily basis, and 5 reported to use it weekly. The tablet was used by 8 respondents and the smart TV by 7 than once a week.

The group of older adults was composed of 8 women and 7 men. The average age of the sample was 70.3 years old ($SD = 7.6$). They received on average 9.3 ($SD = 3.8$) years of education. Concerning participants' usual practices in the kitchen, 10 participants out of 15 reported to cook more than once a day, one reported to cook once a day, three affirmed to cook more than once a week, but not on a daily basis, and one said to cook less than once a week. Furthermore, among the subgroup of ten participants cooking most often, six reported to cook for more than one person. Regarding the level of expertise, all participants but one had an intermediate or a high level of expertise in cooking. Regarding the use of cookbooks, 6 participants out of 15 reported not to use cookbooks. Among those who did, eight reported to consult paper book recipes, five consulted the PC and one the tablet. About technologies employment, in the second group 6 out f 15 reported to use smartphone daily, 9 affirmed to use PC, of which only 6 reported a daily usage.

All participants were recruited by word of mouth and received no compensation for taking part in the experiment (Fig. 3).

Fig. 3. An older and a younger participant during the experimental session.

3.4   Experimental Procedure

On the day of the test, participants were first welcomed in the laboratory and were debriefed regarding the activity and the goals of the experiment. Once participants had signed the informed consent, they were asked to fill in the pre-test questionnaire collecting background information. The experimenter then walked the participant to the kitchen, where s/he was first illustrated how the it was set up. Then the experimenter showed the kitchen apron and helped users to wear it and explained them how to navigate through the digital cookbook contents using the buttons on the apron. When the user was able to operate autonomously the device, the experimenter asked the participant to prepare a pre-selected recipe following the instructions provided by the digital cookbook and the experimental session started. The experiment ended when the participant told the experimenter s/he had finished. At this point, participants were helped to take off the apron and were accompanied in another room, where they filled in the questionnaires assessing user acceptance and the experience of use with the system. Finally, the experimenter greeted and thanked the participant, who was also given the dish s/he had prepared to take away.

4   Results

First, we used a Pearson's correlation test to assess whether and how the variables under examination correlated with each other. We found that Attitude Toward Technology was weakly correlated with the expectancy of the technology being difficult to use, i.e., Effort Expectancy, and negatively correlated with the age, indicating that the older the respondents the lower was their Attitude Toward Technology. Technology Anxiety was moderately correlated with the presence of factors enabling the adoption of the device, namely Facilitating Conditions, and with the Perceived Usefulness of the device. Furthermore, Technology Anxiety correlated moderately with the Behavioral Intention and with the Psychological Attachment. Facilitating Conditions, was moderately correlated with Effort Expectancy and more strongly with Behavioral Intention. In addition, Facilitating Conditions was negatively correlated with Age. Perceived Usefulness correlated moderately with the intention of use the device, i.e., Behavioral Intention, and more strongly with Psychological Attachment. Effort Expectancy was moderately correlated with Perceived Comfort and more strongly with the Perceived Enjoyment. Behavioral Intention was moderately correlated with Perceived Enjoyment and Psychological Attachment and negatively correlated with Perceived Privacy. Psychological Attachment was moderately correlated with Perceived Enjoyment. Finally, we found that Perceived Comfort was strongly correlated with Perceived Enjoyment (Table 1).

A Spearman's correlation test was run to assess whether the gender correlated with any of the factors assessed by the user's acceptance questionnaire. The analysis revealed no significant correlation between the gender and any of the factors investigated (Table 2).

Table 1. The Pearson's correlation matrix. $*p < .05$; $**p < .001$

	ATT	TA	FC	PU	EE	BI	PA	PP	PE	PC	Age
ATT	–										
TA	.065	–									
FC	.158	.402*	–								
PU	−.006	.347*	.164	–							
EE	.029*	.027	.321*	.123	–						
BI	.128	.429*	.605**	.485*	.233	–					
PA	−.022	.418*	.224	.625**	.208	.453*	–				
PP	−.020	−239	−.251	−.172	.103	−.438*	.136	–			
PE	-.016	.288	.227	.483	.601**	.311*	.326*	.107	–		
PC	.079	.042	.254	.321	.415*	.212	.148	.331	.645**	–	
Age	−.50*	−.13	−.401*	.097	−.052	−.111	−.007	.038	.175	−.027	–

Table 2. The Spearman's correlation matrix. $*p < .05$; $**p < .001$

	ATT	TA	FC	PU	EE	BI	PA	PP	P	PC	Age
Gender	.20	−.359	.008	−.202	−.076	−.23	−.248	.076	−.118	−.118	.222

Next, a multiple linear regression was run to test whether the factors assessed by the user acceptance questionnaire predicted the intention of use of the device, i.e., Behavioral Intention. A significant regression equation was found $F_{11,18} = 2.731$, $p = .028$, with an R^2 of .625. In this model, respondents' Behavioral Intention was predicted only by the factor Facilitating Conditions $\beta = .46$ $t = 2.352$ $p = .03$.

Aiming to obtain a more parsimonious model, we replicated the analysis considering only the factors having values of $\beta > .20$, being Facilitating Conditions, Perceived Usefulness and Perceived Privacy. A significant regression equation was found $F_{3,26} = 11.92$, $p < .001$, with an R^2 of .58. In this model (Table 3), Behavioral Intention was predicted by the factors Facilitating Conditions $\beta = .48$ $t = 3.63$ $p = .001$ and Perceived Usefulness $\beta = .36$ $t = 2.78$ $p = .01$.

Table 3. The final regression model. The unstandardized coefficients, the standard errors and the standardized coefficients.

	B	$SE\ B$	β
Facilitating Conditions	.393	.108	.48**
Perceived Usefulness	.356	.128	.36*
Perceived Privacy	−.325	.169	−.25

A further analysis was run to investigate whether there were specific differences between younger and older adults in the average scores of the factors assessed by the user acceptance questionnaire (Table 4). A Mann-Whitney test revealed a statistically significant difference only for Attitude Toward Technology $U = 38$ $p = .001$, with younger adults having a more positive attitude ($M = 5.44$, $SD = .61$, $Mdn = 5.67$) as compared to their older counterparts ($M = 4.35$, $SD = 1.14$, $Mdn = 4.33$).

Table 4. The means and standard deviations values of the scores gained for each factor of the user acceptance questionnaire for younger and older adults and the Mann-Whitney test. *$p < .05$

Factor	Younger adults		Older adults		U
	M(SD)	*Mdn*	*M(SD)*	*Mdn*	
Attitude Toward Technology	5.44 (.61)	5.67	4.35 (1.14)	4.33	38*
Technology Anxiety	3.77 (.44)	4	3.71 (.67)	4	108.5
Facilitating Conditions	4.9 (1.19)	5	3.8 (1.71)	4	66.5
Perceived Usefulness	3.91 (.99)	3.67	4.15 (1.56)	4.33	90
Effort Expectancy	5.56 (.79)	6	5.43 (.72)	5.5	95
Behavioral Intention	4.08 (1.02)	4.33	3.78 (1.49)	3.77	96
Psychological Attachment	4.16 (.79)	4	4.16 (1.27)	4.42	105.5
Perceived Privacy	4.06 (.56)	4	6.02 (2.12)	4	110.5
Perceived Enjoyment	5.17 (.54)	5	5.35 (.69)	5.67	92
Perceived Comfort	4.86 (.67)	5	4.71 (1.06)	5	109

Regarding the post-experience questionnaire, we first investigated whether there were differences between the two groups of users using a Mann-Whitney test, but the analysis revealed no significant difference between the groups for any dimension tested (Table 5).

Table 5. The means and standard deviations values of the scores gained for each factor of the post-experience questionnaire for younger and older adults and the Mann-Whitney test.

Dimension	Young adults			Older adults			U
	M(SD)	*Mdn*	*t*	*M(SD)*	*Mdn*	*t*	
Satisfaction	4.66 (1.54)	6	2.92*	5 (.65)	5	8.87**	109.5
Learnability	5.6 (.48)	6	17.19**	4.6 (1.44)	5	3.12*	67.5
Ease of Use	4.9 (.79)	5	6.9**	4.84 (.82)	5	6.31**	111.5
Navigability	5.54 (.52)	5.8	15.06**	5.4 (.5)	5.6	14.51**	92
Pleasantness	4.76 (.82)	4.75	5.93**	5.08 (.7)	5.25	8.69**	88
Practice	4.73 (.92)	5	5.17**	4.8 (.86)	4.25	5.84**	109
Usefulness	4.98 (.62)	5	9.22**	5.11 (.58)	5.25	10.76**	93.5

After that, we compared the average score of each of the dimension assessed by the post-experience questionnaire against the mid-point of the response scale, i.e., 3.5, which indicates a neutral attitude (Fig. 4). A one-sample t-test highlighted that for both groups all the dimensions received an average score that was significantly above the mid-point of the response scale (Table 5).

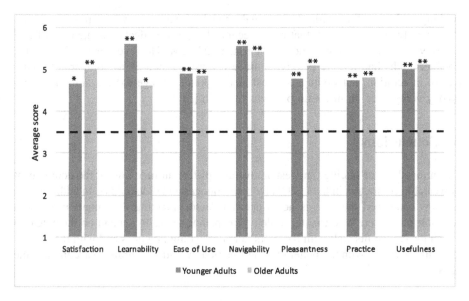

Fig. 4. The average scores of the post-experience questionnaire. $*p < .05$, $**p < .001$ for the one-sample t-test

5 Discussion

In the present research paper, we investigated the user acceptance, the usability and the general experience of use of a wearable device aiming to support cooking activities, namely a kitchen apron, which was conceived to be very simple. Differently from previous studies, in which technology acceptance was assessed after asking respondents to read a scenario or after trying a prototype in a simulation, e.g., [2, 31], we asked participants to use the kitchen apron to complete a realistic cooking task before collecting their opinions. We found that both younger and older adults received positively the device, both in terms of user experience and of usability, supporting our hypothesis regarding the uncomplexity of the interface. This finding is in line with previous research based on a scenario, where it was found that smart wearables are generally perceived positively [32]. Notably, previous studies [10, 31] reported that the use of smart wearables in the kitchen was considered less useful by respondents as compared to other scenarios of use, e.g., the bedroom. However, we found that all participants involved, i.e., both younger and older adults, praised the kitchen apron as a useful tool. This suggests the importance of providing users with a realistic and concrete experience with the prototype under examination before collecting their opinions, especially with older adults, who may struggle to grasp the idea of a new technology [19].

Regarding the user acceptance of the technology, we found that only two factors predicted the intention of use the kitchen apron: Facilitating Conditions and Perceived Usefulness. This model suggests that the adoption of the kitchen apron would depend on the compatibility of the device with the users' typical practices and activities in the kitchen and with their belief that the apron could support them in the unfolding of the cooking tasks, in line with the seminal model of technology acceptance by [7]. Interestingly, it did not seem that users' technical expertise affects the intention of use, contrary to what previous studies suggested [22, 25]. However, we did find that younger adults had a more positive attitude toward technology as compared to older adults. In addition, our findings suggest that respondents' age did not affect the technology acceptance, in line with previous research [31].

6   Conclusions

Taken together our findings suggest an overall positive attitude toward the deployment of wearable computers in the kitchen by both younger and older adults. In addition, our findings confirmed that age is not a decisive factor affecting the intention to use a wearable computer. Whereas, technology acceptance seems to depend on the extent to which the device fits well with the users' already exiting practices and with the tools at their disposal, and with the belief that the wearable would be helpful to accomplish the activity.

References

1. Baber, C., Knight, J., Haniff, D., Cooper, L.: Ergonomics of wearable computers. Mob. Networks Appl. **4**(1), 15–21 (1999)
2. Bodine, K., Gemperle, F.: Effects of functionality on perceived comfort of wearables. In: Proceedings of the Seventh IEEE International Symposium on Wearable Computers (ISWC 2003), vol. 1530, No. 0811/03, p. 17-00, January 2003
3. Boscart, V.M., McGilton, K.S., Levchenko, A., Hufton, G., Holliday, P., Fernie, G.R.: Acceptability of a wearable hand hygiene device with monitoring capabilities. J. Hosp. Infect. **70**(3), 216–222 (2008)
4. Buenaflor, C., Kim, H.C.: Six human factors to acceptability of wearable computers (2013)
5. Chan, M., Estève, D., Fourniols, J.Y., Escriba, C., Campo, E.: Smart wearable systems: current status and future challenges. Artif. Intell. Med. **56**(3), 137–156 (2012)
6. Chen, K., Chan, A.H.: A review of technology acceptance by older adults. Gerontechnology **10**(1), 1–12 (2011)
7. Davis Jr., F.D.: A technology acceptance model for empirically testing new end-user information systems: theory and results. Doctoral dissertation, Massachusetts Institute of Technology (1986)
8. Guo, L., Shan, Y.: Smart clothing system for respiratory monitoring-wearability and user acceptance study. In: 2nd International Congress on Healthcare and Medical Textiles, 25–26 September 2014, Izmir, Turkey. EGE Meditex, September 2014
9. Han, S.H., Yun, M.H., Kwahk, J., Hong, S.W.: Usability of consumer electronic products. Int. J. Ind. Ergon. **28**(3), 143–151 (2001)
10. Hildebrandt, J., Brauner, P., Ziefle, M.: Smart textiles as intuitive and ubiquitous user interfaces for smart homes. In: Zhou, J., Salvendy, G. (eds.) DUXU 2015. LNCS, vol. 9194, pp. 423–434. Springer, Cham (2015). doi:10.1007/978-3-319-20913-5_39
11. Hsu, C.L., Lu, H.P.: Why do people play on-line games? An extended TAM with social influences and flow experience. Inf. Manag. **41**(7), 853–868 (2004)

12. Kaplan, S., Okur, A.: The meaning and importance of clothing comfort: a case study for Turkey. J. Sens. Stud. **23**(5), 688–706 (2008)
13. Kim, S.H.: Moderating effects of job relevance and experience on mobile wireless technology acceptance: adoption of a smartphone by individuals. Inf. Manag. **45**(6), 387–393 (2008)
14. Lee, C., Coughlin, J.F.: Perspective: older adults' adoption of technology: an integrated approach to identifying determinants and barriers. J. Prod. Innovation Manag. **32**(5), 747–759 (2015)
15. Malhotra, Y., Galletta, D.F.: Extending the technology acceptance model to account for social influence: theoretical bases and empirical validation. In: Proceedings of the 32nd Annual Hawaii International Conference on Systems Sciences, 1999. HICSS-32, p. 14-pp. IEEE, January 1999
16. Martin, T., Jovanov, E., Raskovic, D.: Issues in wearable computing for medical monitoring applications: a case study of a wearable ECG monitoring device. In: The Fourth International Symposium on Wearable Computers, pp. 43–49. IEEE, October 2000
17. Meng, Y., Choi, H.K., Kim, H.C.: Exploring the user requirements for wearable healthcare systems. In: 2011 13th IEEE International Conference on E-health Networking Applications and Services (Healthcom), pp. 74–77. IEEE, June 2011
18. Nägle, S., Schmidt, L.: Computer acceptance of older adults. Work **41**(Supplement 1), 3541–3548 (2012)
19. Orso, V., Spagnolli, A., Gamberini, L., Ibañez, F., Fabregat, M.E.: Involving older adults in designing interactive technology: the case of SeniorCHANNEL. In: Proceedings of the 11th Biannual Conference on Italian SIGCHI Chapter, pp. 102–109. ACM, September 2015
20. Perera, G., Holbrook, A., Thabane, L., Foster, G., Willison, D.J.: Views on health information sharing and privacy from primary care practices using electronic medical records. Int. J. Med. Inf. **80**(2), 94–101 (2011)
21. Rapp, A., Cena, F.: Personal informatics for everyday life: how users without prior self-tracking experience engage with personal data. Int. J. Hum. Comput. Stud. **94**, 1–17 (2016)
22. Schaar, A.K., Ziefle, M.: Smart clothing: perceived benefits vs. perceived fears. In: 2011 5th International Conference on Pervasive Computing Technologies for Healthcare (PervasiveHealth), pp. 601–608. IEEE, May 2011
23. Spagnolli, A., Guardigli, E., Orso, V., Varotto, A., Gamberini, L.: Measuring user acceptance of wearable symbiotic devices: validation study across application scenarios. In: Jacucci, G., Gamberini, L., Freeman, J., Spagnolli, A. (eds.) Symbiotic 2014. LNCS, vol. 8820, pp. 87–98. Springer, Cham (2014). doi:10.1007/978-3-319-13500-7_7
24. Steele, R., Lo, A., Secombe, C., Wong, Y.K.: Elderly persons' perception and acceptance of using wireless sensor networks to assist healthcare. Int. J. Med. Inf. **78**(12), 788–801 (2009)
25. van Heek, J., Schaar, A.K., Trevisan, B., Bosowski, P., Ziefle, M.: User requirements for wearable smart textiles: does the usage context matter (medical vs. sports)? In: Proceedings of the 8th International Conference on Pervasive Computing Technologies for Healthcare, pp. 205–209. ICST (Institute for Computer Sciences, Social-Informatics and Telecommunications Engineering), May 2014
26. Venkatesh, V., Davis, F.D.: A theoretical extension of the technology acceptance model: four longitudinal field studies. Manag. Sci. **46**(2), 186–204 (2000)
27. Venkatesh, V., Morris, M.G., Davis, G.B., Davis, F.D.: User acceptance of information technology: toward a unified view. MIS Q. **27**, 425–478 (2003)
28. Wilkowska, W., Ziefle, M.: Perception of privacy and security for acceptance of E-health technologies: exploratory analysis for diverse user groups. In: 2011 5th International Conference on Pervasive Computing Technologies for Healthcare (PervasiveHealth), pp. 593–600. IEEE, May 2011

29. Winckler, M., Bernhaupt, R., Bach, C.: Identification of UX dimensions for incident reporting systems with mobile applications in urban contexts: a longitudinal study. Cogn. Technol. Work **18**(4), 673–694 (2016)
30. Ziefle, M., Röcker, C.: Acceptance of pervasive healthcare systems: a comparison of different implementation concepts. In: 2010 4th International Conference on-NO PERMISSIONS Pervasive Computing Technologies for Healthcare (PervasiveHealth), pp. 1–6. IEEE, March 2010
31. Ziefle, M., Brauner, P., Heek, J.: Intentions to use smart textiles in AAL home environments: comparing younger and older adults. In: Zhou, J., Salvendy, G. (eds.) ITAP 2016. LNCS, vol. 9754, pp. 266–276. Springer, Cham (2016). doi:10.1007/978-3-319-39943-0_26
32. Ziefle, M., Brauner, P., Heidrich, F., Möllering, C., Lee, K., Armbrüster, C.: Understanding requirements for textile input devices individually tailored interfaces within home environments. In: Stephanidis, C., Antona, M. (eds.) UAHCI 2014. LNCS, vol. 8515, pp. 587–598. Springer, Cham (2014). doi:10.1007/978-3-319-07446-7_57

Using Intelligent Personal Assistants to Strengthen the Elderlies' Social Bonds

A Preliminary Evaluation of Amazon Alexa, Google Assistant, Microsoft Cortana, and Apple Siri

Arsénio Reis[1,2], Dennis Paulino[1,2(✉)], Hugo Paredes[1,2], and João Barroso[1,2]

[1] University of Trás-os-Montes and Alto Douro, Quinta de Prados, 5000-801 Vila Real, Portugal
{ars,hparedes,jbarroso}@utad.pt
[2] Campus da FEUP, INESC TEC, Rua Dr. Roberto Frias, 4200-465 Porto, Portugal
dennis.l.paulino@inesctec.pt

Abstract. Social isolation and loneliness are among the important factors for the degradation of the life quality as the persons' aging process advances. These factors can have a pronounced effect on the general health and are caused by the decrease in social interaction by the person with the friends, family and ex-co-workers groups. On the other hand, the software and hardware technologies has reached a maturation point were the electronic assistants can acquire information from the user through camera images, as well as to communicate with the user by means of natural voice language. In this context, a model for the adoption of electronic intelligent assistants by the elderlies has been proposed in previous work. In the current work, it is assessed the possibility of using the current consumer assistants to implement the proposed model. Several assistants are analyzed (Amazon, Google, Microsoft and Apple), assessing their functionalities and how they could be used to assist the elderly in strengthening their social bonds with the family, friends and ex-co-workers groups.

Keywords: Wellbeing · Elderly · Ambient assisted living · Human computer interaction

1 Introduction

Elderly people suffer from an increasing number of problems, mainly due to social isolation and loneliness, requiring support from social agents [1, 2]. These problems, related to loneliness, social isolation, and reduced social activity are linked to the person's mental health, depression, and social bonds [3, 4]. Promoting the social engagement motivates persons to have more complex interactions, mobilizing the cognitive faculties and helping to maintain a good mental health [5].

In our previous work [6], it was proposed a model for the design of an autonomous system, based on the paradigm of the intelligent personal assistant, in order to support the elderly people in maintain their social bonds with the family, friends and colleagues groups. This proposal is focused on tailoring the digital assistant for the specific group of elderlies and for their specific life contexts, which has good perspectives, as the

© Springer International Publishing AG 2017
M. Antona and C. Stephanidis (Eds.): UAHCI 2017, Part III, LNCS 10279, pp. 593–602, 2017.
DOI: 10.1007/978-3-319-58700-4_48

intelligent personal assistants are equipment's that are becoming more interactive and with a more natural language [7].

In this work, we assess the possibility of using the intelligent personal assistants, currently available to the consumer public, accordingly to the previously proposed model. The intelligent personal assistants chosen were: Google Assistant [8], Amazon Alexa [9], Apple Siri [10] and Microsoft Cortana [11]. These are the most popular and readily available from the large, world class, technology companies.

The Google Assistant is an Intelligent Personal Assistant that allows communication with the user through voice commands. It is capable of search online, set reminders and play music using Spotify. This Intelligent Personal Assistant is integrated with Google Home, Google Allo messaging application and Android Wear (e.g. Smartwatches). The Google Assistant is available in English, German, Hindi, Japanese, and Portuguese. In Fig. 1 it is presented the Google Home Smart Speaker which has builtin Google Assistant.

Fig. 1. Google home smart speaker

The Amazon Alexa is an Intelligent Personal Assistant that interacts with the user with voice commands. It is capable of answer questions online, shop online play and read books. This Intelligent Personal Assistant is integrated with Amazon Echo Smart Speaker, Amazon Fire Devices and Amazon Tap Bluetooth Speakers, it can be installed on Android and iOS. It has also some features useful to integrate with smart homes like turning lights on/off or adjusting the temperature at home. The Amazon Alexa is available in English or German. In Fig. 2 it is presented the Amazon Echo Smart Speaker which Amazon Alexa's integrates.

Fig. 2. Amazon echo smart speaker

The Apple Siri is an Intelligent Personal Assistant that allows communication with the user through voice commands. It is capable of search online, make reservations at restaurants, manage email and make calls. This Intelligent Personal Assistant is integrated with iPhone, iPad and Apple Tv. With the Home app, the user can with Apple Siri control lights, thermostats, door locks and other sensors. The user can communicate with Apple Siri in English, French, Dannish, Finish, Spanish, Japanese, Mandarin, Portugusese and others languages. In Fig. 3 it is presented the Apple Siri launched on an Iphone.

Fig. 3. Siri launched on an iPhone

The Microsoft Cortana is an Intelligent Personal Assistant that allows communication with the user through voice commands. It is capable of search online, dictate emails and solve mathematical equations. To answer the questions online, Microsoft Cortana uses the Bing Search Engine. The user can communicate with Microsoft Cortana in English, French, Spanish, Italian, Japanese and Mandarin This Intelligent Personal

Assistant is integrated with Windows 10, Android, Xbox One and iOS platforms. In Fig. 4 it is presented the Microsoft Cortana launched in a Nokia smartphone.

Fig. 4. Microsoft Cortana launched on a Nokia smartphone

2   Background

The model, previously proposed [6], has two main tasks: (1) User identification and data acquisition related to user's personal information, context environment and state of mind assessment; (2) Proposal of a specific interaction activity, accordingly to the user's emotional state and context.

In the first task, the system will identify the user and assess his state of mind using image analysis. It will also gather contextual and personal data, e.g., special personal dates, physical location, or user's preferences.

In the second task, after the user identification and data acquisition phase, the retrieved data will guide the system on selecting and presenting some activities, accordingly to the user profile, current state of mind and context. For example, if the system detects that the user is sad, it can invite him to play one of his favorite games or listen to some of his usual music playlist.

3   Methodology

In this work we assess the usage of the current intelligent personals assistants according to the previously proposed model. We compare the features of each assistant with the relevant requirements of the proposal. The comparison should provide a good assessment, regarding how the intelligent personal assistant provides a set of basic features and requirements, correlated to the interaction of the user with five main features: (1) user identification; (2) state of mind assessment; (3) current context, (4) personal information acquisition; and (5) a set of activity proposals.

The user identification and state of mind evaluation will be made upon the features of image retrieval and analysis. The context and personal information, should include information such as: gender, age, personal preferences, time and date, physical location, etc.

The activity proposals, will be part of the possible interactions with the user. Some activities to be developed are: (a) Basic greeting; (b) Email management; (c) Social Network management; (d) Social and family events management; and (e) Social games. In detail:

- The basic greeting activity is a simple greeting interaction, in which the system meets the user based upon the state of mind, time, and date.
- The email management activity should provide a personal email box to each user and inform the user about the current messages status. In specific dates, such as family anniversaries, the system should offer the user a chance to send a congratulations message.
- The social media management the system monitors the user group of family and friends, regarding their activity in the social networks, e.g., Facebook, Twitter, Instagram, etc., and informs the user about relevant updates.
- The social games activity should provide a set of social games, e.g., cards, trivia, etc., that the user can play in the system.

In Fig. 5, it is shown the system workflow of the proposed model in the previous work.

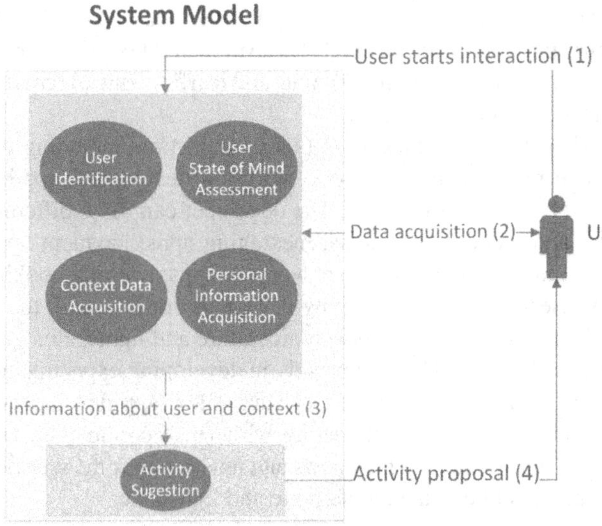

Fig. 5. System workflow

In the Fig. 5, it is presented the system's workflow, displaying the user interaction and the system response, acquiring the user's context and choosing an activity to interact with the user. All the communication is executed through natural language (voice) interactions.

4 Assessment

The following intelligent personal assistants systems were chosen for the assessment: (1) Google Assistant; (2) Amazon Alexa; (3) Apple Siri; and (4) Microsoft Cortana. These systems have Application Programming Interfaces (APIs) providing the functionalities for third party developers to customize some features, which may be used to implement the proposed model.

The assessment results are as follows:

1. The Google Assistant API [12], is divided in two categories: The first one is Conversation Actions, which help the developer to fulfil user requests by letting the developed system have a two-way dialog with users handling the interactions. The second category is Direct Actions that are currently in developing, it will be like Conversation Actions but it will make Google Assistant handle the user interaction, with the developer to be worried only about the handling of the developer's application. With Google Assistant, the user has many features like play news and music, check the weather and traffic, control smart devices like home temperature and lights, etc.
2. The Amazon Alexa API [13] permits developers to make their own application and connect them with users through command voices. Once integrated, the developed systems will have access to the built-in capabilities of Alexa (like music playback package tracking, movie listings, calendar management, and more) and third-party skills developed. The Amazon Alexa for users allows them to play news and music, check the weather and traffic, control smart devices like home temperature and lights, etc.
3. The Apple Siri API [14] handles all the user interaction, including the voice and natural language recognition, and works with the developers' application to get information and handle user requests. The developer can use 6 different categories of apps: audio and video calling apps; messaging apps; payment apps; apps that allow searching through photo libraries; workout apps; and ride booking apps. The Apple Siri for users allows them to play news and music, check the weather and traffic, control smart devices like home temperature and lights, etc.
4. The Microsoft Cortana API [15] is currently in developing expecting to be released in February 2017, which are a set of tools that allow app developers to integrate Cortana into their applications, interacting with voice commands. The Microsoft Cortana for users allows them to play news and music, check the weather and traffic, control smart devices like home temperature and lights, etc.

In Table 1, it is shown a comparison between the assessed intelligent personal assistants, related to the available features that might be used to implement a system for end users.

Table 1. Comparison of several features between the chosen intelligent personal assistants

	Google Assistant	Amazon Alexa	Apple Siri	Microsoft Cortana
Create a shopping list	✓	✓	✗	✗
Check calendar	✓	✓	✓	✓
Manage calendar	✗	✓	✓	✓
Check date and time	✓	✓	✓	✓
Set an alarm	✓	✓	✓	✓
Check weather	✓	✓	✓	✓
Check traffic	✓	✓	✓	✓
Play news	✓	✓	✗	✗
Play music	✓	✓	✓	✓
Search online	✓	✓	✓	✓
Perform calculations	✓	✓	✓	✓
Call an uber	✗	✓	✓	✗
Control home temperature and lights	✓	✓	✓	✗
Lock/unlock doors	✗	✗	✓	✗
Play games	✓	✓	✓	✓
Make a call	✓	✓	✓	✓
Read books	✗	✓	✗	✗
Shopping on Amazon	✗	✓	✗	✗
Order pizza	✗	✓	✓	✓
Manage SMS	✓	✓	✓	✓
Read emails	✗	✗	✓	✓
Send emails	✗	✗	✓	✗
Send posts in Facebook	✓	✓	✓	✗
Send posts in Twitter	✓	✓	✓	✓
Receive Facebook notifications	✗	✗	✗	✗
Receive Twitter notifications	✗	✗	✗	✗

In Table 1, are shown several features that the Intelligent Personal Assistants are capable to provide, and can be used to implement users' interactions.

1. In Google Assistant, there are some important features like playing music, news, and the integration with Smart devices (control home lights and temperatures). But some features that are missing are the calendar and email management with voice commands interaction.
2. In Amazon Alexa, it contains some important features like playing music, news, calendar management, book reader, and the integration with Smart devices (control home lights and temperatures). One feature that is missing is the email management with voice commands interaction.
3. In Apple Siri, it contains some important features like playing music, calendar and email management, and the integration with Smart devices (control home lights, temperature and door locks).
4. In Microsoft Cortana, it contains some important features like playing music, news, and calendar management. Some features that are missing are the email management and the integration with Smart devices (control home lights and temperatures) with voice commands interaction.

In all the Intelligent Personal Assistants, one important feature that was lacking is the social networks notifications.

From the features' set in the Methodology section, the Intelligent Personal Assistants should provide: (1) Basic greeting; (2) Email management; (3) Social Network management; (4) Social and family events management; and (5) Social games.

In the basic greeting activity, all available intelligent personal assistants have a strict greeting, though not allowing the users or other developers to customize. However, in Google Assistant and Amazon Alexa, both provide the possibility for the developer to create and publish their own application in their system, having the freedom to choose the interaction with the user.

In the email management activity, only Apple Siri and Microsoft Cortana can read emails. In specific dates, it is possible for the developer, in Amazon Alexa and Apple Siri, to send in birthday dates messages via Facebook, Twitter or SMS.

In the social network activity, the intelligent personal assistants are only capable of sending posts or update status.

In the playing games activity, all intelligent personal assistants are capable of playing games, e.g., trivia.

5   Conclusion

In this paper, it was presented a comparison of several intelligent personal assistants, with the objective to evaluate how well these services would fulfil the proposed model, based on previous work. This services have many features in common, such as, playing music, search online, or playing games. Although it is important to know what are the features that each service provides, it is also important to understand the extent of how much an third party developer can use and customize these services to accomplish the proposed objectives. These objectives were the user's identification and some data acquisition like state of mind or context information to then propose some activities for voice interaction with the user, based upon the data gathered. These activities should be basic greeting, email management, social network events and social games.

The assessment presented in this paper, shows that it is possible in Amazon Alexa to fulfil the majority of these objectives: Basic greeting, to customize it would be better the Amazon Alexa or the Google Assistant; Email management, to read and send emails like in specific dates it should be used Amazon Alexa; Social Networks events, all services only allow the user's to post or update their status; Social Games, all services have social games like trivia but Microsoft Cortana allows the user's to play some games with other users.

In future work, it will be implemented a scenario, with some of these services and evaluated the effectiveness of the interaction with the users.

Acknowledgements. This work was supported by Project "NanoSTIMA: Macro-to-Nano Human Sensing: Towards Integrated Multimodal Health Monitoring and Analytics/ NORTE-01-0145-FEDER-000016" financed by the North Portugal Regional Operational Programme (NORTE 2020), under the PORTUGAL 2020 Partnership Agreement, and through the European Regional Development Fund (ERDF).

References

1. Fernandes, A.: Velhice, solidariedades familiares e política social: itinerário de pesquisa em torno do aumento da esperança de vida. Sociologia, Problemas e Práticas (36), 39–52 (2001)
2. Reis, A., Reis, C., Morgado, L., Borges, J., Tavares, F., Gonçalves, R., Cruz, J.: Management of surgery waiting lists in the Portuguese public healthcare network: the information system for waiting list recovery programs. In: 2016 11th Iberian Conference on Information Systems and Technologies (CISTI), pp. 1–7. AISTI (2016)
3. Palmer, D., Newsom, J., Rook, K.: How does difficulty communicating affect the social relationships of older adults? An exploration using data from a national survey. J. Commun. Disord. **62**, 131–146 (2016)
4. Reis, A., et al.: Developing a system for post-stroke rehabilitation: an exergames approach. In: Antona, M., Stephanidis, C. (eds.) UAHCI 2016. LNCS, vol. 9739, pp. 403–413. Springer, Cham (2016). doi:10.1007/978-3-319-40238-3_39
5. Bassuk, S., Glass, A., Berkman, F.: Social disengagement and incident cognitive decline in community-dwelling older persons. Ann. Intern. Med. **131**, 165–173 (1999). doi: 10.7326/0003-4819-131-3-199908030-00002
6. Reis, A., Paredes, H., Barroso, I., Monteiro, M., Rodrigues, V., Khanal, S., Barroso, J.: Autonomous systems to support social activity of elderly people - a prospective approach to a system design. In: International Conference on Technology and Innovation on Sports, Health and Wellbeing, TISHW 2016, 1–3 December 2016, UTAD, Vila Real, Portugal (2016)
7. Wobcke, W., Nguyen, A., Ho, H., Krzywicki, A.: The smart personal assistant: an overview. In: AAAI Spring Symposium: Interaction Challenges for Intelligent Assistants, pp. 135–136 (2007)
8. Google Assistant: Google (2017). https://assistant.google.com. Accessed 20 Jan 2017
9. Amazon Alexa: Amazon.com (2017). http://alexa.amazon.com/spa/index.html. Accessed 20 Jan 2017
10. Apple Siri: Apple Inc. (2017). http://www.apple.com/ios/siri/. Accessed 20 Jan 2017

11. Microsoft Cortana: Microsoft (2017). https://www.microsoft.com/en/mobile/experiences/cortana/. Accessed 20 Jan 2017
12. Actions on Google: Google (2017). https://developers.google.com/actions/. Accessed 20 Jan 2017
13. Amazon Alexa Voice Service API: Amazon.com (2017). https://developer.amazon.com/public/solutions/alexa/alexa-voice-service/content/avs-api-overview/. Accessed 20 Jan 2017
14. SiriKit – Apple Developer: Apple Inc. (2017). https://developer.apple.com/sirikit/. Accessed 20 Jan 2017
15. Microsoft Cortana Dev Center: Microsoft (2017). https://developer.microsoft.com/en-us/cortana. Accessed 20 Jan 2017

Designing Autonomous Systems Interactions with Elderly People

Arsénio Reis[1,2(✉)], Isabel Barroso[2,3], Maria João Monteiro[2,3], Salik Khanal[1,2],
Vitor Rodrigues[2,3], Vitor Filipe[1,2], Hugo Paredes[1,2], and João Barroso[1,2]

[1] INESC TEC, Porto, Portugal
salik_khanal@wrc.edu.np
[2] University of Trás-os-Montes e Alto Douro, Vila Real, Portugal
{ars,imbarroso,mjmonteiro,vmcpr,vfilipe,
hparedes,jbarroso}@utad.pt
[3] CIDESD, Vila Real, Portugal

Abstract. Aging is a process inherent to the human condition and part of the human being's life cycle, which can be degraded by the reduction in the individual's physical and social activity. This problem can be augmented by the context in which the person is aging, e.g., family, health and social bonds. The elderly individuals' well-being is related to the strength of their social bonds with their family and friends group, which can be difficult to maintain in some stages of the aging process. A, recently- proposed solution is the adoption of autonomous systems capable of autonomous interactions with the elderly. Such systems are designed to be able to interpret the individual's state of mind and the current context in order to conduct an effective interaction with the elderly person. This study focuses on the interaction design between the autonomous system and the human person, by considering the elderly individual's context and pursuing the type of interaction that will positively influence the reinforcement or maintenance of the person's social bonds with the family and friends groups. The study was carried out by interviewing a group of elderly people, currently living in nursing homes and with limited access to their family and friends.

Keywords: Well-being · The elderly · Ambient assisted living · Human computer interaction

1 Introduction

The aging process is part of the life cycle of every living creature and is inherent to the human condition. Aging can degrade the human life by introducing considerable reductions in the individual's physical and social activities, which may lead to a reduction of the individuals' social bonds with the Family, Friends and former Co-Workers (FFxCW) group [1, 2]. This problem can be further augmented by the specific context of the aging person, e.g., family, health and social bonds [3, 4]. In some stages of the aging process it is difficult to maintain the strength of social bonds, and considering that the individuals' well-being is related to the strength of these social bonds, then acting in order to maintain the individual's social activities is an important issue to address [5, 6].

© Springer International Publishing AG 2017
M. Antona and C. Stephanidis (Eds.): UAHCI 2017, Part III, LNCS 10279, pp. 603–611, 2017.
DOI: 10.1007/978-3-319-58700-4_49

Recently, the use of digital assistants has been proposed to engage and assist the elderly to develop social activities with their FFxWC group [7, 8]. These assistants, proposed as autonomous systems, would be capable of interpreting the individual's state of mind and the current context, as well as to conduct an effective interaction with the elderly person [9]. A component of this model is the catalogue of interactions that would be available to the autonomous systems [10].

In this study we have focused on the current status and motivation of the elderly regarding what they miss the most and how they would accept the interaction with a digital assistant. The objective is to understand the factors that would influence the successful design of human-computer interactions, in particular those types of interaction that will positively influence the reinforcement or maintenance of the person's social bonds with the FFxCW group [11]. A group of elderly individuals, currently living in nursing homes and with limited access to their family and friends, was individually interviewed.

2 The Survey

This study was conducted as a survey, focused on elderly people living in care centres, which might have caused them to experience some form of social deprivation.

2.1 Objectives

The survey was designed in order to comply with the following specific objectives:

1. To characterize the individual population permanently residing in care centres.
2. To determine the current social circumstances of the population regarding their relationship with family, friends and former co-workers.
3. To identify what the individuals miss regarding their relationships with their social peers.
4. To assess the individuals' motivation to accept and use ICT-based systems and applications.

2.2 The Population

The survey was conducted using a set of twenty people, each one individually interviewed.

2.3 The Questions

The survey was designed with twenty five questions, some of which were composed of several sub-questions. The overall questions were arranged in four groups:

1. Characterization;
2. Current situation;

3. Life aspects missed the most;
4. Motivation to use electronic assistants.

3   Survey Analysis

In this section we analyse the survey according to the four groups of questions.

3.1   Characterization

This feature characterises the interviewed population regarding the following categories: Gender, Marital status, Educational level, Mobile phone usage, and Computer usage. They are mostly over 70 years old (50%); more women (65%); and have or had marital relationships (80%).

Regarding the educational level, 20% can't read or write and the other 80% has various levels of education. More than 50% uses a mobile phone daily (53%), but only 5% uses a computer, and only occasionally.

3.2   Current Situation

In this category we analysed the current situation of the individuals, namely: Reason for living in a care centre, Interaction with visitors, Relationship with the family, Relationship with the other residents in the centre, Relationship with the staff, Current health disabilities, and Daily activities.

For all the individuals interviewed, the reason for currently living in the care centre is directly related to some form of loneliness, distributed as follows:

- The family lives in a distant geographical location (10%);
- The family did not have time to take care of them (15%);
- Worsening of health condition (15%);
- Physical dependence (10%);
- Difficulty performing daily tasks (5%);
- Death of spouse (5%);
- Loss of autonomy (10%);
- Fear of loneliness (10%);
- I lived alone (20%).

Most individuals (95%) have some regular visits, mostly from family members (75%) or some other friends (20%). This visits are mainly weekly (60%).

Regarding their current relationships, more that 60% consider to have a good or very good relationship with the others (family, friends centre staff, etc.).

The majority of the individuals have some sort of health problem (95%), distributed as follows:

- Endocrine gland disease, metabolism and immune disorders (31,6%);
- Circulatory System Disease (10,5);
- Respiratory system disease (10,5);
- Disease of the nervous system and sense organs ((10,5);
- Osteomuscular and Connective Tissue System Disease (15,8);
- Neoplasm (10%);
- Mental disorder (10%).

These health issues also manifest as disabilities (75%), mostly causing mobility problems (53%) and sight problems (40%).

Despite the health issues, all individuals classified themselves as active, carrying out the following activities throughout the day:

- Doing activities related to crafts (5,3%);
- Gardening (5,3%);
- Knitting (such as sweaters) (10,5%);
- Outdoor tours (15,8%);
- Playing games (cards, checkers) (5,3%);
- Reading (newspapers or books) (5,3%);
- Watching TV (52,6%).

3.3   The Latest Changes in Life and What Aspects Are Missed the Most

In this group we analysed the life aspects that the individual might miss the most in their current life:

Changes in the social relations with Family, Friends and former Co-Workers (FMxCW);

- Activities missed the most;
- Internet usage by FFxCW;
- Updates from FFxCW;
- Increase in contacts with FFxCW;
- Reasons why they do not have more FFxCW interaction.

A slight majority of the individuals (55%) agrees that their contacts with the FFxWC groups have decreased in the last years, while the others (40%) think they have the same level of contact now as before. The frequency of those contacts is mostly daily (50%) and decreases for more extended periods.

When asked about having more frequent contacts with people from the FFxCW groups, a vast majority was in favor (85%), while a minority (15%) wasn't interested. There wasn't a considerable preference about any of the FFxCW groups.

The main reasons for not getting in touch more often with FFxCWs were:

1. Lack of resources;
2. Lack of reasons or subjects;
3. Other reasons.

When asked about what they miss the most and would like to be currently engaged in, the following list was compiled:

1. Contacting family;
2. Learning to use a computer;
3. Making trips and sightseeing;
4. Growing a vegetable garden;
5. Reading books;
6. Contacting friends;
7. Playing social games;
8. Contacting old co-workers;
9. Working;
10. Listening to music;
11. Playing sports;
12. Hunting or fishing.

To the interviewed individual's knowledge, all of the people from their current FFxCW groups are using some sort of internet service, mostly on a daily basis (85%).

3.4   Motivation to Use Electronic Assistants

In this group we analysed several aspects regarding the acceptance and motivation for the elderly to use a digital personal assistant and some possible types of interaction.

The survey included the following interactions:

1. Interaction with an electronic assistant;
2. Assistance in daily life activities;
3. Email management;
4. Information about activities in social media;
5. Leisure activities (social gaming).

After being explained the concept of a digital personal assistant, a vast majority (85%) considered it "interesting or "very interesting". Half of the individuals (50%) expressed an interest in trying to use a device with a digital assistant.

The following Figs. 1, 2, 3, 4 and 5 describe the motivation for engaging in specific activities with the collaboration of the digital assistant. The numbers, expressed as percentages, clearly show that there is a strong motivation regarding the usage of a digital assistant in all the proposed activities. The column "Positive" reports the cumulative positive answers and is classified as 85% or 95%. We interpret this as strong motivation.

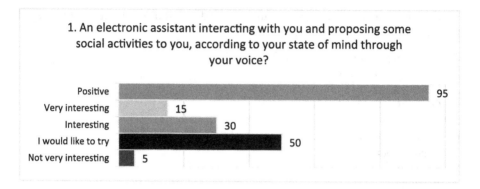

Fig. 1. Interaction with an electronic assistant.

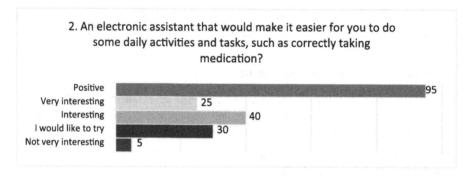

Fig. 2. Assistance in daily life activities.

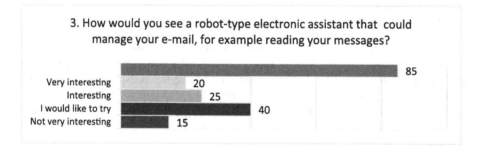

Fig. 3. Email management

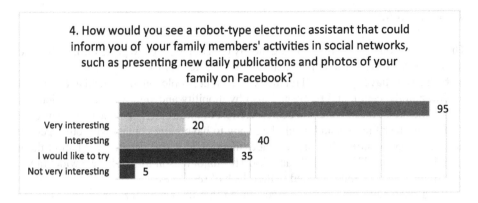

Fig. 4. Social media management.

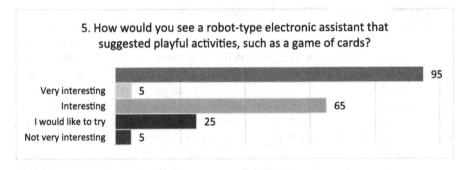

Fig. 5. Social games

In Fig. 1, regarding the adoption of an electronic assistant, there is a strong and positive answer, with half the individuals expressing their will to try and experiment an electronic assistant.

In Fig. 2, there is a strong positive reaction regarding the assistance in the daily life activities, but the majority of the individuals doesn't explicitly expresses their will to try.

In Fig. 3, there is a clear interest in trying an assistive system for mail management, which might be due to the lack of knowledge, by this elderly population, on how to use a mail system.

As in Fig. 3, the answers in Fig. 4, are similar, which might be justified by the fact that the interviewed individuals' don't have the necessary expertise to properly use some common electronic services (e.g., mail, social media, etc.) and would be happy to try with the help of an electronic assistant.

Social games usage, represented in Fig. 5, are a well-known activity, for which the individuals have a clear interest, but don't really have a strong will to try with an electronic assistant. A reason, for this discrepancy between "interesting" and "like to try", might be justified by the fact that, currently, they can use social games whenever they like, and so, don't necessarily depend of the introduction of an assistant.

4   Conclusions

The elderly people in a care centre are mostly old people (over 70 years old), with some sort of chronic health problem, who moved to the care centre due to a loneliness-related problem. They have good social relations with other people, but these tend to be limited by living in the centre and frequently also by mobility and sight problems, which has caused their relationship circle to decrease. Most of these elderly people receive weekly visits from their families and would be happy to have more contact with other people outside the care centre. They also consider themselves active persons, but half of them include "watching TV" as a daily activity. The major reason for not have a wider range of activities and relation is related to their lack of resources.

After analysing this survey, we concluded that the necessary conditions exist for introducing the digital assistant with the main objective of mitigating the problems of social segregation associated with: the residence in the care centre; the lack of mobility and sight; and the lack of resources to engage in activities.

There is a strong motivation for the elderly to adopt the digital assistant option, we think mostly due to the lack of other solutions for the problems of increasing social isolation. However, there is an obstacle related to adopting the technology, which is well expressed by the numbers of about 50% of phone users and only 5% of computer users. Nevertheless, the model of interaction proposed is based on natural language and adaptive interfaces, which should conceal the underlying technology in excellent conditions.

A last conclusion, regarding the motivation to use electronic assistants, can be drawn from the answer pattern in 3.4, in which they express a strong will to try an electronic assistant in scenarios where they don't have the expertise to use electronic systems by themselves. In this cases, e.g., mail management, social media management, the individuals are willing to immediately try an electronic assistant. It is an interesting conclusion, in the sense that shows the individuals' open mind to new technology and devices, although their advance age and isolation.

5   Future Work

The future work will follow-up to test and evaluate specific interactions with the elderly. During the first phase, a set of interactions will be fully developed, by specifying specific interaction scripts and creating digital mock-ups; in a second phase, those mock-ups will be used with the elderly and an assessment will be produced. Another cycle to develop/assess may be necessary in order to proceed to a prototype production scenario.

Acknowledgements. This work was supported by Project "NanoSTIMA: Macro-to-Nano Human Sensing: Towards Integrated Multimodal Health Monitoring and Analytics/ NORTE-01-0145-FEDER-000016" financed by the North Portugal Regional Operational Programme (NORTE 2020), under the PORTUGAL 2020 Partnership Agreement, and through the European Regional Development Fund (ERDF).

References

1. Instituto Nacional de Estatística: Censos 2011 – Resultados Provisórios (2011). http://censos.ine.pt/xportal/xmain?xpid=CENSOS&xpgid=ine_censos_publicacao_det&contexto=pu&PUBLICACOESpub_boui=122073978&PUBLICACOESmodo=2&selTab=tab1&pcensos=61969554
2. Instituto Nacional de Estatística: O Envelhecimento em Portugal. Situação demográfica e socio-económica recente das pessoas idosas, Serviço de Estudos sobre a População do Departamento de Estatísticas Censitárias e da População (2012)
3. Fernandes, A.: Velhice, solidariedades familiares e política social: itinerário de pesquisa em torno do aumento da esperança de vida. Sociologia, Problemas e Práticas [online], n. 36, pp. 39–52 (2001)
4. Reis, A., et al.: Developing a system for post-stroke rehabilitation: an exergames approach. In: Antona, M., Stephanidis, C. (eds.) UAHCI 2016. LNCS, vol. 9739, pp. 403–413. Springer, Cham (2016). doi:10.1007/978-3-319-40238-3_39
5. Conselho Económico e Social: Parecer de iniciativa sobre as consequências económicas, sociais e organizacionais decorrentes do envelhecimento da população. Lisboa (2013)
6. Reis, A., Barroso, J., Gonçalves, R.: Supporting accessibility in higher education information systems. In: Stephanidis, C., Antona, M. (eds.) UAHCI 2013. LNCS, vol. 8011, pp. 250–255. Springer, Heidelberg (2013). doi:10.1007/978-3-642-39194-1_29
7. Sun, H., De Florio, V., Gui, N., Blondia, C.: Promises and challenges of ambient assisted living systems. In: Sixth International Conference on Information Technology: New Generations, ITNG 2009, pp. 1201–1207. IEEE, April 2009
8. Steg, H., Strese, H.: Ambient assisted living–European overview report (2005)
9. Reis, A., Paredes, H., Barroso, I., Monteiro, M.J., Rodrigues, V., Khanal, S., Barroso, J.: Autonomous systems to support social activity of elderly people - a prospective approach to a system design. In: International Conference on Technology and Innovation on Sports, Health and Wellbeing, TISHW 2016, 1–3 December 2016. UTAD, Vila Real (2016)
10. Reza, K., Sima, S., Chu, M.-T.: Socially assistive robots in elderly care: a mixed-method systematic literature review. Int. J. Hum.-Comput. Interact. 30, 369–393 (2014)
11. Reis, A., Reis, C., Morgado, L., Borges, J., Tavares, F., Gonýalves, R., et al.: Management of surgery waiting lists in the Portuguese public healthcare network: the information system for waiting list recovery programs. In: 2016 11th Iberian Conference on Information Systems and Technologies (CISTI), pp. 1–7. AISTI, June 2016

A Systematic Review of the Potential Application of Virtual Reality Within a User Pre-occupancy Evaluation

Kevin C. Tseng[1,2,3,4(✉)], Do Thi Ngoc Giau[1], and Po-Hsin Huang[1]

[1] Product Design and Development Laboratory, Department of Industrial Design, College of Management, Chang Gung University, Guishan, Taoyuan, Taiwan
ktseng@pddlab.org
[2] Healthy Ageing, Research Center, Chang Gung University, Guishan, Taoyuan, Taiwan
[3] Department of Physical Medicine and Rehabilitation, Chang Gung Memorial Hospital, Guishan, Taoyuan, Taiwan
[4] Department of Industrial Design, College of Management and Design, Ming Chi University of Technology, New Taipei City, Taiwan

Abstract. This research aims to discover the potential applications of virtual reality within a user pre-occupancy evaluation. The capability of the VR creates detailed observations, a feeling of immersion, an accurate behaviour measurement and systematic environmental manipulations, which can be controlled in the laboratory. However, previous studies seem to have paid little attention to specific clients when suggesting the most suitable VR approach at the evaluation stage. Moreover, few studies have investigated the use of VR in supporting designers in best practice, and only a limited number of studies focus on the design evaluation from a user's perspective. A systematic literature review is therefore conducted in this study, which focuses on end-user participation. The purpose of this is to explore the extent to which VR is used and to find potential research directions for further studies. The results indicate that VR is a useful aid in a pre-occupancy evaluation which is acceptable and reliable for users.

Keywords: Pre-occupancy evaluation · User experience · Virtual reality

1 Introduction

In an architectural domain, there are various types of design process. Most of these generally start at the briefing stage and end with design drawings [1, 2]. The pre-occupancy evaluation in this process is understood as an environmental evaluation from the user's perspective, prior to the occupation of a building [3]. It plays a crucial role in the design process, aiming to evaluate construction safety [4], customer satisfaction [5], cost effectiveness [4, 6], time and effort prior to the construction phase [7]. In particular, the safety evaluation of the construction site is an important part of planning projects [4]. To be more specific, it supports the reduction of physical risks [5] throughout the communication between designer and client. Client-designer communication is an important part of all these phases of design and is the principal concern of architecture [8].

© Springer International Publishing AG 2017
M. Antona and C. Stephanidis (Eds.): UAHCI 2017, Part III, LNCS 10279, pp. 612–620, 2017.
DOI: 10.1007/978-3-319-58700-4_50

Virtual reality (VR) is explored here in terms of its potential to support the building evaluation. Patel et al. [9] concluded that VR technology has the potential to improve the client design review process within the construction industry. It enhances the communication within the visual presentation of architecture between designers and clients. The related studies suggest that the use of VR tools during the early construction stages is the key theme within 3D visualisation [10, 11].

Some earlier studies have concentrated on methods of researching and applying VR technology. For example, Paes and Irizarry [12] explored the most relevant human factors and cognitive aspects associated with the use of three-dimensional virtual reality models. Lertlakkhanakul et al. [13] applied VR as a platform to simulate a smart home service configuration. In addition, VR has also been applied to evaluate the integrity of occupancy information to close the building energy performance gap [14, 15]. Kuliga et al. [16] demonstrated that in addition to user cognition and behavior, the user experience is analogous to the real and virtual environments. Woksepp and Olofsson [17] explored the credibility and applicability of virtual reality models, which were experienced and assessed within a workforce. Norouzi et al. [7] presented an overview of a design approach focusing on the designer-client relationship. Westerdahl et al. [18] compared the user experiences of employees in a virtual building and the completed building. Another piece of research with a new approach [19] considered a method of virtual pre-occupancy evaluation (VOE) using VR to assess human performance for people with disabilities. Shen et al. [1] enhanced the limited experience of clients by developing a user pre-occupancy evaluation (UASEM) which adopted VR in a case study (a university campus project) including four steps: preparation of the building information model, specification of user activities, simulation of user activities and a pre-occupancy evaluation. A methodology known as VIC-MET [20] has been suggested to include the user in a creative innovation process. VIC-MET has four design spaces that support different functions in the design process: contextual enquiry, a conceptual modeling space, a functional consolidation space and a solution space. The virtual environments are CAVE (Fig. 1) [21], Panorama (Fig. 2) [22], a game console-based solution and a virtual world in second life (Fig. 3) [23].

Fig. 1. CAVE virtual environment

Fig. 2. Panorama

Fig. 3. A scenario in second life

Another methodology has been developed [24, 25] to ensure the usability of virtual environments through user-centered design and evaluation, and has been shown to have a cost-effective strategy which assesses and iteratively improves user interactions in built virtual environments. Santos [26] insisted on user satisfaction in the use of the VR system, and HMD interaction performs better than the desktop setup. Essentially, the architectural design process shows high rates of iteration by design teams [6]; however, the role of the user in this process is also significant. Therefore, an understanding of the user experience with VR tools might to some extent support architectural designers and researchers in being more effective. Nevertheless, the number of studies investigating VR in pre-occupancy evaluations from the user's perspective seems to be low.

This study therefore aims to explore the effectiveness of user participation in the design process using VR and to find potential research directions for further studies of VR.

2   Methodology

2.1   Data Sources and Search Strategy

This study aims to use a meta-analysis method to retrieve articles related to the potential application of VR within a user pre-occupancy evaluation. A search strategy is formulated with filtering rules which focus on exploring related studies that include virtual reality in a user pre-occupancy evaluation, with data drawn from ScienceDirect, Scopus, Web of Science (WOS) and Google Scholar. In addition, the literature review was conducted without a time limit on publications, in order to explore the trends in related studies. There is a great deal of research exploring VR in the engineering field of ScienceDirect, and following the Web of Science and Scopus. The current study also collected related studies published between 2006 and 2016, as more recent changes in commercialized products allow a broader application of VR in engineering and construction [5]. Six main keywords including virtual reality, user experience, pre-occupancy evaluation, designer-client communication, user participation and architectural design were selected for a search strategy related to the application of VR in a user pre-occupancy evaluation.

2.2   Retrieval Methods and Screening Criteria

Retrieval was conducted using ScienceDirect, Scopus and WOS by searching abstracts, titles and keywords to retrieve virtual reality and engineering keywords in all years. The six keywords were used to reduce the insignificantly related results, checking in couples and triples of keywords. Using a publication time limit of between 2006 and 2016 reduces the results of this study. Simultaneously, repeated papers and less relevant papers checked through the abstract were excluded.

The filtering rules were articles that included (1) main keywords and synonyms with a high database reliability; (2) information related to the use of VR in exploring user experience via studies or tests with user participation and methodology in improving client-designer communication; (3) identification of the effects of VR or its contributions in architectural design; and (4) present work clearly related to this study in the abstract. According to these four rules, a total of 17 articles comply with Rules 1 to 3 and finally, a total of eight articles complied with Rules 1 to 4.

3   Results

In order to reduce the numerous results in ScienceDirect when searching all fields to retrieve virtual reality and engineering keywords in all years, we conducted a subsequent search which included the abstract, title and keywords. The following main keywords are the focus of this research: (1) virtual reality (2) user experience (3) pre-occupancy evaluation (4) designer-client-communication (5) user participation and (6) architectural design were combined. However, the search strings in ScienceDirect did not match more than two keywords. A total of 236 articles were eliminated from the three pairs of keywords (1) and (2), (1) and (3), (1) and (5), while 1197 results from the pair (1) and (4) were excluded due to the high quantity of results. Similarly, a search of the article title, abstract and keywords was conducted to retrieve virtual reality and engineering keywords in the Scopus database, reducing the number of articles from 10748 to 444 results. A further 42 were eliminated to reduce the number from 563 to 521 when searching for a topic to retrieve the same keywords in WOS. In particular, Scopus and WOS allow the matching of more than two keywords. Google Scholar launch was also used as an additional search, using the same method of checking the main keywords and excluding the repeated results to retrieve three more related articles.

Following this, the collected articles for each set of keywords were checked to exclude similar and less related papers through the abstract; a total of 17 articles complied with Rules 1 to 3. Finally, a total of 8 articles complying with Rules 1 to 4 were chosen for discussion. Figure 4 illustrates the selection process.

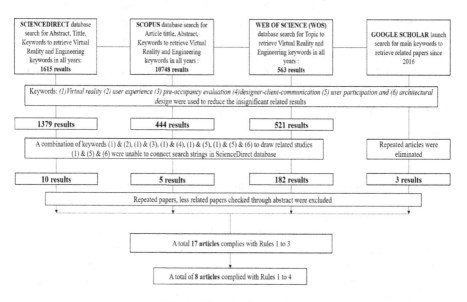

Fig. 4. The selection process

4   Discussion

The related studies discuss a number of useful applications applying VR to meet the demands of clients in the design process. As a result, VR opens up a vast number of opportunities in the innovation of architectural design, with valuable findings. User experience is vital in studies of human–environment interaction, and should be taken into account when examining 'naturalistic' human behaviour in real and virtual environments or the usability of buildings. There is almost no difference between the virtual environment (VE) and the real environment, although there are still some limitations, such as the level of spatial legibility and factors related to atmospherics. VR, for this reason, has the potential to be used as an empirical research tool for architectural researchers and designers. Moreover, the present procedure which distributes information using 2D CAD drawings is assessed as having low effectiveness. Virtual reality itself needs to have a high level of realism in order to obtain a high level of immersion and similarity compared with a real scenario, however. For a better presentation, Spatial Legibility of users, as well as the quality of virtual presentation, should be considered.

A positive result from the user's perspective was that virtual models were useful and well accepted by participants. For instance, by giving a fairly accurate presentation of the real building, VR is a useful aid in the decision-making process concerning the future workplace of employees.

However, virtual simulations are mostly used in the evaluation of environmental performance in relation to people who do not have particular needs. Sometimes, there was a difference in user experience that was believed to be due to a difference in computer experience and the age of the employees. This means that the virtual experience is not similar between users; it varies individually depending on personal characteristics.

Table 1. VR Devices on the Market

Name	Photo
Oculus CV1's Touch [27]	
HTC Vive [28]	
Samsung Gear VR [29]	

Therefore, a focus on specific users would be exhaustively able to resolve certain concerns in post-occupancy evaluation such as the level of safety.

The methods of evaluation of user participation also contribute to an improvement in users' understanding of the design process, users' confidence in expressing comments and an increase in their willingness to work with designers. In this case, VR plays a role as a requirement management technique. Nevertheless, the information of the building simulation model is limited to only basic architectural information. Some users would like to obtain more information, such as the decoration, lighting and details of materials. Furthermore, it seems that the method of presentation and cooperation with the designer is somewhat complicated. For instance, there are limited possibilities for transferring building models from the construction industry's traditional design tools to a 3D representation of Second Life virtual world. This is a significant barrier to an efficient use of the VR tool.

In terms of the virtual devices on the market, several products may be considered. Oculus CV1's Touch and HTC Vive support controllers to users for interaction. These VR devices are more beneficial and easy to use for general users. This would probably be a more simple way, especially for a more popular use. This issue is solved in research which focuses on the evaluation of construction site safety using head-mounted displays (HMDs). With a VR headset and a phone, the designer will be able to present their work to clients easily. Table 1 shows three popular VR devices on the market.

Generally, VR is a useful aid which is acceptable and reliable to customers. It is an empirical research tool, a requirement management technique and a presentation tool providing users with cognition impacts such as spatial perception or orientation, presence or immersion, spatial behaviour, spatial dimension, contextual information and sense of realism. VR also allows for the interaction between users and specific objects

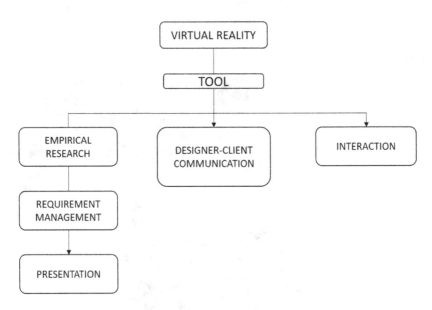

Fig. 5. VR architectural design

in a virtual environment. In pre-occupancy evaluation methods, VR is employed to support end-users in communication with designers regarding their vision of their future work and the building's appearance (Fig. 5).

However, there are several issues related to the quality of representation to users as well as a suitable method applying VR to users in a pre-occupancy evaluation. An investigation of different users with distinguishing characteristics in terms of VR experience, age, physical and psychological concerns is essential for further research.

5   Conclusion

This study conducted a comprehensive literature review to discover the potential applications of VR on a pre-occupancy evaluation. The results indicate that VR is a useful aid in pre-occupancy evaluation, which is both acceptable and reliable for users. In addition, VR brings several benefits not only to designers but also to users. Future studies should focus on investigating users with different physical and psychological characteristics. Research into the VR experiences of these users in terms of the level of realism, human performance and appropriate VR systems and methods for various cases is recommended.

Acknowledgements. This work was supported in part by the Ministry of Science and Technology of Taiwan, ROC under Contracts MOST 103-2628-H-182-001-MY2, MOST 104-2410-H-182-025-MY2 and MOST 105-2632-H-182-001, by the Chang Gung Medical Foundation (grant nos. CMRPD3E0372 and CMRPD2F0211, and by the Healthy Aging Research Centre of Chang Gung University (grant nos. EMRPD1G0221, CMRPD1B0331, and CMRPD1B0332). The funders had no role in the study design, data collection and analysis, decision to publish, or preparation of the manuscript.

References

1. Shen, W., et al.: The user pre-occupancy evaluation method in designer–client communication in early design stage: a case study. Autom. Constr. **32**, 112–124 (2013)
2. Archer, B.L., The structure of design processes. Royal College of Art (1968)
3. Guski, R., Schuemer, R.: Umweltevaluation. Lantermann & V. Linneweber (Hrsg.), Umweltpsychologie **1,** pp. 785–810 (2008)
4. Hilfert, T., Teizer, J., König, M.: First person virtual reality for evaluation and learning of construction site safety. In: Proceedings of the International Symposium on Automation and Robotics in Construction ISARC 2016. Vilnius Gediminas Technical University, Department of Construction Economics & Property (2016)
5. Yang, J.-B., Peng, S.-C.: Development of a customer satisfaction evaluation model for construction project management. Build. Environ. **43**(4), 458–468 (2008)
6. Serginson, M., et al.: Assessing the effectiveness of architectural design communication through public participation methods. Des. Manag. Prof. Pract. **6**(1), 61–84 (2013)
7. Norouzi, N., et al.: A new insight into design approach with focus to architect-client relationship. Asian Soc. Sci. **11**(5), 108 (2015)
8. Kalay, Y.E.: Architecture's New Media: Principles, Theories, and Methods of Computer-aided Design. MIT Press, London (2004)

9. Patel, N.K., Campion, S.P., Fernando, T.: Evaluating the use of virtual reality as a tool for briefing clients in architecture. In: Proceedings of the Sixth International Conference on Information Visualisation. IEEE (2002)

10. Bucolo, S., Impey, P., Hayes, J.: Client expectations of virtual environments for urban design development. In: Proceedings of the Fifth International Conference on Information Visualisation. IEEE (2001)

11. Frost, P., Warren, P.: Virtual reality used in a collaborative architectural design process. In: Proceedings of the IEEE International Conference on Information Visualization. IEEE (2000)

12. Paes, D., Irizarry, J.: Virtual reality technology applied in the building design process: considerations on human factors and cognitive processes. In: Rebelo, F., Soares, M. (eds.) Advances in Ergonomics in Design. Advances in Intelligent Systems and Computing, vol. 485, pp. 3–15. Springer, Cham (2016). doi:10.1007/978-3-319-41983-1_1

13. Lertlakkhanakul, J., Choi, J.W., Kim, M.Y.: Building data model and simulation platform for spatial interaction management in smart home. Autom. Constr. 17(8), 948–957 (2008)

14. Ryu, J., et al.: Application of human-scale immersive VR system for environmental design assessment-a proposal for an architectural design evaluation tool. J. Asian Architect. Build. Eng. 6(1), 57–64 (2007)

15. Niu, S., Pan, W., Zhao, Y.: A virtual reality integrated design approach to improving occupancy information integrity for closing the building energy performance gap. Sustain. Cities Soc. 27, 275–286 (2016)

16. Kuliga, S.F., et al.: Virtual reality as an empirical research tool—exploring user experience in a real building and a corresponding virtual model. Comput. Environ. Urban Syst. 54, 363–375 (2015)

17. Woksepp, S., Olofsson, T.: Credibility and applicability of virtual reality models in design and construction. Adv. Eng. Inf. 22(4), 520–528 (2008)

18. Westerdahl, B., et al.: Users' evaluation of a virtual reality architectural model compared with the experience of the completed building. Autom. Constr. 15(2), 150–165 (2006)

19. Palmon, O., et al.: Virtual environments for the evaluation of human performance: towards virtual occupancy evaluation in designed environments (VOE) (2006)

20. Christiansson, P., et al.: User participation in the building process. J. Inf. Technol. Constr. 16, 309–334 (2011)

21. Wikipedia: Cave automatic virtual environment (2017). https://en.wikipedia.org/wiki/Cave_automatic_virtual_environment

22. Wikipedia: Panorama, 09 March 2017. https://en.wikipedia.org/wiki/Panorama

23. Moi, C.: Chez Moi Furnitures (2017). http://secondlife.com/destination/chez-moi-furnitures

24. Drettakis, G., et al.: Design and evaluation of a real-world virtual environment for architecture and urban planning. Presence Teleoperators Virtual Environ. 16(3), 318–332 (2007)

25. Gabbard, J.L., Hix, D., Swan, J.E.: User-centered design and evaluation of virtual environments. IEEE Comput. Graph. Appl. 19(6), 51–59 (1999)

26. Santos, B.S., et al.: Head-mounted display versus desktop for 3D navigation in virtual reality: a user study. Multimedia Tools Appl. 41(1), 161–181 (2009)

27. Corp, O.: Oculus Rifts (2017). https://www.oculus.com/rift/

28. Corp, H.: HTC Vive (2017). http://store.steampowered.com/app/358040/

29. Corp, S.: SAMSUNG Gear VR (2017). http://www.samsung.com/global/galaxy/gear-vr/

Reconciling Cognitive Reappraisal and Body Awareness in a Digital Mindfulness Experience

Ralph Vacca[(✉)]

New York University, New York, USA
ralph.vacca@nyu.edu

Abstract. This paper focuses on understanding how: (i) the role of cognitive reappraisal can support decentering, and (ii) cognitive reappraisal can be enacted in conjunction with body awareness. From a twelve-day field experience with 13 participants, both quantitative and qualitative data was gathered and analyzed. Findings suggest that an in-situ tracking approach leads to low curiosity scores, and that reminder-only approaches are sensitive to providing insufficient guidance throughout the day. In terms of decentering, findings suggest that there are notable differences in how decentering can be supported through reappraisal and the role of body awareness only serves to support reappraisal and decentering not detract from it.

Keywords: Mindfulness · Situated cognition · Self-reflection · Self-awareness · Emotional health · Persuasive design · Mobile learning

1 Introduction

There is an increasing interest in exploring ways of using interactive design to support mindfulness. This paper explores a mobile design that seeks to support mindfulness in everyday life using prompts to focus on specific mental events throughout the day. The design utilizes a mixed bag of emotion regulation strategies to explore ways in which mental event valence, body awareness, and cognitive reappraisal may play a role in supporting mindfulness states as measured the dual construct of curiosity and decentering. In emotion regulation literature cognitive reappraisal is a strategy that can mediate emotional responses [9], however the strategy may conflict with our conceptions of mindfulness that detract from judgment, that is integral to some forms of cognitive reappraisal [4].

This paper examines the use of body awareness in conjunction with two different forms of cognitive reappraisal – acceptance and forced positive. The research question we are addressing is: what role do different forms of cognitive reappraisal play in how we observe and react to mental events when engaging in mindful awareness operationalized as curiosity and decentering?

© Springer International Publishing AG 2017
M. Antona and C. Stephanidis (Eds.): UAHCI 2017, Part III, LNCS 10279, pp. 621–640, 2017.
DOI: 10.1007/978-3-319-58700-4_51

2 Background for Mindfulness and Cognitive Reappraisal

Mindfulness can be understood as a temporary state that can be induced by an individual with effort [1, 14]. This state can be operationalized in many ways, but one common way is as a two-factor construct – curiosity and decentering – which is understood as being open and inquiring about one's internal mental events, while also maintaining a distance from such mental events, rather than clinging to them. Theoretically, trait-based and state-based approaches may be related in that continued mindfulness state induction and maintenance may lead to changes in mindfulness traits. This study focuses on mindfulness as a state, seeking to use a mobile learning experience to activate the support the induction of the state through individual effort. Lau et al. [10] in devising the Toronto Mindfulness Scale (TMS) operationalized a mindfulness state as consisting of the two factors: curiosity and decentering.

Some research has suggested that a decentered state can promote reappraisal processes [3] – the process of reframing a thought in order to alter the resulting emotional reaction. It is believed that the broadened awareness of the ongoing flow of mental events in a mindfulness state allows for space to reappraise any one mental event in a manner that leverages a greater degree of cognitive flexibility [5]. However the role reappraisal can play in promoting a decentered state, as defined by the Toronto Mindfulness Scale (TMS) is not well understood. The TMS characterizes decentering as a form of disidentification from mental events as representations of reality or an actual self, and more as one of an ongoing flow of mental events. Earlier work on how mindfulness promotes decentering, focuses on the observation of the transience between mental events, and the eventual disconnection at points of uncontrolled rumination or mind wandering back to the meditation object (e.g., breath) [7]. However, it is not clear how a top-down reappraisal may influence one's characterization of identifying with a given mental event. While decentering, as defined by the TMS, encapsulates efforts to change cognition as a form of identification with thoughts, there is little understanding on the phenomenological experience of such as process.

This study incorporates structured reappraisal into three of the challenges provided to a user via a mobile app, so as to explore their influence on decentering – a factor of a mindfulness state. A major challenge with this proposition is the explicit focus on the contents of mental events when enacting the reappraisal process. In focusing on the contents of mental events there is less of a focus on the broader consciousness that is a flow of mental events.

2.1 Different Reappraisal Approaches

There are a large number of different tactics that fall under the umbrella of cognitive reappraisal, each varying in efficacy based on situational relevance [12]. For example distancing is a reappraisal tactic that entails a sense of physical or psychological distance from the events depicted (e.g., this doesn't affect me). Acceptance on the other hand seeks to normalize the negative event (e.g., it was no one's fault, things happen). Being explicitly positive is another tactic that entails the idea that the situation is better than it would have been if the negative event had not happened (e.g., when someone dies saying they are in a better place).

In this study, two different types of appraisal embodiments were implemented: forced positive, and acceptance. While one would guide the user to see the upside of a given mental event, the other would simply guide the user to acknowledge associated thoughts or feelings. In proposing these two variants I sought to further explore if the cognitive reappraisal process occurs, if it will lead to experiences of decentering.

2.2 Breath Awareness and Reappraisal

It is not well understood how breath awareness works in conjunction with reappraisal processes to influence aspects of how decentering is experienced. Some research suggests that the on-going attentional switching towards physical sensations (e.g., breath) that occurs in mindfulness meditation broadens awareness, that in turn supports positive reappraisal mechanisms [3]. In this study, the integration of reappraisal varies amongst the challenges provided to users, specifically on how it is paired with breath awareness. In exploring differences in the absence or presence of breath awareness in conjunction with reappraisal, I sought to further explore how engaging in breath/sensation awareness leads to body awareness, and how it relates to manner in which cognitive reappraisal process occur, and whether it will lead to experiences of decentering.

3   Design Walkthrough

Users were directed to install the SIMA app and complete all six challenges twice in the order presented totaling 12 challenge-completion experiences. Each challenge focused on a different mental event: (1) gratitude, (2) frustration, (3) gratitude journal, (4) self-criticism, (5) envy, and (6) mood tracker. Each challenge starts at the beginning of the day. They receive a reminder notification on his phone throughout the day based on what the user entered as their daily sleep time. The reminders were spaced out in 2-hour increments between 1 h after the start of the challenge (e.g., 10 am) and 3 h before the user said they go to sleep (e.g., 7 pm). At the end of the day, for all the challenges except mood tracker, the user was prompted via a reminder to check-in, which, as illustrated in Fig. 3, varied for each challenge.

3.1 Start

The user was directed to install the SIMA app and complete all six challenges twice in the order presented totaling 12 challenge-completion experiences. Each challenge focused on a different mental event: (1) gratitude, (2) frustration, (3) gratitude journal, (4) self-criticism, (5) envy, and (6) mood tracker.

Table 1. Challenges and directions

Challenge	Directions on start screen
Gratitude	Throughout day observe any thoughts or feelings of gratitude and associated physical sensations. Just observe
Frustration	Throughout day observe any moments of frustration and associated physical sensations. Just observe
Envy	Throughout day observe any thoughts or feelings of envy and associated physical sensations. Just observe
Self-criticism	Throughout day observe moments of self-criticism and associated physical sensations. Just observe
Mood tracker	Throughout day take 5 s to quickly track your current mood
Gratitude journal	Throughout day observe any thoughts or feelings of gratitude and associated physical sensations. Just observe

The user then received a reminder notification at the start of their day that asked them if today they were willing to engage in one of the six daily challenges. It's important to note that challenge completions took place over 15 days, so users were free to skip days if they wanted to, or reenroll in challenges they failed to complete (Table 1).

3.2   Throughout Day

The different challenges included different interactions. As seen in Table 2, the in-action prompts for five of the challenges did not require the user to engage in any action with the app when the mental event is observed, but the mood tracker challenge did prompt the user to track their mood three times throughout the day, which meant an in-the-moment opening of the app to track mood.

Table 2. List of challenges and in-action instructions

Challenge	Notification text
Gratitude	Remember to observe any thoughts or feelings of gratitude and associated physical sensations. Just observe
Frustration	Remember to observe any moments of frustration and associated physical sensations. Just observe
Envy	Remember to observe any thoughts or feelings of envy and associated physical sensations. Just observe
Self-criticism	Remember to observe moments of self-criticism and associated physical sensations. Just observe
Mood tracker	Remember to take 5 s to quickly track your current mood
Gratitude journal	Remember to observe any thoughts or feelings of gratitude and associated physical sensations. Just observe

 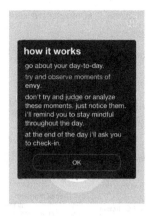

Fig. 1. Daily challenge enrollment screen   **Fig. 2.** Instructions upon challenge start

So imagine that the user started the envy challenge at the start of his day. He would then receive a reminder notification on his phone throughout the day. The reminders were spaced out in 2-hour increments between 1 h after the start of the challenge (e.g., 10 am) and 3 h before the user said they go to sleep (e.g., 7 pm). So the user would receive about 4 reminders throughout the day if she started the challenge at 9 am, and said she usually went to sleep at 10 pm. The prompts were sent and received as local notifications on the mobile device. On the user's phone they would appear on her locked screen, and in the notifications tray (Figs. 1 and 2).

As mentioned, the Mood Tracker challenge was the only challenge that prompted users to engage with the app itself through the notification reminder. For instance, when the user received a notification during the Mood Tracker challenge they would simply click on the notification itself, which would open up the SIMA app to the check-in screen, where they would be able to track his mood by plotting the valence (positive or negative) and the magnitude (strong/weak) of the mood.

3.3   End of Day

At the end of the day, for all the challenges except mood tracker, the user was prompted via a reminder to check-in, which – as illustrated in Fig. 3 – varied for each challenge.

In all of the challenges, users were initially prompted to recall one moment where they observed the mental event. As illustrated in Fig. 3, all of the challenges except Gratitude Journal were instructed to "In your mind recall this moment of [mental event]" and were prompted to tap and hold interaction. The Gratitude Journal challenge engaged in the user in a different kind of recall that was more guided. In a guided recall moment approach, the user selected a context and trigger for the mental event, rather than a broad free form recollection (Fig. 4).

After recalling the moment, all of the challenges except Frustration engaged in a form of breath awareness. For instance, when the user got to this point in the check-in for Gratitude Journal they were prompted with "Savor this sense of gratitude. Where in

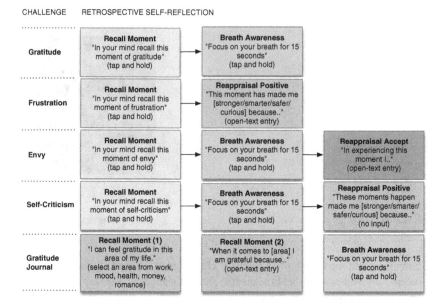

Fig. 3. Mental event and related design embodiments

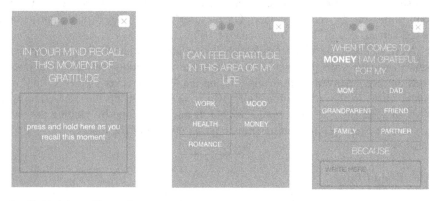

Fig. 4. Check-in: recalling moment through a tap and hold.

Fig. 5. Check-in: guided recall moment – area of gratitude

Fig. 6. Check-in: guided recall moment – analysis.

your body do you feel it?" (see Fig. 8), while for all the other challenges he was prompted with "Focus on your breath for 15 s" (see Fig. 7).

As detailed in Fig. 3, there were two kinds of reappraisals used across three of the six challenges: Frustration, Self-criticism, and Envy. In the Frustration and Self-Criticism challenge, users were prompted to complete a reappraisal interaction

Fig. 7. Check-in: focus on breath.

Fig. 8. Check-in: recalling moment.

Fig. 9. Reappraisal: forced
positive with input.

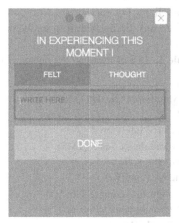

Fig. 10. Reappraisal: acceptance
with input.

Fig. 11. Reappraisal:
forced positive no input

where they prompted to reframe how the moment has made them either stronger, smarter, safer or curious (see Fig. 9). The Envy challenge made use of a different kind of reappraisal approach that prompted the user to simply acknowledge the feeling or thought associated with the moment (see Fig. 10).

Once the user has completed the challenge, they were directed to complete the challenge completion survey, and complete any remaining challenges the following days. It's once again important to note that challenge completions took place over 15 days, so users were free to skip days if they wanted to, or reenroll in challenges they failed to complete.

4 Methods

Thirteen participants were recruited from several New York City universities. Participants were required to have never previously meditated or engaged in cognitive behavioral therapy, as well as have a personal iPhone they can use for the study. The average age was (M = 26.4, SD = 5.5), and 9 out of the 13 participants were female (69.2%).

Participants were asked to complete an initial survey when signing up to ensure they had not engaged in any form of meditation or cognitive-behavior therapy prior to this experience. Each user was then prompted to complete all of the six challenges over one week, and complete a survey each time a challenge was completed.

4.1 Measures

A summary of all of the different measures used in this study is provided in Table 3, categorized by the associated process or outcome (key components of the conjecture map) the measure operationalizes. For each process/outcome we mapped more than one measure to better triangulate any findings during analysis.

Table 3. List of measures by outcome/process

Process/outcome	Measure	Scoring
Curiosity	Toronto Mindfulness Scale (TMS) - curiosity sub-scale	6-item quantitative measure scored from 0 to 24
	Semi-structured interview	
Decentering	Toronto Mindfulness Scale (TMS) - decentering sub-scale	7-item quantitative measure scored from 0 to 28
	Semi-structured interview	
In-action self-reflection	Self-Reflection In-Action (SR-InAct) questions in daily completion survey	2-item Likert questions 0–4
	Semi-structured interview	
Retrospective self-reflection	Self-Reflection Insight Scale – Self-Reflection sub-scale (SRIS-SR)	12-item self-reflection subscale scored 7 to 84
	Semi-structured interview	
Body awareness	Semi-structured interview	
	Body awareness (BA) custom questions in daily completion survey	2-item Likert question 0–4
Reappraisal	Emotion Regulation Questionnaire Reappraisal Subscale Adapted (ERQ-R-A)	Adapted from ERQ. 2-item Likert question 0–4
	Semi-structured interview	

In the challenge completion survey, I included two custom survey questions to get a sense of the role of body awareness in decentering. Each question focused on a different aspect of body awareness – what Mehling [13] referred to as perceived body sensations and awareness of mind-body connection. The two questions are "I noticed some pleasant and unpleasant physical sensations", and "I noticed how my body reacted to recalling a moment I observed throughout the day."

In the Customized Emotion Regulation Questionnaire Reappraisal Subscale (ERQ-RS-A), I created two custom survey questions that were adapted from the reappraisal subscale of the Emotion Regulation Questionnaire [8]. Responses are scored on a Likert scale ranging from 1 = strongly disagree to 5 = strongly agree. The actual ERA-RS-A was not used in that the instrument measures dispositional cognitive reappraisal – reappraisal as a habitual use – rather than cognitive reappraisal as an instance or applied instance.

4.2   Procedure

Participants were asked to complete an initial survey when signing up to ensure they had not engaged in any form of meditation or cognitive-behavior therapy prior to this experience. Each user was then prompted to complete all of the six challenges over one week, and complete a survey each time a challenge was completed.

The survey included questions that span the TMS SRIS-SR measures, as well as customized questions that focused on the frequency of self-reflection (SR-InAct) and body awareness (BA). The order of the challenges completed by users was counterbalanced to minimize any learning effects. After completing all of the challenges, users engaged in an hour-long semi-structured interview (Table 4).

Table 4. Measures by procedure

Stage	Instrument	Measure	Collected	Data points
Pre	Pre-survey	Demographic questions	Start of design cycle	(13 users) = 13 responses
		Five-factor mindfulness Questionnaire (FFMQ)	Start of design cycle	(13 users) = 13 responses
During	Challenge completion survey	Self-reflection Insight Scale (SRIS-SR)	After every completed challenge	(13 users × 6 challenges × 2 runs) = 156 responses
		Emotion regulation questionnaire reappraisal subscale adapted (EQR-A) and body awareness (BA)	After every completed challenge	(13 users × 6 challenges × 2 runs) = 156 responses
		Toronto mindfulness scale (TMS)	After every completed challenge	(13 users × 6 challenges × 2 runs) = 156 responses
		Conjecture survey	After every completed challenge	(13 users × 6 challenges × 2 runs) = 156 responses
		Usage logs	Throughout experience	(936 reminders + 156 check-ins/completions)
Post	Interview	Semi-structured Interviews	End of design cycle	(13 users × [37 – 54] min) = 637 min audio

5 Data Analysis

Analysis was divided into three phases. The first phase entailed drafting single user cases based on the qualitative data gathered so far (surveys and log data), so as to inform the subsequent interview. In my second phase, the interviews were transcribed and analyzed using analytic codes derived from conjecture maps drawn for each of the treatments. The case-study analysis technique Yin [15] referred to as pattern matching was used, which leveraged the conjecture map, since they are patterns of relationships designed to be both measurable and theoretically derived. Once all of the data was collected, it was synthesized using the case-study protocol into a complete single user case. In the last phase of the analysis a cross-case comparison using a word-table [2, 15] that mapped against the conjecture map was conducted.

5.1 Phase 1: Quantitative Analysis

Role of Dispositional Mindfulness. A Pearson's product-moment correlation to assess the relationship between FFMQ scores and TMS scores – averaged across both instances of each challenge – yielded no significant correlation. This indicates that initial dispositional levels of mindfulness as measured by the FFMQ were not significantly related to the different challenges' ability to influence mindfulness states.

Mental Event Types and Mindfulness States. To understand the relationship between mental event types and mindfulness states, a repeated measures ANOVA between the TMS scores – averaged between both instances of each challenge – for all of the six challenges was conducted. Differences between the TMS subscales curiosity and decentering was also investigated. First confirmation that the total TMS, curiosity, and decentering scores were normally distributed was established, as assessed by Shapiro-Wilk's test ($p > .05$). In looking at total TMS scores, significant differences were found between the challenges using the Greenhouse-Geisser correction ($F(5,34.33) = 9.122$, $p < .001$) which corrected for violations in sphericity [11]. Post-hoc tests revealed that the average TMS score for the envy challenge ($M = 41.00$, $SD = 7.05$) was significantly greater than for the gratitude challenge ($M = 34.46$, $SD = 8.67$), frustration challenge ($M = 29.39$, $SD = 7.68$), and mood tracker challenge ($M = 27.46$, $SD = 8.86$). In addition, the TMS score for the self-criticism challenge ($M = 37.23$, $SD = 8.95$) was significantly greater than the frustration challenge ($M = 23.39$, $SD = 7.68$). Lastly, the TMS score for the gratitude journal challenge ($M = 34.01$, $SD = 8.09$) was significantly greater than the mood tracker challenge ($M = 27.46$, $SD = 8.86$). Repeated ANOVA tests on curiosity subscale scores using the Greenhouse-Geisser correction, yielded no significant differences between the challenges. However, there were significant differences in decentering subscale scores differences using the Greenhouse-Geisser correction ($F(5,30.618) = 11.371$, $p < .001$). Post-hoc tests found that decentering subscale scores for the envy challenge ($M = 21.15$, $SD = 4.91$) was significantly greater than both the frustration ($M = 29.39$, $SD = 7.68$) and mood tracker ($M = 27.46$, $SD = 8.86$) challenges. In addition a significant difference between the mood tracker challenge ($M = 27.46$, $SD = 8.86$) and self-criticism challenge was found ($M = 37.23$, $SD = 8.95$) (Tables 5, 6 and 7).

Table 5. Summary of RM-ANOVA of mindfulness states

Challenge	Curiosity	Decentering	Total
All	(F(5, 29.598) = 2.454, p = .093)	(F(5, 30.618) = 11.371, p < .001)	(F(5, 34.33) = 9.122, p < .001)

Table 6. Summary of mean scores of mindfulness states

Challenge	Curiosity M(SD)	Decentering M(SD)	Total M(SD)
Self-criticism	18.23(5.89)	17.85(4.469)	37.23(8.95)
Envy	17.92(5.10)	21.15(4.91)	41.00(7.05)
Mood tracker	13.00(3.39)	12.08(3.97)	27.46(8.86)
Gratitude	17.69(5.02)	16.77(5.02)	34.46(8.67)
Frustration	17.08(5.87)	12.31(3.99)	29.39(7.68)
Gratitude journal	18.01(5.99)	16.02(5.16)	34.01(8.09)

Table 7. Summary of quantitative analysis of self-reflection, body awareness, and reappraisal

Challenge	SRIS-SR
All	(F(2.71, 32.47) = 1.745, p = .181)

To understand the role of mental event types on self-reflection, differences in SRIS-SR scores between the different challenges using a repeated measures ANOVA was investigated. I used the Greenhouse-Geisser correction and found no significant differences between the challenges. SR-InAct questions served the purpose to inform subsequent interview questioning only, rather than be used as part of an inferential analysis. As such only the means were calculated and presented in Table 8.

Table 8. Summary of quantitative analysis of self-reflection, body awareness, and reappraisal

Challenge	SRIS-SR M(SD)	InAct M(SD)
Self-criticism	50.923(5.377)	4.08(1.038)
Envy	49.39(5.32)	2.08(1.04)
Mood tracker	39.23(6.07)	2.23(1.30)
Gratitude	51.15(6.34)	4.231(1.09)
Frustration	43.69(4.64)	3.92(1.66)
Gratitude journal	50.01(6.03)	4.00(1.53)

Questions on the ERQ-RS-A and BA served the purpose to inform subsequent interview questioning only, rather than be used as part of an inferential analysis. As such only the means were calculated and presented in Table 9.

Table 9. Summary of quantitative analysis of body awareness and reappraisal

Challenge	ERQ-RS-A M(SD)	BA M(SD)
Self-criticism	3.69(1.18)	5.308(.8549)
Envy	2.615(1.261)	4.39(1.50)
Mood tracker	1.39(.65)	–
Gratitude	1.54(.519)	5.77(1.36)
Frustration	5.23(1.54)	2.39(1.66)
Gratitude journal	1.77(.725)	6.08(1.19)

The mean ratings on the design conjectures survey completed at the end of each challenge was calculated – the mean ratings are provided in Table 11 (Table 10).

Lastly, I looked for certain patterns in the usage logs. First I looked at the response rate of clicking on reminders. Only the mood tracker prompted users to click on the

Table 10. Design conjectures survey

ID	Question	Self-criticism	Gratitude	Envy	Frustration	Mood tracker	Gratitude journal
U1	It was easy to observe moments of the specific thought/feeling prompted by the challenge	4.12(.61)	4.28(.75)	3.11(.82)	3.91(.52)	4.62(1.1)	3.85(.82)
U2	Recalling a moment at the end of the day was easy	4.76(.73)	4.4(.67)	4.54(1.1)	4.16(.97)	4.32(.87)	4.01(.64)
U3	I was judgmental of my reaction to the recalled moment	4.48(1.2)	2.30(.49)	3.44(.44)	4.72(.59)	–	2.16(.24)
U4	I found the reminders to be intrusive	3.71(.54)	3.16(.58)	3.86(.98)	3.4(.77)	4.4(.71)	3.27(.61)
U5	I was accepting of how I reacted to the recalled moment	2.94(.49)	3.31(.76)	3.11(1.2)	2.10(.44)	–	3.11(.96)
U6	I want to spend more time understanding why I think and feel certain ways	3.8(.71)	3.18(.31)	3.50(.89)	4.64(.91)	4.89(1.1)	3.34(.73)

Table 11. Summarized usage logs

Challenge	Reminder response rate	Time to complete check-in M(SD)	Challenge completion rates
Self-criticism	–	1.21(.76) min	96.3% (1 repeat)
Envy	–	1.65(.38) min	86.7% (4 repeats)
Mood tracker	76% of check-ins at (M = .9, SD = 8.61) min	n/a	100%
Gratitude	–	2.01(.91) min	96.3% (1 repeat)
Frustration	–	1.3(.89) min	89.7% (3 repeats)
Gratitude journal	–	1.52(1.1) min	96.3% (1 repeat)

reminders. Then I looked at the time required to complete the end of day check-in; mood tracker did not require one. Lastly, I looked at challenge completion rates to see the number of failures to complete requiring a re-enrollment in the challenge.

5.2 Phase 2: Individual Analysis

The thirteen semi-structured interviews were transcribed and analyzed using analytic codes that were directly mapped to the design and theoretical conjectures. In line with

Table 12. Selected excerpts of interviews for analytic codes

Conjecture	Code	Sample excerpt	Individual case theme
DC5	Forced perspective; judgment	"It felt a little judgy. Like asking me to look at the bright side. Not just a different way of looking at it"	Reappraisal as managing reactivity (c3)
DC5	Interpretation	"The whole I felt, was interesting because the other one....the um.. the [I help]. Yes this one was like just recognizing how I felt. Without like trying to do anything"	Acceptance
TC6	Suffering	"I was just glad I didn't have to keep doing it. I didn't realize, like… how much I did it, and I don't know if it was good to put in overdrive,.. or at least see how it's kind of already, like in overdrive"	Aversion reactivity user engagement
TC6	Suffering	"I recalled how I had to go back to the bank after forgetting to deposit my check. It was so stupid, but I was so annoyed. And I guess I was more annoyed about how annoyed I was. Does that makes sense. It's like my reaction irritated me"	Attachment in recalling cognitive reactivity

Table 13. Selected examples of significant statements and formulated meanings

Significant phrase	Formulated meaning
"I mean I spent the day punching in all of this stuff, and at the end I wanted to see a graph or like some kind of dashboard. At least tell me something so I don't feel like it was a complete waste of time"	Users displaced value of tracking to retrospective reflection with minimal value towards in-action self-reflection

Yin's pattern matching analytic technique for a valid explanatory approach, the initial codes stemmed from the a priori analytic focus. However, to allow for a concurrent exploratory approach that would serve to both better understand the phenomenological aspects to the conjectures as well as surface alternative patterns that might rival explanatory logic – similar to the previous cycle – I used Colaizzi's (1978) phenomenological method in analyzing participant transcripts (Tables 12 and 13).

5.3   Phase 3: Cross-Case Analysis

Cases were arranged in a word table for cross-comparisons and shared themes [15] across all of the conjectures. From the word table, a review of themes was conducted and a list of the major themes contributing to the research questions were outlined.

6   Findings

6.1   In-situ Tracking Pushes Curiosity to Retrospective Self-reflection

One of the challenges implemented in this design cycle was Mood Tracker. Different from the other challenges, Mood Tracker required an in-the-moment engagement with SIMA rather than end-of-day engagement like the other five challenges. In initial analyses Mood Tracker had a decent click-through rate with 76% of check-ins being clicked and all users completing the required three check-ins throughout the day. This indicated that despite requiring users to interrupt their day more than the other challenges, that provided only a reminder, users did respond to the reminders and completed the challenge. Yet, for Mood Tracker, the average rating from 1–5 on agreement towards the statement, "I found the reminders to be intrusive" was (M = 4.4), the highest of all of the challenges. In the interviews, recurring themes around intrusiveness highlighted that the compensation and formal structure of the study were the primary reasons for app engagement. As one user (p8) put it, "I usually ignore apps that need me to do stuff, but I figured that was the whole point of this challenge, so I just did it." Another user (p2) spoke more towards the feeling of intrusiveness when he shared that, "I'm super connected to my computer. And...you know, the app would literally interrupt me. I liked the whole glance thing. But the whole pick up the phone and do the mood form was a little annoying."

In understanding how curiosity was experienced through this in-situ tracking via reminders I looked at curiosity scores and follow-up during interviews on experiences of present-moment awareness of internal mental events with investigative interest. While there was no significant difference in curiosity scores between any of the challenges, the Mood Tracker challenge did a much lower curiosity score (M = 13.00, SD = 3.39) than all of the challenges. In interviews with users it became clear that there was a fundamental difference in how the reminders were being used that echoed my initial findings during the pilot study. In the Mood Tracker challenge, the reminders served as a prompt to self-reflect, while with the other challenges that specified a mental event (e.g., envy), there was ongoing self-monitoring as result of, and in-between the reminders. For instance, one user (p7) shared that, "I honestly didn't really think about my mood, but after doing it I did", referring to herself thinking about mood throughout the day versus right after the checkin. Another user (p4) described the difference as, "I guess I could just always be thinking about how I'm feeling. But, with the others I was looking for something, like... not as always there." She (p4) went on to share that, "The first time I did it, I thought something was gonna happen at the end, like the others, but then nothing. There should be some kind of summary, or like a graph or something." Other users also eluded to this experience of not self-reflecting in-between reminders and seeing the value of engaging with the check-ins as occurring through some kind of aggregated summary or analysis of the logged entries.

The implication highlighted the value of the approach in prompting users to observe a specific mental event, rather than prompting them to self-reflect on their current thought or feeling at the moment of the reminder. As compared to the Mood Tracker challenge, users described the reminders as re-engaging them in self-monitoring for instances. As one user (p1) put it, "sometimes I would peek at it and, be like oh crap I totally forgot I was doing that today."

6.2   Insufficient Guidance During In-action Self-reflection

In my interviews with users a recurring theme was this sense that during the in-action self-reflection process, there was this feeling that it was not clear what the point was of observing these instances. Even though there was no mention of feeling frustrated with non-reactivity, since the language in the reminders was replaced with body awareness language, there was still a mention of insufficient guidance in early experiences with the challenges, regardless of the challenge itself. As one user (p6) put it, "at times I felt like the reminders were just asking me to do some busy work." Another user (p1) shared with me, "I wanted to analyze the feeling I was having but I know I wasn't supposed to. So I kind of just went back to what I was doing." As one user (p10) put it, "it wasn't until I got to the end of the day thing that I was like. (ohhh). Okay. I get it. Weird but I get it. I mean. I don't know why I have to do it throughout the day, but I understood how it was gonna be used. Now." In short, once the experience was complete, there was a better understanding of the value of the in-action self-reflection. This sense of pragmatic value was most pronounced with the mood tracking challenge that prompted users to simply track their mood throughout the day. As one user (p11) put it bluntly, "I mean I spent the day punching in all of this stuff, and at the end I wanted to see a graph or like some kind of visual. At least tell me something so I don't feel like it was a complete waste of time."

6.3 Guided Recollection Is Limiting

In the Gratitude Journal challenge, SIMA engaged users in a different kind of recalling experience, one that was more guided. Although I did not find any statistically significant differences in SRIS-SR scores between Gratitude Journal and the other challenges, the interviews with users yielded interesting insights into how recalling could be supported. Overall, users preferred the broader, "Recall a moment" rather than a step-by-step scaffolded recollection of the moment as was the case in the Gratitude Journal challenge. One user (p3) described the guided recall approach, "it felt more like analyzing what I remember, instead of trying to recall something." She (p3) went on to also share that, "I liked being able to scan, like, what I spent the day trying to observe, instead of … trying to think about how I'm making sense of what I noticed."

The implication here may be that the generalized approach to recalling a moment may allow for more flexibility in methods of scanning observed instances than a more guided approach that may constrain the way a user goes about thinking back through their day of the effort exerted to observe specific instances of a mental event. The limitation here is clearly that I did not test alternative guided approaches to recall that may have been less constrained than the one designed for Gratitude Journal (see Figs. 5 and 6).

6.4 Breath Awareness Includes Reaction to Moment

In four of the challenges – Gratitude, Envy, Self-Criticism, and Gratitude Journal – breath awareness was incorporated. By far the lowest mean score on the Body Awareness (BA) set of questions was the Frustration challenge (M = 2.39, SD = 1.66). In the BA the questions were, "I noticed some pleasant and unpleasant physical sensations", and "I noticed how my body reacted to recalling a moment I observed throughout the day" rated from 1–5 along the scaled of strongly disagree to strongly agree. Out of all of the challenges Frustration was the only one that did not incorporate the breath awareness embodiment (see Fig. 3).

In interviews with users two recurring patterns emerged. First was a recurring characterization of their body awareness as a reaction to the recalled moment, rather than a distraction. For instance one user (p11) said that, "after tapping and remembering stuff I noticed the breath thing was like… I closed my eyes and tried to feel what I was feeling at that moment. I don't know if that was right, but it's what I did." Another user (p6) described the focusing of breath as "going into" the feeling and another (p10) shared that he, "recalled that feeling of frustration and then calmed down." This indicates that most users did not use the breath awareness as a distraction or explicit attentional shift, but instead as a form of paying attention to the physiological response to recalling a specific moment they observed throughout the day. This experience is line with the how shifting the focus to one's physiological state can be effective in ameliorating mental rumination [7]. However, the sequence after recalling an event implicitly seemed to imply to users that the focus on physiological senses was in noticing physiological reactions to the recalled moment.

In addition, users experienced challenges that focused on positive mental events (e.g., gratitude) differently. While positive feelings took on a characterization of acceptance, the challenges focusing on what are commonly labeled negative mental events (e.g., self-criticism and envy) led to characterizations of wanting to self-regulate.

6.5   Reappraisal as an Approach to Manage Reactivity

The reappraisal embodiment was embedded into three out of the six challenges – Frustration, Envy, and Self-Criticism. The ERQ-RS-A, which consisted of two questions, was used to try to get an understanding on how reappraisal was initially experienced.

While only three of the challenges included the reappraisal embodiment, all of the challenges prompted users to complete the ERQ-RS-A. Mood Tracker, Gratitude, and Gratitude Journal had the lowest scores indicating that most users did not agree that the challenge prompted them to change how they were thinking about the moment they recalled, and did not prompt them to control their emotions by, "changing the way [they] thought about the situation." This makes sense given that these were the three challenges that did not include the reappraisal embodiments.

In looking at the other three challenges, the question was on how reappraisal influenced decentering, and the potential role body awareness played when used in conjunction with reappraisal.

First, I looked at the potential role body awareness played when used in conjunction with reappraisal. The three challenges (Frustration, Envy, and Self-Criticism) where appraisal was implemented all focused on a negative mental event, so it allowed for an understanding on how decentering occurred around such events. Out of the three challenges, the only one that did not include the body awareness embodiment alongside the reappraisal embodiment was Frustration. In this challenge I saw a low body awareness score (M = 2.39, SD = 1.66) and high ERA-RS-A score (M = 5.23, SD = 1.54), broadly indicating that body awareness did not occur, but cognitive reappraisal did. In looking at decentering, Frustration had one of the lowest decentering scores (M = 12.31, SD = 3.99), which was statistically significantly different than the other decentering scores. However, there was only a difference between Frustration and Envy, and not between Frustration and Self-Criticism. While Self-Criticism included body awareness and Frustration did not, it did not seem to be statistically significant. As mentioned earlier, body awareness was less about distracting oneself, but more about paying attention to one's reaction to recalling the moment. In interviews asking about how body awareness played into reappraisal, no consistent themes emerged, but rather users spoke about other aspects of the reappraisal process itself. If anything, users often mentioned that the body awareness experience "calmed them down" or "let them "take a moment", which may have influenced how they went into reappraisal experiences. Language that denoted a state of broadened awareness or cognitive flexibility was not found in in-depth interviews on the relationship.

However, there were pronounced differences between the forced positive and acceptance reappraisal approaches. In looking at the design conjectures survey, after completing the Frustration and Self-Criticism challenges, most users agreed or strongly agreed that they were, "judgmental of [their] reaction to the recalled moment" (M = 4.7 and M = 4.4). For Envy, the rating was lower (M = 3.41), and for the challenges that focused on positive mental events (i.e., Gratitude and Gratitude Journal) the rates hovered around a general disagreement (M = 2.3, and M = 2.1). In interviews, what emerged was a strong sense that the reappraisal process that used a forced positive structure felt like they were judging their reaction to the recalled moment. One user shared with me that, "there was this assumption that I needed to somehow look at things in a better way. like seeing the cup half full was better for me." Another user shared, "it felt a little annoying to have it tell me to look on the bright side." In looking at the acceptance reappraisal approach, that simply prompted a reperceiving of their reaction as it was, users shared that they felt like they were just sharing the mental event itself. One user (p8) stated that, "it felt more clinical, like I was trying to be objective about it." She went to describe the difference as, "the other way was like trying to help me, and this way was just trying to get me to see what it was and move on." Another user (p3) shared that she, "felt like she was writing it down so she could see it for what it was." When pressed to elaborate, she shared that "I saw that there was this feeling that came up when I thought about it and it was nice to feel it and recognize it. You know say hi and then be like, I have other stuff to do."

6.6   Text Entry Prompted Deeper Self-reflection

In the Self-Criticism embodiment of reappraisal, users were prompted to engage in the process in two different ways. The first prompted them to input text in the form of a sentence completion (see Fig. 9), while the other asked them to engage in the reappraisal in their head and double tap on the screen as they engaged in the process (see Fig. 11).

In interview with users there was a surprising preference for the text-entry approach. While I assumed that the no-input approach would be less effortful, and in turn preferred, most users felt the text entry approach allowed them to really take a moment to think it through. As one user (p1) put it, "when I had to write it out, I actually took a moment to phrase what I was thinking." Furthermore, users shared that they anticipated the retrospective self-reflection at the end of the day would entail some kind of deeper reflection. As one user (p10) shared, "I thought it was more like I was thinking about it. Like spending time actually processing what happened, instead of just, quickly considering something."

However, she went on to highlight one core limitation to this finding in that the double tap mechanic may have been frustrating for some users, "I wasn't sure if I was supposed to read it aloud each time I double tapped." Other users also shared this sentiment, for instance one user (p5) shared that he, "was confused about the... I think it said consider the perspective, or like think about it each time you hit the screen. I guess I thought about it and just kept hitting the screen." In my initial usability testing on the double tap mechanic, confusion on what to do did not emerge, suggesting that the clarity of the alternative approaches may helped users contrast against how much clarity users felt was provided in the no text-input embodiment.

The implication here is that users preferred deeper forms of guided reappraisal that more unstructured approaches. Since this input mechanic took place at the end of the day, users did not seem to mind spending time thinking, reflecting, and inputting.

7 Discussion

No initial differences were found between groups on pre-tests, and an analysis of scores during the challenge completion survey yielded differences. Findings suggest that an in-situ tracking approach leads to low curiosity scores, and that reminder-only approaches are sensitive to providing insufficient guidance throughout the day. In terms of decentering, findings suggest that there are notable differences in how decentering can be supported through reappraisal and the role of body awareness only serves to support reappraisal and decentering not detract from it.

To promote decentering, an acceptance-oriented reappraisal approach did not counteract decentering – as defined by the Toronto Mindfulness Scale [10] – as was the case with the forced-positive reappraisal approach. However, despite research positing acceptance as a cognitive reappraisal tactic [12], the extent to which such an approach can really be considered a form of cognitive modification is not clear, in that users did not see the approach as having an embedded form of judgment or alteration of thoughts to manage mood. Integration of a more formal measure of cognitive reappraisal may help contrast such an approach to formal definitions. Furthermore, the use of body awareness in conjunction with reappraisal should be maintained, however the sequence of the two should be further explored. Lastly, a text-input version of reappraisal should be used in place of any no-input embodiment.

In regard to the in-situ tracking exploration, there was limited support for how this approach could promote curiosity as compared to using reminders throughout the day to self-monitor for specific mental events. However, while the tracking approach did not seem to promote curiosity, it is not clear how presenting the data collected within a retrospective self-reflection activity may have translated into a form of investigative interest. If perhaps the data collected was analyzed at the end of the day, it may have led to users feeling like they were curious about their moods more frequently afterwards. Perhaps an extended time beyond engaging with the challenge two times with 3 reminders each may have led to a more engrained awareness of mood, especially if an end-of-day reflection would accompany the throughout the day tracking experience.

8 Conclusion

There are notable differences in how decentering aspects of a mindfulness state can be supported through forms of reappraisal – acceptance oriented forms of reappraisal are superior to forced positive reappraisal approaches. In addition, the incorporation of body awareness only serves to support reappraisal and decentering not detract from it.

References

1. Chambers, R., Gullone, E., Allen, N.B.: Mindful emotion regulation: an integrative review. Clin. Psychol. Rev. **29**(6), 560–572 (2009). https://doi.org/10.1016/j.cpr.2009.06.005
2. Eisenhardt, K.M.: Building theories from case study research. Acad. Manag. Rev. **14**(4), 532–550 (1989). https://doi.org/10.5465/AMR.1989.4308385

3. Garland, E., Gaylord, S., Park, J.: The role of mindfulness in positive reappraisal. Explore (NY) **5**(1), 37–44 (2009). https://doi.org/10.1016/j.explore.2008.10.001
4. Garland, E.L., Gaylord, S.A., Fredrickson, B.L.: Positive reappraisal mediates the stress-reductive effects of mindfulness: an upward spiral process. Mindfulness **2**(1), 59–67 (2011). https://doi.org/10.1007/s12671-011-0043-8
5. Garland, E.L., Fredrickson, B., Kring, A.M., Johnson, D.P., Meyer, P.S., Penn, D.L.: Upward spirals of positive emotions counter downward spirals of negativity: insights from the broaden-and-build theory and affective neuroscience on the treatment of emotion dysfunctions and deficits in psychopathology. Clin. Psychol. Rev. **30**(7), 849–864 (2010). https://doi.org/10.1016/j.cpr.2010.03.002
6. Goldin, P.R., McRae, K., Ramel, W., Gross, J.J.: The neural bases of emotion regulation: reappraisal and suppression of negative emotion. Biol. Psychiat. **63**(6), 577–586 (2008)
7. Grabovac, A.D., Lau, M.A., Willett, B.R.: Mechanisms of mindfulness: a Buddhist psychological model. Mindfulness **2**(3), 154–166 (2011). https://doi.org/10.1007/s12671-011-0054-5
8. Gross, J.J., John, O.P.: Individual differences in two emotion regulation processes: implications for affect, relationships, and well-being. J. Pers. Soc. Psychol. **85**(2), 348–362 (2003). https://doi.org/10.1037/0022-3514.85.2.348
9. Gross, J.J., Thompson, R.A.: Emotion regulation: conceptual foundations. In: Handbook of Emotion Regulation (2007)
10. Lau, M., Bishop, S.R., Segal, Z.V., Buis, T., Anderson, N.D., Carlson, L., Shapiro, S., Carmody, J., Abbey, S., Devins, G.: The toronto mindfulness scale: development and validation. J. Clin. Psychol. **62**(12), 1445–1467 (2006). https://doi.org/10.1002/jclp.20326
11. Maxwell, S.E., Delaney, H.D.: Designing Experiments and Analyzing Data: A Model Comparison Perspective, vol. 1. Psychology Press, Hove (2004)
12. McRae, K., Ciesielski, B., Gross, J.J.: Unpacking cognitive reappraisal: goals, tactics, and outcomes. Emotion (Washington, D.C.) **12**(2), 250–255 (2012). https://doi.org/10.1037/a0026351
13. Mehling, W.E., Gopisetty, V., Daubenmier, J., Price, C.J., Hecht, F.M., Stewart, A.: Body awareness: construct and self-report measures. PLoS ONE **4**(5), e5614 (2009). https://doi.org/10.1371/journal.pone.0005614
14. Mark, J., Williams, G.: Mindfulness and psychological process. Emotion (Washington, D.C.) **10**(1), 1–7 (2010). https://doi.org/10.1037/a0018360
15. Yin, R.: Case Study Research: Design and Methods. Sage Publications, Thousand Oaks (2009)

Author Index

Printed in the United States
By Bookmasters